Eliza Hamilton Dunlop

SYDNEY STUDIES IN AUSTRALIAN LITERATURE

Robert Dixon, Series Editor

The Sydney Studies in Australian Literature series publishes original, peer-reviewed research in the field of Australian literary studies. It offers engagingly written evaluations of the nature and importance of Australian literature, and aims to reinvigorate its study both locally and internationally.

Eliza Hamilton Dunlop

Writing from the Colonial Frontier

Edited by Anna Johnston and Elizabeth Webby

SYDNEY UNIVERSITY PRESS

First published by Sydney University Press

© Individual contributors 2021
© Sydney University Press 2021

Sydney University Press
Fisher Library F03
University of Sydney NSW 2006
AUSTRALIA
sup.info@sydney.edu.au
sydneyuniversitypress.com.au

A catalogue record for this book is available from
the National Library of Australia.

NATIONAL
LIBRARY
OF AUSTRALIA

ISBN 9781743327487 paperback
ISBN 9781743327494 epub
ISBN 9781743327500 mobi
ISBN 9781743327517 pdf

Cover image and frontispiece: Portrait of Eliza Hamilton Dunlop (no date), colour photograph of oil painting (Wollombi Endeavour Museum).
Cover design by Miguel Yamin

Contents

List of Figures

1

"Proud of Contributing Its Quota to the Original Literature of the Colony": An Introduction to Eliza Hamilton Dunlop and Her Writing

Anna Johnston and Elizabeth Webby

Eliza Hamilton Dunlop spiritedly identified her contribution "to the original literature of the colony", when promoting her poem "The Star of the South" in the *Sydney Morning Herald* in 1842.[1] Her new song was "an offering to the people of New South Wales". She celebrated a newly formed society, populated by "sons and daughters of the land" who were privileged to inhabit "happy homes and altars free" where they found refuge and rest. Admiring Australia's opportunities, Dunlop awarded the "moral bulwarks of a nation to this young country". She thought poetry could enable a people to imagine themselves part of a nation, and urged readers into a form of democratic literary appreciation. Quoting great English poets – including John Milton, John Leyden and Alexander Pope – Dunlop wrote self-deprecatingly that a bush hut in "the untrodden ways" of Wollombi or by the lagoons of Watagan Creek might not inspire the same "precious stores of rule and precedent" in poetry when compared to a metropolitan library. Yet she suggested that her poetic inheritance still bore "the lustre of the original gem". Poetry, politics and a new and progressive settler society: these were issues central to Dunlop's writing and core tenets of her personal and public persona.

Dunlop published regularly in colonial newspapers between 1838 and 1873: we have identified about sixty poems from a range of Australian newspapers and periodicals.[2] In the early 1870s, Dunlop put together "The Vase", a fair copy of nearly seventy poems selected from those she had written in Australia, Ireland and India, both published and unpublished. Her poetry was not always popular: the editor of the *Sydney Morning Herald* had agreed with Dunlop's sentiments in "The Star of the South" but deemed it "bad poetry". It was at times controversial, especially "The Aboriginal Mother" (1838).[3] English poetry of the period was understood as being in a state of abeyance, if not decline, after the great Romantic

---

1 Eliza Hamilton Dunlop, "The Star of the South", *Sydney Morning Herald*, 30 August 1842.
2 See Eliza Hamilton Dunlop's Australian Publications, this volume.
3 Editorial comment, *Sydney Morning Herald*, 30 August 1842.

poets. Colonial Australian writers, readers and critics followed these debates closely and they influenced assessments of local writing too. Recently, literary scholars have reassessed early- to mid-nineteenth-century English poetry, noting several important and related features of the period: the increased number of women writing poetry and their publication in new media forms such as annuals and the popular press; a fresh appreciation of sentimental literary modes as vehicles for expressing political ideas; and the place of poetry in exploring ideas about Britain's nineteenth-century colonies.[4] These important questions about poetry, literary history and culture open up new ways to evaluate Dunlop's writing.

No volume of Dunlop's poetry was published during her lifetime, which contributed to its ephemeral status. Twice it seems Dunlop had planned a book: first, as an eighteen-year-old poet in Ireland in 1814, "Ultoniana", a proposed volume of historical poems about Ulster; and then, in late life, "The Vase", Dunlop's own selected edition of her writing, which only exists in manuscript form. In both instances, circumstances conspired to prevent publication.[5] Without a permanent record in book form, Dunlop's writing fell into obscurity, like that of many other colonial and particularly female poets.

This book is the first to restore the *oeuvre* of Dunlop's writing to Australian literary history, following Elizabeth Webby's identification of Dunlop as a colonial poet of note in the 1980s. It includes a new edited selection of Dunlop's poems, and draws upon specialist contributors to reassess the different forms of her writing and collaboration. It brings Dunlop into view as an independent and intelligent woman who determinedly crafted her life and her public contribution through writing. Her Irish childhood and her family's experience across the British Empire profoundly shaped her perspective. Together with her commitment to writing and reading as ways to engage with both social issues and personal experiences, these elements mark a distinctive literary presence. In her Australian writing, Dunlop imagined a new settler society that valued knowledge about Indigenous cultures and thoughtful responses to the environment, as well as having a deeply felt attachment to an Irish homeland that had undergone a violent and ongoing transformation. Dunlop's writing emerges at an important period in literary history in which we can see intensely local issues, places and people linked to global literary concerns. This introduction begins with an overview of Eliza Hamilton Dunlop's life in colonial Australia with her husband David and their children,

---

4   David Stewart, *The Form of Poetry in the 1820s and 1830s: A Period of Doubt* (Cham: Palgrave-Springer, 2018). See also Jerome J. McGann, *The Poetics of Sensibility: A Revolution in Literary Style* (Oxford: Clarendon / Oxford University Press, 1996); Katherine D. Harris, *Forget Me Not: The Rise of the British Literary Annual, 1823–1835* (Athens, OH: Ohio University Press, 2015); Jason R. Rudy, *Imagined Homelands: British Poetry in the Colonies* (Baltimore, MD: Johns Hopkins, 2017).

5   Evidence of Dunlop's intentions lies in two newspaper notices: "Notice", *Freeman's Journal* (Dublin), 7 October 1814; and "Local News", *Maitland Mercury*, 1 June 1871.

before canvassing the reception of Dunlop's writing during her lifetime and more recently.[6] It concludes by introducing the chapters in this volume.

"To seek a new home in a new country is a trying undertaking"[7]: Writing in the Colony

The year 1838 was a tumultuous one to arrive in New South Wales. The Dunlop family travelled aboard the *Superb*: Eliza and David and their four children (Eliza's daughter from her first marriage, Georgina Law, joined them soon after). Captain John Biscoe had made his name for extensive voyaging in the south, including the circumnavigation of Antarctica, for which he received an award from the Royal Geographical Society, and he would have been an interesting interlocutor for the Dunlop family, who were well-read in exploration literature.[8] The new Governor, Sir George Gipps, had arrived only days before the Dunlops, and one of his first acts was to table the House of Commons' 1837 *Report from the Select Committee on Aborigines (British Settlements)*, which has aptly been described as "the most famous statement on the interests of indigenous peoples whose lands came within the [British] Empire's vast territorial claims".[9] Gipps was about to attempt a radically new and contentious legal framework of protection of and jurisdiction over Aboriginal people. Gipps and the Dunlops arrived in Sydney only weeks after a massacre at Waterloo Creek, a punitive expedition of mounted police led by Major James Nunn to suppress Kamilaroi resistance on the north-west frontier.[10] By mid-year, rumours of the June massacre of about thirty Wirrayaraay and Gamilaroi people at Myall Creek, 200 kilometres east, began to filter through official channels. In December 1838, Dunlop's most famous poem, "The Aboriginal Mother", was published in the *Australian*: inspired by the Myall Creek massacre, it was sympathetic to Indigenous survivors and highly critical of settler violence. In 1838, too, the Molesworth Committee formally recommended that convict transportation should be abolished, a decision with major implications for the economy and society of New South Wales. Reforms to convictism, to relations with Aboriginal people, and to land acquisition characterised the first decade of Eliza and David Dunlop's colonial residence, and they were implicated in all three by dint of their personal connections, political interests and public roles.

---

6   A full biographical account of David Dunlop and Eliza Hamilton Dunlop in Ireland appears in Chapter 1.

7   William Hamilton Maxwell, letter to Eliza Hamilton Dunlop, 4 September 1837, qtd Margaret De Salis, *Two Early Colonials* (Sydney: printed by the author, 1967), 34.

8   Ann Savours, "Biscoe, John (1794–1843)", ed. Douglas Pike, *Australian Dictionary of Biography* (Canberra: National Centre of Biography, Australian National University, 1966), https://adb.anu.edu.au/biography/biscoe-john-1784/text2009.

9   Amanda Nettelbeck, *Indigenous Rights and Colonial Subjecthood: Protection and Reform in the Nineteenth-Century British Empire* (Cambridge: Cambridge University Press, 2019), 12.

10   Roger Milliss, *Waterloo Creek: The Australia Day Massacre of 1838, George Gipps and the British Conquest of New South Wales* (Ringwood, Victoria: McPhee Gribble, 1992).

Dunlop's first published poem in the Australian colonial press – "The Dream" – inaugurated a series of ten "Songs of an Exile" published in the *Australian* between November 1838 and October 1840. Conditions for writing were challenging. Dunlop had four children under sixteen; appropriate housing was difficult to secure and they moved around in Sydney from Castlereagh Street to Surrey Hills; and David's work increasingly took him away from the family. Dunlop's thoughts were often on the country, family and friends she had left behind: "What thoughts within this bosom swell, / What tears an Exile's eyes are filling".[11] The early death of a daughter in Ireland in 1835 weighed heavily upon her, and there is no evidence that Dunlop ever returned to visit Jane Wilson Dunlop's grave. Deaths of extended family members or friends regularly provoked Dunlop's colonial poetry, with a melancholy and elegiac mood prevailing.[12] Yet as the paired poems "The Aboriginal Mother" and "The Irish Mother" show (numbers 4 and 5 respectively in the Exile series), Dunlop's writing joined together sentiment and social issues. So too the diasporic locations of the Dunlops' extended Anglo-Irish family remained linked in her imagination and her poetic memorialisation.

Australian places, words and images became part of Dunlop's poetic repertoire, even though her poetry often focused on northern hemisphere topics and events. By 1839 the family had leased the former government house at Emu Plains, which supplied both an aesthetic location and social standing for the Dunlop household. From there, Dunlop was able to write again: poetry in her Exile series and "The Ford of the Emu Plains", her only known published short story.[13] This story follows a party of bullock drivers travelling down the Nepean River who sing Walter Scott ballads and tell personal stories of emigration via America to Australia, marked by grief for a lost homeland and a son drowned due to a father's pride and prejudice. One key protagonist is a dray owner whose life in Ireland had become untenable because, although sympathetic to the politics of the 1798 rebellion, he had through long years of intimacy "learned to love and revere My Orange land lord, the proud-hearted Hamilton". He eulogises the *Personal Narrative of the Irish Rebellion* by Charles Hamilton Teeling. Teeling's eyewitness account remains a valuable source for what is now described as the forgotten history of the revolutionary political movements of Northern Ireland, led by the United Irishmen who mobilised Presbyterian and Dissenter political activity against the English in Ulster during the 1798 rebellion.[14]

---

11   Eliza Hamilton Dunlop, "Songs of an Exile (No. 1): The Dream", *Australian*, 8 November 1838.

12   For example, "Songs of an Exile: No. 3", *Australian*, 29 November 1838 (see Jason R. Rudy's analysis in this volume); "Rosetta Nathan's Dirge", *Sydney Morning Herald*, 25 April 1843 (see Graeme Skinner's analysis in this volume).

13   Eliza Hamilton Dunlop, "Stories of an Exile: No 1 'The Ford of the Emu Plains'", *Sydney Monitor and Commercial Advertiser*, 29 May 1839; "Stories of an Exile No. 1 'The Ford of the Emu Plains Concluded'", *Sydney Monitor and Commercial Advertiser*, 31 May 1839. This story's numbered series title suggests that more might have been planned, although no evidence has been found of their publication to date.

14   Guy Beiner, "Disremembering 1798? An Archaeology of Social Forgetting and Remembrance in Ulster", *History and Memory* 25, no. 1 (2013): 9–50.

This was an important and personal history that Dunlop returned to on several occasions, including her dual eulogy for her husband and father-in-law in her late poem "The Two Graves" (1865), published in Australia and Ireland.[15] "The Ford of the Emu Plains" also revealed Dunlop's new responses to the Australian landscape. The colonial-era fords drew on Darug people's use of the riverbanks along the Nepean River, and the Dunlops would have crossed the ford between their new home at Emu Plains and Penrith regularly.[16] The narrator revels in a late February respite from hot summer winds, and eulogises the Plains:

> bathed in semi transparent vapour, and looked like a waveless sea, bounded by, and blending with the blue firmament. The high land was covered to its topmost ridge with luxuriant sweet flowering shrubs, the wild apple, and the tall gum-trees, and the road, winding far down in front, was a good and smooth one.

Sydney, too, features as "that rising wonder of the southern hemisphere". Dunlop's only "Australian" story reveals her nostalgia for Ireland and her political sympathies, set in closely observed colonial environments. Its affective tone can mask its social, historical and political concerns, yet this connection between poetic feeling, place and politics was central throughout Dunlop's *oeuvre*.

The Police Magistracy and Colonial Poets

David Dunlop was appointed by Gipps to the position of salaried Police Magistrate at Penrith in June 1838, which proved to be a difficult beginning to the family's life in New South Wales.[17] Magistrates in Australian colonies were loosely modelled on the British system: major landholders were expected to serve in an honorary capacity to maintain their districts.[18] In New South Wales, emancipated convicts could not be magistrates, so the position became a powerful one for the Exclusives who were developing vast pastoralist interests. Their business interests were oriented around acquiring land (by dispossessing Indigenous people) and extracting produce and profit (by utilising assigned convict labour); by the 1830s under Governor Richard Bourke it was obvious that such personal interests were often in conflict with their official roles. Introducing stipendiary magistrates was one proposed solution, for these were paid by the Colonial Office on recommendation of the Governor, often to resolve particular problems in districts,

---

15 See Duncan Wu, this volume.

16 Godden Mackay Logan, *Penrith Lakes Scheme: Archaeological Management Plan Draft Report* (Redfern: Penrith Lakes Development Corporation, 2014). See Appendix A: Nepean River Fords and Associated Lanes.

17 On the Dunlops' life in Ireland and motivation for immigration to Australia, see Anna Johnston, this volume.

18 This overview draws upon Hilary Golder, *High and Responsible Office: A History of the NSW Magistracy* (Sydney: Sydney University Press, 1991).

and could serve short to medium terms. David was appointed to "a new kind of magistracy reinforced by paramilitary police", part of Gipps' extension of the powers of Commissioners of Crown Lands to be both protectors and magistrates.[19] This was a daunting prospect for those with pastoral interests, because it promised to combine Aboriginal protection with the existing magistrate's power to grant and withdraw the licences that gave pastoralists conditional rights to depasture cattle temporarily on Crown land, but not any other benefits of tenure.[20] When the honorary magistrates at Penrith had petitioned for a salaried magistrate, they had a favoured candidate in mind (J.C. Lethbridge, "a gentleman of Tory principles").[21] David was appointed instead.

David was assiduous and principled, but probably naive about colonial politics at this early stage and apt to take offence. He was seen as part of a new Whig governmentality that was strongly resisted by powerful pastoralists, whose tendency to evaluate people and issues on "party" grounds – political ideology and adherence – was noted by many officials and visitors. Even those who at first appeared to the Dunlops as allies – such as the Irish-born Member of the Legislative Council, Sir John Jamison, who helped the Dunlops rent the Old Government House at Emu Plains – would undermine officials if their private interests appeared threatened. Dunlop's seventh and eighth poems in the Exile series were written from Emu Plains. In "Songs of Exile No. 8", the protagonist's lament might mirror David's frustrations in his role in Penrith: "What dreary doom is mine! / Unblest 'mid Austral-wilds to roam / A slave at Mammon's Shrine. / What weary lot – to count each link – / Whose rust is on my soul! / To chase life's phantoms; and to sink – Untimely – at the goal".[22]

David Dunlop's decisions as magistrate at Penrith created discord, not least because of his tendency to speak his mind in court. Charles Tompson brought a case of disobedience by his convict servant John Keane, which escalated into the pages of the *Sydney Herald* as a public appeal to the Governor by Tompson, condemning the police magistrate. (Tompson only later wrote personally to the Governor pursuing his complaint.[23]) Tompson refused Keane's request to attend Sunday Mass because he required his services as a cook: Keane had disobeyed. Although supportive of Keane's religious attendance, Dunlop advised Keane that he disbelieved the convict's accusations against his master about poor treatment

---

19 Lisa Ford, "Protecting the Peace on the Edges of Empire: Commissioners of Crown Lands in New South Wales", in *Protection and Empire: A Global History*, ed. Adam Clulow, Bain Attwood and Lauren Benton (Cambridge: Cambridge University Press, 2017), 183.

20 Ford, "Protecting the Peace on the Edges of Empire", 184, 177.

21 "Vox Populi – Vox De", *Australian*, 26 September 1839.

22 Eliza Hamilton Dunlop, "Songs of an Exile – No. 8", *Australian*, 7 May 1840.

23 Dunlop heard the case against Keane on 17 September 1838. Tompson's letter to the *Sydney Herald* was dated 20 September; his formal letter of complaint to the Governor was dated 29 October 1838, responding to the Colonial Secretary's correspondence of 23 October, following a flurry of vituperative correspondence in the newspapers. Tompson to Gipps, 29 October 1838, in Colonial Secretary, CSO 709, "Police – Penrith", NSW State Archives, 38/11.499.

because every person knew that Dunlop "made no distinction between Master and Servant in administering Justice".[24] Inadvisably, Dunlop allowed both the local priest Father Brady and Tompson to address the court, resulting in rancorous exchanges.[25] The religious overtones of the case made Dunlop uneasy. He noted privately to the Governor, "party and sectarian differences exist even more strongly here than in Ireland", a much gloomier interpretation than Eliza's "happy homes and altars free".[26] Tompson declared in the *Sydney Herald* that Dunlop's "belaud[ing] of his own impartiality ... was highly calculated to produce dissatisfaction and insubordination in the men, arising from imaginary grievances ... [I]t is democratical [sic] and levelling to the last degree".[27] Gipps supported Dunlop in the complaint, but advised him that "it would be better to leave the parties and the public to draw a conclusion ... [about your impartiality] from your decisions, and way of disposing of cases brought before you, than to impress it upon them, by any declaration of your own".[28] Gipps' counsel was wise, but both David and Eliza Dunlop were experienced in public debate given their training in Northern Irish politics and they used the newspapers to defend themselves when pushed. The settlers too manipulated the press as a vehicle to protect and promote their own interests.[29] Tompson's vigorous attack on David Dunlop in the *Sydney Herald* was not accidental: the paper promoted settler interests, including campaigning vociferously against the prosecution of men for the Myall Creek massacre, and in this period explicitly urged settlers to commit violence against Indigenous people for their perceived crimes and misdemeanours.[30] Tompson was an experienced colonial bureaucrat: he had been a clerk in the Colonial Secretary's office until 1836. He was also an accomplished poet, having published *Wild Notes, from the Lyre of a Native Minstrel* (1826), the first book of poetry published by a native born Australian.[31] When solicited by Dunlop a year later for a character testimony, Tompson revealed publicly that his complaints had been encouraged

---

24 Dunlop to Gipps, 27 September 1838, in Colonial Secretary, CSO 709, "Police – Penrith", NSW State Archives.

25 Tompson condemned the Catholic Church's "hold" over the "illiterate part of their flock, and the power with which they have been known to wield it": he noted too that the vast majority of agricultural labourers in the region (and many in the public courtroom that day) were Catholic. Charles Tompson, "To His Excellency Sir George Gipps, Governor-in-Chief of New South Wales", *Sydney Herald*, 26 September 1838.

26 Dunlop to Gipps, 27 September 1838, CSO 709.

27 Tompson, "To His Excellency Sir George Gipps".

28 Gipps to Dunlop, Colonial Secretary, CSO 709, "Police – Penrith", 4/2420.3, NSW State Archives.

29 See Duncan Wu, "'A Vehicle of Private Malice': Eliza Hamilton Dunlop and the *Sydney Herald*", *Review of English Studies*, 65(272), new series, (2014): 888–903.

30 See Rebecca Wood, "Frontier Violence and the Bush Legend: The *Sydney Herald*'s Response to the Myall Creek Massacre Trials and the Creation of Colonial Identity", *History Australia*, 6 (2009): 67.1–67.19.

31 Charles Tompson, *Wild Notes, from the Lyre of a Native Minstrel*, ed. G.A. Wilkes and G.A. Turnbull (1826; Sydney: Sydney University Press, 1973).

by "a Whig magistrate": "your QUONDAM thick-and-thin supporter", inspired by "private pique".[32] That was Jamison, whose colonial career was marked by bitter factional disputes that could suddenly reverse: his warm personal letters to the Dunlop family co-exist with this clandestine political campaign against Dunlop.[33] Jamison was primed to respond with suspicion to magisterial reform, having been part of the powerful Parramatta Bench with John Macarthur, responsible for hounding Governor Sir Thomas Brisbane from office for perceived prejudice.[34] Yet so much resentment had been raised, as shown in many letters to the newspapers, that by late 1839 Gipps made a new appointment of David as inaugural Police Magistrate at Wollombi.

Wollombi and Mulla Villa: "The Mulla's emerald banks, in sunny southern clime"[35]

Wollombi, a small township in the Upper Hunter River Valley, was a site of colonial contact between a number of increasingly dispossessed Aboriginal communities (Darkinyung, Awabakal and Wonnarua) and the rough edges of colonial expansion. Initially, conditions were so improvisational that David moved there alone, living in a bark hut that also served as his courtroom. It is likely this second posting was strategic to Gipps' purposes of implementing protection policies, for David undertook the Aboriginal aspects of his responsibilities with seriousness from the start. Gipps' removal of David from Penrith has been interpreted as evidence of David's intractability or indicative of the power of the established magistracy.[36] There is likely some truth in both, but Wollombi was neither a sinecure nor an apolitical and distant placement. Landholders in Wollombi protected and perhaps sheltered John Fleming, the elite pastoralist implicated in the Myall Creek massacre who escaped justice.[37] From Penrith in September 1838, David had already provided some local knowledge when Gipps assiduously (but unsuccessfully) pursued Fleming's whereabouts.[38] The Dunlops' sympathies with Indigenous affairs

---

32 "Vox Populi – Vox Dei", *Australian*, 26 September 1839.

33 G.P. Walsh, "Jamison, Sir John (1776–1844)", *Australian Dictionary of Biography*, National Centre of Biography, Australian National University, https://adb.anu.edu.au/biography/jamison-sir-john-2268/text2907. Letters from Jamison relating to family matters and social occasions in November 1838 reside in Milson Family Papers, Further Papers 1826–1960, Mitchell Library, State Library of New South Wales, MLMSS 9409.

34 Golder, 31–32.

35 Eliza Hamilton Dunlop, "The Mulla, or Wollombi Creek, New South Wales" (1849), "The Vase". See Elizabeth Webby this volume.

36 Even De Salis is critical, drawing a corollary between David and Captain Faunce, who had been an unpopular Police Magistrate at Brisbane Waters in the late 1830s (58).

37 Patsy Withycombe, "The Twelfth Man: John Henry Fleming and the Myall Creek Massacre", in *Remembering the Myall Creek Massacre*, ed. Jane Lydon and Lyndall Ryan (Sydney: UNSW Press, 2018), 38–51.

38 Dunlop to Gipps, 12 September 1838, in Colonial Secretary, CSO 709, "Police – Penrith", NSW State Archives, 38/9591.

were evident, and their posting to Wollombi would not have been welcomed by those who defended the massacre perpetrators. Even before David arrived to take up his post, another newspaper campaign critical of him began, repeating the pattern from Penrith. If anything, the Hunter Valley was a harder posting because it was an amateur magistracy in a convict community, as Hilary Golder describes it, made up of "newly-arrived entrepreneurs anxious for quick returns on the capital they had imported": dependent on harsh physical punishments to control convicts and with a reputation for violent clearance of Indigenous communities.[39] Much of David's daily work involved managing convicts in the region, and resolving tensions between masters and their assigned workers. Bushrangers also plundered the region regularly. Factional troubles continued throughout David's posting, which lasted until 1846, when another set of political campaigns saw him removed from office. Gipps by then was keen on economising. The Legislative Council had successfully decimated policing budgets, priming the return of the honorary magistrates, as advocated by Henry Dangar, owner of the Myall Creek Station, who deplored the "secret correspondence" that police magistrates had with Sydney.[40] Given the association between Eliza Hamilton Dunlop's overt criticism of "supers and stockmen" on Dangar's station in her early poem "The Aboriginal Mother", the proximity of many landholders and agricultural workers who had personal experience of violent conflict between settlers and Indigenous people in the region and the perception of powerful pastoralists that David opposed their interests, the Police Magistracy at Wollombi was inevitably challenging.

Yet the township became the Dunlop family home for forty years.[41] By 1841, the substantial sandstone house Mulla Villa had been built on the Great North Road to provide for the family, for prisoners in cells beneath the house, and for the usual agricultural requirements of a settler family. Rumour has it that Eliza Hamilton Dunlop sheltered Aboriginal women from violence by secreting them in the space between the upper floorboards and the stone cellar.[42] She certainly spent time with Aboriginal people in the region, learning some of their language and customs.[43] The house's name reflected Irish and poetic references.[44] It was set by Wollombi Creek, and the 100-acre holding was fertile, marked by large sandstone rocks and escarpments characteristic of the area; it was also spiritually significant country

---

39 Golder 35.

40 Golder 62.

41 In David's will, the house was for Eliza's usage until her death, when it would be sold and the proceeds divided equally between his son and his daughters' eldest children. "Will and Probate of David Dunlop", State Archives Office NSW, Wills and Probates, 9 May 1859, MSS. 5959. The house was sold in 1881: "Classified Advertising", *Maitland Mercury and Hunter River General Advertiser*, 23 August 1881.

42 The house is privately owned, though recent owners have utilised its historic associations for various small business ventures, including historical tours in which local knowledge is disseminated. See https://www.mullavilla.com.au/.

43 See Anna Johnston and Jim Wafer this volume.

44 See Wafer this volume.

for Indigenous groups. For Dunlop, it was an evocative environment. Poems such as "The Mulla, or Wollombi Creek, New South Wales" (1849) linked her love of landscapes in Ireland and Australia. In some ways, Dunlop considered herself to be isolated, such as when she introduced herself in a letter to the composer Isaac Nathan in 1841: "I who am in the forest far from human habitation of civilized beings".[45] Certainly at Wollombi she was not surrounded by a cultural milieu, although fellow poets such as Tompson had resided at Penrith, and Charles Harpur lived and wrote during the 1840s and 50s at nearby Singleton and Jerry's Plains. John Walker Fulton – editor of the short-lived *Blossom* magazine (1828) and advocate for arts in the Colony – had publicly supported David in his Penrith troubles.[46] While there was a (predominantly male) Hunter Valley literary circle there is little evidence that Eliza engaged with them, although they certainly knew about her work.

Mulla Villa was the site from which Dunlop wrote and published regularly, well into her seventies: poetry, letters to editors about the reception of her poetry, and on local issues. Dunlop's musical collaborations with Nathan – notable and occasionally controversial in the 1840s – were regularly featured in Sydney newspapers, with timely ripostes from Wollombi when she felt a correction or self-defence was warranted.[47] Like many female poets, Dunlop balanced writing with family responsibilities, including the education and marriages of her son and daughters. She was also highly involved in David's career. Anonymous newspaper correspondence suggests that Eliza had a hand in shaping public opinion to support David's initiatives. For example, David relentlessly petitioned the Governor for blankets and clothing rations for the Aboriginal community at Wollombi.[48] Gipps was sceptical of the annual blanket distribution, and withheld supply on the grounds that he wanted to encourage Aboriginal involvement in the colonial economy. David was excoriating about this decision even though he too wanted to employ Indigenous men for police work, declaring to an 1845 inquiry that blankets functioned "as a recognised tie between the ruler and the ruled". They provided "no sufficient recompense" for the loss of Aboriginal land, trees and possums, but

---

45 De Salis, *Two Early Colonials*, 101.

46 Fulton published at least three letters in the *Commercial Journal and Advertiser* in 1838–39 supporting David Dunlop's magistracy at Penrith, drawing fire from detractors as a consequence. On the *Blossom*, see Elizabeth Webby, "Australia", in *Periodicals of Queen Victoria's Empire, an Exploration*, ed. Rosemary VanArsdel and J. Don Vann (Toronto: University of Toronto Press, 1996), 28–29.

47 See Graeme Skinner this volume.

48 This began at least by March 1841, when he requested "50 blankets, 6 shirts 6 pair of trousers" as part of his plan to engage the Aboriginal community with local police work. David Dunlop, "Letter to NSW Colonial Secretary" (1841), in Stan Parkes Papers, State Library of New South Wales, MLMSS 8823. On David Dunlop's understanding of blanket economies, see Anna Johnston, "Mrs Milson's Wordlist: Eliza Hamilton Dunlop and the Intimacy of Linguistic Work", in *Intimacies of Violence in the Settler Colony: Economies of Dispossession around the Pacific Rim*, ed. Penelope Edmonds and Amanda Nettelbeck (Switzerland: Palgrave Macmillan-Springer, 2018), 225–47.

Aboriginal people "accepted [them] from want".[49] In 1846, a correspondent from Wollombi – likely Eliza – reported on sustained cold and frost in the valley: "The sufferings of the helpless and wretched aborigines are … extreme, deprived during the most inclement season, even of their former scanty covering – the 'Government blankets,' – their wretchedness is enhanced ten-fold by the withdrawment of that penurious loan".[50]

Dunlop's involvement in public affairs exposed her to ridicule. When David once again clashed with pastoral interests, she became a target. The *Australasian Chronicle* published a scurrilous letter inferring that David was ruled by his wife. An anonymous correspondent claimed that while David was responding to a plan for secular, state-based education, "Mrs Dunlop mounted the bench, interrupted Mr. Dunlop, and said that for her part she would have 'the bible, the whole bible, and nothing but the bible'", having personally compared the Protestant and Douay versions and found no differences.[51] As intriguing as this vision of Dunlop is, it can only be satirical. The alleged proponent of secular education in this vignette was Richard Alexander Wiseman, son of Solomon Wiseman, the dominant ex- convict landholder of the Hawkesbury. Richard Wiseman's advocacy for education was ironic given that Justice Roger Therry had described his father as "sadly deficient" in literary attainments and dismissive of education: a man who "took unmerciful liberties with the English language and English history".[52] Instituting a national system of education had been controversial and resisted by both Catholic and Anglican churches during this period. Like Governor Sir Richard Bourke, who had first attempted to introduce a new education bill, the Dunlops were liberal and pro-Catholic emancipation. David Dunlop had been involved in the introduction of the Irish national schools system which, in 1831, had enabled state funding of schools that both Protestant and Catholic children could attend while also being instructed by different religious personnel.[53] Other slanderous representations of

---

49   NSW Parliament Legislative Council, *Report from the Select Committee on the Condition of the Aborigines, with Appendix, Minutes of Evidence and Replies to a Circular Letter* (Sydney: Government Printing Office, 1845).

50   "The Wollombi", *Sydney Morning Herald*, 17 July 1846. This letter was reprinted in the *Maitland Mercury*, 22 July 1846.

51   "Wollombi", *Australasian Chronicle*, 22 March 1842. The debate about King James and Douay editions split Protestants and Catholics.

52   Roger Therry, *Reminiscences of Thirty Years' Residence in New South Wales and Victoria*, 2nd ed. (London: Low, 1863), 122. Therry also noted that Solomon Wiseman confused Catholics with Romans, and advised Bishop Polding that the reason for sectarian tension was that the English Protestants had never forgiven Julius Caesar for invading ancient Briton (123). Wiseman remains well known for the ferry service he ran on the Hawkesbury and his corrupt but highly successful business interests: he was the model for the protagonist of Kate Grenville's novel *The Secret River* (2005), based on her own family history.

53   Kelvin Grose, "1847: The Educational Compromise of the Lord Bishop of Australia", *Journal of Religious History* 1, no. 4 (1961): 233–48; Geoffrey Sherington and Craig Campbell, "Middle-Class Formations and the Emergence of National Schooling: A Historiographical Review of the Australian Debate", in *Transformations in Schooling: Historical and Comparative Perspectives*, ed. Kim Tolley (New York: Palgrave Macmillan US, 2007), 15–39.

Eliza continued to be circulated, with derisory comments about her Irish poetry made as a postscript to other politicised criticism of David's duties as Police Magistrate.[54] Reflecting the snobbery inherent in the honorary magistracy, David was sneered at as a "stationer" (he had been a book binder);[55] on other occasions, the Dunlops were criticised as "would-be aristocracy". In 1846, David sued Jonas Morris Townshend for libel over a petition published in *Bell's Life in Sydney and Sporting Reviewer* that contributed to his removal from office. His case was unsuccessful, but elsewhere the presiding Judge Windeyer was scathing about the publications of Thomas Revel Johnson (*Bell's Life* and *The Satirist*) and cited their pernicious effect as part of his reasons for drafting Australia's distinctive *Libel Act* (1847).[56] While David described himself as "unfeignedly averse" to resorting to the media for personal or individual concerns, the colonial press was vociferous and Dunlop certainly asserted herself through that vehicle.[57] Yet the role of women in the colonial public sphere was controversial and, despite Dunlop's active engagement with criticism, the reception she received at times must have rankled.

Mulla Villa was a busy family establishment and the Dunlop children too were involved in the town. The eldest son David Henry was postmaster in the newly established Wollombi Post Office and later Clerk of Petty Sessions in various regions in the Hunter Valley. Augusta was sent to school in Liverpool, although this proved unsuccessful due to her independent temperament, so by 1844 she returned to Wollombi and took over the postmistress role. Dunlop clearly adored her youngest child Rachel Rhoda. She wrote a very fond poem describing her as "my blithsome Irish girl". From her description it is clear that Rachel resembled her mother: "Redundance rich of chestnut hair / Shading a forehead high and fair".[58] By the 1850s, the Dunlop children began marrying into notable settler families, and clearly were seen as good matches. David Henry married Thalia Raine, descendant of Thomas Raine, ship's captain and entrepreneurial merchant in early Sydney. Augusta also married into the Raine family, although the early death of her husband Edmund required her to run the family mill and educate her only surviving son, Thomas, who later established the Raine and Horne real estate business. Wilhemina married Richard Kirk, who with his family had various mercantile interests that spanned the early colonies. Rachel married David Ambrose Milson (the Milson family had been major landholders in early colonial Sydney, then developed substantive business interests): they lived nearby on Byora

---

54 "Wollombi", *Bell's Life in Sydney and Sporting Reviewer*, 17 January 1846.

55 See Johnston this volume.

56 See "Dunlop v J.M. Townshend", *Bell's Life in Sydney and Sporting Reviewer*, 25 July 1846; Paul Mitchell, "The Foundations of Australian Defamation Law", *Sydney Law Review* 28, no. 3 (2006); on Johnson, see 492–93, and *Colonial Australian Narrative Journalism*, Centre for Media History, Macquarie University, https://www.auslitjourn.info/writers/q-z/revel-johnson-thomas/.

57 David Dunlop, "Original Correspondence to Charles Cowper", *Sydney Morning Herald*, 13 June 1848.

58 Eliza Hamilton Dunlop, "A Portrait. Rachel Rhoda", in "The Vase", State Library of New South Wales, B1541.

Station, which David managed for his father. Rachel cared for her mother as she aged, and was the preserver of her mother's papers, hence Dunlop's archives mostly reside within the Milson family papers in the Mitchell Library.[59] Grandchildren proliferated, and the Dunlops' children had become sufficiently financially secure for David Dunlop's will to disperse money directly to his grandchildren for their education. Eliza's first daughter Georgina Law did not marry, but worked as a governess for the Hassall family, at Denbigh Estate at Cobbitty, from the 1840s. She was clearly bright like her mother, and benefited from the association with the Reverend Thomas Hassall, a notable clergyman and educator. By the early 1860s, Georgina was headmistress of Sydney's St Catherine's Church of England School, the first Anglican girls' school in the colonies, established for clergymen's daughters. During all this public service and family life, Eliza and David resided in Wollombi until David's unexpectedly early death in 1863, and Eliza's demise in 1880. Both are buried in the Wollombi Church of England graveyard that they had advocated for from the 1840s.[60]

Eliza Hamilton Dunlop's Poetry: Reception and Scholarship

During her lifetime and for a century after her death, little attention was paid to the poetry of Eliza Hamilton Dunlop. Her now best-known poem, "The Aboriginal Mother", does not seem to have attracted much attention when first published in the *Australian* newspaper in 1838.[61] Three years later, after it had been set to music by the composer Isaac Nathan, it was reprinted in a slightly revised version in a number of Sydney papers as well as in Melbourne's *Port Phillip Advertiser*. This was part of the advertising for a concert Nathan held on 27 October 1841 in which "The Aboriginal Mother" was performed by his daughter Rosetta. Several papers later published reviews of the concert, most of which made favourable mention of the song and its reception by the audience. The *Colonial Observer*, for example, noted that "This beautiful piece, the subject and the language of which are so rich in poetic feeling, was sung by the youngest Miss Nathan with great simplicity and feeling, and called down the plaudits of the assembly".[62] The *Sydney Herald*, however, which in 1838 had condemned the death sentences imposed on some of the men responsible for the Myall Creek murders, ridiculed Dunlop's sympathetic portrayal of the grief-stricken mother:

---

59   See Johnston this volume.
60   De Salis speculated that the following article was penned by Eliza Dunlop, and she is likely correct – noting that "even in the deep wilderness of the Wollombi", Bishop Polding had visited (on David's instigation) and promised a minister and building for the congregation. "Wollombi", *Australian*, 20 October 1840, 2. See Margaret De Salis, "Notebook", in Margaret De Salis – Papers, 1965–1980, Mitchell Library, State Library of New South Wales, ML MSS 5745/1/3.
61   Eliza Hamilton Dunlop, "The Aboriginal Mother", *Australian*, 13 December 1838.
62   *Colonial Observer*, 4 November 1841.

The words are pathetic, and display much poetic feeling, but they ascribe to the aboriginal woman words that might have been used by a North American Indian, but which our very slight acquaintance with the natives of this colony would enable any one to say never issued from the mouth of the woman who escaped from the New England massacre for which, we may remark, seven men were executed in Sydney. The lines will no doubt be copied in England where they are almost sure to be popular.[63]

Eliza Hamilton Dunlop replied to this criticism in a letter to the editor of the *Herald*, confirming that the poem had indeed been written "in the hope of awaking the sympathies of the English nation for a people whom it is averred, are rendered desperate and revengeful by continued acts of outrage".[64] She concluded with a strong condemnation of the attitude displayed by the *Herald* and its correspondents: "the author of the Aboriginal Mother did hope, that, even in Australia, the time was past, when the public press would lend its countenance to debase the native character, or support an attempt to shade with ridicule, ties stronger than death, which bind the heart of woman, be she Christian or savage".[65]

As Duncan Wu noted in an essay on Dunlop's interactions with contemporary newspapers, it was "most uncommon, up to this period, for a female author to bite back".[66] The *Herald*'s animosity towards Dunlop's poetry continued for several months and, he argued, could be linked to its earlier attacks on her husband in his role as Police Magistrate at Penrith. When Isaac Nathan published his setting of "The Aboriginal Mother" in 1842, the *Herald* praised the music but regretted that "the words are not more worthy of the music".[67] It returned to the attack later in the year when Nathan published another setting of one of Dunlop's poems, "The Eagle Chief", with a long critique of the poem published on 18 April 1842, which concluded:

We should not have taken the trouble to show the folly of this second attempt of Mrs. Dunlop's to make the blacks appear a different race of people from what they really are, were it to be circulated in this Colony only, but Mr. Nathan's music is likely to make it known in England, and therefore we thought it a duty to shew the real character of the verse. Mrs. Dunlop appears to have a poetic turn of mind, and we should be glad to see her attempting some subject unconnected with the blacks.

But when Dunlop did so, in the patriotic song "The Star of the South", the *Herald* continued its attack, making the following patronising comments:

---

63   "The Aboriginal Mother", *Sydney Herald*, 15 October 1841.
64   Eliza Hamilton Dunlop, "The Aboriginal Mother", *Sydney Herald*, 29 November 1841.
65   Dunlop, "The Aboriginal Mother".
66   Wu, "A Vehicle of Private Malice", 11.
67   "Domestic Intelligence", *Sydney Herald*, 22 January 1842.

we have nought but delight, as far as the composer is concerned. We wish, for gallantry sake, that we could speak of the poetry in the same terms, but we cannot, even in our most allegorical mood, imagine what the "Star of the South" has to do with either "Soft flowing tresses", or "Proud eagle glances." It is not polite of us, but we do wish that the new "National Melody" had been set to better words.[68]

These comments provoked another letter to the editor from Dunlop, complaining that the newspaper had criticised her poem without printing it to allow readers to make up their own minds: "To have given that poetry to your readers unslurred by prejudicial remark, would have been no more than justice to a pen, not a paid one, but proud of contributing its quota to the original literature of the colony".[69] Wu has noted that Dunlop's response deterred the *Herald* "from persecuting her again. Reviewing 'The Aboriginal Father' in January 1843, it focused exclusively on the music, giving her no cause for comment".[70] Just over a year later, however, it published what was clearly a parody of "The Aboriginal Mother" entitled "Song of the Aborigines" by one S.P.H., otherwise the playwright and minor versifier Samuel Prout Hill.[71] This repeated the extremely negative views of Indigenous Australians that had featured in the paper's earlier attacks on Dunlop's poems.

Although Eliza Hamilton Dunlop continued to contribute poems to newspapers in Sydney – even on occasion to the *Sydney Morning Herald* – these later works do not seem to have attracted much notice, unlike her collaborations with Nathan. In the third of a series of lectures on "Modern Poetry" given at the Sydney School of Arts in June 1846, the Reverend R.K. Ewing mentioned the work of seventeen local poets. "Mrs Dunlop" was the only woman included among them according to a report in the *Spectator*.[72] A long article in the *Band of Hope Journal* for June 1858, entitled "Aborigines of Australia. The Muses – Poetry", quoted Dunlop's transcription and translation of "Native Poetry", originally published in the *Sydney Morning Herald* ten years earlier.[73] Its author, the Reverend Lancelot Threlkeld, added further information about the Aboriginal songman responsible for the original song. Jim Wafer explores all of this in his 2017 essay, "Ghost-writing for Wulatji: Incubation and Re-Dreaming as Song Revitalization Practices".[74]

---

68 *Sydney Morning Herald*, 9 August 1842. Note that the *Sydney Herald* was renamed in August 1842 by its new owner John Fairfax.

69 Dunlop, "The Star of the South", *Sydney Morning Herald*, 30 August 1842.

70 Wu, "A Vehicle of Private Malice", 12–13.

71 *Sydney Morning Herald*, 23 April 1844.

72 *Spectator* (Sydney), 4 July 1846.

73 Eliza Hamilton Dunlop, "Native Poetry: Nung-Ngnun", *Sydney Morning Herald*, 11 October 1848; Lancelot Threlkeld, "Aborigines of Australia. The Muses – Poetry", *Band of Hope Journal and Australian Home Companion*, 5 June 1858, 179–81.

74 Jim Wafer, "Ghost-Writing for Wulatji: Incubation and Re-Dreaming as Song Revitalisation Practices", in *Recirculating Songs: Revitalising the Singing Practices of Indigenous Australia*, ed. Jim Wafer and Myfany Turpin (Canberra: Asia-Pacific Linguistics, Australian National University, 2017), 193–256.

Many years later in 1908, Dunlop's "Native Poetry" was again discussed in an anonymous article in Sydney's *Evening News*, headed "The Australian Aborigines. A Conquered Race. Rude Works of Art and Superstitions".[75] Before this, a certain J.C. Laycock had had the temerity to publish the 1841 version of "The Aboriginal Mother" under his own name in the *Clarence and Richmond Examiner* in 1891.[76] Leo Butler, writing on Isaac Nathan as "Australia's First Musician" in the *Newcastle Morning Herald* in 1951, at least knew that "The Aboriginal Father" had been "versified from the original words by Mrs EK Dunlop", even though he did not get her initials quite right.[77] The link with Nathan is also mentioned in "One of the Old Brigade", about the death of one of Eliza Hamilton Dunlop's grandchildren, R Newby Kirk, which appeared in the *Age* in 1936: "Mrs Dunlop was a cultured woman and a poet and anthropologist".[78] In 1967, one of her great-granddaughters, Margaret De Salis, published a joint biography of Eliza and David Dunlop under the title *Two Early Colonials*.[79] Interestingly, it was Eliza rather than David who was chosen to appear in the first volume of the *Australian Dictionary of Biography*, published in 1966, and her biographical entry was written by Niel Gunson, one of Australia's foremost missionary historians, who brought an appreciation of Eliza's linguistic and ethnographic contributions.[80]

Since the 1980s, increasing attention has been paid to Eliza Hamilton Dunlop's work, mainly in relation to her "The Aboriginal Mother". Elizabeth Webby republished this poem in 1980 in an article in *Southerly* that discussed early colonial poetry about Indigenous Australians and it was later included in a small selection of Dunlop's poems she compiled for Mulini Press in 1981.[81] In 1988, Webby published a short discussion of poems by Dunlop and by three other colonial Australian women entitled "'Born to Blush Unseen': Some Nineteenth-Century Women Poets".[82]

During the 1990s, "The Aboriginal Mother" appeared in a section on "Early Newspaper Poetry", in *The Penguin Book of Australian Ballads*, edited by Philip Butterss and Elizabeth Webby in 1993.[83] In 1995, Susan Lever also included "The Aboriginal Mother" in her *Oxford Book of Australian Women's Verse*.[84] In the

---

75 *Evening News*, 11 February 1908.
76 *Clarence and Richmond Examiner*, 14 February 1891.
77 *Newcastle Morning Herald*, 10 March 1951.
78 *The Age*, 25 August 1936.
79 De Salis, *Two Early Colonials*.
80 Niel Gunson, "Dunlop, Eliza Hamilton (1796–1880)", in *Australian Dictionary of Biography* (Canberra: National Centre of Biography, Australian National University, 1966).
81 Elizabeth Webby, "The Aboriginal in Early Australian Literature", *Southerly* 40, no. 1 (1980): 45–63; *The Aboriginal Mother and Other Poems* (Canberra: Mulini Press, 1981).
82 Elizabeth Webby, "'Born to Blush Unseen': Some Nineteenth-Century Women Poets", in *A Bright and Fiery Troop: Australian Women Writers of the Nineteenth Century*, ed. Debra Adelaide (Melbourne: Penguin, 1988), 41–52.
83 Philip Butterss and Elizabeth Webby, eds., *The Penguin Book of Australian Ballads* (Melbourne: Penguin, 1993).
84 Susan Lever, ed., *The Oxford Book of Australian Women's Verse* (Melbourne: Oxford University Press, 1995), 2–4.

twenty-five years since then it has appeared in seven further anthologies, most of them major historical surveys of Australian poetry, so it could be said to have now achieved recognition as a classic. In 2014, "The Aboriginal Mother" reached an even wider audience when included in a Norton anthology, *Poetry of Witness: The Tradition in English 1500–2001*, edited by Carolyn Forché and Duncan Wu from Georgetown University.[85]

Between 2004 and 2010, John O'Leary, who had completed a PhD on nineteenth-century European writing about Māori at Victoria University of Wellington in 2001, published four essays in Australian and postcolonial journals outlining his further research into nineteenth-century settler poetry about Indigenous peoples.[86] These were followed by a monograph, *Savage Songs and Wild Romances: Settler Poetry and the Indigene, 1830–1880* (2011).[87] Eliza Hamilton Dunlop was one of the poets O'Leary included since, as well as "The Aboriginal Mother", she wrote other poems dealing with Indigenous topics and transcribed Aboriginal songs, with English translations. O'Leary discussed Dunlop's Aboriginal poems in relation to the literary traditions of expressive women's poetry and Romantic primitivism, as well as the historical context of their production.

A few years earlier, Ann Vickery had published an essay entitled "A 'Lonely Crossing': Approaching Nineteenth-Century Australian Women's Poetry".[88] She included a brief discussion of Eliza Hamilton Dunlop, also focusing just on her poems on Aboriginal subjects, while examining the reasons why nineteenth-century women poets had received so little attention in Australian literary history. As she noted: "Even feminist critics of the late twentieth century directed their energies to recovering nineteenth-century novelists, finding in that genre a more accessible form and – as a more acceptable genre for women's writing – the results of a potentially greater freedom for expression".[89] Indeed, even when feminist critics turned their attention to earlier poetry by women, they found very little that they liked. This is well demonstrated by the contents of the first historically based anthology, *The Penguin Book of Australian Women's Poetry*, edited by poets Susan Hampton and Kate Llewellyn, which appeared in 1981.[90] It begins

---

85   Carolyn Forché and Duncan Wu, eds., *Poetry of Witness: The Tradition in English, 1500–2001* (New York: W. W. Norton, 2014).

86   John O'Leary, "Giving the Indigenous a Voice: Further Thoughts on the Poetry of Eliza Hamilton Dunlop", *Journal of Australian Studies* 28, no. 82 (2004): 85–93; "'The Life, the Loves, of That Dark Race': The Ethnographic Verse of Mid-Nineteenth-Century Australia", *Australian Literary Studies* 23, no. 1 (2007): 3–17; "Speaking the Suffering Indigene: 'Native' Songs and Laments", *Kunapipi* 31, no. 1 (2009): 47–60; "'Unlocking the Fountains of the Heart': Settler Verse and the Politics of Sympathy", *Postcolonial Studies* 13, no. 1 (2010): 55–70.

87   *Savage Songs and Wild Romances: Settler Poetry and the Indigene, 1830–1880* (Amsterdam: Rodopi, 2011).

88   Ann Vickery, "'A Lonely Crossing': Approaching Nineteenth-Century Australian Women's Poetry", *Victorian Poetry* 40, no. 1 (2002): 33–53.

89   Vickery, "A Lonely Crossing", 33–34.

90   Susan Hampton and Kate Llewellyn, eds., *The Penguin Book of Australian Women's Poetry* (Melbourne, Penguin, 1981).

with two transcriptions of Aboriginal songs, made by a woman in the twentieth century, and one ballad about a woman convict, which would most likely have been written in England by a man. The earliest colonial poet included is Ada Cambridge from near the end of the nineteenth century. The editors' choices were clearly influenced by a desire to appeal to the interests and concerns of a 1980s readership. As Anne Jamison noted in a recent essay, "Women's Literary History in Ireland: Digitizing *The Field Day Anthology of Irish Writing*", feminist critics have established "a tradition of ideological retrieval which favours explicitly subversive and transgressive writing and which excludes women writers and texts that do not sanction conventional, and often contemporary, feminist thinking".[91] This can lead to a distorted account of what women were actually writing at a particular time.

An additional distortion results from the favouring of poems on local subjects and themes, a natural enough bias when editors are putting together a national anthology. Hampton and Llewellyn were not alone in choosing to present Ada Cambridge as the first Australian woman poet. Two anthologies published over a century apart did the same: *The Golden Treasury of Australian Verse*, edited by Bertram Stevens in 1909, and *Australian Poetry Since 1788*, edited by Geoffrey Lehmann and Robert Gray in 2011.[92] While Cambridge's poetry is not usually about specifically Australian topics, there is a clear bias towards bush themes in the case of other nineteenth-century women poets who have been regularly anthologised, such as Mary Hannay Foott. As Webby noted in her essay in *A Bright and Fiery Troop*, Foott's "Where the Pelican Builds" was, apart from Caroline Carleton's patriotic "Song of Australia", "the only poem by a woman to receive wide recognition in nineteenth-century Australia".[93] "Where the Pelican Builds" was also chosen as the title poem for Foott's first collection although only one other poem in it deals with life in the bush.[94] The others cover a range of themes, including the biblical and memorial poems on great men such as Dickens, W.C. Wentworth and Napoleon III.

It is not surprising then that, with respect to the work of Eliza Hamilton Dunlop, most emphasis has been given to her poetry on Aboriginal subjects, especially as this coincides with postcolonial as well as nationalist critical interests. Many more of Dunlop's poems deal with her love of Ireland, and her feelings of exile from her native land, as well as with other themes. A chapter on Dunlop was included in Katie Hansord's 2012 doctoral thesis, supervised by Ann Vickery, which examined the work of five colonial Australian women poets.[95] Both this

---

91 Anne Jamison, "Women's Literary History in Ireland: Digitizing *The Field Day Anthology of Irish Writing*", *Women's History Review*, 26, no. 5 (2017): 758.

92 Bertram Stevens, ed., *The Golden Treasury of Australian Verse* (Sydney: Angus & Robertson, 1909); Geoffrey Lehmann and Robert Gray, eds., *Australian Poetry Since 1788* (Sydney: UNSW Press, 2011).

93 Webby, "'Born to Blush Unseen'", 51.

94 Mary Hannay Foott, *Where the Pelican Builds and Other Poems* (Brisbane: Gordon and Gotch, 1885).

95 Katie Hansord, "'Spirit-music' Unbound: Romanticism and Print Politics in Australian Women's Poetry, 1830–1905" (PhD diss., Deakin University, 2012).

and an essay on Dunlop that Hansord published earlier focus mainly on "The Aboriginal Mother" in the context of nineteenth-century women poets' support for the anti- slavery movement and interest in the plight of racial others.[96] But Hansord also draws attention to Dunlop's nationalism, as seen in her poems on both Irish and Australian topics. Graeme Skinner has developed an ongoing interest in Dunlop's poetry, initially in relation to her collaboration with Isaac Nathan on his "Australian Melodies", part of the research for his 2011 PhD thesis entitled "Toward a General History of Australian Musical Composition: First National Music 1788–c.1860".[97]

Readings of Dunlop's poems in relation to Indigenous issues continue to be important. This volume reprints the first published Indigenous analysis of "The Aboriginal Mother", Peter Minter's "Settlement Defiled: Ventriloquy, Pollution and Nature in Eliza Hamilton Dunlop's 'The Aboriginal Mother'".[98] Dunlop's work is also discussed in *Imagined Homelands: British Poetry in the Colonies* (2017), in which Jason Rudy argues convincingly for the contribution that colonial poetics made to the global Romantic movement.[99] Questions of memory and memorialisation across diverse cultural forms are raised in Anna Johnston's "'The Aboriginal Mother': Poetry and Politics" as part of the 150-year memorial history of the Myall Creek massacre, edited by Jane Lydon and Lyndall Ryan.[100] She explores Dunlop's collection of Indigenous languages in "Mrs Milson's Wordlist: Eliza Hamilton Dunlop and the Intimacy of Linguistic Work", examining Dunlop's wordlists and considering how they have been used alongside other colonial sources by linguists and contemporary Indigenous communities involved in language reclamation and revitalisation.[101]

---

96 Katie Hansord, "Eliza Hamilton Dunlop's 'The Aboriginal Mother': Romanticism, Anti Slavery and Imperial Feminism in the Nineteenth Century", *JASAL: Journal of the Association for the Study of Australian Literature* 11, no. 1 (2011): 1–12.

97 Graeme Skinner, "Toward a General History of Australian Musical Composition: First National Music, 1788–c.1860" (PhD diss., Sydney Conservatorium of Music, University of Sydney, 2011).

98 Peter Minter, "Settlement Defiled: Ventriloquy, Pollution and Nature in Eliza Hamilton Dunlop's 'The Aboriginal Mother'", in *Text, Translation, and Transnationalism: World Literature in 21st Century Australia*, ed. Peter Morgan (Melbourne: Australian Scholarly, 2017), 137–51. We are grateful to Peter Minter for his collaboration in our project, and to Peter Morgan and Australian Scholarly Publishing for permission to reprint.

99 Rudy, *Imagined Homelands*.

100 Anna Johnston, "'The Aboriginal Mother': Poetry and Politics", in *Remembering the Myall Creek Massacre*, ed. Jane Lydon and Lyndall Ryan (Sydney: UNSW Press, 2018), 225–47.

101 "Mrs Milson's Wordlist". On linguistic uses of Dunlop, see Peter Austin, "The Gamilaraay (Kamilaroi) Language, Northern New South Wales: A Brief History of Research", in *Encountering Aboriginal Languages: Studies in the History of Australian Linguistics*, ed. William B. McGregor (Canberra: Australian National University, Research School of Pacific and Asian Studies, 2008), 37–58; Caroline Jones, *Darkinyung Grammar and Dictionary: Revitalising a Language from Historical Sources* (Nambucca Heads: Muurrbay Aboriginal Language and Culture Co-operative, 2008); Caroline Jones and Shawn Laffan, "Lexical Similarity and Endemism in Historical Wordlists of Australian Aboriginal Languages of the Greater Sydney Region", *Transactions of the Philological Society* 106, no. 3 (2008): 456–86. See also Wafer this volume.

* * *

This book, *Eliza Hamilton Dunlop: Writing from the Colonial Frontier*, brings together Australian and international scholars to provide new perspectives on Dunlop and her writing. Our contributors draw on archival sources and twenty-first-century digital resources to draw public and scholarly attention to Dunlop's significant contribution to colonial literature. Bringing together a variety of disciplinary and interdisciplinary methods in this book provides an approach that aims to account for the range of Dunlop's literary, intellectual and political interests. It also manifests new modes of researching and teaching literary texts, and engaging with colonial and imperial archives, that foreground how literary history sits within historical, social and cultural contexts that shaped aesthetic and political representations such as Eliza Hamilton Dunlop's poetry.[102]

Anna Johnston's chapter provides a literary biography of Dunlop's life and writing in Ireland as a child and young woman, traced through the sources and archives that underpin this research. In "The Poetry of the Archive: Locating Eliza Hamilton Dunlop", Johnston demonstrates how Dunlop's life and writing emerge relationally within archival holdings (like many women's lives), emphasising how we need to read across different kinds of literary and history sources to build a comprehensive picture of the past. She concludes that colonial writers such as Dunlop provide ways to connect nineteenth-century Australian literature with key developments in the literary and cultural history of the British Empire. In doing so, we gain a rich understanding of literature and history that can underpin conversations about difficult colonial histories and pressing contemporary political concerns such as relationships between Indigenous and non-Indigenous Australians.

Drawing together Dunlop's Irish background and her poetry published prior to arriving in Australia with her better-known colonial works, Part 1 of this volume situates Dunlop within global literary trends of the early nineteenth century. Romantic poetry specialist Duncan Wu explores Dunlop's literary sensibility in her 1835 poem " Morning on Rostrevor Mountains" to provide an account of Dunlop's interests and literary influences, based on her exposure to French revolutionary ideas, Indian uprisings against the British, and Irish rebellions. Wu's reading of Dunlop's poem provides evidence about her influences, including the rich literary history of the 1798 Irish Rebellion. Joining this Empire-wide experience to Dunlop's Australian revisions of this poem, Wu provides a compelling pre-history of how Dunlop came to New South Wales in 1838 with a mature and politically engaged poetic voice, ready to respond swiftly to her colonial environment. Katie Hansord's chapter follows

---

102 Ronjaunee Chatterjee, Alicia Mireles Christoff and Amy R. Wong, "Undisciplining Victorian Studies", *Los Angeles Review of Books* (10 July 2020), https://lareviewofbooks.org/article/undisciplining-victorian-studies/#_edn3. For an invigorating repositioning of another settler Australian canonical poet, Henry Lawson, see Manu Samriti Chander, *Brown Romantics: Poetry and Nationalism in the Global Nineteenth Century* (Lewisburg: Bucknell University Press, 2017), Chapter 3.

as a companion piece, focusing attention on Dunlop's childhood reading of Enlightenment philosophers in her father's library. Gender, education and the role of romantic love are brought together with questions of natural rights, ethics and the passions in Hansord's reading of Dunlop's early journals and her poem "To Home and Friends" (1857). Hansord argues convincingly for Dunlop's engagement with eighteenth-century progressive thought, such as that of Mary Wollstonecraft, and shows how reading and writing were political activities for ambitious intellectual women such as Dunlop. Yet she also reveals the uneven complexities of imperial feminism, through which white women painstakingly forged a public role, while colonised and Indigenous women struggled to find platforms to articulate their experience. Jason Rudy's chapter concludes the first section of this book, by tracing how race, genre and sentiment accompanied Dunlop's movements between Ireland, India and Australia, and her engagement with a wide Anglophone literary culture that encompassed the United States. Rudy traces the circulation of Dunlop's "Songs of an Exile – (No. 3)" (1837/38) through its various publication venues to map colonial print culture, especially in the important eighteenth- and nineteenth-century genre of sentimental literature. Drawing attention to Dunlop's intertextual references to key texts of North American settler literature reveals how the poet memorialised family members who had joined the Irish diaspora in the Americas, and how the colonial experience of Native Americans influenced her thinking about Australian settler colonialism. Rudy persuasively shows how different variants of Dunlop's poem accrued meaning in different publication locations, and how diverse readers might have understood and responded to her writing. He argues that Dunlop's poetry confounds assumptions about the supposed universalism of sentiment in the period.

Part 2 focuses on Australian readings and histories of Dunlop's writing. It opens with Peter Minter's Indigenous reading of "The Aboriginal Mother" (1838). Drawing on transnational and postcolonial ecopoetics, Minter links the poem to questions of pollution and defilement in a powerful reading of the ontology of settlement. While not doubting Dunlop's well-intentioned engagement with Aboriginal topics, Minter reminds readers that settler writing emerged in Australia by displacing Indigenous peoples, their voices and their culture. Even sympathetic settler writers like Dunlop "ventriloquised" Indigenous perspectives. The poem's structure of possession and dispossession, he argues, provides a correlation with racial politics, and reveals an alienated relation to nature. The dead bodies created by colonial violence and massacre literally and metaphorically pollute the settler polity and the Australian landscape. This reading of Dunlop's best-known poem advocates for an ecocritical approach to the poet's work.

Situating Dunlop within the context of colonial Australian music history, Graeme Skinner's detailed analysis of the poet's collaboration with the composer Isaac Nathan shows another important aspect of her writing that reveals her musical significance alongside her literary contributions. Dunlop used existing and well-known songs, often from an Irish tradition, to structure her writing. Nathan's English experiences included setting Byron's "Hebrew Melodies" to music and his own *oeuvre* included original compositions alongside adaptations of existing melodies. Nathan's ambitious plan for "Australian Melodies" utilised lyrics from five Dunlop songs, as Skinner outlines, and in collaborating with him Dunlop's public profile increased, even if several of their joint works received a highly critical reception. Understanding Dunlop's active interest in Irish national music reveals another sphere of influence for her Australian work, as well as how aesthetic and political registers worked together during this period. Skinner's meticulous mapping of the "Australian Melodies" uses the lyrics and musicological aspects together to enable us to appreciate this aspect of Dunlop's poetry in new ways.[103]

James Wafer maps Dunlop's work onto local landscapes that connect her house on a tributary of the Hunter River with the beloved Irish landscapes that remained central in the poet's imagination throughout her life. In an extended reading of Dunlop's poem "The Mulla, or Wollombi Creek, New South Wales" (1849), Wafer teases out the speculated reasons for the naming of the Dunlop house "Mulla Villa", connecting the English poet Edmund Spenser's writing about Ireland from his manorial estate in County Cork to Dunlop's location between two Australian watercourses. Wafer draws attention to Dunlop's linguistic abilities and poetic borrowing from both European and Australian languages. He shows how Indigenous languages influenced a range of Dunlop's works, including "The Mulla" and "Erin Dheelish" (1865). The languages of the Hunter River and Lake Macquarie ("HRLM"), Darkinyung, Gamilaraay, the Sydney language and hybrid linguistic forms appear in Dunlop's work, indicating her engagement with a range of Indigenous peoples in the Hunter region. This reveals a persuasive if conjectural reading of Mulla Villa's joint naming: with Indigenous language references and Irish literary allusions that might enable a decolonising reading of time and place.

This volume ends with a new selection of poems by Dunlop with a scholarly introduction by Elizabeth Webby, a fitting conclusion to a collaborative project that seeks to make Dunlop's work better known and more accessible. Webby's meticulous bibliographic scholarship enables a better understanding of Dunlop's poetic work across a long period, and reveals Dunlop's continuing engagement through revision and self-conscious arrangement of her life's work in the unpublished manuscript volume "The Vase" (c. 1873). Read as a literary biography, Webby's selection of poems provides a moving insight into Dunlop's life, her intellectual and poetic preoccupations, and her personal experiences. Fittingly, it concludes with Dunlop's own eulogy, framing the poet's life within her own words.

* * *

Our work on this book has been enormously benefited and enabled by collaboration between the contributors and the editors. We have all benefited from

---

103 This can be heard on Skinner's AustralHarmony website, where he includes audio files of some songs, https://sydney.edu.au/paradisec/australharmony/dunlop-eliza-hamilton.php.

the resources and staff at the State Library of New South Wales, the State Library of Victoria, the National Library of Australia and various regional and community organisations. We are particularly grateful for the support of specialist Mitchell Library staff – especially Rachel Franks, Richard Neville, conservator Kate Hughes and Indigenous curator Ronald Briggs – whose advice has been invaluable. We have worked closely with the Mitchell Library to digitise Dunlop's archives and develop new finding aids that will enable enhanced future access by students, researchers and community members. In this way, we see the current book as beginning new conversations with a diverse range of interested readers and researchers and we welcome future opportunities to extend the work. We have also benefited from conversations with leading Indigenous and colonial historians John Maynard, Victoria Haskins, Jane Lydon, Lyndall Ryan, Lynette Russell and Grace Karskens – each of whose work intersects with the local and global histories of colonial New South Wales – and with members of the Wollombi community, especially Hugh Craig, Donna Snowdon, the Wollombi Endeavour Museum and Stuart Gibson. Thanks also to Dunlop descendants Tom R. Raine and Michéle Celler for their enthusiasm for this book, and to Jenny Johnston for invaluable and exhaustive family history research. Robert Dixon, series editor at Sydney University Press, has been an important interlocutor for the book since its inception, and we thank him and the Press for their support. Earlier versions of the material benefited from feedback from colleagues at the University of Tasmania, the University of Queensland, the University of Melbourne, the University of Newcastle, and University College Dublin, and audiences at conferences including the Association for the Study of Australian Literature and the Australian Historical Association. Several research assistants – notably, Gemmia Burden and Ingrid Finnane at the University of Queensland – have assisted in the research and the book's production. Finally, it has been a pleasure for Anna and Elizabeth to work together commissioning, shaping and editing this book. We are confident that this book demonstrates the strength and longevity of excellent scholarship in Australian literary studies that is enabled by cooperation and mutual respect across generations of academics, committed to engaging Australian material with the best global scholarship and bringing scholarly expertise into mutually stimulating conversations with our readers and publics.

2

The Poetry of the Archive: Locating Eliza Hamilton Dunlop

Anna Johnston

In scrawled pencil, Eliza Hamilton Dunlop jotted down the first two stanzas of a poem on the nearest scrap of paper: it began "O your eyes have the twin stars light *Machree*". On the reverse of the paper is a convict pass – "Permit George Nimbus to pass to Mr John Medhurst and with him to remain for harvest work" – signed by David Dunlop in his role as Police Magistrate at Wollombi, 15 December 1840 (Figure 2.1).[1] In the family papers held in the Mitchell Library, the stanzas are less visible than the convict pass in several senses: faint pencil versus official ink, and a modern archival note about the convict pass but not the verses. Yet Eliza Hamilton Dunlop's poem had a rich publication history that stretched from New South Wales to Northern Ireland. A full three-stanza version of the poem "Songs of Exile No. 5: The Irish Mother" was published in the *Australian* on 12 January 1839.[2] Far away in Belfast, the *Australian*'s version of "The Irish Mother" was read by the Irish nationalist and journalist Charles Gavan Duffy, who included it in his highly popular anthology *The Ballad Poetry of Ireland* (1845), a study of "Anglo-Irish ballads; the production of educated men, with English tongues but Irish hearts". It remained in print throughout the nineteenth century in over forty editions.[3] Even in 1866, Duffy continued to praise "the touching little ballad" for its "freshness and grace". It became more meaningful for him across time because of his extensive travels and long public service in the Australian colonies between 1855 and 1880. Yet he remained unaware of the identity of the author of the poem

---

1   Correspondence and documents of David Dunlop, 1830s–1880s, Mitchell Library, State Library of New South Wales, MLMSS 9409.

2   Eliza Hamilton Dunlop, "Songs of an Exile: (No. 5) The Irish Mother", *Australian*, 12 January 1839. See Elizabeth Webby, this volume.

3   Charles Gavan Duffy, *The Ballad Poetry of Ireland*, Duffy's Library of Ireland (Dublin: J. Duffy, 1845), xv. On Duffy's career, see Joy E. Parnaby, "Duffy, Sir Charles Gavan (1816–1903)", ed. Douglas Pike, *Australian Dictionary of Biography* (Canberra: National Centre of Biography, Australian National University, 1972), https://adb.anu.edu.au/biography/duffy-sir-charles-gavan-3450/text5265.

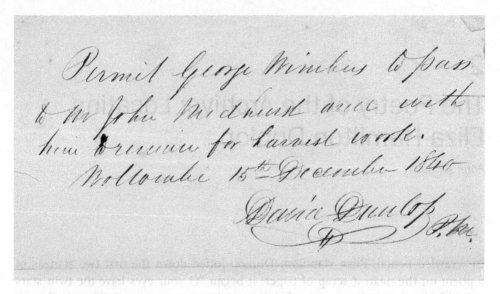

Figure 2.1: David Dunlop, Permit George Nimbus, 1840, paper (State Library of New South Wales, Milson Family Further Papers, 1826–1960, MLMSS 9409).

he had retitled "The Emigrant Mother", perhaps thinking of William Wordsworth's 1807 poem of the same name.[4]

This one item drawn from Eliza Hamilton Dunlop's papers resonates with the romance of archival research, the sense of uncovering past lives and stories, and our retrospective insight into the random nature of opportunities made and missed (did Duffy meet Dunlop in Australia? did Dunlop even know that her poem had been anthologised?). The convict pass written on the back of the poem provides an ideal image of the enmeshment of Dunlop's writing with her family's role in colonial society. This material object reminds us of the vicissitudes of writing under colonial conditions, beginning with the scarcity of paper, which had to be imported for many years, so that one sheet transformed into a palimpsest on which various kinds of writing could be superimposed. The convict pass also works metonymically to represent the distinctive kinds of employment that colonial societies offered Britons who sought financial independence and new lives, allowing David Dunlop, a book binder from Coleraine, and his writer wife Eliza the opportunity for innovative public service, serving and protecting settlers, convicts and Indigenous people, groups who were profoundly changed by the rapid expansion of Britain's second empire. Colonial administrations provided ambitious and curious Britons with opportunities that could combine literary and cultural interests with public service and political work, even if in historical hindsight that work appears

---

4   Duffy's note on an Australian newspaper as the source appears first in the 1866 edition.

mundane at best, and at worst repressive.[5] The movement of these stanzas from convict pass to colonial newspaper to Irish anthology to its final revision in Dunlop's unpublished manuscript volume "The Vase"[6] underscores the constant mobility of writing, ideas and culture around the British Empire.[7] This chapter first canvasses the role of colonial archives in reconstructing Eliza Hamilton Dunlop's life, writing and social context, before considering how we can understand Dunlop's poetic responses to the politics, literature and experiences that shaped her life.

Dwelling in the Colonial Archives

Women writers often struggled to have their literary achievements noted, even though their publications increased exponentially across Europe in the eighteenth and nineteenth century. Eliza Hamilton Dunlop's distinctive initials "E.H.D." identified her authorship of the draft stanzas, as did the published poem in the *Australian*. Yet in Ireland, Duffy did not include the poet's name and renamed the poem, so years later Australian Catholic newspapers "rediscovered" the poem via a Belfast newspaper, lamenting its anonymity but praising the writer: "Whoever he was he had a genuine poetic feeling – and a touch entirely beyond that of the mere facile rhymer".[8] Early twentieth-century readers had forgotten that the colonial newspapers were sites of vibrant poetic and cultural activity, and that women such as Dunlop had participated vigorously in the public sphere. Like many female writers, Dunlop's authorship was elided and her gender mistaken. So, too, some of Dunlop's important writing is in unpublished sources, despite her consistent publication in the colonial press. To take account of this, it is necessary to move beyond traditional literary history that focuses on "an individual's assumed desire for publication and their success or otherwise in achieving it".[9] To create a rich account that both reconstructs a writing woman's life by analysing its archival traces, and subjects it to analysis, requires reading across unpublished and published material, letters, journals and correspondence, and histories and family biographies. Reading relationally is central, because it is often through the

---

5   Ralph Crane and Anna Johnston, "Introduction: Administering Colonial Spaces in Australasia and India", in *Empire Calling: Administering Colonial Australasia and India*, ed. Ralph Crane, Anna Johnston and C. Vijayasree (New Delhi: Cambridge University Press Foundation, 2013), vii–xiv.

6   See Elizabeth Webby, this volume.

7   See Tony Ballantyne, *Webs of Empire: Locating New Zealand's Colonial Past* (Wellington: Bridget Williams, 2012); *Entanglements of Empire: Missionaries, Māori, and the Question of the Body* (Durham: Duke University Press, 2014).

8   Now titled "The Emigrant's Mother", by "an Anonymous Australian": *Freeman's Journal*, 24 December 1914. See Webby this volume.

9   Maryanne Dever, "Photographs and Manuscripts: Working in the Archive", *Archives and Manuscripts* 42, no. 3 (2014): 282–94.

male-dominated public record that we can reconstruct how women such as Dunlop wrote and lived in the margins of mainstream literary culture.[10]

Locating both the obvious and the hidden signs of Dunlop's life and writing has been central to the research that underpins this book, and it has opened up a broader range of sources for analysis. It has required much archival detective work. In the Milson family archives in the Mitchell Library, for example, Dunlop's poetry is mingled with company account books and convict records, records of land purchases and building plans, and family descendants' photographs and ephemera. Much of the material relates to the business dealings of a large and prosperous settler family and its organisation is dominated by the family's founding patriarch James Milson, whose business affairs and private wealth have long been deemed historically significant.[11] Because Rachel Rhoda Milson (née Dunlop) looked after her elderly mother and her affairs, the writer's papers can be found among the many boxes. In one, a handwritten note by Rachel says that it contains "Some Valuable Papers of my dear mother".[12] These include documents that provide insights into David Dunlop's political work in Coleraine, Northern Ireland; Sir George Gipps' original appointment of David to the Police Magistracy; early land allotments in Sydney; and the convict pass poem. The same folder holds a personal letter from Sir John Jamison to David Dunlop, apologising for his absence on the magistrate's bench at Penrith, and his missed opportunity to visit Eliza, due to the "melancholy news" that his daughter's newborn twins had died of influenza soon after birth.[13] From Ireland and New South Wales, both official and personal, signed and anonymous papers are dispersed across a wide range of dated and undated systems that reveal institutional library structures and family enthusiasms: these are the sources through which we can trace the life, thoughts and writing of Eliza Hamilton Dunlop.

---

10 This follows the methodology of a raft of valuable feminist scholarship, including Laurel Thatcher Ulrich, *A Midwife's Tale: The Life of Martha Ballard, Based on Her Diary, 1785–1812* (New York: Vintage, 1991); Natalie Zemon Davis, *Women on the Margins: Three Seventeenth-Century Lives* (Cambridge, MA: Harvard University Press, 1995); Gillian Whitlock, *The Intimate Empire: Reading Women's Autobiography* (London: Cassell, 2000); Carolyn Steedman, *Dust: The Archive and Cultural History* (New Brunswick, NJ: Rutgers University Press, 2002); Arlette Farge, *Allure of the Archives (1997)*, trans. Thomas Scott-Railton (New Haven, CT: Yale University Press, 2004); Lucy Frost, *Abandoned Women: Scottish Convicts Exiled Beyond the Seas* (Crows Nest, NSW: Allen & Unwin, 2012).

11 The Milson Family material was donated successively to the State Library of New South Wales. There are over forty boxes of Milson Family material, and material pertaining to Dunlop is scattered throughout the large collection. Its organisation has been influenced by the family biography written by Roy Goddard in the 1950s, *The Life and Times of James Milson* (Melbourne: Georgian House, 1955).

12 Milson Family Papers, Further Papers 1826–1920, State Library of New South Wales, MLMSS 9409.

13 John Jamison, "Letter to David Dunlop", in Milson Family Papers, Further Papers, 1826–1960, 28 November 1838.

Figure 2.2: Eliza Hamilton Dunlop, untitled landscape, Juvenile notebook, watercolour (Milson Family Papers – 1810, 1853–1862, State Library of New South Wales, MLMSS 7683).

In one box full of company account books, there is an entire volume of juvenile poetry and translations, lightly anonymised but clearly written by the young Eliza in Ireland between 1808 and 1813, and illustrated by her watercolours (Figure 2.2).[14] Each poem is carefully transcribed in exquisitely clear calligraphy, with its date and precise place of composition noted, through which we can map Dunlop's young thoughts and passions. These juvenile poems – together with fragments of a journal that has not been publicly deposited but which was partially transcribed by Margaret De Salis in the 1960s from family sources – provide insights into Dunlop's childhood. Two other important book-length manuscripts are stored separately from the family papers, but remain connected by numerous copies and drafts: Dunlop's fair copy of her poetic *oeuvre* "The Vase, Comprising Songs for Music and Poems by Eliza Hamilton Dunlop" (Figure 2.3); and Dunlop's linguistic collection, donated in 1926 by D. Goddard and (misleadingly) titled "Mrs. David Milson Kamilaroi Vocabulary and Aboriginal songs, 1840".[15] As part of the production

---

14 Milson Family Papers 1826–1895, State Library of New South Wales, MLMSS7948.
15 Eliza Hamilton Dunlop, "The Vase, Comprising Songs for Music and Poems by Eliza Hamilton Dunlop", State Library of New South Wales, B1541; "Mrs. David Milson Kamilaroi Vocabulary and Aboriginal Songs, 1840", State Library of New South Wales, A1688.

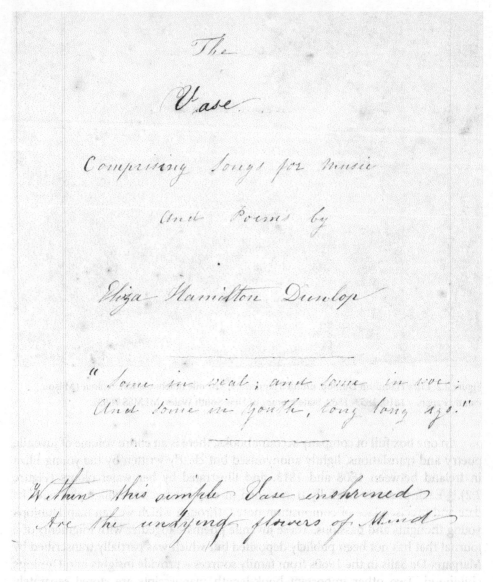

Figure 2.3: Eliza Hamilton Dunlop, Title page, "The Vase", paper (State Library of New South Wales, B1541).

of this book, the State Library of New South Wales has digitised Dunlop's full manuscript of "The Vase", making Dunlop's poems newly available for readers as a comprehensive body of work.[16] For twenty-first-century researchers, these archival riches are supplemented by the digitised colonial newspapers in the National Library

16   Eliza Hamilton Dunlop, "The Vase, Comprising Songs for Music and Poems by Eliza Hamilton Dunlop", https://search.sl.nsw.gov.au/permalink/f/1cvjue2/ADLIB110359904.

of Australia's TROVE, which enable a published Dunlop poem to be traced across various papers, and reviews or responses to it read, alongside Dunlop's own responses to criticism.[17] Digitised databases and family history web sources provide access to dispersed parts of the Hamilton and Dunlop family history.[18] Eliza Hamilton Dunlop's upbringing within a well-educated milieu comprising individuals who were directly involved in various kinds of cultural production means that we can read her own writing alongside that of other family members and her literary contemporaries to build a fuller picture that links archival sources to the public record and to literary history.

Archives are compelling, yet they are not a neutral space of unmediated sources. Rather, archives are highly constructed sites for preserving and creating knowledge, and it is critical to balance what Maryanne Dever rightly describes as the "pleasures of archived paper"against what Nicholas B. Dirks calls the "archival structure of the conditions of historical knowledge".[19] Whose papers, whose donation, and who continues to undertake both the curation and the creation of knowledge from archives are acute (and politically significant) questions. Evidently, gender played a part in how Dunlop's papers were partially retained, even though submerged within a larger family story that focused on preserving the memory of its foundational men. Other parts of Dunlop's archive (especially pertaining to David's work as Police Magistrate) explicitly intersect with the emergence of "the modern colonial state and its documentary apparatus" and are imbued with the power that adhered in settler colonial governance.[20] Traces of Indigenous voices and agencies – including their knowledge and culturally specific modes of authority – have been deposited in this archive in the context of colonial interests, and in our current era these sources can appear tainted by their association with colonial-era ideologies. Yet the personal and political nature of Dunlop's engagement with Indigenous and other colonial actors complicates a reading of her archive as purely hegemonic. We can use these documents to reconstruct the intimate and proximate nature of relationships under colonial conditions, because the archive allows glimpses of the local people who provided information under the conditions shaped by their own agendas and interests. Read this way, Dunlop's archive remains open for new meanings and new interpretations, which this book hopes to open

---

17 Dunlop's writing has been identified in many instances, and transcribed, and tagged in Trove: readers can search public tagged items and lists to find it. Additionally, Graeme Skinner's website lists many of these sources and contextualises them alongside other archival material: "Eliza Hamilton Dunlop, Songwriter", *Australharmony* (an online resource towards the history of music and musicians in colonial and early Federation Australia), https://sydney.edu.au/paradisec/australharmony/dunlop-eliza-hamilton.php.

18 For the Hamilton family, especially Alison Fitzpatrick, *Arborealis*, www.arborealis.ca.

19 Maryanne Dever, "Provocations on the Pleasures of Archived Paper", *Archives and Manuscripts* 41, no. 3 (2013): 173–82; Nicholas B. Dirks, "Annals of the Archive: Ethnographic Notes on the Sources of History", in *From the Margins: Historical Anthropology and Its Futures*, ed. Brian Keith Axel (Durham, NC: Duke University Press, 2002), 50.

20 "Annals of the Archive", 50.

up for its readers and future researchers, including Indigenous researchers and communities. The question then becomes how to locate Eliza Hamilton Dunlop and understand her contributions to literary and cultural history in ways that link local and colonial circumstances to global concerns. In doing so we can enrich understandings of Australia's colonial past, how it was transformed and transported as part of print culture, and its crucial and ongoing role in our literary history.

Eliza Hamilton Dunlop: A Child of Empire in Northern Ireland

Dunlop's childhood was both privileged and precarious. The youngest child and only daughter of Solomon Hamilton and Martha Costly (about whom very little can be learnt), she was brought up by her paternal grandmother Mary Hamilton (neé Speer). The Hamiltons were a large and well-connected Anglo-Irish family; some branches moved to the Ulster Plantations in Northern Ireland from Scotland in the seventeenth century, yet they retained connections across England, Ireland and Scotland. Solomon Hamilton was intellectually curious, ambitious and restless: he was admitted to the King's Inn Society (the Irish Bar) in the 1770s, but by 1781 he applied for admission to the Calcutta Bar and launched a legal career there representing "opulent native clients" and British subjects in Bengal.[21] Attorneys in the English and Irish community in Kolkata were a colourful lot. Hamilton is described in the diary of his fellow attorney William Hickey as "a devilish shrewd, clever fellow, fit for the practice of the villainous profession he belongs to, and fully competent to encounter all the chicanery and dirty tricks of his scoundrel brother attorneys".[22] In the 1780s, Hamilton was also listed in Westminster, London, as an attorney.[23] Legal earnings presumably underpinned Hamilton's acquisition of significant Northern Irish landholdings and tenements around Carlingford and Rostrevor in the 1790s, including Fort Hamilton, later the site of Ballyedmund Castle. His eldest sons Augustus Frederick (c.1788–1871) and George (c.1795–1857) were born nearly ten years after Solomon and Martha's marriage, and Eliza Matilda Harding Hamilton was born c.1796: it is assumed that Martha died soon after Eliza's birth.

---

21 William Hickey, *Memoirs of William Hickey. Vol. III (1782–1790)*, ed. Alfred Spencer, 5th ed. (London: Hurst & Blackett, 1923 [c.1813–14]).

22 Hickey, *Memoirs*, 146; Hickey's biographer describes him as a "self-confessed reprobate, who made good". P.J. Marshall, "Hickey, William (1749–1827), Lawyer in India and Memoirist", in *Oxford Dictionary of National Biography* (Oxford: Oxford University Press, 2004), 10.1093/ref:odnb/37542. Hickey's description of Hamilton is an approving report of words attributed to Colonel Watson, although as Alison Kilpatrick notes, the two lawyers were in competition, so Hickey's disapproval has to be read in context (*Arborealis*, https://www.arborealis.ca).

23 *Bailey's British Directory... for the year 1784 ...* 4 Vols, Vol. 1. London; Printed by J. Andrews, 1784. In 1790, Hamilton was successfully charged with assault upon Thomas Hunt, a hairdressing apprentice. *Whitehall Evening Post*, 12 January 1790.

Figure 2.4: Eliza Hamilton Dunlop, King John's Castle on Carlingford Bay, Juvenile notebook, watercolour and ink (Milson Family Papers – 1810, 1853–1862, State Library of New South Wales, MLMSS 7683).

Dunlop grew up in idyllic landscapes around Carlingford Bay, which she describes as "sublime scenery, where the broad arm of Ocean is stretched between the wildly-romantic hills of Killowen and Carlingford" (Figure 2.4).[24] Her passionate love of local history and the natural environment is evident in her juvenile poems, and she had a wide-ranging self-education, having been given free access to her father's library. Solomon was regularly away: his library was perhaps the way that Eliza best knew her father, and what we know of its contents provides a mapping of Dunlop's literary and philosophical influences.[25] Significantly, the

---

24 Notes to "Fancy", 1810, Milson Family Papers – 1810, 1853–1862, State Library of New South Wales, MLMSS 7683.

25 The full list of Solomon Hamilton's effects upon his death in 1820 provides a fascinating insight into the family's library and interests: "Solomon Hamilton Inventory", in Inventories & Accounts of Deceased Estates – Bengal 1780–1937, British India Office Wills & Probate (Bengal: British Library, 1820), 2051.L-AG-34-27-68. Many thanks to Jenny Johnston for finding this

library also shows the involvement of this branch of the Hamilton family in republican politics and Enlightenment ideas, which underpinned her political interests. Eliza describes herself as having "an early spirit of research", noting that by twelve, she had already read the voyage accounts of James Cook, William Anson and La Perouse, among astronomy, geography and general interest volumes, novels and poetry.[26] The library contained many major republican and philosophical texts, including Mary Wollstonecraft's *A Vindication of the Rights of Woman: With Strictures on Political and Moral Subjects* (1792) and *An Historical and Moral View of the Origin and Progress of the French Revolution* (1795); Thomas Paine's "A Letter Addressed to the Abbé Raynal on the Affairs of North-America" (1782); Voltaire's works in English; and David Fordyce's *Dialogues Concerning Education* (1745). The family library also held a copy of David Collins' *An Account of the English Colony in New South Wales* (1802), which may have influenced Eliza's later choice of immigration to Australia. Philosophical thought and literary study were central to Eliza's unconventional childhood: "'What for' was a question of myself to myself, and my Father's globes which ran on castors and were my jaunting cars and the Planets of my Father's Orrery that were my jackstones early became a subject for the question, 'What for were they made'".[27] The novelist Maria Edgeworth visited Fort Hamilton in 1807, and it is highly likely that Eliza would have met the inspiring writer and advocate for women's education.[28]

Dunlop was brought up an active cultural participant in a notable (if occasionally notorious) family, in a period when literature and poetry were important forms of social commentary through which to explore religious, cultural and political ideas. Her juvenile notebook contains an English translation of *The Temple of Gnide* (1724), a long French classical romance prose poem popular at court for its ornate and suggestive style: purportedly translated from Greek sources, but published anonymously by Montesquieu.[29] At some stage Dunlop attempted

source in 2016, and to Alison Kilpatrick for her partial transcription of this list (*Arborealis*, www.arborealis.ca).

26 Margaret De Salis, *Two Early Colonials* (Sydney: printed by the author, 1967), 15–16.

27 De Salis, *Two Early Colonials*, 15. The orrery – a moving mechanical model of the planets – was listed in Hamilton's effects. It too reflects the wealth and intellectual curiosity of the family.

28 "Undated Letter from Maria Edgeworth to Mrs. Stuart of Rostrevor, Co. Down", National Library of Ireland (Department of Manuscripts), MS49, 419. The Stewarts assumed ownership of Fort Hamilton and became Eliza's guardians around 1807–8. Edgeworth's most famous novel, *Castle Rackrent* (1800), was based on her family's experiences as landholders in Ireland; her views on education were outlined in her own *Letters for Literary Ladies* (1795) and the joint publication with her father Richard Lovell Edgeworth *Essays on Practical Education* (1798). Edgeworth senior is described as "libidinous and abstracted", which suggests that Eliza would have found in Maria many similarities and sympathies: see W.J. McCormack, "Edgeworth, Maria (1768–1849), Novelist and Educationist", *Oxford Dictionary of National Biography* (Oxford: Oxford University Press, 2008), 10.1093/ref:odnb/8476.

29 Eliza Hamilton Dunlop, "Notebook: Translation into English of 'Le Temple De Gnide', a Prose Poem by Charles Louis De Secondat, Baron De Montesquieu", [1810?], Milson Family Papers – 1810, 1853–1862, State Library of New South Wales, MLMSS 7683. The translation is close but not identical to the 1767 English edition, suggesting either another source or that Eliza made

a dramatic adaptation of Mary Russell Mitford's *Blanche of Castile* (1812).[30] The young Eliza wrote what she called "Original Pieces" prolifically from at least 1810: her topics included standard pieces on virtues and vices; poetic responses to her local environment and her emotional attachments (to her family and also love poems); and long narrative poems influenced by history and mythology, often focused on nearby castles. Some early poems were published in local Irish magazines, mostly pseudonymously or under obscure initials.[31] She was precociously intelligent, and believed to be a local beauty. Many years later in New South Wales, an Irish acquaintance still remembered "the beauty and abundance of your hair".[32] She was very close to her cousin William Hamilton Maxwell (1794–1850), whose first anonymously published novel *O'Hara: or, 1798* (1825) addressed the 1798 uprising against English rule. He later became a prolific writer of fairly conservative military-themed fiction and non-fiction, based on his experience of the Napoleonic Wars.[33] The cousins shared a regular correspondence across their life, and at times collaborated. Dunlop wrote verses that were included in Maxwell's own novels, such as *The Dark Lady of Doona* (1834).[34] "Fair as romance our childhood reappears", Dunlop reminisced, near the end of her life.[35] On hearing of his death, she eulogised him as "the gifted one! Inspired with heaven's effulgent flame".[36]

The juvenile poetry also reveals some of the difficulties of Dunlop's youth. These poems are signed "Evelina" or "Evelina Matilda" or "Eliza Matilda". Like other fourteen-year-olds, Eliza was likely experimenting with her persona, but her choice of *nom de plume* reflects the eponymous heroine of Fanny Burney's popular novel *Evelina* (1778). Burney's Evelina is a beautiful and virtuous orphan, cast adrift

---

her own translation: see Charles de Secondat, *The Temple of Gnidos. Translated a Second Time from the French of Mons. De Secondat, Baron De Montesquieu* (London: Printed for G. Kearsley, in Ludgate-Street, 1767). On Rousseau's criticism of the sexual suggestiveness of *Temple*, see Mary L. Bellhouse, "Femininity & Commerce in the Eighteenth Century: Rousseau's Criticism of a Literary Ruse by Montesquieu", *Polity* 13, no. 2 (1980): 285–99.

30 Only an undated typescript of Dunlop's drama remains, although her notes about it are dated 1838.

31 As a consequence, few of these early publications have been identified to date, and most have been located only when Dunlop referenced earlier versions of later poems. See, for example, Rudy, this volume.

32 Mary Isabella Little, Letter to Eliza Hamilton Dunlop, 9 July 1841, State Library of New South Wales, MLMSS 5745.

33 Alfred Webb, *A Compendium of Irish Biography: Comprising Sketches of Distinguished Irishmen, Eminent Persons Connected with Ireland by Office or by Their Writings* (Dublin: M.H. Gill, 1878).

34 W.H. Maxwell, *The Dark Lady of Doona* (London: Smith, Elder and Co., 1834).

35 Eliza Hamilton Dunlop, "Memories of Maxwell", *Australian Town and Country Journal* (1873).

36 Eliza Hamilton Dunlop, "Thoughts of the Last Hours of an Author, the Rev. William Hamilton Maxwell" in "The Vase". Other critics were less effulgent. Maxwell's desertion of his wife, while living mostly in London, aided derisory assessments of his character and writing. On this, see Patrick Maume, "Containing Granuaile: Grace O'Malley in Two Nineteenth-Century Novels", *New Hibernia Review* 19, no. 1 (2015): 101. For a recent and persuasive reappraisal, see James H. Murphy, *Irish Novelists and the Victorian Age* (Oxford: Oxford University Press, 2011). Murphy notes that, until recently, Maxwell had been "generally considered a buffoon and his novels are thought to celebrate the worst kind of male antics" (27).

on the ferocious marriage market of London: "Though motherless, though worse than fatherless, bereft from infancy of the two first and greatest blessings of life", she declares herself blessed by great fortune to have a beloved and dependable guardian.[37] Like Evelina, Eliza had no reliable parental presence and, worse, her guardianship was variable. She writes with great affection of her grandmother, even though she notes that Mary Hamilton insisted upon Christian teaching and feminine occupations that chafed against her independence and intelligence.[38] Those early years she described as ones "of perfect happiness. I was loved, my genius was extolled and I was taught to expect a Father's return who would love me too, visionary expectations".[39] But by 1807–8, her grandmother had died, and from Kolkata her father sold her beloved home Fort Hamilton to Alexander Stewart, who with his wife Sarah assumed some form of guardianship. It appears the property sale was intended to provide Dunlop with an income, but she struggled to access the funds. Unbeknown to Eliza, Solomon Hamilton's life in India was probably focused on his two Indian-born daughters, Charlotte (c.1801) and Mary (c.1804), and their mother Maria. Dunlop's brothers were also in India; her cousin William had entered Trinity College, Dublin.[40] Dunlop probably felt utterly bereft: her 1810 poem "The Tear" laments "a bosom fraught with pain/ ... / When Peace has fled with all her train".[41]

By 1810, aged fourteen, Dunlop had met James Sylvius Law, an astronomer and poet. It is possible he was her tutor. The two exchanged teasing and romantic poetic epistles between "Evelina" and "Sylvius": she deemed him her muse and dramatically declared "'twas a spark of thy poetic fire / First illumined this bosom, and taught it to heave".[42] Law and Dunlop shared many interests; he moved in intellectual circles, read widely and published poetry. Law was politically engaged, and wrote passionately about his favoured causes.[43] By 1812, it appears

---

37 Frances Burney, *Evelina* (1778; Oxford: Oxford University Press, 2002), 219.

38 See Katie Hansord, this volume.

39 De Salis, *Two Early Colonials*, 16.

40 Donald Hawes, "Maxwell, William Hamilton (1791–1850), Writer", *Oxford Dictionary of National Biography* (Oxford University Press, 2009), 10.1093/ref:odnb/18416.

41 Juvenile notebook, Milson Family Papers – 1810, 1853–1862, State Library of New South Wales, MLMSS 7683.

42 Juvenile notebook, Milson Family Papers – 1810, 1853–1862, State Library of New South Wales, MLMSS 7683.

43 In 1813, he published *The Irish Catholic: A Patriotic Poem* (Printed by Joseph Smyth; Dublin; H. Fitzpatrick: Belfast, 1813). Although this is noted in one source as only attributed to Law, consideration of his other poems suggests this is a likely attribution and the copy in the National Library of Ireland is clearly published under his name. (D.J. O'Donoghue, *The Poets of Ireland: A Biographical and Bibliographical Dictionary of Irish Writers of English Verse* (Dublin: Hodges, Figgis & Co., 1912), 244.) In 1831, Law published *The Wrongs of Ireland Historically Reviewed, from the Invasion to the Present Time: A National Poem, in Six Cantos, with Copious Illustrations: To Which Is Prefixed, an Eulogium to Ogyagia* (Dublin: R. Grace, 1831). It argued for Irish independence and condemned the "base qualities of the Saxon Colonists". He dedicated this poem to the "Magnanimous Sons of Irish Independence, who ... have united their energies for a repeal of the Union", celebrating "their public virtues, in befriending human rights" (i).

they had married, although family records suggest that her father was unhappy with the match. The marriage faltered early, but produced two children: James Law (date unknown) and Mary Sophia Georgina Law (1816–1879). James Sylvius Law was unreliable. He first suggested going to India, which Solomon discouraged; and in 1814 and 1815 Solomon wrote expressing serious concern for Eliza and her child given her "unprotected state".[44] It is difficult to trace Law's movements, but in 1816 he was in New York, as evidenced by his poetry and published correspondence.[45] Law learnt much during his "exile" in the United States.[46] His 20-stanza "Valedictory Address" (1817) eulogised "the land of the setting sun" and presented romantic visions of First Nations tribal groups, reflecting the period's poetic preoccupation with the exotic and foreshadowing Eliza's own poetry and research into Indigenous Australian cultures.[47] Despite their shared interests, however, the marriage had failed, and in 1820 Dunlop took a journey to India that had been arranged by her father, leaving her young daughter Georgina with family.[48] On arrival in Kolkata, she learnt that her father had died during her voyage, that her brothers refused to acknowledge their father's Indian family and that she had been left a ninth share of Solomon Hamilton's estate. Importantly, her inheritance was augmented with some funds from her brothers, and it enabled Dunlop to secure her own and Georgina's independence. Although the details of her settlement with Law remain obscure, two years after her return from India Dunlop was able to remarry, to David Dunlop in 1823 in Portpatrick, Scotland, where marriage laws were more favourable to deserted women than in either England or Ireland.[49]

Eliza and David's marriage was fuelled by politics and ideas, too: they had been friends before her trip to India. David was a book binder in Coleraine, and heavily involved in progressive Ulster politics. David's family was embedded in Northern Ireland's turbulent history. This was a dominant part of their family

---

44 See notes in Margaret De Salis, "Notebook", in Margaret De Salis – Papers, 1965–1980, State Library of New South Wales, MLMSS 5745.

45 James Sylvius Law, "Poem by James Sylvius Law on His Return to Ireland", *The Newry Magazine* 3, no. 15 (1817); "Letter", *The Newry Magazine: Or, Literary and Political Register* (1817); Allen Culling Clark, *Greenleaf and Law in the Federal City* (Washington, D.C.: W.F. Roberts, 1901).

46 Law dramatically warned his readers that they could "ill conceive what grief, unmixed with mirth, / Prolongs the misery of an EXILE'S YEAR!" ("Poem by James Sylvius Law on His Return to Ireland").

47 Tim Fulford, *Romantic Indians: Native Americans, British Literature, and Transatlantic Culture 1756–1830* (Oxford: Oxford University Press, 2006).

48 Her son James cannot be traced in the Irish birth or death records, though notices appeared in Australian and Irish papers in 1882 seeking him out after Eliza's death to conclude several family wills and probates. It is possible that he did not survive infancy, or that the Law family took him in, following the failed marriage.

49 Leah Leneman, "'Disregarding the Matrimonial Vows': Divorce in Eighteenth and Early Nineteenth-Century Scotland", *Journal of Social History* 30, no. 2 (1996); Niamh Howlin and Kevin Costello, eds., *Law and the Family in Ireland, 1800–1950* (London: Palgrave, 2017).

story: it informed Eliza Hamilton Dunlop's poetic eulogy for her husband in 1863, and a later dual eulogy that linked David and his father's burial sites.[50] David's great-great-grandfather the Reverend David Dunlop migrated from Ayrshire to Laird Hugh Montgomery's Plantation, the "Ardes" in County Down, in 1616. He was a member of the Covenanters, Scottish Presbyterians who resisted the imposition of the English Book of Common Prayer and refused to recognise the King as head of the church. The Ulster Plantations provided a refuge for Covenanters marked as traitors and persecuted in Scotland, and later were also a departure point for mass Irish immigration to America. David's father Captain William Dunlop was hanged as a rebel in the 1798 Irish Rebellion, when resistance to British rule boiled over into politically complex and violent skirmishes. William Dunlop's house at Priestlands was burned by "The Ancient British Fencibles", a regiment raised by the Welsh Tory MP Sir Watkin Williams Wynn III, whose suppression of Irish independence in the Rebellion was notoriously bloody: Dunlop's "The Two Graves" later characterised this as "the requiem of red ninety-eight!". The bloody history of revolution and its suppression in Ireland remained potent metaphors throughout Eliza Hamilton Dunlop's writing career.[51]

Eliza and David's formative years were profoundly shaped by the subsequent formal Union created by a United Kingdom Parliament and the new Union flag in 1801 (and it was the Union that James Sylvius Law railed against too). Political questions remained highly volatile and they influenced literary and book history. Significantly for both David's occupation as a book binder and Eliza's writing career, the 1801 Union closed a lucrative loophole for the Dublin book trade, which had benefited from exemption from the 1709 British Copyright Act, meaning that throughout the eighteenth century, Irish printers could reprint any book without paying for copy or royalties. Bookbinding had flourished as a high-level craft catering for elite private libraries.[52] After incorporation with Britain under the Union, a new publishing industry had to be built, and it drew on a highly literate element of the population hungry for print culture with local resonances. An increasing number of Irish women joined in a culture where writing was central to articulating a new society for the century, even though it was beset by divisions of the past and unremitting poverty for many.[53] Dunlop's writing of the 1810s can be seen as participating in a pre-Famine literary world that was sidelined because of the relative class privilege of most writers, and the

---

50   Eliza Hamilton Dunlop, "Memorialis", *Empire*, 24 June 1863.
51   See Wu this volume.
52   Máire Kennedy, "'Politicks, Coffee and News': The Dublin Book Trade in the Eighteenth Century", *Dublin Historical Record* 58, no. 1 (2005): 76–85. Thanks to Jean McBain for advice on this question.
53   Riana O'Dwyer, "Women's Narratives, 1800–40", in *The Field Day Anthology of Irish Writing: Irish Women's Writing and Traditions*, ed. Angela Bourke, Siobhán Kilfeather, Maria Luddy, Margaret Mac Curtain, Gerardine Meaney, Máirín Ní Dhonnchadha, Mary O'Dowd and Clair Wills (Cork, Ireland: Cork University Press in association with Field Day, 2002).

distinctively provincial nature of the issues they addressed: laments for a lost Ireland, enthusiasm for Gaelic mythology and rural rediscovery.[54] Through her own reading, Dunlop was well aware of republican sentiment, and her passionate engagement with local histories and places brought together Gaelic antiquity and culture with Enlightenment ideals.[55] Little is known of Dunlop's proposed volume of poetry *Ultoniana*, except an 1814 notice that indicated it would feature "historical Poems, principally confined to the authentic History of Ulster in the days of feudal domination".[56] It likely remained unpublished because the thriving study of antiquity, which had flourished in the political culture of Enlightenment interests in national folk cultures, became in the aftermath of 1798 "a suspect form of sympathy with the rebellious natives".[57] Novelists and poets skirted around the damaging fractures of the past: Maria Edgeworth declared it "impossible to draw Ireland as she is now in a book of fiction – realities are too strong, party passions too violent to bear to see, or care to look at their faces in the looking-glass".[58] Nonetheless, contemporary travel writers perceived that the North remained haunted by the traumatic memory of the defeated United Irish rebellion, and there is evidence that vernacular historiographies, preserved in oral traditions, maintained local knowledges, and transported them within a mobile diaspora.[59] It was not until the 1840s that public culture began to rediscover the events of 1798 for literary audiences, at which stage Romantic sympathies "reconfigured the moral significance of 1798 and its insurgents, first in a tragic, and subsequently in a heroic, light".[60] In New South Wales in 1843, Dunlop published her poem "The Irish Volunteers", eulogising the "150,000 strong, self-constituted, self-supported and effectively disciplined" military body raised in 1780 that prefigured the 1798 Society United Irishman uprising.[61] The Volunteers spurred a popular politics, and gave an emerging, self-conscious public experience in organising and mobilising a "provincial political culture"

---

54 O'Dwyer notes that Irish fiction of this period has traditionally been regarded as inferior: interesting only as a precursor to Famine literature. It was damned as overly interested in an English audience, while on the other hand condemned as too provincial from the viewpoint of London (833).

55 On this alliance more broadly, see Joep Leerssen, "Convulsion Recalled: Aftermath and Cultural Memory (Post-1798 Ireland)", in *Afterlife of Events: Perspectives on Mnemohistory*, ed. Marek Tamm (London: Palgrave Macmillan UK, 2015), 134–53.

56 "Notice", *Freeman's Journal* (Dublin), 7 October 1814.

57 "Convulsion Recalled", 138.

58 Maria Edgeworth, *Life and Letters of Maria Edgeworth*, ed. Augustus J.C. Hare. Vol. 2 (1894; Project Gutenberg, 2005), https://www.gutenberg.org/ebooks/9095.

59 Guy Beiner, "Disremembering 1798? An Archaeology of Social Forgetting and Remembrance in Ulster", *History and Memory* 25, no. 1 (2013): 16, 18; see also Beiner, *Forgetful Remembrance: Social Forgetting and Vernacular Historiography of a Rebellion in Ulster* (Oxford: Oxford University Press, 2018).

60 Leerssen, "Convulsion Recalled", 143.

61 "The Irish Volunteers", *Australasian Chronicle* 1843. The *Australian* also ran a notice, emphasising the interesting history of the tune Dunlop used, which had been composed in the 1780s to celebrate the Volunteers. The *Australian* mentioned the brevity of Dunlop's poem; a longer version appears in "The Vase", which adds lines invoking "Australia's cloudless skies / To blend once more with country's ties" (State Library of New South Wales, B1541).

Figure 2.5: Diamond Coleraine, "The Vase", steel engraving (State Library of New South Wales, B1541).

that was "republican in the classical sense, founded upon the active participation of the arms-bearing citizen".[62] Both political bodies were committed to independence and republican government, inspired by the French Revolution: and both would have engaged strongly with Dunlop's reading of republican writing in her father's library. Through David Dunlop's family history, Eliza's awareness of the Presbyterian component of the Northern Irish resistance to the English was heightened; it also influenced her otherwise Loyalist cousin Maxwell's novel *O'Hara; or, 1798* towards a sympathetic depiction of the Ulster rebels.[63]

Coleraine, where David and Eliza established their family, was a site of intense political activity (Figure 2.5). Coleraine's development was financed by investors in the City of London. The Honourable The Irish Society was established to manage this distinctive business / trading company, and David was active in its early nineteenth-century affairs, including providing education across sectarian divides.

---

62 Ian McBride, *Scripture Politics: Ulster Presbyterians and Irish Radicalism in the Late Eighteenth Century* (Oxford: Oxford University Press-Clarendon, 1998), 161.
63 Beiner, "Disremembering 1798?", 20.

Most importantly, he was involved in post-Union reforms promoted by Ulster leaders that called for an end to absentee landlords and recommended that local residential gentlemen should govern towns.[64] David was part of a seven-member committee representing Coleraine that accused two absentee landlord families – the Jacksons and the Beresfords – of conspiring to dominate the roles of Members of Parliament, and many other local positions of influence, such as Justices of the Peace, Aldermen and Chief Magistrates. The two families had massively profited from this "secret coalition", described by the petitioners as an "unconstitutional and illegal monopoly", contrary to Coleraine's Charter.[65] In 1831, David Dunlop seconded the petition and had a formal role in transmitting copies to members of the House of Lords and the House of Commons known to be open to reform, arguing for parliamentary representation of the people of the town. Eliza Hamilton Dunlop's family connections contributed to this campaign, and she personally made representations in England.[66] Members of the Irish Society stood against the sitting member and after considerable political chicanery the London alderman William Taylor Copeland was elected.[67]

Amid the politics, Eliza and David Dunlop had five children between 1823 and 1829. Dunlop's first daughter Georgina Law became part of a large family with one half-brother, David Henry, and three surviving half-sisters: Eliza Augusta (Bessie), Wilhemina Hamilton Maxwell (likely named after Eliza's cousin, William, as James Wafer notes), and Rachel Rhoda Nevin.[68] In the 1830s, the couple lost their eight-year-old daughter Jane Wilson, whose death Dunlop felt deeply: "She was my dearest one, my pride / For Whom those drops of anguish start".[69] Dunlop was ambitious for David, using her family's extensive contacts to try to secure him a position in London, yet despite determined advocacy this did not come to fruition, perhaps because he had also made powerful enemies during the Coleraine period. Later, Dunlop would describe David's years of service poetically, and perhaps over dramatically, as akin to his father's: "Predestined in life to bend 'under the rod,' / 'Through much tribulation' they passed to their God".[70]

---

64 James Stevens Curl, "Reluctant Colonisers: The City of London and the Plantation of Coleraine", *History Ireland* 17, no. 6 (2009), https://bit.ly/3bhduly.

65 Petition, Meeting of the Inhabitants of the Town and Liberties of Coleraine, 7 January 1831, Correspondence & Documents of David Dunlop, 1830s–1880s, State Library of New South Wales, MLMSS 9409, https://bit.ly/3k2Rr6b.

66 De Salis, 28–30.

67 On Coleraine's complex political history in this period, see Stephen Farrell, "Coleraine", ed. D.R. Fisher, *The History of Parliament: The House of Commons, 1820–1832* (Cambridge: Cambridge University Press, 2009), https://bit.ly/3s3tNtg.

68 Jim Wafer, "Ghost-Writing for Wulatji: Incubation and 'Re-Dreaming' as Song Revitalisation Practices", in *Recirculating Songs: Revitalising the Singing Practices of Indigenous Australia*, ed. Jim Wafer and Myfany Turpin (Canberra: Asia-Pacific Languages 2017), 226.

69 Eliza Hamilton Dunlop, "She Was", in "The Vase", State Library of New South Wales, B1541.

70 Eliza Hamilton Dunlop, "The Two Graves", *Empire*, 15 April 1865; "The Two Graves", *Coleraine Chronicle*, 26 August 1865.

In 1837, the family emigrated to Sydney with some funds and a collection of Spode crockery, a gift of Copeland – their associate since Coleraine, by then MP for Stoke – who also wrote the Dunlops a letter of introduction that would have been well received by the new, liberal Governor of New South Wales, Sir George Gipps.[71] Copeland acknowledged Dunlop's determined pursuit of stability for her large family: "In a pecuniary point of view twenty guineas towards your passage and a tot of crocks are at your service if you decide to go, be not offended at my blunt mode of dealing with this matter … [James] Gribben writes you do not like the Canadas and therefore I have named Sydney. I fear in Hobart Town I could do very little for you".[72] The "tot of crocks" came from Copeland's ownership of Spode pottery, and the china was passed down through the family, as a token of their Anglo-Irish heritage.[73] Dunlop's cousin William counselled her: "Courage and a few years will see you prosperous and happy. You must accommodate yourself to want of comforts, and forgetting that Solomon Hamilton's child was entitled by descent to an easier fate, you must struggle to build up new fortunes in a new land".[74] Settlement in New South Wales offered the best option to establish the Dunlop family independently. Although the colonial political environment proved to be as challenging as Northern Ireland in some respects, it also provided much material for the remainder of Dunlop's writing life.

"Native Poetry", Versified: Dunlop's Collections of Indigenous Languages

In colonial New South Wales, memories of Ireland, feelings of exile, and connections to family and friends now far distant often provided sources for Dunlop's writing, amid her spirited engagement with colonial topics, places and experiences. The conclusion of this chapter on how archival sources can build new understandings of the past turns to the manuscript in Dunlop's archive known as "Mrs. David Milson Kamilaroi Vocabulary and Aboriginal Songs, 1840" (Figure 2.6). The source is misleadingly named, yet Eliza Hamilton Dunlop is not the only unnamed contributor, for the voices of Indigenous informants and interlocutors are also embedded in a scrapbook of valuable linguistic and cultural knowledge. Indigenous communities hold the authority to understand and speak for that knowledge. Before the recent digitisation of Dunlop archival material

---

71   The Dunlops' social connections on arrival included the Irish-born physician and constitutional reformer Sir John Jamison; Lady Gipps, wife of the Governor, who seemingly became Eliza's confidant; and Roger Therry, the Irish barrister who would later become a judge of the Supreme Court of New South Wales. Therry was the junior counsel to John Hubert Plunkett who pursued the Myall Creek perpetrators through two controversial trials.

72   Qtd in De Salis, *Two Early Colonials*, 33. Gribben was a shopkeeper in Coleraine who had supported Copeland's candidacy.

73   The china was specified in David Dunlop's will, and in 1967 De Salis noted that individual pieces were still owned by members of the large descendant family.

74   Qtd in De Salis, *Two Early Colonials*, 34.

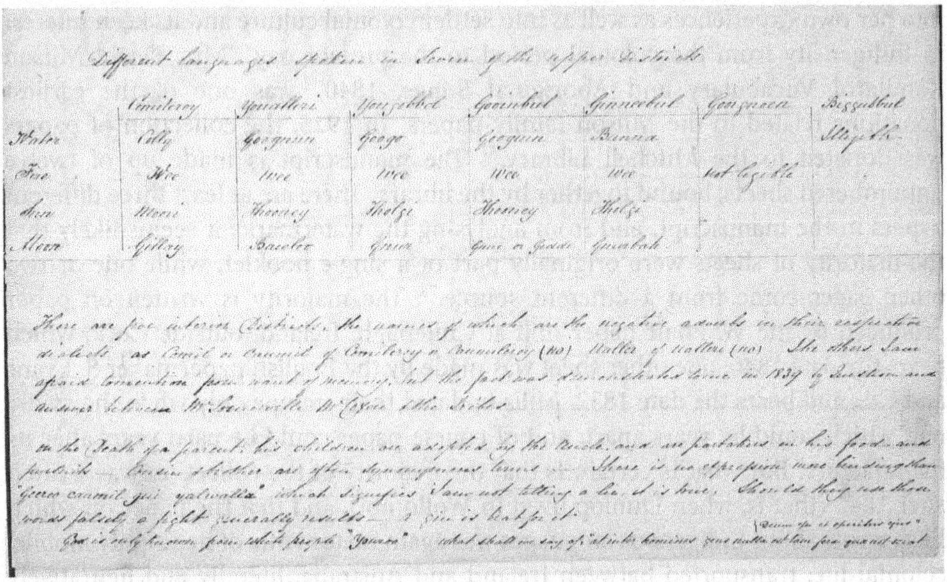

Figure 2.6: Eliza Hamilton Dunlop, "Different languages spoken in seven of the upper districts", Mrs. David Milson Kamilaroi Vocabulary and Aboriginal Songs, 1840–, (State Library of New South Wales, A1688).

that has been instigated by this book, the vocabulary was included in the State Library of New South Wales Rediscovering Indigenous Languages Project, where it has contributed to a rich and growing resource fed by linguists, local Indigenous communities and Indigenous researchers.[75] One powerful public outcome of the broader project has been the promotion of an Indigenous "word of the week", broadcast on national radio and social media alongside a campaign to spread understanding and usage of Indigenous languages. In September 2015, the word of the week was "Batadee. According to 'Mrs. David Milson Kamilaroi Vocabulary and Aboriginal Songs, 1840', Batadee means 'Father'".[76] Together with linguists working on Indigenous languages, this Indigenous-led use of Dunlop's archival collection keeps the knowledge alive, and activated for new and culturally significant purposes.

Yet the same archival source also tells us much about Eliza Hamilton Dunlop, in a similar way to her other writing. Read across Ireland and Australia, relationally, and intergenerationally, Dunlop's language studies provide considerable insight

75 Rediscovering Indigenous Languages, State Library of New South Wales, https://indigenous.sl.nsw.gov.au/ My thanks to Indigenous Librarian Ronald Briggs, State Library of New South Wales, for several discussions about these sources and their role in language revitalisation.

76 Indigenous Services, State Library of New South Wales, Rediscovering Indigenous Languages: Word of the Week, https://bit.ly/3atpFMQ.

into her own experiences as well as into settler colonial culture and its keen interest in Indigeneity from the colonial period to the present day. "Mrs. David Milson Kamilaroi Vocabulary and Aboriginal Songs, 1840" was one of the earliest donations related to the Milson family papers. In 1926, the collection of papers was donated to the Mitchell Library.[77] The manuscript is made up of twelve unnumbered sheets, bound together by the library. There are at least three different papers in the manuscript, and from analysing the watermarks it seems likely that the majority of sheets were originally part of a single booklet, while one or two other pages come from a different source.[78] The majority is written on paper produced by the W. Phair paper mill at Cullenagh, Ireland, outside Cork, which bears the date 1840; one other sheet was made by the English papermaker S. Evans and Co., and bears the date 1832. Mills updated their stamps only when they wore out, which could be years apart; and of course paper could be used years after its manufacture. But what is certain is that the majority of the collection was written after 1840 (that is, when Dunlop lived in Wollombi), and that the paper on which Eliza wrote about Indigenous languages was again metonymic of her highly mobile, colonial life: transported between Ireland and Australia, literally and figuratively stamped with Irish markers, yet animated by engagement with colonial Australian contexts. This archival source reveals how Dunlop's writing and thinking were influenced by engagement with Indigenous people and their culture.

Wordlists and vocabularies provide linguistic evidence, but they also reveal the conditions of collection and exchange, often intimate and interpersonal.[79] Most

---

77 The donor is identified as Rachel Milson's grandchild and the library's name plate acknowledges "D. Goddard". Her daughter Thalia Dunlop Milson married Charles Goddard: their children Roy, Keith and Ida were all keenly interested in their family history, and it is likely that one or all of them donated the material (Ida provided Margaret De Salis access to still undeposited family letters for her biography; the D on the name plate may be a misidentification). Charles' brothers Frederick and Sydney were keen collectors of Indigenous artefacts and they encouraged Roy and Keith to continue those interests: see David Kaus, "The Goddard Family: National Museum Collectors and Collections", *Friends (National Museum of Australia)* June (2003): 16–17. Roy wrote a biography of James Milson (*The Life and Times of James Milson*). He also transcribed some of the Aboriginal songs collected by Eliza Dunlop, and published them: "Aboriginal Poets as Historians", *Mankind* 1, no. 10 (1934): 243–46. Roy was an enthusiastic amateur: some of his methods and analyses of Indigenous sculpture have been questioned in the light of later research, yet his contributions to the Anthropological Society of New South Wales were notable. See Roy H. Goddard, *Aboriginal Sculpture* (Sydney: Australasian Medical Pub. Co., 1939); Glenn R. Cooke, "The Search for Kalboori Youngi", *Queensland Review* 13, no. 2 (2006): 49–64.
78 This information is derived from a conservation assessment provided by the State Library of South Wales: Jane Hughes, email to author, 30 August 2018. Many thanks to Michelle Berry for suggesting this approach.
79 See Hilary M. Carey, "Lancelot Threlkeld and Missionary Linguistics in Australia to 1850", in *Missionary Linguistics: Selected Papers from the First International Conference on Missionary Linguistics, Oslo, March 13th–16th, 2003*, ed. Otto Zwartjes and Even Hovdhaugen, (Amsterdam: John Benjamins, 2004), 253–75; Rachael Gilmour, *Grammars of Colonialism: Representing Languages in Colonial South Africa* (Basingstoke: Palgrave Macmillan, 2006); Hilary M. Carey, "Death, God and Linguistics: Conversations with Missionaries on the Australian Frontier", *Australian Historical Studies* 40, no. 2 (2009): 161–77; Anna Johnston, "Mrs

colonial language collecting was done by amateurs, often missionaries or curious government officials. Joseph Banks wrote down a list of words in what he called the "New Holland Language" from his time on the *Endeavour* in August 1770; early colonial officials such as Lieutenant-Governor David Collins and William Dawes transcribed the languages they experienced under contact conditions and published lists in accounts of the Colony, which became resources for later officials and settlers.[80] Inevitably, linguistics, like ethnography, became part of colonial governance, identifying and classifying communities and rendering Indigenous people subjects of the state.[81] Yet reading vocabularies for the colonial situations in which they were produced can provide glimpses into the ways that people (European and settler collectors and Indigenous interlocutors and informants) operated across and between cultures.

"Yalla murrethoo gwalda[.] moorguia binna / Speak in your own language[.] I want to learn as I am stupid", Dunlop records, in the latter half of the Kamilaroi vocabulary, clearly setting the terms for her instruction.[82] The first nine pages of this archival source are columns of words and phrases set under the title "Murree gwalda or Black's Language of Comileroi". It begins with words for "Blackmen" and "Whitemen", detailed terms for family relationships, and parts of the body, with a footnote explaining "These numbers require the aid of the fingers". Times of the day (by the sun), kinds of trees, native and introduced animals, insects, and varieties of snakes follow. Then come directive statements ("Rub it", "Bring them home"), questions ("Did you eat enough?" "Do you think it will rain?"), and phrases. Terms for Indigenous weapons, tools, and food preparation – and the materials involved – co-exist alongside terms for European domestic and farm labour ("Make the bed", "Milking"). Two pages interrupt the lists: one provides commentary about the process of language learning, noting abbreviations and speculative assessments about the multiple meanings of particular words or phrases. The second contains detailed notes under the heading "Gods and Goddesses", about particular spiritual beings and their function in culture, and then a transcribed song, with a footnote: "I believe these are properly 3 songs". The remainder of the archival object contains

---

Milson's Wordlist: Eliza Hamilton Dunlop and the Intimacy of Linguistic Work", in *Intimacies of Violence in the Settler Colony: Economies of Dispossession around the Pacific Rim*, ed. Penelope Edmonds and Amanda Nettelbeck (Switzerland: Palgrave Macmillan-Springer, 2018), 225–47.

80 David Collins, *An Account of the English Colony in New South Wales from Its First Settlement, in January 1788, to August 1801: With Remarks on the Dispositions, Customs, Manners, &C. of the Native Inhabitants of That Country. To Which Are Added Some Particulars of New Zealand; Compiled by Permission, from the Mss. of Lieutenant-Governor King; An Account of a Voyage Performed by Captain Flinders and Mr. Bass; by Which the Existence of a Strait Separating Van Diemen's Land from the Continent of New Holland Was Ascertained.* 2 vols. (1798; Sydney: University of Sydney Library – SETIS, 2003), http://purl.library.usyd.edu.au/setis/id/colacc2. See Jakelin Troy, "The Sydney Language Notebooks and Responses to Language Contact in Early Colonial NSW", *Australian Journal of Linguistics* 12, no. 1 (1992): 145–70.

81 Johannes Fabian, *Language and Colonial Power: The Appropriation of Swahili in the Former Belgian Congo 1880–1938* (Cambridge: Cambridge University Press, 1986).

82 "Mrs. David Milson Kamilaroi Vocabulary and Aboriginal Songs, 1840".

a table comparing "Different languages spoken in Seven of the Upper Districts", more transcribed songs with notes, and a shorter vocabulary titled "Words of the Wollombi Tribe of Aboriginal Natives New South Wales", written in the distinctive, loose handwriting of Dunlop in late life. Although some linguists have speculated whether Dunlop wrote all these components, a comparison of the juvenile notebook, "The Vase", and the vocabulary suggests it is almost certainly the same hand, writing and revising across time. In my assessment, this confirms Dunlop as the writer, with the slight possibility that Rachel Milson may have assisted as a scribe when Dunlop's handwriting deteriorated in old age.[83]

Dunlop's training as a poet provided her with a distinctive set of skills to analyse cadence and dialect. Her recognition of five to seven different language groups in the region represented by the chart, for example, is notable given that the nearby serious scholar of local languages, Reverend Lancelot Threlkeld, had taken many years to acknowledge the specific nature of the Awabakal language that he was collecting, only eighty kilometres east of Wollombi.[84] Dunlop's understanding of the precision demanded in recording language and the subtlety of how meaning was generated poetically and performatively is notable, as is her appreciation of the quality of Indigenous song and poetry:

> The flights of the lyric Poets are marvellously short perhaps the beauty of sentiment supplies the apparent deficiency – if not, repetition must – for all the aboriginal songs I have heard are frequently repeated, I am told by Mr Somerville who sings all these songs in concert with the Blacks that they are very difficult to be translated.

The source reveals how Dunlop later revised her early attempts to understand Indigenous languages: "N.B. I find I have frequently written Qui and Quia for <u>Gni</u> & gnia. In each poem the resemblance in the original between q and g ... I have corrected some, others remain as when written". Those revisions remain evident in the source, and are suggestive of the care Dunlop took to hear and precisely transcribe linguistic forms. They parallel the different forms of Irish that Dunlop sometimes used in composing her poetry, and the different variants that appear in both her drafts (often with orthography based on aural recollection) and in print (with unreliable availability of the correct print with diacritics).

The comparative table is clearly written out in fair copy, but it is obvious that Dunlop is writing retrospectively: she does not recall some details, noting that the information was gathered from an 1839 "Question and Answer between Mr

---

83 A poignant letter from Dunlop to an acquaintance in later life notes "I write with extreme difficulty not alone from my weak sight but from rheumatism in my arms and consequent tremor of my fingers". Eliza Hamilton Dunlop, Letter to Mrs Dalzell, 18 November 1865, https://www.mullavilla.com.au/hunter-valley-history/.

84 Anna Johnston, *The Paper War: Morality, Print Culture, and Power in Colonial New South Wales* (Crawley: University of Western Australia Press, 2011), especially Chapter Two, Colonial Linguistics.

Somerville, Mr Cox, and the Tribes" (Figure 2.6). This must have taken place at the very beginning of the Dunlops' Wollombi posting. On the settler side, that meeting was witnessed by Eliza and David Dunlop, most likely with Morris Townshend Somerville (a Hunter landowner who had been employed as an overseer in the nearby Wallis Plains since 1828) and William Cox, junior (a pastoralist with stations in Muswellbrook and Warialda, very close to the site of the Myall Creek massacre). On the Indigenous side, it most likely included Boni (a senior man in the Wollombi clan of the Darkinyung people), other unidentified members of the local community (which included Indigenous people displaced from colonial towns such as Newcastle and the violent north-west frontier), and probably also with visiting Aboriginal people, such as the noted songman Wulatji, providing the comparative information.[85] Four words are mapped against the different districts: water, fire, sun and moon. The language descriptions noted are improvisational, but they mostly bear a phonetic relationship to the language groups that are now listed under the designated AIATSIS category Gamilaraay / Gamilaroi / Kamilaroi language (D23) (NSW SH55-12).[86] In the early 1840s, Boni shared information with Dunlop about secret-sacred stones, and gender rules about cultural knowledge, which informed her poem "The Eagle Chief" (1842). In her published and private notes, Dunlop acknowledged Boni's advice about what information she could access, noting that she had to abide by his polite but firm refusal to elucidate certain aspects, explaining that "Ladies' eyes" could bring "bad luck belong it". Dunlop compared Indigenous knowledge protection practices to "hibernian" traditions: "that single phrase comprised a host of argument quite powerful in deterring me from any further effort to obtain view of the magic gem".[87] When published, the *Sydney Herald* condemned the cultural anachronism of sacred stones being brandished in a public ceremony, while the *Australian* instead pointed to "Mrs. Dunlop's well written and interesting note".[88] Dunlop's representation of the "gendered geography" created by men's and women's Dreamings was only partial, yet she made intuitive sense of it and considered this information a contribution to understanding Aboriginal culture, worth communicating to her readers alongside her own poem, which in other aspects was highly influenced by Sir Walter Scott and Robert Burns.[89]

---

85 Jim Wafer's exceptionally rich paper provides the most recent and detailed account of the songman, and the role of song traditions: "Ghost-Writing for Wulatji", 193–256.

86 AIATSIS, "Language Thesaurus", accessed June 2017, https://www1.aiatsis.gov.au/.

87 Notes on "The Eagle Chief", Eliza Hamilton Dunlop, "The Vase"; also published as "The Eagle Chief" *Sydney Gazette*, 21 April 1842.

88 "Domestic Intelligence: New Music", *Sydney Herald*, 18 April 1842; "The Eagle Chief: An Australian Melody by I. Nathan", *Australian*, 19 April 1842.

89 Deborah Bird Rose, "Gendered Substances and Objects in Ritual: An Australian Aboriginal Study", *Material Religion* 3, no. 1 (2007): 37. See John O'Leary's analysis of this poem: "Giving the Indigenous a Voice: Further Thoughts on the Poetry of Eliza Hamilton Dunlop", *Journal of Australian Studies* 28, no. 82 (2004): 85–93.

Dunlop attempted a "versification" of songs that Wulatji shared, despite her comments about the difficulties of translating Aboriginal songs. Those songs provide complex and valuable information about Wulatji as their author / transmitter and the richness of local Indigenous culture, but here I focus on Dunlop's own version: perhaps best considered an adaptation rather than a translation, as Wafer notes.[90] The poetic themes are familiar from Dunlop's *oeuvre* – home places, local environments marked by hills and water, and gendered landscapes deep with history, mythology and meaning – all with specific and rich linguistic markers. These themes mirror those of her Northern Irish writing from the 1810s onwards, but here the linguistic markers are inflected by her understanding of Indigenous words and ideas, so that the home is "the gibber-gunyah", which she glosses for readers as a cave in a rock (distinctive features of the Wollombi / Upper Hunter Valley). The sounds of Wanga (pigeon) fill the air; Makooroo / Makoro (fish) and Kanin (eel) glide in deep shady pools. This is a meaningful, self-sustaining, human and animal landscape, inhabited by Indigenous people, "[t]hat an *Amygest's* (whiteman's) track hath never been near". On the one hand, we can read this poem as a settler fantasy: an appropriation of an autochthonous worldview akin to the Garden of Eden, before the Fall.[91] Yet on the other, it falls within a minority Empire-wide tradition that considered Indigenous culture worth preserving and articulating for new audiences, especially settler colonial readers negotiating their own complex allegiances to place and nationality.[92]

Across the mid to late British Empire, "colonial savants" sought to collect local histories and knowledge. Prior to the advent of anthropology and its explicit imbrication with the colonial state, amateurs and enthusiasts tried to learn what they could about cultures that were being overridden and dismissed by the very colonial enterprises in which many collectors were also involved.[93] It is certainly possible to evaluate Dunlop's "Native Songs" critically within their surrounding colonial system, and to see her archive as implicated within the silencing and erasure of Indigenous voices.[94] Undoubtedly, her writing was shaped by Romantic

90 Wafer, "Ghost-Writing for Wulatji", 199.
91 See Terry Goldie, *Fear and Temptation: The Image of the Indigene in Canadian, Australian and New Zealand Literatures* (Kingston, Ont.: McGill University Press, 1989); Patrick Brantlinger, *Dark Vanishings: Discourse on the Extinction of Primitive Races, 1800–1930* (Ithaca: Cornell University Press, 2003); O'Leary, "Giving the Indigenous a Voice", 92.
92 John O'Leary, *Savage Songs and Wild Romances: Settler Poetry and the Indigene, 1830–1880* (Amsterdam: Rodopi, 2011); Jason R. Rudy, "Floating Worlds: Émigré Poetry and British Culture," *ELH* 81, no. 1 (2014); *Imagined Homelands: British Poetry in the Colonies* (Baltimore: Johns Hopkins, 2017).
93 Dirks, "Annals of the Archive"; on missionary ethnography, see Christopher Herbert, *Culture and Anomie: Ethnographic Imagination in the Nineteenth Century* (Chicago: University of Chicago Press, 1991).
94 On this point broadly, see N. Harkin, "The Poetics of (Re)Mapping Archives: Memory in the Blood", *JASAL: Journal of the Association for the Study of Australian Literature* 14, no. 3 (2014):

literary fashions and global trends in Anglophone writing, which found subjects that appealed to the European taste for the exotic in Indigenous cultures.

Yet Dunlop's literary experiments with Indigenous song also provide a way to map the "critical geography" of settler colonial writing. The Wiradjuri writer Jeanine Leane uses historical fiction that features an Indigenous presence to undertake "more culturally grounded readings of settler and Aboriginal authored works". Leane's call for an Indigenous viewpoint on the "settler cultural terrains" of literature is vibrant and urgent, and already being taken up by Indigenous scholars.[95] In parallel, Dunlop's work can be best understood by following Ann Laura Stoler's exhortation to read archives "along the grain".[96] Mining the Milson family archive for Eliza Hamilton Dunlop's voice and writing connects her Irish childhood and enthusiasms to her mature passions for writing in colonial New South Wales. Despite the privileges of her elite Anglo-Irish family, Dunlop was attuned to countering the pervasiveness of the English language in colonial settings such as Ireland and New South Wales. Her understanding was primed by reading revolutionary writing; she had heard Gaelic and Scottish words and histories that provided counter-narratives to the English presence in Northern Ireland; and she knew that religion and ethnicity could divide communities violently, with long-term effects that societies would struggle to resolve.

Dunlop's linguistic and poetic traces in the archive provide insight into the formation of settler society, including highly visible debates about the morality of colonisation and its devastating effects upon Indigenous people, as evidenced in "The Aboriginal Mother" (1838) in its various guises as poem, song and performance. Alongside the prejudice and racism that accompanied debates about massacre and Dunlop's poetic representation of it, the archive reveals traces of those who were uneasy about settler expansion, questioning its rapidity and dispossessive logic, and who sought to challenge derogatory assumptions about Indigenous people and cultures by studying seriously their languages and cultural productions. Without lapsing into an apologetic account of settler culture, Dunlop's writing provides another way to make meaning from the colonial past as embedded in the archives: one that provides a colonial precursor to reconciliation practices that emerged by listening carefully to different perspectives and interests, and finding common ground through family, history and culture.

1–14; Evelyn Araluen Corr, "Silence and Resistance: Aboriginal Women Working within and against the Archive", *Continuum* 32, no. 4 (2018): 487–502.

95   Jeanine Leane, "Tracking Our Country in Settler Literature", *JASAL: Journal of the Association for the Study of Australian Literature* 14, no. 3 (2014): 1. See also Harkin; Corr; and Peter Minter, this volume.

96   Ann Laura Stoler, *Along the Archival Grain: Epistemic Anxieties and Colonial Common Sense* (Princeton, NJ: Princeton University Press, 2009).

Part 1
Eliza Hamilton Dunlop and Global Literature

3

"Morning on Rostrevor Mountains" and the Making of Eliza Hamilton Dunlop

Duncan Wu

Where did Eliza Hamilton Dunlop come from? The sensibility that produced "The Aboriginal Mother" and other "Songs of an Exile" seems to have sprung fully formed from nowhere when presented with a subject matter that favoured her – the Myall Creek massacre. Yet it is clear, as one reads the outraged responses in Australian newspapers,[1] that her sympathy with the Indigenous people was something for which she had prepared – but how? This is more pressing for the manner in which Dunlop has been portrayed by recent critics. Katie Hansord is exactly right to say that Dunlop "distances herself from the English colonizer",[2] but I'm less certain as to whether Dunlop was ever camped on a "cultural borderland in which Irish writers (like Irish citizens) felt that their incomplete incorporation into British culture (to which they were reminded in various ways that they did not really 'belong') deprived them also of their Irishness".[3] It seems to me that incorporation into a new United Kingdom would have made them more assured of their cultural difference. For a writer such confidence can be a powerful tool. Dunlop's is an interesting case: she was four when Ireland entered the United Kingdom, so grew up when the "cultural borderland" was being mapped out. If any writer should have felt "deprived" of their Irishness, it was her.

"Morning on Rostrevor Mountains", composed probably in the early summer of 1835, reveals her poetic development three years before Myall Creek turned her into the author of "Songs of an Exile" – which would in turn crystallise her opposition to demands for those responsible for the massacre to be exonerated. That makes it hugely valuable because it offers us a profile of Dunlop at the age of

---

1   These are summarised and quoted in my article, "'A Vehicle of Private Malice': Eliza Hamilton Dunlop and the *Sydney Herald*", *Review of English Studies* 65/272 (November 2014): 888–903.

2   Katie Hansord, "Eliza Hamilton Dunlop's 'The Aboriginal Mother': Romanticism, Anti Slavery, and Imperial Feminism in the Nineteenth Century", *JASAL: Journal of the Association for the Study of Australian Literature* (2011): 9.

3   Stephen C. Behrendt, *British Women Poets and the Romantic Writing Community* (Baltimore, MD: Johns Hopkins University Press, 2008), 247.

thirty-nine, enabling us to judge who she thought she was and how sophisticated was her poetic talent. The question of identity is an important one. "The Aboriginal Mother" could have been written only out of confidence, and that in turn depended on a secure sense of self. Her poem "The Star of the South", published in 1842, refers to "Happy homes and free altars", which implies that, though a Protestant, she was sympathetic to the sufferings of Catholic neighbours. That hint, slight as it is, takes additional weight from the knowledge "she wrote in the ancient Irish, i.e., Gaelic".[4] There is an extensive literature dealing with the political implications of speaking and writing in Gaelic, especially in the years preceding and following the uprisings of 1798 and 1803.[5] It anticipated the nationalist impulse that emerged later in the century and was often taken to identify the speaker as Catholic.[6]

"Morning on Rostrevor Mountains" exists in several forms; in chronological order:

1. *The Dublin Penny Journal*, 8 August 1835, 42
2. *The Atlas*, 25 April 1845, 257
3. *Irish Miscellany*, 9 October 1858, 130, as "Morning on Rostrevor Mountain", published anonymously[7]
4. Eliza Hamilton Dunlop, "The Vase, comprising songs for music and poems by Eliza Hamilton Dunlop", manuscript notebook, as "'Morning' on Rostrevor Mountains".

"The Vase" post-dates all published texts; though the latest in a series, it provides the only manuscript of the poem that comes down to us. The *Dublin Penny Journal* provides the earliest of the various versions, and I will refer to that, other than when discussing the Australian stanza.

At the time she composed "Morning on Rostrevor Mountains", Dunlop was resident in Coleraine,[8] but its opening lines place her 100 miles to the south.

> 'Tis morning – from their heather bed
> The curling mists arise,
> And circling dark Slievedonard's head,
> Ascend the drowsy skies.
> 'Tis morning! and beside Cloch-mhor
> In solitude I stand,

---

4   Margaret De Salis, *Two Early Colonials* (Sydney: printed by the author, 1967), 11.
5   See, for a selection of these, *Ireland and Britain 1798–1922: An Anthology of Sources*, ed. Dennis Dworkin (Indianapolis: Hackett, 2012), 49–83.
6   See, for instance, Patrick F. Kavanagh, *A Popular History of the Insurrection of 1798* ("Second Centenary Edition", Cork: Guy, 1898), 11.
7   Elizabeth Webby argues persuasively that this version, being in a Boston paper, is unlikely to have originated with Dunlop; its source appears to have been the text in the *Dublin Penny Journal*.
8   Anna Johnston points out to me that this would explain why Eliza is now "A stranger on my natal shore".

A stranger on my natal shore,
And this, my father-land. (ll.1–8)[9]

She is on the slopes of Slieve Martin, a thousand feet above Rostrevor, next to what is now called Cloughmore, the 50-tonne granite boulder deposited on the mountain during the last Ice Age. The manuscript text provides a prose note: "Clogh-mhor i.e. large stone which according to tradition possesses many wondrous attributes; it is affirmed, that any who touch it, at the precise moment that it catches the first beams of the rising sun will obtain their wish, if a pure and proper one". The note's phrasing is considered: "it is affirmed" – as if the folklore, the magic inherent in the Irish landscape, were as potent as ever. From where she is, she can see the peak of Slieve Donard, nearly twenty miles to the north-east, at 2790 feet the highest mountain in Northern Ireland. This is home, the source of poetic power, from where she can recount her visits to Australia, India and Africa.

The emphasis on her "father-land" is buttressed by the respect accorded Gaelic placenames, even clearer in the manuscript where Slievedonard is "Slieve-dhonard" – as if language were fundamental to its identity. Dunlop is giving us access to a cultural Irishness that means a great deal to her – so that when she enumerates house and placenames, she wants us to be aware of their associations. During her infancy, Rostrevor was home to a number of United Irishmen, thanks partly to Wolfe Tone, who visited twice in 1792.[10] On his first visit, Tone had written: "Beautiful! Mourne, the sea etc. Sit up very late and talk treason".[11] And by 1797, the village was "swarming" with rebels.[12]

There was a price to be paid for joining a proscribed organisation such as the Society of United Irishmen. Dunlop would have heard about the Rostrevor mason Daniel McPolin or McPoland, whose membership got him transported,[13] and would certainly have known about Tom Dunn, Catholic master of the Rostrevor "hedge school", flogged to death for being a United Irishman in August 1798.[14]

In the next stanza, the poem focuses on individual dwellings.

---

9   "Morning on Rostrevor Mountains", *Dublin Penny Journal* 4 no. 162 (8 August 1835): 42.
10 See Jim Smyth, *The Men of No Property* (New York, NY: St Martin's Press, 1998), 94; Leo McCabe, *Wolfe Tone and the United Irishmen* (London: Heath Cranton, 1937), 126; W.E.H. Lecky, *A History of Ireland in the Eighteenth Century* (5 vols., Cambridge: Cambridge University Press, 2010), 3: 223.
11 John McCavitt and Christopher T. George, *The Man Who Captured Washington: Major General Robert Ross and the War of 1812* (Norman: University of Oklahoma Press, 2016), 12.
12 Ibid.
13 Myrtle Hill, Brian S. Turner and Kenneth Dawson, *1798 Rebellion in County Down* (Dublin: Counterpoint Books, 1998), 209.
14 McCavitt and George, *The Man Who Captured Washington*, 12.

> Rostrevor! each illumin'd line
> Of early life's romance,
> Deep in this magic page of thine,
> Is mirror'd to my glance:
> Clonallan's spire, Rosetta's shades,
> From Classic Arno's Vale
> To Ballyedmond's groves and glades, –
> Land of my homage, hail! (ll.9–16)

Eliza spent the first ten years of her life with her grandmother at Fort Hamilton, her father, Solomon Hamilton, having been appointed advocate of the Supreme Court in Calcutta, in 1796. As she grew up, she came to know everyone in the small hamlet. Clonallan is two miles down the road from Rostrevor; Rosetta was the name of a large house "in a very pleasant situation between the road and the shore", owned by the Reverend Holt Waring. (In 1815, and possibly before that, it was rented out to the Misses Taylor.[15]) A minute's walk away was Arno's Vale, owned by James Moore. From some time before 1792, its chief resident was the wealthy merchant-captain Thomas Mercer, who also had a residence in Dublin. He had the distinction of being described by the Marquess of Downshire in private correspondence as "a dangerous man, a great republican & very rich & largely connected about Newry".[16] All of which was accurate. In 1792, Mercer hosted a dinner of thirty Catholic and Protestant Irishmen with Wolfe Tone as guest speaker. ("Ride to Rosstrevor, more and more in love with it", Tone wrote in his diary.[17]) Also that year, Mercer chaired a meeting in Newry at which the Fall of the Bastille was celebrated and £173 collected for citizen-soldiers in France.[18] He was sole signatory to a congratulatory address that meeting sent to the National Assembly in Paris. These were activities for which he risked being found guilty of treason.[19] However, Mercer seems to have remained at Arno's Vale until at least 1813.[20] Ballyedmond townland is a mere two and a half miles along the Lough from Rostrevor; it was the property of Solomon Hamilton from 1792 to 1807, and in the 1790s its castle was visited frequently by William Drennan, co-founder, with Wolfe Tone, of the United Irish Society.[21] Thomas Mercer was a friend of Drennan,[22] so it is reasonable to think Drennan also visited Arno's Vale. In due course, young Eliza Hamilton would

---

15 Réamonn Ó Muirí, "Newry and the French Revolution, 1792", *Seanchas Ardmhacha: Journal of the Armagh Diocesan Historical Society* 13 no. 2 (1989): 116.

16 C.J. Woods, "Samuel Turner's Information on the United Irishmen, 1797–8", *Analecta Hibernica* no. 42 (2011): 208.

17 Ó Muirí, "Newry and the French Revolution, 1792", 105.

18 Ó Muirí, "Newry and the French Revolution, 1792", 103.

19 McCavitt and George, *The Man Who Captured Washington*, 12, 224 n 22.

20 Ó Muirí, "Newry and the French Revolution, 1792", 116–21.

21 Marie McStay, *Carlingford Lough* (Donaghadee: Cottage Publications, 2004), 55.

22 Woods, "Samuel Turner's Information on the United Irishmen, 1797–8", 108–33.

have read Drennan's elegies for William Orr in *The Press* – among the finest poems to emerge from the United Irishmen.[23]

The most important battles of the '98 uprising took place in Ulster. On 9 June, Henry Munro and his rebels routed Colonel Stapleton's yeomanry and took Saintfield (50 miles to the north),[24] though Munro's defeat at Ballynahinch (a mere 25 miles away), on 12 and 13 June at the hands of 2000 troops under General Nugent, Commander of the northern garrison, would bring the rebellion to an end. This was achieved with a threat masquerading as clemency: amnesty was offered to all, on condition that Munro and his men surrender, otherwise the British would "set fire to and totally destroy, the towns of Killinchy, Killeleagh, Ballynahinch, Saintfield, and every cottage and farmhouse in the vicinity of those places, carry off the stock and cattle, and put every one to the sword who may be found in arms".[25] Terrified, every inhabitant of every town and village in County Down rendered arms to the British, apologised, and promised better in future.[26] Munro and Henry Joy McCracken, his Antrim colleague, were executed along with thirty-two leaders of the Ulster rising,[27] Munro being hanged outside his own front door.[28] The lessons of that year would be remembered for a long time to come.[29]

The same tactic led to the capture of Captain William Dunlop, father of the man Eliza would marry; he was hanged from a beech tree in Coleraine on 11 June 1798 and buried beneath it rather than in consecrated ground.[30] That taught David Dunlop and, in turn, Eliza, much about the British, and in 1865 she paid tribute to her father-in-law's courage during "the fierce reign of terror" in " The Two Graves".[31] Such a poem would have been unpublishable in 1798; if, more than

---

23 Guy Beiner, *Forgetful Remembrance: Social Forgetting and Vernacular Historiography of a Rebellion in Ulster* (Oxford: Oxford University Press, 2018), 78.

24 The most detailed account of the skirmish is William M'Comb's *Guide to Belfast* (Belfast: William M'Comb, 1861), 111–13.

25 Quoted in Beiner, *Forgetful Remembrance*, 93. Munro's betrayal to the British forces is recounted by M'Comb, *Guide to Belfast*, 124–25.

26 Beiner, *Forgetful Remembrance*, 93. This was reported in the *Belfast News-Letter*, 15 June 1798, 3.

27 Alvin Jackson, *Ireland 1798–1998: War, Peace and Beyond*, 2nd ed. (Oxford: Wiley-Blackwell, 2010), 19.

28 Thomas Bartlett, "Defence, Counter-insurgency, and Rebellion: Ireland, 1793–1803", *A Military History of Ireland*, ed. Thomas Bartlett and Keith Jeffrey (Cambridge: Cambridge University Press, 1997), 282.

29 Beiner lists a number of Ulster centenarians who, as late as 1889, remembered the events of 1798, including Bridget Brennan of Rostrevor, whom Eliza may have known: *Forgetful Remembrance*, 203–225.

30 Beiner, *Forgetful Remembrance*, 153; De Salis, *Two Early Colonials*, 12; Cliff Hanna, *Bandits on the Great North Road: The Bushranger as Social Force* (Newcastle-upon-Tyne: Nimrod Publications, 1993), 90. Dunlop's corpse was retrieved by friends and buried in the family vault at Derrykeighan; see Barbara Hill, "The 1798 Rebellion in Coleraine and District", *North Irish Roots* 9, no. 2 (1998): 18.

31 I thank Elizabeth Webby for this information. The poem was published in a Sydney newspaper, *The Empire*, 15 April 1865, where date of composition is given as 24 March 1865.

sixty-five years later, there was no danger, Dunlop is still careful to say nothing that might alarm the authorities.

The reference to "Arno's Vale ... / Ballyedmond's groves and glades" is barbed: the association with Mercer, Drennan and – most potently of all – Wolfe Tone reminds us that this picturesque idyll had once been a hotbed of insurrection. This is to be a recurrent feint: Dunlop will name something, or use something, that on the surface appears uncontroversial, by way of articulating an incendiary subtext. Her counters are camouflaged. In that sense, "Morning on Rostrevor Mountains" marks Dunlop's artistic coming of age, its subject being the recognition that injustice and oppression, like the light of the sun, are everywhere.

In stanza 3 she apostrophises the rising sun in a manner reminiscent of loco-descriptive poets of the eighteenth century:

> Yon orb – the beautiful, the bold,
> Hath left his ocean bride,
> And from her couch of wavy gold
> Comes forth in regal pride.
> Fair sun – I've seen that crown of rays
> As gallantly put on,
> And mark'd thy robes of crimson haze
> O'er other waters thrown. (ll.17–24)[32]

The rising sun is code: it means liberty.[33] In 1794, the United Irishmen declared to Dubliners, "There is no truth in any political system, in which the Sun of Liberty is not placed in the centre, with knowledge to enlighten, and benevolence to warm and invigorate; with the same ray to gild the Palace and illuminate the Cottage".[34] In a pamphlet "on behalf of the Catholics of Ireland", Wolfe Tone wrote:

> The dark cloud which has so long enveloped the Irish Catholic with hopeless misery, at length begins to break, and the sun of liberty may once more illuminate his mind, and elevate his heart.[35]

---

32 The manuscript text contains a number of variants, the most important of which makes the subject of the stanza "Morning the beautiful – the bold" (in its first line).

33 The sun had been used in symbolic paintings created before and during the Revolution to symbolise enlightenment; see Susan Maslan, *Revolutionary Acts: Theater, Democracy, and the French Revolution* (Baltimore: Johns Hopkins University Press, 2005), 158, 243–74.

34 *The Society of United Irishmen* (Dublin, 1794), 197. No author or publisher is listed on the title-page.

35 [Theobald Wolfe Tone], *An Argument on Behalf of the Catholics of Ireland* (Belfast: Society of United Irishmen, 1791), 28.

Its significance was taken so much for granted that William Drennan was able to conclude a letter with the assertion that volunteers among the United Irishmen were "Friends to the Rising Sun".[36] Guy Beiner has shown how the poet Mary Balfour elegised Henry Joy McCracken using the rising sun to describe her belief in the ultimate victory of the movement, even though "[s]uch defiance could not be uttered openly".[37]

Many songs of the United Irishmen use the image of the sun: "To your Tents, O Erin!" declares its hope that when union advanced "o'er Erin's green land, / The sun of her Freedom shall vertical stand". And in "London Pride and Shamrock", which appeared in *The Press* on 21 October 1797:

> The sun shoots forth his kindest ray,
> And Shamrock strengthens every day ...

In "Slumbering Ireland", the sun is an image not only of liberty but of armed rebellion:

> Awake from your slumbers – advance and be clever,
> And like rays from the sun, dart forth and deliver
> Your brothers and children from fell tyranny.[38]

Dunlop would not have needed to know these works to be aware that the rising sun implied refusal to surrender to a hostile oppressor. And when she writes that the sun's crimson robe is "O'er other waters thrown", she turns to other contexts in which that liberating urge has resulted in armed conflict. "Yon orb – the beautiful, the bold", she writes, mindful that "bold" (meaning daring, courageous, fearless) was the epithet used by admirers to describe the United Irishmen, not least Robert Emmet.[39]

As the sun "Comes forth in regal pride", the poem extends its thematic reach.

> Rock'd on the billowy bed that heaves
>   Beneath the burning line,
> I've seen where the horizon weaves
>   Its purple threads with thine,
> And hail'd in all their pride of birth,
>   Thy purest lustres given,
> To gladden scenes more fair than earth –
>   The sea – the sea and heav'n! (ll.25–32)

---

36 *The Drennan Letters: Being a Selection from the Correspondence which Passed between William Drennan, M.D. and His Brother-in-law and Sister, Samuel and Martha McTier, During the Years 1776–1819* (Belfast: His Majesty's Stationery Office, 1931), 180.

37 Beiner, *Forgetful Remembrance*, 109, 179.

38 *Literary Remains of the United Irishmen of 1798*, ed. R.R. Madden (Dublin: Duffy, 1887), 55, 292, 90.

39 Tom Maguire's ballad "Bold Robert Emmet" is still widely sung in Dublin.

Dunlop is remarkable for the internationalism of her thought. Her first exposure to oppression was in her "father-land", where the uprisings taught her the importance of armed resistance, even if the oppressor was stronger than oneself. The poem having begun in Rostrevor, it now proceeds to declare a vision for freedom that spans the world: the poet herself has been rocked "Beneath the burning line" (at the equator) and imagines "scenes more fair than earth" on which the sun will shine, "the sea and heav'n" – an image startlingly redolent of St John the Divine 21:1: "And I saw a new heaven and a new earth: for the first heaven and the first earth were passed away". It is tempting also to hear Wordsworth when he writes "The gentleness of heaven broods o'er the sea" in "It was a beauteous evening" (first published in 1807),[40] though Dunlop is as likely to have been exposed to the millenarianism of Irish pamphleteers from the 1790s – John Owen's *The Shaking and Translation of Heaven and Earth* among them.[41] Those resonances are striking because the poem is about to embark on a vision of colonial oppression that demands ultimate justice.

At this point the manuscript contains a stanza published only in the version of the poem in the *Atlas* newspaper:

> Where the wild Emu leads her brood –
> Across the trackless plains,
> And lord of nature's solitude –
> The stately Cedar reigns:
> Even there – through Exile's cheerless hours!
> Beneath Australian skies;
> I've lingered amid orange bowers –
> To catch thy scented sighs.[42]

This was written after Dunlop's arrival in Australia in 1838 – that's to say, at least three years (and quite possibly more) after the rest of the poem, which had appeared in print in 1835. The emu suggests it was written at Emu Plains, Penrith, where emu were, apparently, still to be seen. The "New Holland Cassowary" (as it was sometimes called) thrived on open grassland, managed by Indigenous people.[43] Dunlop's writing is pointed: when white settlers arrived in what would become

---

40 One would like to argue that Dunlop had read Wordsworth's "Recluse" fragments of 1798, which were not of course available to her, or at least *The Prelude* – though that wasn't available either, as it was not published until 1850. The point is that there is every reason she would have been fascinated by Wordsworth's millenarian writings.

41 This is one of a number of similar tracts listed by Myrtle Hill, *The Time of the End: Millenarian Beliefs in Ulster* (Belfast: The Belfast Society, 2001), 23.

42 Elizabeth Webby points out to me the manuscript version dates from c.1870, which means that it post-dates the *Atlas* text.

43 For further discussion of land management by Indigenous people, see Bill Gammage, *The Greatest Estate on Earth: How Aborigines Made Australia* (Sydney: Allen & Unwin, 2011) and Bruce Pascoe, *Dark Emu: Black Seeds: Agriculture or Accident?* (Broome: Magabala Books, 2014).

Sydney, the first thing they did was slaughter emu, regarding them as pests along with kangaroo.[44] In subsequent years, recreational killings of emu became commonplace – as W.C. Wentworth noted in 1824:

> I think that the most fastidious sportsman ... might without moving have seen the finest coursing from the commencement of the chase to the death of the game; and, when tired of killing kangaroos, he might have hunted emus with equal success.[45]

Indigenous people would have been disturbed by this. They associated emu with the spirit of the creator Baiame; emu-figures appear in the Dreaming;[46] they appeared in cave-paintings including "panaramitee", found in rock-shelters in the Blue Mountains.[47] And they were totemic, carved into tree bark as part of Dreaming knowledge.[48] More importantly, emu were a natural resource like any other, valuable for eggs, bones and feathers; not only were settlers' attitudes disrespectful to nature, they were needlessly wasteful.

The poem then mentions a tree. Dunlop could have chosen any number of examples, but selects one with particular significance. As soon as the First Fleet arrived, they began looking for quality timber; most of the available woods being too hard, they were pleased to find the more workable red cedar (*toona ciliate*) along the Nepean and Hawkesbury rivers.[49] These trees were massive. Individual trees were of two to three metres in diameter.[50] Soon colonials were using red cedar to make everything – boats, houses, furniture, even coffins. Dunlop would have seen the offices of Alexander Berry and Edward Wollstonecraft whose business, established in 1822 in George Street, Sydney, had made a fortune shipping red cedar to Britain.[51] The result was devastation. Thanks to them, and other merchants, more than 10,000 acres of red cedar round the Shoalhaven River had been felled – and continued to be felled on an industrial scale. Restrictions had been imposed as early as 1795, but did little to suppress the appetite for "red gold". Trees that had taken two hundred years to mature, and which could live for

---

44 *The Emu: Official Organ of the Australasian Ornithologists' Union* 33–4 (1933), 69.

45 William Charles Wentworth, *A Statistical Account of the British Settlements in Australasia*, 3rd ed., 2 vols. (London, 1824), 1: 269.

46 For instance, "The Emu and the Turkey", William Howell Edwards, *An Introduction to Aboriginal Societies* 2nd ed. (South Melbourne: Thomson, 1988), 29; Val Attenbrow, *Sydney's Aboriginal Past: Investigating the Archaeological and Historical Records*, 2nd ed. (Sydney: UNSW Press, 2010), 128.

47 Attenbrow, *Sydney's Aboriginal Past*, 147.

48 Attenbrow, *Sydney's Aboriginal Past*, 129.

49 Fyfe and Patricia Bygrave, *Growing Australian Red Cedar and Other Meliaceae Species in Plantation* (Canberra: Rural Industries Research and Development Corporation, 2005), 4.

50 Bygrave, *Growing Australian Red Cedar*, 5.

51 The Classified advertisements in the Sydney papers carried regular bulletins from F. Girard who sold "Any quantity of superior Cedar Plank to suit the English market, measuring from 500 to 1000 feet each" (*Sydney Gazette and New South Wales Advertiser*, Thursday, 16 February 1837, 1).

a thousand years, started to disappear from the vast Hunter River floodplains in 1801; by 1819, one visitor to the area noted there was "little timber, only a few trees to an acre".[52] Within a few years of that, cedar stocks in the Illawarra and Hunter River regions were commercially extinct.[53]

At first, some Indigenous workers were complicit in the trade, though not for long. They discovered that whites could be hard, treacherous taskmasters, shooting them dead for the smallest offence, ruthlessness being the order of the day.[54] Many Indigenous people opposed logging because it cut across the delicate balance created by their land management. Besides which they thought of trees as literally alive – as was the land out of which the cedars came. The trees were sacred, and for hundreds of years they had used them as a medicine. Many thousands of red cedars carried carvings, some dating back hundreds of years: those trees were important as a means of communication with older generations.[55] But there was no explaining this to the settlers, and Indigenous groups had little option but to use against cutters the same force used on them. What became a guerrilla war between cedar-cutters and Indigenous people began in November 1804.[56] When cutters moved into the Illawarra in 1815, violence spread, and would continue until the late 1840s.[57] The military expedition of 1816, in which British troops attempted to put an end to raids, implemented Governor Macquarie's policy of inflicting "terrible and exemplary punishment" upon Aborigines, slaughtering them and hanging corpses from the trees.[58]

The red cedar "reigns" – along with its defenders. As in Ireland, the invaders imposed their will by violence, disregarding the beliefs, religious or otherwise, of those who were there first. Dunlop saw the evidence for herself. By the time she arrived in Sydney, the cedar woods north, south and west of the township were

52   John Howe, qtd in Helen Brayshaw, *Aborigines of the Hunter Valley* (Scone: Scone and Upper Hunter Historical Society, 1987), 12.

53   Ian Parsonson, *The Australian Ark: A History of Domesticated Animals in Australia* (Collingwood: CSIRO, 1998), 98; Catherine Warne, *Lower North Shore* (Alexandria: Kingsclear Books, 2005), 19.

54   Christine M. Bramble, "Relations between Aborigines and White Settlers in Newcastle and the Hunter District, 1804–1841" (M.Litt. thesis, University of New England, 1981), 33. For more detailed discussion, see Penny Russell, "Death on a River: Honour and Violence in an Australian Penal Colony, 1826–1827", *Honour, Violence and Emotions in History*, ed. Carolyn Strange, Robert Cribb and Christopher E. Forth (London: Bloomsbury, 2014), 122.

55   See Robert Etheridge, *The Dendroglyphs or Carved Trees of New South Wales* (Sydney: Sydney University Press, 2011).

56   Bramble, "Relations between Aborigines and White Settlers", 32. See also "Contest with the Upper Hunter Blacks in 1804", on the University of Newcastle's Living Histories site, https://livinghistories.newcastle.edu.au/nodes/view/57555.

57   Parsonson, 98; Michael Organ, "C.W. Peck's Australian Legends: Aboriginal Dreaming Stories of Eastern Australia", *Australian Folklore* 29 (2014): 67. C.D. Rowley describes the pre-emptive violence used against Aborigines by cedar-getters on the Clarence River in 1841: *The Destruction of Aboriginal Society* (Canberra: Australian National University Press, 1970), Chapter 7.

58   John Connor, *The Australian Frontier Wars, 1788–1838* (Sydney: UNSW Press, 2005), 51; Heather Goodall, *Invitation to Embassy: Land in Aboriginal Politics in New South Wales, 1788–1972* (St Leonards, NSW: Allen & Unwin, 1996), 28.

gone – as were the emu, which had once nested on the banks of Port Jackson.[59] If the Myall Creek massacre drew her into Aboriginal affairs, the emu and "stately Cedar" remind us of her sympathies. Other Australians with Irish roots felt the same way; two young men, sons of an Irish convict,

> had a sympathetic association with wanton destruction and indiscriminate murder of innocent souls, as their forefathers had suffered similar fates as the result of persecution, greed and murder at the hands of the British nobility and military in the conquest of Ireland. It is said that they showed respect and compassion to the Wiradjuri and were recorded by some as being kind to the Indigenous groups.[60]

The next stanza goes back in time. Dunlop reached Kolkata, then the property of the East India Company, and centre of the British opium trade, in August 1820, to hear that her father had died as long ago as March. She learnt also, for the first time, that she had "two Sisters here, half casts".[61] There must have been many such relatives of British people in India, most regarded as an embarrassment; Dunlop's brothers had severed all connection with them.[62] Typically, Eliza "became very fond of her step-sisters and suggested one of them accompany her back to Ireland".[63] With that in mind, it would be rash to assume the first of her stanzas about Calcutta is merely picturesque.

> Yes! and where Gunga's mighty streams
> Their sacred waters spread,
> I've seen beneath thy worshipp'd beams
> Ten thousands bow the head:
> And by the Brahmin's funeral pile
> In that far hemisphere,
> Sunrise, alas! I've met thy smile,
> Mocking the burning bier! (ll.33–40)

There is little to distinguish Dunlop's adoration of "Yon orb – the beautiful, the bold" from that of the "ten thousands" – and equally little to dispel the millenarianism of earlier stanzas as she views the "sacred waters" of the Ganges and "worshipp'd beams" of the sun. *Ganga Ma*, Mother Ganges, is truly the river of life and death: Indian mythology is full of stories about its healing properties

---

59 John Hunter, *An Historical Journal of the Transactions of Port Jackson and Norfolk Island* (London, 1793), 481.
60 Dennis Foley, "Leadership: The Quandary of Aboriginal Societies in Crises, 1788–1830, and 1966", *Transgressions: Critical Indigenous Australian Histories*, ed. Ingereth Macfarlane and Mark Hannah (Canberra: Australian National University E Press, 2007), 183–84.
61 Letter to David Dunlop, 25 August 1820, qtd in De Salis, *Two Early Colonials*, 21.
62 "My Brothers do not notice them": qtd in De Salis, *Two Early Colonials*, 21.
63 Qtd in De Salis, *Two Early Colonials*, 21.

and powers of ablution and redemption.[64] It has the power literally of washing away one's sins, and to die on its banks, be cremated there, and have one's ashes cast upon its waters is the highest wish of every Hindu.[65] Perhaps Dunlop had seen the old and sick on its banks, hoping that at the moment of death they would be drawn into its waters.[66] This stanza's mood is visionary, even as the sun approaches its author. Irish rebels had once drawn "on the prophecies of Patrick and Columkille to assert the inevitability of the Irish reconquest of their land from the invader";[67] Dunlop invokes an encounter with the sun as a means of suggesting something similar, but in an Indian context – for the sun rises up just as the Indian people will do, sanctified by Mother Ganges, scorning death with a smile. In short, the stanza is about armed revolution.

This was no daydream. Dunlop would have known there had been two major uprisings in recent years – the Vellore Mutiny of 1806 and the Sannyasi Rebellion in Jalpaiguri, West Bengal, ongoing for fifty years prior to her arrival.[68] (As Jalpaiguri was 365 miles to the north, the turmoil was far enough away not to inconvenience anyone in Kolkata, but was a reminder that opposition to the East India Company could spring up at a moment's notice.) In later years, Dunlop would hear about the Indian rebellion of 1857, comparable with those in Ireland because it involved the general population, motivated by longstanding grievances against British rule.

And then the poem's imagery becomes darker.

> In Saugur's sickly jungle met –
>   Met on the arid sand,
> Where the dark domes of Juggernaut's
>   Profane pagoda's stand –
> Met in Calcutta's graveyard gloom,
>   Piercing the tainted air,
> Thy sick'ning rays – a marble tomb
>   Engulfs my memory there. (ll. 41–48)

Dunlop's reference to "Saugur's sickly jungle" is to what is now called Sagar Island at the mouth of the Ganges delta, about 54 nautical miles south of Kolkata, which she would have seen when the boat bringing her from Liverpool entered the Hooghly River. After a "storm wave" laid waste to various clearance and reclamation schemes in 1826, Sagar was allowed to lapse

---

64 Sudipta Sen, *Ganges: The Many Pasts of an Indian River* (New Haven, CT: Yale University Press, 2019), Chapter 1.

65 Eric Newby, *Slowly Down the Ganges* (London: Harper Press, 2011), 2.

66 Sen, *Ganges*, 4.

67 Myrtle Hill, *The Time of the End: Millenarian Beliefs in Ulster* (Belfast: The Belfast Society, 2001), 10.

68 Subhajyoti Ray, *Transformations on the Bengal Frontier: Jalpaiguri 1765–1948* (London: Routledge, 2003), Chapter 1.

back into jungle.[69] It was inhabited but Dunlop would not have set foot there for it had an inhospitable reputation, as Victor Jacquemont recounted in 1834 when he called it "the lowest and most hideous [island] of this vast Delta – the classic region of tigers!"[70] Dunlop's reference to "the dark domes of Juggernaut's / Profane pagoda's stand" is equally specific: she describes the Black Pagoda, a Navratna temple on the Chitpur Road built by Gobindaram Mitra, who had worked as a tax collector for the East India Company.[71] This grand building dated back to 1730, but was in ruins thanks to an earthquake and cyclone that struck on the same day in 1737. A painting by the British watercolourist Thomas Princep, dating from 1829, now in the British Library, shows how it appeared to Dunlop.[72] The surviving fragments were tall enough to be seen by boats approaching the city.[73] The "marble tomb" of the stanza's penultimate line might be that of Dunlop's father, in which case the "graveyard gloom" is that of the South Park Street Cemetery in Kolkata, where Solomon Hamilton was interred.[74] But that would be a very literal reading; "graveyard" is being used as an adjective, not as a noun.

Actual places *are* recalled here, but the "marble tomb" takes us somewhere deeper and darker, as if we are no longer dealing with mere tourist sights but with a symbol of some kind. Dunlop may have had in mind the Black Hole of Calcutta at Fort William, the fortified town that once comprised the main settlement of the East India Company in Bengal. Dunlop would have heard of it and known where it was: in the north-west corner of Tank Square. The remains of the old Fort had been dismantled two years before her arrival,[75] but the location of the Black Hole was marked, as it had been since 1757, by a 50-foot-high obelisk bearing the names of the victims, erected at the urging of one of the few survivors, John Zephaniah Holwell. Dunlop would have been among the last to see it, because it was pulled down in 1821 as the reforming Marquess of Hastings feared "it reminded of a calamity that had befallen the English".[76]

---

69 Lieutenant-Colonel D.G. Crawford, *Roll of the Indian Medical Service 1615–1930*, 2 vols. (London: Thacker, 1930), 1: xlii–xliii.

70 Victor Jacquemont, *Letters from India*, 2 vols. (London, 1834), 1: 83. Even as late as 1887, it was reported that Sagar was "infested by tigers and other wild beasts"; see Sir William Wilson Hunter, *The Imperial Gazetteer of India, Volume XII*, 2nd ed. (London: Trübner, 1887), 110.

71 Krishna Dutta, *Calcutta: A Cultural and Literary History* (Oxford: Signal Books, 2003), 48.

72 See https://bit.ly/34cJwfU.

73 It was seen by Richard Heber on the approach to Kolkata in 1824; see his *Narrative of a Journey through the Upper Provinces of India* (London, 1844), 17.

74 The cemetery opened in 1767 and was the ultimate place of rest for many employees of the East India Company. Besides Solomon Hamilton, it accommodated Sir William Jones; see Keith Humphrey, *Calcutta Revisited: Exploring Calcutta Through Backstreets and Byways* (Tolworth: Grosvenor House, 2014), Chapter 27.

75 Partha Chatterjee, *The Black Hole of Empire: History of a Global Practice of Power* (Princeton, NJ: Princeton University Press, 2012), 4.

76 Qtd in M.L. Augustine, *Fort William: Calcutta's Crowning Glory* (New Delhi: Ocean Books, 1999), 105. See also C.R. Wilson, "A Short History of Old Fort William in Bengal", *Bengal: Past*

Dunlop makes no explicit mention of the Black Hole and perhaps, in a poem styled as a memoir, there is no reason why she should. But this is also about the unstoppability of the revolutionary impulse, and for a poem of that kind there is every reason why, beneath her evocation of the sepulchral atmosphere of the city, there would be a submerged reference to its grim history, and tacit critique of its colonial past. She would have known that the deaths of the British came about only when Shuja-ud-daulah, the last independent Nawab of Bengal, took control of Kolkata, the British having declined to stop work on Fort William.[77] That was the first in a string of "native atrocities"[78] against the colonials, but Dunlop would have realised there was another perspective. Had she not, she might have been prompted by James Mill who in 1818 noted that "the English had their own practice to thank for suggesting it [that is, the Black Hole] to the officers of the Subahdar as a fit place of confinement" – the cause of widespread outrage in the periodicals, not least the *Asiatic Journal*:

> By this schoolboy *tu quoque* logic, the English who perished in the black-hole are made to expiate the atrocities of imprisonment in England; and their destruction by the most lingering death that can be inflicted, is held up to the youthful students of Indian history as a just retribution for the vices inherent in the jurisprudence of their native country, which sanctions personal imprisonment![79]

The idea that Dunlop would align herself with an architect of Utilitarian thought might seem odd, but on this matter, they found common ground. Mill was highly sceptical of colonialism. He thought it beneficial to the aristocracy whose coffers it filled but to no one else. It was the cause of war and a constant drain on the country's resources. At the same time, given that the British were now in India, he thought there was a responsibility to improve the country.[80] Clearly, Dunlop would not have agreed with everything Mill said – he believed, for instance, that only Europeans found it humiliating or shameful to be ruled by colonising forces – but had she come across his views on India, she would probably have approved.

In the years since her visit to India, Dunlop's views on the cost of Empire can only have hardened – not least because, in Ireland and India, she recognised the same one-size-fits-all approach to government. With the Act of Union, the Irish Parliament disappeared and the United Kingdom Parliament exerted its control through magistrates, garrison towns, and the Ordnance Survey of 1824; in India,

---

and Present 2 (January 1908), 10. A detailed description of the obelisk and its inscriptions is in the *Handbook of the Bengal Presidency: With an Account of Calcutta City* (London, 1882), 102. See also Chatterjee, *The Black Hole of Empire*, 65.

77   Anthony Read and David Fisher, *The Proudest Day: India's Long Road to Independence* (New York, NY: W.W. Norton, 1997), 14.

78   Read and Fisher, *The Proudest Day*, 19.

79   Review of James Mill, *History of British India, Asiatic Journal and Monthly Miscellany* 27 (1829) 529.

80   Don Habibi, *John Stuart Mill and the Ethic of Human Growth* (Dordrecht: Kluwer, 2001), 188.

Cornwallis removed Indians from high office and ruled through garrisons and the Great Trigonometrical Survey (1818).[81] As one recent historian has noted, the manner in which the British governed Ireland "would provide a model for British rule in India".[82] Dunlop could have provided detailed comparisons, and probably met Indians who were concerned for the Irish because of their own experiences – indeed, Indian residents of Calcutta collected funds "for the distressed Irish" as early as 1822.[83] Dunlop bore witness to British colonialism in a wider variety of contexts than any woman poet of her day, in addition to which she could claim expertise in reading the behaviour of colonial administrators. It is possible she exerted some influence on the thinking of Sir George Gipps on the matter of how to deal with Indigenous people.

What do we know of Dunlop's political views? As close family members had gone to work in India, she would have felt an investment in the larger colonial enterprise. But she was too percipient not to understand the plight of those oppressed by it. That was why she befriended her half-caste sisters and why, in Australia, she sympathised with the victims of the Myall Creek massacre. We know too little about her education, but her 1820 memoir describes a library-cormorant who feasted enthusiastically on the volumes left by her father which included, *inter alia*, the untranslated works of Voltaire and Rousseau[84] – intellectual godfathers of the French Revolution. (This is one of several clues that Solomon Hamilton was, if not a United Irishman, then at least a fellow-traveller.) Whatever else Eliza Hamilton read in French, she must have tackled Voltaire's novel *Candide* – which, in the words of a recent biographer,

> is a pot-pourri of autobiography, pacifist and anti-clerical satire, anti-providentialist scepticism, and gloriously human good humour and good sense. Look at the facts, and stop relying on philosophical systems (whether Leibnizian or Manichaean); think for yourself and discuss the matter, don't just mouth pre-packaged sound-bites; expect the unexpected; and keep smiling. … Don't rant and rail: just show people what's dumb.[85]

When, many years later, she had to understand for herself the politics behind the Myall Creek massacre, she may have recalled *Candide*, with its built-in scepticism of others' intellectual systems, whether imposed by politicians or by mere prejudice.

---

81   I owe this point to C.A. Bayly, "Ireland, India and the Empire: 1780–1914", *Transactions of the Royal Historical Society* 10 (2000), 386.

82   Kevin Kenny, "Ireland and the British Empire: An Introduction", *Ireland and the British Empire* (Oxford: Oxford University Press, 2004), 11. It is intriguing that, as Alvin Jackson notes, "The British governed Ireland, as they governed India and much of Africa, in conjunction with local élites": Jackson, "Ireland, the Union, and the Empire, 1800–1960", *Ireland and the British Empire* (Oxford: Oxford University Press, 2004), 130.

83   Bayly, "Ireland, India and the Empire: 1780–1914", 387.

84   De Salis, *Two Early Colonials*, 16.

85   Roger Pearson, *Voltaire Almighty: A Life in Pursuit of Freedom* (London: Bloomsbury, 2005), 261.

She would also have recalled Charlotte Smith's *Desmond*, first published in 1792. Smith was a supporter of the French Revolution and, of all her novels, *Desmond* is her most pro-revolutionary. It rebuts the arguments advanced by Burke's *Reflections on the Revolution in France* (1791), making mincemeat of his claim that the aristocracy was the repository of moral virtue,[86] and extends its critique to the British class system and British society. It was not, presumably, recommended reading for a child in the early 1800s, but Eliza Hamilton was left alone for hours at a time, and free to browse her father's books as she pleased. Lionel Desmond, Smith's freedom-loving, French-Revolution supporting protagonist, made such an impression she would remember him as she sailed to India in 1820.[87] But in some ways the most resonant thing about the book was its Preface, in which Smith wrote:

> But women it is said have no business with politics. – Why not? – Have they no interest in the scenes that are acting around them, in which they have fathers, brothers, husbands, sons, or friends engaged! – Even in the commonest course of female education, they are expected to acquire some knowledge of history; and yet, if they are to have no opinion of what *is* passing, it avails little that they should be informed of what *has passed*, in a world where they are subject to such mental degradation; where they are censured as affecting masculine knowledge if they happen to have any understanding; or despised as insignificant triflers if they have none.[88]

In 1792, this kind of talk was radical (it allied its author with Mary Wollstonecraft), and Smith was criticised for it, but I would guess that if Eliza Hamilton read it, it would have resonated with her, and again, years later, when she was attacked in print for sympathising with the sufferings of Indigenous people.

Smith could most accurately be described as "progressive" in her thought, and were we searching for a word to describe Dunlop, that fits better than most others. She was progressive in refusing to think less of someone because of the colour of their skin, their parentage, religion, or submission to a foreign governor. For that reason, she belongs as much in the twentieth-first century as in the nineteenth.

In the *Dublin Penny Journal*, a series of asterisks follows the Indian stanzas, perhaps to indicate a change of subject, for Dunlop now turns to another continent:

> Once, high o'er Afric's southern seas,
> In solitary mood,
> Within the "Vale of silver trees,"
> On Table hill I stood;

---

86   For a more detailed analysis, see the Introduction to Charlotte Smith, *Desmond*, ed. Antje Blank and Janet Todd (London: Pickering and Chatto, 1997).

87   De Salis, 16.

88   Smith, *Desmond*, 6.

The fresh free air, the morning beam,
The vapour crested brow,
Of Caffre-holland – as a dream,
All pass before me now. (ll.49–56)

Just as she began the poem by placing herself on a mountain overlooking Rostrevor, she now ascends Table Mountain above Cape Town. Ships making their way to and from India always stopped here, "remaining only a few days for rest and refreshment".[89] The Cape had been disputed territory for years, fought over by the British and the Batavian Republic, which surrendered it after the Battle of Blaauwberg on 8 January 1806.[90] I have not managed to source the phrase, "Vale of silver trees", but it is clear Dunlop is remembering the many silver trees growing on the eastern side of Table Mountain where, in 1875, one writer described the "hanging woods of silver trees"[91] (a reference to *leucadendron argenteum*[92]).

"Caffre-holland" seems to be Dunlop's own coinage. It edits out the English, prioritising first the blacks (whether or not they originated as slaves), then the Dutch (who affirmed British ownership as long before as 1814). Slavery existed on the Cape at the time of Dunlop's visit. Abolitionist voices were beginning to be heard in 1821, but the trade continued until as late as 1834. She would have known there had been a revolutionary uprising in 1808, when Louis van Mauritius, a former slave who owned a small wine shop by the harbourside,[93] was told by two Irishmen, James Hooper and Michael Kelly, that slavery had ended in Europe and America. According to official reports, Hooper "conceived the idea of emancipating the Slaves and of establishing a Government"; he was "the person with whom the plan originated".[94] They persuaded more than 300 slaves from the Koeberg region to take part in the rebellion, and went on the rampage, looting farms and taking white farmers hostage. As historians have shown, the rebellion was disturbing to the authorities because slaves adopted the trappings of the military, including uniforms, ranks and punishments.[95] The revolt was suppressed, and Mauritius and Hooper executed with eleven others. Dunlop would have known also of the rebellion of 1825 by Galant,

---

89 The observation of Edward Blount, who visited in January 1820; see his *Notes on the Cape of Good Hope: Made During an Excursion in that Colony in the year 1820* (London, 1821), 3.

90 Tim Couzens, *Battles of South Africa* (Claremont: David Philip Publishers, 2004), Chapter 5.

91 "A New Year's Jaunt", *Cape Monthly Magazine* 10 (1875): 92.

92 See *The Botanical Register* 12 (1826): 979.

93 Nigel Worden, "Indian Ocean Slaves in Cape Town, 1695–1807", *Critical Readings on Global Slavery*, ed. Damian Alan Pargas and Felicia Rosu (Leiden: Brill, 2018), 1368–96, 1388.

94 Earl of Caledon to Viscount Castlereagh, 11 November 1808, as qtd in George McCall Theal, *Records of the Cape Colony* (vol. 6, Government of the Cape Colony, 1900), 392.

95 Nigel Worden, "Armed with Swords and Ostrich Feathers: Militarism and Cultural Revolution in the Cape Slave Uprising of 1808", *War, Empire and Slavery, 1770–1830*, ed. Richard Bessel, Nicholas Guyatt and Jane Rendall (Houndmills, Basingstoke: Palgrave Macmillan, 2010), 121–38.

a twenty-five-year-old slave, and twelve slaves and labourers in the Koue Bokkeveld, a sheep-farming area a hundred miles north-east of Cape Town: it was put down and Galant hanged.[96]

Slavery was abolished in the Colony in 1834, just before Dunlop wrote this poem, and that may explain why she describes the landscape in the way she does, its Eden-like perfection the apparent promise of more widespread liberty in future:

> Again, adown the deep ravine,
>   I gaze on fruit and flower –
> A labyrinth maze of silky green –
>   A many-tinted bower:
> Tall aloes crown the rocky steep;
>   Pomegranate blooms are spread,
> And the umkoba branches sweep
>   Across the torrent's bed.
>
> Blushes the crassula, as when
>   Its scarlet blossoms lay
> In the wild fig or sumach glen,
>   That looks on Table Bay;
> And ships bear up by Roben's Isle,
>   From farthest India's shore.
> False dreams, away! ye but beguile –
>   I stand beside Cloch-mhor. (ll.57–72)

Robben Island, where Nelson Mandela would later be imprisoned, is now a World Heritage Site, but was known to Dunlop as the place in which the prophet Makhanda (known also as Nxele) was detained. In the Fifth Frontier War of 1819, Makhanda led a Xhosa army of between 6000 and 10,000 warriors against the settlement of Grahamstown.[97] Defeated by the English, he surrendered in August, realising his people were starving to death and that their best chance was to fall upon the mercy of the enemy. He was not tried, charged or sentenced, but instead imprisoned in Grahamstown before banishment to Robben Island, which would become known as the Isle of Makhanda. While he was detained, the British destroyed all Xhosa huts and kraals, allocating women and children to local farmers as slaves. That knowledge made him determined to escape and he left with thirty other prisoners on 25 December 1820.[98] They overpowered the guards, stole weapons, took three longboats from the whaling station on the island, and sailed

---

96   John Edwin Mason, *Social Death and Resurrection: Slavery and Emancipation in South Africa* (Charlottesville: University of Virginia Press, 2003), 66.

97   See Couzens, *Battles of South Africa*, Chapter 8.

98   Saleem Badat, *The Forgotten People: Political Banishment under Apartheid* (Leiden: Brill, 2013), 12.

for the mainland. Unfortunately, two of the boats capsized in the Atlantic, including the one containing Makhanda, and he drowned.[99] Eyewitnesses report he clung to a rock for as long as he could, shouting encouragement to the others, until "engulfed by the raging surf".[100] Makhanda's body was never recovered and he enjoyed a lengthy afterlife. It was believed he would return, partly because he had preached Christian theology, including resurrection of the dead, condemning witchcraft and adultery.[101] His personal possessions were kept safely for him but he would appear only in dreams and visions.[102]

Dunlop's visit must have taken place some time in the spring or summer of 1821, within months of these events. There is no way she can have been ignorant of them, making her reference to "Roben's Isle" hard to read as other than an allusion to Makhanda – who is not actually mentioned, any more than the Black Hole of Calcutta; the despoiling of Australia; or the '98 rebellion. The poem works as a dream vision inspired by the rising sun seen from Slieve Martin; what Dunlop describes is a fantasia of the places she has visited in what is almost a prelapsarian form, as if the suffering and bloodshed had never taken place. But she depends on the reader to bring their own historical knowledge to a reading of the poem, and to supply the contexts she has omitted. Only when that is done can the reader appreciate the extent to which her account of these places is an act of wish-fulfilment, and how impossible is that wish:

> And ships bear up by Roben's Isle,
> From farthest India's shore.
> False dreams, away! ye but beguile –
> I stand beside Cloch-mhor. (ll.69–72)

The vision is false and beguiling not just because it has transported Dunlop from Ireland to Africa, but because it turns the fallen world into Eden. That glacial rock, Cloch-mhor, signals a return to her roots, the place where she began and which she may never see again. But it also serves as a touchstone for what is real – a reminder of everything that is not in this poem, and which readers must supply. It provides the climactic moment in a poem that has consistently hidden its true opinions behind carefully placed allusive counters. And one can understand why: had it explicitly expressed solidarity with the United Irishmen, then with oppressed peoples in Australia, India and Africa, it would have been unpublishable. Dunlop

---

99 *The Island: A History of Robben Island 1488–1990*, ed. Harriet Deacon (Claremont: David Philip Publishers, 1996), 42–43.

100 David Fleminger, *Robben Island* (Pinetown: 30 Degrees South Publishers, 2008), 45–46; Jacklyn Cock, *Writing the Ancestral River: A Biography of the Kowie* (Johannesburg: Wits University Press, 2018), 60.

101 A.C. Jordan, *Towards an African Literature: The Emergence of Literary Form in Xhosa* (Berkeley: University of California Press, 1973), 50.

102 Jeffrey B. Peires, *The House of Phalo: A History of the Xhosa People in the Days of Their Independence* (Berkeley: University of California Press, 1981), 71.

had no option but to speak through a series of tokens not unlike the spencers or sashes with which the United Irishmen signalled to each other their membership. Her images – whether the rising sun, red cedar, the Ganges or Robben Island – are as concise and articulate as a badge depicting the winged-maiden harp (the official symbol of the United Irishmen[103]) and they are why "Morning on Rostrevor Mountains" is at once more audacious, daring and incendiary than if it aimed merely to recount its author's travels.

Dunlop realised as clearly as any of the Romantic poets that art lives in the realm of the ideal. That was where she found a perfect world that could not exist in reality. "Morning on Rostrevor Mountains" shows us where the beauty of the Irish landscape is untouched by its bloody past; where the flora and fauna of Emu Plains is restored, as if the Indigenous people were still managing it; where the Ganges flows, sacred and unsullied, out of the murk of Calcutta; and where the Cape Colony emerges, fecund and colourful, with no trace of the enslavement that turned it, for so many, into hell. Dunlop knows that her imagined world speaks only because it is what the fallen world is not. It is something we desire but have lost, and which, without the poet, we would lose sight of altogether.

---

103 Barra Boydell, "The United Irishmen, Music, Harps, and National Identity", *Eighteenth-Century Ireland / Iris an dá chultúr* 13 (1998): 48–49.

4

Imperial Feminism and "My Father's Library": Intellectual, Literary and Political Thought in Eliza Hamilton Dunlop's Poetry

Katie Hansord

This chapter examines aspects of Eliza Hamilton Dunlop's poetic relationship to philosophy, particularly that of the Enlightenment, and her ongoing intellectual engagement with late eighteenth-century ideas around natural rights, rational thought and the passions, particularly as they relate to gender. These were ideas that she first encountered in her father's library in Ireland. Ideas about natural rights and behaviour had an important role in the development of feminism, women's poetic traditions and broader cultural representations and understandings of gender over the nineteenth century. I consider the significance of natural rights, virtue ethics, rational thought, and the passions, and the ways these are represented in Dunlop's account of her early education in her journal as well as in examples of her later poetry written in colonial Australia. Dunlop's account both draws on and emphasises key philosophical works of the Enlightenment, but in so doing also frames her own gender-conscious approach. As well as discussing Dunlop's early understandings of these eighteenth-century ideas, I consider how her later uses of them relate to dominant ideological discourses around the domestic ideal and ideas of emigration within settler colonisation in the nineteenth century. These concepts are engaged with alongside the development of cosmopolitan and Enlightenment ideas. As Michael Scrivener suggests, these ideas may best be seen as continuing alongside the later development of Romantic nationalism in the nineteenth century.[1] The Irish nationalist and "emigration" narratives within which Dunlop's later poetry can be contextualised also have complex relationships to her representations of her own experiences of gender identity. Feeling and bodily sensibility as feminised ideals, presented as oppositional to masculinised rational and political thought in much Enlightenment philosophical thinking, are interconnected rather than opposed in her poetry, suggesting that her earlier feminist approaches to philosophy and women's intellectual equality remained important to her later in life. Many of

---

1   Michael Scrivener, *The Cosmopolitan Ideal* (2007; New York: Routledge, 2016).

Dunlop's poems can be described as highly nostalgic and emotionally intense, yet, as I will suggest, this emotional intensity may also be read as connected to the rational mind. Poems published in the *Empire* and the *Town and Country Journal* – such as "To Home and Friends" (1857) – emphasise the passions, particularly as they relate to heartache for her homeland, ongoing articulations of her Irish identity, and the emotional experience of leaving Ireland and arriving in colonial Australia, much as her poems of the 1830s had. Ideas of natural rights and the past–present relationship, as challenges to the political and social order, I suggest, are crucial to Dunlop's feminist poetic practice, yet these Enlightenment feminist ideas must also be understood as part of a wider discourse of enormously damaging impositions in a colonial context.

From an account in her journal of her voyage to India in 1820 we can piece together information about the role of philosophy in Dunlop's early education. The entry, written when she was twenty-four, has important insights about her early childhood experiences in Ireland:

> I loved the open fields, the moon, the stars and my Grandmother. But she wishes me to sew, to knit and to read the Bible. The former she could not easily effect and the latter I had read till I knew the height and length and breadth of the temple and all it contained as well as King Solomon himself could have done. Besides this I was obliged to repeat a Catechism and a few Psalms every Sunday. All this I felt a task, there was no free will in it, but when I found out the treasures of my Father's library I did indeed become the happiest of beings.[2]

It appears Dunlop was strongly aware, from an early age, of rejecting gendered expectations of suitable domestic and religious feminine activities in favour of literary and intellectual preoccupations and a poetic identity, a love of "the open fields, the moon, the stars". This is a self-consciously feminist positioning amid the strong cultural opposition to women's rights at the time, including intellectual rights and literary expression (and especially, women's writing that fell outside gendered parameters).

The journal also provides insights into Dunlop's early reading of a number of significant Enlightenment philosophers including Jean-Jacques Rousseau, Voltaire, Thomas Paine and David Hume. Dunlop's understanding of philosophy, I argue, underpins her feminist poetic practice. As Jane Rendall points out:

> Few writers of the Enlightenment took a deep interest in the relationship between the sexes, and yet the implications of their work were fundamental. The position of women in western Europe was analysed in new terms: it was to be justified by reference to what was natural for their sex, rather than divinely ordained and, at the

---

2   Margaret De Salis, *Two Early Colonials* (Sydney: printed by the author, 1967), 15–16.

same time, set into a particular historical framework. These terms were to dictate the grounds of debate for feminists and their opponents in the nineteenth century.[3]

Dunlop's entry into her father's library is consciously positioned against the feminine domestic activities expected of her, such as needlework and devoutness. Her reading of Bruce, Anson, Lapérouse and Cook, as well as Desmond, Rousseau, Voltaire and Racine, among others, suggests her intellectual engagement with Enlightenment philosophy, literature, geography, history and astronomy as fields of inquiry that were for her a matter of both "free will" and happiness.

Dunlop's recollections of her childhood in the open fields and her father's library, and their contribution to her "early spirit of research", are positioned in terms of gender and intellectual pursuits:

> my Father's globes which ran on castors and were my jaunting cars and the Planets of my Father's Orrery that were my jackstones early became a subject for the question, 'what for were they made?'. My Father's library was open to me and chance threw a work of Astronomy into my hands.[4]

In the library of her absent father, a barrister in Kolkata, she had read Voltaire, Rousseau, Paine and Hume by the age of twelve. These philosophical thinkers were involved in shifting representations of institutions such as church, law and family, and their relationships to personal liberty. These ideas in turn were significant to reframing questions of gender. To reflect on this early reading, as she does in the journal, suggests Dunlop's understanding of how the environment and early education moulded character. Dunlop's familiarity with these philosophers, and her later literary preoccupations with the past and the relationships of emotion and reason to virtue and happiness, can be read as informing a feminist political positioning. Yet Dunlop's emphasis on both "free will" and "happiness" as signifiers of morality in her reading is in many ways at odds with prevailing philosophical ideas on gender, such as Voltaire's view in the *Dictionnaire Philosophique* (1764) that "women, incessantly occupied with the education of their children, and shut up in their domestic cares, are excluded from all these professions, which pervert human nature and render it atrocious. They are everywhere less barbarous than men".[5] Hume too argued "that women and children are most subject to pity, as being most guided by that faculty".[6] As Jane Rendall notes, Voltaire's approach suggested "that women ... had in all societies restricted themselves to the domestic

---

3   Jane Rendall, *The Origins of Modern Feminism: Women in Britain, France and the United States 1780–1860* (Hampshire: Macmillan, 1985), 8.

4   Qtd in De Salis, *Two Early Colonials*, 15.

5   Voltaire [François-Marie Arouet], *A Philosophical Dictionary from the French of M De Voltaire*, trans. unknown, vol. 2 (London: W Dugdale, 1843), 186.

6   David Hume, *A Treatise of Human Nature: A Critical Edition* [1739], eds. David Fate Norton and Mary J. Norton (Oxford: Oxford University Press, 2007), 239.

sphere ... Yet that seclusion meant that women had played no part in the world of wars, atrocities, crime, and that they had preserved a moral advantage through their natural inferiority".[7] These ideas have a clear relationship to the domestic ideology, increasingly imposed on women towards the middle of the nineteenth century, espoused by well-known proponents such as John Ruskin and Coventry Patmore. Such representations of the ideal woman are exemplified in Patmore's narrative poem, *The Angel in the House* (1854). The domestic ideal emphasised wifely and maternal piety, religious devotion, and fervent attention to domestic work and caring upkeep of the home, linking these with "morality".

Dunlop's journal reveals how she constructs her own reading in philosophical terms, as a self-directed, rational and feminist early education within her father's library. Her emphasis on "free will" in her reading choices suggests a natural inclination to intellectual material, and this conceptualises her development in line with Enlightenment philosophical concerns with natural behaviour. Likewise, her framing of this in terms of the happiness it produced engages with an important philosophical concept. Dunlop makes much of her great happiness in both her broad philosophical reading and her physical play outdoors, stating that "these were my years of perfect happiness".[8] This representation of her reading and the strong feelings of happiness it brought is particularly significant given the role that women's reading and writing had in the development of women's rights and feminist philosophy in this period. More than just revealing a familiarity with the major philosophical texts of the period, the way that Dunlop constructs her reading in terms of the relationship of her early education to the domestic and religious duties expected of her as a young woman suggests a close familiarity with Enlightenment ideas on natural rights, personal liberty, critiques of religious authority and happiness as they relate to moral philosophy. Moreover, her emphasis on her own early education and philosophical grounding reflects her knowledge not only of the male philosophers she mentions as examples of her reading, but a personal alignment with and application of feminist ideas, particularly around women's education and intellectual equality, of the kind that were being promoted in radical circles and texts such as Mary Wollstonecraft's *Vindication of the Rights of Woman* (1792).[9] Among the effects of Dunlop's father Solomon Hamilton at the time of his death was a copy of Wollstonecraft's *Vindication*, which was likely part of the library holdings that the young Dunlop read.[10] The central feminist philosophical arguments of the *Vindication* are important in contextualising Dunlop's representation of her own early education, even though she does not overtly reference the work.

---

7   Rendall, *The Origins of Modern Feminism*, 15.
8   Qtd in De Salis, *Two Early Colonials*, 16.
9   Mary Wollstonecraft, *Vindication of the Rights of Woman* (1792), ed. Miriam Brody (Ringwood, Vic: Penguin, 1985).
10 Thank you to Anna Johnston for drawing this inclusion to my attention.

Progressive ideas about women's education, rational womanhood and women's political inclusion are evident in Dunlop's construction of her identity and her reading. She engages with a highly gender-conscious and radical philosophical positioning that had an ongoing significance in her later poetry. Wollstonecraft was arguably the best known and most widely circulated feminist philosopher considering with these questions. Dunlop's journal in this context reflects quite radical values, ones disruptive to the domestic ideal through an emphasis on ideas around moral autonomy, nature, intellectual equality and the passions as they relate to women, and which fundamentally challenge a political and social order which devalues women's natural rights and political voice. Genevieve Fraisse suggests that both reading and writing by women operated as a locus in the philosophical debates around women's capacity for reason and the related significance of reason as foundational to citizenship and to democratic values. Fraise terms this "intellectual equality" and suggests that it is "the emblem of all forms of equality, since it encompassed the issue of human reason".[11] Fraisse asks,

> But why should reading and writing be the locus where a symptomatic contradiction manifested itself? Simply because, before the nineteenth century, having a soul meant having a mind, a mind that could not only be clever but could also reason, like a man's mind ... The question of ontological status, of the soul, lead directly to the question of a being's attributes, in this case the faculty of reason, which led in turn to a consideration of the use or exercise of that faculty, the right to knowledge and the kind of knowledge that entailed.[12]

This connection between women's writing and reading relates, as Fraisse suggests, to questions of gender and reason, as well as involving movements between and across both the public and private spheres. Such an emphasis on women's education, writing and reading, even that which is not necessarily politically radical, is nonetheless important to the reordering of the separate spheres ideology and the relationship of the domestic to the social and political. Dunlop's journal entry and her later poetry take on important feminist implications when read in terms of the developments of the philosophical and political context of women's reading and writing in the late eighteenth and into the nineteenth century.

Wollstonecraft's *The Vindication of the Rights of Woman* was published four years before Dunlop's birth in 1796 and, as Sandrine Bergès suggests, during this period was frequently regarded as a work primarily centred on reform of girls' education. Girls' education reform was also championed by a number of other works (including Wollstonecraft's own earlier writing) such as those by Catherine Macauley and Mary Hays. Republicans also stressed the need for women's

---

11   Genevieve Fraisse, *Reason's Muse: Sexual Difference and the Birth of Democracy*, trans. Jane Marie Todd (Chicago, IL: University of Chicago Press, 1994), 4.

12   Fraisse, *Reason's Muse*, xiv.

educational reform, and in the context of the American Revolution, writers including Judith Sargent Murray and Benjamin Rush advanced similar ideas. As Bergès suggests:

> What would have rattled [Wollstonecraft's] audience would have been the recognition that she meant to achieve what the title stated: namely vindicate women's rights. But this was obviously read by many as an attempt to vindicate women's rights to be educated and not much else. The radical aspect of her work was put down to her revolutionary sympathies.[13]

As Alan Richardson also points out, "most liberal and radical intellectuals of the time viewed education as the cornerstone of any movement for social reform".[14] Certainly, Wollstonecraft's arguments for education reform have been recognised by various scholars as crucial to broader arguments for social reform and gender equality. There can be little doubt that Dunlop's description of her own education as one fitted to the ideas of rational womanhood both reflects and informs her own broader politics. To have been engaging with these ideas in the 1820s, during the ongoing backlash against Wollstonecraft following her death, suggests that Dunlop was far more progressive than has previously been understood. Wollstonecraft's *Vindication* argued as well for the inclusion of women in the political sphere, and Dunlop would, as De Salis points out, go on to be "just as active in politics as her husband" in Ireland.[15] When Wollstonecraft was writing, childhood was understood to be a crucial time in the moral development of character. Dunlop explicitly presents both her past childhood self, and her present self, as precisely the kind of rational woman Wollstonecraft and others had advocated for. That is, a woman who is educated, especially about philosophy, and who is overtly and deliberately far removed from the woman typically idealised for her decorum and unnatural manners rather than for her physical and intellectual strength, rational humanity and attention to moral development.

Dunlop's representation of her personal experiences in nature and in the library is aligned with Wollstonecraft's identification of both the cultivated physical frailty and limited education then deemed suitable for women as social constructs rather than natural behaviours. Wollstonecraft rejected these as constructs that oppress women, physically, intellectually and morally:

> Bodily strength from being the distinction of heroes is now sunk into such unmerited contempt that men, as well as women, seem to think it unnecessary; the latter, as it takes from their feminine graces, and from that lovely weakness, the

---

13 Sandrine Bergès, *The Routledge Guidebook to Wollstonecraft's* A Vindication of the Rights of Woman (London: Routledge, 2013), 12.

14 Alan Richardson, "Mary Wollstonecraft on Education", in *The Cambridge Companion to Mary Wollstonecraft*, ed. Claudia L. Johnson (Cambridge: Cambridge University Press, 2002), 25.

15 De Salis, *Two Early Colonials*, 30.

source of their undue power ... I find that strength of mind has in most cases been accompanied by superior strength of body ...[16]

Miriam Brody notes: "The *Vindication* argues that the rigours of intellectual life, its long hours of study, demand a more sturdy physical constitution than the fashionably delicate standard of femininity would allow".[17] While there is ample evidence of her wide reading of literature and poetry in her epigraphs and her later literary output, Dunlop mentions only a limited number of novels in her early reading, emphasising instead the philosophical, geographical and historical material: "There were few novels, all I recollect was Desmond, Mary – the Racket and Chrysel, Voltaire, Rousseau, and Racine, Cornielle, etc., etc., were all in their originals ... These were my years of *perfect happiness*".[18] Dunlop specifically links her happiness to her access to philosophical reading material. Wollstonecraft argued that the general tendency of girls and young women to read novels (if they read at all), rather than works giving a solid grounding in history and philosophy, produced an "overstretched sensibility" which "naturally relaxes the other powers of the mind, and prevents intellect from attaining that sovereignty which it ought to attain".[19] Wollstonecraft presents the passions and reason as connected and processed through experience to develop knowledge, virtue and happiness.

Philosophical questions about the relationship between intellectual equality and feeling (love, passions, emotional sensitivity and happiness) are crucial to a number of Dunlop's later poems. Dunlop's approach to gender and use of philosophical ideas question what has been regarded as her "feminine morality". Dunlop utilises sentimental and sympathetic feminine modes in much of her poetic work, but she does so in order to dismantle gender inequality and to claim space for women's independence and involvement in key questions about politics, morality and rational thought. Certainly, Dunlop's own political leanings continued in her later life in colonial New South Wales, where she remained intellectually engaged and was acquainted with politically active figures such as Henry Parkes, who as editor of the *Empire* published her later poetry.

The relationship between the domestic ideal and women's intellectual equality and political involvement is an ongoing concern in Dunlop's colonial Australian poetry. Particularly in poems that express her love for Ireland, Dunlop is engaged with feminist challenges to, and negotiations with, the domestic ideal. Fraise suggests that around the time of the French Revolution the intellect was conceptually gendered (masculine) and represented as dichotomised with love, which was being presented as woman's role. While this was a shifting concept, it was

---

16   Wollstonecraft, *Vindication of the Rights of Woman*, 123.
17   Miriam Brody, "Introduction", in Mary Wollstonecraft, *Vindication of the Rights of Woman*, ed. Brody (Ringwood, Vic: Penguin, 1985), 50.
18   Qtd in De Salis, *Two Early Colonials*, 16 (emphasis mine).
19   Wollstonecraft, *Vindication of the Rights of Woman*, 152.

one that was certainly still being challenged in the nineteenth century. As Fraisse points out:

> In the middle of the nineteenth century the issues appeared to have been clarified. Political history and philosophical history changed the nature of the problem. In the aftermath of the Revolution thinking about women was shaped by the realm of rights on the one hand and the sphere of nature on the other. Later it took the form of a discourse on love, human desire and transcendence in some quarters and on the metaphysics of difference in other quarters.[20]

Love was understood to be connected closely to the domestic ideal, in line with understandings of woman's role as confined to marriage and the home, as distinct from intellectual, literary and political participation. In her later poetry, Dunlop problematises the concept of "home". Her expressions of love for a personified Ireland insist upon devotion to home and love, yet they reject the domestic ideal and emphasise women's capacity to encompass both the intellect and emotion as interconnected positions, rather than viewing these as qualities belonging to separate spheres.

Dunlop's Colonial Poetry and Eighteenth-Century Feminist Philosophy

Dunlop's poem "To Home and Friends", published in the Sydney *Empire* in 1857, challenges standard competing colonialist and British ideas of "home" in the nineteenth century and disrupts increasingly conservative narratives around the domestic ideal within broader cultural representations of gender and imperialism.[21]

To Home and Friends

"So shakes the needle, and so stands the pole."

Friends, do ye think, thus far apart –
That, still to home-land feeling true,
The faithful magnet of my heart
Its trembling Index turns to you?

---

20 Genevieve Fraisse, "A Philosophical History of Sexual Difference", trans. Arthur Goldhammer. *A History of Women in the West IV, Emerging Feminism from Revolution to World War*, eds. Genevieve Fraisse and Michelle Perrot (Cambridge, MA: Harvard University Press, 1996), 62.

21 Eliza Hamilton Dunlop, "To Home and Friends", *Empire*, 21 July 1857, 5.

Friends, think you oft, what mem'ries press?
Thick coming thoughts that erst had power
With Sardius tints each hour to bless,
Circling thy minstrel in her bower!

Say, do you think – in days of yore,
What happy influences bound
Our day dreams, by Port Stewart shore,
And on "the Causeway's" classic ground?

Rosstrevor – Carlingford – Killowen –
Proud Down! and Antrim's silvery coast,
Alas! my world hath changed its zone:
Even dear familiar stars are lost.

Bright VEGA, here no sweetness sends;
But fairest of Night's gorgeous train,
The SOUTHERN-CROSS, above me bends,
Pointing my Northward course – in vain.

Could you but think what tears are wept!
For Christian voice – or hallowed fane –
Throughout the hundred Sabbaths, kept –
On lonely rock, and silent plain!

What longings for that old Church-bell,
'Till o'er-strained thoughts the heart beguile,
And on my ear its tollings swell,
As though I trod the sacred aisle.

Here Nature's bounties largely flow,
Her fairest treasures crown our care;
But oh! what aching void may grow
'Mid blessings it were bliss to share.

Then think, my friends, when poet's strain
Sings of the vine, and orange grove;
That one, beyond the Southern Main,
Looks back to Ireland's links of love.

Vega is known as the harp star, and the constellation Lyra formed the harp of Orpheus with Vega its handle. The harp of "Bright Vega" and "orange grove" may both function as Irish political symbolism. According to Belinda Loftus, Irish nationalist taste preferred this imagery to that of the shamrock favoured by unionists; she suggests that orange symbolism was in fact banned around the mid-nineteenth century.[22] The lyre similarly could frequently symbolise a women's lyric tradition through Sappho. Significantly, Dunlop's choice of "Erin" in her manuscript has been replaced by "Ireland" in the *Empire* version of the poem, removing the association with Irish language (Éirinn) common to Romantic Irish nationalist poetry, as well as the suggestion of a feminised personification of Ireland.

"To Home and Friends", like many other poems by Dunlop, resists the pervasive and prescriptive discourses of ideal womanhood in the mid-nineteenth century by writing of her strong emotional response and a disconnection from the domestic ideal in her colonial experiences and in her longing for her Irish home. She expresses instead a nuanced perspective on the complexities of her lived experiences, in which her emotional and rational responses are presented in philosophical and moral terms. In representing passion and feeling as connected with unhappiness, thwarted desire and domestic unease, Dunlop points to the moral significance of their denial. Diana C. Archibald emphasises the uneasy relationship between domesticity and imperialism, suggesting that a number of nineteenth-century texts "show how the ideals of womanhood and 'home' promoted by domestic ideology conflict in many ways with the argument in favour of immigration to imperial destinations".[23] Archibald argues that there is in fact an "implicit conflict of domestic and imperialistic values".[24] Complicating both standard British imperialist and emergent Australian nationalist approaches, Dunlop's Irish nationalism often reads like love poetry to her homeland. This is arguably a strategic move, incorporating an affective sexual politics into the narrative with important feminist implications. The conflict between the domestic ideal and imperialist values in the period is in part addressed through an engagement with an older poetics of sensibility, the passions, reason and virtue ethics. It is also derived from Wollstonecraft's philosophy, as Alan Coffee notes:

> In seeing independence from both an individual and a collective perspective, Wollstonecraft is able to retain the subjective element in which persons are free only where they are able to act on their own terms according to their own lights while recognizing that this necessarily requires a cultural and institutional context that is disposed to bind itself to a genuinely inclusive idea of the common good.[25]

---

22 Belinda Loftus, *Mirrors: Orange and Green* (Dundrum Co. Down: Picture Press, 1990, 70.
23 Diana C. Archibald, *Domesticity, Imperialism and Emigration in the Victorian Novel* (Columbia: University of Missouri Press, 2002), 5.
24 Archibald, *Domesticity, Imperialism and Emigration in the Victorian Novel*, 8.
25 Alan Coffee, "Mary Wollstonecraft, Public Reason, and the Virtuous Republic", in *The Social and Political Philosophy of Mary Wollstonecraft*, ed. Sandrine Bergès and Alan M.S.J. Coffee (Oxford: Oxford University Press, 2016), doi: 10.1093/acprof:oso/9780198766841.003.0011.

"To Home and Friends" engages similarly in a philosophical approach that brings into question both personal freedom and its interconnected cultural and institutional relationships. Anne Mellor points to the significance of Wollstonecraft's philosophical thought for the developments of Romantic women's poetry, noting that: "The rational woman, rational love, egalitarian marriage, and the preservation of domestic affections ... are also the grounding tenets of feminine Romantic ideology".[26] As Isobel Armstrong has noted of nineteenth-century women's poetry more broadly:

> It was this assimilation of an aesthetic of the feminine which enabled the woman poet to revolutionise it from within, by using it to explore the way a female subject comes into being. The doubleness of women's poetry comes from its ostensible adoption of an affective mode, often simple, often pious, often conventional. But those conventions are subjected to investigation, questioned, or used for unexpected purposes.[27]

Dunlop's poem certainly operates similarly and in "To Home and Friends" ideas of "home" and the domestic are conceptualised through her philosophical understandings of subjectivity and personal freedom as they relate to the broader political culture. Virtue ethics, natural rights and women's access to political discourse – important questions expressed by Wollstonecraft and others – operate through Dunlop's gendered poetic modes as points of tension at the increasing expectations around women's attainment of the domestic ideal. "To Home and Friends" engages with discourses of imperialism, national identities and "emigration" and, like many of Dunlop's poems, contains emotional reflections about her own experience.

Dunlop's address to "home and friends" places a social and physical emphasis on "home" that signals a significant departure from gendered domestic discourse as well as a nuanced position in relation to typical examples of "emigration" discourses. The figure of the embowered woman and her relationship to passion and emotional renunciation discourses is linked to Wollstonecraft's cautioning that women should not marry for passion but rather a rational love. Anne Mellor makes the important point that, "given the economic dependence of women upon men, it follows that women cannot obey the impulses and dictates of their feelings ... the leading women writers of the day followed Wollstonecraft in urging their female readers to foreswear passion".[28] Dunlop's persistent passionate feeling expressed as recurrent powerful memories works against such economic constraints. The space given in this poem to friendship is significant too. Friendship, for Wollstonecraft, when compared with romantic love, is presented as "a more sublime affection,

---

26 Mellor, *Romanticism and Gender*, 38.
27 Isobel Armstrong, *Victorian Poetry: Poetry, Poetics and Politics* (London: Routledge, 1993), 324.
28 Mellor, *Romanticism and Gender*, 59.

because it is *founded on principle* and *cemented by time*", aspects which Dunlop reiterates in this poem.[29]

The feminised personification of Erin suggests women's independence as inseparable from ideas of home and love for Dunlop. Likewise, home is a separate concept from the physical house, either Mulla Villa, where she lived in colonial New South Wales, or her physical childhood home in Ireland. Her own sense of home, as she suggests in the title "To Home and Friends", is emotionally distanced. In the domestic ideal, the "Home" encompasses more than the physical home: "home is not a physical space alone but a combination of house and feeling (i.e., home is not constructed merely of brick and mortar but, more important, of 'Peace' and 'love')".[30] The rift between the domestic as a place of being and a place of feeling is tied up with Dunlop's love and memories of her home in Ireland, and all the emotion that evokes. This polarised, spatially and temporally complex relationship to home is particularly important in relation to gender, and the idea of ideal womanhood. "To Home and Friends" suggests that Dunlop is not at home and can never be truly at home (in the sense of feeling) in Australia precisely because she is not able to be physically at home in Ireland. Dunlop's self-identification with the figure of the embowered woman positions her as differentiated from the domestic ideal and occupying a space where she is "in between", generally understood as a waiting space between women's "virginal" and married roles. In Dunlop's application of the trope she is both rationally and emotionally conscious of the moral relationships between the self and wider political culture. So while her longing for her home in Ireland may be read as suggesting a desire to attain the domestic ideal, its Irish nationalist positioning also suggests desire for independence, frustration and unhappiness at multiple levels of financial dependency within imperialist and male-dominated cultures preventing her alignment with that love.

Ireland, Home and Love: Disruption of the Domestic Ideal

A lithograph of the Diamond, Coleraine, is pasted in the inside cover of Dunlop's manuscript collection of poems "The Vase", giving an instant sense of the significance of Irish identity for the poet. Twenty-seven of the sixty-eight poems in "The Vase" contain at least some overt Irish cultural references or are about Ireland or Irish people from Dunlop's past. The first is "I Bless Thy Shores" and, like a number of others, compares Dunlop's love of Ireland somewhat unfavourably to her new life in Australia, as in the line "Unblest mid Austral wilds to roam".[31] In "I Bless Thy Shores", Dunlop articulates a similar position to that of "To Home and Friends", one explicitly at odds with the domestic ideal. Dunlop emphasises

29   Brody, "Introduction", 55 (emphasis mine).
30   Archibald, *Domesticity, Imperialism and Emigration in the Victorian Novel*, 6.
31   Published as "Songs of an Exile no. 8", *Australian*, 7 May 1840, 2.

her own emotional feeling as spatially and temporally located in Ireland through images of the "household hearths ... cold" and her "kindred's graves ... green", disrupting the cultural narrative of the domestic ideal with one in which her past connection to Ireland is conversely brimming with life. It is unclear whether Dunlop is referring to "household hearths" in Ireland or Australia, yet either way this imagery is clearly operating in stark contrast to the domestic ideal of the hearth as emblematising domestic feelings of love and peace associated with the ideal woman, who was expected to keep the metaphoric heart of the home glowing and warm. Dunlop is prioritising rather an ancestrally connected sense of home and ongoing connection in life in which "my kindred's graves are green". As Isobel Armstrong, Joseph Bristow and Cath Sharrock note:

> Women belonged to a poetic culture that welcomed and celebrated intense passions ... The signification of love extended to many forms of passion that we would now no longer recognize. Love poems encompass both sexual and religious experience. An era unembarrassed by affective emotions could move between the erotic and devotional as if they belonged to a continuum.[32]

In articulating her intense love of Ireland, love and particularly rational love are politicised, and the embowered woman – in her waiting and isolation – brings the prevention of her happiness and personal freedoms into question. Such positioning demonstrates the frequent entanglement of feminist ideas with nationalism and imperialism in this period. The separate spheres and their relationship to egalitarian marriage creates a multidirectional pull in "To Home and Friends", since the preservation of domestic affections in Dunlop's poem also signals a problematisation of the preservation of the domestic affections, because it is precisely her preserved love of her home and friends in Ireland that renders the domestic ideal of womanhood an impossible position for her to occupy in colonial Australia.

Faithfulness, emotion, sentimentality and devotion are significantly feminised, and this is reiterated as well by the poem's epigraph from Byron's *Don Juan* (CXCVI):

> My breast has been all weakness, is so yet;
> But still I think I can collect my mind;
> My blood still rushes where my spirit's set,
> As roll the waves before the settled wind;
> My heart is feminine, nor can forget –
> To all except one image madly blind;
> So shakes the needle, and so stands the pole,
> As vibrates my fond heart to my fix'd soul.[33]

---

32 Isobel Armstrong, Joseph Bristow and Cath Sharrock, eds *Nineteenth-Century Women Poets: An Oxford Anthology* (New York, NY: Clarendon Press, 1996), xxviii.
33 George Gordon, Lord Byron, *The Complete Works of Lord Byron* (Frankfort: Joseph Baer, 1846), 689.

"To Home and Friends" was included in "The Vase" under the title "To my Friends / Inscribed to the dearest of any" with an additional epigraph, placed before the Byron: "turns to the touch of joy or woe, but, turning, trembles too" from Frances Greville's "A Prayer for Indifference".[34] Greville (1724–1789) was a well-known woman poet, born in Ireland, and "A Prayer for Indifference" her best-known poem. The rational woman is evoked in Greville's suggestion of an emotional renunciation as false, with Dunlop's poem connecting rational and emotional moral positioning.

Although Dunlop often quoted Romantic poets such as Byron, as well as women poets like Felicia Hemans and Letitia Landon, this second epigraph is significant both in its overt referencing of an Irish woman poet and in the ways it situates "To Home and Friends" in relation to eighteenth-century poetics of sensibility and to ideas of moral philosophy and romantic love. Clare Midgely notes that, more broadly, ideas of the "age of progress" were central to liberal middle-class thought in this period, as well as to feminism and imperial reform. She also points out that

> they perhaps give too tranquil an impression of the politics of an era when the politics of gender occupied a central place in clashes between political radicals and the forces of conservative reaction, and in crises of imperial authority. In the 1790s Mary Wollstonecraft's call for the extension of the 'rights of man' to women was inspired by the American, French and Haitian revolutions, while conservative evangelicals led by Hannah More stressed women's duties in reaction to the perceived threat of social disorder.[35]

The figure of the embowered woman, while still enclosed within the domestic sphere, suggests the isolation, frustration, unhappiness and diminished agency of the unmarried woman who waits, while the idealised figure of the dutiful angel at the hearth by contrast suggests contentment and order through marriage. In representing herself, though married, as an embowered woman poet uneasily positioned in terms of "home", Dunlop clearly problematises the domestic ideal and "home", in which her separation from Ireland resembles a romantic separation.

Deeply personal experiences of love, longing and caring are made visceral and physical: the "trembling" suggested by the epigraph and the sensation of the auditory experience of the church bell – "And on my ear its tollings swell / as though I trod the sacred aisle" – are channelled into a nostalgia that "Looks back to Ireland's links of love", to the culture, friends and memories of her youth. The Byron and Greville epigraphs situate Dunlop's poem in a gendered poetic discourse on reason and emotion, in line with philosophical ideas in which the binary of intellectual rational thought and emotion are represented as gendered masculine

---

34 Frances Greville, "A Prayer for Indifference", *Eighteenth-Century Poetry Archive*, 4 March 2019 (v0.99.10), 29 March 2019, https://bit.ly/34debdb.

35 Clare Midgley, *Feminism and Empire: Women Activists in Imperial Britain 1790–1865* (London: Routledge, 2007), ebook.

and feminine attributes. This dualism is suggested in Byron's lines, "But still I think I can collect my mind", in relation to the embodied and emotional "My heart is feminine".[36] So too the physical trembling associated with intense emotion in Dunlop's own reference in the first stanza of her poem to the compass as a metaphor for personal integrity. Jerome McGann suggests that "the poetries of sensibility and sentiment ... brought a revolution to poetic style exactly by arguing – by 'showing and telling' – that the traditional view of mind and reason would no longer serve a truly reasonable – in eighteenth-century terms a *sensible* – mind".[37] Poems like Dunlop's "To Home and Friends" address such concepts in ways which, in seemingly prioritising the emotional (that is, feminised) over the purely rational, also emphasise personal experience as central to moral development. While women's morality was increasingly connected with the domestic ideal, Dunlop's moral questioning is framed in terms of emotional articulations of love and faithful devotion that can be read as expressing Irish nationalist sentiments that disrupt both British imperialist and emergent colonial nationalist models, as well as problematising the domestic ideal itself.

Dunlop's use of Greville's lines as an epigraph in "The Vase" positions her poem in relation to love and sensibility. Importantly, the epigraph signifies thwarted love as an emotional pain so deep that indifference is preferred, in terms of both gender and Irish identity, signalling the ways in which Dunlop's poem is far from indifferent, and both emotionally and intellectually engaged. Greville's "A Prayer for Indifference" was first published in the *Edinburgh Chronicle* in 1759 and its opening stanza reads:

> Oft I've Implor'd the Gods in vain,
> And Pray'd till I've been weary;
> For once I'll try my wish to gain
> Of Oberon the fairy.

McGann suggests that this "opening mask of playfulness emphasises a need to 'speak' beyond the limits of a semantic or purely rational discourse. And when the mask falls away, Greville's true voice of feeling appears in its naked simplicity".[38] McGann further points out that Greville both allegorises the poem as a Shakespearean and poetic prayer rather than a religious prayer and emphasises the idea of emotional renunciation as one that cannot be taken seriously. Dunlop's use of the epigraph – "turns to the touch of joy or woe, but, turning, trembles too" – reveals the seriousness of emotional feeling.

---

36 Byron, *The Complete Works of Lord Byron*, 689.
37 Jerome McGann, *The Poetics of Sensibility: A Revolution in Literary Style* (Oxford: Clarendon Press, 1996), 5.
38 McGann, *The Poetics of Sensibility*, 52.

Feminine sympathy and feeling are concepts both drawn on and asked of readers in much of Dunlop's poetry. Yet their use often subverts the misogynist underpinnings of much philosophical thought on gender, the separate spheres ideology and the construction of women's morality in exclusion from the mercantile and political public sphere, including literary self-expression. Claire Knowles suggests that many popular women poets expressed emotional distress, leveraging pathos as a strategy for entry into literary spaces hostile to women. She argues that

> it is largely as a result of this association between the physical and the poetic that sensibility, a discourse associated explicitly with women and centred upon physiological sensation, becomes an important medium through which some female poets are able to negotiate this cultural association of femininity with 'embodiedness'. The discourse of sensibility gave women a powerful avenue through which to publicise (and often politicise) their experiences of bodily and emotional suffering.[39]

Mellor suggests moreover that Romantic women poets more often celebrated rational thought, rather than the imagination and overflow of feeling, as being embodied within themselves.[40] Hemans' poems "The Two Homes" and "The Graves of a Household" may be read as important intertexts to Dunlop's conceptualisation of "home" in "To Home and Friends". As Mellor notes of Hemans' "The Graves of a Household":

> This poem stages the dispersal of the home, defining the disparate locations into which it has fragmented. Hemans thus exposes the fictiveness of the very category she valorises – the home – by consigning it to the genre of the memorial. For if the poem creates the gleeful home only to memorialize it, to define it as always already lost, it effectively creates a fiction of the private sphere for the public domain. ... For if domestic love is all, as Hemans' poetry repeatedly insists, then the destruction of that love leaves life without purpose or meaning.[41]

For Dunlop, both time and space present a challenge to domestic ideology, in which the very idealisation of the enduring devotion of woman's love seeds the destruction of that ideology. Dunlop's citation of Hemans and Landon in her poetry, as well as the epigraph from Greville, reveals her knowledge of women writers who were engaging with feminised ideas of sympathy, rational thought and emotion. Hemans brought the domestic and national together in significant ways that Dunlop's complication of the idea of "Home" also suggests. Nationalisms – including Irish, British and emergent Australian – are at play, reflecting the imperial context,

---

39   Claire Knowles, *Sensibility and Female Poetic Tradition* (Surrey: Ashgate, 2009), 10.
40   Mellor, *Romanticism and Gender*, 2.
41   Mellor, *Romanticism and Gender*, 128.

including the imperial context of such feminist thought (that is, an Anglophone, situated perspective rather than a supposed free-floating view). Irish is consciously presented by Dunlop as a more tender language than English, for example: a political comment that is also deeply personal, and based in her emotional experience.

Similar sentiments are expressed by Dunlop in poems such as "Erin Dheelish" where a footnote explains it was written for an "old and somewhat plaintive air, published by Edward Bunting in his Irish Melodies".[42] Here Dunlop moves from description of the Australian landscape in English, and the question of her emotional state, to an answer in Irish Gaelic, suggesting English is the language of imperialism and Irish Gaelic one with a deeper emotional nostalgic longing:

> Why must I sigh in land so fair?
> Mo Erin dheelish gra machree.
> Erin mo cushla, vourneen dheelish ...[43]

The shift in language has a clear emotional significance, suggesting her memory and longing for home are untranslatable. In "The Irish Mother" (1838), too, a footnote explains that the Irish words are "expressions of fondness for which the English tongue offers no sounds half so tender".[44]

Diana C. Archibald emphasises the ideological positions expressed on the subject of the so-called New World in novels, particularly in texts which presented the "Old World and New" (including America, Canada, New Zealand, Australia etc.,) and suggests that the majority are British imperialist texts published in Britain. She notes, "In its most basic form, a virtuous, noble, moral, respectable, comfortable, pretty, and / or trustworthy, old England is contrasted with a savage, rough, wicked, vulgar, indecent, violent and / or hypocritical New World", while "More rarely, a paradisiacal New World appears to advantage against the corrupt Old World".[45] Dunlop's position is slightly more nuanced in terms of its relationship to a simplistic dichotomy of imperialist pro-British or pro-colonial representations, though one certainly also bound up in imperialism. How then does Dunlop's poetry sit in this wider cultural context? She expresses a love of the natural beauty of Australia, which can be read as suggesting morality and virtue. But she retains a deeper love for her Irish homeland, resulting in a position that breaks with the dichotomy Archibald presents, in complicating both British imperialist and emergent nationalist "New World" narratives. Works such as these can be read as love poetry, expressing devotion, yearning and longing to a personified and feminised independent Ireland. Like the reference to Greville's "Prayer for

---

42 Eliza Hamilton Dunlop, "Erin Dheelish", *Empire*, 8 July 1865, 5.
43 For translations of the Irish, see Elizabeth Webby, this volume.
44 Eliza Hamilton Dunlop, "The Irish Mother", *Australian*, 30 November 1838, 4.
45 Archibald, *Domesticity, Imperialism and Emigration in the Victorian Novel*, 4–5.

Indifference" in "To Home and Friends", imperial, national and domestic relationships are situated within a discourse of thwarted and devoted romantic love and embodied emotionality that has both rational and ethical implications. They can be seen as antithetical to expectations of the kind of poetry permissible for a married mid-nineteenth-century woman, suggesting both painful separation from a deep unforgettable love and an inability to be emotionally or otherwise "at home" – a position akin to announcing an inability to be the ideal woman. They express a thwarted desire to enact the virtues associated with the domestic ideal, in their emphasis on a more complex positioning of home, the related emotional feeling and ideas of devotion. The line from "To Home and Friends", "thy minstrel in her bower", signals the significance of Dunlop's poetic identity to her construction of self within the trope of the embowered woman. Far from replicating the domestic ideal of hearth and home, Dunlop instead depicts herself as an isolated and homesick woman poet, embowered within a suspended space in the cultural narrative of women's financial transfer from patriarch to husband, a space at odds with her own free will, agency and personal freedoms.

Dunlop's journal entry and her later poem "To Home and Friends" both work against convention, in particular in relation to gendered representations of conventional behaviour, broadly understood as the separate spheres ideology. Her account of her early education constructs her younger self as having a natural inclination to intellectual reading material and playing outdoors, as well as a disinclination towards needlework. This position suggests a strong desire for and personal application of the kind of reforms suggested by thinkers like Wollstonecraft, who wrote "I have already inveighed against the custom of confining girls to their needle, and shutting them out from all political and civil employments".[46] Dunlop's understanding of Enlightenment philosophical thought and feminist philosophical ideals, particularly as they relate to the relationship of rational womanhood to the emotions, rational thought, the domestic and natural behaviour, can be seen in her early journal writing as well as her later poetry. Her poetry reveals a continued engagement with such philosophical approaches to reason and the passions, particularly in terms of gender and personal liberty, in an increasingly rigid context of imperial gendered expectations around femininity, emotion and the "domestic sphere" in the nineteenth century. Dunlop's grounding in Enlightenment philosophy and its relationship to feminist ideas around education reform and rational womanhood means that her poetry reflects an approach in which passion or the emotions and sensibility are integrated and connected with reason and rational thought in ways that work to undo gender discrimination and emphasise personal liberty. Dunlop's early educational background is crucial to her later Australian poetry, especially in the ways it is positioned in terms of complex interrelationships between narratives of home

---

46 Wollstonecraft, *Vindication*, 288.

and gendered discourses of the "angel at the hearth". Dunlop's approach, while emphatically Irish nationalist, is also grounded in both a feminist cosmopolitanism and imperial feminism. Dunlop's is a Eurocentric and imperial feminism, that both accepts and challenges aspects of the British domestic ideal as a force that excluded women's natural rights, including the capacity for rational thought, personal freedom and political self-expression. Reading Dunlop's poetry through the lens of her earlier understanding of Enlightenment philosophy and virtue ethics demonstrates that she was familiar with much more politically radical feminist approaches than has been recognised and that these philosophical ideas are an important underpinning to her poetic approach. Dunlop's writing may be seen as working in support of European Enlightenment feminist philosophical conceptualisations of natural rights, personal freedoms and the physical and mental relationships of these to ideas of moral growth.

5

Beyond Universalisms: Individuation, Race and Sentiment in Colonial New South Wales

Jason R. Rudy

> they were lovely in their lives,
> And in their deaths had not divided been.
>
> Thomas Campbell, Gertrude of Wyoming (1809)

Sentimental literature requires that we take as axiomatic that the emotional experiences of others are similar to our own. Rest assured, the genre teaches us, other people in similar circumstances will feel roughly the way we feel, even across different times and places. In this way the death of two Irish brothers in Mississippi, recounted in an 1838 poem by Eliza Hamilton Dunlop, should have a similar effect on readers whether they encounter the story in Belfast or in Sydney – or, for that matter, whether they read it in 1838 or the early twenty-first century. As an Irish emigrant newly arrived in Australia, Dunlop situated herself and her readers globally, connecting them imaginatively and emotively to individuals in vastly different locales. Affective sympathy and imagined circulation among readers rest at the core of Dunlop's poetic practice, which enlists both referentiality and sentiment as tools to further readerly association: the fantastical sense of feeling all together, even when far apart temporally and spatially.

Yet the specific contexts of Dunlop's publications challenge the ease of this affective gesture. In what follows, I trace the circulation of Dunlop's "Songs of an Exile – (No. 3)", a poem about the death of two Irish brothers, to show the ways colonial print culture suggests that feeling might not be universal after all. More than that, I argue that the specific politics of race in colonial New South Wales put pressure on the universalising sentimental gesture, questioning the humanitarian value of understanding individuals to be more alike than different. In this way, Dunlop's work anticipates Ronjaunee Chatterjee, Alicia Mireles Christoff and Amy R. Wong's recent critique of nineteenth-century British writers and the scholars who study them insofar as they reflect a "fantasy of an unmarked universality" that is both white and Eurocentric.[1]

---

1   Ronjaunee Chatterjee, Alicia Mireles Christoff and Amy R. Wong, "Undisciplining Victorian Studies", *Los Angeles Review of Books*, 10 July 2020, https://bit.ly/3bh4Mnv.

Both Dunlop's poetry and the newspaper in which she published subtly resist that fantasy, opening up spaces for thinking through differences across geographic spaces (Ireland, the United States, Australia) and among groups of individuals (white settlers, Native Americans, Indigenous Australians).

In late-1830s Sydney, individuation had emerged as a fraught question of law. According to an account in the *Australian* published on the same day as "Songs of an Exile – (No. 3)", the Supreme Court of New South Wales had been asked to determine whether one human being, an Indigenous Australian, might be taken as representative of the group to which he belonged. Under the section "Law" for 29 November 1838, Sydney readers would have encountered the arguments put forth that week about whether a second trial should proceed for the "wilful murder" of Indigenous Australians at Myall Creek on 9 June 1838. The seven white defendants standing before the court had already been tried and acquitted for the murder of an Indigenous man called "Daddy". The question before the court on 27 November was whether the acquittal for the death of one Indigenous man could be taken as an acquittal for the murder of all those killed at Myall Creek, including specifically the murder of a child.

The historical and legal parameters of this exceptional case have been well considered.[2] For the purposes of this chapter, I am interested specifically in the print medium – the *Australian* – and the potential resonances between Dunlop's poem and the court case, a report of which was published on an adjacent page. According to the newspaper, the seven defendants

> were now charged with the murder of an aboriginal black child to the Attorney General [John Hubert Plunkett] unknown, and the simple test as to whether they were not one and the same offence was; whether the evidence which would be given on the second information, might not have convicted them on the first information; whether evidence of the murder of an aboriginal black child would not have convicted them on an information for the murder of a male aboriginal black.[3]

Ultimately, the question of whether the second trial might proceed thus centred on the particularity of identity. Since the Indigenous victims were mostly unknown to the court by name, the defence argued in effect that they were all one and the same. The Supreme Court determined otherwise:

---

2   See, for example, the recent forum in *Law and History* 5.1 (2018): "The Myall Creek Massacre of 1838: Genocide, War Crimes, Crimes against Humanity?"; Lisa Ford and David Andrew Roberts survey the legal history of early-colonial Australia in "Expansion, 1820–1850", *Cambridge History of Australia*, ed. Alison Bashford and Stuart Macintyre (Cambridge: Cambridge University Press, 2015), 121–48.

3   "Law. Supreme Court", *Australian*, 29 November 1838: 2. *Trove*. https://trove.nla.gov.au/newspaper/page/4298611.

His Honor [Justice William Burton] in putting the case to the Jury observed, that although it was a novel case, their duty was simply to determine a plain fact of whether the offence of which the prisoners now stood indicted, was the same for which they had been before tried and acquitted, and as regarded the law of the case, he must premise that where many persons were killed at one and the same time, *the murder of each person was a distinct offence.*[4]

Unspoken but palpable in this framing is an argument about the humanity of the Indigenous victims: an insistence on the part of Justice Burton, who took his lead from the prosecutor, Plunkett, that each individual Indigenous Australian must be considered a human being whose death warranted deliberation before the court.[5]

Having read this account of the Myall Creek hearing, a reader of the *Australian* on 29 November 1838 may have then turned the newspaper's page and encountered the single poem of the issue, printed in the first column: Dunlop's "Songs of an Exile – (No. 3)". The poem offers an immediate, if subtle, connection to violence between settler-colonialists and Indigenous peoples, opening with an epigraph from Thomas Campbell's 1809 long poem Gertrude of Wyoming: "They were lovely in their lives". In Campbell's original the line continues, "And in their deaths had not divided been". The scene referenced is the death of Gertrude and her father, Albert, violently slain in the Wyoming Valley of Pennsylvania at the hands of massacring Native Americans – an event that Campbell eventually admitted was fabricated and historically inaccurate.[6] The lines from *Gertrude* had become popular in newspaper death notices soon after the poem's original publication, detached from their original context and representative of generic grief. The *Aberdeen Journal* of 1810, for example, writes of a widow's death at the same hour her husband had passed away: "They had been married 64 years; and it may be truly said of this ancient pair, that 'they were lovely in their lives, and in their deaths

---

4   "Law. Supreme Court", *Australian*, 29 November 1838 (emphasis mine).

5   According to Mark Tedeschi, "the approach taken by John Hubert Plunkett towards the case … demonstrated an enlightened and visionary attitude that was unparalleled in his time or for more than a hundred years afterwards. Plunkett did not just prosecute eleven men for murder. He prosecuted his entire society for its connivance in the attempted annihilation of the Aboriginal people and their culture". "Speech at the Annual Myall Creek Memorial Ceremony on 11 June 2017 for Those Who Died in the Myall Creek Massacre of 1838", *Law and History* 5.1 (2018): 153.

6   Campbell writes in a note to the poem added subsequently to the original publication, "The name of Brandt, therefore" – the villainous Native American – "remains in my poem a pure and declared character of fiction". See *Gertrude of Wyoming; or, The Pennsylvania Cottage* (London: Routledge, 1857), 80. On the poem, its mis-telling of history, and its reception, see Kate Flint, *The Transatlantic Indian, 1776–1930* (Princeton, NJ: Princeton University Press, 2009), 47–52; Tim Fulford, *Romantic Indians: Native Americans, British Literature, and Transatlantic Culture 1756–1830* (Oxford: Oxford University Press, 2006), 183; and Julia Hansen, "Viewless Scenes: Vividness and Nineteenth-Century Ideals of Reading in and through *Gertrude of Wyoming*", *ELH* 84 (Winter 2017): 943–77, DOI: 10.1353/elh.2017.0036.

they were not divided".[7] We may safely assume the *Aberdeen Journal* author was not thinking of Campbell's massacre when composing this obituary, and was instead imagining only the near simultaneous death of two people who loved one another.

In exactly this mode of detachment from the meaning of the original poem, "Songs of an Exile – (No. 3)" exhibits no clear connection to Campbell aside from the epigraph; Dunlop's use seems entirely generic and universalising, rather than particular to *Gertrude*'s narrative of colonial American violence. The poem instead recounts the death of two brothers in Vicksburg, Mississippi, one a few days after the other. Readers are privy to neither the specifics of the brothers' deaths nor details of the Mississippi setting. A footnote in the *Australian* informs the reader that the two brothers had "died at Vicksburgh [sic], on the Mississippi, within a few days of each other, William, the eldest; and Samuel, the second son of Andrew Dunlop, of Prestlands, Esq., County of Antrim, Ireland".[8] Reference in the poem to "pestilential air" suggests vaguely that the deaths may have been related to infectious disease; Vicksburg was plagued by cholera in the 1830s.[9] In place of concrete details, the poem instead offers an emotional tableau:

> He knelt beside a brother's bed –
> Far in the stranger's land:
> And gently raised the dying head;
> And clasped the lifeless hand.
>
> Alone he knelt! oh kindred love –
> Thy lines are hard to part,
> They err, who call thee – "strong as life,"
> Stronger than death thou art.[10]

Though primarily affective in its register, Dunlop's lyric builds a complex relational network for processing feeling – a network that comes into view in part by tracing its earlier publication history.

Dunlop's Sydney readers would not have known that the poem had first been published in the *Belfast News-Letter* of 3 January 1837, "Inscribed to the Memory of Two Brothers" and signed "E.H.D.".[11] Indeed, I had no notion of the original poem when I began work on this project, and I located it only after searching

---

7   *Aberdeen Journal*, 26 September 1810: 4. *British Library Newspapers, Part I: 1800–1900*. Gale Document Number: BA3205617594.

8   The footnote quotes from 3 January 1837 *Belfast News-Letter*, "Births, Deaths, Marriages, and Obituaries", 3. *British Library Newspapers*. Gale Document Number: Y3202329838.

9   "Cholera", *Workingman's Advocate* 4 (22 June 1833): 2. *American Periodicals*. ProQuest Document ID: 126441872.

10   Eliza Hamilton Dunlop, "Songs of an Exile – (No. 3)", *Australian*, 29 November 1838, 3. *Trove*. https://trove.nla.gov.au/newspaper/page/4298612.

11   Eliza Hamilton Dunlop, "Inscribed to the Memory of Two Brothers", *Belfast News-Letter*, 3 January 1837, 4. *British Library Newspapers*. Gale Document Number: Y3202329841.

for the obituary referenced in the *Australian*'s footnote. We learn from the Belfast periodical that the poem is demonstrably personal: the two brothers, Samuel and William Dunlop, were nephews of Eliza Hamilton Dunlop's husband, David. This becomes evident by way of a death notice for the young men that appears on the third page of the 3 January *Belfast News-Letter*, one page before Dunlop's poem. Whereas the footnote to the *Australian*'s "Songs of an Exile – (No. 3)" identifies the brothers as the sons of Andrew Dunlop of Antrim County, the Belfast newspaper obituary explicitly connects the young men to David Dunlop (they are "nephews to Mr. D. Dunlop, Coleraine, Ireland").

Even in the Irish newspaper, however, the link between the dead brothers and Dunlop's poem is suggestive only. The *Belfast News-Letter* does not openly connect the death notice to the poem; they are printed one page after the other, and a reader would have no way of proving that the brothers of the death notice are the very same addressed in the poem. Only with the *Australian* reprinting can we make a definitive link, as Dunlop quotes the Belfast death notice in her Sydney footnote. In that reprinting, however, she obfuscates her relation to the two brothers by deleting the mention of her husband (that she signs the poem "E.D.H." also obscures a connection between her last name and the "Dunlop" of the death notice).[12] To make full sense of the poem's personal history, then, requires reading both the Sydney and Belfast printings side-by-side, as each fills in the gaps left by the printing context of the other. The Sydney newspaper shows conclusively that the poem and the obituary are linked, and the Belfast newspaper reveals that the brothers were Dunlop's nephews.

We might imagine the ways Dunlop's poem took on new meaning as it moved from Belfast to colonial New South Wales. In its original print venue, the experience of two young men in Mississippi likely seemed quite distant, both to Dunlop and to her readers. Though many Irish recipients of the *Belfast News-Letter* would have had relatives living abroad by the 1830s, Dunlop's Belfast readers themselves had not left their homeland.[13] Vicksburg, if known at all, would have been familiar as a cotton-producing plantation community dependent on enslavement for what one American newspaper called its "unparalleled" growth "in wealth and population" during the mid-1830s.[14] That context remains unacknowledged in either version of "Songs of an Exile – (No. 3)", but with a string of shrewd edits Dunlop reveals her own shifting subject position in the move from Ireland to Australia. In the original *Belfast News-Letter* version, she writes that "We err who call thee 'strong as life' – / Stronger than death thou art". The lines suggest that the two emigrant brothers will not

---

12 "Births, Deaths, Marriages, and Obituaries", *Belfast News-Letter*, 3 January 1837, 3. *British Library Newspapers*. Gale Document Number: Y3202329838.

13 According to David Fitzpatrick, "A million Irish emigrants are estimated to have crossed the Atlantic between 1815 and 1845 … and some 30,000 obtain[ed] state assistance to undertake the much longer journey to Australia". "Emigration, 1801–70", in *A New History of Ireland*, Volume V: *Ireland Under the Union, 1801–1870*, ed. W.E. Vaughan (Oxford: Oxford University Press, 2010), 565.

14 "Cotton Crop of Mississippi", *The Farmer & Gardener, and Live-Stock Breeder and Manager* 3 (18 October 1836): 194. *American Periodicals*. ProQuest Document ID: 90037124.

be parted, even in death. The "we" is a collective of Irish readers in Ireland: those who might underestimate the intimate bond between the dead brothers. In Sydney the "we" becomes a "they": "They err, who call thee – 'strong as life'". In so pivoting from "we" to "they", Dunlop signals her new identification with other Irish emigres; she is now one among them. Similarly, she corrects the original "oh not for *us*, / Whom home and *friendship* cheers" to "oh not for *those* / Whom home and *kindred* cheers" (italics mine), aligning herself and her Sydney readers with the Irish brothers who, living on foreign soil, are thought to lack both a true home and the happiness afforded by friendship.

Less explicit in "Songs of an Exile – (No. 3)" is a shift towards lived knowledge of Indigenous peoples. For Dunlop in Ireland, never having visited North America, Native Americans were – to use Kate Flint's terms – "not real people; they were primarily ciphers".[15] Once in Australia, Dunlop had immediate proximity to and investment in the lives of Indigenous peoples. David Dunlop, Eliza's husband, had been appointed Police Magistrate of Penrith soon after their arrival in 1838, putting the couple in the midst of the Colony's legal world.[16] Dunlop herself was well aware of the Myall Creek massacre, which she would address directly in her very next *Australian* poem, "The Aboriginal Mother (From Myall's Creek)". With this context in mind, the epigraph from Gertrude of Wyoming, which reads as a generic statement of loss in the Belfast newspaper, may have taken on new meaning as it circulated in Sydney at the moment of the Myall Creek trial. Specifically, Dunlop's Sydney readers may have found haunting resonances in the gesture to a well-known poem about violence between settler-colonialists and Indigenous peoples. That the poem was published in the same issue as the account from the Supreme Court on the second trial of the Myall Creek defendants only strengthens the sense that something more is at work here.

The specific line from the epigraph signals in Campbell's poem the experience of communal mourning in the aftermath of a battle. Crucially, both white settlers and Native Americans (peaceful ones, not those portrayed as villainous invaders) contribute to the scene:

> With solemn rites between,
> 'Twas sung, how they were lovely in their lives,
> And in their deaths had not divided been.
> Touch'd by the music, and the melting scene,
> Was scarce one tearless eye amidst the crowd: –
> Stern warriors, resting on their swords, were seen
> To veil their eyes, as pass'd each much-loved shroud –
> While woman's softer soul in woe dissolved aloud.[17]

---

15 Flint, *The Transatlantic Indian*, 51.
16 Margaret De Salis, *Two Early Colonials* (Sydney: printed by the author, 1967), 44.
17 Campbell, *Gertrude*, 73–74.

Campbell here imagines a community united in feeling – a "melting scene" where tears abound. The poem concludes shortly thereafter with the lamentations of an Oneydan chief who, Sir Walter Scott was moved to note, presents a "perfect and powerful ... image of sympathetic sorrow".[18] In expressing strong feelings while contemplating the fallen father and daughter, Campbell's Native American chief articulates a mode of affective sympathy similar to that of Dunlop's "The Aboriginal Mother": the association of feeling among individuals seemingly different but drawn together through emotion. Katie Hansord has suggested that "The Aboriginal Mother" shows Dunlop to have been "very much keyed into transatlantic abolitionist literary conventions".[19] The Campbell epigraph likewise points to broader modes of Anglo print culture, in which referentiality enabled feelings to resonate through texts first between Europe and North America, then triangulated among Europe, North America and Australia.

In Campbell's crying Native American warrior, then, we glimpse a scene that resonates with Dunlop's "The Aboriginal Mother", the poem that follows as fourth in the "Songs of an Exile" series. Each poem features an Indigenous person mourning deeply at the scene of violence between Indigenous and colonising peoples. That we access the scene of Native American mourning via a poem about the death of two Irish brothers emphasises the networks of feeling in which Dunlop situates herself and her readers. Such networks undergird a sentimental tradition whose function was both to create imaginative links among immigrants spread across the globe and, more radically, to insist that feeling crosses cultural and racial lines as well.

Tricia Lootens' important study *The Political Poetess: Victorian Femininity, Race, and the Legacy of Separate Spheres* (2017) helps make sense of this intersection. By the late 1830s, following Britain's 1833 Emancipation Act and its 1838 extension, which liberated enslaved peoples throughout the British Empire, what we have come to think of as "Victorian femininity" had been attached conceptually to the anti-slavery movement: "Henceforth", writes Lootens, "to speak as a patriotic Briton would be, overwhelmingly, to claim very specific national (and increasingly imperial) positions: positions reliant on moral capital derived from conceptions of successful liberation".[20] Of course neither the Native Americans of Campbell's poem nor the Indigenous mother of Dunlop's fits within the discourse of enslavement. Moreover, even though Dunlop's nephews were living in close proximity to enslavement, and perhaps benefiting from it, Dunlop's poem on their death circumvents any direct reference to it. Nonetheless, Dunlop's framing of

---

18 [Sir Walter Scott], Review of *Gertrude of Wyoming*, by Thomas Campbell, *Quarterly Review* 1 (May 1809), 252.
19 Katie Hansord, "Eliza Hamilton Dunlop's 'The Aboriginal Mother': Romanticism, Anti Slavery, and Imperial Feminism in the Nineteenth Century", *JASAL: Journal of the Association for the Study of Australian Literature* 11, no. 1 (2011), https://tinyurl.com/y89r3uaa.
20 Tricia Lootens, *The Political Poetess: Victorian Femininity, Race, and the Legacy of Separate Spheres* (Princeton, NJ: Princeton University Press, 2017), 39.

Indigenous plight would have been recognisable within a broader project of racial justice that in Britain had become attached to notions of femininity. Taking this frame into account makes clear the ways sentimentality in early-colonial New South Wales, and specifically the mode of sentimentality Dunlop inhabits in her "Songs of an Exile" series, was a tool borrowed from a global enterprise and put specifically to anti-colonial and anti-racist uses.

In the "Songs of an Exile" series then, we see an important shifting between universalising sentiment and particular political thought and feeling. I have argued elsewhere that the Victorian sentimental lyric circulated freely through the English-speaking world in part because of its ability to appear universalising. Within this line of reasoning, we might understand Dunlop's "Songs of an Exile" series as formally generic and, as such, recognisable to readers schooled in the affective work of British Romanticism.[21] But such easy access should not be misconstrued as devaluing the specific political work accomplished by the poems' sentimental registers. Consider Kwame Anthony Appiah's caution that cosmopolitan thinking (thinking in relation to other cultures) is not equivalent to universalist thinking: if "cosmopolitans suppose that all cultures have enough overlap in their vocabulary of values to begin a conversation", they still do not "suppose, like some universalists, that we could all come to agreement if only we had the same vocabulary".[22] Similarly, we would be wrong to think that Dunlop's politics read identically in both Australia and Ireland just because we imagine that both Australian and Irish readers responded to the poems' affective work.

By the turn of the nineteenth century, the *Belfast News-Letter* was a mouthpiece for Irish political conservativism, "speaking largely to the Protestant land-owning elite" and "urging all Irish people to bury their political differences within the wider interests of empire".[23] Dunlop's poem contributes quite well to this political frame, drawing together Irish readers through the work of collective mourning. By contrast, the *Australian*, according to Anna Johnston, "was liberal in politics", having been established in 1824 by William Charles Wentworth and Dr Robert Wardell and advocating for "self-government, emancipists' rights, and press freedom" while regularly criticising the colonial administration.[24] For example, immediately below Dunlop's poem on the two brothers, *Australian* readers would have encountered a set of highly critical "Extracts from the Report of the Select Committee of the House of Commons" regarding the treatment of Māori peoples in New Zealand. The *Australian* informs its readers that

---

21   See Jason R. Rudy, *Imagined Homelands: British Poetry in the Colonies* (Baltimore, MD: Johns Hopkins University Press, 2017), 63.

22   Kwame Anthony Appiah, *Cosmopolitanism: Ethics in the World of Strangers* (New York: Norton, 2006), 57.

23   Laurel Brake and Marysa Demoor, eds., *Dictionary of Nineteenth-Century Journalism in Great Britain and Ireland* (Gent: Academia Press, 2009), 44.

24   Anna Johnston, *The Paper War: Morality, Print Culture, and Power in Colonial New South Wales* (Crawley, WA: University of Western Australia Press, 2011), 108.

[t]hese extracts form but a small part of the numerous atrocities which have been investigated and encouraged by the monsters in human shape who have made these islands their rendezvous. It is high time the government of this country interfered, if not for the purposes of commercial interest, at least of the sake of common humanity and christian [sic] charity.[25]

Set alongside the account from the Sydney Supreme Court on the Myall Creek trial, a reader would be unlikely to miss the journal's clear humanitarian agenda.

We know that Dunlop understood herself to be part of this humanitarian agenda, given her subsequent publication of "The Aboriginal Mother" and her later work in translating Indigenous Australian song.[26] Looking back from her more explicitly political work allows us to reframe "Songs of an Exile – (No. 3)" as more political than might first appear. What should be clear among other things is that the poem's political meaning has shifted in its move from Belfast to Sydney. Moreover, we can perceive a humanitarian political advantage to understanding the poem's differences. The Myall Creek hearing raises the question of whether people are interchangeable: whether two or more Indigenous Australians might under the law be considered, in effect, the same. In determining that this was not the case, and that the seven defendants might be tried a second time and ultimately executed for their crimes, the court was making explicit that – from a legal perspective, at least – human beings, be they settler-colonialists or Indigenous Australians, are not one and the same.

Here the politics of the *Australian* and the Sydney Supreme Court run up against and challenge the assumptions that undergird most sentimental literature: the belief that, in fact, human beings are interchangeable insofar as they will respond emotionally with near-identical precision as they encounter strong feeling in works of art. Lauren Berlant identifies the 1830s as the starting point in the United States of what she calls "an intimate public sphere of femininity": the public circulation of feelings through a "mass-mediated, market population of relatively politically disenfranchised people".[27] Like Benedict Anderson's imagined communities, Berlant's intimate publics are abstractions, but no less potent in their intangibility.[28] By the time we arrive in the early 1850s, with Harriet Beecher Stowe's *Uncle Tom's Cabin*, argues Berlant, we find "political optimism ... about the transformation of unjust social institutions through the production of new mentalities".[29] Readers might be

---

25   "Extracts. Colonization of New Zealand", *Australian* (Sydney), 29 November 1838, 3. *Trove.* https://trove.nla.gov.au/newspaper/page/4298612.

26   See, for example, "Native Poetry", *Sydney Morning Herald*, 11 October 1848, 3. *Trove.* https://trove.nla.gov.au/newspaper/page/1514274.

27   Lauren Berlant, *The Female Complaint: The Unfinished Business of Sentimentality in American Culture* (Durham, North Carolina: Duke University Press, 2008), xii.

28   See Benedict Anderson, *Imagined Communities: Reflections on the Origin and Spread of Nationalism* (London: Verso, 1983).

29   Berlant, *The Female Complaint*, 40. Eric Lott offers a counterexample: a politically regressive (and predominantly male) imagined community in the 1830s and 1840s United States whereby the performance of blackface minstrelsy "made possible the formation of a self-consciously white

made to feel in response to texts, and as a result their political identifications might be shifted to humanitarian ends. Personal feeling thus becomes generic: an individual's emotional responses might be understood within a predictable framework of feeling.

Dunlop's "Songs of an Exile" series reflects a process of making the personal into the generic in ways that support Berlant's notion of the intimate public sphere, though the long history of violence against Indigenous Australians following the 1830s points to its limited success. In the case of the Irish brothers in Mississippi, Dunlop distances the tragedy from her own family experience, turning personal loss into a scene of shared loss. Irish readers in Belfast would have mourned not just the death of two young men, but a broader Irish diaspora that resulted in both death and displacement. That sense of shared loss was strengthened as Dunlop moved from Ireland to New South Wales, as the poem's "we" became a "they" and Dunlop, along with her imagined readers, became herself an emigrant. Her poems in the *Australian* mark the shift from individual to communal: for example, in the first of the "Songs of an Exile" poems, "The Dream", Dunlop considers "What thoughts within this bosom swell, / What tears an Exile's eyes are filling".[30] Note the turn across the line break from the particular ("this bosom") to the general ("an Exile's eyes"): a move from individual to type. In so abstracting the personal, in so locating the voice of the poem with a category, Dunlop performs a role that Virginia Jackson and others have identified with female poets, and in particular the figure of the Poetess. "In its heyday", writes Jackson, "the Poetess poem created and was the property of an intimate public sphere … The Poetess was the figure that made the personal generic in the first place".[31] Without question, Dunlop inhabits this abstracting role in colonial New South Wales.

Moreover, the example of Dunlop suggests that the abstracting work of the Poetess amplifies in significance as she moves outward to the colonies. Wordsworth had argued at the turn of the nineteenth century for what he called an "organic sensibility": an "antidote", as John Mullan notes, "to the 'false refinement' of his contemporaries", and also a "guarantee that his feelings are not merely personal, but can be generalized".[32] Romantic women writers, too, valued affection, as Mary Poovey argues, not only because it gave them "an important function in a society increasingly marked by economic competition", but additionally because "sentimentalism was … virtually the only form in which

---

working class". See *Love and Theft: Blackface Minstrelsy and the American Working Class*, 20th Anniversary Edition (Oxford: Oxford University Press, 2013), 9.

30 Eliza Hamilton Dunlop, "The Dream", *Australian* (Sydney), 8 November 1838, 3. *Trove*. https://trove.nla.gov.au/newspaper/page/4298576.

31 Virginia Jackson, "The Function of Criticism at the Present Time", *Los Angeles Review of Books*, 12 April 2015, https://lareviewofbooks.org/article/function-criticism-present-time.

32 John Mullan, "Sensibility and Literary Criticism", in *The Cambridge History of Literary Criticism*, vol. 4: "The Eighteenth Century", ed. H.B. Nisbet and Claude Rawson (Cambridge: Cambridge University Press, 1997), 433.

middle-class women were allowed legitimate self-expression".[33] Dunlop's "Songs of an Exile" series suggests an important social function in the colonies for just the sort of generalised feeling the Poetess was thought to express.

We can see this social function all the more clearly by comparing the 1838 *Australian* version of Dunlop's "The Dream" to the first iteration of the poem, printed anonymously in *The Common-Place Book of Poetry* (1830). Edited by William Clapperton and published in London, the volume included reprinted works by Felicia Hemans, Letitia Elizabeth Landon, Mary Robinson and Joanna Baillie: a veritable who's who of Romantic poetesses. Like the other unknown poets of the collection, Dunlop remained unnamed – "The Dream" is anonymous.[34] In stanzas that echo Wordsworth's "Ode: Intimations of Immortality" (1807), Dunlop recollects her lost childhood: "Of earliest scenes again I bounded; / And long-forgotten joys were mine".[35] The *Australian* version turns these lines into a reflection on emigration: "Of native scenes again I bounded; / And long forgotten joys were mine". Likewise, the final lines of the original poem mourn above all the death of a mother: "That she, the guardian-parent, dead, / Left but of love – *one* relic token".[36] The *Australian* poem more generally speaks to the loss of loved ones: "Hopes buried (with the loved and dead), / And *memories* thus – *atone* – *a token*".

Though we cannot know Dunlop's intent here, one likely effect of her Sydney edits was to make her poems resonate more fully for colonial readers. In this way, "The Dream" becomes less about what might have been Dunlop's particular mourning for her mother, and more an abstracted mourning for those left behind in the process of emigration. The move resembles the distinction between "we" and "they" in "Songs of an Exile – (No. 3)": another instantiation of community through shared emotional experience. Dunlop in other words shifts from one generic frame (the loss of a parent) to another (the trauma of emigration), with the effect in both poems of further abstracting the personal into the generic.

In closing I want to return to the scene of the Sydney Supreme Court, and the obvious political challenges that emerge when navigating between sentimental abstraction and legal individuation. Dunlop's humanitarianism required that settler-colonialists imagine themselves as part of a feeling community: individuals abstracted into a network with moral responsibility that would treat Indigenous Australians with compassion and respect. Such turns to the universal remain characteristic of humanitarian rhetoric. Domna C. Stanton, for example, points

---

33 Mary Poovey, *The Proper Lady and the Woman Writer: Ideology as Style in the Works of Mary Wollstonecraft, Mary Shelley, and Jane Austen* (Chicago, Illinois: University of Chicago Press, 1984), 109.

34 Clapperton writes in the preface that "he is of opinion, that the circumstance of many of the authors being unknown, will not detract from the merit of their poetry". William Clapperton, ed., *The Common-Place Book of Poetry, or British Minstrelsy* (London: Thomas Tegg, 1830), vi. Because the original poem is anonymous, we cannot know with absolute certainty that Dunlop is the author, though she claims authorship of the Sydney reprinting.

35 Clapperton, *The Common-Place Book of Poetry*, 130.

36 Clapperton, *The Common-Place Book of Poetry*, 131.

to the Universal Declaration of Human Rights in her critique of "the unity and coherence of the Enlightenment subject in human rights discourse".[37] Insofar as sentimental poetry participates in the discourse of human rights, it thus tends to transport readers from the particular to the general (we feel similarly, we are encouraged to believe, because we are all human beings). The case before the Sydney court required a different framework for its judgment, determining that each of the Myall Creek victims was an individual worthy of legal protection, and that acquittal for the murder of one Indigenous Australian would not result in acquittal for the murder of another Indigenous Australian. The move in court, then, was from the general to the particular, from a group of Indigenous Australians to one particular murdered individual. The logic of the court is not entirely inconsistent with that of Dunlop's poetry, given that each recognises the fundamental humanity of Australia's Indigenous peoples. But the two documents situate that humanity in distinct terms: the court through individuation, the poem through agglomeration and abstraction.

To some degree, the *Australian*'s layout of court hearing and sentimental poem offers an imaginative training in the shift between self and community, the personal and the generic. These are complementary rather than antagonistic modes. The point is important in drawing out the humanitarian and political exigence of literary sentiment, both in the specific example of Dunlop's isolated lyrics and the broader context of nineteenth-century settler-colonial literary culture. In revising her poems for Sydney readers, Dunlop aided the humanitarian project of the *Australian*, which would succeed in direct relation to the ability of colonialists to think critically about the relationship between self and other. Dunlop's work likewise signals that the "fantasy of an unmarked universality" shaping so much of nineteenth-century literature and criticism (to return again to Chatterjee, Christof and Wong's important formulation) was specious even at the dawn of the Victorian era; Dunlop and her contemporaries recognised the limits of Enlightenment discourse even as they exploited its affective, sentimental power. In juxtaposing the Myall Creek court case with Dunlop's "Songs of an Exile – (No. 3)", then, the *Australian* teaches readers what in an ideal world we would all already know: to wit, that humanitarianism rings hollow if we fail to understand the ways abstracted sentiment might be applied to particular human beings.

---

37   Domna C. Stanton, "The Humanities in Human Rights: Critique, Language, Politics", *PMLA* 121.5 (2006): 1520.

Part 2
Eliza Hamilton Dunlop and Colonial Australia

6

Settlement Defiled: Ventriloquy, Pollution and Nature in Eliza Hamilton Dunlop's "The Aboriginal Mother"[1]

Peter Minter

In her 1980 essay "The Aboriginal in Early Australian Literature", Elizabeth Webby describes a curious rhetorical figure that sheds light on early Australian poetry, the temper and sensibility of the early Australian colonial imagination, and the character of an early Australian landscape aesthetic as it emerged amidst transnational networks of Empire, settlement and race. Webby writes that

> [t]he depiction of aboriginals in early Australian literature, i.e. that written before 1850, resembles in many respects their pictorial depiction as outlined by Bernard Smith in *European Vision and the South Pacific* (1960). Those writers who attempted the longer literary forms on Australian themes – the epic poem or the novel – usually, like the landscape painters, placed the aboriginal to one side.[2]

Of course, Webby is observing a dialectic that can be found in the early art and literature of many settler societies, one where an epic or visionary pictorial centre depicts an imperium in the act of displacing the indigene to pictorial and ideological peripheries. In Australia, like elsewhere, it underpins the embodiment of a crucial part of the settler social imaginary, a procedure aimed at resolving ineluctable environmental, cultural and racial discontinuities. At the heart of Webby's observation is the staging of a gesture, a strophe or a turning, a particular kind of textual or aesthetic movement that produces a choreography between objects as they coincide in material, aesthetic and ideological spaces. This gesture – placing the Aboriginal to one side and producing distance and

---

1   This chapter was first presented as a research paper at the University of Sydney in November 2014 for the Faculty of Arts and Social Sciences Collaborative Research Group "Writing the World: Transnationalism and Translation in Literary Studies". I am grateful for the useful comments and suggestions by colleagues following the presentation and to subsequent reviewers. It was first published in *Text, Translation, Transnationalism: World Literature in 21st Century Australia*, ed. Peter Morgan (North Melbourne, Vic: Australian Scholarly, 2016), 137–51. I thank Professor Morgan and the publisher for permission to republish the essay here.
2   Elizabeth Webby, "The Aboriginal in Early Australian Literature", *Southerly* 40, no. 1 (1980): 45–63.

difference – is pivotal for many reasons, not least for its Levitical demarcation and separation of ontologies into discrete zones of variable iterability. As we shall see, the figuring, possession and dispossession of iterability are central to how the colonial imagination sought to refine senses of voice and place that were undefiled by colonisation and the stigma of its various violences.

To be placed to one side, whether in literature or painting, or indeed within an entire imperial apparatus, is to be subject to a procedure of differentiation and partitioning, a procedure that is central to the production of a particularly ordered, purified political, or aesthetic object. It is a foundational trope in the emergence of early Australian literary representations of nature, especially those that transcribe the unsettling of settlement and the suspense of its interruption in depictions of colonial brutality. The link between aesthetic and existential ruptures follows a deeply rooted aetiology, one that is latent in Webby's use of "depiction" above. To pictorially depict is to place an object, whether a flower or a landscape, to one side of itself. An elementary delineation is always at work. But to depict, in its very archaic sense, is also to "stain" or "destain" in a gesture of disfiguring. In *Troilus and Criseyde*, Chaucer has Criseyde write "I have also seen with tears all depainted, your letter", an expression of blotching or smudging that lingers in the intermediate "depeinct" of the sixteenth century before the more recent "depict".[3] Webby's opening sentence suggests not only that early Australian depictions of the landscape tended to place Aboriginal subjects to one side, but also that colonial sensual and textual environments are structurally destained by gestures of displacement and the movement between states of possession and dispossession.

In this chapter I wish to propose a correlation between the depiction of being placed to one side and the demarcation of colonial attitudes to nature and embodiment as they are affected by a rhetorics of defilement and pollution. Speaking textually, it will be shown that economies of defilement – especially those in which race, gender, nature and settlement are redistributed through transnational imperial externalities and radically local internalities – induce a poetics of ventriloquy in which characters of sympathy and destainment are cross-culturally incarnated and performed: indeed, possessed and dispossessed. I wish to unsettle settlement, and in doing so sanction new readings of the colonial literary sensibility in the earliest phases of its root attachments to the landscape and its modes of aesthetic tenure. My focus here is on Eliza Hamilton Dunlop's poem "The Aboriginal Mother", a watershed piece that ventriloquises an Aboriginal female subject to engender a charged sentimental response in the colonial body politic. Here is the poem, first published in the *Australian* on Thursday 13 December 1838:

---

3   "*Depeint* was connected with depict *adj.* by the transitional forms depeinct *v.*, *depinct*"; *Oxford English Dictionary Online*, Oxford University Press, https://www.oed.com/view/Entry/50182?rskey=LZqzDS&result=2. The citation from Chaucer is given at sense 5: "To stain, distain. 'c1374 G. Chaucer *Troilus & Criseyde* v. 1611, I have eke seyn with teris al depeynted, Your lettre'".

The Aboriginal Mother

(from Myall's Creek)

Oh! hush thee – hush my baby,
    I may not tend thee yet.
Our forest-home is distant far,
    And midnight's star is set.
Now, hush thee – or the pale-faced men
    Will hear thy piercing wail,
And what would then thy mother's tears
    Or feeble strength avail!

Oh, could'st thy little bosom,
    That mother's torture feel,
Or could'st thou know thy father lies
    Struck down by English steel;
Thy tender form would wither,
    Like the *kniven* in the sand,
And the spirit of my perished tribe
    Would vanish from our land.

For thy young life, my precious,
    I fly the field of blood,
Else had I, for my chieftain's sake,
    Defied them where they stood;
But basely bound my woman's arm,
    No weapon might it wield:
I could but cling round him I loved,
    To make my heart a shield.

I saw my firstborn treasure
    Lie headless at my feet,
The goro on this hapless breast,
    In his life-stream is wet!
And thou! I snatched thee from their sword,
    It harmless pass'd by thee!
But clave the binding cords – and gave,
    Haply, the power to flee.

To flee! my babe – but whither?
    Without my friend – my guide?
The blood that was our strength is shed!
    He is not by my side!
Thy sire! oh! never, never
    Shall *Toon Bakra* hear our cry:
My bold and stately mountain-bird!
    I thought not he could die.

Now who will teach thee, dearest,
    To poise the shield, and spear,
To wield the *koopin*, or to throw
    The *boommerring*, void of fear;
To breast the river in its might;
    The mountain tracks to tread?
The echoes of my homeless heart
    Reply – the dead, the dead!

And ever must the murmur
    Like an ocean torrent flow:
The parted voice comes never back,
    To cheer our lonely woe:
Even in the region of our tribe,
    Beside our summer streams,
'Tis but a hollow symphony –
    In the shadow-land of dreams.

Oh hush thee, dear – for weary
    And faint I bear thee on –
His name is on thy gentle lips,
    My child, my child, *he's gone!*
Gone o'er the golden fields that lie
    Beyond the rolling clouds,
To bring thy people's murder cry
    Before the Christian's God.

Yes! o'er the stars that guide us,
He brings my slaughter'd boy:
To shew their God how treacherously
The stranger men destroy;
To tell how hands in friendship pledged
Piled high the fatal pire;
To tell, to tell of the gloomy ridge!
And the *stockmen's human fire*.[4]

Aimed squarely at inducing a sympathetic response in a white readership, "The Aboriginal Mother" addresses the Myall Creek massacre of 10 June 1838, when twenty-eight Aboriginal (Wirrayaraay) men, women and children were hacked to death by swords, beheaded, dismembered, and burnt by a group of ten white men and, curiously enough, one African American, John Johnstone.[5] The poem appeared in print only five days before seven of the men, including Johnstone, were hanged for murder, and has been accurately read by Webby, O'Leary and Hansord as a radical political intervention during an impassioned and at times vehement public debate about the massacre, and whether white men should ever be tried and hung for killing Aboriginal people. I will immediately "place to one side" the serious historical and political consequences of the massacre, an event that after almost two centuries unambiguously endures as a marker for epidemic racial violence. From a discretely literary perspective, one particularly informed by transnational and postcolonial ecopoetics, my focus is on the poem itself, its literary relation to the event, and a set of unambiguous rhetorical figures that emerge in this relation, which together reveal definitive characteristics of the early colonial imagination, its stance towards nature, and the embodiment of the colonial subject.

An opening question: why does one of the first Australian poems, and perhaps the first Australian poem to give voice to an Aboriginal subject, literally enact, in the figure of ventriloquy, the displacement or a "putting to one side" of the voice? How do we understand the poem's structuring of possession and dispossession, its complex relation to race, and its betrayal of an alienated relation to nature? To answer this question, I turn to a transnational rhetorics of pollution, an ecocritical methodology in which scenes and tropes of pollution are appraised not so much for their materiality (although pollution is always inescapably material) but more as figures in literary choreographies of, for instance, defilement, purgation and purification. The scene of "The Aboriginal Mother" – its ethical landscape – is irrevocably polluted, not only by the violent tide of frontier colonisation but crucially

---

4   Eliza Hamilton Dunlop, "The Aboriginal Mother", *Australian*, 13 December 1838, 4. Original italics.
5   On the Myall Creek massacre and other frontier violence in the early colonial period, see Bruce Elder, *Blood on the Wattle: Massacres and Maltreatment of Aboriginal Australians since 1788*, 3rd ed. (Frenchs Forest, NSW: New Holland, 2003) and Bain Attwood and S.G. Foster, eds., *Frontier Conflict: The Australian Experience* (Canberra: National Museum of Australia, 2003).

and ultimately by death, the chthonic defilement of murder and the remains of the corpse. My interpretation of pollution in the poem, focused on the figure of the corpse and its animation or reanimation in a pseudo-Biblical narrative, will draw on a broader project in which I am developing a transnational and transhistorical ecocritical methodology for decoding literary pollutions. Briefly, my methodology emerges from a genealogy of tropes of pollution as they appear across classical, early modern and modern literary texts. Pollution has had many lives, from its earliest depictions in Hippocratic accounts of miasmic defilements caused by breaches in corporeal, communal or cosmological order; to the proto-secular, proto-scientific accounts of seventeenth- and eighteenth-century Europe, in which pollution was waste, plague or infection to be purged or quarantined; to the modern, entirely secular scientific sense of pollution as a synthetic substance that is either toxic or susceptible to material, cultural and aesthetic reassimilation, recycling or compost.[6] Sacred, secular and scientific accounts of pollution can be shown to exploit three prevailing tropes – the cathartic, the (neo-cathartic) quarantine, and the synthetic and integrative – and a set of distinct rhetorical economies that differently cast self, society and nature. Following the cathartic mode, "The Aboriginal Mother" will be shown to dramatise a movement from desecration and alienation to resacralisation and re-embodiment, the tragic interplay of murder, infanticide, and distantiated purification marking the poem as an exemplary moment in early colonial literary representations of the polluting violence of settlement and the refiguring of social, aesthetic and environmental order. Essentially, I propose that Dunlop's iteration of a disembodied, ventriloquised Aboriginal subject produces the classical dramatic figure of the *pharmakos*, whose function is to enact a Levitical demarcation and purgation of the defilement of the massacre and, in an act of disembodied repossession, to sublimate the violence of the colonial dispossession of land.

In focusing on tropes such as "embodiment", "pollution", "voice", and, more generally, "nature", I hope to contribute an ecocritical dimension to the revival of work on Dunlop. "The Aboriginal Mother" has recently enjoyed renewed visibility, especially in transnational and postcolonial readings that relocate early Australian colonial literature, conventionally read through a lens of radical isolation and defamiliarisation, as part of an international network of vibrant cosmopolitan literary cultures that recast English, American and European Romantic and post-revolutionary thought. Such readings of this and other nineteenth-century poems have typically focused on the social and political interplay of modes of imperialism and colonisation and iterations of Romantic and early Victorian humanism. For instance, drawing on the work of Isobel Armstrong, New Zealand scholar John O'Leary has recently described a transnational poetics of cross-cultural

---

6   See Robert Parker, *Miasma: Pollution and Purification in Early Greek Religion* (Oxford: Clarendon Press, 1983); Sophie Gee, *Making Waste: Leftovers and the Eighteenth-Century Imagination* (Princeton, NJ: Princeton University Press, 2010); and Mary Douglas, *Purity and Danger: An Analysis of Concepts of Pollution and Taboo* (London: Routledge & Kegan Paul, 1966).

sympathy that emerged in early Victorian England, the United States, Australia and South Africa. Addressing a pair of "crying mother" poems, Dunlop's "The Aboriginal Mother" and the American poet Lydia Sigourney's "The Cherokee Mother" (1831), alongside "The Bechuana Boy" (1830), an Abolitionist lament by the so-called father of white South African poetry, Thomas Pringle, O'Leary describes how in various English-speaking nations "outpourings of sentiment" aimed at "unlock[ing] the fountains of [the] heart" had the political function of

> carefully crafted propaganda pieces that manipulated the sympathy of their readers in order to achieve practical, political ends (specifically, the amelioration of the treatment of indigenous peoples by white settlers).[7]

O'Leary foregrounds the "crying mother" poem in a transnational and transhistorical genealogy of strategic "fountains of the heart", ranging from Classical and Renaissance "complaint[s] of the desolate nymph" to Wordsworth's "The Idiot Boy" and, "closer to the period in question, British poets such as Leticia Landon and Felicia Hemans", whose 1828 *Records of Women* included poems such as "Indian Woman's Death Song" and "The American Forest Girl".[8] Aptly, Heman's volume is prefaced by epigraphs from William Wordsworth's "Laodamia" and Friedrich Schiller's *Wallenstein*, signalling a figurative threshold in which proto-feminist evangelic impulses are admitted into the moral and aesthetic realm of revolutionary Romanticism. Indeed, as O'Leary points out, by writing poems depicting suffering Indigenous women, women poets in the British colonies and American states were hoping to do more than simply elicit cross-cultural sympathies: they also wanted to subvert "or at least [bring] into question dominant discourses of colonialism and empire".[9]

In Australian criticism, following the work of Fiona Giles in the late 1980s and early 1990s, a contemporary transnational feminist reading of Australian nineteenth-century women's poetry has recently been renewed by Ann Vickery. In her 2002 essay "A 'Lonely Crossing': Approaching Nineteenth-Century Australian Women's Poetry", Vickery observes that, "like their British counterparts", nineteenth-century Australian women poets often served as "moral arbiters" whose otherness refracted normative discourses of class, gender, nation, and literary subjectivity.[10] Writing on Dunlop, Vickery affirms her transnational affiliations:

---

7   John O'Leary, "'Unlocking the Fountains of the Heart': Settler Verse and the Politics of
     Sympathy", *Postcolonial Studies* 13, no. 1 (2010): 66.
8   O'Leary, "Unlocking the Fountains of the Heart", 56. Alongside O'Leary's "crying mother"
     poems, the list could be expanded with poems such as William Cullen Bryant's "The Indian
     Girl's Lament", "An Indian Story", "Monument Mountain", and "An Indian at the Burial-Place of
     His Fathers", as well as Henry Wadsworth Longfellow's "The Song of Hiawatha".
9   O'Leary, "Unlocking the Fountains of the Heart", 56.
10   Ann Vickery, "A 'Lonely Crossing': Approaching Nineteenth-Century Australian Women's
     Poetry", *Victorian Poetry* 40, no. 1 (2002): 33–34.

a migrant Irishwoman whose cultural longing is "projected onto the fate of dispossessed Aboriginal people".[11] Prior to O'Leary, Vickery cites Dunlop's "sympathetic identification" with Aboriginal women, and goes on to remark that for Dunlop and other later women poets, the Aboriginal mother "in her isolation and loss of cultural knowledge, embodied racial discontinuity and would figure only as an 'echo' or trace of those already dead".[12] Vickery's sense of the Aboriginal mother as an echo or trace of the dead is especially poignant, particularly as it correlates with the figure of the corpse in Dunlop's ventriloquy of the Aboriginal subject, which will be discussed further below. More recently, Vickery's emphasis on a transnational feminist imperative has been augmented by Katie Hansord's reading of Dunlop's familiarity with Anglo-European Romanticism, transatlantic anti-slavery poetry, and early international feminism.[13] Writing against Paul Kane's insistence in *Australian Poetry: Romanticism and Negativity* (1996) that there was no tangible emergence of Romanticism in nineteenth-century Australian poetry until the work of Charles Harpur, Hansord situates "The Aboriginal Mother", and Dunlop's *oeuvre* more generally, amidst a deracinated Romantic sensibility that successfully amalgamated, across Europe, North America, Asia and the South Pacific, a set of transnational Romantic impulses in which feminist discourse interrogated, for instance, imperialism, Christian evangelism and slavery. It should be said that Hansord rightly emphasises, via the work of Clare Midgley and Tanya Dalziell, that in some respects the poetics of white feminist sympathy are complicit with an essentialist assumption of the cultural and moral superiority of the Western female subject. Nevertheless, as O'Leary, Vickery and Hansord's work attests, it remains true that "Dunlop's colonial poetry reflects a transnational early feminist discourse, and a transposition of Romantic women's poetry to a specifically Australian context".[14] Dunlop's "The Aboriginal Mother" emerges from the "unlocked heart" of an enlightened political and moral correlation between metropolitan women's suffrage and the suffering of Indigenous women.

And yet, despite the laudable emphasis in these accounts on the social and political aspects of the Romantic sensibility, there is no detailed account of how Dunlop's poem also reckons with that other great pillar of Romantic aesthetics, the representation of nature. Hansord engages briefly with this question: she writes, "we conceive of nature not literally as the Australian landscape but rather as transcendent human nature embodied by the mother".[15] Hansord is again challenging Kane's contention that neither the revolutionary impulse nor a reverence for nature were present in early nineteenth-century Australian verse,

---

11   Vickery, "Lonely Crossing", 34.
12   Vickery, "Lonely Crossing", 35.
13   Katie Hansord, "Eliza Hamilton Dunlop's 'The Aboriginal Mother': Romanticism, Anti Slavery and Imperial Feminism in the Nineteenth Century", *JASAL: Journal of the Association for the Study of Australian Literature* 11, no. 1 (2011): 1–14.
14   Hansord, "Eliza Hamilton Dunlop's 'The Aboriginal Mother'", 3.
15   Hansord, "Eliza Hamilton Dunlop's 'The Aboriginal Mother'", 2.

that for early poets "nature ... no longer corresponded to *Nature* ... not only were the seasons backwards, the plants and animals strange, but the land itself was thought by many to be irredeemably ugly".[16] Hansord rightly observes that Dunlop's representation of nature is shifted through an ideological lens – particularly, as I have shown, her feminist investment in the suffering female Indigene, or, as Hansord writes, "it articulates a maternal nature associated with the protection and love of children that is carried across the Aboriginal Otherness".[17] Even so, until now there has been no engaged account of how Dunlop represents nature or landscape in the poem. Indeed, Hansord contests that "Dunlop's poem offers no description of the natural environment at all".[18] However, keeping in mind Édouard Glissant's affirmation in *Caribbean Discourse* that "landscape is a character in this process",[19] it can be argued that Dunlop's poem yields a far-reaching insight into the depiction (not the description) of nature and landscape in early Australian poetry, especially insofar as it reveals a set of rhetorical formations to do with embodiment, pollution, and the unsettling or defilement of settlement in view of the "placing to one side" of the landscape, like the Aboriginal character. I argue that nature is absolutely present in "The Aboriginal Mother": as the sublimated apparitional ground of the Myall Creek massacre and the destained, spectral Country of the victims, and as the foil or material limit of a ventriloquised Aboriginal woman whose dissociated iterability makes incarnate a simulated relation to nature that, ultimately, underpins a political economy of dispossession and racial purification.

I should briefly emphasise that I do not mean to suggest that Dunlop was personally complicit with a politics of radical dispossession. Indeed, as discussed above, all available evidence shows that Dunlop was deeply committed to a broadly humanist and feminist politics inspired by, among many things, the transatlantic anti- slavery movement and a real concern for the integrity of Aboriginal families and cultures. Vickery emphasises that Dunlop wrote and published "The Aboriginal Mother" in order to publicly argue

> against the view that it was wrong to try white men for the death of creatures considered little more than "monkies", Dunlop describes the Aborigines as a noble people with a distinct culture and strong family ties ... [In "The Aboriginal Mother" Dunlop] extends the feminine capacity for sympathetic identification to a relatively new category of social other.[20]

---

16 Paul Kane, *Australian Poetry*, 11, cited in Hansord, "Eliza Hamilton Dunlop's 'The Aboriginal Mother'", 2. Kane's italics and Hansord's ellipses.

17 Hansord, "Eliza Hamilton Dunlop's 'The Aboriginal Mother'", 2.

18 Hansord, "Eliza Hamilton Dunlop's 'The Aboriginal Mother'", 2.

19 Édouard Glissant and J. Michael Dash, *Caribbean Discourse: Selected Essays*, CARAF Books (Charlottesville: University Press of Virginia, 1989), 106.

20 Vickery, "A 'Lonely Crossing'", 34–35.

From 1840, two years after the publication of the poem, Dunlop lived in Wollombi, a small town north of Sydney, with her husband David, who had been appointed Police Magistrate and local Protector of Aborigines. Here, as O'Leary argues, she put her revolutionary sensibility to work, forming "friendly relations with the Indigenous groups around Wollombi" and producing "Aboriginal poems" that applied her "genuine interest in Indigenous languages ... transliterating and translating songs [and doing] valuable work in preserving Indigenous vocabularies".[21] My reading here is of the poem, not Dunlop, her personality or her attitudes. My purpose is to read "The Aboriginal Mother" as an aesthetic and political object, an object that expresses something of a particular moment in early Australian history and which reveals a great deal about the literary sensibility of the early colonial period. In doing so, I wish to show that such a reading of "The Aboriginal Mother" can add a compelling stratum to the transnational assessment of Dunlop's Romantic, post-revolutionary poetry, and to a transcultural ecocritical reading of early Australian landscape poetry more generally.

The critical factor in the poem is that the theatre of "The Aboriginal Mother" and its environmental sensibility hinges on two principal figures: the ventriloquy of the Aboriginal subject and the polluting desecration of murder. As an example of ventriloquy, like Lydia Sigourney's "The Cherokee Mother" and Thomas Pringle's "The Bechuana Boy", the poem takes possession of the voice of an Indigenous subject to effect a radical sublimation of an elemental and miasmic pollution precipitated by the violence of colonisation. In "The Aboriginal Mother", Dunlop is speaking through the voice of a young Aboriginal woman who runs with her baby from the site of the massacre. As they "fly the field of blood" under "midnight's star", the mother recounts the massacre – her husband "struck down by English steel", her firstborn lying wet with blood, the "the stockmen's human fire" piled high – while grieving for a desecration that has purged the land of Aboriginal people, language and lore/law. The poem's opening line, "Oh! hush thee – hush my baby", establishes the poem's ventriloquial method. The act of ventriloquy is to speak from the belly (Latin "venter") or otherwise reproduce from the belly the voice of another. The line inaugurates the poem's interplay between iterability and displacement, figuring a "putting to one side" or quelling of the voice in the face of death. The Aboriginal mother is beside herself in fear, the cry of the baby is being "hushed" or displaced, and the voice of the poet undergoes a temporal and spatial shift to be beside itself, possessed in the voice of another. As Susan Stewart writes in *Crimes of Writing*, in her discussion of Thomas Percy's *Reliques of Ancient English*

---

21 John O'Leary, "Giving the Indigenous a Voice: Further Thoughts on the Poetry of Eliza Hamilton Dunlop", *Journal of Australian Studies*, no. 82 (2004): 89–90. Vickery and Hansord also emphasise the integrity of Dunlop's political sensibility and her unique contribution to positive relationships with Aboriginal people, especially in the Wollombi and Lake Macquarie regions of the Awabakal people.

Poetry (1765) and the patricidal ballad "Edward", one is immediately immersed in the elaborate "voiced context" of a ventriloquising array.[22] In the Irish, English and Scottish ballad traditions, performative ventriloquy is *de rigueur*, especially as part of the sublimating apparatus in accounts of filial or romantic murder. In an additional transnational turn, the "voiced context" of "The Aboriginal Mother" subsumes something of the ballad tradition's rhetorical armoury. As Hansord reports, Dunlop enjoyed affiliations with literary and political elites in early nineteenth-century London and was clearly no stranger to progressive literary traditions.[23] The liberal Lord Mayor of London, W.T. Copeland, presented Dunlop with a complete dinner service on her departure for Australia, and in Sydney her poems were set to music by the composer Isaac Nathan, who had collaborated with Lord Byron in the production of the famous Hebrew Melodies.[24] Dunlop's ventriloquy was, it could be said, well versed in modes that, as Stewart notes, allow "a world ... to come to life beyond the signature" of the author or the authorial voice.[25]

But significantly in this poem, the figure of ventriloquy is itself established in a deeper and perhaps more ancient rhetoric of defilement. "The Aboriginal Mother" draws to a close with a vision of the spectre of the murdered Aboriginal chief holding his beheaded child aloft to a deity – "*To bring thy people's murder cry / Before the Christian's God*" – an Abrahamic scene of quasi-infanticide that underlines the defilement of the massacre and its miasmic transnational and transhistorical iconography. The Myall Creek massacre and the murder of innocents reverberate with that most primal of pollutants, the remains of the corpse. In *Powers of Horror*, Julia Kristeva writes that "the corpse, the most sickening of wastes, is a border that has encroached upon everything ... Disquieting matter, it is to be excluded from God's *territory* as it is from his *speech*", underlining a rhetorical formation in which the acute defilement of murder produces an elementary demarcation between disembodied iterability and destained, desacralised land.[26] Kristeva writes that the corpse "must not be displayed but immediately buried so as not to pollute the divine earth ... Burial is a means of purification", recalling Sophocles' *Antigone*, in which Creon's hubristic refusal to bury the corpse of Polynices mires him and the Theban social and cosmological order in a miasma of estrangement from self, kin and the sacred Theban estate.[27] It is only with Antigone's precipitous self-sacrificial refusal to submit to Creon's prohibition that, in the end, and after much trauma,

---

22 Susan Stewart, *Crimes of Writing: Problems in the Containment of Representation* (Durham: Duke University Press, 1994), 176.

23 Hansord, "Eliza Hamilton Dunlop's 'The Aboriginal Mother'", 4.

24 See Graeme Skinner in this volume.

25 Stewart, *Crimes of Writing*, 125.

26 Julia Kristeva, *Powers of Horror: An Essay on Abjection* (New York: Columbia University Press, 1982), 3, 109.

27 Kristeva, *Powers of Horror*, 109.

socio-cosmological order is restored. Similarly, in "The Aboriginal Mother", an ancient cathartic procedure emerges in which the pollution of the massacre is rhetorically contained and overcome. In essence, the Aboriginal mother is an early colonial *pharmakos* whose purgative function emerges in Dunlop's ventriloquised choreographing of a scene of defilement and purification. Indeed, Dunlop's rhetorical economy reproduces the aetiology of the ancient Greek *Thargelia*, the annual two-day spring festival held in honour of Apollo and Artemis, and the figure of the scapegoat. Jan Bremmer locates the fullest account of the ritual in fragments by the sixth-century poet Hipponax of Kolophon,

> who wishes that his enemies be treated as *pharmakoi* or 'scapegoats'. This evidently implies that they will be fed with figs, barley cake, and cheese. Then, in inclement weather, they will be hit on the genitals with the squill and with twigs of the wild fig tree and other wild plants … the *pharmakos* was finally [stoned and] burned on 'wild' wood and his ashes strewn into the sea.[28]

Bremmer further writes that *pharmakoi* were typically taken from among "criminals, slaves, ugly persons, strangers … [those] situated at the margin[s] of Greek society".[29] The *pharmakos* is essentially manufactured by the symbolic order's demarcation of corrupt or transgressive elements which are thence systematically ejected as part of the ritualised construction of social and sacred order. The cathartic procedure is aimed not only at expunging the impurity, but at instrumentally organising space. As Mary Douglas writes in *Purity and Danger*, "[e]liminating [pollution] is not a negative movement, but a positive effort to organise the environment".[30] In poetic terms, we might agree with Douglas that pollution is analogical: it can be read as a synecdoche for "designs of hierarchy or symmetry which apply in the larger social system".[31] In "The Aboriginal Mother", Dunlop rehearses the ancient dramaturgy of the *pharmakos* by locating a figure marked as the "criminal, slave, ugly person, stranger" dwelling to one side of the white colonial state, and casting her in a mini-epic of ritualised purgation, her family and kin subject to the final violence of being burnt on the wild wood. As a rhetorical apparatus, the poem positively reorganises the environment by resolving defilement and consecrating an iteration of colonial embodiment. The issue of an undefiled, unpolluted Australian nature is finally settled. The ventriloquy of an Aboriginal subjectivity produces, in the end, a final demarcation between iterability and silence, possession and dispossession. Following Douglas, the effect is much greater than "opening the fountains of the heart", as it also, and perhaps most

---

28   Jan Bremmer, "Scapegoat Rituals in Ancient Greece", *Harvard Studies in Classical Philology* 87 (1983): 300.
29   Bremmer, "Scapegoat Rituals", 303.
30   Douglas, *Purity and Danger*, 2.
31   Douglas, *Purity and Danger*, 4.

importantly, functions to systematise an unsullied relation to the land and a purified ontology of settlement.

Here I conclude by illuminating my core argument: that Dunlop's poem, in a foundational gesture of "placing to one side" and ventriloquising an Aboriginal subject, participates in a rhetorical economy of pollution in which disembodied utterance sublimates the violence of colonisation, thus relieving the colonial imagination of a destained relation to nature. For Dunlop, and, I would argue, her peers at the time, the defilement of the Myall Creek massacre produced an elementary breach in the constitution of the colonial imagination and its bicameral relation to a barely colonised landscape and a transnational imperial polity: a breach that required a sacralising gesture to prepare the ground for the emergence of a "guilt-free" relation to nature. The ventriloquising of the Aboriginal mother is an essential contrivance. Like the *pharmakos* of the *Thargelia*, the tragic Aboriginal mother is a projection that rhetorically sanctions the order of the colonial imagination. This leads me to make one or two final comments about the poem and what it tells us about the early colonial sensibility, especially its stance towards nature. Recalling Webby's depiction of the "placing to one side" of the Aboriginal subject, Dunlop's ventriloquising of the Aboriginal mother, which, as I have shown, is a literary reaction to the violence of the massacre, produces an elementary demarcation between modes of embodiment. The gesture is to make a distance, and to then embody the disembodied across that distance: to possess the dispossessed. In *Poetry and the Fate of the Senses*, Susan Stewart writes that

> ventriloquism per se … is [the projection of] a voice from or across a *distance* spatially (and in the metaphor of possession, temporally as well). This voice is distinguished by its origin in *another place*.[32]

The Aboriginal mother is indeed in another place. She is beside herself, literally and rhetorically, and, as Stewart suggests, her disembodied voice is spatially and temporally distanced, lost in an aesthetic realm in which a "dissociation of voice and gesture … make possession manifest through qualities of distantiation and disassociation".[33] In being "possessed" by the dissociative subjectivity of the author, the Aboriginal mother is singularly "dispossessed" as the object of a spectral literary tenancy that transposes the logic of colonisation and the dispossession of sovereignty, which is then repossessed under the signature of the author. Ultimately, despite the hortatory function of the poem's "outpourings of sentiment" aimed at "unlock[ing] the fountains of [the] heart" and a sympathetic response in a white readership, and despite Dunlop's obvious and very laudable engagements with Aboriginal peoples and cultures, as a poem "The Aboriginal Mother" ultimately results in the reinscription of the logic of colonisation.

---

32 Susan Stewart, *Poetry and the Fate of the Senses* (Chicago, Ill.: University of Chicago Press, 2002), 113.

33 Stewart, *Poetry*, 113.

In *Postcolonial Ecocriticism: Literature, Animals, Environment*, Graham Huggan and Helen Tiffin write that "the proper subject of postcolonialism is colonialism", and that a postcolonial ecocriticism should accordingly look "for the colonial/imperial underpinnings of environmental practices in both 'colonising' and 'colonised' societies of the past and present".[34] Huggan and Tiffin are echoed by Elizabeth DeLoughrey and George B. Handley's introduction to *Postcolonial Ecologies*, "Toward an Aesthetics of the Earth", in which Edward Said's appeal in *Culture and Imperialism* to "historical mythmaking 'enabled by the land'" underwrites "the vital role of the literary imagination in the process of decolonization".[35] A renewed critical appreciation of Eliza Hamilton Dunlop's poem "The Aboriginal Mother", especially from the perspective of contemporary critical work in postcolonial ecocriticism, reveals that the historicisation of a rhetoric of embodiment, settlement and, in this case, pollution, can shed new light on the aesthetic and political conditions of early settler relations to the Australian landscape. Such an approach prompts new and valuable insights into the sensibility of early Australia, the nature of its stance and the orientation of its senses of race, voice, the land and landscapes, among other things. As DeLoughrey and Handley maintain, "[h]istoricisation has been a primary tool of postcolonial studies and … is central to our understanding of the land".[36] In this case, we have observed an elementary ventriloquised displacement or putting to one side of an Aboriginal subject, itself part of a more fundamental suspension of an admission to nature in the wake of the defilement of frontier violence. Nature is historicised as the vanishing point of a transcultural theatre for the possession and dispossession of ontology, a definitively postcolonial ecology that recuperates the alterity of both history and nature without reducing either to the other.

---

34 Graham Huggan and Helen Tiffin, *Postcolonial Ecocriticism: Literature, Animals, Environment* (London: Routledge, 2010), 3.
35 Elizabeth M. DeLoughrey and George B. Handley, *Postcolonial Ecologies: Literatures of the Environment* (New York: Oxford University Press, 2011), 3.
36 DeLoughrey and Handley, *Postcolonial Ecologies*, 4.

7

Eliza Hamilton Dunlop, Irish and Colonial Melodist: Her Songs for Music and Collaborations with Isaac Nathan

Graeme Skinner

More than any other single factor, Eliza Dunlop's collaboration with the composer Isaac Nathan on a series of "Australian Melodies" has ensured that she is a figure of intense literary interest today. Of course, this is principally because of her most widely discussed and anthologised song lyric, "The Aboriginal Mother". Written and first published in 1838 in the wake of the Myall Creek massacre, it appears to have generated no documented response at the time. Yet, three years later, when she offered it to Nathan, and he chose to reset it to original music, its public reappearance sparked controversy, and made the poet and her Aboriginal subject targets of misogynistic and racist ridicule in Sydney's Tory and satirical newspapers.

But Dunlop is, and should be, also a figure of musical interest. Nathan only reset "The Aboriginal Mother". It was already, as Dunlop conceived it, a musical artefact. She told him that she originally "wrote" the song "for" a pre-existing tune.[1] Nor was it an isolated case. As a matter of creative preference as well as technique, Dunlop regularly chose to fit new words and images to the metrical and melodic formats of traditional and popular tunes, and deserves to be considered, in her own right, as one of the generation of "national melodists" that patterned itself on Thomas Moore and his *Irish Melodies* (with John Stevenson as musical collaborator for the first seven volumes).[2] And, as she was well aware, Nathan's own Hebrew Melodies to new lyrics by Byron also formed part of that tradition. Altogether, there are over a dozen identifiable instances where Dunlop either wrote "for" a pre-existing tune, or (and we cannot always be sure which was the case) where she later selected a tune that would allow her new "song" to be sung (see Table 1).[3] And we can reasonably assume there are other unidentified cases (see Table 2). In the full title of her manuscript compendium, "The Vase", Dunlop distinguished "songs

---

1   See her letter to Nathan, Appendix, Document 1.
2   For a comprehensive recent account of Moore's tune selections, see Una Hunt, *Sources and Style in* Moore's Irish Melodies (London and New York: Routledge, 2017).
3   Tables 1–3 are summaries only; full sources appear in the text proper.

Table 1 Eliza Dunlop – 13 songs written for or fitted to specified tunes.

Year	Title / incipit	Tune	Source
1838	"She was – yet have I oft denied"	"I stood amid the glittering throng"	Bishop
1838	"The Aboriginal Mother" ("Oh! hush thee – hush my baby")	"'Twas when the seas were roaring"	Handel
1839	"The Irish Mother" ("Your eyes have the twin-star's light")	"The foggy dew"	Irish
1840	"I bless thy shores, my native land"	"Peggy Ban"	Irish
c.1841	"Oh star of my hope in thy beauty appear" (in "The Cousins of Aledo")	"The guaracha"	Irish
c.1841	"I would not tell a heart so dear" (in "The Cousins of Aledo")	"How oft Louisa hast thou said" ["The birks of Invermay"]	Scottish
1841	"The Eagle Chief" (for Nathan)	"French air"	French
1842-43	"The Aboriginal Father" (for Nathan)	"Kongi kawelgo"	Aboriginal
1843	"The Irish Volunteers" ("For the golden harp on field of green")	"March of the Irish volunteers" [Lord Charlemont's march]	Elfort
1853-57	"The Helleborus niger: The Christmas Rose" ("Stern winter hath no power")	"Eveleen's Bower" ["The pretty girl of Derby O"]	? Irish
1865	"Erin Dheelish" ("The bell birds ring their silvery call")	Unidentified melody from one of Bunting's collections	Irish
Undated	"Echo of 'My ain kind dearie O'" ("Say what avails dim memory's form")	"My ain kind dearie O"	Scottish
Undated	"The Royal Pilosus" ("When the hour of departure is o'er")	"Far, far at sea"	Florio
Undated	"The Evening Star" ("Now Hesper weeps her glistening tears")	"The girl I left behind me"	? Irish

Table 2 Eliza Dunlop – six songs and likely songs without identified tunes.

Year	Title / incipit
1835/45	"Morning on Rostrevor Mountain(s)" ("'Tis Morning! from their heather bed")
1840	"Oh! the limpid streams of my own green land" ("for music")
1847	"To the Memory of … Mary Fitzroy" ("Trembling in agony! faint with amaze!")
1848	"Our home is the gibber-gunyah"
1867	"The spindrift bursts high o'er the cliffs of Clonara"
Undated	"Mo Varia Astore" ("Yes I have wept, to see thus faded")

for music" from her "other poems", and identifying and restoring the "original" music to as many of these as can easily be done (and thus also restoring music to the critical discussion of them) is the main purpose of the first half of this chapter. Moreover, tracing the earlier transmission history of some of the tunes throws up a few cases where earlier lyrics may also have influenced Dunlop's literary decisions.[4]

In a couple of instances, we know from Dunlop's own comments that she relied directly or indirectly on Irish tunes in Moore and Stevenson's widely disseminated volumes, and in the influential but less well-known collections of Edward Bunting (as she put it herself: "Mr. Bunting, although so eminent, was less talented than our great composer, Sir John Stevenson").[5] Probably, given her class and education, most of the tunes she used – and the lyrics she occasionally parodied – originally came her way in print editions, or manuscript copies of print editions.[6] Which is not necessarily to say she still had these copies to hand in Emu Plains or Wollombi; sometimes, her memory alone probably had to serve. At least once, Dunlop called for a tune that had not yet appeared in print anywhere. And yet, in naming it on first publication of her new lyric in Sydney in 1840, she clearly expected that some of her readers would know the tune anyway; if not necessarily in a version with exactly the same melodic details, then still close enough to fit her new lyrics. The printed forms of tunes given

---

4   For more comprehensive documentation on Dunlop's songs with music, along with musical concordances, see Graeme Skinner, "Eliza Hamilton Dunlop, Songwriter", *Australharmony* (an online resource towards the history of music and musicians in colonial and early Federation Australia), https://sydney.edu.au/paradisec/australharmony/dunlop-eliza-hamilton.php.
5   Footnote to "Erin Dheelish", *Empire*, 8 July 1865, 5, https://nla.gov.au/nla.news-article64140758.
6   Another collection she may well have known or even owned was Sidney Owenson's *Twelve Original Hibernian Melodies, with English Words, Imitated and Translated, from the Works of the Ancient Irish Bards* (London: Preston, [1805]), https://books.google.com.au/books?id=VuvZ714xkNcC.

Table 3 Isaac Nathan's published "Australian and Aboriginal Melodies" series 1841–43; those with lyrics by Eliza Dunlop in bold.

No.	Title / incipit	Words	Performances	Published
1	**"The Aboriginal Mother"** ("Oh! hush thee, hush, my baby")	**Dunlop** (1838)	27 Oct 1841 8 July 1842	Jan 1842
2	**"The Eagle Chief"** ("Hark to the sound! along the green hill side")	**Dunlop**	27 May 1842	Feb 1842
3	**"Mable Macmahon"** ("Your eyes have the blackberry's lustre")	**Dunlop**	27 May 1842 8 July 1842	July 1842
4	"Koorinda Braai"	Aboriginal	27 May 1842	July 1842
5	**"Star of the South"** ("Hail, star of the south! Australasia advance")	**Dunlop**	-	Aug 1842
6	"Australia the Wide and the Free"	W.A. Duncan	21 Dec 1842	Dec 1842
7	**"The Aboriginal Father"** ("The shadow on thy brow, my child")	Aboriginal/ **Dunlop**	-	Jan 1843

below should be approached in the same spirit: they fit the words closely enough, but there is no guarantee they are identical to the versions Dunlop or her colonial readers remembered, or – perhaps as often as not – slightly misremembered.

The second half of the chapter looks in closer detail at the creation and reception of the five Dunlop songs in Nathan's "Australian Melodies" series (see Table 3).[7] It is entirely possible that, with "The Aboriginal Mother", Dunlop seeded the original idea for the series, which Nathan enthusiastically pursued by asking her for another Aboriginal lyric for its successor. In due course, he actively promoted the series, variously as "Australian Melodies", and "Australian and Aboriginal Melodies", not only inviting comparisons with, but also suggesting they were worthy successors to, his Hebrew Melodies. The negative as well as the positive press coverage surrounding "The Aboriginal Mother" and its similarly contested successor, "The Eagle Chief", is reconsidered in the context of responses, pro and con, to two later songs, and, in the end, the surprisingly unanimous praise of the fifth song, " The Aboriginal Father", even in the pages of Dunlop's erstwhile antagonist, the *Sydney Morning Herald*.[8] A brief consideration of the genesis of Dunlop's two Nathan poems (not for music), and her three lyrics in his miscellany *The Southern Euphrosyne* brings the chapter to a close. The appendix presents newly corrected editions of two pieces of important correspondence between the two.

---

7   On Nathan, see Graeme Skinner, "Isaac Nathan and Family in Australia", *Australharmony*, https://sydney.edu.au/paradisec/australharmony/nathan-isaac-and-family.php.

8   See also Graeme Skinner, "Whigglings and Tories: David and Eliza Dunlop, Colonial Press Culture and the Contested Reception of Isaac Nathan's 'Australian Melodies' Reconsidered", forthcoming.

Dunlop's Songs with Music

Dunlop's active interest in Irish national music can be traced back to 28 April 1818, when, at the age of around twenty-one, a verse prologue she wrote was read from the stage at a Belfast benefit concert for an elderly invalid harper named Patrick Carolan.[9] She later told Nathan that "a few of my songs" had appeared among the half-dozen characteristic set-piece ballads and love lyrics in *The Dark Lady of Doona*, an Irish gothic novel by her cousin William Hamilton Maxwell, published in 1833/34.[10] But it was not until she arrived in Australia in 1838 that she began to identify tunes and songs together. The earliest of these, in the "Songs of an Exile" series, will be considered separately below, as immediate precursors of her Nathan songs, while her mainly later songs will be considered first here.

Surprisingly, perhaps, there is only one instance of a song where Dunlop nominated a tune that she can only have sourced – directly or indirectly – from one of Moore's collections. This is "The *Helleborus niger*: The Christmas Rose" ("Stern winter hath no power"), fitted to a tune that appeared in the second number of 1807.[11] Dunlop did not mention a tune on publishing her lyric in 1857. But in her earlier manuscript version of 1853, she named her source as "Eveleen's Bower", using the title of Moore's lyric rather than that of the tune itself, which was known in English as "The pretty girl of Derby, O! or The Irish dragoons".[12] Moore acknowledged that its national origins were disputed, but, taking the opinion of those "best acquainted with National Melodies", chose to believe it was Irish nevertheless. The composer Samuel Arnold, arranging it for the ballad opera *Two to One* (London, 1784), marked his setting *Vivace*. Moore and Stevenson, however, opted for *Plaintively*, and, given the melancholy turn of her lyric, Dunlop would probably have done likewise (Figure 7.1).

Likewise, there is only a single late instance of her identifying a tune from Bunting's collections – for "Erin Dheelish" ("The bell birds ring their silvery call"), which she sent to the *Empire* in 1865. Unfortunately, she stopped short of naming the tune, merely explaining that her lyric was "written for an old and somewhat plaintive air" that Bunting had published.[13] Bunting's second collection of 1809

---

9   "Address by Mrs. E.H. Dunlop ...", *Atlas*, 3 May 1845, 269, https://www.nla.gov.au/ferguson/1440365x/18450503/00010023/5-6.pdf; "The Vase", https://digital.sl.nsw.gov.au/delivery/DeliveryManagerServlet?dps_pid=FL9674364; Roy Johnston with Declan Plummer, *The Musical Life of Nineteenth-Century Belfast* (London and New York: Routledge, 2015), 83.

10   Appendix, Document 1; for a discussion of the songs in the novel, see Skinner, "Eliza Hamilton Dunlop, Songwriter".

11   *A Selection of Irish Melodies, with Symphonies and Accompaniments by Sir John Stevenson Mus.Doc. and Characteristic Words by Thomas Moore esq., number 2* (London: J. Power, [1807]), 91–97, https://archive.org/details/MooreIrishMelodies17/page/n129.

12   Papers Mainly Relating to the Raine Family and Eliza Dunlop, 1821–1870; State Library of New South Wales, MLMSS 10156, https://archival.sl.nsw.gov.au/Details/archive/110621176; "Helleborus niger", *Empire*, 11 April 1857, 3, https://nla.gov.au/nla.news-article60277324.

13   "Erin Dheelish", *Empire*, 8 July 1865, 5, https://nla.gov.au/nla.news-article64140758.

Figure 7.1: Musical example "The Helleborus niger" (Dunlop 1857, 1st verse); tune: "Eveleen's Bower" (Moore and Stevenson 2, 1807).

is the volume that Dunlop is most likely to have known well, and perhaps even owned, and there are at least three tunes in it that can be made to fit her lyric. One, "Planxty Maguire", can probably be ruled out for being insufficiently "plaintive" (a *planxty* is, generically, a fairly animated Irish harp tune, and Bunting marked his arrangement of this one *Allegretto spiritoso*). The most promising is "The Dawning of the Day" ("Eirghidhe an lae"), which Bunting presented, moreover, with new lyrics written "from a literal translation of the original Irish" by a Belfast poet, Mary Balfour (c.1778–1819):[14]

> The blush or morn at length appears,
> The hawthorn weeps in dewy tears;
> Emerging from the shades of night,
> The distant hills are tipp'd with light . . .

So that, if Dunlop did indeed set her new lyrics to Bunting's 1809 version of this tune, they can perhaps also be read as a Wollombi bush parody of Balfour's earlier text (see Figure 7.2).

---

14 *A General Collection of the Ancient Music of Ireland, Arranged for the Piano Forte, Some of the Most Admired Melodies are Adapted for the Voice to Poetry Chiefly Translated from the Original Irish Songs by Thomas Campbell Esq. and Other Eminent Poets, to which is Prefixed a Historical & Critical Dissertation on the Egyptian, British and Irish Harp by Edward Bunting, vol. 1st* [sic] (London: Engraved by Williamson, n.d. [1809]) (hereafter "Bunting 1809"), 53, https://archive.org/stream/generalcollectio00bunt_0#page/53/mode/2up.

The bell-birds ring their sil-v'ry call, Clear tink-ling 'midst the myr-tle glades;

The ci-ca-da hath cast its pall, And my-riads throng the ce-dar shades;

The sul-len Mul-la mur-murs bye, Re-flect-ing moun-tain, crag, and tree,

En-chant-ing scene! then whence the sigh? Mo E-rin dhee-lish gra ma-chree.

E-rin mo cush-la'a-vour-neen dhee-lish! A yea yee-lish gra ma-chree.

En-chant-ing scene! then whence the sigh? Mo E-rin dhee-lish gra ma-chree.

Figure 7.2: Musical example "Erin Dheelish" (Dunlop 1865, 1st verse); tune: "The dawning of the day" (Bunting 1809).

If Dunlop had likely recourse once to Bunting's 1809 collection, perhaps we might usefully look there for tunes to other undesignated songs. One case is the ballad-like "Morning on Rostrevor Mountain" ("'Tis morning! from their heather bed / The curling mists arise"), originally published in George Petrie's *Dublin Penny Journal* in 1835, and reworked with some not-quite-despairing Australian allusions for its reappearance in *the Atlas* in April 1845:[15]

> . . . Where the wild Emu leads her brood
> Across the trackless plains,
> And lord of nature's solitude –
> The stately cedar, reigns;

---

15   "Morning on Rostrevor Mountains [sic]", *Dublin Penny Journal*, 8 August 1835, 42, https://www.jstor.org/stable/30003439; "Morning on Rostrevor Mountain . . .", *Atlas*, 26 April 1845, 257, https://www.nla.gov.au/ferguson/1440365x/18450426/00010022/5-6.pdf.

> Even there, through exile's cheerless hours,
> Lighted by Austral skies,
> I've linger'd amid orange flowers,
> To catch thy scented sighs . . .

Bunting's tune of "The song of sorrow" fits it well, and appropriately too, given the words he identifies as traditionally belonging to it are – like Dunlop's original version – a prospective exile's brooding farewell to her native land. Mary Balfour's singing translation begins:[16]

> Adieu! my native wilds, adieu!
> In Spring's green robe array'd,
> Where days of bliss like moments flew
> Beneath the woodland shade.
> Now banish'd from sweet Erin's shore,
> O'er trackless seas forlorn I go,
> In distant climates to deplore
> My Ulican dubh, Oh! . . .

Of all Dunlop's later lyrics without nominated tunes, probably the most likely to carry hidden music is "A Phase of Ireland in the 16th Century" ("The spindrift bursts high o'er the cliffs of Clonara") (1867), a thoroughly bardic ballad, whose opening lines toll resonantly with a litany of Irish placenames:

> The spindrift bursts high o'er the cliffs of Clonara,
> The breakers surge madly around Craignabe;
> Storms hurstle [sic] and howl in the clefts of Knockbara
> And snow-wreaths lie deep in the gorge of Dunro . . .

Dunlop's subject is the disastrous Battle of Kinsale, in 1601, in which the Irish chieftains were finally defeated by the English invaders.[17] Irish ballad tunes fitting the lyric's elaborate structure are few and far between, yet one was reasonably widely known. Moore wrote "The Parallel" ("Yes, sad one of Sion") in his eighth number of 1821 to the tune of "I Would Rather Than Ireland", as previously given by Bunting in 1809 (with the lyric "O lov'd maid of Broka").[18] Dunlop may well have

---

16 Bunting 1809, 4–5, https://archive.org/details/generalcollectio00bunt_0/page/4.
17 Dunlop's notes referred to Leland's *History*, but the passages quoted actually derived directly from John Lawless, *A Compendium of the History of Ireland . . . second edition* (Belfast: Joseph Smyth, 1815), 268–69, https://archive.org/details/compendiumofhist00lawl/page/268.
18 *The Works of Thomas Moore . . . vol. 4* (Paris: A. and W Galignani, 1823), 202–4, https://archive.org/details/worksthomasmoor08moorgoog/page/n218; Bunting 1809, 28–29, https://archive.org/details/generalcollectio00bunt_0/page/29.

Now He-sper weeps her glist - 'ning tears, high o'er the'At-lan - tic o - cean

And its high hea-ving breast ap-pears to sigh with soft — e - mo - tion,

The mur-murs of its cold blue wave With rest - less whi - spers mind me;

That hope is laid in mem' - ry's grave With "the girl I left — be - hind me".

Figure 7.3: Musical example "The Evening Star" (Dunlop undated, 1st verse); tune: "The Girl I Left Behind Me" (Moore 1818).

known it in one or other version, but, even if not, it is clearly the type of musical vehicle she had in mind.

Dunlop parodied the popular song "The Girl I Left Behind Me" in "The Evening Star" ("Now Hesper weeps her glistening tears"), one of her undated lyrics in "The Vase".[19] The tune was so universally known in the Anglosphere that neither she nor her prospective readers/singers would have needed a printed source.[20] Moore had included it in his seventh number in 1818 (with a minor ending), and Bunting, although he did not print it until 1840 (with a major ending), claimed to have collected it from the harper Arthur O'Neill, as early as 1800 (see Figure 7.3).[21]

"Mo Varia Astore" ("Yes I have wept, to see thus faded") ("The Vase", undated) is almost certainly another song, and given Dunlop's title ("Varia" being "Mary", as she elsewhere explained), it is possible she had in mind the tune "O Mary Asthore", which, moreover, fits. If so, it may have reached her by purely oral transmission, as

---

19   *"The Vase"*,
     https://digital.sl.nsw.gov.au/delivery/DeliveryManagerServlet?dps_pid=FL9674337.
20   The epigraph is from Samuel Laman Blanchard's *Stanzas for Evening*, in his *Lyric Offerings*
     (London: William Harrison Ainsworth, 1828), 75,
     https://books.google.com.au/books?id=UlkjTkmNst8C&pg=PA75.
21   Moore and Stevenson, *A Selection of Irish Melodies ... 7* (1818), 7,
     https://books.google.com.au/books?id=PwBfAAAAcAAJ&pg=PA7; *The Ancient Music of Ireland, Arranged for the Piano Forte, to Which Is Prefixed a Dissertation on the Irish Harp and Harpers, Including an Account of the Old Melodies of Ireland by Edward Bunting* (Dublin: Hodges and Smith, 1840), index, and 42,
     https://archive.org/details/ancientmusicofir00bunt/page/42.

Figure 7.4: Musical example "Echo of 'My ain kind dearie O'" (Dunlop undated, 1st verse); tune: "My ain kind deary-O" (Johnson 1787).

there was no printed source until after her death. The earliest identified manuscript transcription is that by George Petrie, who first printed Dunlop's "Morning on Rostrevor Mountain" in Dublin in 1835.[22]

On at least two occasions, Dunlop also had recourse to Scottish melodies. The "Echo of 'My ain kind dearie O'" ("Say what avails dim memory's form"), in "The Vase", uses the tune and the original chorus line of the song also known as "The Lea-Rig", anthologised in the 1787 first volume of James Johnson's *The Scots Musical Museum*, a series to which Robert Burns was a major contributor (Figure 7.4).[23]

One final undated song "The Royal Pilosus" ("When the hour of departure is o'er") is fitted to the tune "Far, Far at Sea".[24] The well-known setting, popularised in Britain by the vocalist Charles Incledon (1763–1826), was composed at the turn of

22 "The Vase", https://digital.sl.nsw.gov.au/delivery/DeliveryManagerServlet?dps_pid=FL9674404; Charles Villiers Stanford (ed.), *The Complete Collection of Irish Music as Noted by George Petrie* (London: Boosey and Co., 1903/04), no. 636, 159, https://archive.org/stream/imslp-complete-collection-of-irish-music-petrie-george/SIBLEY1802.6228.15976.7c20-39087012503696pp127-267#page/n31/mode/2up.

23 "The Vase", https://digital.sl.nsw.gov.au/delivery/DeliveryManagerServlet?dps_pid=FL9674336; *The Scots Musical Museum* (Edinburgh: Johnson & Co., 1787), 50, https://archive.org/details/scotsmusicalmuse12john/page/50/mode/2up.

24 "The Vase", https://digital.sl.nsw.gov.au/delivery/DeliveryManagerServlet?dps_pid=FL9674375; *Far Far at Sea, a Favorite Ballad Sung by Mr. Incledon* (New York: J. & M. Paff, [n.d.]), https://www.loc.gov/item/2014568420.

When the hour of de-par-ture us o'er,   And each ten-der fare-well hath been spo-ken;

The Pi-lo-sus, a-far from our shores;   Shall the love links of mem-'ry be bro-ken;

The Pi-lo-sus, a-far from our shores;   Shall the love links of mem-'ry be bro-ken.

Far,   far   at   sea. ___

Figure 7.5: Musical example "The Royal Pilosus" (Dunlop undated, 1st verse); tune: "Far, Far at Sea" (Florio).

the century by Charles Florio, who fitted the anonymous text's verses of four-lines and refrain to seven phrases of melody by repeating lines 3 and 4.

> 'Twas at night, when the bell had toll'd twelve,
> And poor Susan was laid on her pillow,
> In her ear whisper'd some flitting elve,
> Your love is now toss'd on a billow,
> *In her ear whisper'd some flitting elve,*
> *Your love is now toss'd on a billow,*
> Far, far at sea!

Dunlop probably envisaged a similar repeat for her lyric; unless, by some chance, she knew a shortened four-line and refrain version of the melody (for instance, omitting phrases 4 and 5 – that is: 1, 2, 3, 6 and refrain). This is not impossible or implausible; by the time Dunlop encountered it, Florio's tune had long since passed from being circulated and consumed mainly in print and manuscript, to being transmitted orally, and therefore constantly at risk of being creatively reinterpreted (Figure 7.5).

Music in the "Songs of an Exile" Series (1838–40) and "The Cousins of Aledo"

Dunlop assumed the mantle of colonial poet and song writer with the first four numbers of the "Songs of an Exile" series in the *Australian* in November and December 1838. She indicated no tunes for the first and third songs, although, because of their common metrical and rhyming schemes, any of her readers inspired to sing them could easily have found any number of suitable tunes among traditional national songs and composed settings.

Number 2, "She Was – Yet Have I Oft Denied", which appeared on 22 November, is Dunlop's earliest datable song with its musical source indicated, "adapted to the music" of the concert ballad "I Stood amid the Glittering Throng" (1831) by Henry Bishop, originally with words by F.W.N. Bayley.[25] Dunlop's terminology here – "music" rather than "air" or "tune" – perhaps suggests that she had in mind not just the melody, but also Bishop's piano accompaniment, performed ideally, or actually, from printed sheet music or a manuscript copy that she had access to or some recollection of. Perhaps manuscript or memory are slightly more likely, given she mistook the title slightly: "among" for "amid". The source ballad, popularised in Britain by leading actor-singers Lucia Vestris and Harriet Waylett, is a generic women's song, in which the female vocalist ventriloquises a smitten male, recalling a vision of delicate (female) loveliness on the sidelines at a ball, and reaching its apotheosis with the singer dreaming of leading the lovely girl onto the dance floor. Though Dunlop's new verses are not a direct parody of Bayley's original words, readers and singers would probably have been struck by the parallel trajectory of her post-mortem remembrances of a (female) beloved, finally reposing on (and note the unexpected indefinite article) "*a* Saviour's breast".

The fourth of the series, and Dunlop's best known and most discussed lyric is, of course, "The Aboriginal Mother" ("Oh! hush thee – hush my baby"). Her response to the Myall Creek massacre of June 1838, it was published in the immediate wake of the two November trials, on 13 December, only five days before seven of the perpetrators were executed.[26] No tune was indicated on this first appearance, but Dunlop later informed Nathan privately that she wrote the verses to the tune of "'Twas When the Seas Were Roaring".[27] The well-known melody was probably associated with the original lyrics from their first documented outing in John Gay's farce, *The What d'ye Call It?*, in London, 1715, although only somewhat later were they first published together (1740) and attributed to Handel (1746), the setting also known as "The Melancholly Nymph", or "The Faithful Maid". The tune meanwhile also reappeared, fitted out with new words ("How cruel are the traytors"), in Gay's *The Beggar's Opera*.

However much, or little, Dunlop knew of this pre-history, she was almost certainly aware of the original ballad's melancholic association with a

---

25 "Songs of an Exile (No. 2)", *Australian*, 22 November 1838, 3, https://nla.gov.au/nla.news-article36860702; *I Stood amid the Glittering Throng, a Ballad, the Poetry by F.W.H. Bayley esq., the Music by H.R. Bishop* . . . 4th ed. (London: Goulding and D'Almaine, [1831]), https://archive.org/stream/hartley00535542#page/n78/mode/1up.
26 "Songs of an Exile (No. 4)", *Australian*, 13 December 1838, 4, https://nla.gov.au/nla.news-article36861275.
27 See Appendix, Document 1.

woman-in-distress. There is nothing in her new verses to suggest a direct parody of Gay's lyrics, although there is a likely indirect influence by way of an intermediate ballad written for the same tune, called "The Forsaken Damsel" ("It was a Winter's evening"), the third verse of which, somewhat clumsily fitted to the melody, reads:[28]

> Hush, hush, my lovely baby, and warm thee in my breast;
> Ah little thinks thy father how sadly we're distrest;
> For cruel as he is, did he know but how we fare,
> He'd shield us in his arms from this bitter piercing air.

Dunlop can be excused for opting not to identify her original source tune on its first print appearance, or later in "The Vase". Clearly, on other occasions, and for other pieces of verse, she was happy not only to name tunes, but also to be seen to draw on lyric traditions attached to them. However, doing so amid the unfolding public drama of late 1838 might have risked diluting the song's impact, by conjuring exotic and other unintended associations, and setting readers off in a vain search for parodies. In this, it was not the tune itself that was the potential distraction, but – from the author's point of view (and perhaps also that of the *Australian*'s editor) – its uncontrollable associations.[29] On the other hand, the tune deserves consideration alongside the other poetic inputs in Dunlop's compositional process. And, if imagining ourselves in her shoes is of any critical use at all, trying to sing it is probably a useful analytical tool. By comparison, Nathan's later, very different setting – however earnestly Dunlop invited it and came to value it – should probably be seen as an authorial after-thought (Figure 7.6).

The fifth of the series, "The Irish Mother" ("Your eyes have the twin-star's light, ma croidhe"), followed closely on the previous four.[30] It is one of two lyrics in the set for which Dunlop nominated melodies anthologised by Bunting. However, in the case of this tune, "Foggy Dew", Bunting did not publish his version – the first in print – until 1840. In fact, when Dunlop's new lyric for it appeared in Sydney on 12 January 1839, Bunting was yet even to collect the melody, doing so in Belfast, that very year, from J. McKneight, probably Dr James McKnight (1801–1876), the Protestant nationalist leader and newspaper editor, who presumably knew the song from childhood in rural County Down. Bunting anyway concluded that it

---

28 James Plumtre, ed., *A Collection of Songs, Moral, Sentimental, Instructive, and Amusing . . . vol. 2* (London: F. C. and J. Rivington, 1806), 133, https://books.google.com.au/books?id=NYBEAAAAcAAJ&pg=PA133; it was also later widely anthologised (usually without reference to the tune) as "A Winter Piece".

29 Another well-known lyric composed to be sung to the tune was Reginald Heber's hymn "From Greenland's Icy Mountains", of 1817; compare, also, a typical satirical parody "'Twas When a New Election" [from the *Morning Chronicle*, 6 August 1811], *The Spirit of the Public Journals for 1811* (London: James Ridgway, 1812), 297, https://books.google.com.au/books?id=StsXAQAAIAAJ&pg=PA297.

30 "Songs of an Exile (No. 5)", *Australian*, 12 January 1839, 4, https://nla.gov.au/nla.news-article36862585.

Figure 7.6: Musical example "The Aboriginal Mother" (Dunlop 1838, 1st verse): tune: "The Melancholy Nymph" (Handel, HWV 228:19).

was "Very ancient, author and date unknown". McKnight's rather elaborate melody (printed by Bunting without any words) is probably close, though not necessarily identical in every detail, to the tune that Dunlop knew, either from a manuscript copy, or – perhaps more likely – from memory (Figure 7.7).[31]

Dunlop mentioned in her 1841 letter of introduction to Nathan that she had been intending to use the last two "Songs of an Exile" series in a verse drama, "The Cousins of Aledo", based on Mary Russell Mitford's *Blanch, a Poem in Four Cantos*.[32] This certainly makes sense of the nostalgic subject matter and romantic style of the songs, in the context both evidently to be sung by the medieval heroine herself, Blanch of Murcia, during her enforced exile further south in Spain's drier "Austral lands" towards Granada, notwithstanding that their first newspaper readers – knowing nothing of this scenario – probably imagined that the singer was the author herself, exiled in Emu Plains. The fact that, on its 1840 first publication, "Oh! the Limpid Streams of My Own Green Land" was designated as "stanzas for music", perhaps indicates that Dunlop had not yet discovered a pre-existing tune that suited her, and was actively canvassing musical assistance in anticipation of her play being published or produced.[33] But finding or devising a strophic tune to

31 Bunting 1840, x (note), 109,
   https://archive.org/stream/ancientmusicofir00bunt#page/109/mode/1up.
32 See Appendix, Document 1.
33 "Songs of an Exile (No. 7)", *Australian*, 11 April 1840, 4,
   https://nla.gov.au/nla.news-article36862149; "Song of an Exile", *Empire*, 24 December 1862, 4,
   https://nla.gov.au/nla.news-article60520671.

Your eyes have the twin-star's light, *ma croi-dhe, Mo Cui - sle___ ING-HEAN ban;*

And your swan-like neck is__ dear to__ me, *Mo Cai - lin___ og a - lain:*

And dear is your fai - ry__ foot so__ light, And your daz - zling milk - white hand,

And your hair! it's a thread of the gol - den light That was spun__ in the rain-bow's band.

Figure 7.7: Musical example "The Irish Mother" (Dunlop 1839, 1st verse); tune: "The Foggy-Dew" (Bunting 1840, down a minor third).

fit her lyric would not have been a straightforward task. The rhetorical repeat of the first line as the second (a blemish Dunlop slightly masked on republishing it much later), and the irregular scansion (feet variably of two, three or four syllables) would most likely have confused all but the most intrepid composers or arrangers, of whom there were few in the Colony anyway.

Meanwhile, for no. 8, "I bless thy shores, my native land", she had already found a tune. The new lyrics are a stylish, if doleful, fit for the old melody "Peggy Ban (barn/bawn)", as Bunting gave it in his 1809 volume, probably anyway the printed iteration of the tune that Dunlop was most likely either to have had in mind, or even in hand at Emu Plains (Figure 7.8).[34]

But neither of these songs appears in the mid twentieth-century typescript copy of "The Cousins of Aledo" preserved in the State Library of New South Wales. Rather, there are two entirely different songs, both (as dramatised) for the singer accompanying him/herself on the guitar, and both for named tunes. That for "Oh star of my hope in thy beauty appear" (for Almanzor, in act 1 scene 2) is "the Juaracha", probably the "guaracha" (a "Moorish" or "Spanish dance") widely known in the Anglosphere in the arrangement in John Baptist Cramer's popular piano method, that, directly or indirectly, was also plausibly Dunlop's source.[35] For "I would not tell a

34 "Songs of an Exile No. 8", *Australian*, 7 May 1840, 2,
    https://nla.gov.au/nla.news-article36862754; Bunting 1809, 56,
    https://archive.org/stream/generalcollectio00bunt_0#page/56/mode/2up.
35 State Library of New South Wales, MLMSS 6011/4/2, typescript of "The Cousins of Aledo", 5,
    https://digital.sl.nsw.gov.au/delivery/DeliveryManagerServlet?dps_pid=FL8980873; *J.B. Cramer's*

Figure 7.8: Musical Example "I Bless Thy Shores, My Native Land" (Dunlop 1840, 1st verse); tune: "Peggy Ban" (Bunting 1809).

heart so dear" (for Blanch, act 4 scene 2), the tune is that of "How oft Louisa hast thou said". In the context, this probably seemed a suitable national choice, since the original lyric also comes from a Spanish play, Sheridan's comic opera *The Duenna* (London, 1775). However, the dramatist's father-in-law and brother-in-law, composers Thomas Linley senior and junior, fitted it to a Scottish tune, "The Birks of Invermay".[36] Dunlop evidently chose to play up the geographical dissonance by introducing a Burnsian "sair" into the second line of her new lyric, the result an effective – if unexpected – "Scottish melody" in the wilds of southern Spain.[37]

"The Aboriginal Mother" (1841–42)[38]

Isaac Nathan was close to the age of fifty when he arrived in Sydney in April 1841. He was still, and would remain, best known as a composer for his early

---

Instructions for the Piano Forte (London: Chappell, 1812), 24,
https://digital.staatsbibliothek-berlin.de/
werkansicht?PPN=PPN84855101X&PHYSID=PHYS_0032&DMDID=DMDLOG_0001.

36 "The Cousins of Aledo", 20,
https://digital.sl.nsw.gov.au/delivery/DeliveryManagerServlet?dps_pid=FL8980888; *The Duenna; or, The Double Elopement, a Comic Opera as Performed at the Theatre Royal in Covent Garden for the Voice, Harpsichord, or Violin* (London: Printed for C. and C. Thompson, [1776]), 50,
https://archive.org/details/duennaordoubleel00linl/page/50.

37 Notably, Burns' well-known lyric "My heart is sair".

38 *The Aboriginal Mother, an Australian Melody Respectfully Inscribed to Lady Gipps, the Poetry by Mrs. E.H. Dunlop, the Music by I. Nathan* (Sydney: published for the composer, Ada Cottage, Prince Street, [1842]), https://trove.nla.gov.au/work/24305488.

collaboration with the poet Byron on the series Hebrew Melodies, which the pair originally published in two numbers in 1815–16, emulating the format, and hoping to share in some of the success, of Moore and Stevenson's *Irish Melodies*. Nathan was generally well received by the Sydney press, with high hopes expressed for the benefits that might accrue to the Colony by the leading role he seemed so eager to take in its musical affairs. But by early September, he also had a few vocal detractors, who were accusing him – as was all too usual for recent arrivals with public reputations at "Home" – of overreaching with his plans and for allowing himself to be too ardently promoted by his admirers. His troubles crystallised in a fawning editorial, on 7 September, in which the *Australian*'s Wickham Hesketh claimed that Nathan was a direct descendant of the late king Stanislaus of Poland.[39] "God protect us from our friends", the *Gazette* counselled in response, hoping (but evidently not fully trusting) that Nathan himself had no "part in this superlative piece of puffery".[40]

It is unlikely that Dunlop was yet aware of these last developments when she first wrote to Nathan, introducing herself, probably no later than the beginning of September, and enclosing the texts of at least one, and possibly three lyrics for his consideration.[41] Evidently, of these, Nathan chose to set "The Aboriginal Mother", for already, on 25 September, one of his closest confidants, William Augustine Duncan, editor of the Catholic newspaper the *Australasian Chronicle*, reported that it was to be on the program of Nathan's forthcoming concert.[42] To publicise both the event and his new setting itself, Nathan arranged for Dunlop's lyric to be printed by the *Herald* on 15 October, the *Chronicle* a day later, the *Gazette* on the 19th, and the *Monitor* on the day of the concert itself, the 27th.[43] Only the *Herald*, in an editorial footnote, probably added by the leader writer Ralph Mansfield, distanced itself from Dunlop's sympathetic characterisation:

The words are pathetic, and display much poetic feeling, but they ascribe to the aboriginal woman words that might have been used by a North American Indian, but which our very slight acquaintance with the natives of this colony would enable

---

39 [Editorial], *Australian*, 7 September 1841, 2, https://nla.gov.au/nla.news-article36852702.

40 [Editorial], *Sydney Gazette*, 9 September 1841, 2, https://nla.gov.au/nla.news-article2554422; the *Gazette* was in the last stages of the management of Robert Howe, junior (1820–1875); he sold it to Patrick Grant in October.

41 Appendix, Document 1.

42 "Nathan's Subscription Concerts", *Australasian Chronicle*, 25 September 1841, 3, https://nla.gov.au/nla.news-article31732969; "Select Poetry", *Australasian Chronicle*, 16 October 1841, 2, https://nla.gov.au/nla.news-article31733155; "The Aboriginal Mother", *Sydney Gazette*, 19 October 1841, 2, https://nla.gov.au/nla.news-article2554757; "The Aboriginal Mother", *Sydney Monitor*, 27 October 1841, 2, https://nla.gov.au/nla.news-article32191166.

43 "The Aboriginal Mother", *Sydney Herald*, 15 October 1841, 2, https://nla.gov.au/nla.news-article12871688; in 1838, Mansfield had told the committee of inquiry in the wake of the massacre that he had no knowledge "of the Aborigines" from direct personal contact; "Extracts from the Minutes of Evidence on the Aborigines Question", *Colonist*, 29 December 1838, 4, https://nla.gov.au/nla.news-article31722278.

any one to say never issued from the mouth of the woman who escaped from the New England massacre for which, we may remark, seven men were executed in Sydney. The lines will no doubt be copied in England where they are almost sure to be popular.

The *Herald* had taken a strong editorial position back in 1838 opposing the execution of the Myall Creek perpetrators, and as late as 1844, Duncan, one of the paper's most strident critics, accused it of continuing to abuse the Governor, George Gipps, "because he would not allow the Squatters to shoot the blacks".[44] In October 1841, however, the paper's new owners, Kemp and Fairfax, with Mansfield as leader writer, had been in charge for only nine months, and were still inclined to be, as the editorial collective, more circumspect. Nevertheless, the judicious pairing of the massacre and the executions was a polite warning shot across Dunlop's bows, and having made its point, the *Herald*'s own generally supportive review of the 27 October concert made no further mention of the song at all.[45] But this omission was instantly remedied – too conveniently for it to be by mere chance – in a second "review", run directly below it, from a "correspondent". Signing himself as "P.P." (Paul Pry, a generic satirical commentator of the day), the plain-speaking author regretted that, as sung by Nathan's daughter Rosetta, the song had appeared to create so little interest with the audience:

Perhaps some excuse may be said for the song itself. And it will serve Mr. Nathan as a hint for the future, not to attempt putting into music what is unintelligible in verse: that, having no meaning in itself, not Handel himself could have made any thing of it . . . had this been got up in the character of a *black Gin* with a ghastly, toad-like looking brat, gnawing a raw oppossum – the house would have been in a roar of applause, and no end of *encore* . . . truly it is utterly impossible that out of "nature's own" the pretty Rosetta could have undertaken the part.[46]

Dunlop and her "mother" were not the only targets of this Tory satirist, however. Clearly, he also intended to take down Nathan a peg or two, not least by gloating that the Whiggish Governor's non-attendance (Gipps was visiting Melbourne) resulted in "the absence from the concert of 'follow-my-leader clique' and the cabbage-tree *oi polloi*", thus, presumably, curtailing Nathan's takings. The *Herald*'s editors themselves would never have adopted the insinuating tone towards the seventeen-year-old Rosetta, yet were evidently not deterred from facilitating, and

---

44 "The Aborigines", *Weekly Register*, 12 October 1844, 183, https://nla.gov.au/
nla.news-article228134802; "The Squatters, the Governor, and the Blacks", *Weekly Register*, 19
October 1844, 193, https://nla.gov.au/nla.news-article228135328.

45 "Nathan's Grand Concert", *Sydney Herald*, 29 October 1841, 2,
https://nla.gov.au/nla.news-article12871965.

46 "Mr. Nathan's Concert (From a Correspondent)", *Sydney Herald*, 29 October 1841, 2,
https://nla.gov.au/nla.news-article12871963.

perhaps even commissioning, this nasty, but strategically effective piece of journalistic overreach.

The *Herald*, as the town's only daily news sheet, almost inevitably influenced, one way or another, the content of its nearest competitor, the thrice-weekly *Gazette*, as of October under the new editorship of Patrick Grant.[47] On this occasion its review, which appeared a day later, chimed in neatly with the *Herald*'s, though its ostensibly fulsome praise of the music and Rosetta's performance now only further underlined the incongruity it, too, alleged:

> We had seen the verses in the public prints; we had also seen Gins, and from our acquaintance with the gyneocracy of Australia, we could but regret that these thrillingly touching lines should have been so misplaced. Disconnect them however, from their present black heroine – fancy her any one else, and a treat awaits you. By the time the few first bars of the symphony were played, we were totally absorbed in the composition. The song was sung by Miss R. Nathan with a simplicity, chastity, and pathos truly thrilling – never was poetry recited to greater advantage, the accompaniments were most appropriate – the melody touching and effective. We were in spite of ourselves affected even to tears, and most of our neighbours from a similar state, were prevented observing our weakness. Since *Jeptha's Daughter* [sic], we have not had such a treat, and we shall conceive no concert complete for months to come without a repetition of the "Aboriginal Mother." In England the song *must* become a favorite.[48]

The well-observed comparison with "Jephtha's Daughter", one of the best known of Nathan's Hebrew Melodies and warmly applauded at his recent concerts, probably seemed genuine enough, and construed as such by disinterested readers. Yet others, remembering the *Gazette*'s hard line a month earlier, under its previous editor, on Nathan's penchant for self-promotion, may have been a little more suspicious. And was it the music that the *Gazette* felt would appeal back in homeland England? Or – as the *Herald* had first suggested – the misplaced sympathy of the lyrics?

A fourth salvo appeared in a letter to the *Herald*, signed "Thorough Bass", on 3 November, although, in the context of yet another complaint against the continued "puffing" of Nathan's reputation, the composer, not the lyricist, was the immediate target:

---

47   A Scot, who married into the family of Charles Grant, Lord Glenelg (1788–1866), Patrick Grant had edited several incarnations of the radical paper, the *Sun*, in London in the early 1830s. In Australia he was police magistrate at Maitland 1837–40; see Andrew Messner, "Contesting Chartism from Afar: Edward Hawksley and the *People's Advocate*", *Journal of Australian Colonial History* 1, no. 1 (April 1999): 77–78, https://search.informit.com.au/documentSummary;dn=200009595;res=IELAPA.

48   "Mr. Nathan's Concert", *Sydney Gazette*, 30 October 1841, 2, https://nla.gov.au/nla.news-article2554858; the review mentions an instrumental introduction ("symphony"), not included in Nathan's published version.

the Aboriginal Mother (*proh pudor!*) is a very – very indifferent song – "another failure" in fact – is praised as equal to the sublime, superhuman pathos of Jephtha's Daughter. How much farther than this could absurdity go? "From the sublime to the ridiculous is but a step." I do sincerely wish Nathan every success.[49]

As he later intimated to Dunlop, Nathan was almost certainly right in believing that the author of this diatribe was the polymathic "professor" James Rennie (1787–1867) – like Nathan, another recent arrival and, by the Colony's exacting standards, also too ardent a self-promoter, and very briefly editor of the *Herald* in the months before the Fairfax and Kemp takeover.[50]

Meanwhile, as might be expected, Duncan in the *Chronicle* warmly greeted the work itself ("equal to any thing that Mr. Nathan has yet written"), and Hesketh's *Australian*, likewise, the performance:[51]

Miss Rosetta, though evidently wanting a due share of confidence, imparted to the *Aboriginal Mother* a peculiar degree of pathos – indeed, her very tremulousness harmonised most happily with the subject.

Reviews in the lower-circulation papers, Robert McEachern's *Free Press* (30 October) and James Noble's double-sheet weekly *Observer* (4 November), were also positive as to the song and Rosetta's singing.[52] However, one other informal "review" sent in to the *Free Press* by "a Bushman", fortuitously in town for the concert, might have led seasoned readers to suspect it was another strategic journalistic plant:

The "Aboriginal Mother" no doubt is very good music, but the young lady must have been timid at the first starting off, as I could easily see she could have sung it *ten times as well at home*; and the House, not much understanding these matters … never encored her, so that they are in perfect ignorance *what the song is* after all.[53]

Musically, Nathan's setting of "The Aboriginal Mother" is as distinct from Dunlop's "original" – with Handel's tune – as he could possibly have reimagined it. He

49 "Original Correspondence", *Sydney Herald*, 3 November 1841, 2, https://nla.gov.au/nla.news-article12872050; the other target was the painter Maurice Appleby Felton (1803–1842).
50 Appendix, Document 2.
51 "Nathan's Grand Concert", *Australasian Chronicle*, 28 October 1841, 2, https://nla.gov.au/nla.news-article31733245; "Concert", *Australian*, 30 October 1841, 2, https://nla.gov.au/nla.news-article36849358.
52 "Mr. Nathan's Concert", *Sydney Free Press*, 30 October 1841, 3, https://nla.gov.au/nla.news-article226356910; "Mr. Nathan's Concert", *Colonial Observer*, 4 November 1841, 6, https://nla.gov.au/nla.news-article226359780.
53 "Original Correspondence", *Sydney Free Press*, 30 October 1841, 2, https://nla.gov.au/nla.news-article226356914.

Figure 7.9: Musical Example "The Aboriginal Mother" (Dunlop and Nathan, published January 1842), words and melody of first stanza only.

was a dab hand at pastiches of Arne, Shield, Handel and even Purcell; indeed, his first Australian opera, *Merry Freaks in Troublous Times*, composed a couple of years later, would be generously supplied with them. Yet Nathan lit here upon a modern melody of disarming simplicity, naturally pathetic rather than theatrically lachrymose, and original enough to defy easy stylistic categorisation or comparison. In his own large output, the two early settings composed, thirty years earlier, for insertion into Caroline Lamb's novel *Glenarvon* (1816), perhaps come closest to a family resemblance to this song, and its immediate successor.[54] As we shall see, the melody he used in "The Eagle Chief" was borrowed, as he claimed were most of his Hebrew Melodies (tunes commonly sung in Hebrew ceremonies, if not all originally Jewish). And it is not impossible that here Nathan also inaugurated what he later dubbed the "Australian Melodies" with an appropriation that may yet be identified. The simple accompaniment is virtually unchanged in each of the three stanzas (of Dunlop's nine) underlaid with music in the print edition, and three of its four phrases harmonically static apart from piquant chromatic inflections (see Figure 7.9).

For all that they were unwelcome and unfortunate, the negative reviews and letters had appeared in only two of the four major Sydney newspapers, the *Herald* and *Gazette*, and in one also-ran, over no more than three weeks surrounding the 27 October first performance.[55] And there the matter probably would have

54 For instance, the song "Farewell", see *Glenarvon . . . volume 2* (London: Printed for Henry Colburn, 1816), page following 192 (the other song on page following 170), https://archive.org/stream/glenarvon02lambc#page/192/mode/2up.

55 Dunlop's lyric was also published in Melbourne, with a note that dismissed the *Herald*'s: "It has been said that the words as ascribed to an aboriginal woman are somewhat overdone, although they might be used by a Mingo or a Delaware, but that is taking by far a too matter-of-fact view of the question"; see "The Aboriginal Mother", *Port Phillip Patriot*, 29 October 1841, 2, https://nla.gov.au/nla.news-article226510582.

rested, had not Dunlop claimed right of reply, in the *Herald*, late in November. She admitted having been captive to the forlorn hope:

> that, even in Australia, the time was past, when the public press would lend its countenance to debase the native character, or support an attempt to shade with ridicule, ties stronger than death, which bind the heart of woman, be she Christian or savage.[56]

And defending herself from the charge of "deficiency in poetical imagery", she allowed the *Herald* further opportunity to clarify its position:

> We complained of her having by means of poetical talent, of no mean order, given an entirely false idea of the native character, and that opinion we see no cause to alter.

Yet when the sheet music appeared in January 1842, the *Herald* refined this to a simpler regret "that the words are not more worthy of the music".[57] Understandably keen to be associated professionally with the Colony's Crown representatives, Nathan had previously dedicated his first colonial publication, a "new national air", "Long Live Victoria" (to words by W.A. Duncan), to George Gipps.[58] And, aware that Dunlop also counted the Governor's wife as a confidant, he dedicated the print of the "Mother" to Elizabeth Gipps.

The *Gazette* had predicted many further public performances, but it was wrong. Only one more outing was advertised, at the first of Nathan's many charity concerts (this one for the Benevolent Asylum, this time with the Gipps in attendance), on 8 July 1842, when it attracted no further critical comment, positive or negative. Both the *Gazette* and the *Herald* were correct, however, that the song would be picked up by a homeland English press sympathetic to its subject matter. Evidently copied directly from the Sydney papers, Dunlop's lyrics were reprinted by the anti-transportation, pro-emigration lobbyist Henry Capper, in his *Australian and New Zealand Monthly Magazine* in May 1842, immediately following an article on the treatment of "the Aborigines", critical of the lack in the colonies of systematic action towards "communicating with and preserving the aborigines of Australia … from aggression".[59] Nathan continued to advertise the original sheet music edition

---

56 "Original Correspondence", *Sydney Herald*, 29 November 1841, 2,
    https://nla.gov.au/nla.news-article12872517.

57 "New Music", *Sydney Herald*, 22 January 1842, 2, https://nla.gov.au/nla.news-article12873433;
    but see also "New Music", *Australasian Chronicle*, 22 January 1842, 2,
    https://nla.gov.au/nla.news-article31734813.

58 In fact, Duncan, who was also a leading member of Nathan's choir at St. Mary's, wrote new
    words for existing music, Nathan having previously published it, in 1831, as *Long Live Our
    Monarch*, with words by W. Montague addressed to William IV.

59 "Australian Lays", *Australian and New Zealand Monthly Magazine* (May 1842): 296; [Henry
    Capper], "The Aborigines, and Their Treatment Considered", [same issue], 294.

of the song until mid-September 1842, but thereafter it disappeared almost entirely from record.[60]

"The Eagle Chief" (1842)[61]

Neither collaborator appears to have been cowed by their critics, who may, rather have egged them on. When Nathan wrote to Dunlop in December, he reported that his printer, Thomas Rolfe, was still being tardy with the sheet music of "The Aboriginal Mother", and took the opportunity to ask her, meanwhile, for a second set of lyrics, for:

> a simple French air which I would like to have sung at my next concert, to English words ... I would rather make it an aboriginal subject, an Australian subject connected with native dance or festival

and promised,

> I shall not set a line of my music to any words of the Sydney writers whilst I may calculate on receiving productions from your powerful pen.[62]

In the manuscript copy that Nathan evidently sent her, the "simple French air" was probably even simpler than it appeared in his final arrangement. Dunlop would have imagined her lyrics fitted to a melody identical in each stanza, without divisions between solo and chorus singers, and the transpositions in and out of the dominant that Nathan so effectively imposed upon it.[63] The end result, "The Eagle Chief", is an attractive song with chorus, with majestically rolling verses and more exuberant tolling refrains, European in sound and style, but exotic enough in the

---

60 Dunlop's lyrics, on the other hand, did not entirely disappear. Charles Harpur closely reworked the theme as "A Wail from the Bush", *Weekly Register*, 26 July 1845, 41, https://nla.gov.au/nla.news-article228135712, later reused as "An Aboriginal Mother's Lament" in *The Bushrangers* (1853). And a shortened version of Dunlop's original, otherwise largely intact, much later reappeared attributed John Connell Laycock (1818–1897), as "Aboriginal Mother's Lament", *Clarence and Richmond Examiner*, 14 February 1891, 2, https://nla.gov.au/nla.news-article61236615.

61 *The Eagle Chief, an Australian Melody, Respectfully Inscribed to Lady O'Connell, the Poetry by Mrs. E. H. Dunlop, the Music (From a French Subject) Composed Expressly for the Cecilian Society, by I. Nathan* (Sydney: published for the Composer, Ada Cottage, Prince Street [1842]), https://trove.nla.gov.au/version/29359459 (lacks title-page).

62 For full text, see Appendix, Document 2.

63 I have not yet been able to find the melody, which probably dates from the eighteenth century, among the smattering of French melodies in likely English printed sources; nor, to give an idea of the immense territory in France itself, is it among the 891 in Capelle's *La clé du Caveau, à l'usage de tous les chansonniers français* (Paris, 1811), https://archive.org/details/lacléducaveau00cape/page/n7, or the many hundred in Doche's *La musette du vaudeville, ou, Recueil complet des airs* (Paris, 1822), https://archive.org/details/lamusetteduvaude00doch/page/n7.

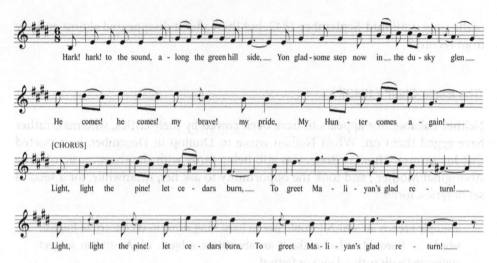

Figure 7.10: Musical Example "The Eagle Chief" (Dunlop and Nathan, April 1842); words and melody, first stanza only.

British colonial context to appeal to its first hearers on its musical merits, free of its original national attachments. Of the reviewers, only Duncan reported that the melody was a "popular French air" – in this case, "popular" in the generic sense, without necessarily implying that the tune was well known (see Figure 7.10).[64]

Nathan first advertised "The Eagle Chief" in early February, but it did not come off Rolfe's press until mid-April. Nathan dedicated it to Mary O'Connell (1783–1863), daughter of William Bligh, and wife of the commander of troops in the Colony, Maurice O'Connell, to whom Dunlop dedicated her song "The Irish Volunteers" the following year. Reviews referred to the inferior quality of the engraving and printing, a problem with the series from first to last, which must have discouraged some buyers and affected the long-term survival of copies sold, contributing to the extreme rarity of all the Dunlop-Nathan prints today. According to the cover, which survives uniquely with the State Library of New South Wales exemplar, Nathan composed it for the Cecilian Society, a club of amateur professional vocalists and instrumentalists that opened its rehearsals to visitors once a month. The society probably gave at least one unadvertised performance, in addition to the fully public premiere at Nathan's concert on 27 May 1842, in the hall of Sydney College (now Sydney Grammar School). Nathan again advertised copies for sale, along with the rest of the "Australian and Aboriginal Melodies", later in the year. But there were no further reported performances, even in Nathan's own concerts in future years, so that the impact of the song on the

---

64 "New Music", *Australasian Chronicle*, 16 April 1842, 2, https://nla.gov.au/nla.news-article31735630.

historical record rests almost solely on the April reviews of the sheet music, and follow-up mentions in the concert reviews in May.

Noticing the print, Grant's *Gazette*, surprisingly, seemed to have overcome its earlier scruples over Dunlop's characterisation, and greeted both the poetry and the music enthusiastically; the latter combining "the rare desiderata of beauty – simplicity, and learning", and the former:

> what an Australian melody should be, characteristic of the aborigines, it is therefore free from the objections we made against No. 1 of these Australian melodies – the "Aboriginal Mother" … We hope that our fair and gifted poet will continue her labours, and that Mr. Nathan will give us a set of Australian Melodies not unworthy the composer of the Hebrew Melodies.[65]

In a longish review, the low-circulation *Examiner* regretted that "such a trifle as this can give us no very exalted notion" of Nathan's gifts as a composer, nor were they convinced of the collaborators' claims to have produced "an *Australian* melody":

> The Irish melodies, as all the world knows, are a series of songs, written by one THOMAS MOORE and adapted to airs which had existed in the country for a long time anterior to the birth and reputation of the Irish poet. But in the present case, Mrs. DUNLOP writes some very pretty verses – which are without a single local association – and Mr. NATHAN makes a tune for them, and forthwith they are exalted, under distinguished patronage, into the style and title of *Australian Melodies!* The Public have had quite enough of this sort of pretension and quackery, and we say reform it altogether.[66]

But the *Herald*'s response no doubt captured the widest attention. Praising Nathan's music (the melody "simple, pretty, and appropriate", the harmonies "rich and classical"), it yet again regretted that Dunlop's poetry was:

> entirely out of character, and instead of giving any idea of the habits of the black natives of this Colony, it is calculated to mislead, indeed did we not know that Mrs. Dunlop resides at the Wollombi, where she has every opportunity of studying the habits and characters of the natives, we should imagine from her poetry that she was a cockney, and that her only knowledge of the aboriginal natives, was acquired by reading the *Last of the Mohicans*.[67]

---

65 "New Music", *Sydney Gazette*, 16 April 1842, 3, https://nla.gov.au/nla.news-article2556255.

66 "New Music", *New South Wales Examiner*, 20 April 1842, 3, https://nla.gov.au/nla.news-article228247845.

67 In 1838, Mansfield told a committee of inquiry in the wake of the Myall Creek massacre that he had no knowledge "of the Aborigines" from direct personal contact, unlike the writer in this case, who appeared well informed of traditional customs of the people in the Wollombi area; see

After demonstrating at length that some of Dunlop's ethnographic details were misobserved, the writer (in this instance, probably not Mansfield) concluded:

> We should not have taken the trouble to show the folly of this second attempt of Mrs. Dunlop's to make the blacks appear a different race of people from what they really are, were it to be circulated in this Colony only, but Mr. Nathan's music is likely to make it known in England, and therefore we thought it a duty to shew the real character of the verse. Mrs. Dunlop appears to have a poetic turn of mind, and we should be glad to see her attempting some subject unconnected with the blacks.

But the sadder reality is that the *Herald*'s fears of the "melodies" influencing public opinion in Britain were almost certainly unfulfilled. Apart from the words of "The Aboriginal Mother" appearing in Capper's journal, there is no evidence that any of them came to the attention of the British or Irish press.

Did Dunlop reply to the *Herald*'s criticism a second time? No letter from her was printed, and perhaps she hadn't bothered to write one. This left the *Herald* to take a bet each way in its review of the 27 May performance ("sweetly sung by a young lady, and the effect of the chorus and accompaniments was very rich"), supportive of Nathan, but directing readers back to its earlier takedown of Dunlop.[68] The *Australian* did not run a review of its own, but printed one from a "correspondent" eager to appear even-handed:

> A new Australian Melody by Mrs. Dunlop followed, which was very well sung by a Young Lady, and as it would seem, her first appearance in public. Without a book of the words, much of a song is lost, and the "Eagle Chief" might have been an excellent subject, but without this concomitant, it was not to be discovered; the melody was pretty, but reminded us of certain symphonies in Macbeth . . .[69]

"Evidence ... on the Aborigines Question", *Colonist*, 29 December 1838, 4, https://nla.gov.au/nla.news-article31722278.

68 "Mr. Nathan's Concert", *Sydney Herald*, 30 May 1842, 2, https://nla.gov.au/nla.news-article12875453.

69 "Concert. To the Editor", *Australian*, 31 May 1842, 2, https://nla.gov.au/nla.news-article37115169. Though then attributed to Matthew Locke, the standard setting of the witches' music used in productions of Shakespeare's play ("Locke's music in Macbeth") was composed by Richard Leveridge (1670/71–1758); the "symphony" (instrumental movement) referred to is that at the opening; see *The Introductory Symphony, Airs, Recitatives, Dance, and Choruses in the Tragedy of Macbeth* ... (London: Goulding and D'Almaine, [1829]), 2–4, https://archive.org/details/lockesmacbethand00addi/page/n11.

"Mable Macmahon" (1842)[70]

The third of the Dunlop-Nathan series, "Mable Macmahon", perhaps seemed an unlikely successor to the previous "Australian Melodies", for the lack of any local reference in the lyrics. However, if Dunlop had wanted to avoid further animosity from the *Herald*, she could hardly have done better than by addressing her lyric, instead, to the "bold and beautiful" beloved of a seventeenth-century northern Irish chieftain. The fact that it was written and composed by Australians was probably enough, and if not, in "The Vase" Dunlop recalled that Nathan, "with good taste", had dedicated it "to one of the most worthy and most esteemed Irishmen in Australia", Roger Therry. A native of Cork in the deep south, and a leading Catholic, Therry was then acting Attorney General, while the incumbent, his co-religionist J.H. Plunkett, was back in Ireland on leave. But four years earlier, Therry had been Plunkett's junior prosecuting the Myall Creek perpetrators, and so, as Dunlop herself might have added, doubly worthy of a dedication in a series begun with "The Aboriginal Mother".[71]

As to precedence, it is hard to imagine that Dunlop's lyric did not come first, and that Nathan's appropriately lovely treatment was composed specifically for it. Unless, as for "The Eagle Chief", Nathan again borrowed the tune; for it certainly sounds little like any other melody of his colonial years, and little like anything at all in his earlier output. Where "The Eagle Chief" does indeed sound French, "Mable Macmahon" sounds like a cross between a genuine Irish original and one of Bellini's opera tunes, or a "sin" of Rossini's old age. If it was borrowed, again, no one went on record saying so at the time. Duncan, in the *Chronicle*, thought that this easy, catchy, almost infectious song was "of the Australian Melodies, and, so far as respects the melody itself ... perhaps the best of the series" (see Figure 7.11).[72]

Had a song like this appeared a few years later, Nathan's vocalist friends at Sydney's Victoria Theatre might have helped it achieve popularity and a modest circulation in print. As it was, after its first outing on 27 May there was only one other advertised concert performance (8 July), neither of which merited more than a simple mention in the mostly supportive reviews. The sheet music of "Mable", drawn and printed by the ex- convict lithographer Thomas Liley in July 1842, is as unattractive physically as Rolfe's two previous prints, and no more likely to have appealed to those Sydneysiders used to more elegant imported sheet music.[73] As

---

70 *Mable Macmahon, an Australian Melody, Respectfully Dedicated to Roger Therry, Esq., Attorney General, Written by Mrs. E.H. Dunlop, Composed by I. Nathan* (Sydney: published for the composer, Ada Cottage, Prince Street, [1842]), https://trove.nla.gov.au/work/16497075.

71 For Therry's recollections of the case, see his *Reminiscences of Thirty Years' Residence in New South Wales and Victoria* (London: Sampson, Low, Son, and Co., 1863), 282, https://books.google.com.au/books?id=rFJZAAAAcAAJ&pg=PA282.

72 "New Music", *Australasian Chronicle*, 21 July 1842, 2, https://nla.gov.au/nla.news-article31736598.

73 From similarities in the hands, it is possible that Liley or his colleague Thomas Bluett may also have drawn the music and text for the two earlier prints.

Figure 7.11: Musical Example "Mable Macmahon" (Dunlop and Nathan 1842); words and melody of first stanza only.

with the rest of the series, the song's preservation would have been doubtful, were it not for a couple of strategic copies in public collections.

"Star of the South" (1843)[74]

The fourth Dunlop-Nathan joint production was also lithographed and printed by Liley in August 1843. "Star of the South" ("Hail, star of the south! Australasia, advance") had the added commercial drawback of not being a solo song, but a less saleable "glee" or part-song. Nathan registered the patriotic tone of both lyrics and music by calling it not just an "Australian Melody", but an "Australian National

---

74 *Star of the South, an Australian National Melody, Written by Mrs. E.H. Dunlop, the Music Composed and as a Small Token of Grateful Recollection of the Hospitality Experienced on His First Landing in Australia Felix, Respectfully Inscribed to his Honor Mr. La Trobe, and the Inhabitants of the District, by I. Nathan* (Sydney: Printed by Thos. Liley, Litho. &c. &c., Brougham Place, [1842]), https://trove.nla.gov.au/work/15080814.

Melody". He dedicated it to Charles Latrobe, superintendent of the Port Phillip district, whose hospitality he and his family enjoyed during their first two months on Australian soil at Melbourne in February and March 1841. Dunlop's immediate inspiration, however, was the prospect of the first Sydney municipal election, which finally came off on 1 November 1842 (those for Melbourne's municipality followed shortly afterwards), and, in devising her lyrics, had freer rein, Nathan's music almost certainly being composed for them, rather than the other way around.

Nathan's setting is a choral march that probably reminded some of its first hearers of similar examples in Bellini's and Donizetti's operas; though it was nothing he could not have dreamt up unassisted, as evidenced by its audible kinship to "Warriors and chiefs" from the Hebrew Melodies, and to the second act finale ("Hail to the star that in glory appears") of his 1847 Sydney opera *Don John of Austria*. Nathan separated off Dunlop's first two lines to create an opening chorus, and set the remaining two lines of the first stanza as a short first verse. The other two stanzas he kept intact, set to different melodies, with the opening chorus recurring after each. Duncan, less enthusiastic than previously, described the result aptly as "rather a bundle of melodies" with a chorus "in the Maestoso style". Nevertheless, he predicted "a hearty encore on whatever occasion it shall be well performed".[75] No such performance, however, is known to have taken place; which is a pity, because the words and music – separately and in combination – are more interesting and attractive than those of Duncan and Nathan's resoundingly conventional attempt, a few months later, at a "national song" celebrating the newly elected city council, "Australia the Wide and the Free" (number 6 of the series).[76]

Again, the music struck entirely the right note for the *Herald*:

> the composition pleases us much, and we allow it to possess no small amount of beauty and merit in pronouncing it to be one of Mr. Nathan's best. The air is what a national air should be – Majestic, but it is at the same time flowing and pleasing, and is enriched throughout with most effective communications.[77]

Yet despite having "nought but delight, as far as the composer is concerned", and no Aboriginal allusions to dispute, the columnist still could not summon the gallantry to compliment Dunlop's lyrics, or:

---

75 "New Music", *Australasian Chronicle*, 11 August 1842, 3,
    https://nla.gov.au/nla.news-article31736838.

76 *Australia the Wide and the Free! A National Song Written by W.A. Duncan, esqr., as Sung at the Great Civic Dinner, December 21st, 1842, Composed and Respectfully Inscribed to the Right Worshipful John Hosking, Mayor of Sydney, by I. Nathan* (Sydney: published by the composer, Elizabeth St. Sth.; T. Bluett, lithographer, Brougham Place, n.d. [1842/43]),
    https://trove.nla.gov.au/work/16495344.

77 "New Music", *Sydney Morning Herald*, 9 August 1842, 3,
    https://nla.gov.au/nla.news-article12419051.

even in our most allegorical mood, imagine what the "Star of the South" has to do with either "Soft flowing tresses," or "Proud eagle glance." It is not polite of us, but we do wish that the new "National Melody" had been set to better words.[78]

Having held her peace over "The Eagle Chief", Dunlop now let off a spirited reply, complaining that, contrary to the new democratic spirit, the *Herald* had not:

> faithfully discharged its duty to the reading public or to its numerous patrons. The song, an offering to the people of New South Wales, should have been published by the *Critic* to enable the many to form their own judgment of its fitness for the period when we can for the first time be truly designated A PEOPLE ... But has not the author added to a former offence, against a formidable clique, by saying that Australia possesses *"happy homes and altars free?"*[79]

Since Dunlop appeared "to wish that her song should have a place in the columns of the *Herald*", it happily obliged her by doing so, immediately under her letter, confident that:

> most of our readers will concur in the judgment we passed on its merits when it was first published. We admire, as much as Mrs. Dunlop can possibly do, "happy homes and free altars," but it does not follow that we should admire bad poetry written in their praise.

"The Aboriginal Father" (1843)[80]

Between numbers 3 and 5 of the "Australian Melodies" – "Mable Macmahon" and "Star of the South" – in mid-1842 Nathan published number 4, "Koorinda Braai", to which Dunlop made no contribution. It was based on an Aboriginal song fragment, originally sourced from speakers of the Ngarigu language in the Monaro area near present-day Canberra by Henry Tingcombe (1810–1874), a pastoralist and musical amateur (later an Anglican clergyman) who had worked on the Monaro in the late 1830s.

The seventh and last of what Nathan was now billing as the "Australian and Aboriginal Melodies", "The Aboriginal Father" was also sourced from Ngarigu speakers. The Aboriginal melody and words had been transcribed and printed previously by Polish naturalist and explorer John Lhotsky in 1834, under the title

---

78 "New Music".

79 "The Star of the South. To the Editors", *Sydney Morning Herald*, 30 August 1842, 3, https://nla.gov.au/nla.news-article12426027.

80 *The Aboriginal Father, a Native Song of the Maneroo Tribe ... Versified From the Original Words ... by Mrs. E.H. Dunlop, the Melody, as Sung by the Aborigines, Put Into Rhythm & Harmonized with Appropriate Symphonies & Accompaniments, Respectfully Inscribed to the Lady Mayoress, by I. Nathan* (Sydney: [Nathan], Elizabeth Street; T. Bluett, Litho., Brougham Place, [1843]), https://trove.nla.gov.au/work/16497064.

"A Song of the Women of the Menero Tribe".[81] But Nathan justified the need for a second edition in a long introductory note:

> On my arrival in Australia, I felt anxious for the honor, pride and glory of musical tradition, to make myself acquainted with the characteristic peculiarities of the native Aboriginal airs. I was favored with a lithographic copy of this beautiful pathetic melody, so deformed and mutilated by false rhyme, so disguised in complete masquerade, by false basses and false harmony, that I cast it from me with no small share of regret at the poor chance thus afforded me of adding any thing in favor of the claim of the Aborigines to the pages of musical history. My astonishment, however, a short time afterwards, was only equalled by the delight I experienced at hearing the same melody sung in all its genuine purity and simplicity, by one of the Maneroo tribe. I at once discovered the key to its latent rhyme and excellent scope for good basses and rich transitions and progressions of harmony.[82]

Lhotsky's edition is certainly unusual, a rare example of a transcription of a non-European melody that falls conspicuously outside the diatonic system. Its three phrases end successively on D, G and C, closing a note shy of the upper octave D. To Nathan, who believed that the octatonic system applied universally, Lhostky's ending on C can only have been an error, which he, Nathan, had a responsibility anyway to correct to D. Having since, he claimed, heard for himself the melody sung "by one of the Maneroo tribe", he also felt justified in extending Lhotsky's first phrase, correcting the "false rhyme" by making three regular 8-bars phrases. The song thus restored, Nathan claimed:

> There is in the first four bars of this melody, so striking an affinity to one of Handel's compositions, that those who are acquainted with the works of that great master might find difficulty in divesting themselves of the belief, that the Aborigines had been guilty of piracy.[83]

Rather, he argued, "no stronger proof of the musical powers of these beings, nor of the nature of Handel's compositions" was required than the affinity itself, evidence that the music of all cultures derived ultimately from a common source.[84]

---

81 *A Song of the Women of the Menero Tribe Arranged with the Assistance of Several Musical Gentlemen for the Voice and Pianoforte, Most Humbly Inscribed as the First Specimen of Australian Music, to Her Most Gracious Majesty Adelaide, Queen of Great Britain & Hanover, by Dr. J. Lhotsky, Colonist N.S. Wales* (Sydney: Sold by John Innes, [1834]), https://digital.sl.nsw.gov.au/delivery/DeliveryManagerServlet?dps_pid=IE3727874.
82 *The Aboriginal Father.*
83 *The Aboriginal Father.*
84 *The Aboriginal Father.* Duncan was also reminded of a melody by the composer Sigismund Neukomm; and, in 1834, Lhotsky had to assert that the melody was not "(as some of my enemies say) a Portuguese air, nor any thing else than a wild air, carrying however a great depth

Whether Nathan's new version satisfied the "honour, pride and glory" of musical tradition remains open to question. But we can certainly question its merits on a practical level. The fortuitous first-hand confirmation of his corrections "by one of the Maneroo tribe" sounds almost too good to be true, unless someone like Tingcombe organised the encounter for him (and if so, we might ask: with whom, where and when?). And even if we accept that the performance took place, and that the song Nathan heard was substantially the same song Lhotsky had transcribed, is Nathan's version necessarily to be preferred? Might not the irregularities of Lhotsky's original merely reflect a different performance? Or another way of attempting to notate a melodic feature difficult to interpret in European musical syntax? Especially in the final phrase, might not Lhotsky's version better represent a phrase that seemed to end up high, but not on the key note? Figure 7.12 compares Lhostky's version of the melody (in grey on the upper staff), with that of the first stanza of Nathan's setting, below.[85]

According to Nathan's title-page, Dunlop's English lyrics ("The shadow on thy brow, my child") were "versified from the original words". But Jim Wafer argues elsewhere in this volume that her only likely access to the original was through Lhotsky's English version, there being no evidence that Dunlop had a working knowledge of the Ngarigu language. Dunlop and Nathan also altered the gender of the singers artificially, from Lhotky's women, to their Aboriginal father. The obvious and only reason for this was to pair it with "The Aboriginal Mother".

Nathan released the lithographed sheet music of "The Aboriginal Father" in January 1843.[86] He dedicated it to Martha Hosking, wife of the first Mayor of Sydney, making it a pair of another sort with the previous number of the series, "Australia the Wide and the Free", dedicated to her husband John, on the occasion of his election as first Mayor of Sydney. Nathan himself had sung John's song (to Duncan's words) at the inaugural mayoral dinner, on 21 December. However, there does not appear to have been any public performance of Martha's song, and there is no record of its private reception, even by its dedicatee. Victims of the colonial financial crisis of the 1840s, the Hoskings withdrew from public life in mid-1843, and thereafter also largely from public record.

Whether gallantry finally won out, or perhaps for the Hoskings' sake (they were, like Ralph Mansfield, also Methodists), the *Herald* review avoided any

---

of feeling", [Advertisement], *Sydney Monitor*, 29 November 1834, 1, https://nla.gov.au/nla.news-article32147713.

85   For more on colonial transcriptions of Aboriginal melodies, see Graeme Skinner, "Recovering Musical Data from Colonial Era Transcriptions of Indigenous Songs: Some Practical Considerations", in Jim Wafer and Myfany Turpin, eds, *Recirculating Songs: Revitalising the Singing Practices of Indigenous Australia* (Canberra: Asia-Pacific Linguistics, 2017), https://hdl.handle.net/1885/132161.

86   The cover named Thomas Bluett as lithographer. Bluett appears to have worked out of the same Brougham Place premises as Liley; they produced at least one map together, and a common text hand appears in some of the Nathan (and other) prints bearing one or other of their names.

Figure 7.12: Musical Example "Kongi kawelgo" (Lhotsky 1834), words and melody, on upper stave; "The Aboriginal Father" (Dunlop and Nathan 1843), first stanza, words and melody, on lower stave.

comment at all, negative or positive, on Dunlop's versification. And, now apparently running counter to the prejudices of the "clique", the paper judged that, of all Nathan's Australian compositions, "none has pleased us more than the above song: it is in every respect worthy of the composer of the Hebrew Melodies". If the melody was as worthy of Handel, Nathan's arrangement was "no less so", and even casual comparison, it felt, bore out its superiority to Lhotsky's original: "We hope to see the 'Aboriginal Father' an universal favourite, as the study of music of this sort must beget a correct taste for the science".[87]

How many copies Nathan printed or sold is unknown, but, as with all the preceding "Australian Melodies", almost certainly far fewer than he had hoped. Nathan evidently decided by early 1843 against giving any further public concerts for the time being, probably for financial reasons – the newly proclaimed city was

---

87 "New Music", *Sydney Morning Herald*, 19 January 1843, 2, https://nla.gov.au/nla.news-article12411279; see also "New Publication", *Australasian Chronicle*, 19 January 1843, 2, https://nla.gov.au/nla.news-article31738598.

in the depths of a depression – and, as a result of this, the piece did not receive even a single advertised performance. Still a year away from his first colonial insolvency, Nathan refocused his professional attention on teaching, and was in the last stages of composing an opera, *Merry Freaks in Troublous Times*, that he hoped would be staged, lucratively, at the Royal Victoria Theatre in the second half of 1843.

If the *Herald*'s unqualified support for "The Aboriginal Father" suggested that the mainstream press had decided, judiciously, to give no further oxygen to the past controversies, the anti-*Melodies* "clique" quickly found an alternative outlet in a scabrous new weekly, the *Satirist and Sporting Chronicle*. In February and March, the editor, Thomas Revel Johnson, let off a series of squibs against Nathan and his daughter Rosetta. One lampooned the "Old music master" for straining the young throats of his singing class "in the attempt to give effective deliverance to 'Koorinda Braia,' or some other equally fine national song or melody", which "unutterable nonsense", by contrast, even "Rosy", it claimed, could no longer be prevailed upon to sing. There was another pointedly obscene reference to Rosy two pages later, and a third piece of "gossip", only slightly less salacious, in the next week's issue.[88]

Tragically, the morning the last of these appeared, 1 April 1843, Rosetta Nathan died. Inexplicably, according to the family's death notice she was only in "her sixteenth year".[89] In fact, she was over nineteen, and admired enough to attract heartfelt eulogies in the next week's press from at least five amateur poets, including John Rae (the town clerk) and Henry Halloran, both in the *Herald*, and Samuel Prout Hill.[90] To these, also in the *Herald* – and without the slightest editorial demur – Dunlop later added her own "Rosetta Nathan's Dirge".[91]

Another Dunlop song was, coincidentally, already in the press, and appeared the same month. The sheet music of "The Irish Volunteers" ("For the golden harp on field of green") was her only known solo venture into music publishing, and was dedicated to Maurice O'Connell (1768–1848), the Irish-born commander of the colonial troops. No copy of the edition itself has yet been identified, but Dunlop's words (printed in the *Chronicle*) and the original march tune (published as *Lord*

---

88   "Elizabeth Street", *Satirist*, 25 March 1843, 1, https://nla.gov.au/nla.news-article228065539; "Sayings and Doings", *Satirist*, 25 March 1843, 3, https://nla.gov.au/nla.news-article228065543; "Get Along Rosy", *Satirist*, 1 April 1843, 3, https://nla.gov.au/nla.news-article228065415.

89   "Deaths", *Sydney Morning Herald*, 3 April 1843, 3, https://nla.gov.au/nla.news-article12413592; her mother, the novelist Eliza Nathan, died as a result of giving birth to Rosetta early in January 1824.

90   [John Rae], "Stanzas Suggested By the Recent Death of a Beautiful Girl", *Sydney Morning Herald*, 4 April 1843, 3, https://nla.gov.au/nla.news-article12412062;
"Lament on the Untimely Death of a Young, Beautiful, and Accomplished Girl . . . [by] T. C.", *Australasian Chronicle*, 4 April 1843, 2, https://nla.gov.au/nla.news-article31739378;
[Samuel Prout Hill] "Stanzas. On the recent sudden death of a beautiful and accomplished Young Lady", *Colonial Observer*, 5 April 1843, 5, https://nla.gov.au/nla.news-article226361300; "Original Poetry. Rosette, by H.H. [Henry Halloran]", *Sydney Morning Herald*, 5 April 1843, 4, https://nla.gov.au/nla.news-article12419641; "Lines on Hearing of the Untimely Death of Miss R. Nathan", *Australian*, 7 April 1843, 4, https://nla.gov.au/nla.news-article37118078.

91   "Rosetta Nathan's Dirge", *Sydney Morning Herald*, 25 April 1843, 2, https://nla.gov.au/nla.news-article12417841.

Charlemont's March, in Dublin c.1782) both survive separately, allowing a fairly reliable reconstruction to be made.[92]

After "The Irish Volunteers", neither Dunlop nor Nathan – together or separately – published anything further for the remainder of 1843 and all of 1844. This did not entirely end the commentary on their joint enterprise, however. The *Herald*, in April 1844, allowed one of poor Rosetta's eulogists, Samuel Prout Hill, to add a postscript to the controversy, with his own "Song of the Aborigines". Cleverly fitted to the tune of "Tambourgi" (besides the Hebrew Melodies, Nathan's best-known Byron setting), it was an elaborate riposte to the views of the "clique", in the format of an imagined Indigenous warrior's song. As Hill wryly explained:

The following song has been written out of sheer compassion for the narrowed intellects of the blacks: the "EAGLE CHIEF," "ABORIGINAL MOTHER," &c., being considered of too flighty and exalted a nature to be comprehended by the dark and benighted understandings of our brethren of the woods: *Damnant quod non intelligunt.*[93]

Nathan's last public dealings with Dunlop's work were in his literary and musical "ladies' miscellany", *The Southern Euphrosyne*. He initially hoped to publish it in the new year of 1848, but did not finish printing it until early 1849. Dunlop's Aboriginal lyric "Pialla Wollombi" ("Our home is the *gibber-gunyah*") appears at the beginning of over forty pages dedicated to Aboriginal music and culture.[94] She published the same lyric in the *Herald* on 11 October 1848 and later copied it into "The Vase", both of which also include her transcriptions of original Aboriginal song words. But none of the three sources indicates whether or not she anticipated her verse translation being set to music. No transcription of a corresponding Aboriginal melody has been identified (or, at this remove, is ever likely to be), and, even had there been one, it is doubtful that Dunlop's metrical versification can have followed it closely.[95] She may instead have imagined it sung to a suitable European tune,

---

92   The *Chronicle* gave the full title, *The Irish Volunteers, Dedicated to Captain M.C. O'Connell, H. M. 28th Regt., the Poetry by Mrs. E.H. Dunlop; The Music Composed by a Professor in Dublin, in 1780*; "New Music – An Irish Melody", *Australasian Chronicle*, 13 April 1843, 2, https://nla.gov.au/nla.news-article31739492; see also [Review], *Australian*, 10 April 1843, 2, https://nla.gov.au/nla.news-article37115124.

93   "Original Poetry", *Sydney Morning Herald*, 23 April 1844, 4, https://nla.gov.au/ nla.news-article12409847; a month after Rosetta's death, in May 1843 for the Sydney Debating Society, Hill spoke for the affirmative to the question "Have the Aboriginal Blacks of this Colony an indefeasible right to the soil of Australia?"; see "Sydney Debating Society", *Australian*, 12 May 1843, 2, https://nla.gov.au/nla.news-article37115312.

94   Nathan, *The Southern Euphrosyne*, 94, https://books.google.com.au/books?id=ziwieom4lBQC&pg=PA194.

95   The melody of "The Aboriginal Father" is exceptional among colonial transcriptions of Aboriginal songs for the metrical regularity that was, almost certainly, imposed upon the original, and it is unlikely that a traditional singer would have recognised it, unprompted, from a performance of either Lhotsky's or Nathan's arrangements.

pre-existing or newly composed. But providing one is unlikely to have appealed to Nathan, who used this section of the *Euphrosyne* to print as many arrangements of "genuine" Aboriginal melodies as he could. Nathan also reprinted Dunlop's versified text for "The Aboriginal Father", substantially as it appeared in 1843, though adding another page and a half of commentary.[96] However, time and an insufficient supply of type, he said, prevented him from including a new edition of the music itself, or of several other "beautiful native melodies" that he had collected, and which he hoped to publish later. But, alas, after the *Euphrosyne*, nothing more was heard of them.

Dunlop's third contribution was her elegy "To the memory of ... Mary Fitzroy" ("Trembling in agony! faint with amaze!"), who died in a carriage accident on the Domain at Parramatta on 8 December 1847.[97] Nathan also printed Dunlop's short covering letter, written from Wollombi on 20 December, in which she hoped that he "could create a melancholy melody to embody the sad thoughts I offer you". But, again, Nathan was unable to comply, probably because, when he received her letter, he was still hoping to issue the *Euphrosyne* early in 1848 and had simply run out of time. When the collection did finally come off the press a year later, the moment for such a musical memorial had long since passed. At least, the *Euphrosyne* ensured that a few more pieces of Dunlop's work were seen in Britain. A copy that belonged to the English musician Edwin Matthew Lott (1836–1902) is now in the British Library and digitised by Google.

There is no record yet identified of any later contact or correspondence between Dunlop and Nathan. Her unpublished ode, "Nathan" ("Sweet voice of song! Australia's shores / Have hailed thee as, a newborn gladness! . . ."), in "The Vase", almost certainly dates from the time of their close association in the 1840s, when her idealised description of him there bore most resemblance to reality, and the colonial renown she imagined for him still seemed within his grasp.

> ... Be this thy country "Son of Song"
> Australian pearls shall gem thy name
> On Time's bright current wafted on
> Blending with Byron's waves of fame.[98]

---

96 Nathan, *The Southern Euphrosyne*, 104–5.
97 Nathan, *The Southern Euphrosyne*, 136.
98 "The Vase", https://digital.sl.nsw.gov.au/delivery/DeliveryManagerServlet?dps_pid=FL9674377T; the epigraph is from John Bowring's 1828 translation of the Hungarian ballad "Lovely Lenka" (*Szép Lenka vár a' part fellet*), by Ferenc Kölcsey.

APPENDIX

Document 1

Letter draft or sender's copy, Eliza Hamilton Dunlop, undated (Wollombi, NSW, before October 1841) to Isaac Nathan, Sydney; unidentified original, transcribed in Margaret De Salis papers, State Library of New South Wales, MLMSS 5745; incomplete ed. in Margaret De Salis, *Two Early Colonials* (Sydney: printed by the author, 1967), 101–2.[99]

Isaac Nathan, Esq.
Ada Cottage, Prince Street
Sydney
It is not I feel assured that to a mind so gifted as Mr. Nathan's I need to make apologies that without formal introduction present myself to his notice – if my poetry lines have merit they will require no other usher, and I who am in the Forest far from human habitation of civilized beings, may well be forgiven the want of due observance in this matter, should my poetry be honored by your acceptance, pray do me the favor of a reply addressed Wollombi.

The Dark Lady of Doona, written by a relative, has a few of my songs published in it. A lady, a stranger in this land, but one to whom your eminent universal fame as an author and composer has long been known, thus begs permission to offer the accompanying poetry for your kind consideration. They are my favourites of a Collection which I hope to get published by Bentley of Broad St., but were I so honored as to find those few worthy of acceptance to go forth into the world, – [with] the seal of your genius, it would be to me a source of pride and pleasure greater than I can say. I wrote

the Aboriginal Mother for the air, "When the seas were roaring". [*]

"I bless thy shores my native land" and "Oh the limpid streams" [+]

[*] The massacre it commemorates took place a short period after my arrival in the Colony.

[+] Were intended to be introduced in a Drama (the Cousins of Aledo) which I have arranged for the stage from Mary Mitford's "Blanch", and which as it has not been seen by any individual with the exception of Lady Gipps, I will if you give permission submit for your opinion.

My publications at home were confined to the magazines, but altered circumstances in this country where my husband has only £250 as Police Magistrate, induces my attempt to make my pen an aid for my numerous family, but more than this it would aid my way to future favor with the public. If my poetry be honoured by your acceptance pray do me the favor of a reply, addressed Wollombi.

---

99 In *The Southern Euphrosyne*, 136, Nathan published the short text of a second letter from Dunlop, dated 20 December 1847, which she wrote as a covering note with her elegy for Mary Fitzroy.

I am sir respectfully
Eliza Hamilton Dunlop.

Document 2

Letter, Isaac Nathan, Sydney, NSW, 3 December 1841, to Eliza Hamilton Dunlop; unidentified original, transcribed in De Salis papers; incomplete ed. in De Salis, *Two Early Colonials*, 104–5.[100]

Sydney, Ada Cottage
3rd Dec'br 1841
I fear my dear Madam my long silence will not place me at no. 1 in your estimation. The truth therefore must out. The same day that I did myself the honour to forward you the music of your beautiful aboriginal mother, I gave a copy to an engraver here, that I might testify by its immediate publication the delight I really felt in connecting my humble music with the words, & it was my intention to surprise you with a copy – unfortunately the engraver (who is infected I imagine with the gross air of Sydney), has not yet done his work, & puts me off from day to day, & I fear will do so for some months to come.

I now take leave to hand to your notice a simple French air which I should like to have sung at my next concert, to English words, so that it may be published – if you can spare the time & will write on any subject you please, I shall feel highly flattered; do not confine yourself to French words – I would rather make it an aboriginal subject, an Australian subject connected with native dance or festival. My object is to publish all I can in England as well as in Sydney and you may be certain that I shall not set a line of my music to any words of the Sydney writers whilst I may calculate on receiving productions from your powerful pen.

I have not forgotten your wish to have set to music
[blank]
but I have been much harassed with an approaching law suit – & other worldly affairs so that I have had no musical sounds to command. You may however depend on my setting the words to music the first moment that I can command for melody.

I will lose no time in forwarding your "aboriginal mother" as soon as the engraver brings <u>her home</u>.

Dear Madam,
Yours respectfully & obliged,
I. Nathan.
<u>Private</u> I suppose you know that Professor Rennie [&] "Thorough Bass" to be one & the same – I have no doubt on the subject.

---

100 De Salis also noted that she saw a second original letter from Nathan to Dunlop, dated 10 January 1843 (nine days before the first review of "The Aboriginal Father"); however, she did not transcribe it or summarise its contents.

8
Unmapping the Mulla: Dunlop and the Villa on Wollombi Brook

Jim Wafer

For Donna Snowdon

Figure 8.1: "Mulla Villa" in the nineteenth century, as seen looking south along the Great North Road. (Courtesy of Cultural Collections, University of Newcastle.[1] Original photographer and date unknown.)[2]

---

1   https://www.flickr.com/photos/uon/8111475973/in/photolist-dmMrd2-CsHTkm.
2   The current whereabouts of the original photograph are also unknown. It was once held by Wollombi resident Mrs Ida D. Stephenson, née Andrews (1904–2000); cf. Wollombi Valley Progress Association, *Wollombi Valley Description and History* (Laguna NSW: 1981 rev. ed), 41;

"Mulla Villa" stands on a hill above Wollombi Brook – a tributary of the Hunter River – and was built by David Dunlop and his crew of convict labourers in 1841. The original sandstone structure is, today, partly shaded over by verandahs, which were a later addition. Margaret De Salis – great-granddaughter of David and Eliza – tells us it was David who named it "Mulla Villa".[3] But De Salis leaves room for a suspicion that Eliza may have had some say in the matter – indeed, it is hard to imagine that such an accomplished multi-lingual wordsmith would not have.

Eliza Hamilton Dunlop was already a published poet at the time she and her husband left Ireland for Australia, in 1837, and she continued to write verse until quite late in her life. Her earliest Australian poems, published in 1838, were written while the Dunlop family was quartered at Old Government House (Emu Plains, near Penrith). In 1840 they moved to Wollombi, and from 1841 "Mulla Villa" was their home. It also provided Eliza, for the next thirty or so years of her writing life, with an address she could use on her publications.

The extent of her known literary *oeuvre* amounts to more than 100 poems,[4] and many of these include, in their published versions, not just Eliza's by-line but also the date and location. Her last poem may have been "Faith", which appeared on 15 November 1873. The formula that comes after the poem is typical of the way she had situated her literary voice over the preceding three decades: "Mulla Villa, September 25, 1873". She would have been about seventy-seven at the time, and appears not to have published anything else between then and her death in 1880.

Margaret De Salis offers two potential etymologies for the building's name.[5] One derives it from the Northern Irish placename "Mulla Villy",[6] and the other links it to Edmund Spenser's use of the name "Mulla" in his 1595 poem "Colin Clouts Come Home Againe", where it designates a legendary river, personified by an eponymous nymph.[7] While it is certainly not impossible that the Dunlops could have had some connection with the Ulster parish of Mullavilly (Co. Armagh),[8] there is no evidence available to support this. In the case of Spenser's usage, on the other hand, it is quite clear that Eliza was aware of it. At the head of one of her

---

and https://soundcloud.com/uoncc/060b-stephenson. The standing female figure in the foreground appears to be looking towards the standing (male?) figure on the east-facing balcony in the mid-ground. Could this be Eliza looking towards David (dating the photograph before 1863), or perhaps the next generation of the Dunlop family visiting with grandchildren? Photographic technology was introduced to Australia in the 1840s, gaining popularity from the 1850s onwards (Helen Ennis, *Photography and Australia*. London: Reaktion, 2007, 13–30).

3   Margaret De Salis, *Two Early Colonials* (Sydney: printed by the author, 1967), 98.
4   Plus one short story: "The Ford of Emu Plains".
5   De Salis, *Two Early Colonials*, 98.
6   Today spelt "Mullavilly". Google recognises it as "Mullavilly, Craigavon BT62 2NJ, UK" and provides this link: https://goo.gl/maps/J8AeBgSPPbJ2.
7   The river is introduced at line 59, and the nymph at lines 108–9.
8   See Brett Hannam, *Mullavilly – Portrait of an Ulster Parish* (Mullavilly, Ulster: Lulu and Select Vestry of Mullavilly Parish Church, 2010).

Figure 8.2: "Mulla Villa" in 2018, as seen looking west from the left bank of Wollombi Brook. (Photo by the author, 30 August 2018.)

poems, as the epigraph, she actually quotes a verse from *Colin Clout* (lines 56–59) that refers to the Mulla.

The Dunlop poem in question, "The Mulla, or Wollombi Creek, New South Wales", was first published in *The Month* in December 1857, but the manuscript version is dated "25th Sep'tbr 1849". Aside from quoting Spenser in the epigraph, Dunlop also makes allusions to his work in the body of the poem. The quoted phrase "sweet Mulla mine" suggests a reference to Spenser's line "Mulla mine, whose waves I whilom taught to weep", in book IV of *The Faerie Queene*.[9] (This occurs in the same stanza where Spenser writes of "the fishy fruitfull Ban".[10]) Further, the quotation "Mole with all his mountain woods" is borrowed from Robert Southey's homage to Spenser in the proem to "Carmen Nuptiale. The Lay of the Laureate" (1816, stanza 20).

Spenser used the figure of the Mulla not just in "Colin Clout" (1595) and *The Faerie Queene* (1596)[11], but also in "Epithalamion" (1595).[12] Dunlop likewise wrote

---

9   Book IV, Canto xi, stanza 41.

10   The River Bann, in Ulster. See Patrick Joyce, "Spenser's Irish Rivers", in Joyce, *The Wonders of Ireland, and Other Papers on Irish Subjects* (Dublin: Longmans, Green, 1911), 76, 85, 113.

11   This is the publication date of books IV–VI. The first three books were published in 1590.

12   "Ye Nymphes of Mulla", line 56. This plurality of nymphs is no doubt explained in *The Faerie Queene* (VII, vi, 40), where Mulla has a sister called "Molanna" – both are daughters of the mountain that Spenser refers to as "Mole".

about the Mulla more than once. But before I turn to what the name might have meant to the Mulla Villa poet, let me clarify its usage in Spenser.

Spenser and the Mulla

In 1590, after some years of legal wrangling, Edmund Spenser received a royal grant of "the manor, castle and lands of Kylcolman, Co. Cork".[13] He had occupied Kilcolman possibly as early as 1588,[14] and lived there until 1598, when he and his family were obliged to flee due to a rebellion in the Munster Plantation. He died in London in the following year.[15] Elizabeth I's grant of Kilcolman occurred shortly after Spenser and Sir Walter Raleigh (Spenser's neighbour in Ireland) had visited the Queen in London, in 1588–89.

Kilcolman Castle – today a ruin, but viewable as it might have been in Spenser's time via a digital reconstruction[16] – stands in the fork created by the confluence of two small rivers, the Awbeg and the Bregoge. These come together about three kilometres south of the castle, a little to the west of the town of Doneraile.[17] This fluvial relationship provided Spenser with the basis for his account, in "Colin Clouts Come Home Againe", of the ill-fated romance between two legendary rivers that he called "Mulla" and "Bregog".

> [Mulla] lov'd and was beloved full faine
> Of her owne brother river, Bregog hight,
> So hight because of this deceitfull traine
> Which he with Mulla wrought to win delight.[18]

---

13   Willy Maley, *A Spenser Chronology* (London: Macmillan, 1993), 55.
14   Ray Heffner, "Spenser's Acquisition of Kilcolman", *Modern Language Notes* 46, no. 8 (1931): 497.
15   Eric Klingelhöfer, "Edmund Spenser at Kilcolman Castle", *Post-Medieval Archaeology* 39, no. 1 (2005): 134. See also Thomas Herron, "Spenser and Raleigh", in East Carolina University's "Centering Spenser" project (2014–16), https://bit.ly/3d2qOv6.
16   http://core.ecu.edu/umc/Munster/virtual-tour.html.
17   Doneraile lies mid-way between Limerick (to the north) and Cork (to the south).
18   "Colin Clout", lines 116–19. On the trope of "river marriages" in Spenser, see Graham Atkin, "Raleigh, Spenser, and Elizabeth", in *Edmund Spenser: New and Renewed Directions*, ed. J.B. Lethbridge (Madison: Fairleigh Dickinson University Press, 2006), 212–13.

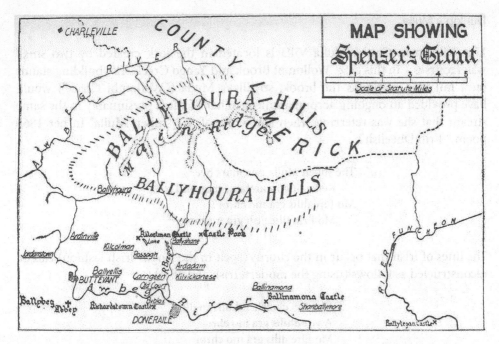

Figure 8.3. Map of "Spenser's Grant" in northern County Cork, showing mountains, rivers and townland names around Kilcolman Castle. From Pauline Henley, *Spenser in Ireland*.[19]

According to Patrick Joyce, Spenser's use of the name "Mulla" was based on a misinterpretation of the etymology of "Kilnemullah" – as the town of Buttevant, which straddles the Awbeg, was once called. Spenser took this placename to mean "church on the Mulla", whereas in fact "the old name is *Cill-na-mullach, ecclesia tumulorum,* [or] as O'Sullivan Beare translates it, 'the church of the summits or hillocks'".[20] Nonetheless, as Joyce observes, "having got the name Mulla, [Spenser] used it ever after for the river, and loved it and multiplied it in every direction".[21]

It is certainly true that Spenser referred to the Mulla numerous times, and in several poems; but the only extended elaboration is in "Colin Clout". When he mentions the Mulla (or its nymph) in other poems, he takes the (purportedly) legendary material in "Colin Clout" as his reference point. The same applies to his introduction of related characters, such as Mulla's father, Mole (the Ballyhoura Range).

---

19   Pauline Henley, *Spenser in Ireland* (Cork: Cork University Press 1928), 61. Online at
     http://core.ecu.edu/umc/Munster/maps.html.
20   Joyce, "Spenser's Irish Rivers", 108, footnote.
21   Joyce, "Spenser's Irish Rivers", 108. Note that the morpheme rendered here as *mullach* occurs
     also in the original Irish name of Mullavilly and has the same meaning ("hill"): Mullavilly "is an
     anglicisation of the Irish place name *Mhullach an Bhile* meaning 'the hill of the ancient tree'"
     (Hannam, *Mullavilly*, 9).

Dunlop's Mulla

Like Kilcolman Castle, Mulla Villa is located in the fork created by two small watercourses – in this case, Wollombi Brook and Yango Creek. The building stands on a hill that overlooks the brook, so Eliza's Mulla ("Wollombi Creek") would have provided an ongoing accompaniment to her life. It is presumably to the same stream that she was referring when she wrote of the "sullen Mulla" in her 1865 poem " Erin Dheelish".

> The sullen Mulla murmurs bye,
>> Reflecting mountain, crag, and tree,
> Mo Éire dílis grá mo chroí
>> Mo Erin dheelish gra machree.[22]

The lines of Irish that occur in the chorus (spelt in the Anglo-Irish fashion) can be reconstructed as follows (using the modern Irish alphabet):

> Éire mo chuisle mhuirnín dílis
> A yea dhílis grá mo chroí
> Mo Éire dílis grá mo chroí

An approximately literal translation would be:

> Ireland my pulse, faithful sweetheart
> O yea, true love of my heart
> My Ireland, faithful love of my heart

In these lines, as in the rest of the poem, we see a reversal of the sentiment expressed in "The Mulla, or Wollombi Creek". There, the River Bann (in Dunlop's home province of Ulster) "Would half the homage claim, my heart bestows on thee" (the addressee being Wollombi Brook). But in "Erin Dheelish", the Mulla is "sullen", and the poet despondent and sighing for Ireland.

Two things are clear: first, that Dunlop used the name "Mulla" to refer to Wollombi Brook; second, that, in doing so, she was drawing an analogy between herself and Spenser: Spenser "exiled" from England to Ireland, herself "exiled" from Ireland to Australia; Spenser, master of the manorial residence near the Awbeg, herself, mistress of the manorial residence on Wollombi Brook; both enchanted by the spirit of their own local river, but still dreaming of the land of their origins; both using their time of exile to compose poetry in which this tension provides a kind of thematic ostinato.

---

22   Eliza Hamilton Dunlop, "Erin Dheelish", *Empire*, 8 July 1865, 5.

All this is evident on the surface of the two Dunlop poems under consideration here.[23] But we are still left with a question. Why, of all the legendary river-names she might have applied to Wollombi Brook, did Eliza choose precisely the one that was invented by Spenser? There are a number of possible answers to this question; but the one I want to explore here concerns her interest in, and knowledge of, languages other than English.

Dunlop as translator

Eliza Hamilton Dunlop was not just a poet but also a translator. Her poetic output includes translations from Irish,[24] Spanish[25] and the Australian language spoken in the Hunter River and Lake Macquarie region.[26] As well, she interspersed her poems with words and phrases from these and other languages, including a number of additional Australian ones. In this she was not unlike Spenser, whose poetry is written in a version of English he invented for the purpose. His style was partly archaic and "rustic", derived from Chaucer (who had died a century and a half earlier) and the regional languages and dialects of the United Kingdom and Ireland;[27] but it was also self-consciously "learned", and drawn from the Latin and Greek classics and mediaeval chronicles and romances.[28]

Describing this aspect of Spenser's art, Anthony Esolen refers to "its affected homeliness, its odd mixture of rusticity and polish".[29] And just as Spenser is said to have borrowed it from Chaucer, we could perhaps suggest that Dunlop has borrowed an analogous style from Spenser. Another aspect of the "oddness" of such mixtures is their affinity with older verse forms that were intended to be sung.

---

23 These are reproduced in Webby this volume.

24 "Mable Macmahon" (1842).

25 "Rendirse a la Razon" (1863). Dunlop provides no information about her Spanish original. The epigraph appears to come from a Spanish version of Alain-René Lesage's picaresque novel *Histoire de Gil Blas de Santillane* (1715) – possibly the translation by Padre Isla published in 1828 (Chapter 11, 30). Dunlop's poem "A Problem" (1867) also includes a two-line epigraph in Spanish – a translation of John 1:3. Similarly, the epigraph to "Aphorisms" (1868) is a Spanish translation of Revelation 21:4.

26 "Native Poetry" (1848). See also Jim Wafer, "Ghost-writing for Wulatji", in *Recirculating Songs*, ed. Jim Wafer and Myfany Turpin (Hamilton NSW: Hunter Press, 2017), 193–201.

27 Including Irish and Welsh. See Roland Smith, "The Irish Background of Spenser's 'View'", *The Journal of English and Germanic Philology* 42, no. 4 (1943): 499–515, and "More Irish Words in Spenser", *Modern Language Notes* 59, no. 7 (1944): 472–74. Also Donald Bruce, "Spenser's Welsh", *Notes and Queries* (1985) 32(4): 465–67. See as well Willy Maley, "Spenser's Languages: Writing in the Ruins of English", in *The Cambridge Companion to Spenser*, ed. Andrew Hadfield (Cambridge: Cambridge University Press, 2001), 162–79.

28 See Edwin Greenlaw, "Spenser's Fairy Mythology", *Studies in Philology* 15, no. 2 (1918): 105–22; Colin Burrow, "Spenser and Classical Traditions", in Hadfield, *Cambridge Companion to Spenser*, 217–36; William Blackburn, "Spenser's Merlin", in *Merlin: A Casebook*, ed. Peter H. Goodrich and Raymond H. Thompson (New York: Routledge, 2003), 342–60.

29 Anthony Esolen, "The Disingenuous Poet Laureate: Spenser's Adoption of Chaucer", *Studies in Philology* 87 no. 3 (1990): 287.

Dunlop wrote her own lyrics for a number of older melodies, and Isaac Nathan set several of Dunlop's poems to music.[30]

My present focus is on one particular component of this mixture, namely, Dunlop's borrowings from Australian languages. These occur in "The Aboriginal Mother" (1838), "The Eagle Chief" (1842), "The Aboriginal Father" (1843), "Native Poetry" (1848) – and, I would argue, also in the two poems that provide the foundation of this chapter: "The Mulla, or Wollombi Creek" (1849) and "Erin Dheelish" (1865).

In an earlier publication,[31] I analysed the languages Dunlop drew from in "Native Poetry" (including her English adaptations of the original transcription) and came to the conclusion that, aside from the language of the Hunter River and Lake Macquarie ("HRLM") in which the song was composed, she used words from Darkinyung, Gamilaraay, the Sydney language and New South Wales Pidgin. At the end of the present chapter I have included an appendix that glosses her borrowings in the other poems just mentioned, and the words are almost all derived from languages that were spoken at or in the vicinity of Wollombi (Darkinyung, HRLM, Gathang, Gamilaraay and its related dialects, and Wiradjuri).[32] So it seems likely that Dunlop learnt most of these terms from conversations she heard in and around Mulla Villa, whether from Aboriginal people or other colonial settlers.[33]

What is surprising is that only a minority of the words can be positively attributed to Darkinyung, even though Darkinyung people are said to have occupied Wollombi Brook.[34] The "Wollombi tribes" had been greatly reduced in the 1840s,[35] so it is quite possible that other peoples had moved to the region to compensate for Darkinyung population loss. On the other hand, the Wollombi

---

30   For details of these musical concordances, see Skinner this volume and the entry for "Eliza Hamilton Dunlop, Songwriter" in Graeme Skinner's "Australharmony" website, at https://sydney.edu.au/paradisec/australharmony/dunlop-eliza-hamilton.php.

31   Wafer, "Ghost-writing for Wulatji", 216–17.

32   It is less likely, though of course not impossible, that speakers of more distant languages in which some of these words occur, such as Dhanggati, Ngiyampaa or the Yuin languages (Dharawal, Walgalu, Ngunawal etc.) could have contributed to Dunlop's word-store.

33   Only two of the words in the list ("myall" and "boommerring") were in common circulation among the colonisers.

34   For a summary of the data, see Caroline Jones, *Darkinyung Grammar and Dictionary* (Nambucca Heads NSW: Muurrbay, 2008), 3–7; Jim Wafer and Amanda Lissarrague, *A Handbook of Aboriginal Languages of New South Wales and the Australian Capital Territory* (Nambucca Heads: Muurrbay), 143–45.

35   In 1845, David Dunlop reported that there were only twenty-seven Aboriginal residents of the township of Wollombi; quoted in Denis Mahony, "Changing Patterns of Landuse and Decision-making in the Wollombi Valley", in *The Way of the River: Environmental Perspectives on the Wollombi*, ed. Denis Mahony and Joe Whitehead (Wollombi NSW: Wollombi Valley Landcare Group, 1994), 123. W.A. Squire provides the figure of fifty-four for the total population of the "Wollombi tribes" in 1848, in *Ritual, Myth, and Customs of the Australian Aborigines* (Maitland NSW: Mercury Print, 1896), 83.

region includes such an abundance of ceremonial sites that it may have always hosted regular visits by a number of different groups.[36]

The Mala

It is theoretically possible that Dunlop applied the name "Mulla" to Wollombi Brook only because of its use in Spenser. But this seems unlikely, given that the word *mala* occurs in one of the languages that were probably spoken at Wollombi, and that its meaning could be interpreted as referring to a geographical feature. In Gamilaraay, it means "fork", and the compilers of the standard dictionary of Gamilaraay (and its related dialects Yuwaalaraay and Yuwaalayaay) add the following note: "The main meaning seems to be 'fork', as in the 'fork of a tree' or anything that branches into two, as the body branches into two legs".[37]

As mentioned already, Mulla Villa stands in the fork created by the confluence of Wollombi Brook and Yango Creek. But it is also located close to another fork straddled by the village of Wollombi, at the point where Wollombi Brook is joined by Congewai Creek. It is difficult to tell which of these two forks the Gamilaraay name "Mala" might have referred to. The fork at Wollombi was probably better known, being the centre of a small settlement. But Mulla Villa is closer to the conjunction of the brook and Yango Creek, and it is there that Dunlop wrote the poem she entitles "The Mulla, or Wollombi Creek, New South Wales".

Whichever the original referent, there are good reasons to conjecture a double meaning in Dunlop's use of the name "Mulla". She appears to have taken advantage of a lucky coincidence, namely, that Spenser's "Mulla" is homophonous with Gamilaraay "Mala". Evidently, she understood the latter to be the local Indigenous name for Wollombi Brook, and she was probably right. It would be consistent with Aboriginal place-naming practices for the name of a major landmark, such as a junction of watercourses, to be applied to related features in the surrounding region.

Mala has not been recorded with the meaning "confluence" in Gamilaraay, but this almost certainly means that the original sources reported only the most obvious parts of the word's full semantic range. There are many other sites in New South Wales where the morpheme *mala* forms part of a documented placename, and all of the locations are at or near the junction of streams (rivers, creeks, brooks).[38] One of these places is Mallabula, located at the confluence of Tilligerry

---

36 William Needham, *A Study of the Aboriginal Sites in the Cessnock–Wollombi Region* (Cessnock NSW: W.J. Needham, 1981), 4; see also 35–40.

37 Anna Ash, John Giacon and Amanda Lissarrague, *Gamilaraay, Yuwaalaraay and Yuwaalayaay Dictionary* (Alice Springs: IAD Press, 2003), 106.

38 These include: Mulla Mulla Creek (Gamilaraay?), Bungemullagalarno Mountain (Gamilaraay?), Mulla Mulla Cowal (Ngiyampaa?), Mullamuddy Creek (Wiradjuri?), and Mallabula (Gathang).

Creek and Bobs Farm Creek,[39] where Gathang was spoken. The word *mala* has not been recorded with this meaning in Gathang, but the weight of evidence suggests that the placename could be reconstructed as *mala-bula* and translated as "confluence of two streams".[40] If *mala* carried this sense in Gathang, there is a strong likelihood that it occurred with the same meaning not just in Gamilaraay but also in at least one of the other languages spoken at Wollombi, namely the HRLM, which shared about two-thirds of its vocabulary with Gathang.[41]

The evidence suggests fairly strongly that *mala*, as used in Dunlop's historical environment, meant at least "fork" and "confluence". It also seems likely that Dunlop would have been aware of both meanings.

Through "the mighty telescope of Time"

In "The Mulla, or Wollombi Creek", Dunlop conjures up an image of the Virgin Queen peering through "the mighty telescope of Time". The object of Elizabeth's investigation lies at the fringes of a later world, where her successor, Victoria, rules over not just the United Kingdom and Ireland, but also lands unknown in Gloriana's own day. When the device comes into focus, adjusting to a distance of three centuries ahead, an indecipherable topographical squiggle has resolved itself into "Mulla's emerald banks, in sunny southern clime".

This is one of Dunlop's more startling metaphors, perhaps because it strikes one as being both disproportionate (in relation to the Queen's physical stature) and anachronistic (in relation to the history of the telescope). But it is nonetheless highly effective, not just in the way it juxtaposes the two eras Dunlop is invoking through her punning on the word "Mulla", but also because it reverses the direction of "translation". Instead of discerning in the Spenserian term a reference to the Irish past, the Queen has pointed the telescope the opposite way, to "the Globe's bright boundaries" (specifically, the Colony of New South Wales) in 1849.

The phrase "the Globe's bright boundaries" could in fact be an allusion to Merlin's scrying device in *The Faerie Queene*:

> Merlin's mirror, in which Britomart first, glimpses Artegall . . . is elevated by Spenser into an image of the great globe itself

---

39 These streams then join the Karuah River, which flows into Port Stephens. See William Howard et al., *A History of the Tilligerry Peninsula* (Newcastle, NSW: Newcastle City Printers, 1996).

40 In Gathang the suffix *-bula* (*~bularr*) means, as it does in many other Aboriginal languages, "two, pair, couple"; cf. Amanda Lissarrague, *A Grammar and Dictionary of Gathang* (Nambucca Heads: Muurrbay, 2010), 189–90.

41 Wafer and Lissarrague, *Handbook of Aboriginal Languages*, 159. See also Amanda Lissarrague, *A Salvage Grammar and Wordlist of the Language from the Hunter River and Lake Macquarie* (Nambucca Heads: Muurrbay, 2006) and Lissarrague, *A Grammar and Dictionary of Gathang*.

Forthy it round and hollow shaped was
Like to the world it selfe, and seem'd a world of glas. (III, ii, 19)

This world of glass is no ordinary crystal ball. Since it shows all things truly, the
mirror is an image of prelapsarian Eden, of a world free of illusion and error . . .[42]

That Dunlop might be suggesting a link between the Virgin Queen's telescope and
Merlin's glass is not implausible, when one considers that John Dee (for a time
Elizabeth's adviser and astrologer, and a probable model for Merlin in *The Faerie
Queene*[43]) collaborated with his pupil,[44] Thomas Digges, on the construction of
what was arguably the world's first reflecting telescope.[45] Elizabeth almost certainly
knew about it, though there is no evidence that she ever used it, or even saw it.

However that may be, the telescope of Dunlop's poem is not the common
variety designed for the eye, but evidently a *faerie* telescope that facilitates (inner)
vision by means of words. The poem thus functions like a spell cast over Elizabeth,
enabling her to see a slow-winding brook that flows three hundred years in the
future. At times this vision seems to her familiar, and reminds her of people (like
Raleigh and Spenser) and projects (such as the domestication of untamed lands
with olives, grapes and limes) in her own life. But there is also much that is
strange about it – strange enough that the spell-caster wonders whether even the
river's name might cause a start. For the word *mala* comes not from any of the
languages with which the skilled linguist Elizabeth was familiar,[46] but is related to
a music of "sweet sylvan sounds" and "melodies 'mid laughing leaves" – the kind of
soundscape that the Queen might be culturally predisposed to hear as the language
of "Faery lond".

---

42 Blackburn, "Spenser's Merlin", 352. Blackburn's text includes a misprint ("for thy"), which I have
    corrected here. Spenser's text has "forthy" (Middle English, meaning "because").
43 As William Sherman observes, "in both the scholarly and the popular imagination Dee has
    become the reincarnation of Merlin at the Tudor court". Sherman, *John Dee: The Politics of
    Reading and Writing in the English Renaissance* (Amherst: University of Massachusetts Press,
    1995), xii.
44 After the death of Digges' father, Leonard, the younger Digges may also have become Dee's
    ward. See Peter French, *John Dee: The World of an Elizabethan Magus* (London: Routledge and
    Kegan Paul, 1972), 99.
45 Colin Ronan, "The Origins of the Reflecting Telescope", *Journal of the British Astronomical
    Association* 101, no. 6 (1991): 339.
46 See Donatella Montini and Iolanda Plescia, *Elizabeth I in Writing* (New York: Palgrave
    Macmillan, 2018). There is little information about Elizabeth's knowledge or use of Irish, but see
    Pádraig Ó Macháin, "Two Nugent Manuscripts", *Ríocht na Midhe: Records of the Meath
    Archaeological and Historical Society*, 23 (2012), 132–38. Elizabeth also commissioned the first
    Irish typeface – see Dermot McGuinne, *Irish Type Design* (Blackrock [Ireland]: Irish Academic,
    1992), 7. As well, she was known to be fond of Irish music and musicians – see William Flood,
    A History of Irish Music (Dublin: Browne and Nolan, 1906), 113, 164, 168.

Unmapping the Mulla

The Virgin Queen with her mighty telescope of Time is a remarkably succinct image of the colonial project. Elizabeth I not only played a major role in the Tudor reconquest of Ireland and the first British attempts to invade and settle the east coast of North America; as noted above, she was also directly implicated, through her association with John Dee, in the invention of the reflecting telescope. This development was a major step in the standardisation of time for navigational purposes, so one might argue that the Queen's most brilliant long-term achievement was the colonisation of Time itself.

In his day, Dee was one of Europe's foremost mathematicians and astronomers, and the Queen drew heavily on his advice in matters of maritime and military strategy. As well, Dee helped her formulate plans for a worldwide empire based on British culture.[47] But it took a few more centuries for the colonisation of Time to become global. The theoretical basis was provided when Isaac Newton decreed that time was absolute,[48] and the concept finally achieved universal institutionalisation when Greenwich Mean Time was declared in 1884.[49]

But, as Giordano Nanni puts the matter:

> [T]he path towards global temporal standardisation was not paved solely through global events and grandiloquent gestures of imperialism, such as the proclamation of GMT. The process also entailed a series of world-wide, localised assaults on alternative cultures of time.[50]

Nanni has made a persuasive case that the colonisation of Australia depended for its success on the thoroughgoing imposition of a culture of time that was radically different from the temporal concepts and practices of the peoples being colonised. But to date there has been little attention given to understanding the linguistic underpinnings of Aboriginal temporal cultures. The most helpful formulations have come from Deborah Rose, who summarises the time ethos of Yarralin people thus:

> [W]e here now, meaning we here in this shared present, are differentiated from early days people by the fact that they preceded us and made the conditions of our existence possible. In relation to them, we are the "behind mob" – those who come after. From

---

47 Ken MacMillan, "Discourse on History, Geography, and Law: John Dee and the Limits of the British Empire, 1576–80", *Canadian Journal of History* 36, no. 1 (2001): 1–26.

48 In Scholium I of *Principia Mathematica*. See also Deborah Harkness, "Alchemy and Eschatology: Exploring the Connections between John Dee and Isaac Newton", in *Newton and Religion: Context, Nature, and Influence*, ed. James E. Force and Richard H. Popkin (Dordrecht: Kluwer, 1999), 1–15.

49 Kristen Lippincott, ed. *The Story of Time* (London: Merrell Holberton, 1999), 7–8.

50 Giordano Nanni, *The Colonisation of Time* (Manchester: Manchester University Press, 2012), 3. For a close-up satirical take on the issues, see Turkish novelist Ahmet Tanpinar's *The Time Regulation Institute* (London: Penguin, 2013).

our perspective, they are the old or olden time people, the first people. Sequence and succession are the salient features. The future is the domain of those who come after us. They are sometimes referred to as the new mob, or simply as those "behind to we": those who come after. It is our job to ensure that those who come behind us are taught the Law and have a place and responsibilities to take over from us.[51]

Aboriginal Australians are not alone in conceptualising time in terms of spatial relations. This is so common in the world's languages that it is often regarded as a universal.[52] What is less common, or at least less commonly attested, is the notion that the past lies *ahead* and the future *behind*. But there is evidence for similar alternative ways of understanding the directionality of the relationship between time and space in at least the Apache,[53] Aymara,[54] Amondawa[55] and Yucatec Maya[56] languages of the Americas and the languages of Pormpurraaw, on the west coast of Cape York Peninsula.[57]

It is hard to know whether Dunlop's knowledge of the Aboriginal languages spoken at Wollombi was fluent enough for her to have comprehended something of the local Indigenous culture of time. But the fact that she has counterposed the figure of the Mulla and the image of Good-Queen-Bess-with-the-Time-and-Space-Conquering-Telescope is at least suggestive. For the word *mala* (or a semantic equivalent) is used in a number of Australian languages in a way that has implications, some of them probably significant, for an understanding of temporal concepts in Aboriginal cultures.

There is a trope in the Yolngu languages that associates the junction of watercourses with the relationship between the phenomenal world and "the Dreaming".[58] Similar usages in other Australian languages have a common abstract

---

51 Deborah Bird Rose, *Dingo Makes Us Human: Life and Land in an Aboriginal Australian Culture* (Cambridge: Cambridge University Press, 1991), 206.

52 A position challenged by Sinha and his collaborators, who nonetheless concede that it is a "quasi-universal". Chris Sinha, Vera da Silva Sinha, Jörg Zinken and Wany Sampaio, "When Time Is Not Space", *Language and Cognition* 3, no. 1 (2011): 165.

53 Keith Basso, "'Speaking with Names': Language and Landscape among the Western Apache", *Cultural Anthropology* 3, no. 2 (1988): 112; Nancy Munn, "The Cultural Anthropology of Time: A Critical Essay", *Annual Review of Anthropology* 21 (1992): 113. For a more recent overview of the issues, see Andrea Bender and Sieghard Beller, "Mapping Spatial Frames of Reference onto Time: A Review of Theoretical Accounts and Empirical Findings", *Cognition* 132 (2014): 342–82.

54 Rafael Núñez and Eve Sweetser, "With the Future Behind Them: Convergent Evidence from Aymara Language and Gesture in the Crosslinguistic Comparison of Spatial Construals of Time", *Cognitive Science* 30 (2006): 401–50.

55 Sinha et al., "When Time Is Not Space", 146–65.

56 Chris Sinha and Peter Gärdenfors, "Time, Space, and Events in Language and Cognition: A Comparative View", *Annals of the New York Academy of Sciences* 40 (2014): 1–10.

57 Lera Boroditsky and Alice Gaby, "Remembrances of Times East: Absolute Spatial Representations of Time in an Australian Aboriginal Community", *Psychological Science* 21, no. 11 (2010): 1635–39.

58 On the use of this term, see Howard Morphy "Australian Aboriginal Concepts of Time", in Lippincott, *The Story of Time*, 264–68.

sense of "connection or connectivity",[59] even though the semantic range of the relevant words may vary. In north-eastern Arnhem Land, for example, the word for "confluence" (likan) has the basic meaning of "elbow",[60] but is also used in the sense of "the connection between the physical world and the Ancestral domain".[61] In a number of more southerly languages, however, the sense of "confluence" is rendered by a word that means "barb" or "hook" (as in the barb on a hook-spear). In Gurindji, for example, the word for "junction in a river" (also "fork of a tree", "fork in a road") is *jarra* (~*jarrapaly*); but the same word also means "hook on a hook-spear".[62]

In fact, the geographical spread of a semantic connection between "confluence" and "spear-hook" is surprisingly wide. In Gumbaynggirr, for example, *garraabula* is glossed as "fork in a river or track; junction"; but *garraa*'s primary referent is "barb" or "fishhook", with secondary meanings given as "fork, clip, peg".[63] There are a number of other languages where *garra(a)* is part of a word that has been recorded as referring either to "hook"[64] or to "confluence",[65] but is not attested with the alternative meaning. In these cases, it seems at least plausible that the semantic range of *garra(a)* was wider than the documenters realised and could have extended at least to the other of the two meanings.

A similar argument can be made in relation to the morpheme *mala*, which occurs as part of the word for "spear-hook" in at least some of the Western Desert

---

59 Howard Morphy, *Ancestral Connections: Art and an Aboriginal System of Knowledge* (Chicago: University of Chicago Press, 1991), 189.

60 Fiona Magowan, "Waves of Knowing: Polymorphism and Co-Substantive Essences in Yolngu Sea Cosmology", *The Australian Journal of Indigenous Education* 29, no. 1 (2001): 26. The same morpheme has a number of other meanings as well, all of them based on the notion of "joint~junction~connection". See R. David Zorc, *Yolngu-Matha Dictionary* (Darwin: School of Australian Linguistics, Darwin Institute of Technology, 1986), 159; also Beulah Lowe, *Yolngu-English Dictionary* (Darwin: Aboriginal Resource and Development Services Inc., 2004), 102.

61 Howard Morphy, *Journey to the Crocodile's Nest* (Canberra: Australian Institute of Aboriginal Studies, 1984), 26. See also Ian Keen, *Knowledge and Secrecy in an Aboriginal Religion* (Oxford: Oxford University Press, 1994), 71 and "Ancestors, Magic, and Exchange in Yolngu Doctrines", *Journal of the Royal Anthropological Institute* (N.S.) 12 (2006): 518.

62 The same word also means "line of verse" and "different meaning of a word". Felicity Meakins et al., *Gurindji to English Dictionary* (Batchelor NT: Batchelor Press, 2013), 90.

63 Steve Morelli, *Gumbaynggirr Dictionary and Learner's Grammar* (Nambucca Heads: Muurrbay, 2015), 48. The suffix -*bula* means, "two, pair, couple" (Morelli, *Gumbaynggirr Dictionary*, 25).

64 For example, in the Sydney language, *garraba* means "prong" [of the three-pronged muding harpoon] – see Jakelin Troy, *The Sydney Language* (Canberra: the author/AIATSIS, 1994), 45; see also illustration (c), 111. And in Wiradjuri, *garraan* mean "fish-hook, grub-hook, shepherd's crook"; Stan Grant and John Rudder, *A New Wiradjuri Dictionary* (O'Connor, ACT: Restoration House, 2010), 367.

65 For example, "Gurrabulla" (the name of a waterhole on the Wollondilly River) is glossed as "junction of watercourses". Jim Smith, "New Insights into Gundungurra Place Naming", in *Aboriginal Placenames: Naming and Re-Naming the Australian Landscape*, ed. Harold Koch and Luise Hercus (Canberra: Australian National University E Press 2009), 102. And according to Jen Willetts, Kurrahboolya (the name for the junction of the Crawford and Myall Rivers, Bulahdelah) means "fork, two gullies, two streams etc.", https://www.jenwilletts.com/hunter_valley_place_names_K.html.

languages. Wilf Douglas has recorded *malapirtu* as "spear head" – that is, the mulga-wood barb that is bound to the tip of a *kurlarta* spear.[66] This suggests that the conceptual link between "hook" and "confluence" is probably mediated by the similarity in their geometric configuration. The hook (or "barb") is bound to the tip of a spear in such a way that it creates a narrow angle, as a tributary typically does when it joins a main watercourse. The underlying geometrical sense of *mala* is made most explicit in Ngiyampaa of western New South Wales, where it functions as an adverb and is glossed as "sideways on".[67] That is, it pertains to events that happen at an angle to each other.[68]

What is of interest for present purposes is the word's potential relevance to the temporal culture mediated by the languages spoken at Wollombi. The matter can be approached conveniently through a consideration of the contrasting perspective that a speaker of English is liable to bring to the matter. In English (and many other languages that propagate similar concepts), the metaphor of time as "flow" is taken so much for granted that Newton was able to use it in his famous definition of "true" time.[69] It also provides the underlying logic for the trope of time as a river.[70] But this flow has only one significant direction: downwards. That the English-speaker's viewing point is oriented towards the river's outflow is clear from geographical terms such as "left bank" and "right bank", which are based on the perspective of a viewer looking downstream.

I conjecture that Australian languages, by contrast, may have an "upstream" orientation to flowing water – that is, towards the source rather than the outflow. This would fit very neatly not just with the notion of the past as "ahead" and the future as "behind", but also with the idea of "the Dreaming" as originary.[71]

---

66   Wilf Douglas, *An Introductory Dictionary of the Western Desert Language* (Perth: Institute of Applied Language Studies, Western Australian College of Advanced Education, 1988), 27; cf. 19, 90. The morpheme *pirtu* means "thumb" or "big toe" (Douglas, *Introductory Dictionary*, 70).

67   Tamsin Donaldson, *Ngiyambaa, the Language of the Wangaaybuwan* (Cambridge: Cambridge University Press, 1980), 76.

68   In the light of Hoffmann's work on "Path salience" in Jaminjung, I suggest that *mala* could be a candidate for analysis as an uninflecting coverb in some Australian languages. Dorothea Hoffmann, "Path Salience in Motion Descriptions in Jaminjung", in *Space and Time in Languages and Cultures: Linguistic Diversity*, eds. Luna Filipovic, Kasia M. Jaszczolt (Amsterdam: John Benjamins, 2012), 460. The work of Bill Palmer and his collaborators on "sociotopography" and the OzSpace Project is also relevant to this discussion. See B. Palmer, Jonathon Lum, Jonathan Schlossberg and Alice Gaby, "How Does the Environment Shape Spatial Language? Evidence for Sociotopography", *Linguistic Typology* 21, no. 33 (2017): 457–91; and https://c21ch.newcastle.edu.au/eldta/ozspace/.

69   "Absolute, true and mathematical time, of itself, and from its own nature flows equably without regard to anything external, and by another name is called duration" (Newton, Scholium I of *Principia Mathematica*, in the translation of 1729 by Andrew Motte, based on Newton's 3rd edition of 1726). See also Huw Price, "The Flow of Time", in *The Oxford Handbook of Philosophy of Time*, ed. Craig Callender (Oxford: Oxford University Press, 2011), 276–311.

70   J.J.C. Smart, "The River of Time", *Mind* 58, no. 232 (1949): 483–94.

71   In English (and no doubt most "Western" languages), it is clear that we take "wakefulness" to be originary. See Thomas Crowther and Matthew Soteriou, "Time in the Dream", in *The Routledge Handbook of Philosophy of Temporal Experience*, ed. Ian Phillips (London: Routledge, 2017), esp. 195–97.

Unfortunately, if the data for "confluence" are gappy, the data for "orientation to flow" are, as far as I can tell, non-existent; so I am unable to make the case on the basis of currently available linguistic evidence. Still, there are a few hints in the literature that are worth mentioning. Howard Morphy, for example, writes of Yolngu mortuary rituals that they

> are concerned in part with the journey of the souls of the dead from the place of death to their conception sites . . . At various stages people sing songs of all the clans present to show their relationship to the deceased . . . Frequently river systems provide a symbolic linking theme, people are said to be "singing the waters of the clan". By selecting tributaries appropriately and occasionally bringing in songs from places which are related on a different basis, all the clans present can be included in a sequence of ritual action which organizes the landscape so that an individual's life seems to flow directly out of it.[72]

In a similar vein, Fiona Magowan notes that in the Yolngu languages, where ancestral water is lexically determined as anatomical parts, "the source of freshwater is referred to as the eye (*mangutji*), while its stream is the neck (*mayang*). Adjoining tributaries are the arms (*wana*), and the points of confluence are known as the elbows (*likan*)".[73]

Unmapping Time

The indecipherable topographical squiggle has turned out to be something more – and no doubt other – than the Virgin Queen, with her massive scrying implement, might have expected. She could scarcely have foreseen that the wizardry of the likes of Dee and Newton, who were both alchemists, would enable the British, then Europe, then the world, to succeed in the experiment of materialising Time.

And what could the fantasy of alchemical gold be if not this? Time is undoubtedly "of the Essence", and in its materialised form has produced the kind of wealth and power that would have been unimaginable in Elizabeth's own day. But the end result of the experiment has, in the twenty-first century, turned out

---

72 Howard Morphy, "Landscape and the Reproduction of the Ancestral Past", in *The Anthropology of Landscape*, ed. Eric Hirsch and Michael O'Hanlon (Oxford: Clarendon, 1995), 203.
73 Magowan, "Waves of Knowing", 26. The conception of a river system as "embodied" may be widespread in Australia. I note, for example, that in the south-east, the creation of rivers is attributed to a water creature called "Waway" in a number of languages. See Ngiyampaa texts 3 and 4 in Donaldson, *Ngiyambaa*, 315–19 (cf. 20, 92, 99, 205, 374). See also Jim Wafer, "Why Waway? The Proctor Map and the Getting of Song in New South Wales", in *Language, Land and Song: Studies in Honour of Luise Hercus*, ed. Peter Austin, Harold Koch and Jane Simpson (London: EL Publishing, 2016), 287–303. On Aboriginal cognitive engagements with waterscapes generally, see Marcia Langton, "Earth, Wind, Fire and Water", in *The Social Archaeology of Indigenous Societies*, ed. Bruno David, Bryce Barker and Ian J. McNiven (Canberra: Aboriginal Studies Press, 2005), 139–60.

to be a horror story with such a grotesque denouement that Donna Haraway has dubbed our era "the Chthulucene".[74] The dream of gold has actually furnished the framework of the Iron Cage[75] from which we witness the ludicrous final act.

We may not be able to escape this cage in any practical sense,[76] but at least we have the option of withholding belief. A number of scholarly fields are providing support for this process, and the one I have found most useful in my own work is the transdiscipline known as "counter-mapping".[77] The intent of this approach, at least in part, has been to decolonise and relativise the taken-for-granted categories that "we moderns" conventionally use to describe space and topography. And the inspiration for the deconstruction of these categories has most often come from the alternative perspectives offered by the world's surviving Indigenous languages.

But, in spite of a number of moves to develop a "culture of temporal diversity",[78] the counter-mapping project has not yet been explicitly extended to time.[79] The present chapter, then, could be regarded as a very preliminary step in that direction. But instead of using the expression "counter-mapping", I have borrowed the term "unmapping" from the artist and curator Jonathan Kimberley, who devised and led a project called "Unmapping the End of the World" for the Mildura Palimpsest Biennale in 2015.[80]

The creek at the heart of this chapter, the Mulla~Mala, or Wollombi Brook, has already outlived Elizabeth Tudor and Eliza Hamilton Dunlop; and the fluvial regeneration projects currently being undertaken there mean it will probably outlive me and my contemporaries.[81] But its name will not last beyond the disappearance of the human species. In the interim, the toponym provides us with

---

74   Donna Haraway, *Staying with the Trouble: Making Kin in the Chthulucene* (Durham NC: Duke University Press, 2016).

75   Max Weber, *The Protestant Ethic and the Spirit of Capitalism* [1905], trans. Talcott Parsons (New York: Scribner, 1930), 181.

76   As implied in the work of Michel Foucault and his followers – see, for example, Sam Binkley, "Discipline, Civilization and Temporality: The Rise of Abstract Time in the Constitution of Modern Subjectivity", in *Care or Control of the Self?*, ed. Andrea D. Bührmann and Stefanie Ernst (Newcastle-upon-Tyne: Cambridge Scholars, 2010), 36–50.

77   A good overview of the growing literature on this topic is provided by the special issue of *Geographica* devoted to "Indigenous Cartographies and Counter-Mapping" (vol. 47, no. 2, 2012); see in particular the introduction by Renee Pualani Louis, Jay T. Johnson and Albertus Hadi Pramono, 77–79. See also Mac Chapin, Zachary Lamb and Bill Threlkeld, "Mapping Indigenous Lands", *Annual Review of Anthropology* 34 (2005): 619–38.

78   Karlheinz Geißler, "A Culture of Temporal Diversity", *Time & Society* 11, no. 1 (2002): 131–40. See also Bernhard Albert, "'Temporal Diversity': A Note on the 9th Tutzing Time Ecology Conference", *Time & Society* 11, no. 1 (2002): 89–104.

79   Even though, as noted already, the intimate relationship between spatial and temporal concepts is widely attested.

80   As reported on the ABC Radio National program "Earshot", 19 October 2015. See Daniel Browning, "Unmapping the End of the World: Is Art a Time Machine?" at https://ab.co/2ZvKYr2.

81   See Mahony and Whitehead, *Way of the River*; G.J. Brierley and K.A. Fryirs, "The Use of Evolutionary Trajectories to Guide 'Moving Targets' in the Management of River Futures", *River Research and Applications* 32, no. 5 (2016): 827–31.

some clues as to how we might proceed in the task of decolonising the time that is left to us.

Acknowledgements

Many thanks to Anna Johnston and Elizabeth Webby for their helpful feedback; also to the other colleagues and friends who read and corresponded with me about the various drafts of this chapter. These include Greg Bork, Grace Karskens, Marie Makinson, Donna Snowdon, Petronella Vaarzon-Morel and Peter Lamborn Wilson.

Appendix: Words from Australian Languages Used in Eliza Hamilton Dunlop's Poetry

The works cited as sources (following a forward slash in the Language and source line, or bracketed in the Notes) are included in the bibliography at the end of this volume.

"The Aboriginal Mother"

Myall (in subtitle "From Myall's Creek")

Language and source: Yuwaalaraay, Yuwaalayaay, Gamilaraay / Ash et al. 104

Reconstruction and gloss: *maayaal*, "myall tree" (*Acacia pendula*)

Notes: As borrowed into Australian English, the word "myall" has two quite distinct meanings. Most commonly, it means "a stranger" or "hostile, wild, ignorant" and is said to be derived from Dharuk (Dixon et al. 172). But in the present context, where it refers to the site of the Myall Creek massacre, the second meaning is more plausible. Dixon et al. (144) gloss it thus: "Any of several *Acacia* trees, especially *Acacia pendula* ('weeping myall')". The massacre site is in Gamilaraay country, and it is from this language (or a closely related one) that the English name for the "myall tree" is derived. Ash et al. (104) reconstruct the tree name as *maayaal*. (See also Parker, 123, 124, 146.) For an overview of the literature on the massacre itself, see Maynard,[82] and other essays in the same volume.

goro (line 27, stanza 4)

Language and source: Wiradjuri / Grant & Rudder 393

Reconstruction and gloss: *guruwu*, "tomahawk"

Notes: The word is spelt "goro" in the version of the poem originally published in the *Australian* in 1838, but the manuscript version in " The Vase" has "gooroo" – which is also the way De Salis (65) spells it.

Toon Bakra (line 38, stanza 5)

---

82   John Maynard, "Myall Creek Memories", in *Remembering the Myall Creek Massacre*, ed. Jane Lydon and Lyndall Ryan (Sydney: NewSouth, 2018), 114–15.

Toon

Language and source: Darkinyung / Jones 155; Wiradjuri/ Grant & Rudder 350; Yuwaalayaay, Gamilaraay/ Ash et al. 66

Reconstruction and gloss: *dhun*, "tail"

Bakra

Language and source: Wiradjuri / Grant & Rudder 292

Reconstruction: *bagadaa*, "wedge tailed eagle, eaglehawk, *Aquila audax*"

Notes: Forché and Wu (392, n.2) are undoubtedly correct in glossing the name "Toon Bakra" as "hawk's tail". Compare also the following line of the poem: "My bold and stately mountain-bird" (line 39).

koopin (line 43, stanza 6)

Language and source: Gathang / Lissarrague 2010: 236, Mathews 20–21; cf. Lissarrague 2007: 145

Reconstruction and gloss: *gupiyn*, "fighting hook, wooden instrument used for warding-off spears, and also to hinder the flight of an opponent"

Notes: Mathews provides an illustration of this instrument (item 19 on p. 20).

boommerring (line 44, stanza 6)

Language and source: Sydney language (Dharuk) / Troy 43; Dixon et al. 175–77

Reconstruction and gloss: *bumarit* (Troy)~*bumariny* (Dixon et al.), "boomerang"

"The Eagle Chief"

Maliyan (line 6, stanza 1)

Language and source: Darkinyung / Jones 164; Yuwaalaraay, Yuwaalayaay, Gamilaraay / Ash et al. 106; Wiradjuri/ Grant and Rudder 400; Ngiyampaa/ Donaldson 28; Dharawal, Walgalu, Ngunawal/ Besold Part A 133, Koch 149

Reconstruction and gloss: *maliyan*, "wedge tailed eagle, eaglehawk, *Aquila audax*"

"The Aboriginal Father"

Wheeguon-Eura (footnote to Nathan's score, 1844, pp. 1, 3)
Wheeguon

Language and source: Gamilaraay / Ash et al. 141

Reconstruction: *wiigun*, "back log – a large log put at the back of the fire"

Notes: From Gamilaraay *wii*, "fire; firewood; spirit light" (Ash et al. 140). Dunlop has added to her footnote a guide to pronunciation: "Fire Clouds. Pronounce the (g) hard in 'Wheeguon'".

Eura

Language and source: Darkinyung / Jones 174; Hunter River-Lake Macquarie language (HRLM)/ Lissarrague 2006 146; Gathang / Lissarrague 2010 283; Dhanggati/ Lissarrague 2007 170

Reconstruction and gloss: *yurra*, "cloud(s)"

batwan (line 8, stanza 2)

Language and source: Hunter River-Lake Macquarie language (HRLM) / Lissarrague 2006 132, Wafer 2017 216, n. 67; possibly also Sydney/ Troy 48; Darkinyung / Jones 148

Reconstruction and gloss: *patu-wan*, "big water"

Notes: From its use in other HRLM texts,[83] I conjecture that the suffix *-wan* is an augmentative in that language – as it is in Yuwaalaraay and Yuwaalayaay (Ash et al. 138).

Batwan-mian (footnote to Nathan's score, 1844, pp. 1, 4)
Batwan – see previous entry.
mian

Language and source: Gamilaraay / Ash et al. 110

Reconstruction and gloss: *mayan*, "waterhole, creek"

Original words of "A Native Song of the Maneroo Tribe" (from which " The Aboriginal Father" was versified).

The words of this song were originally transcribed by John Lhotsky (1834),[84] as follows:

> Koon-gi koon-gi kawel-gho yueree, koon-gi kawel-gho yueree,
> Kooma-gi ko ko kawel-gho koomagi ka-ba kooma-gi ko ko –
> Kooma-gi ko ko kawel-gho koomagi ka-ba kooma-gi yue-ree.

Lhotsky translated this as

> Unprotected race of people, unprotected all we are; and our children shrink so fastly, unprotected why are we?

---

83 For example, as part of the word *katja-wan*, "sated", in Threlkeld's translation of Luke 9:17. Lancelot Threlkeld, "Gospel of St. Luke [Evangelion Unni ta Jesu-ūm-ba Christ-ko-ba Upatōara Louka-ūmba]" (Auckland: Auckland Public Library, Grey MSS 82, 1857). Compare *katjaway*, "satiety" (Lissarrague, *Salvage Grammar and Wordlist of the Language from the Hunter River and Lake Macquarie*, 116).

84 Lhotsky also transcribed the melody. See Graeme Skinner and Jim Wafer, "A Checklist of Colonial Era Musical Transcriptions of Australian Indigenous Songs", in Wafer and Turpin ed., *Recirculating Songs*, 372–73.

Dunlop's versification is almost certainly based on Lhotsky's English version rather than on whatever the original words may have meant. There are no indications that she had any familiarity with the Ngarigu language spoken in the Monaro region, and Lhotsky's "translation" itself gives scant evidence of any deep understanding of it. I leave it to those with a specialist interest in the Yuin languages to attempt a more accurate version, but offer a few preliminary observations.

In a number of the South Coast languages, a word that can be reconstructed as *gundji* means "camp, hut" (Besold part B 256). The other words in the song are less immediately recognisable, but I note that *gawa* is glossed as "talk", *yuwa* as "how?" and *gumari* as "wind" (Besold part B 255, 273, 255). The form *guuguu* ("dead relative") occurs in Gamilaraay (Ash et al. 98), at some distance from the Yuin languages, but could well have had a wider distribution. This might suggest that the first line is a question, such as "who is now talking in the camp?", followed by a response in the second and third lines which, if translated as something like "it is only the ghostly wind", would at least not be inconsistent with the sense of Lhotsky's English version.

Part 3
Poems

9

A Selection of Eliza Hamilton Dunlop's Poems

Elizabeth Webby

In the 1960s, while reading through early Australian newspapers during research for my PhD thesis on literary culture in Australia before 1850, I came upon several poems by Eliza Hamilton Dunlop and was especially impressed by "The Aboriginal Mother" and her other work on Indigenous themes and issues. In 1981, I arranged a small selection of her poems, with this particular emphasis, for publication by Mulini Press in their Colonial Poets Series. At the time I was not aware of the full range of Dunlop's work, especially poems published after 1850, and had not made a close study of those in her unpublished manuscript "The Vase", now in the Mitchell Library. Nor did I know that some of the first poems she published after arriving in Sydney had already appeared in books and journals in Britain. The larger selection of poems included here aims to give a better representation of what she wrote, while also indicating the more substantial changes she made to many of her poems during her lifetime.

One initial difficulty was deciding which version of the poems selected for inclusion here would be the best to use as my copy text. I was initially drawn to the idea of using the first version to be published in Australia as the one that had been known to her contemporary readers. But a number of her earlier poems had in fact been published in Britain or Ireland before Dunlop arrived in Sydney. I finally decided to use the final version written during her lifetime, incorporating revisions she made when preparing her poems for a hoped-for published volume which never eventuated. A brief note in the *Maitland Mercury* for 1 June 1871 refers to Dunlop as "having some intention of collecting these works and publishing them in a more permanent form". As her last published poem appeared in 1873, this would suggest that "The Vase" was prepared between 1871–73. In *Two Early Colonials* (1967), Margaret De Salis refers to a family story that the manuscript "had been despatched by the mail coach from Wollombi to Sydney and was lost on the way".[1] This seems unlikely given that the manuscript is now in the Mitchell Library.

---

1   Margaret De Salis, *Two Early Colonials* (Sydney: printed by the author, 1967), 64.

The rumour may have developed because "The Vase" was never published. Since Australian poets usually had to pay for the printing of a volume of their poetry in either Australia or Britain at the time, the most likely reason was that Dunlop was unable to afford to have it published, since after her husband's death in 1863 she may have been left without regular income.

Most poems included here take the version in "The Vase" as the copy text with the exception of a few that were not included there. Any substantive changes of wording from earlier versions of each poem are indicated although changes in capitalisation and punctuation have not been noted. In most cases changes in punctuation mainly consisted of substituting dashes for commas or vice versa, together with adding or deleting exclamation marks. Explanatory notes have been included for places, people, events and terms that might not be familiar to twenty-first-century readers. In the case of some poems, especially those revised for "The Vase", Dunlop herself wrote notes to explain aspects of her earlier work with which she could not expect contemporary readers, whether in Australia or overseas, to be familiar. These have all been included in the selection, together with notes attached to earlier versions of some poems, such as "The Aboriginal Mother". I am grateful to all the contributors to this volume for their extensive research on a number of these poems, as specifically indicated in my notes on each of them.

Many of the changes Dunlop made when revising her poems for "The Vase" were fairly minor in nature, with by far the most substantial occurring in a poem originally entitled "The Irish Mother". This was published in the *Australian* early in 1839 as No. 5 in the series "Songs of an Exile" and signed "E.H.D.". In 1845, Charles Gavan Duffy, who ten years later was to migrate to Australia, included it in his highly popular anthology *The Ballad Poetry of Ireland*, as an anonymous poem entitled "The Emigrant Mother". In a note to the forty-second edition of his anthology in 1866 he claimed to have found "this touching little ballad in an Australian newspaper, long before I contemplated visiting that country, and was charmed with its fresh feeling and grace. I have not been able to discover the writer's name". Apart from the change of title and the spelling of one word, "The Emigrant Mother" is identical to Dunlop's "The Irish Mother" so the newspaper in question must have been the *Australian*. Early in the twentieth century, under the slightly different title of "The Emigrant's Mother", Dunlop's poem was reprinted in Australia in the *Catholic Press*, the *Freeman's Journal* and the Melbourne *Advocate*, with reference to Duffy's 1866 comments and regrets that he had not mentioned the newspaper's name so that it was not possible now to identify the author. "The Emigrant Mother" was also reprinted in at least seven Irish newspapers between 1901 and 1953, in most cases without any reference to Duffy and his anthology.[2]

---

2   See *Freeman's Journal*, 24 December 1914; *Advocate*, 18 September 1915; *Catholic Press*, 4 November 1915; *Southern Star*, 14 September 1901; *Nationalist* (Tipperary), 1 January 1916; *Strathbone Chronicle, Donegal News, Fermaugh Herald*, all 1 April 1939; *Leitrim Observer*, 25

While Dunlop was no longer alive at the time of these later newspaper reprintings of her poem, given her continuing interest in Irish affairs one wonders if she was aware of its inclusion in Duffy's anthology. If so, was this a reason for the extensive changes she made when rewriting "The Vase" version of "The Irish Mother"? As Katie Hansord has noted, the poem was originally published in the *Australian* immediately after "The Aboriginal Mother", so "Dunlop clearly intended this poem to be read alongside 'The Aboriginal Mother,' suggesting her personal experience as a factor weighing heavily in her ability to empathise".[3] Yet by retitling "The Vase" version as "The Irish Nurse, to a Foster Child", Dunlop removed any suggestion of personal experience as well as substituting a difference in class rather than in locality as the explanation for their separation. Whatever the reason for the extensive changes in this poem, when revising it in the 1870s, Eliza Hamilton Dunlop chose to remove any autobiographical references.

Dunlop had begun writing poetry in her teens and my selection begins with one written in 1810 which is preserved in a manuscript now in the Mitchell Library.[4] Before she emigrated to Sydney, a number of her poems were published in Irish magazines, including the *Dublin Penny Journal* and the *Belfast Magazine*. Her cousin William Hamilton Maxwell was a best-selling novelist of the 1830s and some of her songs also appeared in his *The Dark Lady of Doona* (1834). She began publishing poems in local newspapers soon after her arrival in Sydney and continued to do so for much of her long life, before dying aged eighty-four at Wollombi in 1880.

While I had earlier found twenty-three poems by Eliza Dunlop published before 1850, thanks to Trove we now know that her poetry appeared in Australian journals until 1873.[5] She continued her earlier practice of sending poems to a particular newspaper for a time and then favouring another, with her post-1850 poems appearing mainly in the *Empire* and the *Australian Town and Country Journal*. The AustLit database lists forty-five poems by Dunlop, with links to Trove, though a search of Trove has revealed a few additional ones. And it is possible that more were published in post-1850 newspapers and magazines that have not yet been digitised. While Dunlop's earlier poems were often on Australian topics, her later ones rarely dealt with local matters. Though she still returned frequently to Irish subjects she appears to have written nothing more on Indigenous ones after 1850. Instead, she chose more abstract themes such as "Ambition", "Destiny", and the consolations of poetry and religious belief. After her husband died in March

---

July 1953. My thanks to Anna Johnston for drawing this to my attention as well as to Jenny Johnston for her additional research.

3   Katie Hansord, "Eliza Hamilton Dunlop's 'The Aboriginal Mother': Romanticism, Anti Slavery and Imperial Feminism in the Nineteenth Century", *JASAL: Journal of the Association for the Study of Australian Literature* 11, no. 1 (2011): 7.

4   Juvenile notebook, Milson Family Papers – 1810, 1853–1862, State Library of New South Wales, MLMSS 7683.

5   See "Eliza Hamilton Dunlop's Australian Publications", this volume.

1863, many later poems had an understandable emphasis on her loss of him, as in "Memorialis", published in the *Empire* on 24 June that year, and "The Two Graves", published in the same paper on 15 April 1865, which contrasted Dunlop's grave in Australia with that of his father in Ireland. A rare description of her natural surroundings, with accompanying prose notes, which leave one regretting she did not write more in this vein, can be found in "Erin Dheelish", published in the *Empire* on 8 July 1865. Dunlop's use of Irish in a number of her poems, together with her use of local languages in "The Aboriginal Mother" and other poems on Indigenous themes, allowed her to assert a non-English identity even while writing predominantly in English.

The following abbreviations have been used for periodical and other publications in which the poems were originally published, with the dates referring to the years in which Dunlop's poems appeared:

Atl	*Atlas* (1845)
AC	*Australasian Chronicle* (1843)
Aus	*Australian* (1838–40)
AM	"Australian Melodies" (1842–43)
ATCJ	*Australian Town and Country Journal* (1872–73)
BNL	*Belfast News-Letter* (1837)
BPI	*The Ballad Poetry of Ireland* (ed. Charles Gavan Duffy, 1845)
DPJ	*Dublin Penny Journal* (1835)
Emp	*Empire* (1846–69)
IM	*Irish Miscellany* (1858)
MFP	Juvenile notebook, Milson Family Papers – 1810, 1853–1862, SLNSW, MLMSS 7683
Mon	*Month* (1857)
SMH	*Sydney Morning Herald* (1842–43)

The poems are listed in chronological order of either first publication or date of composition for unpublished poems. Notes included with "The Vase" version are reproduced under the relevant poem. This is followed by collations with earlier versions of the poem, which are indicated with reference to line numbers in "The Vase" versions. Explanatory notes provided by me are given at the end of each poem.

Fort Hamilton

The place of the Author's nativity, now in the possession of another family.
"Here are the voices of rocks, – and the bright tumbling of waters." OSSIAN

I

Near the base of those hills,* whose blue tops kiss the skies,
    Stands a mansion embosom'd in trees;
And tho' no lofty dome meets the traveller's eyes,
    Nature's charms to advantage he sees.

II

Here the eye may delightfully visit each scene,
    Which can please a contemplative mind;
Where alternately mountain and vale intervene,
    And in each some grand beauty we find.

III

Oh! how well can I picture from Memory's page!
    Scenes of many an infantine year;
When Fancy's bright beams my light heart could engage,
    And my sorrows were lost in a tear.

IV

Oh! scenes which in fond Recollection still dwell,
    Where life's early morning first smiled:
Cold dews damped my heart when I bade you farewell;
    And sadness then marked me her child!

V

Yes! dearest Fort H! still with rapture I view,
    Thy woodlands and lawns every green,
Where the sweet-scented Eglantine spangl'd with dew,
    And the wild-woven woodbine are seen.

VI

There Carlingford hills roundly bend o'er the deep,
    On whose brink their dark castles still stand,
Where the sea-boy oft fearless hangs o'er the dread steep,
    A full view of the coast to command.

VII

Here *Health*, *Peace*, and *Competence* rule o'er the land,
    Where each social endearment is known;
And rural Simplicity's innocent band,
    Erect in *Killowen* their throne.

VIII

But why should I joy those loved scenes to pourtray,
    When each charm that endeared them is fled? –
When no longer for me the fair flowrets bloom gay.
    E'en the *name* is low laid with the dead.

IX

Ah! 'twas Mem'ry that bade me awaken the strain,
    Which so long had forgotten to flow;
Yet each pleasing sensations she mingles with pain,
    And delights in augmenting my woe.

Then adieu dear Fort H! *Nature's* favorite retreat,
Where her charms bloom luxuriantly wild; –
Yet reluctantly sad the farewell I repeat,
    To those charms ever dear to thy child,

And thou, dearly loved! for a season adieu,
    Fairest flowret of Albion's blest clime:
May the virtues that find a protector in you,
    Their patroness hail thee thro time!

Fort Hamilton – March 1810 *Evelina*
* Fort-Hamilton is situated at the base of the wildly romantic hills of Killowen; on the beautiful Bay of Carlingford.

Copy-text: MFP

Collated states: None.

For discussion of Eliza Hamilton Dunlop's juvenile poems and her childhood at Fort Hamilton, see Anna Johnston this volume.

'Morning' on Rostrevor Mountains

'Tis morning! from their heather-bed –
    The curling mists arise,
And circling, dark *Slieve-dhonard's* head
    Ascend the drowsy skies:
'Tis morning, and beside *Cloch-mhor* –
    In solitude I stand,
A stranger on my natal shore;
    And this, my father-land!

Rostrevor! each illumin'd line
    Of early life's romance!
Within this beauteous page of thine,
    Lies mirrored to my glance:
Clonallen's spire – *Rossetta's* shades,
    From classic *Arno's-Vale* –
To *Ballyedmond's* groves and glades;
    Land of my homage, hail!

Morning the beautiful – the bold,
    Hath left his ocean-bride,
And from her couch of wavy gold
    Comes forth in regal pride.
Ah me! I've seen that crown of rays,
    As gallantly put on.
And watched thy robe of crimson haze –
    O'er other waters thrown.

+ Rocked, on the billowey bed that heaves –
    Beneath the burning Line –
I've marked the far horizon weave –
    Its purple threads with thine!
And hail'd in all their pride of birth,
    Thy purest lustres given,
To gladden scenes more fair than Earth;
    The boundless Sea! and Heaven!

Where the wild Emu leads her brood –
    Across the trackless plains,
And lord of Nature's solitude –
    The stately Cedar reigns:
Even there – through Exile's cheerless hours!
    Beneath Australian Skies;
I've lingered amid orange bowers –
    To catch thy scented sighs.

Yes, and where *Gunga's* mighty streams –
    Their sacred waters spread,
I've seen beneath thy worshipped beams,
    Ten thousands bow the head:
And by the Brahmin's funeral pile,
    In that far hemisphere:
Young Morn! Have I not met thy smile –
    Mocking the burning bier!

In Sangor's sickly jungle met!
    And on the arid sand,
Where the dark domes of Jaghernaught's
    Profane Pagodas stand!
Aye met, even 'mid the graveyard gloom
    Piercing the tainted air –
Thy sickening rays! – a marble tomb –
    Engulphs my memory there.

Once, high o'er Afric's southern seas,
    In solitary mood:
Within the "glen of silver trees"
    On *Table-hill* I stood.
The fresh free breeze, the morning beam,
    The vapour-crested brow –
Of Caffre-holland; as a dream –
    All, come before me now.

Again adown that deep ravine,
I gaze on fruit and flower:
A labyrinth maze of silky green
A many-tinted bower.
Tall *aloes* crown the rocky steep,
Pomegranate blossoms spread;
And the *umkobas'* branches sweep –
Across the torrent's bed!

Blushes yon *crassula*, as when
Its scarlet blossoms lay –
In the *wildfig*, or *sumach* glen;
That looks on Table-bay!
And bearing up by *Roben* Isle
From farthest India's shore,
That Ship – false dreams! ye but beguile –
I stand beside *Clogh-mhor.**

+ This poem, with the exception of one verse, was published when written, many years since, in the Dublin Penny-journal.

+ I know of no view in nature so impressively grand as that of the rising sun in the calm of tropical seas, beautiful, how exceedingly beautiful! are the different tints of the very richest purple and yellow, varied by deep and glowing crimson – alike spread over an horizon of sea and sky.

The waves around our Ship just breathing and no more than breathing – seem as if afraid of awaking the glorious Luminary who will then quit their ruby couch for the radiant heaven, that blushing smiles his welcome.

He does awake! and that sea, and that heaven, are sparkling with ten-thousand new, and dazzling fires; one long track of brilliantly transparent gold marks his ascent, a moment more and softening drapery falls from the form of the conqueror, and our gaze, is blinded by the glory of his rays. E.H.D.

Note from a journal

*Clogh-mhor i.e. large stone which according to tradition possesses many wondrous attributes, it is affirmed, that any who touch it, at the precise moment that it catches the first beams of the rising sun will obtain their wish, if a pure and proper one. [Note in *Atlas* version reads "CLOCH-MHOR (i.e. large rock) of which it is said that, like the *Fons Solis*, it is warm at the rising of the sun."]

Copy-text: Vase

Collated states: *DPJ* (8 August 1835), as "Morning on Rostrevor Mountains", signed E. (*A*); *Atl* (25 April 1845), as "Morning on Rostrevor Mountain, in Ulster, Ireland", signed Mrs. E.H. Dunlop (*B*); *IM* (9 October 1858), as "Morning on Rostrevor Mountain" (*C*).

11 Deep in this magic page … (*A,C*) 13 Clonallan (*A,C*) 17 Yon orb – the beautiful (*A,C*) 21 Fair sun – I've seen … (*A,C*) 23 And mark'd thy robes … (*A,C*) 27 I've seen where the horizon weaves (*A,C*); I've marked where the horizon weaves (*B*) 32 The sea – the sea and … (*A,C*); The sea! the sea, and … (*B*) 33-40 omitted (*A,C*) 38 Lighted by Austral skies, (*B*) 39 orange flowers (*B*) 47 Sunrise, alas! I've met … (*B*) 49 Sangur's (*A,C*); SAUGUR'S (*B*) 50 Met on … (*A,C*) 51 Jughernaught's (*A,C*) 52 pagoda's (*A,C*) 53 Met in Calcutta's graveyard … (*A,C*) 56 Engulfs (*A,C*) between 56 & 58 line of asterisks (*A*) 59 "Vale of … (*A,B,C*) 61 The fresh free air, … (*A,C*) 64 All pass … (*A,C*) 65 Again, adown the deep … (*A*); Again, adown and deep … (*C*) 70 blooms are spread (*A,C*) 71 umkoba branches … (*A,C*) 73 the crassula, (*A,C*) 77 And ships bear up by Roben's Isle (*A,C*) 79 False dreams, away! ye … (*A,C*) 80 Cloch-mhor. (*A,C*).

For a detailed analysis of this poem, which includes additional explanations of many of its place references, see Wu this volume.

Ballyedmond: Eliza Hamilton was born at Fort Hamilton, Ballyedmond, County Down, Northern Ireland. **silver trees**: *Leucadendron argenteum*, endangered plant species in the family Proteaceae, endemic to a small area of the Cape Peninsula. **umkoba**: The yellow-wood tree, *Afrocarpus latifolius*, now the national tree of South Africa. **crassula**: Genus of succulent plants, many originating from Eastern Cape of South Africa. **sumach**: A flowering plant belonging to the *Rhus* genus.

The Brothers

"It matters not, what distant clime,
    Receives the Body's mouldering clay
For it shall rise when Death and Time
    No more shall triumph."

He knelt beside a brother's bed –
Far in the stranger's land,
And gently raised the dying head,
And clasped the lifeless hand.

Alone he knelt! – oh kindred love!
Thy links are hard to part;
They err, who call thee "Strong as Life".
Stronger than Death thou art.

That precious clay – with what fond care
He laid it, "*earth to earth*,"
    And wept – where pestilential air
And fever-fangs have birth.

    Wept o'er his dead! oh not for those
Whom home, and friendship, cheers,
To taste, or tell the bitter source
Of a lone Exile's tears.

Grief barbed its arrows, to destroy
To slay, *yet not divide* –
That, young and fair, and noble boy
Rests, by his brother's side.

* At Vicksburg, on the Mississippi on the 7th and 30th Sept. – 1836 Samuel, aged 23, and William aged 25 years the second and eldest sons of A. Dunlop, of Priestsland, Esq., Co. of Antrim, Ireland.

Copy-text: Vase

Collated states: *BNL* (3 Jan 1837) as "Inscribed to the Memory of Two Brothers", signed E.D.H. and dated Coleraine, 26th Dec. 1836 (*A*); *Aus* (25 Nov 1838) as "Songs of an Exile – No. 3", signed E.D.H., Penrith (*B*); *Atl* (17 May 1845) as "The Brothers" by Mrs E.H. Dunlop (*C*).

1 "They were lovely in their lives". (*B*); "They were lovely in their lives, and in death they were not divided". (*C*). 9 Alone he knelt! (*B, C*) 10 *Stronger ... art* (*C*) 17 not for us (*A*) 18 kindred cheers (*B*) 21 Death barbed his (*B*) Death barbed its (*C*) 22 "yet not divide (*B*); "To slay but not divide" (*C*) 23 A young – a fair – a noble (*B*); That true, and brave, and gentle (*C*) 24 Sleeps by (*B*) 25 (*B*) reprints a slightly different note, attributed to the "Belfast News Letter" although somewhat different to the one that appeared there on 3 June 1837, which included the information that the dead brothers were "nephews to Mr. D. Dunlop, Coleraine, Ireland".

See Jason R. Rudy this volume for discussion of this poem. The epigraph comes from the final stanza of "The Stranger's Funeral" by Alpha, published in *The Sacred Lyre: Comprising Poems, Devotional, Moral and Preceptive* (Glasgow, 1824). The last line originally ended "triumph o'er decay".

The Dead

She was – although my lip denied
    Veiling the secret in my heart:
She was my dearest one – my pride
    For whom these anguish'd tear drops start.

Young gladsome footsteps throng around
    And mirthful voices fill my ear!
Her, joyous voice, hath left no sound,
    Her, bounding step, I may not hear!

Bright wavy ringlets, by my knee
    Like floating sunbeams come and go:
But one, shorn tress, alone I see!
    And whence it came too well I know.

Copy-text: Vase

Collated states: *Aus* (22 Nov 1838) as "Songs of an Exile – (No. 2)", signed E.H. Dunlop and with the note "Adapted to the music of *I stood among the glittering throng*".

1 SHE was – yet have I oft denied (*A*) 3 SHE (*A*) 3 those bitter tear drops (*A*) 5 Now happy voices fill mine ear (*A*) 6 And dancing footsteps throng around (*A*) 7 Yet hers amid them all I hear! (*A*) 8 A sound of music from the ground (*A*) 9 Still MY lorn spirit, seeks the clay, (*A*) 10 Where her young limbs in darkness rest – (*A*) 11 While her's in light of endless day, (*A*) 12 Reposes on a Saviour's breast. (*A*).

On the Dunlops' daughter Jane who died in Ireland in the 1830s aged eight, see Anna Johnston this volume.

The Aboriginal Mother*

Oh! hush thee, hush my baby – I may not tend thee yet,
Our forest-home is distant far, and midnight's star is set:
Now hush thee, or the pale-faced men will hear thy piercing wail
And what would then thy mother's tears, or feeble strength avail!

Ah! could thy little bosom that mother's torture feel,
Or could'st thou know – thy father lies struck down by English steel;
Thy tender form would wither, like the *Kniven* on the sand,
And the Spirit of my perish'd Tribe would vanish from our land.

For thy young life – my precious, I fly the field of blood!
Else had I, for my Chieftain's sake, defied them where they stood;
But basely bound my woman arm, no weapon might it wield:
I could but cling round him I loved, to make my heart a shield.

I saw my firstborn treasure lie headless at my feet
The *gooroo* on this hapless breast, in his life's stream is wet!
But thou! I've snatch'd thee from their sword, the stroke it aimed at thee
Severed the binding cord, and gave the coward-boon, to flee.

To flee my Babe, but whither, without my friend, my guide?
The blood which was our strength is shed – he is not by my side.
Thy Sire? Oh never, never can *Toonbacra* hear thy cry.
My bold and stately mountain-bird! I thought not he could die.

Now who will teach thee, dearest, to poise the shield, and spear,
To wield the *koopin*, and to throw the boommerang void of fear?
To breast the river in its might – the mountain-tracks to tread:
The echoes in my homeless heart – reply, the dead – the dead!

Oh! ever must these murmurs, like the ocean torrent flow:
The *parted-voice* comes back no more, to cheer our lonely woe,
Even in the region of our Tribe – beside our mountain streams,
'Tis but a hollow symphony – from the shadow-land of dreams.

Nay hush thee dear, for weary and faint I bear thee on:
His name is on thy gentle lips – my child! My child! he's gone
Gone to the golden plains that lie above the rolling cloud
To bring thy people's murder-cry, before the Christian's God.

Yes! o'er the stars that guide us, he bears my slaughter'd boy,
To show their God how treacherously those stranger-men destroy;
How hands of whitemen pledged in peace piled high the gory pyre
Of dying shrieks of the *Myal* race, on that fatal ridge of fire.

*This lament is set to sweetly impressive music by Nathan, the composer of "Byron's Hebrew melodies".

Copy-text: Vase

Collated states: *Aus* (13 Dec 1838) as "Songs of an Exile (No. 4) The Aboriginal Mother (From Myall's Creek)", signed E.H.D., with stanzas made up of eight shorter lines (A); *SG* (19 Oct 1841) as "THE ABORIGINAL MOTHER". With the epigraph: "Only one female and her child got away from us". – *Evidence before the Supreme Court*. (B); *AM* (1842) as "The Aboriginal Mother; An Australian Melody" (C). 2 forest-land (B) 5 Oh, could'st (A) could … anguish (B, C) 7 kniven (B, C) 9 fields (B, C) 12 his shield (B, C) 14 goro (A) gooroo (B, C) his mother's breast … with his (B, C) 15 And thou! I snatch'd thee … It harmless pass'd by thee! (A) 16 But clave the binding cords – and gave, / Haply, the power to flee. (A) 17 To flee! my babe (A) our friend, our guide (B, C) 19 *Toon Bakra* hear our cry (A) can *Toonbahra* (B, C) 20 my stately (B, C) 22 and to throw ... *boommerring* (A) 23 in its height (A) 24 echoes of (A) 24 And ever must their murmur/ Like an ocean (A) For ever (B, C) 26 *The parted voice comes never back* (A) 27 E'en in (B, C) summer streams (A) 28 'Tis as … (B, C) In the (A) 29 Oh hush thee (A) 30 *His name* (A) 31 Gone o'er the golden fields that lie/Beyond (A) 32 *To bring thy people's murder cry /Before the Christian's God* (A) 33 He brings (A) slaughtered (B) 34 The stranger (A) 35 To tell how hands in friendship pledged / Piled high the fatal pire; (A) To tell of hands, the cruel hands, that piled the fatal pyre (B, C) 36 To tell – to tell of the gloomy ridge; /And the *stockmen's human fire*. (A) To show our blood on Myab's ridge, our bones in the stockmen's fire. (B, C).

Kniven: "A sweet purple berry", note in *AM* version. *gooroo*: "An opossum cloak", note in *AM* version. *Toonbacra*: Eagle tail. See Jim Wafer this volume for further discussion of the Indigenous words used in this poem. *koopin*: "Battle-axe", note in *AM* version.

"The Vase" version includes a long note attributed to the *Monitor* for 19 November 1838:

In the evidence given in the Supreme Court Sydney, New South Wales to the massacre of the *Myal-Creek* Tribe of Aborigines, Edward Day Police Magistrate states "I went accompanied to where the fire had been. The place appeared to have occupied a space of fourteen yards in circumference, we found fragments of bones, a rib of a child, jaw bones of human beings, and human teeth." W. Holls states, "I saw several heads with the flesh on; but I could not recognize the features of any; there were female heads among them. I cannot say by what means the heads were taken off, but the hair was not singed on *some* of them, I endeavored to count the children's skulls, but the smell prevented me, the Natives had not been on the offensive in any way – The fire had been made on the side of a ridge – The Native-dogs had pulled the bodies about and great numbers of Eagle-hawks were hovering over them." G. Anderson states, "I heard the Blacks crying and moaning when they were tied, their hands were tied together, two little *Boys jumped into the creek*. One female and Infant escaped".

A different note had been included in the *AM* version of 1842:

In 1838 a tribe of *Balka Gal* (i.e. a mountain tribe), to the number of seventy, were lured by convict stockmen, shepherds, and hut keepers (eleven of whom were brought to trial), to congregate at a cattle station on Myall Creek, outside the territory of New South Wales; their *gins* (wives) were interfered with, and it was stated by one of the murderers that the blacks "*threatened*" him. No other cause was adduced for a massacre thus spoken of by Judge Burton: – "The circumstances of the case presented a fearful barbarity, which perhaps had rarely been equalled. Several human beings had been *tied together*, and shot, and cut, and burned in the most barbarous manner. They had been peaceably encamped for the night when they were driven away to be slaughtered." – *Charge to the Jury*. Charles Reid sworn – "I saw the place where the fire had been. I saw bodies and heads lying about, but I walked away as quick as I could. I knew this tribe; they were very peaceable, and had been about Mr. Wiseman's and Mr. McIntyre's stations for some time." Mr. Hobbs sworn – "I knew a little boy, we called him Charley; his father and his mother were with their tribe at Myall Creek when I proceeded to the Big River. *There were more than forty or fifty*. The men went away every morning hunting, and returned with opossums and other food, enough to keep them; I sometimes gave them food … The footmarks I speak of were of persons who appeared to have been rolling logs to the fire. Unless a person went close up, and stirred about the ashes, he could not see the bones and sculls [sic]; I judged by the size of the heads as to their being adults or children. About twenty sculls were collected, men, women, and children. One woman escaped."

The Irish Nurse, to a Foster Child

Air, "The foggy-dew".

Your eyes have the twin-star's light; mo croidhe
Mo Cuisle-Inghean, ban;
And your swan-like neck is dear to me,
"Mo Varia" oig aluin:
And dear is your tiny foot so light,
And your milk-white lady hand;
And your hair! oh fair! as the threads of light
That were spun in the rainbow's band.

No more may your voice with its silver-sound,
Come like music in a dream!
Or your heart's sweet laugh, gush merrily 'round:
Like the dancing mountain stream.
But green! ever green be the distant shore
Where you bloom like the "ubhae tree";
Mo Varia astore, we meet no more –
Yet the pulse of my heart is with thee.

For "Mo Varia", the pillar'd halls are high
Where *Ullin's* splendors shine!
And all too proud for the humble sigh –
Your heart would send back to mine!
Like a misty wreath on a craggy steep
Keeping watch for the rising sun
I lonely mourn, and watch; and weep:
Mo chreach! Mo thruaidh! och on!

Irish	English
Mo. chroidhe	i.e. My heart
Mo. Cuisle Inghean Ban	i.e. My darling fair daughter
Mo. Varia og aluin	– My young Lady Mary
Mo. Varia astore	– My Mary dear
Ubhal	– apple
Mo Chreach! Etc. etc.	Expressing the grief of a breaking heart

Copy-text: Vase

Collated states: *Aus* (12 Jan 1839) as "Songs of an Exile – No 5. The Irish Mother", signed E.H.D., November 30, 1838 (*A*); *BPI* (1845) as "The Emigrant Mother", anonymous (*B*).

1–2 Note translates Irish as "My pulse, my white daughter". (*B*) 4 *Mo Cailin og alain*; (*A*); *Mo caillin og alain*; (*B*) 5 your fairy foot … (*A*, *B*) 6 And your dazzling milk-white hand (*A*, *B*) 7 And your hair! it's a thread of the golden light (*A*, *B*) 8 That was spun … (*A*, *B*) 9 *"Oh! green be the fields"* of my native shore (*A*, *B*) 10 Where you bloom, like a young rose-tree; (*A*, *B*) 11 *Mo* VARIA *astore* – we meet no more! (*A*, *B*) 12 But the pulse of my heart's with thee. (*A*, *B*) 13 No more may your voice with its silver sound, (*A*, *B*) 14 Come, like music in a dream! (*A*, *B*) 15 Or your heart's sweet laugh, ring merrily round, (*A*, *B*) 16 Like the gush of the summer's stream. (*A*, *B*) 17 O! *Mo* VARIA, the stately halls … (*A*, *B*) 18 Where ERIN'S … (*A* ,*B*) 19 Yet their harps shall swell to the wailing cry (*A*, *B*) 20 That my heart sends forth to thine. (*A*, *B*) 21 For an Exile's heart is a fountain deep, (*A*, *B*) 22 Far hid from the gladsome sun – (*A*, *B*) 23 Where the bosom's yearning ne'er may sleep: (*A*, *B*) 24 * Mo thruaidh! Mo chreach! Och on! (*A*); note translates this as "My pity! my plunder! och on!" (*B*).

* The last line is the *Irish-ery* of a broken heart, of which there can be no adequate translation. The name *Varia*, is MARY. The other Irish words are expressions of fondness for which the English tongue offers no sounds half so tender.

I Bless Thy Shores

(Air, Peggy Bawn)

I bless thy shores – my native land –
'Mid nature's parting strife,
I hail thee of the powerful wand
Which moves the pulse of life.
Alas! The shadows of thy hills –
Lie dark across my heart;
And the gurgle of thy gushing rills –
Can never thence depart.

I know that household hearths are cold;
That my kindred's graves are green;
I know I know, the Churchyard mould –
Tells where my race have been.
But organ-peals are sounding there –
And Choral Anthems swell!
There the holy voice of Christian prayer –
And sounds of the Sabbath-bell.

Oh birth-rights of my Island home,
What dreary doom is mine!
Unblest 'mid Austral-wilds to roam –
A slave at Mammon's Shrine;
What weary lot – to count each link –
Whose rust is on my soul!
To chase life's phantoms; and to sink –
Untimely – at the goal.

Copy-text: Vase

Collated states: *Aus* (7 May 1840) as "Songs of an Exile – No. 8", signed from "Government House, Emu Plains, New South Wales" (*A*) 2 parting nature's (*A*) 6 Are thrown (*A*) 7 thy gushing (*A*) 8 Doth never (*A*) 9 I know that (*A*) 15 Where the holy (*A*) 16 Ascends with Sabbath (*A*) 18 dreary lot (*A*) 21 weary doom (*A*) 22 on my soul (*A*) 23 Thus woo … phantoms but (*A*).

Go Dia leat Slan

The fragrant west-wind sighs –
Through stately orange-bowers:
    And my natal star; from midnight skies
Woos the pale *night-blowing flowers.

    Meet hour, for minstrel strains –
On the perfumed breeze to dwell:
    Meet time for the Harp of Emu=plains
To breathe its sad "farewell".

    Farewell! sweeps thrilling round
Like the rush of withered leaves,
    And our empty halls send forth the sound
O'er all the lofty eaves!

    But thoughts of long-past-years –
Unnerve the minstrel's hand!
    And the mute farewell; of gushing tears
Falls cold in a foreign land.

* *Oenothera biennis* of the class Octandria.

Copy-text: Vase

Collated states: *Aus* (13 Oct 1840) as "Songs of an Exile. *Go Dia Lest Slan.* – (Irish Song.)" (*A*) 1 fragrant and (*A*) 2 Thro' stately (*A*) 3 natal star (*A*) 7 harp of Emu Plains (*A*) 8 a sad (*A*) 9 It sweeps in murmurings 'round (*A*) 10 wither'd (*A*) 11 And empty halls give back … (*A*) 12 From all the lofty eaves (*A*) 13 But a grief too deep for tears (*A*) 14 Unnerves (*A*) 15 And the sad 'farewell' of other years (*A*) 16 Is breathed in the stranger's land (*A*)

Go Dia leat Slan: "Goodbye" or "farewell" in Irish. **Oenothera biennis**: The evening primrose.

The Eagle Chief – melodized by *Nathan*

Hark to the sound – along the grey hill side,
Yon gladsome step – now in the dusky glen;
   He comes! he comes! my brave – my pride!
   My swift one comes again:
     Light, light, ye cedars! pine trees burn –
     Spread wide *Bibija's* glad return.

Proud-bounding dancers, fill your honey-shells!
Drink to the bold, beneath our own bright sky;
   Drink to the plains where the *Emu* dwells,
   Where the *Ibis* floats on high.
     Light, light, ye cedars! pine trees burn:
     Spread wide Bibija's glad return.

Wave high his glancing plumes! To him you bring
The lustrous +gem, that lights the spirit's bower!
   Sons of the land; laud loud your king,
   In our festal midnight hour!
     Light, cedars! light, and pine trees burn.
     Spread wide my Eagle-Chief's return.

* Bibija, name given to the Falcon-Hawk by the Tribe of the *Wollombi*. The bird is of snow-white plumage it is a noble looking, strong and bold bird.

+ The *Braves*, *Kings*, or *boldest fighters* of a Tribe amongst the various aborigines wear in a secret nook of their girdle a piece of crystal on which none of their females are ever permitted to look, it has been described to me as "one bit of the sun's eye" same as "make every body shut eyes when it looks at them".

I have pray'd for a peep at one, worn by the Old Wollombi King Boni, who not refusing absolutely yet evaded compliance, by sundry "wreathed smiles" and mysterious sentences, implying a secret and indefinable affinity between "Ladies eyes" and "*bad luck* belong it." To my hibernian ear that single phrase comprised a host of argument quite powerful in detering from any further effort to obtain view of the magic gem, which is I believe either a symbol of the right to govern; or else an object of reverence, as being to the privileged holder, a means of communication with a great mysterious Power, whose anger they dread.

Copy-text: Vase

Collated states: *SG* (21 Apr 1842), as "The Eagle Chief" (*A*) *AM* 1842 (*B*) 1 green hill side (*A*, *B*) 3 my bride (*A*) 5 Light, light the pine! Let cedar burn; (*A*, *B*) 6 To greet Maliyan's* glad return! (*A*, *B*) 7 Bid joyous dancers fill the honied shell, (*A*, *B*) 8 our own blue sky (*A*, *B*) 9 Drink to the land (*A*, *B*) 10 And the Ibis (*A*, *B*) 11 Light, light the pine! Let cedar burn; (*A*, *B*) 12 To greet Maliyan's glad return! (*A*, *B*) 13 Wave high the glancing plume – and proudly bring (*A*, *B*) 14 That dazzling gem+ which lights (*A*, *B*) 15 Ye sons of the soil, proclaim your King (*A*, *B*) 16 In the festal (*A*, *B*) 17 Light, light the pine! Let cedar burn; (*A*, *B*) 18 To greet my Eagle Chief's return! (*A*, *B*) 19 *The Maliyan, or great Eagle Hawk. (*A*) 21ff +Many variations in wording of Dunlop's note on this special "gem" although substance is much the same. (*A*)

The Star of the South*

Hail Star of the South! fair Australia advance,
With thy soft flowing tresses, thy proud eagle glance,
Happy homes and free altars – broad-lands and bright skies.
All, are thine! all are thine – star of beauty, arise!

Advance, for the Sybil hath written thy name,
And Futurity opens the volume of fame
Wit, valour, and virtue, the heart's treasured ties
All, are thine, all are thine: fair Australia, arise.

Advance! bid the righthands of fellowship join
Let faith, be the plummet – and truth, be the line
There are rights we could die for, and blessings we prize
They are thine! they are thine! Star of beauty, arise!

* Published in Nathan's "Australian Melodies".

Copy-text: Vase

Collated states: SMH (30 Aug 1842) (*A*); *AM* 1842 (*B*) 1 Australasia advance (*A, B*)
2 Advance with thy (*B*) 8 Australasia arise (*A, B*) 9 let the right hand (*A*) let the
right hands (*B*) 10 Bid faith (*A, B*) 12 Australasia arise (*A, B*).

The Aboriginal Father, a translation of a *Maneroo* dirge versified also for I. Nathan

The Shadow, on thy brow my child:
    A mist o'er a clear Lagoon,
Steals on with presage – dim and wild;
    Of the *death-god's* direful doom.

Our Tribes are falling by their streams,
    Each fount, that fed, is dry!
And the White-man's fire sends forth its gleams
    O'er the *batwan* where they die.

And thou beloved! the last – the first –
    Green branch, of a withering tree
The Stranger's mock will drown the burst
    Of my Spirit's Lament o'er thee.

Copy-text: Vase

Collated states: *AM* 1843, as "The Aboriginal father, a native song of the Maneroo Tribe … versified from the original words … by Mrs. E. H. Dunlop" (*A*) 2 Like a mist (*A*) 4 *death-clouds** (*A*) 5 Our Tribes droop by each native stream (*A*) 6 Where the founts which have fed them lie (*A*) 7 And white man's fire … gleam (*A*) 8 *Bat-wan** (*A*) 9 And thou my boy! (*A*) 10 Green leaf of a smouldering tree (*A*) 11 A stranger's eye will crush (*A*) 12 Of a Warrior's (*A*)

"Australian Melodies" version includes the notes: "Death-clouds 'The unseen Power' has many names and forms, and is a Spirit of evil only: living within 'Wheeguon-Eura' – Fire-clouds. Batwan-mian The water of the creek."

Dirge of Rosetta Nathan

Way for my grief – give way!
Shroud not that beauteous form!
I would but kiss the brow that yesterday
With life's young pulse was warm:
    And, now – oh God! 'tis clay.

Those lips unclose no more –
Even tho' I name her name;
Oh! broken heart, hath that rich tide ebb'd o'er,
And I yet live – the same?
    Come back sweet voice of yore.

Back to me from the dead!
Doth voice of love dwell there?
No, no – I am bereaved –
Thus from my head I rend the flowing hair!
Go – leave me with my dead:
    Give way, for my despair!

Cutting from newspaper describing Rosetta Nathan's death is pasted in below poem: "On Saturday morning, at the residence of her father, Elizabeth street, in the sixteenth year of her age, Rosetta Nathan, daughter of J. [sic] Nathan, Esq. This highly accomplished, amiable, and virtuous young-lady, who was but a few hours ago the pride and delight of her family and friends, calmly slept in death after two short days' illness, leaving her afflicted family inconsolable for their sudden but irreparable loss".

Copy-text: Vase

Collated states: *SMH* (25 Apr 1843), as "Rosetta Nathan's Dirge", signed E.H.D. Wollombi, April 18 (*A*). 3 which yesterday (*A*) 13 None – none (*A*) 14 see from … the waving hair (*A*) 16 to my despair (*A*).

Native Poetry

Song 1.   Nung-ngnun.
Nge a runba wonung bulkirra umbilinto bulwarra;
Pital burra kultan wirripang buntoa

Song 2.   Nung-ngnun.
Nge a runba turrama-berrambo, burra kilkoa,
Kurri wi, raratoa yella walliko
Yulo moane, woinyo, birung bulliko.

Song 3.   Nung-ngnun.
Nge a runba, kan wullung, makoro, kokein.
Mipparai, kekul, wimbi murring kirrika:
Nge a runba, murra kè-en kulbun kulbun Murrung.

There is a God of Poesy, *Wallatu*, who composes music, and who, without Temple, Shrine or, Statue is as universally acknowledged as if his oracles were breathed by *Belus* or *Osiris*. He comes in dreams! and transports the favoured individual wrapped in visioned slumber, to some bright, warm hill; where he is inspired with the rare and Supernatural Gift. Songs in general are a few words of praise, or anger, often repeated in a variety of cadence.

Native Song (the foregoing) translated and versified.

Our home, is the gibber-gunyah,
    Where hill joins hill, on high;
Where the Turruma, and berrambo,
    Like twisted serpents lie!
And the rushing of wings, as the *Wangas* pass,
Sweeps the *Wallaby's* prints, from the glistening grass.

Ours, are the Makoro gliding,
    Deep in the shady pool:
For our spear is sure, – and the prey secure –
    Kanin, or the bright gherool!
And Lubras sleep by the batoo clear –
That an *Amygest's* track hath never been near.

Ours, is the Koolemon flowing,
    With precious *Kirriku* stored:
And fleet the foot – and keen the eye,
    That tracks the *nukkung's* hoard!
And glances as bright, as the footstep is free
Light our dancers that rest by the karakan tree.

Gibber gunyah – cave in the rock. Turrumu and berramboo i.e. war-arms. Wanga a species of pigeon. Makooroo – fish. amygist – white fellow. Kanin – eel. gherool – mullet. bato – water. Kirriku – honey. Nukkung – wild bee. Karrakan – oak tree.

Copy-text: Vase

Collated states: SMH, 11 Oct 1848 (*A*). 7 birung poro bulliko (*A*) 9 rumba (*A*) 10 Mip-pa-rai (*A*) 11 mura (*A*) 15–17 transports the individual to some sunny hill, where he is inspired with the supernatural gift. (*A*) 22 sleeping serpents (*A*) 29 Our lubras ... bato (*A*) 30 the Amygest's (*A*) 31 koolema (*A*) 34 That seeks the (*A*) 35 And the glances are bright, and the footsteps are free (*A*) 36 When we dance in the shade of the karakun tree (*A*)

For discussion of this poem, see Jim Wafer, "Ghost-Writing for Wulatji: Incubation and Re-Dreaming as Song Revitalisation Practices", in *Recirculating Songs: Revitalising the Singing Practices of Indigenous Australia*, ed. Jim Wafer and Myfany Turpin (Canberra: Asia-Pacific Linguistics, Australian National University, 2017), 193–256 and Anna Johnston this volume.

Ode to Gold – 1851

Avaunt! pale meteor of the mine –
Perfidious Sprite! our steps misleading –
To Mighty Moloch's demon-shrine!
Where human hearts lie – pierced and bleeding.
Vain yellow dross! when Time was young
And Earth was cursed for Adam's sinning;
Volcanic thunders, echoing rung,
To herald thy unbless'd beginning!

Forth issuing, from thy caverned bed;
With arms around the globe extending,
A thirst for blood – how early shed!
While "Sin and Death" thy spells were blending!
Blending the spells that since have been
Warring with man's, sublimer, Spirit:
Chimeras! shapeless – and unseen!
Born, of the curse, thy powers inherit

And craving still, like that "Dead Lake"
That gulps old Jordan's sacred river,
Not seas of liquid ore would slake
The burning thirst – insatiate ever!
Yes! subtle Fiend! I know thee well,
Yet deemed not, till I saw thee gleaming,
That "Spirit of the Hartz" could dwell
Where fair Australia's bowers were beaming.

I dreamt not, of thy twinkling ray
Or glimmering lamp of Tomb-fire lighted
Deeming, afar, thy kindred clay; –
In Californian gloom benighted!
Delusive form, what would'st thou here?
Where plenty weds with peaceful-quiet.
Alas! thy Tocsin fills my ear – !
And Ravens croak, and Vultures riot!

Copy-text: Vase

Collated states: SMH (27 Feb 1852), as "Ode to Gold", signed E.H. Dunlop, Mulla
Villa, Wollombi, 1852 (*A*) 9 cavened bed (*A*)

"Spirit of the Hartz": In Walter Scott's "The Fortunes of Martin Waldeck" (1813),
a German man steals gold from a demon in the Hartz mountains, an action which

eventually leads to his death. Like others at the time, Dunlop feared the problems the discovery of gold in New South Wales and Victoria in 1851 may bring to the colonies.

To My Friends Inscribed to the dearest of any.

"Turns to the touch of joy or woe, but, turning, trembles too.
So shakes the needle, and so stands the pole."

Friends, do ye think – thus far apart,
    That still, to homeward feeling true,
The faithful magnet of my heart
    Its trembling index turns to you?

Friends, do you think what memories press!
    Thick-coming thoughts, that erst had power
With rainbow-tints, each hour to bless,
    'Circling your minstrel in her bower.

Say do you think – in days of yore
    What happy influences bound
Our day-dreams; by *Port Stewart* shore?
    And on the *Causeway's* classic ground!

Rostrevor – Carlingford – Killo'en –
    Proud *Down*, and *Antrim's* silvery coast!
Alas, my world hath changed its zone,
    Even dear familiar stars are lost.

Bright Vega, here no sweetness sends!
    But, fairest of the nightly train;
The *Southern-Cross* above me bends,
    Pointing my homeward course in vain.

Friends, do ye think what tears are wept
    For Christian voice or hallowed fane!
Throughout the hundreds Sabbaths kept,
    On lonely-rock and silent plain!

What longings for our old church bell,
    'Till o'erstrained thoughts the heart beguile!
And on my ear its tollings swell,
    As though I trod the sounding aisle.

True, nature's bounties largely flow:
    Her rarest treasures crown our care!
But oh! what aching void may grow
    'Mid blessings! it were bliss to share.

Then think my friends; when poet's strain
    Sings of the vine and orange grove.
That one, beyond the southern main
    Looks back to Erin's links of love.

Copy-text: Vase

Collated states: *Emp* (21 July 1857) as "To Home and Friends", signed ELIZA HAMILTON DUNLOP, Mulla Villa, N.S.W. (*A*) 1 First line of epitaph omitted (*A*) 4 to home-land (*A*) 7 Friends, think you oft, what mem'ries press? (*A*) 9 With Sardius tints (*A*) 10 thy minstrel (*A*) 14 "the Causeway's" (*A*) 15–16 Placenames not in italics (*A*) 19 VEGA (*A*) 20 fairest of Night's gorgeous train (*A*) 21 SOUTHERN-CROSS (*A*) my Northward course (*A*) 23 Could you but think (*A*) 25 Sabbaths (*A*) 27 that old Church-bell (*A*) 20 sacred aisle (*A*) 31 Here Nature's bounties (*A*) 32 Her fairest (*A*) 37 Southern Main (*A*) 38 Erin's links (*A*).

See Katie Hansord this volume for discussion of the epigraph and other references in this poem.

Port Stewart: Small town on the north coast of Northern Ireland, near the Giant's Causeway. **Rostrevor – Carlingford – Killo'en**: Killowen, County Down, Northern Ireland, is a small village near the town of Rostrevor and on the shore of Carlingford Lough. **Vega**: The brightest star in the northern constellation of Lyra.

The Mulla, or Wollombi creek, New-South-wales

> I sate as was my trade:
>> Under the foot of *Mole*; that mountain hoar,
>> Keeping my sheep amongst the coolly shade
>> Of the green Alders, by the Mulla's shore.
> Spenser, 1596

Deep, silent water – water dark and still,
Bowered in the desert, lonely lot is thine!
For thee, no courtly Bard, essays his skill
At thy cool fount inspired – "sweet Mulla mine".

But thou hast melodies 'mid laughing leaves,
Of blossom'd myrtles, on each craggy steep:
Sweet Sylvan sounds, far up amongst the caves,
Where coy rock-lilies, throned – their proud dominion keep.

Shaded by countless broidered canopies,
Clematis, silvery-wreathed, festoons thy course:
And girt with odorous gums, and radiant dyes!
Well mayest thou lingering turn – back to thy mountain source.

Slow-winding River! had the Virgin Queen –
Looked through the mighty telescope of Time!
And at the Globe's bright boundaries have seen
The Mulla's emerald banks, in sunny southern clime;

Would clustering olives, ripening on thy brink –
Would grapes, or golden limes have charm'd her eye
Or would she of the *Poet's Alders* think,
Where, "*Mole* with all his mountain woods", was nigh?

Thy name, dusk water, would it cause a start,
Or fling a shadow o'er the Sovereign's brow?
Her valorous Raleigh! Spenser's broken heart!
Well might She image both, in thy dim grottos now?

Soft thoughts come stealing – as you calmly glide
They waft me to fair bowers, beyond the sea;
And murmuring Bann; in sparkling summer pride
Would half the homage claim, my heart, bestows on thee.

25th Septbr 1849.

Copy-text: Vase

Collated states: *Mon* (Dec 1857) as "The 'Mulla,' or Creek of Wollombi". By E.H.D. (A) 10 'mongst laughing leaves, (A) 14 'broider'd canopies, (A) 16 orient dyes, (A) 17 may'st thou ling'ring turn … (A) 18 slow, winding river, could the … (A) 19 Have grasped the magic telescope … (A) 23 charmed that eye? (A) 29 thy deep channel now. (A) 30 Soft thoughts … (A) 34 Mulla Villa. (A) The *Month* version includes the note:

* *Mulla*, in the Irish language, signifies the patena of a chalice or a height-top, or summit, as *Mulluige na Sleibte*, the tops of the mountains. The letter L is one of the only three consonants in the language which are ever written double. Mrs. Hall, who has, as an Irish Tourist, so gracefully rescued from oblivion much of the beautiful – eulogizes "the Mulla, rendered classic by the pen of Spencer, and by numberless fascinations, influencing his muse in many of his most sublime descriptions of scenery." Sir Walter Raleigh, as well as Spencer, held in this neighborhood, by patent from Elizabeth, large grants of Earl Desmond's forfeited estates; and there, from 1596 until 1598, the most tranquil years in the eventful lives of both rolled away. But rapine and bloodshed were rife in the Tyrone Wars – and, the tragical catastrophe of *Kilcoleman* still serves "to point a moral." We are aware that the "Faërie Queene" was written in Ireland, and it was believed that the concluding parts were lost in the disastrous fire which left the poet destitute; but a late author says that more than a mere rumor exists for a belief that the "lost books" have been preserved and that the manuscript was in the possession of a Captain Garrett Nagle, within the last fifty years. – E.H.D.

See Jim Wafer this volume for detailed discussion of other references in this poem.

The Two Graves

> "Cut off from the land that bore us,
> Deceived by the land we find:
> The brightest are gone before us,
> And left but blanks behind!"
>   DE WARRIEN.

On her bold northern coast, where the Isle of the West
Owns the last solemn cell of her martyr'd one's rest,
In Benvarden's grey grave-yard, envelop'd in gloom,
His name, and his story, is graven on a tomb:
    Shed a tear on the name, as you look on the date,
    And let sighs ring the requiem of red ninety-eight!

But the fierce reign of terror hath passed from the land,
With the clang of the bayonet, and glare of the brand,
And he sleeps where young shamrocks make verdant the sod,
Near the homes and the hills where his forefathers trod.
    Oh better that grave in our Emerald Isle,
    Than a long life of anguish in dreary exile.

But alas! *for the love of that Patriot* – laid
Where branching acacias are spreading a shade,
In "the land of the stranger," a deep narrow bed
Hides tho woe-stricken heart, and the time-silver'd head,
    In that love-guarded area, enclosed from the crowd
    The truthful and trustful lies sealed in his shroud.

Tombs parted as wide as the span of the sphere;
Yet father and son have had widowhood's tear!
Predestined in life to bend "under the rod," &
"Through much tribulation" they passed to their God:
    And star's rays fall bright on the homes of their rest,
    From the "Cross of the South," and the "Lyre of the West."

ELIZA H. DUNLOP
Mulla Villa, N. S. W., March 21, 1865.

Copy-text: *Emp* (15 Apr 1865)

Collated states: None.

DE WARRIEN: This popular quotation has been attributed to several authors but seems originally to have come from a poem called "Indian Revelry" by W.F. Thompson, published in India in the *Bengal Annual*, ed. David Lester Richardson (Calcutta, 1835), 123–25 where it appears as "Cut off from the land that bore us,/Betrayed by the land we find,/Where the brightest have gone before us, /And the dullest remain behind". **red ninety-eight:** Captain William Dunlop, David Dunlop's father, had taken part in the unsuccessful Rebellion of United Irishmen in 1798. He was later captured and hanged in punishment. (See De Salis, 12.) **sealed in his shroud:** David Dunlop died in 1863 and was buried at Wollombi.

Erin Dheelish

The bell birds ring their silvery call,
    Clear tinkling 'midst the myrtle glades;
The cicada† hath cast its pall,
    And myriads throng the cedar shades;
The sullen Mulla murmurs bye,
    Reflecting mountain, crag, and tree,
Enchanting scene! then whence the sigh?
    Mo Erin dheelish gra machree.
        Erin mo cushla, avourneen dheelish!
        A yea yeelish gra machree.
        Enchanting scene, then whence the sigh.
        Mo Erin dheelish gra machree.

With ruby breast and emerald wing,
    The gorgeous lory flashes near;
Sweet mocking birds their carols sing,
    Till hearts lie listening in the ear.
Spinosa's‡ odours load the air,
    The fragrance stays the wandering bee.
Why must I sigh in land so fair?
    Mo Erin dheelish gra machree.
        Erin mo cushla, vourneen dheelish,
        A yea yeelish! gra machree!
        Why must I sigh in land so fair?
        Mo Erin dheelish gra machree.

Mulla Villa, Wollombi, New South Wales, 12th May.

* Erin dheelish is written for an old and somewhat plaintive air, published by Edward Bunting in his "Irish Melodies." Mr Bunting, although so eminent, was less talented than our great composer, Sir John Stevenson.
† The cicada septendecim bursts from its shroud, which retains the perfect form of the insect, except the wings. The hollow cast off cover is left adhering to dry branches or rails of fences. The chirp of the cicada is not unpleasing.
‡ The spinosa odorato of Sir T. Mitchell is the most enjoyable and the most lasting perfume of any shrub or flower that I have met with in any land.
E.H.D.

Copy-text: Emp, 8 July 1865, p. 5.

Collated states: None.

Thanks to Katie Hansord, Katie Fleet, Val Noone, Colin Ryan and Greg Byrnes, for translations of the Irish:

> Mo Erin dheelish gra machree
> *Mo Éirinn dhílis, grá mo chroí*
> My dear Ireland, my heart's beloved

> Erin mo cushla, mavourneen dheelish!
> *Éirinn mo chuisle, mo mhuirnín dhílis*
> Beloved Ireland, my dear darling

> A yea yeelish gra machree
> *A Dhia dhílis, grá mo chroí*
> Dear God, My heart's beloved

See Jim Wafer this volume for explanatory notes on Dunlop's notes.

Memories of Maxwell

Author of "Stories of Waterloo", "Dark Lady of Doona", "Hector O'Haloran" etc.
"There take thy stand my spirit – nay – the trance of poesy is o'er."
    Salis.

Fair, as romance, our childhood reappears
With swift-wing'd step amongst the purple heather
Or eager, gazing, down that stream of years
    Where our light shallops held their course together

Appears – like pearls on ice-incrusted spray;
Or feathery snowflakes, on green leaves of holly,
Phantoms of loveliness, that drop away
    As bubbles on the sparkling wine of folly!

Then, even then, when our high mountain top
Might well have seemed the boundary of thy daring
Scorning upon its utmost ridge to stop
    You rushed, where other peaks their brows were rearing

How buoyant, frank, and fearless, was thy youth
Onward! still onward, heart to lip repeating
Thy world – a thing of beauty, fervor, truth!
    And hopes, proud hopes, that keep young pulses beating.

Magician of the mind! its inmost vein –
Its mazy deeps – its lights and shades unveiling.
Thine own a thrilling chord! a silken skein –
    Leading thro labyrinths of human feeling.

A Maxwell – thy proud heritage, the sword.
A Hamilton, what did'st thou not inherit!
All, that the wealth of genius might afford:
    All, ancestry could guarantee of merit.

And thine, the boasted boon, to one of old
The ear, "the listening, ear that heard thee, blessed thee"
And eyes were turned upon thee, to behold
    The seal of beauty, with which God imprest thee.

His love hath called thee early, to thy rest,
While yet the sun was high – and fame the sweetest,
Oh! meetest time! to summon such a guest –
    Since blooms that shew the fairest, fade the fleetest.

The sharpest steel soon wears its sheath away –
The lustrous diamond wears away its setting –
And purest essence pent in mortal clay –
    Soon bursts the barrier-bounds its course besetting

Yet, mind leaves footprints on the sands of time,
Itself resolved again to light undying!
Stamping the past with imagery sublime;
    And with the cloud-world of the future vying.

Copy-text: Vase

Collated states: *ATCJ* (6 Sept 1873), signed "ELIZA HAMILTON DUNLOP. Mulla Villa, Sep. 1, 1873". (*A*) 1 includes "Late Prebendary of Balla, and Rector of Roslea, Ireland … Wild Sports, Life of Wellington, &c., &c."; omits "Hector O'Haloran" (*A*) 2 Omits epitaph (*A*) 5 blooming heather (*A*) 6 Or restless, lounging by that stream (*A*) 11 Melting, like day-dreams, on the lap of Folly. (*A*) 12 There, even there, when our bold mountain (*A*) 15 You'd rush where (*A*) 17 heart and lip (*A*) 19 which keep (*A*) 21 many deeps (*A*) 23 Leading through (*A*) 28 gracious boon (*A*) 32 thy sun (*A*) Ah! meetest (*A*) 35 The sharp-edged steel, its sheath soon wears away; (*A*) 36 The purest diamond still outlasts its setting, (*A*) 37 And heaven-born spirit pent (*A*) 39 But mind (*A*) 41 Stamps the great past (*A*) 42 And lives, the mystic future still outvieing. (*A*)

Maxwell: William Hamilton Maxwell (1791–1850) was Eliza Hamilton Dunlop's cousin and author of some twenty books. The most popular were *Stories of Waterloo* (1829), *Wild Sports of the West* (1832), and *Life of Wellington* (1839–41). Other titles mentioned by Dunlop include his *The Dark Lady of Doona* (1834) to which she contributed poems and *Fortunes of Hector O'Halloran and his Man, Mark Antony O'Toole* (1842–43). In 1820, after taking holy orders, he was appointed to two beneficiaries in the area of Ballagh, Connemara, Ireland. For further details, see Donald Hawes, "Maxwell, William Hamilton (1791–1850)", *ODNB*, https://doi.org/10.1093/ref:odnb/18416.

My own Epitaph – E.H.D.

Bow low the veiled head –
Suppress thy head – be still –
Ask not how grief doth kill;
That secret's of the dead!
Enough – the feel of *time*
Through thorny ways had striven.
Now, they have reached the gates, that shut out Earth from Heaven.

A last faint lingering sigh
Struggling, as loth to part;
Told of a broken heart –
Ere Death had sealed the eye!
'Tis past! the Spirit cleansed from human stain
Hath soared, to seek the realms, of its Redeemer's reign.

Yet! are there bonds of earth!
'Tis said, "Love never dies" –
That essence of life's holiest ties
Is perfume, mingling with our second-birth:
A Lamp! that burns before the Eternal's throne,
Lighting the Vale of death! for the returning one.

Copy-text: Vase

Collated states: None.

10
Eliza Hamilton Dunlop's Australian Publications

This table provides a list of all currently known publications by Dunlop in Australian newspapers and magazines. We welcome additional information and references.

Year	Title	Publication	Issue Date
1838	Songs of An Exile (No. 1) The Dream	*Australian*	8 Nov 1838
1838	Songs of An Exile (No. 2)	*Australian*	22 Nov 1838
1838	Songs of An Exile (No. 3)	*Australian*	29 Nov 1838
1838	Songs of An Exile (No. 4) The Aboriginal Mother	*Australian*	13 Dec 1838
1839	Songs of An Exile (No. 5) The Irish Mother	*Australian*	12 Jan 1839
1839	Stories of An Exile (No. 1) The Ford of the Emu Plains	*Sydney Monitor and Commercial Advertiser*	29 May 1839
1839	Stories of An Exile (No. 1) The Ford of the Emu Plains Concluded	*Sydney Monitor and Commercial Advertiser*	31 May 1839
1840	Songs of An Exile (No. 7) For music	*Australian*	11 Apr 1840
1840	Songs of An Exile (No. 8) Air "Peggy Barn"	*Australian*	7 May 1840

Year	Title	Publication	Issue Date
1840	Songs of An Exile: Go Dia Leat Slan	*Australian*	31 Oct 1840
1840	Songs of An Exile: Lights of the Past	*Australian*	5 Nov 1840
1842	The Eagle Chief	*Sydney Gazette and New South Wales Advertiser*	21 Apr 1842
1842	Mable MacMahon	*Australasian Chronicle*	21 July 1842
1842	Star of the South	*Sydney Morning Herald*	30 Aug 1842
1843	The Aboriginal Father	*Australasian Chronicle*	19 Jan 1843
1843	The Irish Volunteers	*Australasian Chronicle*	13 Apr 1843
1843	Rosetta Nathan's Dirge	*Sydney Morning Herald*	25 Apr 1843
1847	Elegy	*Sydney Morning Herald*	21 Dec 1847
1848	Native Poetry: Nung-Ngnun	*Sydney Morning Herald*	11 Oct 1848
1849	Inscribed to the Memory of E.B. Kennedy	*Maitland Mercury and Hunter River General Advertiser*	8 Aug 1849
1852	Ode to Gold	*Sydney Morning Herald*	27 Feb 1852
1853	The Shamrock	*Sydney Morning Herald*	17 Mar 1853
1853	Caritas	*Sydney Morning Herald*	29 Mar 1853
1856	Poesy	*Empire*	22 Dec 1856
1856	Destiny	*Empire*	27 Dec 1856
1857	Helleborus Niger: The Christmas Rose	*Empire*	11 Apr 1857

Year	Title	Publication	Issue Date
1857	Carlingford Bay	*Empire*	18 Jun 1857
1857	To Home and Friends	*Empire*	21 Jul 1857
1857	Hope's Nativity	*Month: A Literary and Critical Journal*	Sep 1857
1857	The Mulla, or Wollombi creek, New-South-wales	*Month: A Literary and Critical Journal*	Dec 1857
1860	Stanzas [From a self-exiled Lady to a dear Friend in England]	*Month: A Literary and Critical Journal*	Oct 1858
1863	Rendirse a la Bazon: Translado del Espanol	*Empire*	23 Feb 1863
1863	Memorialis	*Empire*	24 Jun 1863
1863	Ambition	*Empire*	24 Aug 1863
1863	The Past	*Empire*	17 Oct 1863
1863	Life	*Empire*	20 Nov 1863
1864	Reminiscences of Byron	*Empire*	8 Jan 1864
1864	Time's Album	*Empire*	2 Dec 1864
1865	The Two Graves	*Empire*	15 Apr 1865
1865	Erin Dheelish	*Empire*	8 July 1865
1867	A Phase of Ireland in 16th Century	*Empire*	18 May 1867
1867	A Problem	*Empire*	17 Jun 1867
1867	Past and Present	*Empire*	5 Aug 1867
1867	Death	*Empire*	10 Sep 1867

Year	Title	Publication	Issue Date
1868	Aphorisms	*Empire*	15 Jul 1868
1869	The Desert Pea	*Empire*	11 Jan 1869
1872	Emblems	*Evening News, Australian Town and Country Journal*	18 May 1872
1872	Mind	*Evening News, Australian Town and Country Journal*	15 Jun 1872
1872	Tears: A Sonnet	*Australian Town and Country Journal*	10 Aug 1872
1872	Poesy	*Australian Town and Country Journal*	5 Oct 1872
1873	Memories of Maxwell	*Australian Town and Country Journal*	6 Sep 1873
1873	Faith	*Australian Town and Country Journal*	15 Nov 1873

Works Cited

Anderson, Benedict. *Imagined Communities: Reflections on the Origin and Spread of Nationalism*. London: Verso, 1983.

Appiah, Kwame Anthony. *Cosmopolitanism: Ethics in the World of Strangers*. New York: Norton, 2006.

Araluen Corr, Evelyn. "Silence and Resistance: Aboriginal Women Working within and against the Archive." *Continuum* 32, no. 4 (2018): 487–502.

Archibald, Diana C. *Domesticity, Imperialism and Emigration in the Victorian Novel*. Columbia: University of Missouri Press, 2002.

Armstrong, Isobel. *Victorian Poetry: Poetry, Poetics, and Politics*. London: Routledge, 1993.

Ash, Anna, John Giacon and Amanda Lissarrague. *Gamilaraay, Yuwaalaraay and Yuwaalayaay Dictionary*. Alice Springs: IAD Press, 2003.

Attenbrow, Val. *Sydney's Aboriginal Past: Investigating the Archaeological and Historical Records*. 2nd ed. Sydney: UNSW Press, 2010.

Attwood, Bain and S.G. Foster, eds. *Frontier Conflict: The Australian Experience*. Canberra: National Museum of Australia, 2003.

Augustine, M.L. *Fort William: Calcutta's Crowning Glory*. New Delhi: Ocean Books, 1999.

Austin, Peter. "The Gamilaraay (Kamilaroi) Language, Northern New South Wales: A Brief History of Research." In *Encountering Aboriginal Languages: Studies in the History of Australian Linguistics*, edited by William B. McGregor, Pacific Linguistics Ser., 37–58. Canberra: Australian National University, Research School of Pacific and Asian Studies, 2008.

Badat, Saleem. *The Forgotten People: Political Banishment under Apartheid*. Leiden: Brill, 2013.

Ballantyne, Tony. *Entanglements of Empire: Missionaries, Māori, and the Question of the Body*. Durham: Duke University Press, 2014.

Ballantyne, Tony. *Webs of Empire: Locating New Zealand's Colonial Past*. Wellington: Bridget Williams, 2012.

Bartlett, Thomas. "Defence, Counter-Insurgency, and Rebellion: Ireland, 1793–1803." In *A Military History of Ireland*, edited by Thomas Bartlett and Keith Jeffrey, 247–93. Cambridge: Cambridge University Press, 1997.

Bayley, F.W.H. and Henry Bishop. *I Stood amid the Glittering Throng, a Ballad, the Poetry by F.W.H. Bayley esq., the Music by H.R. Bishop*. 4th ed. London: Goulding and D'Almaine, [1831].

Bayly, C.A. "Ireland, India and the Empire: 1780–1914." *Transactions of the Royal Historical Society* 10 (2000): 377–97.

Behrendt, Stephen C. *British Women Poets and the Romantic Writing Community*. Baltimore, MD: Johns Hopkins University Press, 2008.

Beiner, Guy. "Disremembering 1798?: An Archaeology of Social Forgetting and Remembrance in Ulster." *History and Memory* 25, no. 1 (2013): 9–50.

Beiner, Guy. *Forgetful Remembrance: Social Forgetting and Vernacular Historiography of a Rebellion in Ulster*. Oxford: Oxford University Press, 2018.

Bellhouse, Mary L. "Femininity & Commerce in the Eighteenth Century: Rousseau's Criticism of a Literary Ruse by Montesquieu." *Polity* 13, no. 2 (1980): 285–99.

Bergès, Sandrine. *The Routledge Guidebook to Wollstonecraft's* A Vindication of the Rights of Woman. London: Routledge, 2013.

Bergès, Sandrine and Alan Coffee. *The Social and Political Philosophy of Mary Wollstonecraft*. Oxford: Oxford University Press, 2016.

Berlant, Lauren. *The Female Complaint: The Unfinished Business of Sentimentality in American Culture*. Durham, NC: Duke University Press, 2008.

Besold, Jutta. "Language Recovery of the New South Wales South Coast Aboriginal Languages." PhD thesis, Australian National University, 2013.

Blanchard, Samuel Laman. "Stanzas for Evening." In *Lyric Offerings*. London: William Harrison Ainsworth, 1828.

Blount, Edward. *Notes on the Cape of Good Hope: Made During an Excursion in that Colony in the Year 1820*. London, 1821.

Boydell, Barra. "The United Irishmen, Music, Harps, and National Identity." *Eighteenth-Century Ireland / Iris an dá chultúr* 13 (1998): 44–51.

Brake, Laurel and Marysa Demoor, eds. *Dictionary of Nineteenth-Century Journalism in Great Britain and Ireland*. Gent: Academia Press, 2009.

Bramble, Christine M. "Relations between Aborigines and White Settlers in Newcastle and the Hunter District, 1804–1841." B.Litt. thesis, University of New England, 1981.

Brantlinger, Patrick. *Dark Vanishings: Discourse on the Extinction of Primitive Races, 1800–1930*. Ithaca, NY: Cornell University Press, 2003.

Brayshaw, Helen. *Aborigines of the Hunter Valley*. Scone: Scone and Upper Hunter Historical Society, 1987.

Bremmer, Jan. "Scapegoat Rituals in Ancient Greece." *Harvard Studies in Classical Philology* 87 (1983): 299–320.

Brody, Miriam. "Introduction." In *Mary Wollstonecraft: Vindication of the Rights of Woman*, edited by Miriam Brody, 7–84. Ringwood: Penguin, 1985.

Bunting, Edward. *A General Collection of the Ancient Music of Ireland, Arranged for the Piano Forte, Some of the Most Admired Melodies Are Adapted for the Voice to Poetry Chiefly Translated from the Original Irish Songs by Thomas Campbell Esq. and Other Eminent Poets, to which is Prefixed a Historical & Critical Dissertation on the Egyptian, British and Irish Harp by Edward Bunting*, vol. *1st [sic]*. London: Engraved by Williamson, n.d. [1809].

Bunting, Edward. *The Ancient Music of Ireland, Arranged for the Piano Forte, to Which is Prefixed a Dissertation on the Irish Harp and Harpers, Including an Account of the Old Melodies of Ireland*. Dublin: Hodges and Smith, 1840.

Butterss, Philip and Elizabeth Webby, eds. *The Penguin Book of Australian Ballads*. Melbourne: Penguin, 1993.

Bygrave, Fyfe and Patricia Bygrave. *Growing Australian Red Cedar and Other Meliaceae Species in Plantation*. Canberra: Rural Industries Research and Development Corporation, 2005.

Byron, George Gordon. *The Complete Works of Lord Byron*. Frankfort: Joseph Baer, 1846.

Campbell, Thomas. *Gertrude of Wyoming; or, The Pennsylvania Cottage*. 1809. London: Routledge, 1857.

Capelle, Pierre Adolphe. *La clé du Caveau, à l'usage de tous les chansonniers français*. Paris, 1811.

Carey, Hilary M. "Death, God and Linguistics: Conversations with Missionaries on the Australian Frontier." *Australian Historical Studies* 40, no. 2 (2009): 161–77.

Carey, Hilary M. "Lancelot Threlkeld and Missionary Linguistics in Australia to 1850." In *Missionary Linguistics / Lingüística Misionera: Selected Papers from the First International Conference on Missionary Linguistics, Oslo, March 13th–16th, 2003*, edited by Otto Zwartjes and Even Hovdhaugen. Studies in the History of the Language Sciences, 253–75. Amsterdam: John Benjamins, 2004.

Chander, Manu Samriti. *Brown Romantics: Poetry and Nationalism in the Global Nineteenth Century*. Lewisburg: Bucknell University Press, 2017.

Chatterjee, Partha. *The Black Hole of Empire: History of a Global Practice of Power*. Princeton, NJ: Princeton University Press, 2012.

Chatterjee, Ronjaunee, Alicia Mireles Christoff and Amy R. Wong. "Undisciplining Victorian Studies." *Los Angeles Review of Books* (10 July 2020). https://lareviewofbooks.org/article/undisciplining-victorian-studies/#_edn3

Clapperton, William, ed. *The Common-Place Book of Poetry, or British Minstrelsy*. London: Thomas Tegg, 1830.

Cock, Jacklyn. *Writing the Ancestral River: A Biography of the Kowie*. Johannesburg: Wits University Press, 2018.

Coffee, Alan. "Mary Wollstonecraft, Public Reason, and the Virtuous Republic." In *The Social and Political Philosophy of Mary Wollstonecraft*, edited by Sandrine Bergès and Alan M.S.J. Coffee. Oxford: Oxford University Press, 2016. doi: 10.1093/acprof:oso/9780198766841.003.0011.

Collins, David. *An Account of the English Colony in New South Wales from Its First Settlement, in January 1788, to August 1801: With Remarks on the Dispositions, Customs, Manners, &C. of the Native Inhabitants of That Country. To Which Are Added Some Particulars of New Zealand; Compiled by Permission, from the Mss. of Lieutenant-Governor King; an Account of a Voyage Performed by Captain Flinders and Mr. Bass; by Which the Existence of a Strait Separating Van Diemen's Land from the Continent of New Holland Was Ascertained*. 2 vols. [1798]. Sydney: University of Sydney Library – SETIS, 2003.

Connor, John. *The Australian Frontier Wars, 1788–1838*. Sydney: UNSW Press, 2005.

Cooke, Glenn R. "The Search for Kalboori Youngi." *Queensland Review* 13, no. 2 (2006): 49–64.

Couzens, Tim. *Battles of South Africa*. Claremont: David Philip, 2004.

Cramer, Johann Baptist. *J.B. Cramer's Instructions for the Piano Forte*. London: Chappell, 1812.

Crane, Ralph and Anna Johnston. "Introduction: Administering Colonial Spaces in Australasia and India." In *Empire Calling: Administering Colonial Australasia and India*, edited by Ralph Crane, Anna Johnston and C. Vijayasree, vii–xiv. New Delhi: Cambridge University Press Foundation, 2013.

Crawford, D.G. *Roll of the Indian Medical Service 1615–1930*. 2 vols. London: Thacker, 1930.

Curthoys, Ann, ed. "The Myall Creek Massacre of 1838: Genocide, War Crimes, Crimes against Humanity?" Special Forum in *Law and History* 5.1 (2018): 146–49.

Davis, Natalie Zemon. *Women on the Margins: Three Seventeenth-Century Lives*. Cambridge, MA: Harvard University Press, 1995.

De Salis, Margaret. Margaret De Salis – Papers, 1965–1980. Sydney: State Library of New South Wales.

De Salis, Margaret. *Two Early Colonials*. Sydney: printed by the author, 1967.

Deacon, Harriet, ed. *The Island: A History of Robben Island 1488–1990*. Claremont: David Philip, 1996.

DeLoughrey, Elizabeth M. and George B. Handley. *Postcolonial Ecologies: Literatures of the Environment*. New York: Oxford University Press, 2011.

Dever, Maryanne. "Photographs and Manuscripts: Working in the Archive." *Archives and Manuscripts* 42, no. 3 (2014): 282–94.

Dever, Maryanne. "Provocations on the Pleasures of Archived Paper." *Archives and Manuscripts* 41, no. 3 (2013): 173–82.

Dirks, Nicholas B. "Annals of the Archive: Ethnographic Notes on the Sources of History." In *From the Margins: Historical Anthropology and Its Futures*, edited by Brian Keith Axel, 47–65. Durham, NC: Duke University Press, 2002.

Dixon, R.M.W., W.S. Ramson and M. Thomas. *Australian Aboriginal Words in English*. Melbourne: Oxford University Press, 1990.

Doche, Joseph Denis. *La musette du vaudeville, ou, Recueil complet des airs*. Paris, 1822.

Donaldson, Tamsin. *Ngiyambaa*. Cambridge: Cambridge University Press, 1980.

Douglas, Mary. *Purity and Danger: An Analysis of Concepts of Pollution and Taboo*. London: Routledge, 1966.

Drennan, William et al. *The Drennan Letters: Being a Selection from the Correspondence which Passed between William Drennan, M.D. and His Brother-in-Law and Sister, Samuel and Martha McTier, during the years 1776–1819*. Belfast: His Majesty's Stationery Office, 1931.

Duncan, W.A. and I. Nathan. *Australia the Wide and the Free! A National Song Written by W.A. Duncan, esqr., as Sung at the Great Civic Dinner, December 21st, 1842, Composed and Respectfully Inscribed to the Right Worshipful John Hosking, Mayor of Sydney, by I. Nathan*. Sydney: published by the composer, n.d. [1842/43].

Dunlop, Eliza Hamilton. "Inscribed to the Memory of Two Brothers." *Belfast News-Letter*, 3 January 1837: 4. *British Library Newspapers*. Gale.

Dunlop, Eliza Hamilton. Letter to Mrs Dalzell, 18 November 1865. https://www.mullavilla.com.au/hunter-valley-history/

Dunlop, Eliza H. "Morning on Rostrevor Mountains." *Dublin Penny Journal* 4, no. 162 (8 August 1835): 42.

Dunlop, Eliza Hamilton. "The Two Graves." *The Coleraine Chronicle*, 26 August 1865: 6.

Dunlop, Eliza Hamilton. "The Vase, Comprising Songs for Music and Poems by Eliza Hamilton Dunlop." Sydney: State Library of New South Wales, B1541.

Dunlop, E.H. and I. Nathan. *The Aboriginal Father, a Native Song of the Maneroo Tribe . . . Versified From the Original Words . . . by Mrs. E.H. Dunlop, the Melody, as Sung by the Aborigines, Put Into Rhythm & Harmonized with Appropriate Symphonies & Accompaniments, Respectfully Inscribed to the Lady Mayoress, by I. Nathan*. Sydney: [Nathan], Elizabeth Street; T. Bluett, Litho., Brougham Place, [1843].

Dunlop, E.H. and I. Nathan. *The Aboriginal Mother, an Australian Melody Respectfully Inscribed to Lady Gipps, the Poetry by Mrs. E.H. Dunlop, the Music by I. Nathan*. Sydney: published for the composer, Ada Cottage, Prince Street, [1842].

Dunlop, E.H. and I. Nathan. *The Eagle Chief, an Australian Melody, Respectfully Inscribed to Lady O'Connell, the Poetry by Mrs. E.H. Dunlop, the Music (From a French Subject) Composed Expressly for the Cecilian Society, by I. Nathan*. Sydney: published for the composer, Ada Cottage, Prince Street [1842].

Dunlop, E.H. and I. Nathan. *Mable Macmahon, an Australian Melody, Respectfully Dedicated to Roger Therry, Esq., Attorney General, Written by Mrs. E.H. Dunlop, Composed by I. Nathan*. Sydney: published for the composer, Ada Cottage, Prince Street, [1842].

Dunlop, E.H. and I. Nathan. *Star of the South, an Australian National Melody, Written by Mrs. E. H. Dunlop, the Music Composed and as a Small Token of Grateful Recollection of the Hospitality Experienced on His First Landing in Australia Felix, Respectfully Inscribed to his Honor Mr. La Trobe, and the Inhabitants of the District, by I. Nathan*. Sydney: printed by Thos. Liley, Brougham Place, [1842].

Dutta, Krishna. *Calcutta: A Cultural and Literary History*. Oxford: Signal, 2003.

Dworkin, Dennis, ed. *Ireland and Britain 1798–1922: An Anthology of Sources*. Indianapolis, IN: Hackett, 2012.

Eastwick, Edward B. *Handbook of the Bengal Presidency: With an Account of Calcutta City*. London, 1882.

Edgeworth, Maria. *Life and Letters of Maria Edgeworth*. 1894. Ed. Augustus J.C. Hare. Vol. 2. Project Gutenberg, 2005.

Edgeworth, Maria. "Undated Letter from Maria Edgeworth to Mrs. Stuart of Rostrevor, Co. Down." Dublin: National Library of Ireland.

Edwards, William Howell. *An Introduction to Aboriginal Societies*. 2nd ed. South Melbourne: Thomson, 1988.

Elder, Bruce. *Blood on the Wattle: Massacres and Maltreatment of Aboriginal Australians since 1788*. 3rd ed. Frenchs Forest, N.S.W.: New Holland, 2003.

Etheridge, Robert. *The Dendroglyphs or Carved Trees of New South Wales*. Sydney: Sydney University Press, 2011.

Fabian, Johannes. *Language and Colonial Power: The Appropriation of Swahili in the Former Belgian Congo 1880–1938*. African Studies Series. Cambridge: Cambridge University Press, 1986.

Farge, Arlette. *Allure of the Archives*. Translated by Thomas Scott-Railton. New Haven: Yale University Press, 2004.

Fitzpatrick, David. "Emigration, 1801–70." In *A New History of Ireland*, Volume V: *Ireland Under the Union, 1801–1870*, edited by W.E. Vaughan, 562–622. Oxford: Oxford University Press, 2010.

Fleminger, David. *Robben Island*. Pinetown: 30 Degrees South, 2008.

Flint, Kate. *The Transatlantic Indian, 1776–1930*. Princeton, NJ: Princeton University Press, 2009.

Florio, C.H. *Far Far at Sea, a Favorite Ballad Sung by Mr. Incledon*. New York: J. & M. Paff, [n.d.].

Foley, Dennis. "Leadership: The Quandary of Aboriginal Societies in Crises, 1788–1830, and 1966." In *Transgressions: Critical Indigenous Australian Histories*, edited by Ingereth Macfarlane and Mark Hannah, 177–92. Canberra: Australian National University E Press, 2007.

Foott, Mary Hannay. *Where the Pelican Builds and Other Poems*. Brisbane: Gordon and Gotch, 1885.

Forché, Carolyn and Duncan Wu, eds. *Poetry of Witness: The Tradition in English, 1500–2001*. New York: W.W. Norton, 2014.

Ford, Lisa. "Protecting the Peace on the Edges of Empire: Commissioners of Crown Lands in New South Wales." In *Protection and Empire: A Global History*, edited by Adam Clulow, Bain Attwood and Lauren Benton, 153–74. Cambridge: Cambridge University Press, 2017.

Ford, Lisa and David Andrew Roberts. "Expansion, 1820–1850." In *Cambridge History of Australia*, edited by Alison Bashford and Stuart MacIntyre, 121–48. Cambridge: Cambridge University Press, 2015.

Fraisse, Genevieve. "A Philosophical History of Sexual Difference." Translated by Arthur Goldhammer. In *A History of Women in the West IV, Emerging Feminism from Revolution to World War*, edited by Genevieve Fraisse and Michelle Perrot, 48–60. Cambridge, MA: Harvard University Press, 1996.

Fraisse, Genevieve. *Reason's Muse: Sexual Difference and the Birth of Democracy*. Translated by Jane Marie Todd. Chicago: University of Chicago Press, 1994.

Frost, Lucy. *Abandoned Women: Scottish Convicts Exiled Beyond the Seas*. Crows Nest, N.S.W.: Allen & Unwin, 2012.

Fulford, Tim. *Romantic Indians: Native Americans, British Literature, and Transatlantic Culture 1756–1830*. Oxford: Oxford University Press, 2006.

Gammage, Bill. *The Greatest Estate on Earth: How Aborigines Made Australia*. Sydney: Allen & Unwin, 2011.

Gee, Sophie. *Making Waste: Leftovers and the Eighteenth-Century Imagination*. Princeton, NJ: Princeton University Press, 2010.

Giles, Fiona. "Finding a Shiftingness: Situating the Nineteenth/ Century Anglo/ Australian Female Subject." *New Literatures Review*, no. 18 (Winter 1989): 10–19.

Gilmour, Rachael. *Grammars of Colonialism: Representing Languages in Colonial South Africa*. Basingstoke: Palgrave Macmillan, 2006.

Glissant, Édouard and J. Michael Dash. *Caribbean Discourse: Selected Essays*. CARAF Books. Charlottesville: University Press of Virginia, 1989.

Goddard, Roy H. "Aboriginal Poets as Historians." *Mankind* 1, no. 10 (1934): 243–46.

Goddard, Roy H. *Aboriginal Sculpture*. Sydney: Australasian Medical Publishing, 1939.

Goddard, Roy H. *The Life and Times of James Milson*. Melbourne: Georgian House, 1955.

Godden Mackay Logan. *Penrith Lakes Scheme: Archaeological Management Plan Draft Report*. Redfern: Penrith Lakes Development Corporation, 2014.

Golder, Hilary. *High and Responsible Office: A History of the NSW Magistracy*. Sydney: Sydney University Press, 1991.

Goldie, Terry. *Fear and Temptation: The Image of the Indigene in Canadian, Australian and New Zealand Literatures*. Kingston, ON: McGill University Press, 1989.

Goodall, Heather. *Invitation to Embassy: Land in Aboriginal Politics in New South Wales, 1788–1972*. St Leonards, NSW: Allen & Unwin, 1996.

Grant, Stan and John Rudder. *A New Wiradjuri Dictionary*. O'Connor, ACT: Restoration House, 2010.

Greville, Frances. "A Prayer for Indifference". (1759) *Eighteenth-Century Poetry Archive*. https://www.eighteenthcenturypoetry.org/works/o5089-w0150.shtml.

Grose, Kelvin. "1847: The Educational Compromise of the Lord Bishop of Australia." *Journal of Religious History* 1, no. 4 (1961): 233–48.

Gunson, Niel. "Dunlop, Eliza Hamilton (1796–1880)." In *Australian Dictionary of Biography*. Canberra: National Centre of Biography, Australian National University, 1966.

Habibi, Don. *John Stuart Mill and the Ethic of Human Growth*. Dordrecht: Kluwer, 2001.

Hamilton, Solomon. Inventories & Accounts of Deceased Estates – Bengal 1780–1937. British India Office Wills & Probate, 1820. London: British Library.

Hampton, Susan and Kate Llewellyn, eds. *The Penguin Book of Australian Women's Poetry*. Melbourne: Penguin, 1981.

Hanna, Cliff. *Bandits on the Great North Road: The Bushranger as Social Force*. Newcastle-upon-Tyne: Nimrod, 1993.

Hansen, Julia. "Viewless Scenes: Vividness and Nineteenth-Century Ideals of Reading in and through *Gertrude of Wyoming*." *ELH* 84 (Winter 2017): 943–77.

Hansord, Katie. "'Spirit-music' Unbound: Romanticism and Print Politics in Australian Women's Poetry, 1830–1905." PhD diss., Deakin University, 2012.

Hansord, Katie. "Eliza Hamilton Dunlop's 'The Aboriginal Mother': Romanticism, Anti Slavery and Imperial Feminism in the Nineteenth Century." *JASAL: Journal of the Association for the Study of Australian Literature* 11, no. 1 (2011): 1–14.

Harkin, N. "The Poetics of (Re)Mapping Archives: Memory in the Blood." *JASAL: Journal of the Association for the Study of Australian Literature* 14, no. 3 (2014): 1–14.

Harris, Katherine D. *Forget Me Not: The Rise of the British Literary Annual, 1823–1835*. Ohio: Ohio University Press, 2015.

Heber, Richard. *Narrative of a Journey through the Upper Provinces of India*. London, 1844.

Hemans, Mrs [Felicia]. *Records of Woman*. 1828. Oxford: Woodstock, 1991.

Herbert, Christopher. *Culture and Anomie: Ethnographic Imagination in the Nineteenth Century*. Chicago: University of Chicago Press, 1991.

Hill, Barbara. "The 1798 Rebellion in Coleraine and District." *North Irish Roots* 9, no. 2 (1998): 14–19.

Hill, Myrtle. *The Time of the End: Millenarian Beliefs in Ulster*. Belfast: The Belfast Society, 2001.

Hill, Myrtle, Brian S. Turner and Kenneth Dawson. *1798 Rebellion in County Down*. Dublin: Counterpoint, 1998.

Howlin, Niamh and Kevin Costello, eds. *Law and the Family in Ireland, 1800-1950*. London: Palgrave, 2017.

Works Cited

Huggan, Graham and Helen Tiffin. *Postcolonial Ecocriticism: Literature, Animals, Environment.* London: Routledge, 2010.

Hume, David. *David Hume: A Treatise of Human Nature: A Critical Edition.* 1739. Edited by David Fate Norton and Mary J. Norton. Oxford: Oxford University Press, 2007.

Humphrey, Keith. *Calcutta Revisited: Exploring Calcutta Through Backstreets and Byways.* Tolworth: Grosvenor House, 2014.

Hunt, Una. *Sources and Style in* Moore's Irish Melodies. London: Routledge, 2017.

Hunter, John. *An Historical Journal of the Transactions of Port Jackson and Norfolk Island.* London, 1793.

Hunter, William Wilson, Sir. *The Imperial Gazetteer of India, Volume XII.* 2nd ed. London: Trübner, 1887.

Jackson, Alvin. "Ireland, the Union, and the Empire, 1800–1960." In *Ireland and the British Empire,* edited by Kevin Kenny, 123–53. Oxford: Oxford University Press, 2004.

Jackson, Alvin. *Ireland 1798–1998: War, Peace and Beyond.* 2nd ed. Oxford: Wiley-Blackwell, 2010.

Jackson, Virginia. "The Function of Criticism at the Present Time." *Los Angeles Review of Books,* 12 April 2015. https://lareviewofbooks.org/article/function-criticism-present-time

Jacquemont, Victor. *Letters from India.* 2 vols. London, 1834.

Jamison, Anne. "Women's Literary History in Ireland: Digitizing *The Field Day Anthology of Irish Writing*." *Women's History Review* 26, no. 5 (2017), 751–65.

Johnson, James. *The Scots Musical Museum.* Edinburgh: Johnson, 1787.

Johnston, Anna. "'The Aboriginal Mother': Poetry and Politics." In *Remembering the Myall Creek Massacre,* edited by Jane Lydon and Lyndall Ryan, 68–84. Sydney: UNSW Press, 2018.

Johnston, Anna. "Mrs Milson's Wordlist: Eliza Hamilton Dunlop and the Intimacy of Linguistic Work." In *Intimacies of Violence in the Settler Colony: Economies of Dispossession around the Pacific Rim,* edited by Penelope Edmonds and Amanda Nettelbeck, 225–47. Switzerland: Palgrave Macmillan-Springer, 2018.

Johnston, Anna. *The Paper War: Morality, Print Culture, and Power in Colonial New South Wales.* Crawley, Western Australia: University of Western Australia Press, 2011.

Johnston, Roy and Declan Plummer. *The Musical Life of Nineteenth-Century Belfast.* London: Routledge, 2015.

Jones, Caroline. *Darkinyung Grammar and Dictionary: Revitalising a Language from Historical Sources.* Nambucca Heads: Muurrbay Aboriginal Language and Culture Co-operative, 2008.

Jones, Caroline and Shawn Laffan. "Lexical Similarity and Endemism in Historical Wordlists of Australian Aboriginal Languages of the Greater Sydney Region." *Transactions of the Philological Society* 106, no. 3 (2008): 456–86.

Jordan, A.C. *Towards an African Literature: The Emergence of Literary Form in Xhosa.* Berkeley: University of California Press, 1973.

Kane, Paul. *Australian Poetry: Romanticism and Negativity.* Melbourne: Cambridge University Press, 1996.

Kaus, David. "The Goddard Family: National Museum Collectors and Collections." *Friends (National Museum of Australia)* June (2003): 16–17.

Kavanagh, Patrick F. *A Popular History of the Insurrection of 1798.* 2nd ed. Cork: Guy, 1898.

Kennedy, Máire. "'Politicks, Coffee and News': The Dublin Book Trade in the Eighteenth Century." *Dublin Historical Record* 58, no. 1 (2005): 76–85.

Kenny, Kevin. "Ireland and the British Empire: An Introduction." In *Ireland and the British Empire,* edited by Kevin Kenny, 1–25. Oxford: Oxford University Press, 2004.

Knowles, Claire. *Sensibility and Female Poetic Tradition.* Surrey: Ashgate, 2009.

Koch, Harold. "The Methodology of Reconstructing Indigenous Placenames: Australian Capital Territory and South-Eastern New South Wales." In *Aboriginal Placenames,* edited by Harold Koch and Luise Hercus, 115–71. Canberra: Australian National University E Press, 2009.

Kristeva, Julia. *Powers of Horror: An Essay on Abjection.* New York: Columbia University Press, 1982.

Lamb, Caroline. *Glenarvon*. London: Printed for Henry Colburn, 1816.

Law, James Sylvius. *The Irish Catholic: A Patriotic Poem*. Belfast: H. Fitzpatrick, 1813.

Law, James Sylvius. *The Wrongs of Ireland Historically Reviewed, from the Invasion to the Present Time: A National Poem, in Six Cantos, with Copious Illustrations: To Which Is Prefixed, an Eulogium to Ogyagia* [in English]. Dublin: R. Grace, 1831.

Lawless, John. *A Compendium of the History of Ireland*. Belfast: Joseph Smyth, 1815.

Leane, Jeanine. "Tracking Our Country in Settler Literature." *JASAL: Journal of the Association for the Study of Australian Literature* 14, no. 3 (2014): 1–17.

Lecky, W.E.H. *A History of Ireland in the Eighteenth Century*. 5 vols. Cambridge: Cambridge University Press, 2010.

Leerssen, Joep. "Convulsion Recalled: Aftermath and Cultural Memory (Post-1798 Ireland)." In *Afterlife of Events: Perspectives on Mnemohistory*, edited by Marek Tamm, 134–53. London: Palgrave Macmillan UK, 2015.

Lehmann, Geoffrey and Robert Gray, eds. *Australian Poetry Since 1788*. Sydney: UNSW Press, 2011.

Leneman, Leah. "'Disregarding the Matrimonial Vows': Divorce in Eighteenth and Early Nineteenth-Century Scotland." *Journal of Social History* 30, no. 2 (Winter 1996): 465–82.

Lever, Susan, ed. *The Oxford Book of Australian Women's Verse*. Melbourne: Oxford University Press, 1995.

Lhotsky, J. *A Song of the Women of the Menero Tribe Arranged with the Assistance of Several Musical Gentlemen for the Voice and Pianoforte, Most Humbly Inscribed as the First Specimen of Australian Music, to Her Most Gracious Majesty Adelaide, Queen of Great Britain & Hanover, by Dr. J. Lhotsky, Colonist N.S. Wales*. Sydney: John Innes, [1834].

Linley, Thomas and Richard Brinsley Sheridan. *The Duenna; or, The Double Elopement, a Comic Opera as Performed at the Theatre Royal in Covent Garden for the Voice, Harpsichord, or Violin*. London: Printed for C. and C. Thompson, [1776].

Lissarrague, Amanda. *Dhanggati Grammar and Dictionary*. Nambucca Heads: Muurrbay, 2007.

Lissarrague, Amanda. *A Grammar and Dictionary of Gathang*. Nambucca Heads: Muurrbay, 2010.

Lissarrague, Amanda. *A Salvage Grammar and Wordlist of the Language from the Hunter River and Lake Macquarie*. Nambucca Heads: Muurrbay, 2006.

Locke, Matthew. *The Introductory Symphony, Airs, Recitatives, Dance, and Choruses in the Tragedy of Macbeth*. London: Goulding and D'Almaine, [1829].

Loftus, Belinda. *Mirrors: Orange and Green*. Dundrum, Co. Down: Picture Press, 1990.

Lootens, Tricia. *The Political Poetess: Victorian Femininity, Race, and the Legacy of Separate Spheres*. Princeton, NJ: Princeton University Press, 2017.

M'Comb, William. *Guide to Belfast*. Belfast: William M'Comb, 1861.

Madden, R.R., ed. *Literary Remains of the United Irishmen of 1798*. Dublin: Duffy, 1887.

Maslan, Susan. *Revolutionary Acts: Theater, Democracy, and the French Revolution*. Baltimore: Johns Hopkins University Press, 2005.

Mason, John Edwin. *Social Death and Resurrection: Slavery and Emancipation in South Africa*. Charlottesville: University of Virginia Press, 2003.

Mathews, R.H. *Notes on the Aborigines of New South Wales*. Sydney: William Applegate Gullick, Government Printer, 1907.

Maxwell, W.H. *The Dark Lady of Doona*. London: Smith, Elder, 1834.

McBride, Ian. *Scripture Politics: Ulster Presbyterians and Irish Radicalism in the Late Eighteenth Century*. Oxford: Clarendon-Oxford University Press, 1998.

McCabe, Leo. *Wolfe Tone and the United Irishmen*. London: Heath Cranton, 1937.

McCall Theal, George. *Records of the Cape Colony*. Vol. 6. Government of the Cape Colony, 1900.

McCavitt, John and Christopher T. George. *The Man Who Captured Washington: Major General Robert Ross and the War of 1812*. Norman: University of Oklahoma Press, 2016.

McGann, Jerome. *The Poetics of Sensibility: A Revolution in Literary Style*. Oxford: Clarendon Press, 1996.

McStay, Marie. *Carlingford Lough*. Donaghadee: Cottage, 2004.

Mellor, Anne. *Romanticism and Gender*. New York: Routledge, 1993.

Messner, Andrew. "Contesting Chartism from Afar: Edward Hawksley and the *People's Advocate*." *Journal of Australian Colonial History* 1, no. 1 (April 1999): 62–94.

Midgley, Clare. *Feminism and Empire: Women Activists in Imperial Britain 1790–1865*. London: Routledge, 2007.

Milliss, Roger. *Waterloo Creek: The Australia Day Massacre of 1838, George Gipps and the British Conquest of New South Wales*. Ringwood, Victoria: McPhee Gribble, 1992.

Milson, David Mrs [Eliza Hamilton Dunlop]. *Mrs. David Milson Kamilaroi Vocabulary and Aboriginal Songs, 1840*. Sydney: State Library of New South Wales.

Milson Family Further Papers, 1826–1960. Sydney: State Library of New South Wales, MLMSS 9409.

Milson Family Papers 1810, 1853–1862. Sydney: State Library of New South Wales, MLMSS 7683.

Milson Family Papers 1826–1895. Sydney: State Library of New South Wales, MLMSS 7948.

Milson Family – Newscuttings and other Miscellaneous Material, 1880–1955. Sydney: State Library of New South Wales, MLMSS 6011.

Minter, Peter. "Settlement Defiled: Ventriloquy, Pollution and Nature in Eliza Hamilton Dunlop's 'The Aboriginal Mother." In *Text, Translation, and Transnationalism: World Literature in 21st Century Australia*, edited by Peter Morgan, 137–51. Melbourne: Australian Scholarly Publishing, 2017.

Mitchell, Paul. "The Foundations of Australian Defamation Law." *Sydney Law Review* 28, no. 3 (2006): 477–504.

Moore, Thomas. *The Works of Thomas Moore*. Paris: A. and W. Galignani, 1823.

Moore, Thomas and Sir John Stevenson. *A Selection of Irish Melodies*. London: J. Power, [1807].

Moore, Thomas and Sir John Stevenson. *A Selection of Irish Melodies*. Vol. 7. London: J. Power, 1818.

"On Mr. Mill's 'History of British India." *Asiatic Journal and Monthly Miscellany* 27, no. 161 (1829): 525–38.

Mullan, John. "Sensibility and Literary Criticism." In *The Cambridge History of Literary Criticism*, vol. 4: "The Eighteenth Century," edited by H.B. Nisbet and Claude Rawson, 417–33. Cambridge: Cambridge University Press, 1997.

Nathan, I. *The Southern Euphrosyne and Australian Miscellany*. London: Whittaker, 1848.

Nettelbeck, Amanda. *Indigenous Rights and Colonial Subjecthood: Protection and Reform in the Nineteenth-Century British Empire*. Cambridge: Cambridge University Press, 2019.

"A New Year's Jaunt." *Cape Monthly Magazine* 10 (1875): 91–96.

Newby, Eric. *Slowly Down the Ganges*. London: Harper Press, 2011.

NSW Parliament Legislative Council. *Report from the Select Committee on the Condition of the Aborigines, with Appendix, Minutes of Evidence and Replies to a Circular Letter*. Sydney: Government Printing Office, 1845.

Ó Muirí, Réamonn. "Newry and the French Revolution, 1792." *Seanchas Ardmhacha: Journal of the Armagh Diocesan Historical Society* 13, no. 2 (1989): 102–20.

O'Donoghue, D.J. *The Poets of Ireland: A Biographical and Bibliographical Dictionary of Irish Writers of English Verse*. Dublin: Hodges, Figgis, 1912.

O'Dwyer, Riana. "Women's Narratives, 1800–40." In *The Field Day Anthology of Irish Writing: Irish Women's Writing and Traditions*, edited by Angela Bourke, Siobhán Kilfeather, Maria Luddy, Margaret Mac Curtain, Gerardine Meaney, Máirín Ní Dhonnchadha, Mary O'Dowd and Clair Wills, 833–49. Cork: Cork University Press, 2002.

O'Leary, John. "Giving the Indigenous a Voice: Further Thoughts on the Poetry of Eliza Hamilton Dunlop." *Journal of Australian Studies* 28, no. 82 (2004): 85–93.

O'Leary, John. "'Unlocking the Fountains of the Heart': Settler Verse and the Politics of Sympathy." *Postcolonial Studies* 13, no. 1 (2010): 55–70.

O'Leary, John. "Speaking the Suffering Indigene: 'Native' Songs and Laments." *Kunapipi* 31, no. 1 (2009): 47–60.

O'Leary, John. "'The Life, the Loves, of That Dark Race': The Ethnographic Verse of Mid-Nineteenth-Century Australia." *Australian Literary Studies* 23, no. 1 (2007): 3–17.

O'Leary, John. *Savage Songs and Wild Romances: Settler Poetry and the Indigene, 1830–1880*. Cross/ Cultures 138. Amsterdam: Rodopi, 2011.

Organ, Michael. "C.W. Peck's Australian Legends: Aboriginal Dreaming Stories of Eastern Australia." *Australian Folklore* 29 (2014): 53–69.

Owenson, Sidney. *Twelve Original Hibernian Melodies, with English Words, Imitated and Translated, from the Works of the Ancient Irish Bards*. London: Preston, [1805].

Parker, K. Langloh. *The Euahlayi Tribe*. London: Constable, 1905.

Parker, Robert. *Miasma: Pollution and Purification in Early Greek Religion*. Oxford: Clarendon Press, 1983.

Parkes, Stan. Stan Parkes Papers. Sydney: State Library of New South Wales.

Parsonson, Ian. *The Australian Ark: A History of Domesticated Animals in Australia*. Collingwood: CSIRO Publishing, 1998.

Pascoe, Bruce. *Dark Emu: Black Seeds: Agriculture or Accident?* Broome: Magabala, 2014.

Pearson, Roger. *Voltaire Almighty: A Life in Pursuit of Freedom*. London: Bloomsbury, 2005.

Peires, Jeffrey B. *The House of Phalo: A History of the Xhosa People in the Days of Their Independence*. Berkeley: University of California Press, 1981.

Percy, Thomas. *Reliques of Ancient English Poetry: Consisting of Old Heroic Ballads, Songs, and Other Pieces of Our Earlier Poets*. London: J. Dodsley, 1765.

Plumtre, James, ed. *A Collection of Songs, Moral, Sentimental, Instructive, and Amusing*. Vol. 2. London: F.C. and J. Rivington, 1806.

Poovey, Mary. *The Proper Lady and the Woman Writer: Ideology as Style in the Works of Mary Wollstonecraft, Mary Shelley, and Jane Austen*. Chicago: University of Chicago Press, 1984.

Pringle, Thomas. *African Sketches, with a Narrative of a Residence in South Africa*. London: E. Moxon, 1834.

Raine Family. Papers Mainly Relating to the Raine Family and Eliza Dunlop, 1821–1870. Sydney: State Library of New South Wales, MLMSS 10156.

Ray, Subhajyoti. *Transformations on the Bengal Frontier: Jalpaiguri 1765–1948*. London: Routledge, 2003.

Read, Anthony and David Fisher. *The Proudest Day: India's Long Road to Independence*. New York: W.W. Norton, 1997.

Rendall, Jane. *The Origins of Modern Feminism: Women in Britain, France and the United States 1780–1860*. Hampshire: Macmillan, 1985.

Richardson, Alan. "Mary Wollstonecraft on Education." In *The Cambridge Companion to Mary Wollstonecraft*, edited by Claudia L. Johnson, 24–41. Cambridge: Cambridge University Press, 2002.

Rose, Deborah Bird. "Gendered Substances and Objects in Ritual: An Australian Aboriginal Study." *Material Religion* 3, no. 1 (2007): 34–46.

Rowley, C.D. *The Destruction of Aboriginal Society*. Canberra: Australian National University Press, 1970.

Royal Australasian Ornithologists' Union. *The Emu: Official Organ of the Australasian Ornithologists' Union* 33, no. 4 (1933).

Rudy, Jason R. "Floating Worlds: Émigré Poetry and British Culture." *ELH* 81, no. 1 (2014): 325–50.

Rudy, Jason. *Imagined Homelands: British Poetry in the Colonies*. Baltimore, MD: Johns Hopkins University Press, 2017.

Russell, Penny. "Death on a River: Honour and Violence in an Australian Penal Colony, 1826–1827." In *Honour, Violence and Emotions in History*, edited by Carolyn Strange, Robert Cribb and Christopher E. Forth, 107–26. London: Bloomsbury, 2014.

[Scott, Sir Walter]. Rev. of *Gertrude of Wyoming*, by Thomas Campbell. *Quarterly Review* 1 (May 1809): 241–58.

Scrivener, Michael. *The Cosmopolitan Ideal*. New York: Routledge, 2016.

Secondat, Charles de. *The Temple of Gnidos. Translated a Second Time from the French of Mons. De Secondat, Baron De Montesquieu*. London: printed for G. Kearsley, in Ludgate-Street, 1767.

Sen, Sudipta. *Ganges: The Many Pasts of an Indian River*. New Haven, CT: Yale University Press, 2019.

Sherington, Geoffrey and Craig Campbell. "Middle-Class Formations and the Emergence of National Schooling: A Historiographical Review of the Australian Debate." In *Transformations in Schooling: Historical and Comparative Perspectives*, edited by Kim Tolley, 15–39. New York: Palgrave Macmillan US, 2007.

Skinner, Graeme. "Eliza Hamilton Dunlop, Songwriter." *Australharmony*. https://sydney.edu.au/paradisec/australharmony/dunlop-eliza-hamilton.php.

Skinner, Graeme. "Isaac Nathan and Family in Australia." *Australharmony*. https://sydney.edu.au/paradisec/australharmony/nathan-isaac-and-family.php.

Skinner, Graeme. "Recovering Musical Data from Colonial Era Transcriptions of Indigenous Songs: Some Practical Considerations." In *Recirculating Songs: Revitalising the Singing Practices of Indigenous Australia*, edited by Jim Wafer and Myfany Turpin, 349–74. Canberra: Asia-Pacific Linguistics, 2017.

Skinner, Graeme. "Toward a General History of Australian Musical Composition: First National Music, 1788–C.1860." PhD diss., Sydney Conservatorium of Music, University of Sydney, 2011.

Skinner, Graeme. "Whigglings and Tories: David and Eliza Dunlop, Colonial Press Culture and the Contested Reception of Isaac Nathan's Australian Melodies Reconsidered", forthcoming.

Smith, Charlotte. *Desmond*. (1792) Edited by Antje Blank and Janet Todd. London: Pickering and Chatto, 1997.

Smyth, Jim. *The Men of No Property*. New York: St Martin's Press, 1998.

The Society of United Irishmen. Dublin, 1794.

Stanford, Charles Villiers, ed. *The Complete Collection of Irish Music as Noted by George Petrie*. London: Boosey, 1903/04.

Steedman, Carolyn. *Dust: The Archive and Cultural History*. New Brunswick, NJ: Rutgers University Press, 2002.

Stevens, Bertram, ed. *The Golden Treasury of Australian Verse*. Sydney: Angus and Robertson, 1909.

Stewart, David. *The Form of Poetry in the 1820s and 1830s: A Period of Doubt*. Cham: Palgrave–Springer, 2018.

Stewart, Susan. *Crimes of Writing: Problems in the Containment of Representation*. Durham: Duke University Press, 1994.

Stewart, Susan. *Poetry and the Fate of the Senses*. Chicago: University of Chicago Press, 2002.

Stoler, Ann Laura. *Along the Archival Grain: Epistemic Anxieties and Colonial Common Sense*. Princeton, NJ: Princeton University Press, 2009.

Tedeschi, Mark. "Speech at the Annual Myall Creek Memorial Ceremony on 11 June 2017 for Those Who Died in the Myall Creek Massacre of 1838." *Law and History* 5.1 (2018), 150–54.

Therry, Roger. *Reminiscences of Thirty Years' Residence in New South Wales and Victoria*. 2nd ed. London: Sampson, Low and Son, 1863.

Tompson, Charles. *Wild Notes, from the Lyre of a Native Minstrel*. 1826. Edited by G.A. Wilkes and G.A. Turnbull. Sydney: Sydney University Press, 1973.

Tone, Wolfe [Theobald Wolfe Tone]. *An Argument on Behalf of the Catholics of Ireland*. Belfast: Society of United Irishmen, 1791.

Troy, Jakelin. *The Sydney Language*. Canberra: the author/AIATSIS, 1994.

Troy, Jakelin. "The Sydney Language Notebooks and Responses to Language Contact in Early Colonial NSW." *Australian Journal of Linguistics* 12, no. 1 (1992): 145–70.

Ulrich, Laurel Thatcher. *A Midwife's Tale: The Life of Martha Ballard, Based on Her Diary, 1785–1812*. New York: Vintage, 1991.

Vickery, Ann. "A 'Lonely Crossing': Approaching Nineteenth-Century Australian Women's Poetry." *Victorian Poetry* 40, no. 1 (2002): 33–53.

Voltaire [François-Marie Arouet]. *A Philosophical Dictionary from the French of M De Voltaire*. Vol. 2. London: W. Dugdale, 1843.

Wafer, Jim. "Ghost-Writing for Wulatji: Incubation and Re-Dreaming as Song Revitalisation Practices." In *Recirculating Songs: Revitalising the Singing Practices of Indigenous Australia*, edited by Jim Wafer and Myfany Turpin, 193–256. Canberra: Asia-Pacific Linguistics, Australian National University, 2017.

Warne, Catherine. *Lower North Shore*. Alexandria: Kingsclear, 2005.

Webby, Elizabeth. "The Aboriginal in Early Australian Literature." *Southerly* 40, no. 1 (1980): 45–63.

Webby, Elizabeth, ed. *The Aboriginal Mother and Other Poems*. Canberra: Mulini Press, 1981.

Webby, Elizabeth. "Australia." In *Periodicals of Queen Victoria's Empire, an Exploration*, edited by Rosemary VanArsdel and J. Don Vann, 19–58. Toronto: University of Toronto Press, 1996.

Webby, Elizabeth. "'Born to Blush Unseen': Some Nineteenth-Century Women Poets." In *A Bright and Fiery Troop: Australian Women Writers of the Nineteenth Century*, edited by Debra Adelaide, 41–52. Melbourne: Penguin, 1988.

Webby, Elizabeth. *Early Australian Poetry: An Annotated Bibliography of Original Poems Published in Australian Newspapers, Magazines & Almanacks before 1850*. Sydney: Hale & Iremonger, 1982.

Wentworth, William Charles. *A Statistical Account of the British Settlements in Australasia*. 3rd ed. 2 vols. London: G.B. Whittaker, 1824.

Whitlock, Gillian. *The Intimate Empire: Reading Women's Autobiography*. London: Cassell, 2000.

Wilson, C.R. "A Short History of Old Fort William in Bengal." *Bengal: Past and Present* 2, no. 1 (January 1908): 1–16.

Withycombe, Patsy. "The Twelfth Man: John Henry Fleming and the Myall Creek Massacre." In *Remembering the Myall Creek Massacre*, edited by Jane Lydon and Lyndall Ryan, 38–51. Sydney: UNSW Press, 2018.

Wood, Rebecca. "Frontier Violence and the Bush Legend: The *Sydney Herald*'s Response to the Myall Creek Massacre Trials and the Creation of Colonial Identity." *History Australia*, 6 (2009): 67.1–67.19.

Woods, C.J. "Samuel Turner's Information on the United Irishmen, 1797–8." *Analecta Hibernica* no. 42 (2011): 181–227.

Worden, Nigel. "Armed with Swords and Ostrich Feathers: Militarism and Cultural Revolution in the Cape Slave Uprising of 1808." In *War, Empire and Slavery, 1770–1830*, edited by Richard Bessel, Nicholas Guyatt, and Jane Rendall, 121–38. Houndmills, Basingstoke: Palgrave Macmillan, 2010.

Worden, Nigel. "Indian Ocean Slaves in Cape Town, 1695–1807." In *Critical Readings on Global Slavery*, edited by Damian Alan Pargas and Felicia Rosu, 1368–96. Leiden: Brill, 2018.

Wu, Duncan. "'A Vehicle of Private Malice': Eliza Hamilton Dunlop and the *Sydney Herald*." *Review of English Studies* 65, no. 272 (November 2014): 888–903.

Contributors

Katie Hansord completed her PhD, on settler women's poetry in colonial Australia, at Deakin University. She has published work on the poets Caroline Leakey, Eliza Hamilton Dunlop and Louisa Lawson, and co-edited a special issue of *New Scholar* Cosmopolitanism and its Critics. She is the author of *Colonial Australian Women Poets: Political Voice and Feminist Traditions* (2021).

Anna Johnston is Deputy Director of the Institute for Advanced Studies in the Humanities and Associate Professor in English Literature in the School of Communication and Arts at the University of Queensland. She has been an Australian Research Council Future Fellow and a Queen Elizabeth II Research Fellow. She has published widely in colonial and postcolonial studies. Her books include *Missionary Writing and Empire, 1800–1860* (2003), *The Paper War: Morality, Print Culture, and Power in Colonial New South Wales* (2011), and *Travelling Home*, Walkabout *Magazine and Mid-Twentieth-Century Australia* (with Mitchell Rolls, 2016).

Peter Minter is a poet, poetry editor and writer on poetry and poetics. His books include *Rhythm in a Dorsal Fin, Empty Texas, blue grass* and *In the Serious Light of Nothing*. He was a founding editor of *Cordite* poetry magazine, poetry editor for leading Australian journals *Meanjin* and *Overland*, and has co-edited anthologies such as *Calyx: 30 Contemporary Australian Poets* and the *Macquarie PEN Anthology of Aboriginal Literature*. He teaches at the University of Sydney in Indigenous Studies, Creative Writing and Australian Literature.

Jason R. Rudy is a Professor of English at the University of Maryland, College Park, in the United States. He is the author of *Imagined Homelands: British Poetry in the Colonies* (2017) and *Electric Meters: Victorian Physiological Poetics* (2009). He is currently writing an authorised biography of the Indigenous Australian painter Gordon Syron.

Graeme Skinner is a musicologist and music historian. He is author of the biography *Peter Sculthorpe: The Making of an Australian Composer* (2007/2015), and has published widely on Australian music history. He is an Honorary Associate, University of Sydney, and curator of *Australharmony* (https://sydney.edu.au/ paradisec/australharmony), an open access resource on Australian colonial music. He also curates a virtual colonial music archive inside the National Library of Australia's Trove, currently consisting of over 19,000 items. (https://trove.nla.gov.au/search?l-publictag=Australian+colonial+music)

Jim Wafer is a linguist-anthropologist with a background in literature and religious studies, and a conjoint senior lecturer in anthropology at the University of Newcastle. His books include *Recirculating Songs: Revitalising the Singing Practices of Indigenous Australia*, (co-editor, 2017), *A Handbook of Aboriginal Languages of New South Wales and the Australian Capital Territory* (co-author, 2008), *Out in the Valley: Hunter Gay and Lesbian Histories*, (co-editor, 2000), and *The Taste of Blood: Spirit Possession in Brazilian Candomblé*, 1991. He is currently working on a critical edition of Lancelot Threlkeld's translations into the language of the Hunter River and Lake Macquarie.

Elizabeth Webby is Professor Emerita of Australian Literature at the University of Sydney. She has had a longstanding interest in colonial Australian literature. Her publications include *Early Australian Poetry* (1982), *Colonial Voices* (1989), *Modern Australian Plays* (1990), *The Cambridge Companion to Australian Literature* (2000) and, as joint editor, *Happy Endings* (1987), *Goodbye to Romance* (1989), *The Penguin Book of Australian Ballads* (1993) and *Australian Feminism: A Companion* (1998). She has also published numerous book chapters, articles and reviews and been a contributing editor of *The Penguin New Literary History of Australia* (1988) and *The Macquarie PEN Anthology of Australian Literature* (2009).

Duncan Wu is Raymond Wagner Professor of Literary Studies Georgetown University, Washington DC. He has authored or edited a number of books, principally in the areas of Romantic Studies and Contemporary British Drama. These include *Romanticism: An Anthology* (four editions, 1994, 1998, 2007, 2012); *A Companion to Romanticism* (1998); Wordsworth's *Reading 1770–1815* (two vols., 1993, 1995); *Wordsworth: An Inner Life* (2000); *Selected Writings of William Hazlitt* (nine vols., 1998); and *Making Plays: Interviews with Contemporary British Playwrights and Directors* (2000).

Index

Corporate
Travel Management

James M. Poynter
Metropolitan State College

A NATIONAL PUBLISHERS BOOK
PRENTICE HALL
Englewood Cliffs, New Jersey 07632

Library of Congress Cataloging-in-Publication Data

Poynter, James M.
    Corporate travel management / James M. Poynter.
      p. cm.
    ISBN 0–13–176140–4
    1. Business travel. I. Title.
  G156.5.B86P68 1990
  658.3′83—dc20   89–28421
                         CIP

Editorial/production supervision and
   interior design: Fred Dahl and Rose Kernan
Cover design: George Cornell
Manufacturing buyer: David Dickey

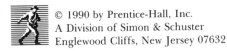 © 1990 by Prentice-Hall, Inc.
A Division of Simon & Schuster
Englewood Cliffs, New Jersey 07632

Printed in the United States of America
10 9 8 7 6 5 4 3 2 1

ISBN 0-13-176140-4

Prentice-Hall International (UK) Limited, *London*
Prentice-Hall of Australia Pty. Limited, *Sydney*
Prentice-Hall Canada Inc., *Toronto*
Prentice-Hall Hispanoamericana, S.A., *Mexico*
Prentice-Hall of India Private Limited, *New Delhi*
Prentice-Hall of Japan, Inc., *Tokyo*
Simon & Schuster Asia Pte. Ltd., *Singapore*
Editora Prentice-Hall do Brasil, Ltda., *Rio de Janeiro*

To

Carol Duerr, CCTE,
Business Travel News' Corporate Travel Manager of the Year for 1988

and to

The Association of Corporate Travel Executives

Contents

CHAPTER 3

The Multiple Functions of Corporate Travel Departments, 23

CHAPTER 4

The Roles of the Corporate Travel Manager, 33

CHAPTER 7

Basic Financial Management and Corporate Travel Payment Systems, 74

CHAPTER 8

Managing for Profits, 91

CHAPTER 9

Saving Money, 125

CHAPTER 10

Money-making Affiliations, 149

CHAPTER 11

The Corporate Travel Profit Center Business Plan, 162

CHAPTER 15

The Proposal and Contracting Process, 263

CHAPTER 16

Internal Considerations, 297

CHAPTER 17

Group and Leisure Travel, 309

CHAPTER 18

Corporate Travel Policies, 318

CHAPTER 19

Professionalism, 327

Preface

Corporate Travel Management is the first comprehensive book on corporate travel management to be published. Therefore, it meets several needs. The book is designed to provide travel educators with a text for a standard one-semester or one-quarter course devoted to corporate travel management. It is also designed to meet the needs of a new corporate travel manager who has recently been assigned the task of managing most or all corporate travel for a business, government entity, or an association. Finally, this book is designed to meet the needs of experienced corporate travel managers who are undertaking new or different aspects of corporate travel management and who seek a reference publication to guide them in undertaking these new tasks.

To meet the multitude of needs of the student, teacher, new and experienced corporate travel manager, this book moves from the presentation of elementary aspects of corporate travel management to the more intricate and precise tasks. Chapters 1 through 4 present a background for the field of corporate travel management. Chapters 5 and 6 discuss the interrelationships between the corporate travel department and others in the industry. Financial management is the theme for Chapters 7 through 12. Chapter 13 stands alone in discussing the intricacies of automation. The process of undertaking a corporate travel study, developing a Request for Proposal, reviewing Requests for Proposal, and selecting a travel agency vendor constitutes the subjects of Chapters 14 and 15. The last part of the book, Chapters 16 through 19, detail corporate travel operations and emphasize professionalism.

Complementing the chapters themselves are end-of-chapter summaries, end-of-chapter discussion questions, role plays, and case situation discussions. Both corporate travel managers and students will find the case situation discussions and the role plays beneficial in considering the direct applications of the corporate travel management principles presented.

Several special features of the book make it particularly valuable as a resource document for those currently working in the field. Most corporate travel managers have started their jobs since deregulation. The discussion of deregulation presents a historical viewpoint which provides the answers to questions many corporate travel managers ask regarding why the systems in effect in the industry exist the way they do. This historical presentation can remove some of the confusion found by many in the industry who do not understand why the industry operates the way it does.

The discussion of interrelations provides corporate travel managers who plan to undertake direct vendor negotiations with an understanding of the sensitivities in the industry and negotiation approaches that can be considered to provide the best possibility for success.

The financial management section of the book has two special features that corporate travel managers and students will find of unique value. The formulas for travel agency profit determination are presented along with formulas for airline computer reservation profitability. One corporation with a $10 million travel budget obtained automation on a totally gratis basis after being exposed to the financial formulas in these chapters and utilizing them in direct automation negotiations. In addition, an entire chapter is devoted to moving the corporate travel department from a cost center status to a profit center. An increasing number of corporate travel managers are looking at this as a direction in which to go in order to obtain greater internal security and to provide greater benefits to their companies.

The automation discussion is comprehensive. It provides for the first time an analysis of the AOS Telephone system charges which have recently plagued corporate travelers and corporate travel budgets.

The Request for Proposal and proposal review process presents a unique approach toward obtaining funding for corporate travel manager continuing education. This effective approach should be of considerable value to those currently working in the field of corporate travel management.

The operations and professionalism section of the book provides answers to the many questions corporate travel managers ask about adding group, leisure, and incentive travel to their menu of services. It presents both the pros and cons in a unique treatment of this often controversial addition to corporate travel management. In addition, the chapter on professionalism provides an overview of professional opportunities for growth in the corporate travel management field today. These are just a few of the unique aspects of this book. There are many more.

In the belief that books should be fun, as well as educational, the case situations are presented in a frequently humorous format. Although they may be funny, they are based on serious, and in almost all cases, real-life examples of often controversial corporate travel business concerns. Although the names have been changed with an often-humorous slant, case situations are real enough that those corporate travel managers who lived through the situations discussed, will frequently be able to recognize them as their own. Many other corporate travel managers will be able to identify with a large number of the case situations presented.

For the student or the new corporate travel manager, it is suggested that this book be read in the normal manner of progressing from Chapter 1 through Chapter 19. After reading the chapter, stop and consider the main points in the chapter. Review the end-of-chapter summaries and answer the end-of-chapter discussion questions. This summary and question combination will provide an excellent review for the entire chapter. Next, read the role play and attempt to pick up on the role play either in your own mind or, even better, through a discussion with another student or another corporate travel manager. This will provide another opportunity to review major points in the chapter. Finally, turn to the case situation. After reading the case situation, give some thought as to how you would handle the situation and what recommendations you would make. You may even wish to detail these in writing.

An alternative approach for the student or the new corporate travel manager is to start each chapter with a review of the summary and the end-of-chapter questions. This will provide an overview of the major points in the chapter and some of the most important questions that are answered in the chapter. After utilizing the review and end-of-chapter questions as an introduction to the chapter, read the chapter looking for the answers to the questions as you go. This is not to suggest that this is the only purpose of reading the chapter, but it is suggested that you consciously think about the questions and perhaps even write down the answers to questions as you come to them in the reading of the chapter. After the chapter reading, again go back over the summary and the questions before moving on to the role play and the case situation.

For the experienced corporate travel manager, this book presents an excellent resource. The experienced manager may not wish to read the book from cover to cover, but may want to delve into specific chapters on an "as needed" basis. It is suggested that you utilize the table of contents and the index to identify those sections of the book that meet your specific needs and you may wish to go directly to those sections when the need arises.

This book is the result of the input and concerns of literally scores of corporate travel managers and it is the outgrowth of industry certification courses, corporate travel management seminars, and a multitude of industry and student courses. It was reviewed by and bears the strong imprint of Carol Duerr, CCTE, Robert Vaiden, Elisabeth Van Dyke, Keith Powell, and Jeanie Harris. It is designed to bring together the contributions of all for the professional development and the additional corporate travel management expertise of its readers. It will be updated on a regular basis.

If you have suggestions or recommendations that will make the book better, please do not hesitate to write to the author accordingly at the following address: 6994 East Heritage Place, Englewood, Colorado 80111. There is a strong probability that your suggestions will be included in the next revision and I thank you in advance for your contributions.

Acknowledgements

It takes many contributions to build a quality book. This book is dedicated to the person who consistently provided contributions to its development, Carol Duerr, CCTE. Others who watched over it for lengthy periods of its development and who are thanked for that are: Ellen Coleman, Paul Corey, Elisabeth O'Brian, and Rose Kernan. Don Hawkins of George Washington University contributed considerable information and material. Other educator contributors who provided essential material and contributions include Christina Navis of Cloud County Community College, Scott Feinerman of West Los Angeles College, Katherine Heiligmann of Salem State College, Shelly Friedland of Kingsborough Community College, Elisabeth Van Dyke of the University of New Haven, Keith Powell of Coastline Community College, Cord Hansen-Sturm and Richard Selden of the New School for Social Research, and Jeanie Harris of Long Beach City College. Certainly the book could not have the educational quality it has gained without the contributions of these educators.

Major contributions have come from corporate travel managers and those who work closely with corporate travel managers. There were so many who contributed that I cannot thank them all. However, special thanks go to the late Peter Jensen of the Association of Corporate Travel Executives who was so supportive throughout the project. I had planned to dedicate this book to both Carol Duerr and Peter Jensen. Shortly before his death, however, Peter asked that the dedication be to Carol and ACTE. Bowing to his wishes, the dedication reads accordingly. Also special thanks to Judith Dettinger-Gardner, Vice President of Consulting Services with American Express Travel Management Services; Jeanie Thompson-Smith, President of Topaz Enterprises; John Seng, Account Supervisor with Henry J. Kaufman and Associates; Robert Vaiden, Manager, General Services with Ciba-Geigy, Pharmaceuticals Division; and Sheryl Hanson, Administrative Services Section Manager with Hewlett Packard. They have all contributed in their own special ways.

Other corporate travel managers who have given considerable assistance in the development of this book include Mary Bittrich with AT&T; E. J. Hewitt with Libbey Owens Ford; Lynn Hutto formerly with the University of Michigan Travel Services; Carol Cooper with AT&T; Helen Leopold, CCTE, with Citicorp Diners Club; Donna Peterson with the National Cattleman's Association;

xx

Nancy Rowley, CCTE, with U.S. West; Diane Hawkins with AT&T; Eileen Wingate with Harvard University; Adrienne Marchese, CCTE, with Barclays Bank; Lowell Vieman with Cedarapids; Maureen Sober with Adolph Coors; Betty Atwood, CCTE with the Manville Corporation; Boyd Kessler with Sundstrand Fluid Handling; Kathleen Peterson with Storage Technology Corporation; Chris Johnson, CCTE with Ball Aerospace Systems Division; Betty Pepper with the Platte River Power Authority; Loretta Martin with Gates Rubber; Linda Neese with Autotrol; Joann Goddard, CCTE with Petroleum Information; Treva Hankins with the Boy Scouts of America; Elisabeth Lima with Columbia Pictures; and Anna Schultz with Cypress Minerals.

Thanks are also extended to students who have researched the field of corporate travel management and whose research has contributed to the literature in the field of corporate travel management, as well as to this book. These are Paige Curtis with Uniglobe Travel and Mischa Bettis with American Express.

Travel industry executives have made substantial contributions. Thanks are extended to Andy Menkes with Forster-Joyce Travel; Jim Alkon with Business Travel News; Kevin Ficco with Delta Airlines; Bill O'Conner with The Trinity Group; Jan Haver with Destination Travel; Dan Bicker with Classic World Travel; Richard Eastman with The Eastman Group; Bob Graze with ACTE, Joanne Davis with Ask Mr. Foster; Robert Montgomery with Polk World Travel; Walter Maschmeyer with Lufthansa; Mike Cedar with Master Travel; and Linda Chambers with Thomas Cook Travel.

Special thanks go to my wife, Sorore, and my sons, Lewis, Robert, and Michael for living with several years of research, typing at all hours, and all the other inconveniences that go along with living in the same place where a book is being developed.

CHAPTER 1

Deregulation and Corporate Travel

Introduction

Since the revitalization of American business and industry during and after World War II, there has been a recognition among an increasing number of companies that travel is, or can be, a major corporate cost. Together with this recognition has come a desire to "manage" corporate travel or, perhaps better put, a desire to "manage" corporate travel costs.

Jack Witherspoon, President of the National Business Travel Association, points out the reason corporate travel management is important, saying,

> "The importance of the business travel manager really surfaces when one considers that the three highest costs incurred by any organization are salaries, data collection, and travel and entertainment. The only one of these three expenses that can be fully controlled through strident management is travel and entertainment." (*Business Travel Review*, July, 1988)

Indications are that more than twice the number of business travel managers are employed in industry today than prior to deregulation. In fact, the *1988 American Express Survey of Business Travel Management (Fourth Edition, Executive Summary)* page 10 finds that twenty-nine percent of all companies it surveyed now, ". . . have an employee with the title of Travel Manager, . . ." This is more than a seventy percent increase in two years (since the 1986 study was undertaken). However, just a few years ago there was far less to manage. This was the era before deregulation.

This chapter, and the five that follow it, clearly set the stage for corporate travel management. They identify the reasons why a corporate travel department is created, the political structure within which the corporate travel department operates, and the importance of corporate travel department mentors. These chapters also identify the roles and functions of corporate travel managers and of the corporate travel department. They identify the standard roles which tend to be found in every corporate travel department (although there are a very few exceptions) along with optional roles which are sometimes found in a number of corporate travel departments and, in some cases, are found in only a few departments. In addition to the roles, the functions of managing travel services, offering financial services, budgeting travel, and organizing travel expense and other reports are discussed. This section of the book also addresses the interrelationships between the corporate travel department and travel vendors. The travel agency and airline interrelationships are explored in detail, but hotel and ground transportation interrelationships are also discussed.

However, before the current status of corporate travel can be understood and appreciated, it is helpful to see why corporate travel management has expanded so rapidly. In order to do this, one needs some historical perspective. Just a few years ago, there were far fewer corporate travel management opportunities. This was the era before deregulation.

Pre-deregulation

Prior to the deregulation of airlines and travel agencies, airlines were *regulated*. Regulation meant that airlines operated under strict policies and guidelines set by the *Civil Aeronautics Board* (CAB) in what were called *CAB Orders*. Airlines and, to some extent, travel agencies were exempt from anti-trust laws. They were able to operate in ways in which other businesses, because of the danger of violating federal anti-trust laws, could not operate. They were also unable to do many of the things other businesses could do because of CAB limitations.

There were both good and bad aspects to the CAB regulated air travel environment. By any measure, the United States air travel system was a smooth, well-integrated, comfortable, and well-working system for travelers and for the industry. It was a system copied by other countries and other carriers all over the world. If a passenger flew frequently between cities, he knew the schedules, the carriers, and the fares because none of them changed with any degree of frequency. He knew his ticket would be accepted by every air carrier on which he flew (there was total *interlining* between air carriers (i.e., they accepted one another's tickets and baggage)) and he knew his baggage would probably arrive at the final destination with him. Service was excellent and so were the meals.

Historical Airline/Agency Markets

Looking at the history of the travel agency business in the United States, one finds that travel agencies started out as steamship agencies. Even until World War II, most companies called themselves *steamship agencies* and saw their business as being mainly the transport of immigrants to the United States paid for by family members currently working in America. Each payday, the men currently residing in America would give the steamship agency money toward passage of a relative coming to the United States from the "old country." Although steamship agencies handled air travel reservations and tickets before the war, it was only after World War II that air travel became a major part of their business. With the increase in the popularity of travel by air, the development of larger, safer aircraft, the reduction in air travel costs, and the desire of many to vacation in Europe, steamship agencies changed their names to travel agencies and travel agencies started to grow in number.

While airlines appointed travel agencies to sell air tickets, the air carriers maintained from the beginning that corporate travel was the sole domain of the airlines. Travel agencies were to handle leisure travel only, leaving the air carriers to handle business travel. Airline city ticket offices were set up in downtown business locations and the *Universal Air Travel Plan* (UATP) credit card payment plan was established with cards issued to corporate accounts. Corporate travelers could use the card to pay for air tickets on all major air carriers, but travel agencies were barred from accepting the cards. In addition, to make sure travel agencies concentrated on handling leisure travel, a two-tier commission structure was established. Airlines paid travel agencies two percent less on the business travel they booked than on their leisure travel bookings.

Corporate travelers were encouraged to book directly with air carriers in other ways as well. Airline sales representatives were assigned to major corporate accounts and free airline VIP room memberships were provided to many corporate frequent fliers until government regulations prohibiting this were passed. With the CAB authorizing only a maximum of two carriers to serve any city pair, it was easy for business travelers to remember the air carriers serving any particular destination. Air fares and flight schedules changed infrequently due to the lengthy and difficult CAB approval process. Both carriers serving a city pair had to fly at agreed-upon times and charge the same air fare. All of this meant that corporate travelers, travel managers, and booking secretaries found it very easy to make air travel arrangements through air carrier reservation offices.

Air System Concerns

But as good as everything seemed to be, there were concerns. The *National Business Travel Association* (NBTA) raised questions about the cost of air travel. The NBTA also noted that the system allowed travel agencies to receive a commission from air carriers, but it would not allow corporate travel departments to receive a commission on the air travel that they, themselves generated. Tour operators also had concerns. Airlines were setting up in-house tour companies and giving blocked air space only to their own in-house tours. This sometimes left no space for independent tour companies and some tour operators went out of business. Pan American World Airways expressed concern because the CAB route authorization system did not give it a feeder system for its international flights. And a growing number of people in government maintained that government monies were not being spent well in regulating the air travel sector of the economy. Free enterprise, they argued, would lessen government dependency, reduce government airport subsidies, and lower government costs. Jimmy Carter ran for President on a campaign that included the deregulation of an entire government department—the Civil Aeronautics Board.

The system President Carter deregulated had both flaws and benefits. To appreciate both, it is important to understand the CAB system and how it worked. To understand the effects of deregulation, it is important to know what the Civil

Aeronautics Board has done, to know the difference between agent exclusivity and marketing exclusitivy, to know the mandated alterations affecting exclusivity and affecting the accreditation system, to understand the ruling relating to the *Area Settlement Plan* and its anti-trust immunity, and to know how the Civil Aeronautics Board interpreted the act that authorized its own demise.

Few corporate travel managers, airline executives, or travel agents have read Public Law 95-504, commonly called the *Airline Deregulation Act of 1978*. It was designed to deregulate the airline industry, not the travel agency industry, and few of its forty-seven sections were designed to affect travel agencies either directly or indirectly. Almost none were designed to affect corporate travel managers directly. But the few Deregulation Act sections that do either affect travel agencies and corporate travel departments or that have the power to affect travel agencies and corporate travel departments provided the Civil Aeronautics Board with a tool that resulted in altering some of the most important relationships between airlines, travel agencies, and corporate travel departments. Many airlines and travel agencies were affected to such a degree that they went out of business.

Anti-trust Immunity and the Exclusivities

For an understanding of the effects of the Deregulation Act, it is necessary to go back to obtain an understanding of the provisions of the Federal Aviation Act of 1958. Under this act, any agreements between carriers which affected air transportation had to be filed and approved by the Civil Aeronautics Board. The Board's Bureau of Operating Rights had a department known as the Agreements Section. This section kept the filings of all *Air Traffic Conference* (ATC) agreements dealing with or affecting travel agencies with the Board. The key point of the 1958 law, however, was that any agreement approved by the Board was automatically given immunity from anti-trust laws. This meant that any agreement between the Air Traffic Conference and travel agencies, which the Board approved automatically, received anti-trust immunity. This immunity was extended to agency exclusivity, agency marketing exclusivity, the operation of the system of accrediting travel agencies, and the *Area Settlement Plan* (a central ticket payment processing arrangement through regional banks). The crux of the Deregulation Act related to the continuation or cessation of anti-trust immunities granted by extension under the *1958 Federal Aviation Act*.

To understand what happened, it is important to understand how the system worked. With most items of importance, international route awards excepted, the process followed was the initiation of a case through hearings conducted by a CAB-approved law judge. The judge would make a recommendation to the Civil Aeronautics Board as a whole and the Board issued a ruling. Board rulings had the effect of law in the air travel industry, but airline interpretations of the rulings did not have the same effect. In the case of route awards, the system added a step. The CAB made recommendations of the carrier(s) to serve new or abandoned routes to the President. He either approved or disapproved. This gave aviation power to the President and some Presidents used that power to a considerable degree. Under one President, for example, every route award went to an air carrier based in his home state.

The Agency Deregulation Ruling

In the case of travel agency deregulation, Judge Yoder heard the case. Testimony was conducted, as in any civil law case, and Judge Yoder made a recommendation to the entire Civil Aeronautics Board in the early Fall of 1982. Judge Yoder's recommendations were generally favorable to the travel agency industry cause (namely, the agency's desire to continue holding limited anti-trust regulation immunity), but the final determination had to be made by the full Board. Although it is customary for the Board to act directly upon the findings and recommendations of the hearing law judge, in December, 1982, the release of the preliminary decision of the full Board reflected considerable changes from Judge Yoder's recommendation. The Board's preliminary decision was detrimental to the travel agency cause. The final decision on the case in CAB ruling number 336 issued in January, 1983 was almost identical to the preliminary one. Like the air carriers, travel agencies lost almost all anti-trust immunity.

Exclusivity Distinctions

Understanding some of the key elements of the CAB competitive marketing case decision will help to clarify how deregulation as it has evolved (and continues to evolve) directly affects corporate travel. Judge Yoder found a distinction between agency exclusivity and marketing exclusivity. Agency exclusivity, he noted, prohibits a principal/sales agency relationship between an airline and any person (or business) other than an accredited agent. This is crucial, since Judge Yoder's interpretation of "agency exclusivity" would eliminate a possible principal/sales agency relationship to exist or to come about between an airline and a corporate travel department. Marketing exclusivity, on the other hand, prohibits the payment of sales remuneration or commission to any person (or business) except accredited agencies. Again, this would eliminate the payment of commissions to corporate travel departments.

It is generally agreed that Judge Yoder would have had the agency exclusivity continued under anti-trust waiver, but that he would have opened up marketing exclusivity by disallowing anti-trust waivers and allowing commissions to be paid to corporate travel departments. The full Board, however, disallowed continuation of both agency exclusivity and marketing exclusivity by eliminating anti-trust waivers in both of these areas. This allowed each airline to appoint its own sales outlets and to pay commissions or other remuneration as they see fit to any marketing entity they wish to have sell their tickets. However, a two-year phase-out period was mandated.

Travel agencies continued to be protected by anti-trust waiver on the sale of *interline tickets* (tickets on flights where two or more carriers were involved). For the sale of *on-line tickets*, the anti-trust waiver was eliminated in January, 1983. Effectively, what this meant was that each airline could appoint any vendor of its choice to sell tickets only on its airline and could remunerate them in whatever way they wished. The term *vendor* could apply to a corporate travel department, thus opening the way, for the first time, for a corporate travel department to receive commissions on the tickets it generates for itself. However, any non-travel agency vendor (including corporate travel departments) would not have the approval to sell, nor would such a vendor receive remuneration for the sale of tickets when the passenger would change from one airline to another on his scheduled itinerary.

Travel agencies were concerned that airlines would immediately offer commissions to corporate travel departments after the phase-out period, in 1984. Because almost all tickets issued before deregulation were interline tickets (the CAB made it a general policy not to allow more than two carriers to serve any city pair prior to deregulation), they were not fearful of direct corporate travel department appointments prior to the end of the phase-out period. Meanwhile, they pushed for a permanent extension to both agency and marketing exclusivity by trying to get a new law enacted by Congress, the *Air Travelers' Protection Act* (which really was an act designed to protect travel agencies). Although it came close to being passed, airlines pulled their support for the act at the last minute and the act failed to pass in Congress.

The travel agency retention of anti-trust immunity on interline ticket sales could well have proven to be only a hollow victory for travel agencies. Another provision of the ruling allowed any two or more airlines to agree to accept tickets and pay commissions for writing tickets by non-agency vendors (if those two or more airlines were in agreement). This additional provision could have taken away the two-year protection of continued anti-trust immunity for travel agencies in regard to the sale of interline tickets. However, it was a moot point. Ticket sale exclusivity was taken away completely from travel agencies in 1984.

The Threat of Travel Agency Booking Power

Something happened outside of the official regulations and rulings that effectively continued travel agency marketing exclusivity far beyond the two years agents thought they had. Shortly after airline deregulation became effective in January, 1982, airlines realized that they were no longer bound by the CAB-imposed commission levels. They started offering more and more commissions to travel agencies in order to get agencies to sell tickets on their carriers. Each carrier watched the competition and hastened to meet its competitor's commission payment percentage. A settling out rapidly occurred, leaving all major carriers paying ten percent commissions on domestic air travel.

Then a major carrier announced in the trade press that a ten percent commission was too expensive for the carrier and it would reduce the commission level. Only two other carriers followed suit. Two things immediately became obvious. First, no other carrier followed in reducing its commission level. Of much greater importance, however, was immediate booking level drops on the three carriers which had announced plans to lower commissions. All three carriers saw a disasterous drop in travel agency bookings the same day the plan to pay lower commissions was announced in the trade press. And each day that passed reflected even steeper drops in travel agency bookings for the three carriers. Within a week all three carriers had announced that they would continue paying commissions of ten percent. The result was a solid recognition in the airline world of the power of travel agencies to switch carriers if one or several carriers did something travel agencies considered to be detrimental to their economic health. Although the CAB ruling left the door wide open for commission payments to corporate travel departments, the economic impact of travel agency wrath felt by an airline when travel agencies stop booking that carrier, combined with the inability of airlines to act together (they now face potential prosecution under anti-trust laws if they all get together to appoint corporate travel departments or to pay corporations a commission) resulted in no major carrier being willing to be the first to pay commissions to businesses. While the vehicle to get commissions continues to stand ready to be used, no major air carrier has used it.

Adding to the difficulty for corporate travel departments in receiving appointments and thereby possibly being paid commissions, is the wording of the CAB ruling. Much was nebulous about the full Board ruling that eliminated travel agency anti-trust waivers with the phase-out elimination of both agency exclusivity and marketing exclusivity. It was open to considerable interpretation in relationship to various practical aspects of administration. In relation to the accreditation system, the CAB ruling did not find fault with the appointment standards and the criteria for appointing travel agencies to sell airline tickets, but it did not set any standards or criteria for non-agency vendors (i.e., corporate travel departments) appointment. If such standards or criteria were to be set, they would be determined on an individual airline-by-airline basis. The Board ruling pointed out that,

> "The need for indefinite antitrust immunity has not been fully established. The public interest arguments that have been raised are founded on the view that carriers will abandon the ATC and IATA systems because of the cost of lawsuits. Their argument makes sense only if any accreditation program would be found to be anti-competitive. It is clear, however, that with the exception of a handful of anti-competitive provisions the agreements are on balance pro-competitive."

The Board had no doubt that with modifications, the agreements could be conformed to the standards of the anti-trust laws. The Board, therefore, considered it highly unlikely that carriers would abandon the, ". . . substantial benefits of common accreditation to avoid the cost of defending it against frivolous lawsuits." Therefore, anti-trust immunity for the accreditation system was withdrawn, but the continuation of accreditation standards and the appointment system for travel agencies was not disallowed. The system, of course, has continued with the establishment of the Airline Reporting Corporation (ARC) and the International Airlines Travel Agent Network (IATAN), but as expected, the appointment standards for travel agencies have become far less rigorous than if they were mandated and protected under anti-trust laws. A similar finding resulted in relationship to the Area Settlement Plan. The protection of anti-trust immunity was lifted, but the Settlement Plan, itself, was allowed to continue.

Case Ramifications for Corporate Travel Departments

Although the Board rulings on agency exclusivity, marketing exclusivity, the accreditation system, appointment standards, and the Area Settlement Plan were the major areas of concern to corporate travel managers and to travel agents, there were many areas of the CAB ruling that have affected corporate travel. These rulings continue to affect corporate travel departments depending on their pre-deregulation working arrangements, the airline/travel agency working arrangements that both prefer, and the degree to which corporate travel departments expect to participate in commission sharing. For those wishing to read the CAB *Competitive Marketing Case* decision in its entirety, it can be found in many library archives or purchased from the Government Printing Office. Refer to CAB Transmittal Number 336.

Deregulation Confusion

After having gained a basic understanding of what the major immediate aspects of the marketing case decision were in relationship to corporate travel managers and retail travel agencies, it is important to identify the longer-term results that have come about. Most agree that deregulation has both helped and hurt corporate travel. There has been a reorientation of the traditional airline supplier/ travel agency vendor relationship as it relates to corporate travel, but there is still confusion. Two factors have contributed to the confusion. The first is that much of the final ruling was not expected, especially the difference between marketing exclusivity for off-line sales and the waiver of anti-trust immunity for the marketing of on-line sales. The second, and more important, factor was the very large movement of corporate travel business from direct airline bookings to travel agency bookings during the first few months of airline deregulation. To understand how this major change in booking patterns came about, it is necessary to go back to the pre-deregulation era to determine why most air travel was booked through air carriers until the advent of deregulation. (See the previous section entitled "Historical Airline/Agency Matters.")

Air Deregulation Confusion and a Switch to Travel Agencies

Everything changed in January, 1981. Between January and August, when the air controllers' strike stopped immediate air-carrier certification, over one thousand new carriers were authorized to start flying between states. This compares with only eleven air carriers holding such authorization prior to deregulation. In the first week of deregulation, some carriers changed their schedules twenty times in an hour. Scheduled carriers increased their flights so rapidly that by the end of the first five days of deregulation, one carrier found itself flying to twice the number of destinations it had served the previous week. Prices went up and down so fast that some airline reservationists admitted they did not know what the price was at times.

Confusion reigned. Everybody wanted to fly because prices were coming down almost daily. Airline reservation offices were so busy that corporate travelers and booking secretaries had to spend long periods of time calling to get through. And once information was provided, there was no guarantee it would not change by flight time. Air carriers started merging and started heading for bankruptcy. The immediate result was a massive move by corporate travelers to book air travel with travel agencies. Instead of spending long periods calling one airline after another only to get information that frequently changed, travel agencies would make the reservation, issue the tickets, take on the responsibility of getting the best fare, and deliver the tickets. In a matter of months travel agencies began booking the major portion of tickets for almost every air carrier in the market.

Corporate Travel Department Expansion

Deregulation also meant an increase in the number of corporate travel departments throughout corporate America. The changing prices, the marketing options now made available by air carriers and travel agencies alike, the start-up of wholesale rebating, and the general confusion meant that air travelers could get frequent flier bonuses, first-class upgrades, drink coupons, and a myriad of other benefits for the traveler, but not necessarily for the company. These new factors also meant that the company could get volume discounts (or rebates), additional services, and cost-saving reports like they had never had before. However, companies found that to get all the benefits for the company, to keep travelers from taking options beneficial to the traveler and not to the company, and to consistently find the best "deals" for the company, it was necessary to have a person responsible for corporate travel. As more and more companies came to this conclusion, and as more and more companies compared their corporate travel expenses/benefits with other companies that had corporate travel departments, *business* or *corporate travel departments* (BTDs/CTDs) began to be created.

Summary

The desire to manage corporate travel dates back to, at least, World War II. Since the deregulation of the airline industry, managing corporate travel has become even more important. Prior to deregulation, the Civil Aeronautics Board regulated travel and, by extension, the ways in which both airlines and travel agencies worked. There was much that was good about the pre-deregulation system. Travelers knew which airline would fly between cities because no more than two carriers were allowed to fly between each city pair. All major carriers were interlined with one another and, therefore, accepted both tickets and baggage from each other. Service was considered to be very good and there were regular flights into even very small cities throughout the United States.

There were concerns, though. Many, especially corporations, felt that the cost of air travel was far too expensive. Corporate travel managers wanted to receive commissions and issue tickets themselves instead of working through travel agencies and allowing agencies to get the commission. Tour operators were sometimes locked out of group space because airlines started developing their own tour companies. And, an increasing number of government executives came to the conclusion that greater benefits would accrue to all if air travel was deregulated.

An understanding of how the Civil Aeronautics Board regulated air travel can be beneficial. Immunity from anti-trust laws was extended to air carriers and travel agencies when there was an agreement which the Board approved between the Air Traffic Conference and travel agencies. This primarily affected travel agency exclusivity, travel agency marketing exclusivity, the operation of a system of accrediting travel agencies, and a central bank ticket payment processing plan. As it related to air carriers, the Civil Aeronautics Board made recommendations relating to new route awards (these had to be approved by the President), air fares, and flight schedules. Free price competition was not allowed.

Although airline deregulation went into effect in January, 1981, travel agency deregulation was delayed until January, 1983. Travel agents fought to retain anti-trust immunity and the recommendations of the initial hearing judge were very positive. The judge's interpretation of agency exclusivity would have eliminated a possible air carrier/sales agency relationship to exist between an airline and a corporate travel department. Also it would have prohibited the payment of sales remunerations or commissions to corporate travel departments. The full Board did not go along with the judge's recommendations, but they did agree to a phase-out period which delayed the opportunity for airlines to pay commissions directly to corporate travel departments until January, 1984. Although travel agencies attempted to get a bill passed in Congress to retain their anti-trust waiver (and commission exclusivity), air carriers pulled their support for the act at the last minute and Congress did not pass the bill. With deregulation, therefore, airlines can now pay commissions directly to corporate travel departments. They may appoint corporate travel departments to sell tickets on behalf of the airline(s). However, the threat of travel agencies not booking a carrier which might pay commissions directly to a corporate travel department is substantial. In 1982, several carriers attempted to reduce commissions and found that the level of travel agency bookings for their carriers fell substantially. As a result, the commission levels were reinstated and the travel agencies were able to show air carriers the substantial power that they could levy when a carrier acted in a manner that was detrimental to travel agency economics. Many agree that it is for this reason that no major air carrier has started paying across-the-board commissions to corporate travel departments.

Meanwhile, other aspects of deregulation have resulted in the proliferation of corporate travel departments. Historically, airlines encouraged direct booking of corporate travel with air carriers rather than going through travel agencies. Prior to deregulation, air carriers paid travel agencies a lower commission for booking air travel than they paid for leisure bookings. They allowed businesses to charge airline tickets on Universal Air Travel Plan (UATP) credit cards but they did not allow travel agencies to accept UATP cards for ticket payment. Airline sales representatives called on corporate accounts and provided many corporate frequent fliers with free VIP room memberships. But perhaps the main reason why travelers booked their flights directly with air carriers was the ease with which they could make reservations and obtain tickets.

Under the Civil Aeronautical Board regulations no more than two carriers could fly between city pairs and flight schedules and air fares tended to be the same. Therefore, it was easy for travelers to remember which two carriers flew between any particular pair of cities and, since they could charge their tickets to the company's UATP card and have them either available for pick up at the airport or mailed to their offices, the convenience resulted in almost all corporate travelers booking directly with air carriers.

With deregulation, however, confusion reigned. Over one thousand new airlines started flying during the first year of deregulation. Carriers that were currently certified to fly, increased their flights during the first week of deregulation so much that one carrier doubled its destinations. Air fares changed so rapidly that some airline reservationists admitted that they did not know what the price of a ticket was. Changes were frequent and it was difficult to get through to airline reservation offices. As noted earlier, in a matter of just a few days, travel agencies were booking the majority of corporate travel and they have continued to book most corporate travel ever since.

Deregulation also spurred the establishment of many more corporate travel departments. As air fares went up and down, airlines merged or went into bankruptcy. Marketing schemes proliferated and companies found that not only could their travelers receive better service, but the companies could save money by having a single department within the company responsible for all corporate travel. The creation of these corporate travel departments was sometimes haphazard and, at other times, it was carefully planned. Internal politics often entered into the creation decision and, although the structure may have looked similar from corporate travel department to corporate travel department, the power, often created at inception, differed. This is the subject of Chapter 2—the creation of a business or corporate travel department.

Discussion Questions

1. What organization regulated airlines and, by extention, travel agencies prior to deregulation?
2. What were the beneficial aspects of the air travel system in the United States prior to deregulation?
3. What is meant by the term *interlining?*
4. Why did the National Business Travel Association, tour operators, and government executives want airline deregulation?
5. What had to happen to an agreement between the Air Traffic Conference and travel agencies for travel agencies to automatically receive anti-trust immunity?
6. For what reasons is the 1958 Federal Aviation Act important?
7. What role did a law judge play in effecting a ruling which would have the effect of law in the air travel industry?
8. What role did Presidents play in determining the award of new or abandoned air routes for service by air carriers?
9. What role did Judge Yoder play in travel agency deregulation?
10. What is the distinction between agency exclusivity and marketing exclusivity?
11. What happened in January, 1983 that opened the way for a corporate travel department to receive commissions for the tickets that it generates for itself?

12. What was the Air Travelers' Protection Act designed to do?

13. How did the changing of commission levels relate to the possibility of airlines paying commissions directly to corporate travel departments?

14. Is there a ruling that has set standards or criteria for non-travel agency vendors (corporate travel departments) as they relate to their direct appointment?

15. What kind of confusion occurred during the first week of deregulation?

16. What happened after World War II to change agencies from being steamship agencies to travel agencies?

17. Prior to deregulation in what ways did airlines discourage travel agencies from selling air travel to corporate travelers?

18. Prior to deregulation, in what ways did air carriers encourage corporate travelers to make reservations directly with the airlines rather than through travel agencies?

19. By August, 1981 how many new air carriers were certified to fly between states in the United States?

20. At the end of December, 1980 how many air carriers were authorized to fly between states in the United States?

21. Why did air travelers move from booking air travel directly with air carriers to obtaining their airline tickets through travel agencies during the first three months of 1981?

22. What factors resulting from deregulation resulted in an expansion of corporate travel departments?

Role Play Exercise

Two students may participate in this role play either out-of-class, as a fun way to review the chapter, or as an in-class exercise. One plays the role of the new corporate travel manager and the other plays the role of the experienced corporate travel manager. Please read the script and then pick up the conversation in your own words.

New Corporate Travel Manager: You have been a corporate travel manager for a good many years, haven't you?

Experienced Corporate Travel Manager: Yes, I was first in the marketing division of a major air carrier and then I worked for a travel agency. About four years before deregulation, I became a corporate travel manager and I have been in corporate travel management ever since. There have been a number of changes and it is often gratifying to be able to look at the historical perspective.

New Corporate Travel Manager: There are a good number of things I do not understand. Why does the industry work the way it does? Why do airlines pay commissions to travel agencies and not to corporate travel departments? I suppose these things have some kind of historical basis. What kinds of things happened in the past that have any bearing on the way we operate today?

13

Group
Discussion
Situation:
Updating the
CTM at
International
Productions

Experienced Corporate Travel Manager: It may take a few minutes to explain, but the historical perspective is important. Let me try to explain . . .

CONTINUE ON YOUR OWN

Group Discussion Situation:
Updating the CTM at
International Productions

International Productions is an international meeting industry supplier which supplies audiovisial equipment and other supplies for meetings in major cities throughout the world. The company has bases on four continents and major city distribution offices in twenty cities throughout the world. Its headquarters is in New York City with major overseas division offices located in London and Hong Kong. Jim Grayson started the corporate travel department for International Productions in the 1960s. This was Jim's first executive position with International Productions reporting directly to the President of the company. Jim was able to save International Productions twenty percent on its travel during the first year he was the corporate travel manager. He continued saving the organization a considerable amount of money on its travel as he served in the position of corporate travel manager throughout the years. Due to his excellent work, Jim was offered a liaison position in the London division office where he was responsible for purchasing audiovisual equipment in England and shipping it to offices throughout the world.

For family reasons, however, Jim needed to return to the United States and be based in New York City again. His request for a transfer resulted in Jim's being reappointed to the position of corporate travel manager. He will be reporting to the President again, as he did before. The former corporate travel manager is being transferred to a position outside the country.

Because Jim has been in London for a good number of years, the current corporate travel manager wishes to have Jim receive a complete briefing on the major changes in corporate travel management since deregulation. Since the current corporate travel manager will be leaving two days before Jim's arrival, the corporate travel staff has been asked to brief Jim.

You are meeting today to finalize a written briefing for Jim. You are expected to reach agreement and to write a two-page summary briefing of the major changes since deregulation and how you see these changes affecting the operation of International Productions.

In your group session, select one person to chair the group. All will have an equal vote on decisions. In the group session, you are expected to reach agreements on the structure and basic content of the briefing paper and to prepare the two-page paper to be presented to the entire class by the chair of your committee.

CHAPTER 2

The Creation of a Corporate Travel Department

Introduction

In the Summer of 1987, the participants enrolled in Metropolitan State College's Corporate Travel Management course studied how corporate travel departments come into existence and how the "mentor" for the creation of the department can determine the department's initial structure and the department's corporate power. Indeed, it was hypothesized that the department's mentor may even determine the department's ultimate demise. Much of this chapter is based on the thinking, reasoning, hypotheses, and examples brought out by the corporate travel managers, travel agency owners, agency sales executives, and others enrolled in that program.

Who Initiates Corporate Travel Departments

When asking who initiates corporate travel departments, one must recognize that the "who" may be either singular or plural. It is important to identify who, whether it is one person or a group of people, takes the initiative in a business to initiate the idea of having a travel department. The executive study group analyzing this question came up with four "whos" (i.e, four groups and/or individuals within businesses that mentor the concept of having a corporate travel department). From the top of the organization down these are:

1. the CEO (chief executive officer);
2. the CFO (chief financial officer);
3. One or more of the travelers; and
4. One or more of the booking secretaries.

Each has his or her reason or set of reasons for wanting to have a corporate travel department and it is these reasons or sets of reasons that, to some extent, determine the structure and power of the resulting corporate travel department.

The CEO as CTD Mentor

Although there are exceptions to the rule, three factors are important to chief executive officers in a corporate travel department. These are:

1. service;
2. cost savings; and
3. equality in the treatment of travelers.

To be able to make certain that these three factors are considered with something of an equal degree of weight and that all in the corporation do their best to cooperate in making certain that these goals (factors) are realized, the CEO frequently mandates the creation of a corporate travel department, appoints the corporate travel manager (although not always using this title), and mandates the reporting line (often directly to the CEO). Often, initial directives from the corporate travel department may be drafted by the corporate travel manager, but are signed by the CEO. Sometimes, this process does not stop after the initial stage, but continues for some time into the future of the corporate travel department.

Because service is important to the CEO, the best financial "deal," perhaps the one with the highest level of rebates, is sometimes passed up in favor of one with good cost savings and excellent services. Quality control offered by the vendor is reviewed closely and frequently and may make the difference between retaining a vendor and leaving a vendor. Service is expected, demanded, and received.

Because cost savings (perhaps even profits) are important to the CEO, the best financial "deal" is studied with careful consideration. Savings reports are expected and are reviewed to make sure vendors are providing the best possible savings. Often, direct negotiations are entered into with car rental and hotel vendors. Not infrequently, travel department financial reports are routed to the CEO for review on a routine basis.

Because equality is important to the CEO, those who feel slighted are encouraged to come to the CEO with their complaints and/or concerns. Travel policies are written early in the history of the corporate travel department and copies are circulated to all travelers and potential travelers, thereby ensuring that everyone knows the policies in advance. Strong efforts are made to abide by the policies on an equal basis for all travelers or at least for all travelers in each status category. Suggestions are solicited from travelers and the corporate travel manager is expected to study, consider, and report back on each suggestion.

While one or two of these three factors may outweigh the others in the mind of the chief executive officer, a balancing of all three is much more often the norm.

The CFO as CTD Mentor

The chief financial officer is concerned about money. He is expected to lead his company to profits. Therefore, cost savings are of paramount importance. Making a profit is ideal, but most CFOs settle with the corporate travel department saving money. The corporate travel department manager is sometimes treated just like any other corporate buyer. The best financial deal is usually the only deal the CFO is interested in. Maximum rebates and frequent detailed financial reporting are two strong expectations. The CFO may look to the corporate travel department to be a profit center. While service is important, as it is to most corporate buyers, it is often less important than financial benefits. Equality is considered only to be able to make operations smoother within the finance department.

Structurally, the corporate travel department is often housed within the financial division of the organization when the CFO is the corporate travel department mentor. In fact, the development of a corporate travel department sometimes comes about through an evolutionary process starting with centralizing travel purchasing through a single person or section in the purchasing department or division. Depending upon the importance of travel as a cost factor in the business, the corporate travel manager may report directly to the chief financial officer or will report through one or more intermediaries to the chief financial officer. When there is direct reporting, there is sometimes the same or similar referred power, as in the case with CEO mentoring. In other words, the CFO sends out the travel policies and procedures under his name rather than under the name of the corporate travel department. He fields the concerns and complaints rather than the corporate travel manager and he makes the decisions regarding travel conflicts—often siding with the position that will be more economical for the company. Chief financial officers in many companies report directly to Board officers, the treasurer of the company or of the Board, and sometimes directly to the lenders and/or bankers. This provides them with power similar to that held by the CEO and sometimes with greater power. The referred power of the corporate travel manager can be considerable under such circumstances.

On the other hand, when the corporate travel manager reports to or through intermediaries (and especially if there are several intermediaries), the financial power of the CFO will often be felt less in the corporate travel department—especially if the corporate travel manager reports to vice presidents and other executives in other departments. Under such circumstances one can expect to see much more negotiation and compromise on the part of the corporate travel manager.

Corporate Traveler(s) as CTD Mentor(s)

One or more of the company's travelers may also act as the mentor(s) for the establishment of a corporate travel department. Typically, traveler(s) find that travel agency and air carrier service are not what the traveler(s) believe they should be. Harried secretaries do not give enough time to the task of transmitting accurate data regarding the traveler's needs to the travel agent and perhaps the agency has begun to take the company and its travel for granted. Service problems erupt into a decision to have one person in the company responsible for corporate travel and the traveler(s) make certain that this person is the secretary who is best at making travel arrangements. Often the traveler(s) are not sure what is wanted. Generally, service is of primary concern. While equality may be voiced, the policies that insure equality are usually hard to get agreement on. If policies are drawn up under this scenerio, the corporate travel manager often lacks the clout to make the policies work. When a person in another division fails to follow policy, there is nothing to ensure that the failure will not continue.

Like equality, cost savings may be voiced as a desire, but when cost savings interfere with convenience or personal benefits, there is no authority on the part of the corporate travel manager to make sure the least expensive fare is used or that the less expensive carrier (on which there is no frequent flier program) is used. Convenience, ease of travel, and frequent flier points are often the major concerns to the traveler(s) who through their mentoring created the corporate travel department and the department reflects these priorities.

Booking Secretary(ies) as CTD Mentor(s)

Some corporate travel departments have been established as a result of the secretaries who phone in travel bookings getting together and determining that it will be easier for all concerned if all travel arrangements are made by one secretary. In such circumstances, the initial corporate travel department is more of a coordination function performed along with a myriad of other duties. Seldom is cost savings or equality a major concern in making travel arrangements. Usually the travel agency offering the easiest, fastest service will be selected as a vendor. Rapid service, a friendly travel agent, and speedy, efficient ticket delivery are often the prime concerns in interfacing with an agency vendor. Policies are seldom established by the corporate travel manager and there is no power to enforce policies if they are developed.

The life of corporate travel departments established by one or more booking secretaries is often short. The department lasts as long as it is accepted by management and/or as long as a strong secretary is in a position to run the department. If and when the secretary is transfered or leaves the company, the corporate travel department function often leaves with her.

What Happens First

What happens first in the creation of a corporate travel department depends upon who the mentor is. If the mentor is the CEO or the CFO, typically a study is undertaken initially to determine whether or not a corporate travel department is needed and, if so, whether such a department would be cost effective. The request for such a study can be given to any person, group, or department in the company. Typically, it is given to the personnel department, research and development, finance, or the president's office.

Other sections of companies have been known to handle initial studies as well. The initial study usually gathers statistics on:

- cost of travel (broken down into the components of air, hotel, car rental, meals, entertainment, and other costs);

- the percentage of travel costs to other corporate costs;
- who travels (executives and non-executives and the reasons for their trips);
- how they travel (corporate jet, first class, economy, discounted fares, hotel suites, expensive hotels, economy hotels, inexpensive rooms, the class of cars rented, how often rented, if there is car sharing, what car rental company, and so on);
- vendors and their cost or cost-effectiveness; and
- other details relating to the company's travel.

It is usually expected that the study includes some specific recommendations, one of which might be to establish a corporate travel department. If such a recommendation is an outcome of the study, it is usually based upon cost reduction, service increases, or both, which could and should come from having centralized travel arrangements and travel responsibility. Chapter 14 discusses the company travel study in detail.

If the corporate travel department mentor is a group of travelers or of secretaries, what usually happens first is a discussion of the concept among the travelers or secretaries (sometimes both), agreement among a significant segment of the travelers or secretaries, clearance from appropriate authorities to establish a corporate travel department, and then the routing of travel requests to the person designated to handle travel.

From Initial Study to Departmental Status

Even before a person is selected to become the corporate travel manager and head up the corporate travel department, it is often beneficial to bring in a corporate travel management consultant. This consultant can advise the firm of the pros and cons of the structure and reporting options. The consultant can help bring about a transition between the committee, company executives, and the establishment of a full-fledged corporate travel department. This can reduce the initial political pressure often facing newly-appointed corporate travel managers. This is especially true when the corporate travel management consultant undertakes the role of bringing together agreement on corporate travel policies, distributing the policies, and making certain that all travelers are aware of the policies. Executives and the corporate travel manager can transfer any animosities that travelers may feel regarding the pressure associated with new policies to the corporate travel management consultant, leaving the corporate travel manager free from initial restrictive policy enforcement blame.

When a CEO- or CFO-mandated study recommends that a corporate travel department be established, one of the first steps is to appoint a person to head the department. Often this is an in-house person. It frequently is a clerical person assigned to the committee that helped undertake the study of the corporation's travel. Sometimes, it is the person who has handled most of the travel bookings within the company. Often it is a travel agent who handled much of the corporation's travel and is hired away from the travel agency. Infrequently, a search is undertaken through a recruitment firm to find a person who will best serve the needs of the business.

Often, once a person is named to the position of corporate travel manager (other terms are used as well), that person is given the responsibility to put together and to run the corporate travel department. Three jobs face the corporate travel manager immediately:

1. to develop a departmental budget and to get it approved (sometimes this is done by the committee and included in their study report);
2. to develop, get agreement on, and disseminate a comprehensive travel policy (though it is often drawn up by the corporate travel manager with assistance and input from other key individuals in the company, it is often signed by the CEO or the CFO and distributed from the office of the CEO or CFO preferably *before* the corporate travel department goes into operation); and
3. to develop a *Request for Proposal* (RFP) (usually with the assistance of a committee that will also evaluate vendor proposals).

The initial months of a corporate travel department are usually occupied with getting these three tasks completed.

The following chapters will go into the details of putting together a departmental budget, developing and dissiminating a corporate travel policy, and preparing a Request for Proposal.

Summary

For most corporate travel departments, there are four initiators/mentors who cause the department to be developed. These are the CEO (chief executive officer), the CFO (chief financial officer), one or more corporate travelers, and one or more corporate secretaries who make travel arrangements. Each of these department development mentors has a set of outcomes or expectations from the corporate travel department. There are three major outcomes or expectations including:

1. service;
2. cost savings; and
3. equality in the treatment of travelers.

To some extent the CEO often wants an equal balance of all three expectations. The CFO will concentrate on cost savings. Service and equality are important to corporate travelers. Service is the major expectation of the corporate secretaries who make travel arrangements. Structurally, the corporate travel department will be located in the finance division if the mentor is the CFO, but it may be found in a wide range of divisions if the sponsor is the CEO, corporate traveler(s), or corporate secretary(ies). Considerable power to enforce corporate travel policies is often available to corporate travel managers heading departments for which the mentor is the CEO and/or the CFO. Almost no power can be expected to be found in the corporate travel department depending upon corporate traveler(s) or corporate secretary(ies) for sponsorship.

When the traveler(s) or secretary(ies) are the mentors, clearance for having a corporate travel function is sought and obtained and the responsibility for centralizing bookings is given to a designated individual. Although most often it is an add-on job, the maintenance of the corporate travel manager function is often informal in nature.

When the CEO or the CFO is the mentor, the first step is usually to undertake a comprehensive study of the company travel and how that travel is currently being handled. The committee undertaking the study makes a written report with one of the recommendations being the establishment of a corporate travel department. Often the report also suggests who should head up the travel department (i.e., become the company's corporate travel manager) and sometimes it even recommends a travel department budget.

After action is taken on the study and the resulting report and a corporate travel manager is named, three tasks are generally undertaken during the first few formative months of the corporate travel department's existence. These are to develop:

1. a departmental budget and get it approved;

2. a comprehensive travel policy, get it agreed upon and distribute it; and

3. a Request for Proposal.

Then, the corporate travel manager must distribute the request, review the proposals that come in (in conjunction with an appropriate committee), and award a vendor contract to handle the company's travel.

Discussion Questions

1. What four persons or groups may act as mentors for the establishment of a corporate travel department?

2. What three outcomes or expectations are expected from corporate travel departments?

3. Which of the expectations or outcomes might one expect the CFO to place as of higher priority than the other two major outcomes? Why?

4. How might most CEOs be expected to prioritize outcomes and expectations?

5. What mentor might place service above all outcomes and expectations in importance? Why?

6. In terms of corporate travel department power, which mentors would be most desirable? Why?

7. What happens first in the creation of a corporate travel department when the mentor is a senior executive?

8. What types of people are often appointed to head a new corporate travel department?

9. What three jobs face a corporate travel manager immediately after the creation of the corporate travel department?

10. What senior executives often sign the corporate travel policy cover letter when it is distributed within the company? Why?

Role Play Exercise

Two students may participate in this role play either out-of-class, as a fun way to review the chapter, or as an in-class exercise. One plays the role of the company's chief executive officer (CEO) and the other plays the role of the company's chief finance officer (CFO). Please read the script and then pick up the conversation in your own words.

CEO: You were with me when we talked with the travel consultant last week about setting up a corporate travel department. He has just called and wants us to draw up a priority list of expectations or outcomes for the department. I have listed the top three as service, equality of treatment of our travelers, and cost savings in that order. What do you think?

CFO: I met with the bankers and the Chairman of the Board yesterday afternoon. Again, they want to see some positive evidence of our cutting costs. I don't see how we can let anything go out that doesn't show cost reduction as our number one priority.

CEO: But if we don't emphasize service first and we stress costs, we could really be buying ourselves false economy. Let me explain why. If we get an agency that gives us an eight percent rebate, then . . .

CONTINUE ON YOUR OWN

Group Discussion Situation:
The Violating VPs

Barbara Brislin worked as an executive secretary in the comptroller's office at Greater Louisiana Refineries for six years. When there was a structural change and the corporate comptroller was promoted to Vice President Finance, each division of the corporation got its own controller and Barbara was assigned to work with the controllers in a small group that managed cross-division, corporate-wide expenses. Barbara was asked to take charge of managing travel expenses. Within a year she held the title of corporate travel manager. Barbara still handled some of the Vice President of Finance's other responsibilities as well. For example, she coordinated all top-level Finance Department meetings and she always covered for the Vice President of Finance's personal secretary while his secretary was out to lunch. Two and a half years ago, the Vice President of Finance had a massive heart attack and passed away quite rapidly. A new Vice President was brought in from another company and he brought key staff people with him. Barbara was not happy and looked for another job.

    Almost two years ago, Barbara was hired to head the clerical support staff for the production team in the news department at KJJK Television in New Orleans. Along with other duties, Barbara is responsible for the travel arrangements for those in the news department who travel. Because of her previous experience, Barbara does an excellent job in handling all their travel arrangements. Other secretaries at the station have turned to Barbara for help in solving travel problems for their travelers and Barbara has enjoyed helping them.

Barbara recently suggested to the other secretaries that she take on the travel function for the entire station so that the benefits of having centralized travel will be enjoyed by KJJK. The other secretaries readily agreed and Barbara's boss, the news production manager, said it would be okay as long as it did not interfere with Barbara's other responsibilities.

Barbara drew up an announcement indicating the formation of a corporate travel department and sent it to all KJJK staff members. The announcement detailed the benefits of having a corporate travel department and especially stressed the cost savings that could now be expected for KJJK. There was no response to the announcement. Most of the company's travelers started calling Barbara when they wanted to make travel arrangements. A few still wanted their secretaries to make the arrangements, but did not complain when their secretaries in turn called Barbara and let Barbara handle the arrangements. Barbara spoke with the production manager, her boss, about the inefficiencies of executives telling their secretaries what they wanted and then the secretaries going to Barbara. She had hoped he would advise the executives that they should call Barbara directly. Instead, the news production manager told Barbara she should give it more time. That was about three weeks ago.

Two weeks ago, Barbara distributed a travel policy she drew up. In the cover letter she outlined the cost saving benefits the company would receive by having everyone fly on economy or discounted fares and by using the hotels listed in the policy, since these are the hotels that are extending corporate rates to KJJK. Again, there has been no response back to Barbara and almost everyone is using the fares she gets for them and staying in the hotels Barbara has identified. The Vice President of Marketing, however, has begun to bypass Barbara altogether and is having his own secretary make his travel arrangements. He has flown first class twice in the last week and a half and he stays in more expensive hotels than Barbara has authorized. Barbara spoke with him on the phone about bypassing the corporate travel policy and he told Barbara that his travel is none of her business. Barbara then spoke to her boss. He told Barbara he was sure the Vice President of Marketing was concerned about company costs, but that he (the Vice President of Marketing) probably had some very good reasons for flying first class and for using other hotels. Her boss advised Barbara to be patient.

A few hours ago Barbara learned that the Vice President of Administration bypassed the corporate travel department yesterday and had his secretary call an airline directly (not the travel agency Barbara had selected for KJJK) and make first-class reservations for a flight next week. Barbara checked with the travel agency and found that there are a number of discounted seats available on the same flight. She is unsure of what she should do next. What do you suggest?

CHAPTER 3

The Multiple Functions of Corporate Travel Departments

The Range of Functions

It goes without saying that corporate travel departments run the gamut of size, functions, and structure. They vary from very small departments consisting of a fraction of the total assignments given to a corporate secretary with only air arrangements made for those corporate travelers (normally only the CEO (chief executive officer) and perhaps the CFO (chief financial officer) who wish to have arrangements for their flights made) to the large, multi-person staff performing all the duties of an internal travel agency (often with many additional duties).

Although some would say that the secretary who makes an occasional air reservation hardly qualifies to call herself a corporate travel manager, the determination of the title of corporate travel manager and the designation within a company of a corporate travel department lies with the company, not any outside observer. In reality, most of those who are designated within companies as corporate travel managers are people who undertake some of the functions described in this chapter, but not all of them. They are people who undertake these functions as only a part of their total job responsibility. The range, therefore, can be very broad, but, in reality, tends to be very narrow.

Travel Service Functions

Making travel arrangements either directly with air, hotel, car rental, and other vendors or through a travel agency constitutes the single most important and the single most often performed function of corporate travel management. Making air travel arrangements is the most important and the most often performed function within the travel services function. In undertaking the function of making travel arrangements, corporate travel managers may work in several ways, but tend to adopt one of three approaches.

The Most Common Approach—
Direct Traveler/Agency Interfacing

The most common and the most often-used approach is for the traveler or the traveler's secretary to phone the travel agency that has been selected as the corporate agency, arrange bookings with the agency, and report the arrangements to the corporate travel manager. The manager's function is to determine whether or not the arrangements have been made in accordance with established corporate policy. Although the manager may discuss the individual travel arrangements with the agency owner and/or staff members, the corporate travel manager seldom initiates travel arrangement requests under this scenerio.

The Second Most Common Approach—
Manager/Agency Interfacing

A second very common approach, found almost as often as the one where a traveler or a traveler's secretary contacts the travel agency directly, is the routing of all travel requests through the office of the corporate travel manager. The manager then phones the travel agency, makes travel arrangements herself in accordance with established policy, and advises the traveler or the traveler's secretary of the details regarding the travel arrangements that have been made.

The Multi-agency Variation

A variation of both of the above approaches is to use more than one travel agency. In some corporations, the traveler is given the freedom to select an agency of his/her choice, the only requirement being that the travel arrangements are made in accordance with established travel policy. Other businesses select two travel agencies in order to provide the traveler with a choice, at the same time limiting the number of vendors the organization must deal with. Still other organizations select travel agencies on the basis of the agency specializations.

In many cities today, there is a wide choice of agencies that specialize in serving commercial clients. In addition, there are a growing number of cities in which there are international-only agencies. Companies that have a respectable amount of international travel may select one agency to handle the international portion of their travel and another agency to handle the domestic portion of their business. Some firms expect the travel department to offer company-sponsored leisure trips for those in the firm who are planning vacations. There are even some large companies that have weekend bus tours put together almost every weekend for those employees who wish to participate in such off-time leisure activities.

In many cases, the corporate travel manager will turn to a travel agency that specializes in tours or leisure travel for these arrangements. Still other reasons for the selection of more than one travel agency vendor are:

- internal politics (a company executive may have a good friend who owns a travel agency);
- convenience (there may be an agency around the corner that is more convenient to use for the occasional rush trip); or
- area specialization (some agencies specialize in serving clients going to particular parts of the world—Middle Eastern oil countries, for example).

Manager/Carrier Interfacing

The interfacing between air carriers, car rental companies, hotels, and other vendors, on the one hand, and the corporate travel manager on the other hand, is increasing. The reasons for this are many, with most of these reasons explored in depth in other parts of this book. However, it has given rise to a return to direct vendor/corporation relationships that tend to eliminate the travel agency middle man. Unlike the structure where every traveler or his secretary calls a travel agency, the vendor/corporation relationships tend to be strictly between the corporate travel manager and the vendor.

Other Interface Patterns

A few other interface patterns are beginning to exist—primarily so that corporations can get a larger reduction in price, share in the commissions traditionally paid to travel agents alone, or a combination of both. Several corporations have bought travel agencies, mandating that all corporate travel of non-travel corporate-owned businesses be routed through the corporate-owned agencies. This pattern not only exists locally, but is being found on a national and on an international level.

Another non-traditional pattern is the establishment of an "in plant" or an internal travel agency. Both pay commissions back to the corporation. The "in plant" pays a lower commission, but does not have to sell to the general public. The internal travel agency presumably sells to the general public, but gets a full commission. For a complete explanation of the difference between "in plants" and internally owned travel agencies, see Chapter 5.

A final non-traditional interface pattern is the multi-corporate-owned travel agency. To gain greater leverage with suppliers, a few combinations of related or non-related businesses have gotten together to buy or to start a travel agency. Not only do they obtain full commissions from vendors, but the combined buying power gives them greater leverage in terms of special assistance being rendered when needed and larger override commission payments being extended when vendors are sold with a prejudice. Some of these large agencies perform the roles traditionally undertaken by corporate travel managers, thus eliminating the corporate travel manager position. With others, the corporate travel manager interfaces directly with agency management, sometimes sitting on the board of directors of the agency and directly affecting both agency management and the agency's day-by-day direction.

Air Travel Service Functions

No matter what interface structure has been established, it is the function of corporate travel managers and their departments to obtain the best possible air arrangements for corporate travelers. This means working in two directions at the same time. On the one hand, it means knowing the flexibility of travelers and getting corporate travelers to qualify for discounted rates as often as possible. This usually means that early ticket purchases should be made whenever possible with a selection of flights that have discounted seats (these are often at non-peak times) whenever possible.

On the other hand, it means working closely with air carriers and travel agents to make sure the best "deal" possible is obtained from or through vendors. An increasing number of corporate travel managers are requiring savings reports from travel agency vendors showing the amount of money saved as a result of selecting fares at less than a full economy fare level.

They also hold seminars or other training sessions for those who make travel arrangements, usually corporate secretaries, advising these key employees of techniques to use in getting the very lowest fares possible. Sometimes seminars are held for corporate travelers letting them know how they can reduce air fare costs—especially when changes are needed in flight arrangements after they have already started a series of flights. But close monitoring, often with their own computer reservation system CRT, remains the favored way with many corporate travel managers to make sure they are getting the very lowest possible fares for their travelers.

Hotel Travel Service Functions

Hotel costs for corporate travelers can be substantial. In many cases, especially when a corporate traveler spends two or more nights in a hotel, the hotel cost can exceed the air travel cost. The corporate travel manager is faced with a conflict. The traveler must stay in accommodations that are sufficiently comfortable to allow the traveler to get the job done, but the cost must be as reasonable as possible. Circumstances vary. Obviously, a more expensive hotel can save the company money if it provides free transportation to and from the airport and is within walking distance of the location where the corporate business will be conducted. A less expensive hotel, the location of which is in an area where a rental car would be needed, may be a false economy. The combination of car and hotel cost could be much higher than the more expensive hotel.

To control hotel costs corporate travel managers attempt to find properties that are comfortable, close to their factories, offices, and other places of business in destination cities, and obtain rates that are at, or below, corporate hotel rates. To get these rates, they often use travel agencies that have negotiated less than corporate rates for their clients or they may undertake direct negotiations with hotels. Some travel agents split their commissions with their corporate travel accounts, allowing for another way of reducing hotel costs. Still another approach is to monitor expense reports to make sure the rates charged were the rates quoted.

The other half of the hotel problem is the quality of hotel rooms provided. Some hotels give discounted corporate rate clients inferior rooms, reserving the better rooms for clients who may pay greater room night rates. Judy Albright, former travel coordinator for the State of Colorado, points out that one Colorado mountain hotel gave a state employee a room with no heat because he was on a state corporate rate. Obviously, if the room is of inferior quality and the corporate employee is unable to perform his work adequately, the savings from getting a discounted rate may well be lost in employee productivity. Therefore, a large part of the corporate travel manager's function is to obtain a comfortable, quality accommodation for the corporate traveler.

Car Rental Service Functions

Often automobiles are rented by corporate travelers when they travel and when they are needed. This becomes a responsibility assigned to the corporate travel manager. As with hotel rooms, the corporate travel manager has the responsibility of obtaining a car of reasonable quality at the best price possible. Some car rental companies will extend a national discounted rate to a company if there is substantial business to be obtained from the company. However, many corporations do not have a sufficient amount of car rental business to qualify for national discounted rates. Under such circumstances, the corporate travel manager often expects the travel agency it works through to obtain the best possible car rental rate by checking the rate with all destination airport car rental companies and getting the best rate available. Since most airport car rental companies are franchisees of national car rental companies (Hertz, Avis, National, Budget, and so on), it is sometimes possible for corporate travel managers to negotiate directly with a destination franchisee and obtain a better rate than can be obtained in any other way.

Again, the second half of the car rental equation is to obtain a good quality car. Most corporate travelers expect to drive new cars (not more than about eighteen-months old), cars that are well-serviced, and cars that will be replaced with other automobiles if a mechanical problem occurs. Although some companies maintain that luxury cars (usually the more expensive cars available at car rental locations) may not be rented because of the additional expense of such cars, others may require that only economy cars be rented. This policy varies, often within the company, depending upon the status of the traveler and the needs of the traveler. The corporate travel manager is expected to understand these quality differences and to arrange for appropriate car rentals accordingly.

Other Service Functions

While the arrangement of air travel, hotels, and car rentals constitute the bulk of the travel service functions, corporate travel managers are sometimes called on to make other travel service arrangements as well. Sometimes rail tickets (especially for travel in other countries) are needed. In other cases, the corporate travel manager makes ferry crossing or other ship arrangements. Still other types of

28

Chapter 3:
The Multiple
Functions of
Corporate
Travel
Departments

travel arrangements are made on rare occasions. Finally, some corporate travel managers have the responsibility of arranging vacation or other leisure trips for company employees who want help planning their holidays. There are even a few corporate travel managers who run tours for employees. Some of these are weekend jaunts, while others are multi-day international trips. The vacation travel aspect of corporate travel management is discussed in detail in Chapter 12.

Financial Services

Five financial functions may fall within the responsibility area of corporate travel managers. These are:

1. Advising in regards to expense level criteria;
2. Handling expense allocations as they relate to travel;
3. Obtaining and reviewing expense reports;
4. Budgeting for corporate travel and for the corporate travel department; and
5. Financial reporting.

Advising in Regards to Expense Level Criteria

Although advising on the setting of travel policies is usually considered the responsibility of the corporate travel manager to some extent, almost all travel departments are expected to monitor travel expense levels in the destination cities of corporate travelers. They are then able to determine expense ranges appropriate for business trips to these cities and, in most cases, they are expected to recommend expense caps with the status of the corporate traveler. By providing this data, departments within the business can more easily budget their departmental travel and the corporation will have guidelines for determining reasonable travel expense levels.

Handling Expense Allocations

Corporate travel managers often handle expense allocations as they manage travel. This means communicating. Once expense levels are determined, they usually are announced to the corporation by the comptroller or another senior officer of the corporation. At the same time, they usually are transmitted to the corporate travel manager so that the manager may set up files and records accordingly. The corporate travel manager frequently is given the responsibility of advising corporate travelers of all policies, including expense allocation policies, prior to their taking a trip, filing expense allocation data, and retrieving the data when needed.

Processing Trip Expense Reports

Many corporate travel managers also process trip expense reports. Since a number of corporate travel departments are in the finance division of the business, it is logical for these corporate travel departments to obtain expense reports, review the reports, as well as process trip expense approvals, waivers, and other matters having to do with travel expense report filings.

Travel Budget Preparation

Corporate travel managers are usually expected to prepare annual budgets for the operation of the corporate travel department itself. However, in many businesses, the corporate travel manager and other travel department employees are expected to assist both line and staff management in preparing their individual departmental travel budgets. Sometimes this is carried even further by the company requiring the corporate travel department to prepare monthly status reports for the travel budgets of each department within the business.

Financial Reporting

Financial reporting is also important. Chapter 7 discusses these financial responsibilities in detail. One of the major requirements of most corporate travel departments is to provide financial reports which show the savings in air travel and, to a lesser extent, the savings in hotel costs, car rental costs, and other travel costs realized for the business through the monitoring of travel expenses by the corporate travel department. Reports range from simple "savings" reports to lengthy, detailed reports on all aspects of air, hotel, car rental, and other travel.

Other Functions

Some of the other functions that corporate travel managers are expected to undertake include:

1. Keeping up with new developments in the field of corporate travel management and advising senior management of change recommendations;
2. Working with the sales department in developing and running incentive travel programs;
3. Handling relocation arrangements;
4. Taking the responsibility for corporate-owned aircraft (sometimes including corporate aircraft scheduling); and
5. Performing the functions of an internal meeting planner.

Summary

The functions of a corporate travel department depend upon the structure of the business itself and the desires of each business' management. Although a large number of corporate travel managers share the responsibility for corporate travel with other duties they perform, there is an increasing number of corporate travel managers who perform the function of corporate travel management on a full-time basis. Overseeing the making of travel arrangements is a primary function of

30

Chapter 3:
The Multiple
Functions of
Corporate
Travel
Departments

corporate travel management. The most important of the travel arrangements is usually air travel. This can be arranged in one of three different ways. The first is for the traveler or the traveler's secretary to call a travel agency or an air carrier and make flight reservations, advising the corporate travel department after flight arrangements have been made. Another common approach is for all travel requests to go through the corporate travel department and for the corporate travel department to make the arrangements through a selected travel agency vendor. Sometimes corporate travel departments will have more than one travel agency vendor because of either internal or external reasons. As travel agencies specialize to an increasing degree, many corporate travel departments are taking advantage of the specializations and contracting with agencies based upon the specialized needs of the corporate traveler.

Although much of the interfacing between the corporate travel department and vendors is with travel agencies, there is some direct interfacing with air carrier representatives, company-owned travel agencies, parent company-owned travel agencies, and multi-corporate-owned travel agencies. The special arrangements tend to provide either the parent company or the corporation itself with both financial and other advantages through such approaches as shared commissions and shared override benefits. The corporate travel department attempts to get the best prices in terms of air travel, hotels, and car rentals, but the corporate travel department is usually also concerned with quality. Therefore, they must balance out the best prices with making certain that a reasonable degree of quality is obtained.

Financial services are also important. Most corporate travel managers are expected to advise the corporation regarding expense levels, handle travel expense allocations, review trip expense reports, assist business departments in their own budgeting for travel, prepare the corporate travel department budget, and report financial data relating to travel costs.

In addition, corporate travel departments are often expected to undertake responsibilities in the areas of incentive travel, relocation of employees, corporate aircraft, and meeting planning.

Discussion Questions

1. Does the designation within a company of a corporate travel department and/or the determination of the title of a corporate travel manager lie within the company or with an outside observer?

2. What constitutes the single most important and the single most often performed function of corporate travel management?

3. What is the most often performed function within the travel services functions?

4. What is the most common and the most often used approach regarding corporation/travel agency interfacing as it relates to the business and the travel agency working together?

5. Why might some businesses prefer to work with more than one travel agency rather than to have only one travel agency handle all of their business?

6. Is the interfacing between air carriers, car rental companies, hotels, and other vendors on the one hand and the corporate travel manager on the other hand increasing or decreasing?

7. What are some of the newer and non-traditional interface patterns that are beginning to be found in the industry?

8. Obtaining the best possible air arrangements for corporate travelers means working in two directions at the same time. Explain what these directions are.

9. How many nights must a business traveler spend in a hotel to start equaling the cost of what is spent on air transportation for the trip?

10. In what way might the location of an expensive hotel make that hotel a better choice for a business traveler than a less expensive hotel located some distance away?

11. What are some of the quality of hotel room considerations with which a business travel manager might be concerned?

12. With whom might the corporate travel manager negotiate better car rental rates rather than the car rental company's sales representative?

13. What kind of rental cars do most corporate travelers expect to drive?

14. What types of leisure travel benefits are sometimes offered by corporate travel departments to the employees of the company?

15. What are some of the financial functions which may fall within the responsibility area of corporate travel managers?

16. Is it more common to find corporate travel managers setting travel expense level criteria or advising on travel expense level criteria?

17. How might corporate travel managers assist business department heads in budgeting for their departmental travel?

18. What type of financial reports are corporate travel managers often expected to make?

19. What add-on or "additional" functions are sometimes performed by corporate travel departments and/or corporate travel managers?

Role Play Exercise

Two students may participate in this role play either out-of-class, as a fun way to review the chapter, or as an in-class exercise. One plays the role of the first corporate travel manager and the other plays the role of the second corporate travel manager. Please read the script and then pick up the conversation in your own words.

First Corporate Travel Manager: In our company, my job is pretty straight forward. I work with the traveler to help clarify travel needs and with the vendors to make sure our travelers obtain a reasonable quality of service. I make sure the total cost of travel is as low as possible. I don't get into anything else. I understand that your job entails a lot more than this. I guess you do the same kind of things that I do. But what other kinds of functions do you undertake?

32

Chapter 3:
The Multiple
Functions of
Corporate
Travel
Departments

Second Corporate Travel Manager: I perform a wide range of financial reporting, negotiating, and other functions.

First Corporate Travel Manager: Why don't you explain the details of some of these. Perhaps I should be doing more in my job.

Second Corporate Travel Manager: Okay, let's start with the financial functions.

CONTINUE ON YOUR OWN

Group Discussion Situation: Justifying Bretten's Travel Management Position

Amplified Audiotronics has employed Bretten Brutter as their corporate travel manager for approximately seventeen months. Since undertaking the role, Bretten has reduced travel expenses considerably and has established a very good interface with the travel agency vendor. Financial reports are submitted on a regular basis by the travel agency vendor and Bretten has routed these through all appropriate levels of the company. Bretten feels that she has done an excellent job and she is becoming complacent in her role as corporate travel manager.

Yesterday, Bretten's direct supervisor, Stringley Miserly, the chief financial officer, told Bretten that he is seriously considering eliminating her position as a separate position within the company. A study of functions performed indicates that the job can be given to a senior corporate secretary as an add-on responsibility. Miserly advised Bretten that this action will probably be taken unless she can justify the need for a full-time corporate travel manager. Bretten has called together some of the department heads who seem to appreciate her work. You, the department heads, are meeting today to finalize a written justification for Bretten's position. As involved and concerned department heads, you have agreed to prepare a one or two-page justification report.

In your group session, select one person to chair the group. All will have an equal vote on decisions. In the group session, you are expected to reach agreement on the justifications and the basic content of the justification report. You are expected to prepare the one to two-page paper to be presented to the entire class by the chair of your group of concerned department heads.

CHAPTER 4

The Roles of the Corporate Travel Manager

The Felt Roles of the Corporate Travel Manager

At the inaugural meeting of the Rocky Mountain Business Travel Association in February, 1986, the inaugural presentation treated lightly the very difficult roles of a corporate travel manager. Such roles as "magician" and "tightrope walker" were discussed. Of course, the humorous presentation was meant to make light of some of the major concerns and constraints relating to the corporate travel manager. However, the titles of "tightrope walker" and "magician" point out some of the unrealistic expectancies relating to corporate travel management.

The Real Roles of the Corporate Travel Manager

But what are the real roles of a corporate travel manager? Seldom has this question been addressed. Corporate travel managers are found in so many different corporate settings and their roles vary to such a considerable degree, that it is very hard to understand what the exact roles of a specific corporate travel manager are, or will be, without looking at that individual's unique corporate setting. It must be understood that a vast majority of the people who perform the role of corporate travel manager do not do this in isolation. The corporate travel management function in many corporations is shared with other functions. In discussing corporate travel management with members of the *National Business Travel Association* (one of the national associations of corporate travel managers), one manager after another pointed out that she shares the job of corporate travel manager with other job responsibilities and one finds that relatively few have the position of corporate travel manager alone as a responsibility. Since the corporate travel management duties are shared with so many other responsibilities and since these "other responsibilities" vary to a considerable degree from business to business, there are those who say that attempting to identify specific corporate travel management roles is a futile process.

Major, Optional, and Subordinate Roles

Nevertheless, the corporate travel management function carries with it limited specific roles that tend to stay the same for the vast majority of those who hold the position. It is these roles that will be addressed first. Because they are shared by almost all corporate travel managers, we will call these the "major roles." While reviewing the major roles, optional roles will be discovered. Some of the most frequently found optional roles, therefore, will also be discussed.

Major Roles

In reviewing roles, a group of corporate travel managers was asked: "What do you see as the major roles in your job?" As they responded, groupings started appearing so that it became possible to identify major roles and subordinate (or minor) roles. Six major roles were identified. These are:

1. Management;
2. Technical;
3. Compliance;
4. Financial;
5. Negotiation; and
6. Educational.

Some aspects of the major roles tend to overlap. For example, in the managerial function, one may be performing a management role, but at the same time educating or training an assistant or a client (traveler working within the corporation). Subroles also tend to overlap major roles, but in most cases the subroles can be classified as predominantly belonging to a specific major role.

Although the major and subroles discussed in this chapter include all of the important roles identified by the group of corporate travel managers who assisted in the development of this chapter, there may well be additional roles that are major or minor and are of considerable importance in specific organizations. Therefore, this listing should not be considered exclusive.

Managerial Role

The title of "corporate travel manager" infers that the person holding this title is a manager and performs managerial functions. Nevertheless, one of the complaints from a number of those working as corporate travel managers is that they do not manage. Although this may at first appear to be a contradiction in terms (i.e., a manager who does not manage), looking at the role closely, it becomes possible to identify why corporate travel managers complain they do not manage and some of the reasons why they still carry a management title. If one is considered a manager in most organizations, one can expect to see that there will be subordinates or people who are managed. However, in a large number of corporate travel management sections or departments, the corporate travel manager exists alone, with no staff. To suggest that this person is a manager may be stretching the imagination, at best. However, the corporate travel manager who does not have subordinates, nevertheless, does manage corporate travel policies and programs. In many ways, the corporate travel manager manages those in the corporation who travel. In almost all corporations in which corporate travel managers are found, the corporate travel manager assists in the development of, or by herself determines corporate travel policy. To the extent that this policy is managed within the corporate travel department, the corporate travel manager is performing a management role. In most corporations, the corporate travel manager is the policy setter or performs some aspect of policy setting.

MANAGERIAL COMPLIANCE SUBROLE

Management can also be seen in the compliance role, although in many corporations the corporate travel manager is not allowed to tell a superior that he or she may not travel on a certain flight. Even in those corporations, in many cases, the corporate travel manager has a reporting function when violations of travel policy occur—even when policies are violated by top corporate executives. To the extent that the corporate travel manager plays some role in the compliance function, this can be considered a managerial function and the corporate travel manager is acting in a management role.

MANAGERIAL FINANCE SUBROLE

Financial management is another key role for the corporate travel manager. The purpose of establishing a corporate travel department in the first place, for many corporations, is to control or "manage" travel expenses. The corporate travel manager is expected to work with other departments of the corporation in establishing travel budgets (obtaining travel cost estimates, making certain that actual travel costs are the lowest possible, and reviewing individual traveler travel costs, for instance).

MANAGERIAL NEGOTIATION SUBROLE

In the negotiation arena, the corporate travel manager is also functioning as a manager of the corporation when she performs the function of making the final decision and when she speaks on behalf of the corporation and signs contracts as a responsible corporate executive.

MANAGERIAL EDUCATION SUBROLE

Finally, the educational role can be considered to be a managerial role when the corporate travel manager is educating travelers on corporate policy, advising them of what can be done, what can be done only on an exceptional basis, and what can not be done.

By looking at the above managerial functions, it can be argued that a corporate travel manager does, indeed, perform in a managerial role even when there is no immediate staffing in the corporate travel department below the corporate travel manager.

Technician Role

Probably every corporate travel manager performs the role of technician, to some extent. Many work as technicians the majority of the time. A technician is a person who actually does a task rather than the person who manages that task. In the technician role, four subroles have been identified. These are the:

1. Reservations and ticketing role;
2. Reviewing role;
3. Reporting role; and the
4. Miscellaneous task role.

RESERVATIONS AND TICKETING SUBROLE

Reservations need to be made and tickets need to be issued for all corporate travelers. Airline reservations and ticketing may require more time and expense, but making car rental reservations and hotel reservations is vital as well. How these arrangements are made differs from corporation to corporation. However, many corporate travel managers work actively in the reservation and ticketing subrole. The extent may be a very large one or it may be small. In the case of a large reservations and ticketing subrole, the corporate travel manager may have a CRT on her desk. When she receives a request for travel within the corporation, she may make all reservations and issue all tickets for the travelers herself. In this major reservations and ticketing subrole she is acting very much in the same manner as a travel agent would act.

On the other hand, the corporate travel manager may have an arrangement with a travel agency whereby the functions of making reservations and of ticketing are taken care of by the agency. When the reservations and ticketing functions are handled by a travel agency, the corporate travel manager, nevertheless, performs some of the ticketing and reservations subrole as well. This may be as small as making certain that reservations are made and that the tickets are issued in a timely manner by contacting the agency and checking on a periodic basis. Or, it may be as major as having all reservation requests flow through the corporate travel manager to the travel agency and back from the agency to the corporate travel manager to the traveler. The corporate travel manager may identify options or spot-check to make certain that the reservations and ticketing are done in the correct manner and for the best fares. She usually makes certain that the trip has been authorized and that the corporate travel policy has been followed. In the latter reservations and ticketing subrole, the corporate travel manager is performing an auditor or a compliance, role as well as reservations and ticketing. Nevertheless, to whatever extent, whether it be to a major or a minor extent, the reservations and ticketing subfunction is a technician function that to some degree is performed by most corporate travel managers.

REVIEWING SUBROLE

A second subrole of the corporate travel manager as a technician is a reviewing function. As suggested above, corporate travel managers are expected to review tickets to make certain that these tickets are issued at the lowest fare possible. In addition, they also review agency reports when they work with a travel agency. The reports are reviewed to make certain that the agency is doing its job in a timely manner and that it is obtaining the tickets at the lowest possible price. A part of the reviewing process is to make certain that policies are adhered to. This is both an internal and an external function.

REPORTING SUBROLE

A third technician subrole is that of reporting. Both internal (within the corporate travel department) and external (normally within the corporation) reports are prepared, usually by the corporate travel manager. These reports may range from savings reports (which show how much savings have been obtained by the corporate travel department) to a review of actual expenses verses budgeted expenses on a month-by-month and a year-by-year basis for corporate travel for each cost and/or profit center in the corporation. Often a part of the reporting process involves developing departmental travel budgets with each department in the corporation for which travel is to be budgeted. These budgets typically are drafted prior to the fiscal year. Going along with this series of departmental travel budgets is a similar series of reports that are prepared by the corporate travel manager showing what each cost and/or profit center has actually spent on a month-by-month and on a year-to-year basis for the current year.

MISCELLANEOUS TECHNICIAN SUBROLES

Miscellaneous technician functions can be quite wide. Two of these are the delivery of tickets and setting up for negotiation meetings. In many corporate travel departments, tickets are not delivered by the corporate travel manager, but by a contracted agency. However, even in this situation, the contracting agency may sometimes deliver tickets to the corporate travel manager's office and the corporate travel manager is responsible for either delivering the tickets to the traveler or arranging for the traveler to come to the corporate travel office to pick up tickets.

NEGOTIATION MEETING SET-UP SUBROLE

Setting up meetings to negotiate travel is also a technician task performed by many corporate travel managers. If the corporate travel manager expects to receive a better rate from the car rental company, a hotel, an airline, or a travel agency, and if a corporate travel manager expects to receive service beyond what is customarily delivered by a vendor, negotiation needs to be entered into. There are a series of activities typically encountered in the setting up of negotiation meetings by corporate travel managers and these are activities of a technician-type. In many cases, they are performed by the corporate travel manager.

FIVE SUBROLES

Five subroles, therefore, have been identified for the technician role. These subroles are roles performed by many corporate travel managers, but not by all in all cases.

Compliance Role

Some corporate travel managers complain that they are seen as policemen, policing what travelers do. They say this is their major function. Certainly in many organizations making certain that travelers comply with the regulations is a key responsibility of the corporate travel manager. However, the degree to which the corporate travel manager undertakes the role of compliance officer varies considerably from organization to organization. In some companies the corporate travel manager is not expected to play any compliance role other than to report any policy variations through a reporting process. If any steps are taken to encourage travelers to follow the regulations, they are taken only by the senior departmental executives in the departments of the travelers affected.

On the other hand, there are corporations where the corporate travel manager is expected to handle all policy-compliance matters herself, contacting the traveler who would or has violated the regulations, and initiating disciplinary steps.

The compliance role can be broken down into four subroles as follows:

1. Policy administrator;

2. Travel monitor;

3. Auditor; and

4. Referee.

Policy Administrator Subrole

As a policy administrator it is the responsibility of the corporate travel manager to make certain that policies, prepared in writing, are distributed to all travelers or potential travelers, clarified for travelers, and followed by corporate travelers. Often the corporate travel manager will initiate policy recommendations, get clearance by senior executives, and publish the policies in a travel policy manual or booklet. Sometimes these booklets are small enough to fit in a jacket pocket or as an insert into a ticket jacket and, therefore, are easily distributed and carried with the traveler.

The compliance role comes when policy is violated or there is a potential violation of policy. This can occur in regards to many aspects of policy. Most policy violations occur when a traveler takes a more expensive flight than the one he is authorized to take. A traveler could attempt to fly first class rather than economy or the traveler might take a more convenient flight rather than a less expensive, less convenient one. Still other travelers might wish to travel on another airline in spite of the fact that it is more expensive, because they participate in a frequent flyer program with that carrier and may wish to accumulate enough coupons to earn tickets for their personal use. In each of the above cases, as well as in less common policy violation cases, the corporate travel manager may be expected to flag violations and react in a number of different ways ranging from reporting the violation to taking disciplinary action.

Because of the frequency of violations, and the concern over reporting them by both the corporate travel manager and the traveler, it is easy to see why many corporate travel managers view their jobs as corporate policemen. Often this "policing" function is a major part of the job in the beginning stages of developing the corporate travel department. Once the entire corporation is aware of and starts following policies, the violations are less frequent and the policy administration/policing tasks occur, therefore, equally less frequently.

TRAVEL MONITOR SUBROLE

The travel monitoring aspects of the compliance role are closely related to policy administration aspects. The corporate travel manager is expected to review either selected tickets or every ticket to make certain that the travel agency vendor is obtaining the best possible flights at the least possible cost. By reviewing tickets on a selective basis, or by reviewing each ticket, the corporate travel manager is able to discover these variations from least expensive and most convenient. However, as a travel monitor, the job goes beyond just looking at tickets. Most corporate travel managers are also expected to initiate and review hotel contracts, car rental contracts and contracts with other vendors. They are expected to monitor the effectiveness of these contracts, making certain that they are totally fulfilled. Hotels, for example, may put contracted rate employees into less desirable rooms than the contract calls for. This is an example of the type of situation that the corporate travel manager is expected to monitor, find out about, and correct in future situations.

AUDITING SUBROLE

When working in the auditing subrole, corporate travel managers are often expected to perform in a wider compliance role than when acting as a corporate travel monitor. They may be asked to go into a specific department within the corporation and review every travel transaction. In the auditing subrole they may be asked to continuously keep track of travel expenses for each department in the corporation and report back on a monthly basis the amount of expenses and the year-to-date balance left in the departmental travel budget for each department where travel is undertaken.

REFEREE SUBROLE

A final compliance subrole of referee is undertaken by some corporate travel managers. Corporate travel managers are sometimes asked to interpret policy and to make a policy determination as to whether or not a traveler has followed policy or violated it. As with the policy administration subrole, the referee subrole tends to lessen as instances of policy variation become fewer with the experience of operation. Therefore, frequently one will find the referee subrole almost non-existent in a corporation that has had a corporate travel department for a number of years. On the other hand, it may be a daily situation in a new corporate travel department.

COMPLIANCE ROLE—DEPARTMENTAL JUSTIFICATION

The compliance role is a very important one for the corporate travel manager. It justifies the existence of the department, since without compliance, there may well be no savings occuring to the corporation in relation to travel and it is the savings that justify the corporate travel management position. However, for a healthy corporate travel department it is beneficial that the compliance role be handled very diplomatically and on a very low-key basis.

Financial Management

In the role of financial manager the corporate travel manager plays an especially important role, since travel expenses are found to be the second largest expense in many corporations. Because of this major cost, saving money on travel is the most important corporate travel management responsibility. Therefore, the corporate travel management function often comes under the chief financial officer's position and reports directly to the chief financial officer in many organizations. The financial role is mainly a budgeting and a controlling role. This means that the corporate travel manager has the responsibility of developing a travel budget that is appropriate as a whole and in many instances assisting each department in the development of its travel budget. Once that budget has been developed and approved, the corporate travel manager has the responsibility of controlling the budget (i.e., monitoring the expenses on a regular basis and reviewing actual versus authorized expense throughout the year).

Negotiation Role

In the role of negotiator, the corporate travel manager has the responsibility of identifying those areas where costs can be reduced while maintaining quality service. Three major areas are identified in most corporations. These are:

1. airline tickets;
2. hotels; and
3. car rentals.

The corporate travel manager negotiates for best fares and airline services by developing a *Request for Proposal* (RFP) from travel agencies working directly with airlines for bartered and/or contract agreements on fares, or working on arrangements between agencies and airlines for undertaking the ticketing function in-house. Some corporate travel departments negotiate in all three directions and make a determination as to what would be best for the organization after determining what can be obtained from travel agencies and/or airlines.

Hotel negotiations tend to be ongoing in the corporate travel department. Typically, the corporate travel manager identifies those destinations where there are a number of corporate travelers spending one or more hotel nights. Hotels that have been used and are satisfactory to the travelers are approached and negotiations are initiated in order to obtain favorable corporate rates. Sometimes the corporate travel manager will agree to a guaranteed block of room nights for a specific short period (or for a one-year period) in exchange for a more favorable rate per room night. Often the quality of the room and sometimes the location of the room enter into negotiations.

Car rental negotiations are similar to those undertaken with hotels. Again, a corporate travel manager identifies destinations where corporate travelers rent cars on a regular basis. Since most car rental outlets at airports are franchisees, and since most of these franchisees have considerable control over establishing rates, the corporate travel manager will approach major franchisees which offer the range of services and the types of cars required by the corporation and will enter into negotiations. Again, the corporate travel manager will often guarantee a specific number of car rental days for a specific period of time (normally a one-year period) in exchange for obtaining a more favorable corporate rate. Preferred vendor status is then established. In very large corporations a corporate travel manager can spend a substantial amount of time negotiating airline fares and services, hotel, and car rental agreements. On the other hand, corporations with smaller corporate travel budgets and fewer trips have less to negotiate with and, therefore, the corporate travel manager will usually spend much less time in a negotiation role.

Educational Role

As in the case of negotiation, a corporate travel manager finds education an ongoing role. There are two broad areas of education:

1. educating the corporate travel department on new facets within the industry; and
2. educating the corporation regarding travel.

Since deregulation, the travel industry has changed substantially with many new educational opportunities available to corporate travel managers and corporate travel departments almost every day. It is essential, therefore, for corporate travel managers to educate themselves and their staffs on an ongoing basis by attending seminars, reading the trade press, and meeting with other corporate travel managers.

Educating the corporation regarding travel is often a difficult task. Two groups within the corporation require ongoing education. These are:

1. corporate management; and
2. corporate travelers.

Corporate management needs to be educated regarding the savings or the potential savings that are available to the corporation through a well-run corporate travel department. This requires periodic briefings and finding vehicles to encourage top management to understand the options that are available.

Corporate travel managers use a number of vehicles to accomplish this educational task. These include: memos and letters, newsletters to the entire corporation (including top management), management briefings, taking top management executives into negotiation meetings, travel seminars, and proposal reviews.

Educating the corporate traveler can also be accomplished through a wide range of vehicles. Again newsletters within the corporation, letters, and memos are one approach. Departmental briefings are often held. Meetings with secretaries who make travel arrangements for executives who fly on corporate business also helps to educate the traveler. Many corporate travel managers will attempt to schedule one-on-one meetings with those who travel frequently.

Summary

As can be seen, the major roles of corporate travel managers are time consuming, often frustrating, and sometimes nebulous. Both managerial and technical roles are carried out on a day-by-day basis and in many corporations the compliance, financial, and educational roles occupy a substantial amount of the day-to-day activities of a corporate travel manager. In the more travel-oriented organizations, negotiations are entered into requiring a substantial amount of the corporate travel manager's attention.

As pointed out, corporations vary to a considerable extent regarding how corporate travel departments are set up and what their total responsibilities are. In addition, corporate travel managers often share the travel management function with some other functions within the corporation and, therefore, often can give less attention to corporate travel management than they might wish to provide. Nevertheless, the above six corporate travel management roles tend to be the major roles that are undertaken by corporate travel managers in most corporations today. Specific aspects relating to the carrying out of these roles will be discussed in later chapters.

Discussion Questions

1. Some say that attempting to identify specific corporate management roles is a futile process. What is their justification for this position?

2. Six major corporate travel manager roles were discussed in this chapter. What are they?

3. Do subroles ever overlap major roles? If so, provide an example.

4. On what basis do some corporate travel managers complain that they are not managers and why might they be considered managers anyway?

5. What are some of the managerial subroles performed by corporate travel managers?

6. What four subroles have been identified within the corporate travel manager technician role?

7. What are some of the different ways corporate travel managers perform the reservations and ticketing technician subrole?

8. What is meant by saying that the reviewing and reporting subroles are both internal and external functions?

9. What do corporate travel managers do that makes them complain that they are seen as policemen?

10. Why is the role of financial manager considered an especially important role?

11. What are the major negotiation areas in most corporations as they relate to corporate travel? Are they ongoing or one-time negotiations?

12. There are two broad areas of corporate travel education. In what ways do corporate travel managers manage corporate travel education?

Role Play Exercise

Two students may participate in this role play either out-of-class, as a fun way to review the roles of the corporate travel manager, or as an in-class exercise. One student plays the role of an outgoing corporate travel manager (i.e., the corporate travel manager who has worked for XYZ Company for a number of years, recently resigned, and will be moving to another company as its corporate travel manager at a considerable increase in salary). The other student plays the role of the incoming corporate travel manager (i.e., the person recently hired to be the new corporate manager for XYZ company).

Incoming Corporate Travel Manager: The new position seems simple enough, Mr. Anderson. All I do is keep track of the travel that is authorized, make sure the travel agency is doing its job right by investigating them a lot, and giving a report to the company's comptroller about how much money we are saving the company. Isn't that about it, Mr. Anderson?

Outgoing Corporate Travel Manager: It's a little more complicated than that, Mr. Newtsome. There are several roles that corporate travel managers undertake in all companies that have travel departments. And there are some unique corporate travel roles we take on here at XYZ Company. To get a complete picture of the corporate travel management job here, it will be beneficial to know what these roles are.

Incoming Corporate Travel Manager: Well maybe it is a little more involved than I thought. Tell me about these roles.

CONTINUE ON YOUR OWN

Group Discussion Situation: Justifying Salary to Fit The Corporate Travel Position

Elaine Ellis started working for Industrial Containers when she was eighteen-years old. She has been working for the company for twenty years. Elaine started out preparing documents in the warehouse. By going to school at night, she learned to be a secretary and got a job in the secretarial pool. Over the years, Elaine worked her way up to a position of executive secretary. About ten years ago Elaine started handling the travel arrangements for several of the training division travelers who conducted seminars at company sites throughout the United States. Elaine became so good at making travel arrangements and she seemed to enjoy it so much that other secretaries asked her to make the travel arrangements for their bosses as well. When the Vice President of Finance decided that saving money on travel was something the company needed to do and that a current company employee would be given the task, Elaine was the logical choice.

Elaine has managed the corporate travel department for five years now. Her savings for the company is well documented. Elaine has proven that several hundred thousand dollars a year has been saved in her efforts to manage corporate travel. In addition, her handling of emergency travel arrangements has resulted in the company beating the competition in getting to key bids and this has been part of the reason Industrial Containers has won several important contracts. Elaine has received three letters of commendation from the President of the company and several from other executives.

Elaine wants a raise. She is being paid $27,000 per year, but has identified that new MBAs coming in to the company who are given far less responsibility are being paid over $30,000 a year. When Elaine approached the Vice President of Finance asking why she is being paid less money than newly-hired MBAs, she was told that she is only a glorified secretary making travel arrangements. The Vice President of Finance advised Elaine that he would consider giving her an increase if she could show on paper that her knowledge and skills are important to the company and that the role she plays is one that any other secretary could not undertake in a few months of on-the-job training. "In other words . . . ," he said, ". . . justify the salary by showing that you can do what the MBAs do, and I will give you the salary."

You are meeting today to help Elaine prepare the written role justification paper required by the Vice President of Finance. You are expected to reach agreement and to write a two-page justification paper.

In your group session, select one person to chair the group. All will have an equal vote on decisions. In the group session you are expected to reach agreement on the roles and justifications and to prepare the two-page paper to be presented to the entire class by the chair of your committee.

CHAPTER 5

Travel Industry Interrelationships

In the chapter on the background and history of corporate travel departments, a picture of the close relationships between travel agencies, airlines, and corporate travel departments was presented. To understand this interrelationship and how it affects a corporation's travel department, it is necessary to understand some basics about what travel agencies do (and do not do), how agencies interrelate with air carriers, the travel agency commission earning structure, agency specialization(s), services travel agencies provide to corporate clients, airline/corporate travel interrelationships and the services airlines provide to corporate clients. As the chapter on history pointed out, airline and agency interrelationships with one another and with corporate travel departments are constantly changing. Therefore, in this chapter, some movements and directions will be pointed out so that the industry observer will have a foundation on which to forecast future planning.

What Travel Agencies Do

Travel agencies provide a wide range of travel services for a wide range of travel clients. However, most travel agencies spend most of their time making air travel arrangements. They seek out the best itinerary for the client based on what the client indicates are important factors. They then seek the best fare unless the client has indicated that first class or some other higher than best fare is preferred. Most agencies will request seat assignments when advanced assigning is allowed by the air carrier involved. And they will process a boarding pass for the client whenever this is allowed by the air carrier. This gives the client a better chance of getting the seat of his or her choice and keeps the client from having to get a ticket or a boarding pass after getting to the airport. Most travel agencies will deliver the ticket to the client if the client is a business (most do not deliver to residences). Larger travel agencies provide accounting reports to larger corporate accounts.

A number of additional services are provided by selected agencies, but since travel agencies tend to be small businesses, the range of services is decided upon by each agency. The range of services provided may vary from client to client within an agency depending upon how important the client is to the agency. All of the above services are usually provided at no cost to the client. Airlines pay a commission of usually ten percent domestic and eight percent international to travel agencies, so the cost to the client is the same as it would be if the client purchased the ticket from an air carrier. In some cases, the ticket will be less expensive than if it is purchased directly from a carrier, since larger agencies can sometimes convert economy fared seats to discounted fares and provide a rebate to the corporate client. Some travel agencies do charge service charges for a few of their services. Most agencies, for example, pass on the airline imposed service charge of $15 to $25 for processing prepaid tickets and some agencies levy a service charge for handling a corporate account's frequent flier program paperwork.

There are some things that travel agencies do not do. Most do not have charter aircraft and many do not work with charter operators. Some agencies, however, will arrange charters for corporate clients and a very few travel agencies have their own charter aircraft. Travel agencies are not air carriers and, therefore, they cannot maintain quality control standards as they relate to scheduled air carriers. If a plane is late or a flight is cancelled, the agency has no control over correcting the situation. The agency can, however, identify air carrier service trends and it can avoid booking travel on a carrier that is not providing an acceptable level of service on a routine basis.

Travel agencies are appointed sales representatives of air carriers. Most interstate air carriers flying within the United States belong to the *Airline Reporting Corporation* (ARC) which appoints travel agencies to sell tickets for their domestic carrier members. IATAN, the international carrier organization paralleling the appointment process of ARC, represents most major carriers that fly between the United States and other countries. This organization appoints travel agencies to sell tickets on its member international carriers.

Most travel agencies have at least one computer reservation system. These systems are owned by individual airlines or small groups of airlines. Although the vendors represent that their computerized reservations systems are not biased, usually there is a strong correlation between the airline booked most often and the carrier whose system the agency has adopted.

Some agencies and airlines have worked out special arrangements. For example, ethnic travel agencies can sometimes build up such a large volume of travel on the ethnic airline that the carrier will provide the agency with higher commissions, special payment arrangements, rebates, and other benefits not normally extended to the average travel agency. Large commercial agencies may be extended rebates, computer credits for hotel or other non-air bookings, and ticket conversion ability by individual air carriers—especially the carrier whose computer system they use. Therefore, the travel agency/airline interrelationship may run the gamut from being somewhat superficial to being very close often depending upon the volume of sales an agency makes on the specific carrier, and whether or not the agency works with the carrier's computer system.

The official remuneration program of travel agencies by airlines is based upon a percentage of the cost of the air ticket. As pointed out above, this is normally ten percent for domestic airline tickets and eight percent for international tickets. However, overrides can reach a much higher level. Even agencies with as little as a million dollars of business have been given one half percent commission override by carriers when they sell the carrier with a preference or when they beat a quota established by the carrier. Larger agencies can obtain much higher overrides (up to a total of fifteen percent of airline ticket cost).

Recently many carriers have moved to a "market share" formula to determine override percentage payments. The carrier determines the total sales of an agency and then determines what its (the airline's) share of the market is. The percentage share of the market is divided into the agency sales volume to determine the quota level for each agency. When the agency exceeds its quota level for several months at a time, the agency receives an override. Many agencies are provided "soft" overrides (i.e., free and/or reduced rate airline tickets) based upon their volume of business with carriers. In some cases, these can be used by agency personnel, resold, and/or given to corporate travel accounts. Benefits, and other remuneration, however, are usually closely tied with sales and productivity.

Travel Agency Specialization(s)

Although they are not required to do so, a growing number of travel agencies are beginning to specialize. Knowing the specializations of travel agencies can help a corporate travel manager learn where to turn for the best help at any specific point in time. It can also help a manager narrow down the field of potential travel suppliers.

The two main categories of travel agency specialization are:

1. corporate; and
2. leisure.

Some travel agencies sell travel to business and industry accounts exclusively or almost exclusively. Other agencies sell vacation or "leisure" travel exclusively or almost exclusively. There are some breakdowns of specialization within these two broad areas, especially within the leisure specialization. Destination or "ethnic" specialization is especially common. Most major cities have agencies that sell travel to certain countries or regions. Almost every major city has at least one agency specializing in travel to Scandinavia. Latin American travel agencies are also found in most major cities. There are agencies specializing in travel to Russia and Eastern block countries. Others specialize in travel to Korea, Japan, and the Far East. There are agency specialists for just about every major area of the world.

Another leisure specialization breakdown relates to the type of trip. For example, there are agencies that specialize in offering such things as their own bus tours. Others specialize in package tours. Still others are cruise specialists. And some are foreign independent tour (FIT) specialists.

In the corporate area, there are fewer who specialize. Almost all corporate travel agencies offer a full range of corporate travel services. Some of the larger agencies will have special desks (for example, the international desk or the incentive travel desk), but even these agencies tend to offer a wide range of services to all business travelers. In the few agencies that have specialized within the corporate travel general area, one finds that the special "desks" have been turned into whole-agency specializations. Therefore, in larger cities one may find corporate agencies specializing in international corporate travel and corporate agencies specializing in incentive travel programs for businesses, industry, and associations.

FIGURE 5.1. This LIFECO TRAVEL MANAGEMENT reservations office in California reflects the efficient surroundings in which many corporate travel oriented travel agents work.

FIGURE 5.2. Reservation "Bays" need not be cold and crowded as this photo of a LIFECO TRAVEL MANAGEMENT reservations office in California shows. Note the clocks which show the time in various parts of the country.

Services Provided By Agencies

Earlier in this chapter an overview of the services provided by travel agencies for their commercial accounts was presented. However, these were only the major services. A menu of possible services include the following:

Negotiate corporate hotel rates—identify high frequency travel cities and negotiate with one or two hotels to get corporate rates or better-than-corporate rates for the commercial account(s).

Educate corporate travelers, booking secretaries, and the corporate travel manager by holding seminars, funding local and national corporate travel manager membership dues and association conference attendance, meeting individually with those having travel booking problems, preparing and distributing educational newsletters, and so forth.

Provide a best-fare guarantee and document that the best possible fare was obtained (including conversion rate) except during authorized exceptions through an agreed-upon exception report.

Negotiate individual franchisee car rental rates—identify high frequency car rental cities and negotiate with car rental franchisees to obtain a better-than-published corporate daily and weekly car rental rate.

Tailored invoices with data designed specifically to meet the internal needs of the corporation.

Customer service representatives who will research customer-reported problems and present solution options in a short-time frame.

Agency branch location either in-house or at a location convenient to the client if client travel volume justifies same.

Bookings made on preferred carriers when the client specifies one or more specific carriers that provide a desired service level.

Provide total automation including boarding pass printers capable of issuing boarding passes on all carriers that will allow boarding passes to be issued in advance, hard copy printers, itinerary printers, and automated accounting interface system reports.

Long-term billing, credit card annual fee payment, or other credit incentives.

Automated reports tailored to the needs of the corporate client.

Updated and well-briefed agents dedicated to the corporate account. Very experienced agents should be handling only the individual client account or at best handling only two corporate accounts.

Twenty-four hour, seven-day-a-week, toll-free (800 number) booking and reservations service provided at no cost to the client and available at any major airport in the world.

Twice-a-day (or more frequent) signed for uniformed ticket delivery service plus two-hour guaranteed ticket generation and delivery.

Quality control services (sometimes called pre-ticket audits) checking to make sure the price has not gone down since it was quoted so that the lowest fare since the reservation was made is attained. Checking to make certain that all aspects of the reservation, the ticket, and the documents are accurate.

Third-party audits reviewing all documents to determine that the lowest fares were indeed obtained, the number of times the best possible fare was not obtained (and why), and quality control checks to determine if and when the agency's quality control department missed in catching all possible errors. Third party audits are often paid for by the travel agency, but report to the commercial client.

Frequent Flier Management Program—the travel agency systematically collects, sorts, files, stores, documents, and calculates frequent flier bonuses and coupons for the corporation and/or the corporation's travelers, handling all aspects of the program so that the client is given an accounting of frequent flier status for each traveler and for each carrier on a once-a-month basis.

Visa and health record information and documentation—the agency provides visa information and works with a visa service to obtain visas at the best possible price in the most timely manner and provides published information on innoculation requirements as well as copies of shot record forms, visa application forms, and passport application forms on a gratis basis.

Travelers checks issued by or for the agency for commercial clients either without an issuance fee or for a reduced fee.

Passport photos taken by the agency and provided to the agency's clients on a gratis basis.

Inflight accidental death/life insurance provided for the agency's clients on a gratis basis.

Immediate refunds to the corporate client even when air carriers, hotels, or other vendors may take months to reimburse the travel agency for the refund.

Computer terminals, printers, and other appropriate equipment installed and maintained in the client's offices (if ticket volume warrants) at no cost to the client.

Foreign currency exchange services at no cost to the client.

A bond, irrevocable letter of credit, or other indemnification in the case of an agency bankruptcy, default, sale, merger, or other action that may affect current travel transactions and future travel transactions between the client and the travel agency.

Contracts, policies, authorization procedures and systems protecting the client against unauthorized or misuse of travel by a client employee, ex-employee, or other person for billing against the commercial client.

Saturday, weekend, and/or evening service based upon the needs of the client.

Rapid call processing. Some agencies guarantee to answer incoming calls on the third ring. Others provide dedicated lines for larger clients with guarantees that these lines will be answered first. Still others provide dedicated lines to the desks of dedicated agents. However it is handled, providing rapid call answering and not putting clients on hold once the phone has been answered is essential.

Traveler security protection—security training for travelers flying outside the
United States, security retention of the names of commercial travelers, and
so on.

Communications—Regular sales and service representative calls, newsletters directed to travelers and booking secretaries, regular training manual updates,
and frequent client training sessions.

While this is not meant to be a comprehensive list of the services provided by
travel agencies for commercial accounts, it presents the major services expected
by many corporate travel managers. In addition, however, there are many non-
service benefits and programs provided by travel agencies for their commercial
accounts. These will be discussed in future chapters.

Airline/Corporate Travel Interrelationships

As noted in the historical section of the book, considerable progress has been
made with the advent of deregulation in terms of the air carriers being able to
openly work with corporate travel departments. While no major carrier is openly
paying corporate travel departments the same commissions they pay travel agencies across the board, deregulation opened the doors to being able to do so. And,
an increasing number of corporate travel departments are receiving some monetary and considerable non-monetary compensation directly from air carriers
(these monies are not normally called commissions) and a travel agency belonging
to the *National Business Travel Association* (NBTA) was paid a full commission level
during the time of its appointment.

The interrelationship between air carriers and corporate travel departments has a history of being close, but sometimes volitale. Aside from the corporate travel departments continuously pushing for full commissions and the air
carriers continuously avoiding appointment of corporate travel departments and
payment of full commissions for corporate travel to corporate travel departments, the relationship has generally been a good and a close one.

For major air carriers commercial accounts are an important target market.
Airline sales representatives are assigned to call on corporate travel managers and
do so on a regular basis. Some larger corporate accounts receive more sales calls
from airline representatives than many travel agencies. During these calls new
routes, schedules, fares, and other facts relating to the airline are discussed, but
many corporate travel managers also take these opportunities to discuss service
problems, accounting difficulties (as it relates to air carrier refunds, exchanges,
and so on), scheduling inconveniences, and other factors that would make the life
of the corporate travel manager easier if the airline assisted in resolving the
problems. One of the major benefits of the interrelationship between corporate
travel managers and air carriers is that when a corporate traveler has a problem, it
can often be resolved by having the corporate travel manager make a call to the
airline sales representative or the district sales manager for the air carrier. This
leverage that air carriers provide to and for corporate travel managers is important in resolving many problems—often before they become serious problems.

Services Airlines Provide To/For Corporate Travelers

Airlines offer pre-trip, enroute, and post-trip services for corporate travelers. Pre-trip service includes the assignment of seats usually at the time reservations are made, upgrades, free, or reduced rate trips with the use of frequent flier coupons, VIP treatment in some cases (especially when requested by a corporate travel manager), reduced rate airline lounge usage (sometimes free coupons to use the airline frequent flier lounge), and meeting rooms for groups. During the flight, seating upgrades are sometimes provided, with an advanced request from the corporate travel manager, special meals and free or reduced rate liquor coupons are sometimes provided. Important messages can sometimes be transmitted to corporate travelers, inflight, usually without cost. Excess luggage can sometimes be taken on board at no extra cost if arrangements are made in advance. Post-trip services include VIP handling upon arrival and customs clearance assistance if requested in advance.

Although many of the above services can and are provided to clients other than corporate travelers, the frequency with which they are extended to other categories of clients tends to be less. In many cases special services, however, will not be provided unless requested well in advance, usually by the corporate travel manager.

Summary

Travel industry interrelationships are constantly changing, but appear to be growing stronger since deregulation. Travel agencies provide a wide range of services to corporate travelers and since deregulation the range of services has expanded considerably. Travel agencies sell all types of travel, packaging travel so that customers can get the combination of travel products and services that they desire. They charge no more than air carriers charge for their services and products, often charging less when one considers the rebates and additional services provided on a gratis basis by so many of today's agencies.

Travel agencies receive a ten percent commission on domestic tickets and eight percent on international tickets by and large. The price they charge to the client (corporate or otherwise) is the same as or less than the client would have to pay if he/she would have purchased the same tickets from the airline counter. Travel agencies, however, have limited or no control over the quality of the travel services they sell. They act as agents and do not control air carrier services.

Travel agencies are appointed by two associations of air carriers to sell tickets on their behalf. The domestic appointing airline association is ARC (Airline Reporting Corporation). Its international equivalent is IATAN (International Air Traffic Association Network). While ARC member airlines normally pay travel agents a ten percent commission, some pay more based on the volume of air travel sold or based on the percentage above the carrier's market share tickets sold. Part of this override commission is sometimes passed on to corporate travel accounts by travel agencies in a revenue sharing arrangement that can result in income generation for the commercial account.

Travel agencies tend to specialize in either the leisure travel area or in commercial travel. Leisure agencies may specialize further into specific destinations or types of travel, such as cruises, tours, or FITs. Commercial travel agencies tend not to specialize further, but those few who do may offer specializations in international commercial travel or incentive travel for business and industry. There are many services provided by travel agencies and these tend to fall into the categories of rate or fare negotiation, corporate reports, education, financial services, booking and documentation services, delivery services, and services for international corporate travelers.

Although most corporate travelers book travel through travel agencies in order to benefit from the range of services that they provide, there is still a close relationship between air carriers and corporate travel departments. All major carriers have identified corporate travel as a major target market and sales representatives are assigned to call on corporate travel managers on a regular basis. New and updated product information is reviewed during these sales calls, but they also offer the opportunity for corporate travel managers to request direct action on air carrier problems as they relate to the company, as well as to request special services if they are needed. The services provided by air carriers can be broken down into pre-flight, inflight, and post-flight services and they are designed to give special attention to corporate travelers and resolve their unique air travel problems.

Discussion Questions

1. What are some of the things a travel agency does for its clients?
2. What are the standard domestic and international commission levels travel agencies are paid by air carriers?
3. Is it more expensive to buy air tickets from a travel agency? Why?
4. For what kinds of things might travel agencies normally levy a service charge?
5. What kinds of things can travel agencies not do?
6. What airline associations appoint travel agencies?
7. What is meant by the term "airline appointment?"
8. Why might a corporate traveler want to have his travel arranged by an ethnic agency when traveling to the country of the agency's ethnic specialization?
9. What is meant by the term "override?"
10. What are "market share" formulas?
11. What are the two major areas of travel agency specialization?
12. How might a corporate travel agency further specialize?
13. For what kinds of things might a travel agency negotiate on behalf of its corporate travel accounts?
14. What types of educational services might a travel agency provide for its corporate accounts?
15. What financial services and benefits might a travel agency provide to and for its corporate accounts?

16. What types of booking, ticketing, and delivery services might a travel agency provide for its corporate accounts?

17. What kinds of quality control might a corporate travel manager ask for and/or expect from the travel agency handling the corporation's account?

18. How might a travel agency help a corporation handle its frequent flier coupons to the benefit of both the corporation and the traveler?

19. What kinds of services might a travel agency provide to corporate travelers flying to destinations outside the U.S.?

20. What other types of service might a travel agency provide to a corporation and its travelers?

21. To what extent do airlines pay a full commission to corporate travel departments for corporate travel business?

22. How do airline sales representatives provide a foundation for the airline/corporate travel interrelationships?

23. What are the three categories of services provided by air carriers to corporate travelers?

24. What are some of the services an airline can provide to a corporation and/or a corporate traveler while the traveler is in the air traveling?

25. What are some of the other services an airline can provide to corporate travelers and/or corporate travel departments?

Role Play Exercise

Two students may participate in this role play either out-of-class, as a fun way to review the chapter, or as an in-class exercise. One plays the role of a travel agency manager and the other plays the role of a corporate travel manager. Please read the script and then pick up the conversation in your own words.

Travel Agency Manager: I appreciate your taking the time to meet with me today. As you know, we would like to handle your account. I sent you a packet of information on our agency. We provide a wide range of services and benefits. How will these match your current needs?

Corporate Travel Manager: Your services seem to be comprehensive. I have a concern about how our relationships with the air carrier representatives might be affected if we work with you. I am also not sure how comprehensive your services really are. Tell me how we can continue to work directly with air carriers to solve our unique air problems and review your services for me so that I can note any differences between what you propose to provide and what our current agency is providing, if you don't mind.

Travel Agency Manager: I'll be happy to. Let's start with . . .

CONTINUE ON YOUR OWN

Group Discussion Situation:
Prissy's CFO Upgrade

American Widgets has been dealing with the largest travel agency in town, but recently changed to Personalized Travel (a small agency that prides itself on providing very personal service). The reason for the change is that the large agency was just too large for the liking of American Widgets' corporate travel manager, Prissy Prentice. Prissy found that service varied considerably depending upon who handled the transaction. Also, the large agency made several mistakes. Prissy has been happy with the way in which Personalized Travel has handled her account since she changed agencies. However, yesterday the chief financial officer called and asked Prissy to use one of his Frequent Flier Coupon eligibilities to upgrade his flight to Europe, scheduled a week from Tuesday, to first class. Personalized Travel just called back saying the air carrier refused to confirm the upgrade and the CFO will just have to take his chances on getting it when he gets to the airport. Prissy is disturbed. The large agency always got upgrades almost automatically. She knows the CFO won't be happy. What suggestions do you have for Prissy?

CHAPTER 6

Airline Industry Overview and Interrelationships

Balanced Airline Interrelationships

Many who are new to corporate travel management view the interrelationship between a corporate travel manager and airlines as being minimal. They are correct when there is relatively little corporate travel (i.e., when few air trips are taken by anyone in the company or the dollar amount spent on travel is insignificant). However, most organizations that have a corporate travel department also have a sufficient volume of air travel that air carriers are very much interested in receiving their business. Again, some who are new to corporate travel management may feel that all aspects of airline interfacing are routed through their travel agency vendor. Although the day-to-day air reservation arrangements may very well be handled routinely by the travel agency that may be under contract to the corporation, airline executives will want to receive at least their "fair share" of the corporation's air travel business and they will usually take the initiative in establishing a rapport with corporate travel managers, their departments, and others within the corporation to make sure that they get their "fair share." Therefore, the initial belief of many new corporate travel managers that they will interface with airlines seldom and only through travel agencies is usually fallacious. This is not to suggest that the average corporate travel manager is constantly on the phone with airline executives dealing directly on all matters relating to air travel. However, a balance is struck.

Airline executives want corporate travel business and corporate travel managers often have special needs which can be fulfilled by airline marketing executives. It is this mutuality of needs and interests that brings about what often is an extremely good rapport between airline marketing executives and corporate travel managers. However, the rapport is not always positive. Sometimes airline marketing programs bypass the corporate travel manager or make the manager's job harder in their efforts to appeal directly to the traveler. In some cases the relationship can be adversarial and can even result in a boycott of a carrier by the company and/or the corporate travel department.

The Air Carrier Sales Structure

To explore the rapport that can be developed and to identify the parameters of the working relationships between corporate travel managers and airline marketing executives, it is important to identify how airlines work in relationship to obtaining corporate travel. The vehicle or catalyst for corporate travel manager interfacing is the airline's sales manager and/or the sales manager's sales staff (airline sales representatives). All major air carriers have a marketing and sales structure, but it can change from carrier to carrier depending on the location, the size of the city, and the airline's position in the market (usually determined by the number of flights into or through the city each week). These factors determine who in the airline calls on corporate travel managers and the degree of power or influence the airline sales contact has. This degree of power or influence can often spell the difference between the ability of the corporate travel manager to get what is needed or not to get it.

The local airline marketing structure typically starts with a regional manager. The regional manager may have either a large territory or a small one and may have either a large staff or a small one. Pan American World Airways, for example, at one time had a regional manager who covered all of Europe and the Middle East. He had a large staff of district managers and sales representatives. At the same time, Pan Am had a Denver-based district manager who was responsible for all of Colorado. She had no staff support.

Domestic carriers who fly into a major U.S. city with a large number of flights each week may have a large marketing staff consisting of at least a district manager and a number of sales representatives. Sales representatives are typically assigned geographical territories and will be responsible for all airline business (for their carrier) generated within their assigned territory.

Typically, this will be broken into business from travel agencies, large cargo shippers, and corporate travel. The sales representative will call on corporate travel managers on a regular basis in the same way that regular calls are made to cargo shippers and travel agencies in the assigned territory. When the corporate travel manager needs direct interface with the air carrier, a call can be placed to the sales office and the sales representative assigned to the corporate travel manager's territory will get back to the manager and make an effort to assist the corporate travel manager.

It must be remembered, however, that air carriers are usually strict in their reporting regulations and a sales representative may have relatively little influence on the outcome of a request or of negotiation with a corporate travel manager. Unless the matter is something the sales representative has a predetermined authority to provide, it will have to be referred to a higher level sales manager. The airline will expect the corporate travel manager to interface with the sales representative and if the matter is not agreed to at that level or if the sales representative refers the matter to the district manager and it is not agreed to at that level, the airline expects the matter to be dropped. Many corporate travel managers do drop requests or negotiation points at this level, but since they are not working for the air carrier, they are not locked into the airline's reporting structure.

A large number of corporate travel managers go higher than the district manager level for their requests and negotiations. Not infrequently, they find that higher management will approve requests or will negotiate important areas that the district manager, and/or the sales representative, feels uncomfortable about. In many cases, airline regulations make agreement difficult.

A few carriers organize sales representatives differently. They assign sales reps on the basis of client type. Again, in a large city a carrier with many weekly flights may assign sales representatives to either the entire city or to a much larger territory, but their responsibility will be for only one client type. In other words, the sales representative calling on corporate travel managers may call on only corporate travel managers but may be assigned to all large corporations in the city. In this way sales representatives can begin to specialize. Of course, another sales representative will be assigned to the cargo shippers and still another will cover the travel agencies in the city. Sometimes sales representatives who are specialized are given more latitude in solving problems or negotiating with clients than are geographically-based sales representatives. The reasoning is that, being specialized, they have a better understanding of the situation than a district manager might. However, there are still definite limits to what can be agreed to by a specialized sales representative.

In cities where the air carrier has fewer flights (or no flights), airlines will typically have coverage by either a district sales manager or a regional sales manager. If it is a large city, the district sales manager will usually live in the city. The regional sales managers will normally work out of the largest city in the region. District and regional managers will usually call on only the largest clients or potential clients. They will seek out those clients and potential clients who are currently giving them a substantial amount of business. For example, they might call on a corporate travel manager whose travel business is smaller than that of many other corporate travel managers in other companies, but whose company has a factory, sales office, home office, or other entity in a city to which the airline flies, resulting in a large amount of the company's travel going to that city. In dealing with district and regional sales managers two points are important to keep in mind:

1. fewer corporate travel managers are called on by district and regional managers; and
2. the authority of district and regional sales managers for airlines is usually considerably greater than the authority of airline sales representatives.

Even when a corporation's air travel volume is relatively low and/or the corporation has few flights between city pairs served by a carrier represented by a district or a regional sales manager, a call to the office of the district or regional sales manager will usually result in a return call and the district/regional sales manager will often be able to make a positive decision without having to refer the matter to any higher level in the airline.

New corporate travel managers and corporate travel managers controlling a small amount of air travel frequently never get called on since airline sales representatives can often only reach quota levels by concentrating on big travel budget firms. Corporate travel managers can call sales offices, however, and if their air travel budget increases, a positive welcoming of airline sales representatives plus the increased air volume to justify sales calls may be enough to change the situation around.

Major Corporate Travel Negotiation Factors

Several factors affect a corporate travel manager's ability to negotiate with air carriers in addition to the level of the airline marketing person who calls on the corporate travel manager. Primary among these factors is the amount of air travel purchased by the company on city pairs served by the carrier. The larger the amount of annual air travel purchased for travel between these city pairs, the greater the interest of the air carrier to obtain and negotiate for the company's travel.

Another factor of importance is competition. When two or more carriers are competing for business, the airline will usually try very hard to get the company's business. However, if there is no competition, the carrier will know that the market is locked in and there will be little, or no, negotiation.

A final factor of major importance is the position of the corporate travel manager within the company. If travelers go through many different travel agencies, the CEO or the CFO make all the decisions as to the carriers that will be used, or if the company's travelers make their reservations by calling airline reservation offices, the airline marketing sales person will make calls on the corporate travel manager out of courtesy considerations only or will simply bypass the corporate travel manager. However, if all travel decisions are routed through the corporate travel manager, the ability to get special assistance when needed or to negotiate with an air carrier will be considerably better.

Agency Versus Airline Assistance

Sometimes it is difficult to determine what types of requests should be routed through a company's travel agency vendor and what types should go to the airline marketing person. After all, most day-by-day travel arrangements for most corporate travel departments are routed through the travel agency vendor under contract to the company. However, even some travel agencies will agree that there are some requests that will be acted on faster and with a greater degree of certainty if the request goes directly from the corporate travel manager to the air carrier—especially if the airline is trying to get more business from the corporation. VIP handling is the primary example of this type of request. If VIP service is needed, the corporate travel manager could call the travel agency. However, the agency would need to relay the request to the air carrier and it would normally go through the airline's reservations office and then to the airport.

On the other hand, if the corporate travel manager contacts the airline marketing person calling on the agency, that individual can often send a message to the appropriate airport service executive directly. At least two middle men are cut out of the request and the request will have originated within the airline. The chances of getting the service will be much better and the chances of getting a high quality of service will be much better.

Another type of request that can often be handled better by going directly to the air carrier is fare restriction exceptions. Occasionally, a corporation will encounter a situation where a traveler is booked on a discounted fare requiring restrictions and, for one reason or another, the corporation is unable to meet the restrictions. To cancel the ticket may result in paying a penalty or paying a much higher price for a replacement ticket. It is possible that this will result in the price being beyond the budget of the department involved. Although corporations seldom run into these types of problems, they can occur. A typical example is an advance-purchase fare. Although the traveler may have requested the ticket in time, the corporate travel manager may have slipped in getting the request transmitted to the travel agency in time to meet the date restrictions. Under such a circumstance, the corporate travel manager can often call the airline sales contact and obtain a waiver of restrictions. Obviously, this cannot be done on a routine basis, but most airline sales representatives have the authority to waive restrictions on a case-by-case basis.

Price/Benefits Direct Negotiation

Corporate travel managers with large volumes of air travel constantly make choices regarding where to turn in terms of negotiations for better services and prices. Since deregulation, everything is negotiable. Obviously a corporate travel manager can negotiate with the travel agency vendor and can often get rebates and special services. However, increasingly corporate travel managers can and do negotiate directly with air carriers for price reductions, free tickets, upgrades, and direct rebates. In a recent issue of, *Runzheimer Reports On Travel Management*, over half of the companies responding to a survey of airline interrelationships indicated that they had negotiated direct arrangements with air carriers and had obtained either discounts or special services, or both. Although many of these corporate travel managers did involve their travel agencies in the negotiations, so that when sitting down at the table to discuss arrangements with the airlines, the travel agency, the corporate travel manager, and the airline executive were all present, almost as many negotiated without their travel agency representative being present.

City-Pair Analyses

When negotiating price reductions, it is important to keep in mind that the air carrier will want to increase its profits by switching a large percentage of the corporation's business from competing air carriers to their carrier. Therefore, they will normally only discuss specific city pairs (i.e., the number of trips that the corporation has had and future projects between the various combinations of "two cities" in their system) on a city-pair by city-pair basis. And, they will expect the corporate travel manager to have exact statistics when sitting down at the negotiation table.

At a minimum, the statistics will include:

- the number of trips taken by the corporation's travelers between these city pairs last year (and preferably every year for a five-year period);
- the budget projections for trips on every city pair for the future year;
- the amount of travel booked for each city pair with their carrier last year (and every year for the last five years); and
- the amount of travel booked on each competing carrier on each of these city pairs last year and for each year in the past for the last five years.

With this data, the corporate travel manager is in a position to negotiate moving some or all of the business expected for next year which historically has been given to competing carriers. According to a reference in *Travel Agent,* Barney Kogin, President and chief executive officer of LIFECO Travel Services, indicates that discounts of up to fifty-five percent have been applied to negotiated city pairs.

Off-peak Flight Negotiations

In addition to switching carriers on city pairs, corporate travel managers may also offer to assist carriers in filling their planes during off-peak time flights. Although this must be looked at carefully because many of these off-peak flights will get the traveler to the destination at a most disadvantageous time, there are some off-peak flights that may well fit into the schedules of corporate travelers without creating any inconveniences. When off-peak flights can be utilized, there can be advantages to the air carrier and the carrier is usually willing to offer return reductions in price and/or amenities.

Special Ticketing Arrangements

In working with air carriers, it is usually better to consider all potential options. Some carriers will prefer to make special ticketing arrangements available to the corporation, often bypassing the travel agency. When this is the case, the corporate travel manager needs to look closely at the restrictions and the lack of travel agency services (i.e., those services from the agency that will be given up). While there may be substantial reductions in cost to the corporation, the fare reduction benefits may be outweighed by the service reductions and/or services that are eliminated. Most corporate travel managers believe that service is paramount and, while cost is important, the major consideration is to make sure that the traveler gets to the destination on time and in a condition that the traveler will be ready for work upon arrival.

Some special deals which bypass travel agencies can sometimes make this difficult to accomplish. For example, a large organization in Florida negotiated a direct arrangement with an air carrier several years ago. They bypassed the travel agency and saved as much as sixty percent on every ticket. However, after the "deal" was struck, they found that they had to order tickets two weeks in advance, that no changes could be made to the ticket, and that some of their executives were placed on a stand-by basis when they went to the airport to board flights. They found that last-minute changes were impossible, and the corporate travel manager came close to being fired because the service problems became so considerable.

Carrier Lump-sum Rebates

Some air carriers will prefer to make lump-sum payments of direct rebates to the company, normally on a quarterly basis. In this way, tickets can be issued showing the full fare and there will be no evidence on the tickets themselves of any type of direct rebating. This helps to eliminate competitor knowledge of the "deals" that are struck. In addition, it helps the traveler. When special "negotiated" fares are shown on an airline ticket, airport check-in desk agents sometimes do not understand the codes and/or fare reduction notes printed on the tickets and will either treat the traveler as a stand-by or require additional payment prior to allowing the traveler to board the plane. Although these misunderstandings are rare, when it happens to a top corporate executive, the corporate travel manager will hear about it.

Other Corporate Travel Areas of Negotiation

In addition to discounts, it is possible to negotiate a number of other items/areas that may be of importance to both the traveler and the company. These include automatic upgrades to first class, fare restriction elimination, and special services.

Group and Meeting Travel

Many corporate travel managers also have the responsibility for group travel. When the groups are large in size and there can be benefits to the air carrier, the potential for negotiation becomes good. Most air carriers have group desks, but it is usually better to negotiate special group benefits, services, and prices with a senior executive of the air carrier. The group reservation desk manager is normally severely limited in terms of what can be negotiated. Airlines can, and do, compete hard for corporate meeting business. If one is able to speak to the right person with an air carrier, it is often possible to obtain substantial financial and nonfinancial benefits.

It is always wise to reach an airline executive who has the authority to negotiate. In other words, find a person who can commit the airline to something beyond those regulation guidelines that are distributed to all stations and all group desks in print format. This usually means getting to a very high level.

A corporate travel manager who has considerable experience with large groups states that she always starts with trying to contact the President of the airline in her efforts to find someone to negotiate with on behalf of the carrier. Although she is seldom able to negotiate directly with the President, by starting at that level, she is usually able to find someone at a high enough level that specific commitments can be made and fulfilled. It should be kept in mind, however, that senior executives with air carriers move and often are no longer with the carrier at the time that the travel actually starts. Therefore, all oral agreements should be agreed to in writing.

Breakdown of Negotiation Areas

The areas for negotiation can be broken down into pre-departure, enroute, and post-arrival services and benefits. Obviously, in addition to the services and benefits, ticket price reduction is an area for negotiation as well. The range of negotiation possibility in each of these three areas will be discussed in detail.

Site Selection

One of the most important areas of pre-departure often is site selection. This is an area in which many airlines are most cooperative. Free tickets to and from potential on-line meeting sites are often provided to corporate travel managers who plan meetings. The old Republic Airlines even offered a "wish list" of destinations to those who plan meetings. However, before providing free tickets for site selection, the air carrier will usually expect that the corporate travel manager provide proof of numbers and commitment. They want documentation showing how many people attended the last meeting of this type and they will want some type of indication that most of the "attendees" at the next meeting will be flying with their air carrier.

Group Fares

The issue of group fares is usually the first point of negotiation. The corporate travel manager has a choice. One option is to work with a "best existing fare," even if all fare restrictions are not met. Often this is the easiest option, since, if the group that is traveling does not meet the exact fare requirements, a waiver of the unmet requirements can sometimes be negotiated. For example, for a group traveling to Europe for a sales meeting, the corporate travel manager found that one of the regulations for an excellent fare was a minimum stay of seven days. The meeting, however, was scheduled to conclude after only four days. Through negotiations the corporate travel manager was able to obtain a reduction in the minimum stay requirement and was able to save the corporation approximately $50 per ticket.

The second option is to negotiate a "special" fare. This is a fare that may bear little or no resemblence to an existing fare. Although many carriers will initially advise that they cannot negotiate a special fare, several corporate travel managers have been successful in obtaining special fare quotes as much as two years prior to the travel of a corporate group. Often the air carrier will want to do the ticketing when a special fare has been negotiated. This should present no problem, but it is advisable to get the fare quote in writing once it has been negotiated. For associations that are negotiating special fares for conventions or meetings, it is especially important to obtain agreement from the air carrier that the same inexpensive fare will be provided to all attendees. An association executive recently noted a case in which the association received the number of inexpensive seats normally allocated by the carrier for its supersaver fare. The carrier expected all others in the association who were planning to attend the meeting to pay normal economy fares. They did not. They flew with another carrier using that carrier's supersaver fare. The original carrier lost passengers and the association had to contend with attendees arriving at different concourses.

Deposits

A special fare problem encountered by some who are able to negotiate special fares is the concern relating to advanced deposits. Often air carriers state that in order to provide a good advanced special fare quote, they will require a deposit which may range from a low of fifteen percent up to as much as 100 percent. Sometimes these deposits are non-refundable. It is advisable to negotiate away from such a deposit if at all possible. Although deposits are usually refundable, they sometimes are not and they can tie up a considerable amount of the company's cash, sometimes for several months. Obviously, the company would prefer to earn the interest on its money rather than allowing the air carriers to do so.

Trip Marketing Materials

For companies running incentive travel programs and associations holding meetings and conventions, obtaining marketing materials from air carriers constitutes another potential area for negotiation. For years airlines have provided shells, flyers, and destination material on a gratis basis to both corporate travel managers and travel agencies. Some airlines are levying a charge for these items today in a move to cut costs. A corporate travel manager recently advised that she changed air carriers when the carrier of first choice advised she would have to pay for shells. The carrier of second choice offered them free. This may seem like a small reason to change carriers, but when the cost of marketing materials such as shells is added to other costs, one can soon discover a substantial difference between the total cost of utilizing one air carrier for a group movement as compared to utilizing another one.

Seat Selection

Something most airlines will readily agree to, because it costs them nothing, is advanced seat selection. If the corporate travel manager has a group traveling together, a request for a block of seats at the back of the non-smoking section and at the front of the smoking section can be made, thereby allowing all travelers in the group to sit next to or near one another. It is suggested that the corporate travel manager make seat assignments herself and advise the travel agency who will be sitting where a week or more prior to the date of travel. This advice should be sent by letter to the group sales department.

Corporate travel managers can obtain a supply of airline seating charts from each of the air carrier sales representatives at no cost. These can help considerably when selecting seats for those traveling as a group, but they can also be particularly advantagous when working with a corporate traveler who may be either handicapped or particularly tall and needing more leg room. In both cases, special attention may need to be given to selecting an appropriate seat.

Free Tickets

Obtaining free tickets is sometimes possible when working with group travel. Some carriers will provide one free pass for each fifteen paid passengers. However, the ratio can go as high as one to fifty. Obviously, this is also an area for negotiation. Often the number of free tickets one obtains for those who are traveling in a group is a direct indicator of how good a negotiator the corporate travel manager is. However, it is important that such tickets not be *space available,* but be *positive space* tickets.

Free of Charge/Shipping Assistance

Airlines can also provide shipping documentation on a gratis basis. Though the shipment of material may be of limited value for those traveling domestically, it can be invaluable for employees attending a group function or holding a group function outside the U.S. Not only is it vital that documents be accurate for clearing items into the foreign country, but anything returning to the U.S. will need accurate documentation as well. When negotiating for shipping documentation assistance, it is also possible to request free shipping containers and the free shipment of materials. The containers will often be provided on a gratis basis without hesitation. The shipment of materials will probably be an area of negotiation. If the air carrier chooses to negotiate this area, it is suggested that a number/poundage ratio be utilized. For example, one might try asking for twenty pounds of material shipped free for every forty corporate travelers flying with the sponsoring carrier.

VIP Lounges

For corporate travelers departing from, transiting through, or arriving at major airports the utilization of group VIP or club lounges is an amenity the travelers will appreciate—and the use of these lounges for corporate groups is usually free. Often the air carrier will provide coffee, tea, and/or soft drinks without charge.

FIGURE 6.1. Negotiating for benefits, like "Upgrades" can be beneficial for both the company and the corporate traveler.

Sometimes cocktail parties can also be arranged. These can be negotiated to be provided without charge or at a small fee.

Inflight Services and Benefits

In addition, to the services and benefits that one can negotiate for those individuals and groups who travel relating to pre-flight travel, there are also a number of inflight services and benefits that one can request. If possible, the corporate travel manager should always try to get advanced check in with boarding passes issued on a round-trip basis and for connecting cities. If the corporate traveler starts his trip with all his boarding passes, the waiting time in several lines at the various gate counters will have been eliminated.

Upgrades

With a sufficient amount of business provided to an air carrier upgrades can sometimes be negotiated. With international trips the normal upgrade will be to business class from economy and for domestic trips to first class from economy.

Special Meals

Special meals for those travelers who prefer them can usually be obtained without difficulty. If a group of corporate travelers are flying together, it is sometimes possible to negotiate additional special touches to the meals. Little extras can often be added without cost and first class meals can sometimes be provided at little or no additional cost. Almost all carriers can provide corporate travelers with free or reduced rate drink coupons and sometimes it takes little negotiation to receive a substantial supply of these. It is even possible to negotiate complimentary headsets on long flights. Usually this is an amenity that is requested only for those traveling in a group, but some corporate travel managers ask for headset coupons and occasionally receive them on a gratis basis.

Give-aways

Give-aways provide another area for corporate travelers to receive additional comfort while flying.

Post-arrival services and products provide a third general area for negotiation. Japan Airlines started the custom of providing arriving U.S. businessmen with Japanese–English business cards. Some other carriers have followed the JAL lead on their flights destined for Tokyo.

VIP Arrival Service

VIP arrival service, with an escort through customs at the arrival airport is a small touch that can be very meaningful to the busy corporate traveler and it is a touch that costs the airlines nothing in additional fees in most cases.

Prioritize Negotiation Areas

In all, the range of services and products that a corporate travel manager can address in direct negotiation with air carriers is quite considerable. It is suggested that corporate travel managers give some thought to those areas to be negotiated. Prioritize those items that are most important and list them in order from those that are most important down to least important. One should not ignore an item just because other areas have been agreed to in the negotiation. Sometimes, an air carrier will be happy to offer or to provide a service or a benefit even when a number of other services and benefits have been agreed to. It is noted that air carriers tend to respect those corporate travel managers who do negotiate with them and it is suggested that corporate travel managers experiment by negotiating a full range of services and products when meeting with their sales representatives.

Air Carrier Concerns

Having developed an understanding of the areas that are of importance to corporate travel managers, it is important to focus on the areas of concern for air carriers. Of course, the major concern of an airline is to fill its seats as much as possible on as many flights as possible at as high a ticket price as possible. Usually this translates into a theme of encouraging corporate travel managers to arrange travel for their travelers on the sales representative's carrier. However, carrier representatives will undertake efforts to educate corporate travel managers to the advantages of higher priced fares and first-class travel benefits as well, since maximizing profits is important. Frequent flier programs and other gimmicks that encourage selection of one carrier over another are other areas of discussion between air carrier representatives and corporate travel managers.

Ticket Validation

A point that is not brought up often, but one that can be profitable for an airline, is ticket validation. When a ticket involves travel on two or more air carriers, it is validated or endorsed on only one carrier. What this means is that the carrier on which the ticket is endorsed, becomes the "sponsoring" carrier for that ticket. This means that all payments are routed to the carrier on which the ticket was validated and this carrier in turn pays the other carriers for that part of the travel that is on the other carriers. However, the validated carrier also deducts a profitable service charge for processing the payment and it also enjoys the use of the float of the money during the processing time. Therefore, all carriers encourage corporate travel managers to have tickets validated on them.

In many cases, especially for domestic flights, it will not make any major difference for a client or for a business whether the ticket is validated on carrier "A" or carrier "B." Therefore, the validation preference of carriers becomes a point of beneficial negotiation for the corporate travel manager. However, when it comes to international travel, the corporate travel manager needs to keep in mind that the traveler may have difficulty making changes to his ticket, cancelling a flight, or switching to later/earlier flights if the carrier of validation is not available in the city where the change is being attempted. If the businessman wants to change a ticket while he is in Africa and the ticket was validate on a U.S. domestic-only carrier, the airline in Africa can refuse to make a change. Therefore, for international tickets it is often wise to validate tickets on a carrier with an office or a representative in as many of the airports in the destination countries as possible. The general validation rules that apply state that an international ticket should be validated on the air carrier that is taking the traveler out of the U.S. While this is the general practice, if it results in validating on a carrier that does not have sufficient representation abroad, and not validating on a carrier that has excellent representation in the countries the business traveler will be visiting, it is suggested that the general rule be reconsidered and the validation be made with the carrier with the best representation.

A second general rule also needs to be considered. This is that the carrier of validation should be one of the carriers on which the traveler is flying (at least one leg of the trip). However, this too can leave the traveler with a ticket that is validated on a carrier with no representation in a destination airport (especially if there are one or more surface trips on the itinerary). In such a case, a carrier with representation in as many airports on the itinerary as possible should be found and a request should be made to that carrier for permission to validate the ticket on their carrier.

The validation issue becomes a stronger one when it comes to automated reservations equipment. As pointed out in Chapter 13 on computerization, the utilization of a carrier's computerized reservations system will usually result in a natural tendancy to book on that carrier and to validate tickets on the sponsoring carrier.

Summary

The larger the amount of corporate air travel, the greater the amount of interface a corporate travel manager is likely to have with airlines and their representatives. While much of the day-by-day air activity will be handled by, and with, the corporation's travel agency, airlines want to obtain their "fair share" of corporate business and will often take the initiative in meeting with corporate travel managers to assist them in handling special air travel concerns. Their mutuality of needs often results in good relationships between corporate travel managers and airline marketing executives.

The airline person with whom corporate travel managers interface can hold different positions depending upon the air carrier structure. For a carrier with a large presence in the company's home city, the probability will be that a sales representative will be assigned to work with the corporate travel manager. For a carrier with few flights into the city, either a district manager or a regional manager will cover the territory. The sales representative will make more frequent calls and will usually be more accessible, but usually has less influence with top airline management and less power to cut special deals. The district manager, and especially the regional airline sales manager, will have much more power and ability to negotiate, but they will be harder to contact when needed.

While several factors affect a corporate travel manager's ability to negotiate with an air carrier, two factors are of greatest importance:

1. the volume of the company's air travel; and
2. the competition between carriers.

For a company with several million dollars of annual air travel based in a city where three or four air carriers are fighting for market share, the ability to negotiate should be excellent. On the other hand, if one carrier controls the market or if the company generates very little air travel, negotiation opportunities for the corporate travel manager will be slim. Of course, the ability of the corporate travel manager to commit the company in negotiations is also vital.

Some negotiation points will be better handled by the company's travel agency while others are negotiated better directly with the air carrier. Obtaining VIP service and handling corporate groups are two of the major areas of negotiation with air carriers. A large number of corporate travel managers negotiate directly with air carriers regarding pricing. In doing so, they need to have exact figures on city-pair historical volume and the carriers to which this business has historically been given. If the corporate travel manager can agree to switch carriers to some degree, utilize off-peak flights, and allow special air carrier ticketing, the opportunity for negotiated cost-savings can be considerable. Keep in mind that ticket prices may show no special fares. However, lump-sum rebates may be included in the negotiation.

Other areas of negotiation include upgrades, fare restriction elimination, group travel meeting site selection, marketing materials for associations or companies running incentive travel programs, advanced seat selection, free tickets, shipping assistance, advanced boarding passes, special meals, give-aways, dual-language business cards, and international arrival escort service through customs. Corporate travel managers often search for a person as high in the airline as possible with whom to negotiate and getting written commitments is considered essential since the person conducting the negotiations may move on to another position before the negotiated benefits can be used.

In negotiation, focusing on the areas of concern for the air carriers is also important. Carriers will want as much of the company's air travel business as possible. However, even when not all of the flights are on their airline, having a ticket validated on their carrier is also important since they get the float on the use of the money paid for the ticket and can charge other participating carriers on the ticket a service charge for processing the ticket accounting. While validation is often a point corporate travel managers are comfortable negotiating, it should be remembered that travelers can make changes easier when the carrier of validation has representation in the airport where the change is to be made. Therefore, especially for international tickets, many corporate travel managers have tickets validated on carriers with an office or a respresentative in as many of the airports in the destination countries as possible.

Discussion Questions

1. Why do airline executives usually take the initiative in establishing a rapport with corporate travel managers?

2. Explain the "mutuality of needs and interests" that often brings about a good rapport between airline marketing executives and corporate travel managers.

3. On what factors might an air carrier's marketing and sales structure depend on any specific city and how might these factors determine who in the airline calls on corporate travel managers in that city?

4. Why might the person representing an off-line air carrier be in a better position to negotiate with a corporate travel manager than the person representing an on-line carrier?

5. Are there airline sales representatives who call on corporate travel managers exclusively? Explain.

6. What aspects of travel volume affect a corporate travel manager's ability to negotiate with an airline executive regarding rates and fares between two specific cities? What documentation is considered important by airline marketing executives?

7. What types of requests should a corporate travel manager bring to airline marketing people rather than the company's travel agency? Why?

8. Since deregulation, what is negotiable?

9. Approximately what percentage of companies, responding to a survey of airline interrelationships, reported they had negotiated direct arrangements with air carriers and had obtained either discounts or special services or both according to the, *Runzheimer Reports On Travel Management?*

10. Discounts of up to what percent have been applied to negotiated city pairs according to Barney Kogen?

11. How can carrier-issued tickets, sold at a negotiated discounted price, create problems for a corporate traveler and/or for a corporate travel manager?

12. What are some of the group and/or meeting travel services and benefits that can be negotiated for by corporate travel managers?

13. With what person in an airline (title) should a corporate travel manager initiate negotiation discussions?

14. What are the two options available to a corporate travel manager wishing to negotiate for the best possible group air fare?

15. What can airlines provide that can benefit businesses undertaking incentive travel programs?

16. Why might a corporate travel manager wish to obtain a supply of airline seating charts?

17. For what kind(s) of cargo and/or shipping assistance might corporate travel managers negotiate?

18. Can VIP lounge usage be obtained free? What type(s) of VIP lounge amenities might have to be paid for?

19. What is the normal upgrade from economy class on international flights?

20. What airline started the practice of providing its business passengers with dual-language business cards?

21. Almost all carriers provide what kind of free or reduced rate coupons for use by corporate travelers inflight?

22. What assistance does VIP arrival service provide on arrival at an international airport?

23. Why is it important to prioritize negotiation areas?

24. Why is ticket validation important to an air carrier? Why should it be important to a corporate travel manager?

Role Play Exercise

Two students may participate in this role play either out-of-class, as a fun way to review airline industry interrelationships, or as an in-class exercise. One student plays the role of the corporate travel manager and the other plays the role of the airline executive. Please read the script and then pick up the conversation in your own words.

Corporate Travel Manager: Thank you for meeting with me. Let me get right to the point. Fares are increasing rapidly and our travel budget has already been exceeded by over thirty percent. The only justification for a corporate travel department at this company is cost savings. Although I know I have saved the company money, convincing the top floor is hard when expenses exceed budget and the year isn't even over. I have been told to cut air travel costs and I plan to start by getting better fares from your carrier. I'll give you more business in return.

Airline Executive: We would like to get more business from you, but . . .

Corporate Travel Manager: Last year over eighty percent of our flights were between five city pairs. You fly between four of these. However, we used your carrier only thirty-two percent of the time. If you give me the right fares, we will switch to your airline for 100 percent of these flights. Counting the increased flight plans based on our new factory due to open in three months, we could triple our business with your carrier next year.

Airline Executive: You are talking my language. Let's get down to specifics. Where did you fly last year? What carriers did you use? And what did you pay?

CONTINUE ON YOUR OWN

Group Discussion Situation:
Negotiating Air Arrangements
for the
International Beer Drinkers' Association,
Munich Convention

Grindle Grundle is the corporate travel manager for the International Beer Drinkers' Association. The association is having its annual convention in Munich, in October, and Grindle is getting ready to negotiate with air carriers flying from U.S. gateways in an effort to get the best "deal" for the association and for its U.S. members. Review the laundry list of areas for negotiation in this chapter and identify those that Grindle may want to consider in her negotiations. What documentation should Grindle bring with her for her meetings with the carrier representatives? What suggestions do you have for Grindle?

Group Discussion Situation:
Gertie Gospit's Concern
Over Plungit's Validation

Plungit Enterprises takes special pride in their Supra Plunger, tailor-made for the Islamic market. In recent years, their Supra Plunger has sold better than any other plunger in all but two countries of the Middle East and North Africa. As a result, travel from East Evans, Idaho, where the home office and factory for the production of the Supra Plunger are located, to the Middle East and North Africa has been considerable. This constitutes well over eighty percent of Plungit Enterprises' 3.4 million dollar air travel budget for the next year. Gertie Gospit, the corporate travel manager for Plungit Enterprises, is justly proud of the way she has managed Plungit's travel. She has documented a twenty-two percent savings in air travel alone. In addition, the travelers are happy because Gertie makes sure travel arrangements are set up so that they can perform their job as easily and comfortably as possible within the constraints of corporate travel restrictions.

About a month ago, Gertie was visited by Happy Goshen, the district sales manager for America America Airlines. Happy offered Gertie a free FAM trip on America America to San Diego. The trip would be first class all the way and Gertie could bring her family. America America would put them up in the presidential suite of the America America-owned Americana Americana Resort located right on the border between the U.S. and Mexico with an excellent view of the border crossing area. The entire week-long vacation would be free for Gertie and her family. All Happy wanted in return was to have all airline tickets validated on America America Airlines when America America was used as a carrier to Portland, Maine (the gateway used to connect with Middle East Africa Airways for flights to the Middle East and Africa). After all, Happy had argued, ARC regulations require tickets to be validated on the originating carrier. Gertie refused the FAM trip on the grounds of ethics and refused to have her travel agency validate tickets on America America since validation on Middle East Africa Airways provides much greater convenience for Plungit's travelers.

About a week ago, the President of Plungit, Chris Cross, had asked Gertie to find a hotel for him in Tripoli that will be close to government headquarters so that he can walk to the Golden Plunger Award ceremony when he is in Libya next month. Gertie called to give Cross the information yesterday and was told that he and his family were vacationing in San Diego and would not return until the thirteenth of the month. Later yesterday, Gertie called the America America sales office to find out when the new schedules would be ready for distribution. She was told that only Happy knew about it and he was in San Diego at the Americana Americana entertaining a corporate client. He would not return until the thirteenth.

Today is the thirteenth and it is about four in the afternoon. Gertie just received a call from Cross saying that the agency should be told to validate all international tickets for Plungit on America America in the future.

Gertie is concerned. She is considering discussing the matter with Merrie Dreadly, a friend in Gertie's garden club and a next-door neighbor. Merrie is single and she and Gertie talk a lot. Merrie is also the sister of Dread Dreadly, the Chairman of the Board of Plungit Enterprises.

73   What advice do you have for Gertie?

CHAPTER 7

Basic Financial Management and Corporate Travel Payment Systems

Introduction

Making money is the purpose or goal of businesses. Saving money, or making a profit, is the purpose or goal of corporate travel departments. The few studies that have been undertaken that review the reasons why corporate travel departments are established, with few exceptions, identify saving money as one of the two overriding reasons. Reflecting savings, as the justification for a corporate travel department is the strong predominance of companies which place corporate travel management in the financial reporting structure. Studies vary, but it is safe to say that somewhere between one-third and two-thirds of all corporate travel departments are housed in the purchasing department, or some other area of the finance division structure of businesses. In addition, there is a strong tendency for the ultimate reporting of corporate travel department executives to the chief financial officer (CFO) of the organization.

While saving money was the original goal that prompted the creation of many corporate travel departments, making money is the goal of an increasing number of corporate travel departments. Obviously, making money rather than spending it, being a profit center rather than a cost center or a service center is preferable to most chief financial officers and can provide a stronger power position for the corporate travel manager.

This chapter and the next several chapters will concentrate on saving money and making money. The basic financial management contributions of the corporate travel department to the company will be discussed in this chapter. More sophisticated financial management approaches will be the subject of Chapter 8. The many approaches used by corporate travel managers to save money will be discussed in Chapter 9. Chapter 10 reviews travel agency interfaces as they relate to financial management. Chapter 11 focuses on making the corporate travel department a profit center, while Chapter 12 closes the financial management section of the book with a discussion of international financial management.

Since documenting savings and earnings is vital to corporate travel management, a part of the finance section will be an analysis of savings and earnings documentation and reports. There will be three documentation and reporting discussions. The first will relate to basic reports and these will be identified after reviewing the basic financial management contributions of the corporate travel department. The next documentation/reporting discussion relates to savings documents and reports. It follows the chapter on savings. The final documentation and reporting part of this section of the book discusses profit reporting. This follows the discussion of structuring the corporate travel department in order to create profits.

The finance section of the book will next turn to Chapters 10 and 11, making money through corporate travel management. The several approaches that have been utilized will be discussed together with the pros and cons of each. Again, documentation is important. Therefore, profit reports, return on investment reports, and similar types of profit-oriented documentation will be reviewed. Because so many corporate travel managers are striving to convince management of the need to move from cost center structures to profit center structures, the development of business plans designed to convince top management will be explored.

The last chapter of the finance section discusses financial management as it relates to international travel. This is a short chapter, but a pertinent one, since managing a company's international travel offers the potential for saving substantial amounts of money.

The Services Model vs. the Savings Model

Most corporate travel managers would agree with Sheryl Hansen of Hewlett Packard who says, "Our job is to get them there on time and ready to do business." Her position is that the first job of the corporate travel manager is to get the traveler to the destination on time (arriving in sufficient time to get from the airport to the meeting or business site) ready to do business (not so tired or hassled that the beneficial conduct of business is impossible). Sometimes, in the effort to save money on travel, corporate travel managers lose sight of why the corporate traveler is undertaking the trip. Indeed, if the traveler is burdened down with travel problems or the cheapest possible facilities (middle seat in the discounted section of a plane that makes several stops enroute, a hotel room in a cheap hotel with no amenities and far from the site of business, or the cheapest possible rental car picked up from an off-airport location, then the company can be short-changed because the traveler may be so concerned with working out the mechanics of travel arrangements that the business to be conducted may become a secondary concern.

To understand this further, one can look at *Maslow's Hierarchy of Needs*. According to Maslow, man puts priority on the needs that are of greatest importance at any particular point in time. Security is one of these needs and man will place more importance on this than on psychological or self-fulfillment needs. Having a place to stay and food to eat, according to this theory, will take priority over the satisfaction of striking a good business deal. In other words, concentrating on the business at hand can only be done effectively if the mechanics of getting the person to the destination, having reasonably good meals, and a reasonably comfortable place to stay will free up the mind of the executive to concentrate on the business to be undertaken.

76

Chapter 7:
Basic Financial
Management
and Corporate
Travel Payment
Systems

A tightrope-walker balance must be struck between the importance of having the needed services available to the corporate traveler and our *raison d'etre* (reason for being) (i.e., saving money on corporate travel). The tightrope between having good, needed service and saving money is a very fine line. There are those in companies who say the most important job of the corporate travel manager is to serve the corporate traveler. This pure service model of corporate travel management can be expensive. On the other hand, there are those who believe the only duty of a corporate travel manager is to save or to make money on travel. This pure savings model of corporate travel management can leave the traveler unable to concentrate on business and unable to do the job for which the trip was undertaken. Most corporate travel managers agree that a good "balance" is the best model.

Departmental Travel Debit/Credit Systems

In order to understand how the financial management of a corporate travel department can assist and affect the financial management of a business as a whole, it is important to understand the concept of travel expediture debit and credit systems within a business. Each department in a business is considered, for financial purposes, to be either a cost center or a profit center. Each department is given an appropriate cost center number or profit center number and is provided with a budget. When a department within a business expects to incur travel costs during its next fiscal year, it includes the travel costs in its budget. The departmental cost center or profit center budget will include an allocation of money for the trip, or trips, to be undertaken by the department's employees.

When the employee who works in a department initiates the processing of paperwork for the trip, the department head normally approves a trip request form which indicates to both the employee and to the corporate travel department that the supervisor has approved of spending the money allocated in the budget for the trip. When an airline ticket is issued, the corporate travel department normally debits the account of the cost center or profit center relating to the department in which the traveling employee works and a transfer of funds is made from the employee's department to the corporate travel department so that the corporate travel department can pay airline and/or other travel expenses that are owed as a result of the trip.

Although fund transfers may be only paper transfers of money from one department to another in the initial stages, at some point in time, the airline ticket and other travel expenses must be paid and the transfer of funds becomes a reality. While the funds are normally paid for from one central department of the business (normally the accounts payable department), the ability of the corporate travel department to make a profit (to be a profit center) or not to make a profit (to be a cost center) can sometimes depend upon when the actual transfer of funds takes place.

As noted later in this chapter in the discussion of "float," if the transfer of funds from the department that incurred a travel expense to the corporate travel department takes place at the time that the ticket is issued and delivered to the employee who is traveling, there may be a period of time in which the corporate travel department can invest these funds into an interest-earning account and (therefore, the corporate travel department) may be able to function as a profit center). If, on the other hand, the transfer of funds is made directly from the business's accounts payable department to an airline, travel agency, or credit card company at the time a bill for payment is rendered, then the corporate travel department handles these funds on paper only and has no opportunity to invest the funds in an interest-bearing account. This latter situation leaves less opportunity for the corporate travel department to become a profit center.

Cash Flow, Liquidity, and Float

Cash flow, liquidity, and float are all terms, concepts, and considerations that the professional travel manager deals with on a daily basis. All of these refer to aspects of financial management. In many ways they are closely related and interrelated. *Cash flow* refers to a literal flow of money (cash) into the company on a steady basis so that there is always a sufficient amount of funds to pay for ongoing expenses. Managing cash flow starts by identifying the amount of cash or funds held, in a readily available manner, by the company to pay for current bills (debts).

Companies have conflicting concerns relating to paying debts. On the one hand, they can earn more money by placing funds in investments or interest-earning financial instruments. On the other hand, in many cases investments and interest-earning financial instruments cannot be converted to cash easily and will lose their interest-earning ability, or at least a part of their interest-earning ability, if they are converted into cash. Therefore, a business attempts to manage financial resources in such a way that a maximum amount of interest or profit is earned through the investment of money, while at the same time, they hold out or keep readily available a sufficient amount of money to pay for current debts. But the key factor is the cash flow relationship. The more money that is kept in readily available funds to pay suppliers means there is less money available to earn interest on investments and vice versa.

Liquidity is closely related to cash flow in that liquidity refers to the total amount of money that is available in "liquid" funds (or funds that can be spent immediately at any particular point in time). Obviously, funds that are in checking accounts may actually cost a business money to maintain the account, while monies that are kept in certificates of deposit can earn money for a business. There are, of course, many other financial instruments that businesses use in addition to certificates of deposit. This instrument is mentioned to provide a financial management investment (interest-earning) example.

The money that is kept in a checking account is extremely liquid in that it can be spent at any time. Although convenient, it is expensive to the business in that it can actually cost the business money to keep it and to use it since a bank may charge a fee for check processing. On the other hand, money that is in a certificate of deposit is not available except at the time the certificate matures. However, CDs (certificates of deposit) earn the company money because the company can earn interest on the certificates. Liquidity (keeping money available in a form that is

78

Chapter 7:
Basic Financial
Management
and Corporate
Travel Payment
Systems

readily spendable), therefore, is needed by a company, but it can also be expensive for a company.

The third financial term with which corporate travel managers work on a daily basis is *float*. Float refers to money, time, and interest. It is the total amount of money that is currently being held from client payments (or any other resource) prior to the time that it is spent. In the travel industry the term float normally refers to money that belongs to a supplier. In the case of a travel agency, after a client pays the travel agency for an airline ticket, it is some time before the travel agency pays the air carrier. The amount of time between taking in money for the ticket and paying the air carrier for the ticket is considered to be *float time*. The average amount of money being held at any particular point in time by the travel agency for the airline is considered float. As noted before, the term, float refers to two things, money and time. However, float also refers to the actual amount of money that is earned by investing the money that has been received for a supplier and earning interest on that money prior to the payment to the supplier.

For example, if a company purchases $10,000 worth of airline tickets from a travel agency and purchases these tickets using a credit card for payment, the amount of time between the time that the tickets were actually delivered to the business by the travel agency (at which time payment is due), to the time the credit card company cashes the travel payment check of the business purchasing the tickets is considered to be the *travel float time*. However, if the business which purchased the tickets immediately takes the money that they would otherwise utilize to pay for the tickets, and places that money in an interest-bearing account, the interest earned on the money owed to the airlines for the airline tickets accrued between the time that they placed the money in the account and the time the credit card company cashed the travel payment check drawn against that account, is considered float.

Controlling Cash Flow

Corporate travel managers can assist their companies by financially managing their business's money by maximizing the benefits of cash flow, liquidity, and float for the company for which they work. By working closely with the comptroller or other appropriate financial manager, the corporate travel manager can help to identify those times in the annual history of the company when the company has what is referred to as a *tight cash flow situation*. Almost all businesses have an up and down swing to their business. They may sell more of a product or service at one season of the year than at another season. This normally results in an uneven flow of money coming into the business. With the uneven flow of incoming money, financial managers need to be careful about spending money at some periods of the year. However, they can have more money coming into the company in the form of receipts at other times of the year.

Obviously, there is always a concern about the extent of expenditures, but when the company has very little money coming in, and knows that it must draw from an interest-bearing account to stay even during a particular season, there will be a desire to lower expenditures and delay payments during this period of time in order to maximize the utilization of interest-earning investments and not have to break them in order to cover current expenditures.

At the same time, paying bills on time is important. If a business fails to pay on time, its reputation among suppliers is effected, employees receive dunning calls, and interest penalties can be levied.

Once the company's cash flow cycle is known, the corporate travel manager can manage corporate travel payments in such a way that the payments can fit with the cash flow and current liquidity situation of a company at all times. This does take talent and it takes cooperation from suppliers, but by "managing" travel payments, the corporate travel manager can provide substantial help in the overall financial management of the company's resources. In addition, if a substantial amount of money can be earned from float, the corporate travel manager can provide the company with an additional source of income. Sometimes this becomes a very important income-generating source for a company.

DUAL-AGENCY UTILIZATION TO BALANCE CASH FLOW PAYMENTS AND FLOAT EARNINGS

Several approaches can be used in managing financial resources by the corporate travel manager. Some corporate travel managers work on a dual-agency arrangement. One of the two agencies may provide considerable rebates, but in exchange for the rebates, the agency will usually expect rapid payment. A second travel agency, on the other hand, may provide lower rebates, but it allows the business to pay for its tickets after sixty days or in some cases even ninety days from the date of the use of the ticket. After identifying the tight liquidity times for the business, the corporate travel manager may move from working with the travel agency that provides large rebates and has immediate payment requirements, to utilizing a company that provides for long-term payment and offers little or no rebates during those times when the business has little money coming in.

Alternatively, when the cash flow situation is better and the liquidity of the company is strong (i.e., sales are high and payments from buyers are flowing in at a peak time of the year), the corporate travel manager may want to be more concerned with getting a high rebate since immediate payment will not be a problem. The dual-travel agency arrangement, therefore, can give corporate travel managers a maximum degree of flexibility in managing travel payments as a part of total corporate financial management.

THE THREE TRADITIONAL PAYMENT OPTIONS

Three corporate travel payment options have traditionally been available to businesses. These are *extended billing* by travel agencies, *credit card payment*, and *payment by either cash or check* (usually check).

For many years travel agencies carried business accounts and it was not at all unusual for a business to expect a travel agency to carry its account for a period of at least thirty days. It was not uncommon to find travel agencies carrying larger accounts for sixty days. And, in a few cases, an agency carried accounts that provided very good profits for a period of ninety days or more.

80

Chapter 7:
Basic Financial
Management
and Corporate
Travel Payment
Systems

However, this form of long-term settlement with travel agencies tended to be much more popular prior to deregulation. At that time, neither travel agencies nor airlines were allowed by Civil Aeronautics Board regulations to compete on a price basis. Therefore, one way travel agencies could compete with one another for commercial accounts was to offer generous delayed payment options. Since deregulation, however, there are no airline ticket pricing limitations and commercial-oriented travel agencies have developed a stronger tendency to offer rebates and other services rather than to carry an account for a long period of time.

They have found that carrying accounts can be risky and it can tie up substantial amounts of money which a travel agency may very well need for expansion purposes or for other uses. Although there still are a large number of travel agencies which will bill a business client and not ask for payment for thirty or even sixty days, the frequency of this type of arrangement is far less than it once was.

Float Examples

It should be remembered when negotiating with a travel agency that if the travel agency carries the company account, the corporate travel department is in a position to earn approximately one half of one percent of the cost of the airline tickets for each month in interest or float. Although this may not be real earnings in that the business may not have taken the money that would otherwise be paid for the airline tickets and put it into a bank, one half of one percent per month represents a rough approximation of the money that would have been earned by the company if it had taken the money and put it into a bank. In fact, the business may actually earn considerably more than one half of one percent per month by not having to break certificates of deposit or other long-term higher-interest-earning financial instruments in order to pay for the airline tickets at an earlier time.

Float, therefore, can be considered a savings when it is internal or within the company. In other words, it is a savings to the company when the company does not have to pay right away. On the other hand, float is a profit when it is external or outside the company. In other words, if the company actually transferred the money for an airline ticket from the cost center (or profit center) that incurred the travel debt (normally the department for which the traveler is working) to the corporate travel department, and then from the travel department to a bank account belonging to the company, and if the business kept that money in that bank savings account (or other interest-bearing financial instrument) until the vendor (the airline, the travel agency, or the credit card company that is carrying the account) is paid, a profit (interest) is earned by the corporate travel department from the savings account or other interest-bearing account.

A good example of the second way in which float operates (i.e., accruing interest by holding money that is received for someone else), is the travel agency that receives payment in cash for an airline ticket that it issues. After deducting its commission, the balance of the airline ticket cost is owed to the air carrier which will provide air transportation. Because of the travel agency-airline financial payment cycle, the airline never draws from the agency's account for a sale less than ten days from that sale. If the agency puts all its cash payments into an interest-earning account, the interest earned off of the sale of each ticket (that has been paid for in cash during the ten or more days between when the agency put the money into the interest-bearing account and the date the airline withdrew the money) is float.

Credit Card Programs

Because of the financial benefits that interest, liquidity, and cash flow can provide a company by having airline tickets and other travel expenditures paid for thirty days or more after incurring the costs, credit card travel management programs have become popular with corporate travel managers.

The Three Credit Card Programs

Although there are many credit card programs in existence today, by far the majority of businesses utilize one or a combination of three major credit card programs designed for corporate travelers and their companies. Each program has its benefits and drawbacks. In order to maximize financial and other benefits and to compensate for individual program drawbacks, an increasing number of corporate travel managers are combining the utilization of two credit card programs or even adopting all three of the major programs.

The three credit card programs that are most popular are:

1. The Universal Air Travel Program (UATP) Air Travel Card;
2. The Citicorp Diners Club Business Travel Management Program; and
3. The American Express Corporate Card Program.

The *Universal Air Travel Card Program* is the oldest corporate travel card program. It is also the least expensive. There are no annual fees. It is a program that is owned by the air carriers. Therefore, it is accepted by more air carriers for charging of air tickets than any other credit card system. Unlike the other major credit card programs, the air travel card has both the advantage and, perhaps, the disadvantage of limiting its usage to charges for air travel only. The advantage is that by limiting its use to air travel, air travel management and air travel ticketing may be easier to track than with other credit card systems. In addition, air travel security is often better. Travelers cannot charge unauthorized other business or personal expenses to the card since it is limited only to usage for air travel. If the corporate travel manager wishes to screen travelers, it is possible to select out cards based on the travel patterns allowed for each corporate traveler. For example, the red card is limited to use for air travel in North America only, while the green card is designed for international corporate travel purposes.

Financially, the air travel card provides several benefits. Although other credit cards may require an initial set-up charge to businesses, the air travel card requires none. Some carriers, however, do ask for a one-time deposit when initially starting usage of the air travel card on their carrier. However, all one-time deposits are fully refundable. A major financial advantage for some businesses is that there is neither a floor limit nor a credit limit. Whereas some credit

82

Chapter 7:
Basic Financial
Management
and Corporate
Travel Payment
Systems

FIGURE 7.1. The AIR TRAVEL CARD is one of three travel card systems designed to help the company track and control travel costs. Photo courtesy of Air Travel Card.

card systems have a severe floor limit and credit limits, while often generous, are sometimes difficult to get increased to a workable level, the air travel card starts with these financial benefits in place.

The *Citicorp Diners Club Business Travel Management Program* is more comprehensive than the air travel card program in that travelers may charge their hotel expenses, car rental costs, and air travel to the card. This is convenient for both the air traveler and the corporate travel department, but it carries with it the potential danger of a traveler spending money for unauthorized and, perhaps, non-travel expenses. The Citicorp Diners Club Business Travel Management Program provides a sophisticated accounting report which allows the corporate travel manager to balance authorized expenditures with actual expenditures in every major corporate travel category.

Perhaps the major disadvantage of the Citicorp Diners Club Business Travel Management Program is its cost and its limitations. There is an annual fee ranging between $30 per card for up to twenty-four cards down to $5 per card for 5,000 or more cards. Although most users feel that these per card annual fees are reasonable, there are some businesses that simply are not able to receive approval to pay the fees. In some cases, travel agencies pay the fee costs in order to obtain business travel clients without having to carry the client account themselves. However, some businesses are reluctant to allow travel agencies to pick up such costs as they feel that this is an informal commitment from the business to the travel agency and that it obligates the company to work with a travel agency for at least a reasonable enough time to make the financial commitment on the part of the travel agency worthwhile.

The Citicorps Diners Club requirements for Business Travel Management Program card member acceptance are also limiting. To meet application requirements, a business must:

1. have a $250,000 net worth;
2. submit audited financial statements for the past two years;
3. have been in business for three years; and
4. project $120,000 annual travel and entertainment expense.

Other advantages of the Citicorps Diners Club card program include a vendor tracking information system which can be used for rate negotiations with hotels, car rental firms, and air carriers. In addition, a client company is provided with options to either have central billing or individual billing. There are advantages and disadvantages to both. When tickets are cancelled, if the cancellation occurs prior to the billing time, they are automatically erased from the bill. This reduces accounting time and problems and it eliminates tying up interest or funds for airline tickets that are never used. With the Citicorps Diners Club program, travelers automatically receive $150,000 in travel accident insurance, $1,250 of baggage insurance for checked or carry-on baggage on both domestic and international flights, an access system provides cash advances twenty-four hours a day, and up to $25,000 of car rental liability reimbursement coverage is provided if the car rental is charged to the traveler's Diners Club account and if other conditions are met.

The *American Express Corporate Card* program is similar to the Citicorp Diners Club Business Travel Management program. It also allows the traveler to charge hotel, car rental, air travel, and other business trip expenses.

The American Express Corporate Card system levies a cost per card that ranges from $45 for as many as nine cards down to $5 per card for 10,000 or more cards, but there is no pre-set spending limit. The American Express program claims to, "Eliminate or reduce cash advance by plus/minus seventy-five percent." They have 1,500 travel service offices throughout the world to assist card holders and also they offer a twenty-four hour referral service for legal, medical, and dental problems. Personal check cashing privileges are extended and there is an automatic $100,000 travel accident insurance as well as an automatic $1,250 lost, stolen, or damaged baggage insurance coverage. American Express provides companies, ". . . with uniform IRS accepted receipts for all business related expenditures. Corporate liability is protected one hundred percent for employee misuse of American Express card retroactive seventy-five days from notification. (The) corporation has a maximum exposure for fifty dollars if (the) AMEX Card is lost or stolen; liability is zero if notification is made prior to use of the card." American Express quotes a thirty-seven to forty-seven day float for travel expenses charged on their card system. They estimate that ninety-five percent of all travel and entertainment expenses can be charged to the American Express card because it is accepted by so many airlines, car rental companies and restaurants. In addition, they provide emergency check cashing at most travel offices of American Express and at some participating hotels and airlines.

84

Chapter 7:
Basic Financial
Management
and Corporate
Travel Payment
Systems

Perhaps the major benefit for corporate travel managers is a series of management information reports that present a, "Macro to micro view of (the) company's spending patterns." These present tools for budget forecasting and vendor discount negotiations. They provide monthly and year-to-date activity reviews by industry, vendor, and by city.

Add-on Benefits

There are add-on, optional cost benefits provided by all three of the major credit card programs. These tend to be the same as the standard benefits for which no additional fee is charged, but the benefits are greater. Most relate to insurance: life, medical, car rental, and baggage. Several programs offer evacuation and repatriation assistance and the Air Travel Card offers both traveling dependent assistance and reduced rate trip and/or frequent flier free ticket trip coverage.

Multi-card Plan Options

Because of the considerable benefits that are available and the variation of the benefits between each of the three credit card programs, businesses are opting to adopt two or, in rare cases, all three of the credit card programs. Often businesses will start with the air travel card because there is no cost for this program. However, with the extensive benefits provided through the American Express and the Citicorp Diners Club card programs, one of these is often also added. When the selection of the American Express or the Citicorp Diners Club program is made, often it is paid for either by the travel agency as a part of the contractual agreement or the cost is deducted from agency rebates that have been contractually negotiated.

Credit Card Benefits and Travel Department Image

Corporate travel managers are often seen by corporate travelers as policemen enforcing restrictive travel policies. The benefits that a corporate traveler can obtain by having one or more of the major credit card programs offer the corporate travel manager an opportunity to show the company's travelers how their corporate travel department can be of direct benefit and assistance to the traveler. This can go a long way toward changing the negative image that many corporate travel departments have inherited. Even more important, the opportunities for corporate travel managers to manage travel payments through credit card programs provide unequalled opportunities to positively contribute to the financial health of a business through the financial management of float, liquidity reduction, and cash flow.

Summary

While making money is the purpose or goal of businesses, saving money or making a profit is the purpose or goal of corporate travel departments. In fact, the possibility of bringing about substantial savings is the justification for the creation of most corporate travel departments. This is reflected by the fact that a substantial number of corporate travel departments are housed in the financial department, or in some other area of the finance divisions of businesses. However, as important as saving money is, earning money is also important. Therefore, there is a growing tendency toward an increase in corporate travel departments becoming profit centers rather than cost centers.

At the same time, service is important. The concentration on savings can sometimes be so substantial that corporate travel departments lose sight of the fact that if the business traveler must suffer through substantial inconvenience and hardships, the purpose of the business trip may be jeopardized and the company can lose more money than it saves through business travel cost cutting and corporate travel savings efforts. Therefore, a tightrope-walker balance must be struck between the importance of having the needed services available to the corporate traveler and saving money or making money on corporate travel.

Corporate travel systems within companies normally start with a travel budget being prepared by each department which expects to have one or more persons undertake travel during the next year. After obtaining budget approvals, when an employee wishes to prepare for a trip, a trip request is submitted and approved by the department head and/or higher management. In some companies, the traveler or the traveler's secretary makes travel arrangements by calling the company's travel agency. In other cases, all travel arrangements are made by the corporate travel department interfacing with the company's travel agency. After all arrangements are finalized, payment is made by the company by deducting the authorized amounts from the budget of the traveler's department and either transferring funds to the corporate travel department for payment or paying the vendor travel agency directly. If the transfer is made to the corporate travel department at the time the trip is authorized, the corporate travel department has a good opportunity to become a profit center. However, if payment is made by the company's accounts payable department directly to the company's travel agency vendor sometime after the trip has been completed or if the accounts payable department pays a credit card company on the date the monthly credit card bill becomes due, the corporate travel department is left out of the payment cycle and the corporate travel department has less of an opportunity to become a profit center.

Cash flow, liquidity, and float are all terms worked with by the corporate travel department in the financial management of corporate travel. Because businesses receive money on an uneven basis throughout the year and must pay vendors on an uneven basis throughout the year, managing the flow of its cash is important. The key factor cash flow relationship is that the more money that is kept in readily available funds to pay suppliers, the less money that is available to earn money from interest and investments and vice versa. Liquidity, therefore, is also important. Because money that is invested can earn money for a business, but that which is kept in a checking account earns no money and sometimes costs money, financial managers are concerned about keeping only the smallest amount of funds possible in liquid (readily available) funds. Float, therefore, becomes a technique for managing liquidity and cash flow. Float normally refers to money that belongs to a supplier. If the business can delay paying a supplier, it may be able to use funds that will come in at a later time (cash flow) and not have

86

Chapter 7:
Basic Financial
Management
and Corporate
Travel Payment
Systems

to use funds that are currently earning money (liquidity control). However, by delaying payments to vendors, the vendor may have trouble paying its suppliers and therefore the close control of cash flow is often a consideration of major importance to financial managers. A corporate travel manager can assist in the financial management of a company by understanding the company's cash flow cycle. By working with two or more travel agencies, it is sometimes possible for a corporate travel manager to balance the receipt of rebates when there is sufficient money available through cash flow to pay suppliers right away and maximize float benefits by paying a travel agency sixty or ninety days after a cost has been incurred when the cash flow provides less readily available income for the company.

One of the ways in which companies can manage travel financial payments is by managing travel payments. There are three traditional payment options. These are cash, check, and credit card. Although few companies with large volumes of travel have ever used cash to pay for their travel, prior to deregulation it was not at all unusual for travel agencies to extend credit and for businesses to expect long-term payments of sixty and sometimes ninety days. This allowed the business to invest the money and earn float income. However, with deregulation rebates are possible and corporate travel departments are moving increasingly toward rebating agreements that do not include long-term payment arrangements.

For this and other reasons, credit card travel payment programs are becoming popular. The Universal Air Travel Program (UATP) air travel card, the Citicorp Diners Club Business Travel Management Program, and the Amercian Express Corporate Card Program are the three major travel credit card programs. Each has its advantages and disadvantages. The UATP card is limited to use for air travel only, but it requires no up-front or annual fees. It issues one card for domestic travel (North America) and one for international travel. It also provides several add-on benefits. The Citicorp Diners Club card requires an annual fee that decreases with the number of cards issued. However, both the Citicorp Diners Club and the American Express card programs allow charges for air travel, hotel expenses, car rental expenses, and other travel expenses to be charged to the card. In addition, they both offer a wide range of reports and other benefits. Some insurance is available automatically through both the Citicorp Diners Club and the American Express travel payment programs and all three credit card programs provide optional add-on insurance benefits. The American Express Corporate Card program quotes a thirty-seven to forty-seven day float and estimates that ninety-five percent of all travel and entertainment expenses can be charged to their card. Because the benefits vary from one card program to another, multi-card programs have been adopted by several corporate travel departments.

Basic financial management is important to any company and corporate travel provides unique opportunities to complement and add to the financial management of the business as a whole. By managing such areas as cash flow, liquidity, and float, negotiating with vendors, and taking maximum advantage of credit card programs, the corporate travel manager has an opportunity to provide substantial assistance in the financial management of the company as a whole.

Discussion Questions

1. What is the purpose or goal of businesses?

2. What is the purpose or goal of corporate travel departments?

3. What percentage of all corporate travel departments are housed in the purchasing or some other area of the finance division structure of businesses?

4. Is the corporate travel manager in a stronger power position if the corporate travel department is a cost center or if the corporate travel department is a profit center?

5. What is the first job of the corporate travel manager according to Sheryl Hansen?

6. Use Maslow's Hierarchy of Needs to explain the following quote,

   "Concentrating on the business at hand can only be done effectively if the mechanics of getting the person to the destination, having reasonably good meals, and a reasonably comfortable place to stay will free up the mind of the executive to concentrate on the business to be undertaken."

7. Is it easy to provide good services for the corporate traveler and to save money on travel for the company at the same time? Provide examples.

8. Why does the ability of the corporate travel department to make a profit, and therefore to be a profit center, or not to make a profit, and therefore to be a cost center, sometimes depend upon when the actual transfer of funds takes place?

9. Managing cash flow starts by identifying what?

10. What is the key factor cash flow relationship?

11. Why is it that liquidity can be expensive for a company?

12. What is the difference between *float time* and *float*?

13. What is meant by the term *tight cash flow situation*?

14. What might happen to a business which fails to pay its bills on time?

15. For what financial reasons might a business work with two travel agencies rather than only one?

16. Was it more popular for travel agencies to "carry" business accounts for sixty days or longer prior to deregulation or has it been more popular for travel agencies to carry business accounts sixty days or longer since deregulation?

17. Why might float be considered a savings when it is internal or within the company and a profit when it is external or outside the company?

18. The majority of high travel volume businesses utilize one or a combination of three major credit card programs designed for corporate travelers and their companies. What are these three major credit card programs?

19. Which is the credit card program that limits its usage to charges for air travel only?

20. What color is the card that is limited to use for air travel in North American only and what color is the card designed for international corporate air travel purposes?

88

Chapter 7:
Basic Financial
Management
and Corporate
Travel Payment
Systems

21. What are the benefits and the drawbacks of each of the corporate credit card programs that are designed for travel payment purposes?

22. Which one of the three major credit card payment programs does not require an annual fee or a set-up charge from businesses?

23. Which credit card program(s) carries with it (them) the potential danger of a traveler spending money for unauthorized and, perhaps, non-travel expenses?

24. Which credit card program charges an annual fee ranging from thirty dollars per card for up to twenty-four cards down to five dollars per card for five thousand or more cards?

25. Why might travel agencies pay credit card fee costs?

26. Why are some businesses reluctant to allow travel agencies to pay credit card fee costs?

27. Compare the credit card programs and their abilities to track vendor information which can be used for rate negotiations with hotels, car rental firms, and air carriers.

28. Compare the insurance (life, accident, baggage, and so on) benefits included in each of the credit card programs.

29. Which credit card program levies a cost per card that ranges from forty-five dollars for as many as nine cards down to five dollars per card for ten thousand or more cards?

30. Compare the legal, medical, dental, and other referral services offered through each of the credit card programs.

31. What personal check cashing privileges are offered by each of the credit card programs and how do these operate?

32. Which credit card program quotes a thirty-seven to forty-seven day float for travel expenses?

33. Which credit card program estimates that ninety-five percent of all travel and entertainment expenses can be charged to their credit card?

34. Which credit card program offers reduced rate trip insurance coverage?

35. Why might a business utilize more than one credit card program for its travelers?

36. What provides an opportunity for corporate travel managers to provide unequal opportunities to positively contribute to the financial health of their business through the financial management of float, liquidity reduction, and cash flow?

Role Play Exercise

Two students may participate in this role play either out-of-class, as a fun way to review the chapter, or as an in-class exercise. One plays the role of the chief financial officer (CFO) and the other plays the role of the corporate travel manager (CTM). Please read the script and then pick up the conversation in your own words.

89

Group
Discussion
Situation: Best
Banks'
Reduction in
Costs

Chief Financial Officer: Every year we lose thousands of dollars by having to pay vendors during our very worst income months. We have negotiated some excellent long-term interest percentages with high-quality financial institutions. This year I want us to be able to set up arrangements with vendors so that we pay them during our high cash flow months and don't have to break these long-term high-interest income instruments. Can you help us?

Corporate Travel Manager: As you know, since we moved to working with our current travel agency, we have started to get good rebates back from them and by charging all travel expenses to credit cards, our float now is in the range of thirty-four to forty-two days. I don't think we can get any more than this from the travel agency we are using now. However, there might be a way to get even better float. But we will have to give up some of the money received in rebates.

Chief Financial Officer: Tell me about it. What are the exact trade offs?

Corporate Travel Manager: I will have to get in touch with the vendor principals to get the exact figures, but by working with two travel agencies, we should be able to . . .

CONTINUE ON YOUR OWN

Group Discussion Situation:
Grabitol Grabs It All

Gretta Grabitol, the corporate travel manager for Fanny's Friendly Financial Management got a call from Freddy Fearless, the company's chief financial officer, saying:

> "Frequent Flier coupons, individual rebate checks made out to me personally, hotel gift packs, . . . Ms. Grabitol, our travelers are making out like bandits on their travel, and they are doing it at our expense. Control it, Grabitol! Get all these benies for the company instead. Live up to your name, Miss Grabitol. Grab it all back. All of it. It's our money, not theirs. Save us money by getting all these things for us, the company. Report back to me in a week and tell me, we, the company, have gotten it all. Goodbye, Ms. Grabitol."

What suggestions do you have for Ms. Grabitol? You are meeting today to finalize a list of written suggestions for her. In your group session, select one person to chair your group. All will have an equal vote on suggestions. In your group session, reach agreement on suggestions and prepare a paper to be presented to the entire class by the chair of your group.

Group Discussion Situation:
Best Banks' Reduction in Costs

Jane Jones works as the corporate travel manager with Best Banks, the largest bank chain in Birmingham. She reports to the bank's comptroller, who has told Jane that she must contribute more to the reduction of bank costs. There was no

90

Chapter 7:
Basic Financial
Management
and Corporate
Travel Payment
Systems

problem last year when the average ticket price was much lower, but since many departments based their travel budgets on last year's figures, several have already exceeded their travel budgets this year. Everyone is looking to Jane for answers and for help. In addition, the comptroller has advised Jane that she must interact with other bank departments to help cash flow, increase float, and bring departmental travel budgets into balance. Keeping in mind that Best Banks' budget for travel is a little more than a million dollars; twenty percent of travel is in-state, eighty percent is in-country (this includes the twenty percent that is in-state), and twenty percent is to other countries (mostly to Canada and Europe), the bank charges travel to its own bank credit card, and written policies have been distributed to all bank travelers, what suggestions do you have for Jane? You are meeting today to finalize a list of written suggestions for her. In your group session, select one person to chair your group. All will have an equal vote on suggestions. In your group session, reach agreement on suggestions and prepare a paper to be presented to the entire class by the chair of your group.

CHAPTER 8

Managing for Profits

Introduction

Managing for profits means constantly keeping in mind that in dealing with all aspects of corporate travel, the desire to create a profit for the company is most important. Cost cutting is emphasized, but there are many ways in which the corporate travel department can cut costs. In addition to cutting costs, however, profits can be realized by bringing money back to the company in the form of rebates or other financial incentives received from vendors. Although this chapter does not pretend to be comprehensive relating to covering all aspects of managing for profits, (all of the other chapters dealing with financial management also relate to the development of management strategies for profits), it will identify some of the more specific profit management approaches. Since management often starts with financial plans, this chapter starts by identifying travel budget cost development. Many consider budgets to be financial instruments and the corporate travel manager is expected in many organizations to provide expertise in developing accurate travel budget cost projections for all areas of the business.

Although Chapter 18 relates specifically to corporate travel policies, this chapter discusses travel expense policy distribution and the relationship of the distribution to profit management. Tax considerations provide an opportunity for planning profits. The tax considerations relating to travel are discussed in this chapter.

One of two major sections in this chapter relates to financial reports. Financial reports are an outgrowth of travel expense monitoring and can be classified in two broad categories, departmental reports and corporate travel reports. The bulk of the reports relate to corporate travel. Those discussed in this chapter include monthly expense budgets, air travel exception reports, and vendor expense reports for hotels and car rentals. In addition, expense reports for meals, entertainment, and other expenses are discussed.

Because most corporate travel departments find that the largest amount of vendor financial management opportunity comes in dealing with travel agency vendors, over half of the chapter relating to managing for profits is concerned with travel agency interfaces as those interfaces relate to corporate travel financial management. This section of the chapter starts by discussing how travel agencies make money. Major agency costs are reviewed, and the variables open to a travel agency in dealing with corporate travel to obtain its own profits are discussed. Three tools that travel agencies utilize in obtaining profits when working with corporate travel accounts are discussed. These are the commercial account commissions report, the personnel productivity analysis, and the travel agency break-even/profit formulas. Recognizing how travel agencies can make profits by specializing in business travel, the corporate travel manager is placed in a better position to negotiate and work with travel agencies in order to maximize profits so that corporate travel expenses are minimized and profits for the corporate travel department (and its parent company) are also maximized. One of the major factors considered by corporate travel managers in selecting travel agency vendors is agency size. A significant discussion of agency size and the financial pros and cons of working with large agencies verses small agencies is included in this chapter.

Perhaps the most important financial relationship between corporate travel departments and travel agencies relates to the financial effect on the business as a whole (and the corporate travel department, specifically) while using preferred vendor agreements negotiated by travel agencies in working with air carriers, hotels, car rental firms, and other suppliers. A discussion of preferred vendor agreements and both the financial benefits, as well as the drawbacks that are possible for corporate travel departments is discussed.

It is stressed that while those opportunities for the corporate travel department and the corporate travel manager to contribute to the profits of the company are important, many additional tools are provided in the other financial management chapters as well, and should be considered in the development of a total strategy for managing for profits.

Travel Budget Cost Projections

An important way many corporate travel managers assist their companies is through providing budgeting expertise for each of the business' cost centers and profit centers that expect to have travel in their budgets for the coming year. The mechanics of this may vary from one business to another, but most line and staff executives are aware that they have limited knowledge in travel budgeting and most appreciate having corporate travel manager expertise available for assistance. This assistance can be financially valuable to the business. The corporate travel manager should keep accurate records reflecting percentage of average company-used air fare ticket price changes on a city-pair basis from year to year. The corporate travel manager should also be able to obtain price change projections from airline executives. By reviewing on a city-pair by city-pair basis, an average change history can emerge. By comparing that average change history with projected changes from the industry, the corporate travel manager will be able to determine a very close approximation in most years of next-year air fare costs for any single trip, as well as for multiple trips. The same type of approach can be utilized in projecting hotel costs, car rental costs, and other travel costs. By lending this expertise to both line and staff managers, the corporate travel manager not only reduces the uncertainty in travel cost projecting, but saves the individual managers considerable time in what, in many cases, would be duplicative research.

It is important to recognize that accurate budget projections for travel costs can, in themselves, provide a substantial savings for the business. After budgets are finalized, businesses can plan cash flow around total projected expenses. When travel is such a substantial expense for many companies, having inflated travel budgets can result in keeping too much money in current accounts and not enough money in interest-bearing accounts, thus losing float income for the business.

The mechanics that are generally utilized in most businesses to affect travel budget cost projections is to send a memo to all executives within the business who have the responsibility of preparing budgets. The memo would advise that assistance will be rendered at no cost. Include forms with the cover letter on which the executive who will be preparing the budget can insert the city pairs for the projected flights, the duration of stay, whether or not car rental(s) are required, and other appropriate expense indicators. The return of the forms provides the corporate travel manager with an instrument base that can not only give each person who will be preparing the budget a good projection of costs, but it will give the corporate travel manager a good indication of projected total corporate travel costs.

Travel Expense Policy Distribution

One of the costs incurred in businesses is a cost that travel expense policies can reduce or come close to eliminating. This is the cost of individual travelers exceeding policy travel expense limits. There are times when such excesses are accepted for various administrative reasons, but there are other times when such excesses may occur because of policy ignorance. When excesses occur because of policy ignorance, some companies absorb the cost coverage while other companies require individual travelers to pay back the difference. In either case, there is an expense, either in time or in money, to the business. This expense can be reduced considerably or eliminated by the wide distribution of travel expense policies. One of the major ways of undertaking this distribution is to reproduce the travel expense policies in a flyer or booklet and insert the policies with the airline ticket when it is given to the traveler.

Tax Considerations

The 1986 Tax Reform Act reduced considerably the deductibility of several major travel expenses. Meals and entertainment, which are subject to a new 80/20 rule, not only allow less deductibility, but could easily increase costs to the business. Most corporate travel managers are addressing this concern through the development of new expense report forms that require specific identification of meal and entertainment expenses, as well as justification for same. Separate expense account numbers are assigned to meal and entertainment expenses. Many of the forms are broken down into separate columns for meals and entertainment.

A cost saving option considered and utilized by some corporate travel managers is *computerized expense reporting*. Under a computerized expense reporting system, account numbers and addition are checked prior to submission of the expense report both by the traveler and by the traveler's supervisor, who customarily signs off on the expense report.

Per diems are allowed under the new regulations, but can cost companies both money and traveler concern. Flat per diems for meals are both convenient and encourage travelers to stay below them. However, because of the wide range of differences between the cost for meals in one part of the country as compared to other parts, geographical per diems are becoming more popular. It should be noted that if per diems are paid to an employee and are tax deductible from the company, the per diems are taxable to the employee as a part of his/her income. This can create a concern as it could result in being a major cost to employees if they travel substantially throughout the year. Per diem expenses can be deducted by employees in many cases, but they must provide appropriate documentation with their annual income tax filings.

Expense report item analyses and averaging can provide the business with good guidelines for travel costs in all cities to which travelers normally make trips throughout the year. This is especially beneficial for corporate travel managers who are utilizing an automated expense report system. With a strong data base kept on file over a long period of time, such a system has the capability of averaging hotel costs, meal costs, limo costs, other transer costs, and so on. These averagings, compared from one year to the next, will assist the corporate travel manager in providing budgeting assistance and will give the business solid guidelines for exception reporting and cost projections.

Travel Expense Monitoring

Almost all corporate travel departments undertake travel expense monitoring. Often this is coordinated or combined with efforts from an auditing or other accounting department within the business. Not only are meal expenses and entertainment monitored in accordance with the 1986 tax law, but all other reimbursable expenses are monitored as well. Monitoring, itself, can reduce travel expenses considerably, but combining monitoring with travel policies and individual traveler counseling has been documented to reduce total travel expenditures considerably. Normally, monitoring is undertaken on an exception reporting basis. In other words, if the traveler spends more than was allocated to the budget or the policy, that increased expense is flagged and reported as being outside of the policy limitation.

Basic Financial Report Types

There are three types of basic financial reports developed and worked with by most corporate travel departments. These have been classified under the categories of *departmental reports*, *corporate travel reports*, and *travel vendor expense report(s)*.

Departmental Reports

Departmental reports consist of departmental *receipts and disbursements reports, revenue improvement reports,* and *cost reduction reports.* Receipts and disbursements reports are normally prepared on a monthly basis and reflect all receipts coming into the corporate travel management department during a month and all payments made out from that department during that same month. There is normally a year-to-date column in the report, as well as a current month column. In this way, comparisons can be made from one month to another and from one year to another. Charts of accounts may vary from one corporate travel department to another.

Revenue improvement reports are utilized by some corporate travel departments, but not by all. The revenue improvement report is normally prepared in paragraph form. It reflects the contributions of the corporate travel department to the revenues of the business as a whole.

The *accounts payable report* shows those monies owing to vendors. This will often be an ageing report which will show the number of weeks or the number of months that the money has been owed. Typically, this reflects monies owed to travel agencies or credit card companies. The utilization of the accounts payable report can assist a corporate finance executive to determine a total corporate financial status or a corporate travel financial status (or both) at any particular point in time.

The *cost reduction report* is similar to the revenue improvement report in that it is normally a paragrapy-by-paragraph report rather than a report consisting solely of figures. The cost reduction report identifies those areas within the business relating to travel where costs have been reduced over what they would have been if corporate travel were not managed. Most reports of this type concentrate on air savings, but many will also emphasize hotel, car rental, and other aspects of travel as well.

Corporate Travel Reports

Three types of reports are normally included in the corporate travel reports. These include a *cost/profit center travel expense forecast,* a *monthly corporate travel expenditures budget,* and *exception reports.* The cost/profit center travel expense forecast attempts to project total expected travel expenses by cost or profit centers for the balance of the fiscal year. The corporate travel department keeps a running analysis on average ticket price by city pair, average hotel price by city and hotel, and average car rental price. Utilizing these changing average prices, a monthly report on expected travel expenses is developed by applying current average costs to balance of the year projected trips so that the report reader will rapidly know whether or not overexpenditures or underexpenditures on the annual travel budget can be expected. Obviously, if either is the case, an early projection of a potential problem will provide the maximum time necessary to make adjustments.

A monthly corporate travel expenditures budget shows the total amount of money spent on travel during the current month and year to date. With many of these reports, a comparison to the money budgeted for travel is provided so that a column in the report will show overexpenditures and underexpenditures in each category on a month-by-month basis and also on a year-to-date basis. Again, this report helps to project potential overexpenditures and underexpenditures for travel on a timely basis so that management can take appropriate actions at an early date.

Exception reports are utilized by almost all corporate travel managers. These reports identify travel expenditure policy exceptions. They reflect each instance when an expenditure has been made which is not in accordance with corporate travel policy. In other words, if a trip was undertaken at a first-class fare, whereas only economy or discounted fares are allowed in policy, this trip will be shown in the exception report. Also if a full-economy ticket was issued where discounted fares are required by policy, again the exception report will show this expenditure. Like air travel, hotel, car rental, and other expenses that are incurred which are not in accordance with corporate travel policy are shown in the exception report. The exception report goes beyond simply listing those travel expenditures that exceed the amounts or types authorized by corporate travel policy. They customerily also reflect reasons by category for why the exception occurred. Between ten and twelve reasons are provided on the normal computerized exception report. (See Figure 8.1.) By studying exception reports, management can make a decision whether or not the exception was warranted. Management may then take the appropriate action. It is also possible for management to identify patterns of exceptions so that possible changes in corporate travel policy can be made based on the extent of the patterns that occur.

Travel Vendor Expense Reports

Travel vendor expense reports are normally prepared for all major vendors. They are categorized by type of vendor and then by vendor itself. In the case of air expenditures, the vendor expense report will normally be broken down by air carrier and then again within each carrier by city pair. An alternative is to break down air travel expenses by city pair and then by air carrier. Many air travel expense reports are broken down both ways (i.e., by carrier and then by city pair and also by city pair and then carrier).

Hotel vendor expense reports are normally broken down by chain and then by property and city. As with air carrier reports, some corporate travel managers will break out hotel expense reports by city and then by property.

Car rental vendor expense reports are normally broken out by chain, then by franchisee, and then by city. An alternative approach is to break out car rental expenses by city and then by car rental franchisee.

Entertainment, meals, and other aspects of corporate travel management are sometimes reported on vendor expense reports as well. However, because the vendors for these reports may be so numerous that specific vendor patterns cannot be established and will be of little value if they are established, many corporate travel managers limit their travel vendor expense reports to air, hotel, and car rental only.

ASSOCIATED TRAVEL SERVICES, INC.
1241 EAST DYER ROAD, SUITE 110
SANTA ANA, CALIFORNIA 92705

```
12/05/89              ASSOCIATED TRAVEL SERVICES, INC              7:54 am
                              CUSTOMER REPORT
                                                                 PAGE 1 OF 5

Customer: 028630  A.B.C. Corporation

Name:  DOKES/BRAD MR
       QPGRSV   01DEC          CS  Code: C     Fare Quote:  $628
                                               Lowest Fare: $416
CO 738Y  06DEC W SANIAH HK1  730A 1241P                         Difference: $212
CO 505B  08DEC F IAHPHX HK1  940A 1128A
US1051H  08DEC F PHXSAN HK1  1225P 1229P

Name:  MIRANDA/JENNY MS
       RRHGKT   01DEC          CS  Code: C     Fare Quote:  $420
                                               Lowest Fare: $234
CO 738Y  11DEC M SANIAH HK1  730A 1241P                         Difference: $186
WN 709Y  12DEC T HOUPHX HK1  400P 540P
WN 394Y  12DEC T PHXSAN HK1  625P 630P

Name:  GARDNER/SAM
       RRJEWD   01DEC          CS  Code: C     Fare Quote:  $420
                                               Lowest Fare: $234
CO 738Y  11DEC M SANIAH HK1  730A 1241P                         Difference: $186
WN 709Y  12DEC T HOUPHX HK1  400P 540P
WN 394Y  12DEC T PHXSAN HK1  625P 630P

Name:  BOLER/WILL MR
       QRL2HG   28NOV          CS  Code: A     Fare Quote:  $148
                                               Lowest Fare: $98
UA1176Q  06DEC W SANSFO HK1  650A 818A                          Difference: $50
UA1083M  08DEC F SFOSAN HK1  640P 802P
UA1083Q  08DEC F SFOSAN HL1  640P 802P

Name:  CAMPBELL/CLARENCE MR
       QVNWUD   29NOV          CS  Code: A     Fare Quote:  $148
                                               Lowest Fare: $98
UA1176Q  06DEC W SANSFO HK1  650A 818A                          Difference: $50
UA1083M  08DEC F SFOSAN HK1  640P 802P
UA1083Q  08DEC F SFOSAN HL1  640P 802P

Name:  GISHOP/CHRIS MS
       QJRLMI   30NOV          CS  Code: G     Fare Quote:  $872
                                               Lowest Fare: $830
AA 550Y  04DEC M SANDFW HK1  903A 148P                          Difference: $42

-----------------------------------------------------------------------
A = LRF SOLD OUT                       I = INTERNATIONAL
B = AP PENALTY FARE USED               M = MGMT APPROVAL NO LRF
C = REF DUE SCHEDULING                 N = NEGOTIATED FARE
D = RQST SPECIFIC ARLN                 P = PROMOTIONAL FARE
E = AUTH FIRST OR BUSINESS CLASS       Q = ADV PURCH W/O PENALTY
F = LOWEST REASONABLE FARE             U = ADV PENALTY REFUSED
G = REF CONN/MULTI STOP                V = SPEC REQ/UPGRADE
H = REF ALTERNATE ARPT                 Y = NOT IN TIME FOR ADV PURCH
```

FIGURE 8.1. Sample exception report. Report reprinted with permission from Associated Travel Services, Inc.

Customer: 028630   A.B.C. Corporation

Name: GISHOP/CHRIS MS   CS Code: G   Fare Quote: $872   Difference: $42
     QJRLMI   30NOV   Lowest Fare: $830

AA 199Y 08DEC F DFWSAN HK1 1108A 1218P

Name: PUNT/JED MR   CS Code: G   Fare Quote: $872   Difference: $42
     QQSFYK   28NOV   Lowest Fare: $830

AA1010Y 05DEC T SANDFW HK1 710A 1157A
AA1413Y 08DEC F DFWSAN HK1 244P 353P

Name: PEDERSON/JACK MR   CS Code: G   Fare Quote: $882   Difference: $42
     RQGIWU   04DEC   Lowest Fare: $840

AA 550Y 14DEC Q SANDFW HK1 903A 148P
AA 67Y 15DEC F DFWSAN HK1 635P 745P

Name: ANDERSEN/MEREDITH   CS Code: G   Fare Quote: $872   Difference: $42
     SLQIIF   27NOV   Lowest Fare: $830

AA 550Y 04DEC M SANDFW HK1 903A 148P
AA 251Y 05DEC T DFWSAN HK1 404P 514P

Name: KOETLER/FRED MR   CS Code: G   Fare Quote: $872   Difference: $32
     RGSUYC   04DEC   Lowest Fare: $840

AA 550Y 11DEC M SANDFW HK1 903A 148P
AA 251Y 15DEC F DFWSAN HK1 404P 514P

Name: SNOWMAN/NANCY   CS Code: G   Fare Quote: $872   Difference: $32
     RLKJIV   04DEC   Lowest Fare: $840

AA1110Y 05DEC T SANDFW HK1 215P 704P
AA 251Y 07DEC Q DFWSAN HK1 404P 514P

```
A = LRF SOLD OUT                        I = INTERNATIONAL
B = AP PENALTY FARE USED                M = MGMT APPROVAL NO LRF
C = REF LRF DUE SCHEDULING              N = NEGOTIATED FARE
D = RQST SPECIFIC ARLN                  P = PROMOTIONAL FARE
E = AUTH FIRST OR BUSINESS CLASS        Q = ADV PURCH W/O PENALTY
F = LOWEST REASONABLE FARE              U = AP/PENALTY REFUSED
G = REF CONN/MULTI STOP                 V = SPEC REQ/UPGRADE
H = REF ALTERNATE ARPT                  Y = NOT IN TIME FOR ADV PURCH
```

Customer: 028630   A.B.C. Corporation

Name: LEWIS/NED MR   CS Code: G   Fare Quote: $872   Difference: $32
     RSTDOH   01DEC   Lowest Fare: $840

AA1010Y 06DEC W SANDFW HK1 710A 1157A
AA 251Y 17DEC S DFWSAN HK1 404P 520P

Name: ROCOCO/S L MR   CS Code: G   Fare Quote: $872   Difference: $32
     RUWQSG   01DEC   Lowest Fare: $840

AA 550Y 06DEC W SANDFW HK1 903A 148P
AA 251Y 08DEC F DFWSAN HK1 404P 514P

Name: RINGS/J MR   CS Code: A   Fare Quote: $151   Difference: $23
     RFOMOH   04DEC   Lowest Fare: $128

HP1282K 04DEC M SANPHX HK1 810P 1010P
HP 456L 04DEC M PHXTUS HK1 1100P 1135P
US2163Q 08DEC F TUSLAX HK1 655P 722P
US 29Q 08DEC F LAXSAN HK1 805P 844P

Name: MARLER/ROBERT A MR   CS Code: 1   Fare Quote: $-WS   Difference: $0
     QVKTAI   29NOV   Lowest Fare: $0.00X

DL5745Y 18DEC M SANLAX HK1 310P 355P
BA 282M 18DEC M LAXLHR GK1 600P 1220P

Name: SMITH/E B MR   CS Code: B   Fare Quote: $1333   Difference: $0
     QGCGBU   30NOV   Lowest Fare: $1333

AA 900H 06DEC W SANORD HK1 645A 1249P
AA1024H 06DEC W ORDDCA HK1 125P 420P
NW 810B 06DEC F DCAMEM HK1 620P 745P
NW 859B 10DEC S MEMBOS HK1 730P 1110P
CO1049Y 12DEC T BOSCLE HK1 800A 950A
US 149B 14DEC Q CLESAN HK1 650P 1016P

```
A = LRF SOLD OUT                        I = INTERNATIONAL
B = AP PENALTY FARE USED                M = MGMT APPROVAL NO LRF
C = REF LRF DUE SCHEDULING              N = NEGOTIATED FARE
D = RQST SPECIFIC ARLN                  P = PROMOTIONAL FARE
E = AUTH FIRST OR BUSINESS CLASS        Q = ADV PURCH W/O PENALTY
F = LOWEST REASONABLE FARE              U = AP/PENALTY REFUSED
G = REF CONN/MULTI STOP                 V = SPEC REQ/UPGRADE
H = REF ALTERNATE ARPT                  Y = NOT IN TIME FOR ADV PURCH
```

FIGURE 8.1. (cont.)

Customer: 028630 A.B.C. Corporation

```
Name: PEDERSON/MANNY                                Fare Quote: $498
      QHENJO   30NOV     CS Code: B                 Lowest Fare: $498     Difference: $0
UA 432H 11DEC M SANORD HK1   715A 1259P
UA 506H 11DEC M ORDALB HK1   141P  428P
UA 715H 22DEC F ALBORD HK1  1024A 1142A
UA 477H 22DEC F ORDSAN HK1  1244P  252P

Name: PEREZ/JOSE MR                                 Fare Quote: $681
      QIQDKL   30NOV     CS Code: B                 Lowest Fare: $681     Difference: $0
AA  76Y 14DEC Q SANLAX HK1   715A  759A
AA  31Y 14DEC Q LAXHNL HK1   900A 1237P
AA 294Q 20DEC W HNLLAX HK1   430P 1142P
AA 137Q 21DEC Q LAXSAN HK1  1220A  106A

Name: WHITE/DONALD MR                               Fare Quote: $478
      QWRQTE   29NOV     CS Code: B                 Lowest Fare: $478     Difference: $0
TW 844Q 26DEC T SANSTL HK1  1228P  420P
TW 586Q 26DEC T STLMDT HK1   128P  420P
TW 563Q 05JAN F MDTSTL HK1   717A  840A
TW 203Q 05JAN F STLSAN HK1   915A 1117A

Name: STUKE/ROBERT L                                Fare Quote: $477
      SKQIVV   27NOV     CS Code: F                 Lowest Fare: $477     Difference: $0
DL 105B 04DEC M SANHNL HK1  1050A  220P
AQ 114V 06DEC W HNLKOA HK1   441P  515P
AQ 127B 08DEC F KOAHNL HK1   800A  830A
DL  72B 08DEC F HNLLAX HK1   945A  450P
DL1710B 08DEC F LAXSAN HK1   520P  559P

Name: ADAMS/R S MR                                  Fare Quote: $1063
      QARPWL   17NOV     CS Code: F                 Lowest Fare: $1063    Difference: $0
AA 550Y 04DEC M SANDFW HK1   903A  148P
AA1123X 05DEC T DFWATL HK1   516P  819P
AA1153Q 07DEC Q ATLDFW HK1   155P  309P
AA 251Q 07DEC Q DFWSAN HK1   404P  514P
```

```
A = LRF SOLD OUT                          I = INTERNATIONAL
B = AP PENALTY FARE USED                  M = MGMT APPROVAL NO LRF
C = REF LRF DUE SCHEDULING                N = NEGOTIATED FARE
D = RQST SPECIFIC ARLN                    P = PROMOTIONAL FARE
E = AUTH FIRST OR BUSINESS CLASS          U = ADV PURCH W/O PENALTY
F = LOWEST REASONABLE FARE                V = AP/PENALTY REFUSED
G = REF CONN/MULTI STOP                   Y = SPEC REQ/UPGRADE
H = REF ALTERNATE ARPT                      = NOT IN TIME FOR ADV PURCH
```

Customer: 028630 A.B.C. Corporation

```
Name: ADAMS/R S MR                                  Fare Quote: $1063
      QARPWL   17NOV     CS Code: F                 Lowest Fare: $1063    Difference: $0

Name: BARD/M X MR                                   Fare Quote: $582
      QAUBNC   17NOV     CS Code: F                 Lowest Fare: $582     Difference: $0
AA101Q 05DEC T SANDFW HK1   710A 1157A
AA 504Q 05DEC T DFWATL HK1 1251P  349P
AA1153Q 07DEC Q ATLDFW HK1  155P  309P
AA 251Q 07DEC Q DFWSAN HK1  404P  514P

Name: HILLER/LEONARD MR                             Fare Quote: $582
      QAXDGL   17NOV     CS Code: F                 Lowest Fare: $582     Difference: $0
AA101Q 05DEC T SANDFW HK1   710A 1157A
AA 504Q 05DEC T DFWATL HK1 1251P  349P
AA1153Q 07DEC Q ATLDFW HK1  155P  309P
AA 251Q 07DEC Q DFWSAN HK1  404P  514P

Name: ORLESEN/JAMES MR                              Fare Quote: $1063
      QAZAVW   17NOV     CS Code: F                 Lowest Fare: $1063    Difference: $0
AA 550Y 04DEC M SANDFW HK1   903A  148P
AA 222Y 05DEC T DFWATL HK1   516P  819P
AA1153Q 07DEC Q ATLDFW HK1   155P  309P
AA 251Q 07DEC Q DFWSAN HK1   404P  514P

Name: THOMPSEN/RICHARD MR                           Fare Quote: $981
      QDAHQW   12SEP     CS Code: F                 Lowest Fare: $981     Difference: $0
TW 240Y 20DEC W SANSTL HK1   215P  752P
TW 656Y 20DEC W STLPIA HK1   851P  941P
AA4091Y 22DEC F PIAORD HK1  1255P  157P
AA 897Y 22DEC F ORDPSP HK1   250P  513P
```

```
A = LRF SOLD OUT                          I = INTERNATIONAL
B = AP PENALTY FARE USED                  M = MGMT APPROVAL NO LRF
C = REF LRF DUE SCHEDULING                N = NEGOTIATED FARE
D = RQST SPECIFIC ARLN                    P = PROMOTIONAL FARE
E = AUTH FIRST OR BUSINESS CLASS          U = ADV PURCH W/O PENALTY
F = LOWEST REASONABLE FARE                V = AP/PENALTY REFUSED
G = REF CONN/MULTI STOP                   Y = SPEC REQ/UPGRADE
H = REF ALTERNATE ARPT                      = NOT IN TIME FOR ADV PURCH
```

FIGURE 8.1. (cont.)

Travel Agency Interfacing as Related to Financial Management

Even before deregulation, one of the most popular approaches toward saving money utilized by corporate travel managers was to negotiate with travel agency vendors to obtain, not only the best possible fares and routings, but to obtain cost-saving benefits as well. Since deregulation, travel agency negotiation has become the main way corporate travel managers effect cost savings. It also has become one of the best ways of initiating a move from the status of a cost center to a profit center by obtaining a sufficient amount of money from the travel agency to more than cover all corporate travel management departmental costs.

Before negotiating with travel agencies relating to the financial arrangements and "deals" that might be possible, it is important for a corporate travel manager to understand how valuable his or her company's business is to its travel agency or potential travel agency. One must clearly understand the answer to the question: How important is your account to your travel agency? To reach this answer one must understand both the extent of one's travel and how travel agencies make money. Several aspects of agency profitability need to be understood as they relate to travel agencies. You should know the amount of money an agency makes on a transaction and what makes one account more valuable to a travel agency than another commercial account when both spend approximately the same amount of money on travel. Clearly, if a corporate travel manager understands exactly how valuable his or her account is to an agency, it will be possible to determine the exact parameters within which one can negotiate. Without this knowledge, it is far too easy to ask for and expect either too much or too little from travel agencies. With a complete understanding, it is possible to negotiate for the maximum financial and other benefits possible. It is possible to work with the ultimate travel agency vendor on a continuing basis so that the vendor is able to make a reasonable profit and render good service, while the maximum financial benefits are accrued by the corporate travel department.

A starting point in understanding how travel agencies make money is to recognize that they are paid a commission by the vendors they represent. Approximately sixty percent to eighty percent of an average corporate business-oriented travel agency's commissions come from the sale of airline tickets. Hotel booking commissions and car rental booking commissions constitute other major income sources for travel agencies. When a travel agency completes the travel arrangements for a business traveler, they typically issue an airline ticket, make a hotel reservation, and book a rental car. The commission levels paid by air carriers to travel agencies vary with the carrier and the type of ticket sold. However, since deregulation, the average commission earned by a travel agency for domestic airline ticket sales has hovered right at ten percent for the base fare (before taxes are added).

Although it is important for a corporate travel manager to understand the exact amount of commission paid for airline tickets issued, for the purposes of this explanation, the average ten percent commission will be utilized. On average, hotels also pay a ten percent commission. Car rentals can be anywhere from a base of $2.00 per transaction to ten percent of base rental cost. Therefore, if the corporate travel manager calculates the cost of the airline ticket and the hotel for the trip undertaken by a corporate traveler, ten percent of the total figure (plus

101

Travel Agency
Interfacing as
Related to
Financial
Management

$2.00 each car rental) would be the approximate average amount earned by the travel agency for arranging the trip.

Costs

It must be recognized, however, that the travel agency is given the ten percent commission for:

- issuing the ticket;
- making hotel and car rental reservations;
- providing boarding passes, itineraries, and other documents;
- delivering the tickets, hotel confirmations, and car rental reservations; and
- providing additional services.

The cost of providing these services can be substantial and a travel agency must always determine whether or not the costs of serving a commercial account will outweigh the commissions earned. Many travel agencies have given up what appeared to be substantial amounts of corporate travel business after having found the business cost them money rather than made them money. Major costs for a travel agency are:

- personnel (approximately fifty percent of total travel agency costs);
- computers; and
- ticket delivery services.

Variables

If a travel agency can reduce some of its costs in serving a corporate client, it can either make more money or it can move from a position of losing money on an account to a position of making money on it. There are really only two ways of altering the financial arrangements with a commercial account in order to create or to increase profitability. These are:

1. to increase the sales (unit sales, average ticket price to total sales, or number of tickets); or
2. to reduce the costs (less expensive personnel handling the account, less expensive computers, less frequent ticket delivery, and so forth).

Obviously, there is a trade-off between service and costs. Almost any travel agency can make money on almost any corporate account if that account is sold full economy priced tickets (or preferably first class tickets). Money may be saved by using agents who are paid minimum wage to book travel as well as by utilizing the least expensive computer reservation system, and making ticket delivery only by mail. All of these arrangements are unsatisfactory to corporate travel managers, but corporate travel managers need to be aware that these are some of the major factors that travel agencies deal with in reviewing the profitability of corporate accounts.

Commercial Account Commissions Report

To make it easier for travel agencies to evaluate the value of their commercial accounts, the American Society of Travel Agents has developed a form as a part of its travel agency accounting package. This form is the *Commercial Account Commissions Report*. A sample of a completed report for a one month period appears in Figure 8.2.

In completing that report, the travel agency listed the airline bookings for each of three accounts for the month of January and it took the actual dollar commissions paid by the air carriers involved listing these as air commissions. Car rental, hotel, and other bookings for the clients were listed under the "Other Bookings" category and again the actual dollars received in commissions for these other bookings were listed. The "Total Commission" figure was calculated by adding the "Air Commission" and the "Other Commission" for each of the commercial accounts. To determine an "Average Commission Per Sales Hour," the total number of sales hours was divided into the "Total Commission." If the travel agency has calculated the percentage of cost it incurs for personnel costs, it can rapidly look at the "Average Commission Per Sales Hour" to determine whether or not a profit has been made on a particular account. For example, if "Total Personnel Costs" constitutes fifty percent of a travel agency's total costs, and if the agency is paying $20 per hour of total remuneration to a travel agent to handle an account, then the total operating cost per hour for the travel agency is $40 and the agency would make a profit from each of the three accounts shown in Figure 8.2. However, if the average total compensation per agent is $40 per hour, then the total cost to the travel agency for operations on an hourly basis is $80 and the agency has lost money on each of the accounts shown.

Personnel

People are important in either making a travel agency profitable or in creating a loss. As pointed out earlier, total personnel costs in travel agencies, on an average national basis, constitute approximately fifty percent of the total costs for an agency. Although other factors are certainly important as well, two of the key factors involved in determining profitability are *sales hours* and *employee cost per hour*. Although sales hours can certainly be affected by such factors as the number of changes in an average booking, cancellations, and reissues, they are also affected by the degree of efficiency of an agent. It is not at all uncommon to find that one agent in an agency is twice as efficient as another (when defining efficiency as the amount of time it takes to earn a dollar in travel sales.)

Of considerable importance is an understanding of the employee cost per hour factor (as it relates to the profitability of an agency and as that cost relates to the service provided to the corporate travel account). If the corporate travel manager insists on using a *dedicated agent* (an agent that will work on a specific commercial account only or is one of two or three people who work on that account and no others, depending upon its size, then the corporate travel man-

COMMERCIAL   ACCOUNT   COMMISSIONS   REPORT

Period Ended_____ January 1986 _____

ACCOUNT NAME	AIR BOOKINGS	AIR COMM.	OTHER BOOKINGS	OTHER COMM.	TOTAL COMM.	# SALES HOURS	AVG. COMM. PER SLS. HR
KLIM ENTERPRISES	920.00	98.20	308.00	24.18	122.38	2.10	58.28
MIGHTY MIDGETS INC.	190.00	19.00	-0-	-0-	19.00	.25	76.00
TELEGRAPHICS ASSOC.	2,612.00	248.00	973.00	86.50	334.50	5.50	60.82
							+
TOTAL							

FIGURE 8.2. Example of a Commercial Account Commissions Report.

ager must understand that the dedicated agent(s) will be either good or bad. This rating is directly related to the agent(s)' ability to produce profits for the travel agency. The corporate travel manager should understand that the dedicated agent(s)' ability to produce a profit will vary to a considerable degree depending upon the type of travel handled, the number of changes that occur, and other factors that are often more within the control of the corporate travel manager and his business or personnel rather than within the control of the travel agency's management.

To get a clearer picture of personnel productivity, review the *Personnel Productivity Analysis* for Jane Doe at XYZ Travel (see Figure 8.3). A key factor is the total compensation received by Jane. As can be seen, with all other factors being the same, when one looks at Jane's contribution to the travel agency's break-even point or profitability, if one considers only her salary, her contribution is $3,350 for booking $62,500 worth of travel. Since personnel costs constitute approximately fifty percent of a travel agency's costs, Jane would have covered her salary (($3,000), the other fifty percent of agency costs her sales must cover (if the agency is to obtain a break-even point) ($3,000), and $350 will be left over to apply toward profits.

Salary $12,00 yr.
Benefits 2,600 yr.
Contributed Tax 960 yr.
Edu illow 1,140 yr
Bonus 1,000
—————
17,700 yr
4,425 Quarter

XYZ Travel

Agency Name

PERSONNEL PRODUCTIVITY ANALYSIS

Quarter Ending 3/31 198__

Salesman Name	Bookings (1)	Commissions (2)	Sales Salary (3)	Contribution (4)=(2)-(3)	# of Sales Hours (5)	Avg. Comm. per Sales Hr (6)=(2)÷(5)	Avg. Comm. % (7)=(2)÷(1)	No. of Transactions (8)	Avg. Comm. per Transaction (9)=(2)÷(8)
JANE DOE	62,500	$6,350	3,000	$3,350	520	$12.21	10.16%	191	$33.25
			sales cost						
JANE DOE	$62,500	$6,350	4425	$1,925	520	$12.21	10.16%	191	$33.25
TOTAL									

FIGURE 8.3. Example of a Quarterly Personnel Productivity Analysis for the quarter ending March 31, 198X for XYZ Travel and the effect on personnel productivity by adding agent sales costs.

However, in adding a benefits and tax package to Jane's salary, there is an increase of almost fifty percent in terms of what the agency must pay to have Jane work for them (i.e., Jane's total compensation package). Jane's contribution to break-even or profitability is almost cut in half. Taking all of this into account, her earnings are now only $1,925 (less than half that needed to cover the other fifty percent of operating costs which need to be covered if the travel agency is to reach a break-even status).

Obviously, the amount of salary and benefits paid to the agent or agents who handle the commercial account is a key factor in a travel agency's ability to make a profit or to have a loss as a result of handling that account. However, a closely related factor to agency profitability, as it relates to the productivity of the agents working in the agency, is the ability of the agency to provide continuous and profitable work for each agent. Since most travel agencies pay their personnel on a salary basis or a salary plus bonus basis, it is expected that agents work a full forty-hour week (they are paid for working whether or not they do work that number of hours). If the travel agency has few accounts, it may have agents sitting

104

around much of the time not producing profitable bookings for the travel agency. What this means is that a greater percentage of the income needed to pay the salary of an employee comes from the few commercial accounts that the agency may have.

As a result, on a per contract-hour basis with the corporate travel manager or with the corporate travel manager's business, the compensation paid is far greater than the quality of the agents being utilized. As a result, corporate travel managers will often find that the large travel agency, which can keep each of its agents fully productive throughout every business day, can afford to provide agents with greater experience, more knowledge, and generally a higher quality level and it can offer a larger range of services than can a travel agency that is small and, therefore, unable to fully utilize its agency staff. This will be clarified to a much greater degree later in the chapter.

The Travel Agency Break-even Formula

Having determined how personnel productivity affects a travel agency's profitability and how travel agencies are able to take one measure of commercial account profitability by utilizing the Commercial Account Commissions Report, it will be beneficial to understand how travel agencies apply a formula to determine their own break-even point and extend this formula to project their own profitability. The basic formula is a very simple one. By dividing the travel agency's average commission into the travel agency's operating expenses, the agency is able to determine its break-even point.

For example, if the travel agency had $200,000 of expenses and if its average commission is ten percent, then by dividing ten percent into $200,000, one can determine that the agency has a break-even point of $2 million in sales. In other words, the agency would have to sell $2 million of ten percent commissionable travel (airline tickets, car rentals, hotel bookings, and so on) in order to cover its costs of $200,000. This simple formula for determining a break-even point can be expanded to project costs, sales, and profits.

However, the formula is somewhat misleading and very much over simplified from the real-world expenditure decisions and income-generation decisions agency managers face every day. Before analyzing the ramifications of the formula and its impact as it relates to corporate travel management, it is important to agree on some basic financial terms.

A Definition of Terms

Several terms are utilized in determining the profitability of travel agencies. The following basic ones require an understanding:

1. Break-even;
2. Profit;
3. Commission;

4. Earnings;

5. Capitalizing; and

6. Override.

The most fundamental concept to understand is the difference between *sales, earnings, commissions,* and *overrides.*

One must be careful not to confuse *earnings* with *sales.* When a one-hundred dollar ($100) airline ticket is sold, an eight (8%) percent tax ($7.41) is deducted and a commission of ten percent is paid on the balance ($92.59). The eighty-three dollars and thirty-three cents which is sent to the air carrier cannot be considered a part of the agency's earnings. Only the ten percent commission ($9.26) belongs to the travel agency and only the nine dollars and twenty-six cents of commission can be considered in the earnings of the travel agency.

Overrides, however, can contribute to earnings as well. Although the average commission earned for selling an airline ticket in the U.S. approximates ten percent, many airline carriers pay travel agencies an additional amount of money if the agency sells a large dollar volume of tickets on that particular carrier or if the agency moves a large percentage of its sales from other carriers to the carrier that is paying an overrride commission. The override can be looked at as a type of bonus paid to the travel agency for being a good producer for the airline. This override is usually not very large, but in a few cases it can make the critical difference between a travel agency showing a profit or a loss at the end of its fiscal year.

Capitalization is the amount of money the owners of a travel agency put into the business in order to create the business. Ideally, capitalization is paid into the business at the time the business is created. If it is capitalized sufficiently and managed well, there may be no additional money paid into the agency by the owners in the form of capital. However, if the business has lost money, the owners may have to put additional money into the travel agency in order to keep it solvent. Whatever money is put into the company by owners is considered *capital.*

In exchange for capitalizing a business, owners customarily expect to obtain a return on their investment. This return on investment is sometimes considered *profit,* but some travel agency managers do not consider the business to have made a profit until the owners have received a pre-determined percentage or dollar figure return on investment for their capitalization. Any additional monies made during the fiscal year by the company is considered profit. In some other cases, profit is considered any amount of money that is earned after the business has broken even.

Therefore, the definition of profit often hinges on the definition of *break-even.* The traditional definition of break-even is that point in time or income level where the amount of earnings for the travel agency is exactly the same as the amount of expenses. As noted above, some of those in the travel agency industry consider break-even to be a point in time when the expenses not only equal earnings, but equal sufficient earnings to include the amount of money paid to the owners for the capital which they have invested (i.e., the return on investment). Both definitions of break-even are used in the industry and used considerably. Unless specified otherwise, the term break-even will be used, in this textbook, as the point in time when earnings equal expenditures without considering return on investment for capitalization as being a part of those earnings which must equal expenditures.

Converting the Break-even Formula to a Profit Formula

A corporate travel manager recently noted that she had netotiated a good financial arrangement with the travel agency vendor serving her account. She pointed out that she was receiving good service and substantial rebates. But she also noted that within a few months, the agency owner came to her and explained that he was losing money on her account. He showed her the figures indicating that his costs for computers, personnel, and other factors were so high that it cost him more to generate and deliver a ticket than he was able to receive in terms of the commissions that were left after paying his rebates. He asked if the rebate level could be lowered so that he could afford to continue serving the account. The corporate travel manager agreed, but questioned whether or not her decision was a correct one.

In determining a break-even point for many travel agencies working with corporate accounts, the corporate account manager reviewing an agency's financial status needs to watch out for an agency determination of a break-even point which really is a profitability point rather than a break-even point. As noted earlier, there are several ways of calculating a break-even point. However, if a travel agency has identified all of its costs and all of its earnings, as well as its average commission level, it is possible to identify a true break-even point by dividing the average commission into expenses in order to determine the amount of sales needed for break-even.

To obtain a profitability formula from this basic break-even formula, the agency manager need only to determine either the percentage or the dollar amount of the profit that is projected to be earned. By adding this *profit* amount to the travel agency total costs, the agency owner is able to divide the average commission level into the figure (which is a result of both costs and profit projection) to determine the total amount of sales needed to break-even. In reality, the total amount of sales needed is not to just break-even (utilizing the formula in this structure), but it is to break-even and make a profit.

The earlier example of the travel agency that had $200,000 of expenses and an average commission level of ten percent, calculated that their break-even point would be $2 million (based upon dividing the $200,000 of expenses by the ten percent average commission). Taking the same agency, if one determines that a $20,000 profit is desired, then the expenses are no longer $200,000, but $220,000. By dividing the ten percent into the $220,000 of expenses, one calculates that the travel agency needs to sell $2.2 million in sales in order to break-even and make a $20,000 profit.

It should be pointed out that this is a simplistic approach because anytime sales are increased, costs are also increased to some extent. For example, in order to sell $20,000 more of air, hotel, car, and other travel products, the agency may need to hire an additional staff person, add another computer, or create other needed services that will add to costs. Therefore, instead of just adding projected profit to projected costs to get a figure into which to divide average commission, the agency manager will need to review all costs and then add those costs needed to maintain sufficient services and programs in order to keep customers happy in order for the additional sales to be realized. Therefore, the real cost figure, in the above example, would be considerably more than $220,000 and, therefore, the real amount of sales needed to reach break-even and obtain a $20,000 profit would be considerably more than $2.2 million.

Therefore, when an agency professes that it has difficulties in terms of meeting the financial agreements it has agreed to with a corporate account, the corporate travel manager needs to first determine whether or not the figures quoted by the travel agency are figures designed to reach a true break-even point or figures designed to reach a break-even point based on having a profit as well as breaking even.

As noted earlier, override commissions also affect the break-even formula and the profitability formula. In addition, they affect the financial aspects of working arrangements between travel agencies and corporate travel managers. The two factors that airlines are looking for from a travel agency, in providing that agency with an additional income in the form of override commissions, are the volume of sales with that air carrier along with the amount of air sales that have been converted from other air carriers to the air carrier that would be paying the override commission.

Recently, a travel agency executive advised that one of the top volume air carriers was paying his agency a fifteen percent override for producing a forty-eight percent market share on that carrier. *Business Travel News*, in reporting the results of the 1988 Department of Transportation CRS industry report noted that:

> The CRS vendors reported 1986 override commissions paid to more than 12,000 travel agencies. They paid almost $43 million, in 1986, in cash inducements to attract or retain subscribers, plus $151 million in free travel or hotel accommodations. (*Business Travel News*, June 20, 1988, p. 61).

Based on 13,000 agency recipients (far less than half the total number of appointed agencies in the U.S.), this averages more than $3,300 in override commissions per agency recipient and more than $11,100 per agency recipient in free travel and accommodations.

Obviously, the tickets that a travel agency would sell in order to reach a volume level sufficient to earn an overide commission, and the tickets a travel agency would sell in order to convert sales on traditional carriers to one or more carriers paying override commissions are, in fact, sales to corporate account travelers. Recognizing this, some corporate travel managers have tracked airline bookings made by their travel agency for their business and have become proficient in identifying when a substantial amount of ticketing is converted from one carrier to another. In addition, corporate travel departments have asked for a share of the traditional commissions and of the override commissions in what is known in the industry as a *commission or revenue sharing arrangement*.

The Financial Pros and Cons of Working with Large Agencies vs. Small Agencies

There are efficiencies of scale in the travel agency business, just as there are in many other businesses. Going back to the example discussed earlier of the corporate travel manager whose travel agency wanted to change their financial arrangements because the agency was losing money on an account, a major factor in this situation turned out to be that the agency with which the corporate travel department was contracting was a small agency as compared to several others in that community. The statistics prove how a larger agency can be in a better financial position to provide a wide range of services, whereas a smaller agency cannot.

As noted earlier, the average agency sells approximately $1.1 million of travel annually. This means that that agency has approximately $110,000 of operating income. After deducting approximately fifty percent of the income for personnel (in many cases, more than this must be spent on personnel expenses, especially in small agencies), the agency is left with only $55,000 with which to pay all other expenses. This also means that this average agency pays approximately $55,000 in salaries, taxes, and benefits to all of its employees.

Obviously, $55,000 as a total payroll (including salary, payroll taxes, and benefits) is not substantial and it is not possible to obtain a large number of employees with such a limited personnel budget. Someone in the agency must handle all accounting, all business management functions, and ticket deliveries, in addition to making reservations and issuing tickets. Agencies need more than two full-time employees. However, at a total compensation of $55,000 for personnel costs, if the agency employs two full-time employees, this means that each full-time employee is allocated only approximately $27,500 per year for salary, benefits, and payroll taxes. If a part-time person is hired to handle ticket delivery, even at minimum wage, the monies to pay such a person must be taken from the total $55,000 of the personnel budget, thus substantially reducing the income of the two full-time employees.

Not only does the average travel agency have problems in attracting good personnel and an adequate number of personnel to handle commercial accounts (considering the limited budget with which the average travel agency is working), but it also has limited monies available in order to purchase computers, pay rent, and provide cost-saving services (such as special rates negotiated with hotels and car rental companies, airport parking, and so on). It also has limited funds available to attend continuing education seminars and other programs designed to keep the agency staff up-to-date with trends in corporate travel.

Looked at another way, there is a minimal expense level involved in operating any travel agency. Just to keep an agency open for business, there *must* be two employees. One of these two must be a *qualifier* (i.e., a person who meets the airline requirements to "qualify" the agency for airline ticketing appointments). In addition, at least two CRTs and two printers (one for tickets and one for itineraries) are needed. Rent and other expenses are mandatory and can be substantial. Some feel that the following represent the bare minimum range of annual expenses just to keep a travel agency open for business.

		Yearly	*Yearly*
Personnel:	Qualifier	$16,000–$20,000 +	
	Agent	$10,000–$15,000 =	$26,000–$35,000
Computers:	2 CRTs and 2 Printers		$ 9,000–$12,000
Rent			$12,000–$18,000
Other Expenses			$18,000–$24,000
Total Minimum Annual Expenses			$65,000–$89,000

Obviously, the "average" travel agency in the U.S., which is selling $1.1 million in travel annually and earning a 9.9 percent average commission, is receiving $108,900 in annual operating income and is just barely clearing these minimum operating expenses.

Part of the problem with an average-size agency is that if it is selling only $1.1 million of travel in a year, even two full-time employees will not be kept busy, in terms of constantly selling travel. The volume of travel bookings simply is not sufficient to keep them productively making reservations and issuing tickets throughout the day. Two reservations agents in a large agency usually are booking $1 million in travel apiece, and many book more than this annually.

In comparing the average travel agency with a large commercial travel agency, one can see how the larger agency is able to provide considerably more in terms of services and benefits for the corporate account. An agency that has sales of $25 million to $50 million per year is able to hire employees who have more experience. They can also pay these employees a better salary. A travel agency that sells an annual $50 million in travel is also no longer earning an average ten percent commission. This agency should be in a position to earn override commissions with a number of its vendor suppliers.

While the average agency has $110,000 of annual operating capital with which to pay all its expenses, the agency selling $50 million in corporate travel has approximately $6 million with which to pay its expenses. When such an agency expects each agent to sell a minimum of at least $1 million in travel bookings per year, this $50 million volume agency is employing a reservations staff of perhaps forty-five agents. If this agency allocated ten percent of its personnel costs to administrative and support staff, it would have 4.5 additional staff members and rounded off, it would have a total staff of fifty people.

If this large agency also allocated fifty percent of its income to personnel costs, its fifty person staff would have a total personnel compensation base of $3 million which would provide every employee a compensation of approximately $60,000. Obviously, in reality, this does not occur. Agency reservation experts working in large agencies are able to book substantially more than $1 million in travel sales per year and their total compensation packages (including payroll taxes and benefits) are much closer to $30,000 annually on the average. Meanwhile, the support staff, many of whom are paid considerably less than the agent experts, is much more than ten percent.

However, even if half of the operating income was allocated to personnel expenses in large travel agencies (and it seldom is), this still leaves approximately $3 million in this hypothetical example agency for other operating costs. With a

111

Agency
Preferred
Vendors and
the Financial
Effects on
Commercial
Accounts

$3 million annual operating base to cover all expenses except personnel, a substantial number of additional services and benefits can be provided for the commercial accounts of the agency, especially when this is compared with the average agency in the U.S., which has approximately $55,000 to cover the same types of operating costs, client services, and client benefits. This substantial difference in terms of monies available in a large travel agency to provide services and benefits for corporate accounts means that a very large agency can provide their own computer hardware, tailored software, reports designed by their own in-house programmer, ticket deliveries throughout the day, dedicated agents who specialize in international travel, meetings, group travel, and so on, plus many additional service programs for their commercial accounts. The agency can still earn a substantial profit.

Perhaps most important, however, is that the large travel agency can employ people and can buy systems that will provide for true continuous "best fare" searches and it has clout with airline carriers. This results in the ability to give their corporate accounts far less expensive average ticket prices than the small- or average-sized travel agency has the economic ability to provide. In other words, all travel agencies are not created equal and cannot provide the same types of services or cost-saving benefits to a corporate account.

Some argue that the other side of this picture is the ability of the small travel agency to provide dedicated agents who work only on specific corporate accounts and, because any business's travel which is substantial can well be the mainstay of a small travel agency, that agency will bend over backwards to provide every possible service for the corporate account. The reality, however, is that a large agency has the buying power, the negotiating power, and the staff that can get, on the average, much lower air fares and provide much more service. In addition, even large agencies can, and usually do, provide dedicated agents for corporate business. In selecting a travel agency, therefore, it is important to recognize the economies of scale that can, and do, exist in selecting a vendor who has the economic ability to provide the best possible air fares and the widest possible range of services since these factors are of such considerable importance to most corporate travel departments.

Agency Preferred Vendors and the Financial Effects on Commercial Accounts

Several years ago, airlines concluded that they could effect the amount of sales generated from travel agencies in several ways. Obviously, if they could encourage travel agencies to sell more of their carrier as compared with competing carriers, the airline's share of the total market out of a city might increase significantly. One way airlines found to encourage travel agencies to sell their carrier, as compared to other options, was to offer financial incentives in the form of overrides. The original concept of an override was to encourage high-producing agencies to produce more and, more importantly, to hold out an offer for lower producing agencies to produce more. However, in recent years, the emphasis has not been as much on producing more total travel by the agency, but to encourage the travel agency to produce more travel with the particular carrier. This is a significant difference in that, under the prior emphasis, travel agencies

AN OVERVIEW OF THE FINANCIAL ADVANTAGES AND DISADVANTAGES OF WORKING WITH A LARGE VERSUS A SMALL TRAVEL AGENCY

Large Agencies

Financial Advantages	*Financial Disadvantages*

1. Lower fares—best fare guarantees
  a) Standard best fare guarantee
  b) Best fare reimbursement guarantee
  c) Quality control best fare process guarantee
  d) Guaranteed discount best fare
  e) Continuous low fare check best fare guarantee
2. Rebates
  a) Larger
  b) Selection—soft or hard rebates
3. Fee-based service option
4. Conversion ability
	1. No float—typically agencies won't "carry" the account
	2. Commission agents may push favored vendors at client's expense

Non-financial Advantages	*Non-financial Disadvantages*

1. Service representatives employed with many agencies
2. More experienced agents
3. Dedicated agents
4. Quality control checks
5. Agency paid education for the corporate account
6. More computer systems—multiple reservations systems
7. More up to date computers
8. Back office computer systems
9. Reports
  a) Savings report
  b) Other reports
  c) Tailored reports by in-house programmer
10. Last seat availability with more carriers
11. Automatic "policy based" fare selection
12. Limited travel benefits for corporate travel staff
  a) Airline "give away" free tickets
  b) ARC list travel benefits in a few cases
13. More frequent scheduled ticket delivery
14. Parking program
	1. Factory-type "mechanical" process (agents usually have quotas to meet and do not spend substantial time with clients)
	2. Ticket delivery is scheduled—not "on demand"
	3. Free tickets from vendors may have restrictions
	4. Agency expertise often allocated on the basis of the client company's profits for the agency

FIGURE 8.4. Large vs. small travel agencies: advantages and disadvantages.

113

Agency
Preferred
Vendors and
the Financial
Effects on
Commercial
Accounts

Small and Medium-Sized Agencies	
Financial Advantages	*Financial Disadvantages*
1. Rebates—the smaller agency may give greater rebates in order to obtain the commercial account 2. Float—the smaller agency may be willing to "carry" the corporate account for two months or more whereas the larger agencies seldom do or do so for only a short time	1. Rebates—the smaller agency is too small to earn large overrides. Therefore it has less ability to offer substantial rebates 2. If high rebates are offered, higher ticket prices may be obtained to offset the effect of high rebates and to earn at least a small profit 3. Unable to offer conversion ability 4. Unable to provide low fare monitoring
Non-financial Advantages	*Non-financial Disadvantages*
1. Specialization—may result in the best possible prices to and from specialized destinations and better prices for specialized services 2. Each corporate account is very important 3. Convenient locations 4. Ticket delivery sometimes offered "On Demand" 5. More personalized service 6. Dedicated agents—in some medium-sized agencies	1. Parking programs are seldom offered 2. Dedicated agents rare—especially in small agencies due to shortage of agents 3. Less experienced agents who are paid less 4. Reports—none or only pre-structured savings report 5. Seldom any quality control—almost never any comprehensive quality control

FIGURE 8.4 (cont'd.). Large vs. small travel agencies: advantages and disadvantages.

were encouraged to go out and get additional accounts and build up their business, primarily through leisure travel. The emphasis now encourages agencies to move business from one carrier to another carrier.

For example, if airline "A" has received $2 million in travel bookings from a travel agency in the previous twelve months and the records indicate that airline "B," a direct competitor, received $5 million of bookings from that same agency during the same time period, airline "A" might approach the agency and offer an override commission or an additional commission if the agency moves some of its traditional bookings from airline "B" to airline "A." This percentage can result in a substantial amount of additional money. Therefore, many agencies seriously pursue it. The problem is, it can affect the ability of a corporate traveler to obtain the best possible travel arrangements.

An agent working with one of the top twenty corporate travel-oriented travel agencies in Denver recently made the following comment:

When a client calls, unless there is more than a $15 difference in air fare, I book them with our preferred carrier rather than any other carrier. If they ask for another carrier, I usually tell them that that airline's flight is full. We get agent bonuses for producing business with our preferred carrier and I always earn the bonus.

This agent received over $2,000 in bonuses in one month for having sold a large number of preferred vendors ranging from the preferred air carrier to the preferred car rental company, preferred hotels, and even the preferred travel insurance carrier.

Because travel agencies selling preferred vendors can increase their earnings, the agents working for those agencies are often encouraged to sell preferred vendors. One way of encouragaing agents to select preferred vendors is to pay a bonus to the agent if the preferred vendor is utilized. Although most agencies claim that they sell a preferred air carrier only when the price is the same or less expensive and when there is no measureable difference in flight departure or arrival time or other factors that would affect service to the client, the corporate travel manager needs to be sensitive not only to the service differences between carriers (when one with an inferior service standard is the preferred carrier of its travel agency) but also to the financial ramifications.

One of the financial ramifications is *revenue sharing*. The revenue sharing concept is simply that the travel agency provides a percentage of its override commissions to a corporate account when that account agrees to be included in preferred carrier sales strategies. In other words, if the corporate account agrees that it will be willing to utilize a preferred carrier when all other factors are equal, then a percentage of the override commission is paid to the account. Corporate travel managers reason that unless there is a major difference in services, there is no reason why they should not obtain a percentage of override commissions. This is especially true when the preferred air carrier has a reputation for providing superior service and amenities. However, the corporate travel manager has an obligation to make certain that there is no additional cost factor involved. Although an agency's management may very well state that they will not sell a preferred air carrier if the price is greater than a competing carrier's price, when that travel agency offers bonuses to its agent employees, there is always a danger that the employee will be like the one quoted above who makes certain that she obtains the bonus even at an expense of up to $15 per booking to the client.

A variation of the revenue sharing concept is one whereby the corporate travel manager approaches competing airlines and, having the statistics in hand, offers to have a certain percentage of the business's travel switched from one carrier to another in exchange for a direct payment. In this way, the corporate travel manager is able to receive all of the override commission rather than having to share a percentage of it with the travel agency. Some airlines are hesitant to make a direct payment to corporate travel managers and, therefore, they work out arrangements to make out the check for the override commission directly to the travel agency (with the agency signing the check over to the corporate account). This arrangement bypasses the travel agency altogether (in terms of an override commission being paid on the travel for personnel where the corporate travel manager has reached direct negotiation agreement with the air carrier). Obviously, travel agencies are not pleased with such an arrangement, but some have accepted such an arrangement in order to retain the commercial account.

Still another arrangement is a cooperative airline/agency approach. When an air carrier approaches a travel agency with an override offer if that agency moves a large percentage of its travel to it from a competing carrier, sometimes

115

Agency
Preferred
Vendors and
the Financial
Effects on
Commercial
Accounts

the airline lets the agency approach the agency's corporate accounts on behalf of the airline with a corporate account override package designed to get the corporate account to change preferred vendors also. Figure 8.5 shows pertinent paragraphs in a letter to a corporate travel executive encouraging such a change.

Although corporate travel managers may audit the savings report submitted by the travel agency on a month-by-month basis to make certain that the best fares were obtained, if the agent has requested best fares by carrier from the computer rather than overall best fare, many of the reports will not reflect that a fare other than the best fare has been obtained. The reason is that the computer will respond to the agent request with the best fares on the designated carrier. It will not reflect that there might have been a better fare on another carrier. The result is that the computer-generated saving report will show that the best fare was obtained.

To overcome this potential for bias, the corporate travel manager either needs to do an independent spot check fare search or contract with a fare check company to do a periodic audit. Otherwise, there is a strong potential for the travel agency to consistently sell higher priced tickets that are reflected as the best fares simply because the agent only accessed the best fare with the preferred carrier(s). Obviously, the same concerns apply to car rental bookings, hotel bookings, and other services or products obtained from travel agencies.

Agency bias also is affected when it comes to selecting one airline as compared to another by a computer reservation system. All of the major travel agency computer reservation systems are affiliated with airlines or airline groups. They are as follows:

- American Airlines—SABRE computer system;
- United Airlines—APOLLO computer system;
- Trans World Airlines and Northwest Orient Airlines—PARS reservation system;
- Delta Airlines—DATAS II reservation system; and
- Eastern Airlines and Continental Airlines—SYSTEM ONE.

Although airlines may emphasize in their literature that their systems are not biased, most analysts agree that there is at least some bias in every system. Whether or not the systems are biased, the airlines, and the industry as a whole recognize that every study has shown that travel agencies book more of the flights offered by the airline whose computer reservation system they are utilizing, than they book of any competing carrier.

Recognizing this, there has been a strong effort on the part of airlines to encourage travel agencies to buy and utilize their systems as compared to competing airline systems. Major price breaks have been offered to travel agencies and some airlines offer substantial amounts of free and/or reduced rate tickets to the travel agency when the agency selects their computer system. Some in the industry suggest that this is another form of rebating or of paying an override to the travel agency by an airline because the airline is absorbing many of the costs of the computer system and not passing those costs along to their travel agency computer subscribers. Whether or not this is a form of rebating, the corporate

Dear

Per our phone conversation today, I wanted to provide more detail, for your consideration, pertaining to the _____ offer we have negotiated with _____ Airlines for a 20% reduction of the normal coach airfares to your most frequently traveled destinations. Following is a listing of the cities involved and a comparative analysis of how the 20% relates to "typical" discounted rates currently in the market along with a brief description of what is required with regard to advance purchase and penalty applications for those particular fares:

City	20% Discount	Market Discount	Fare Requirements
	$480.00	$530.00	7day—25%
	644.80	510.00	none-limited seats
	512.00	564.00	7day—25%
	704.00	550.00	none-limited seats
	456.00	504.00	7day—25%
	512.00	518.00	none-limited seats
	512.00	564.00	7day—25%
	512.00	564.00	7day—25%
	158.40	138.00	none-limited seats
	217.60	160.00	none-limited seats

If this program appeals to you, _____ would propose to have you sign a contract that would extend the offer through the end of the year. The program would then be extended into _____ if it has resulted in a 50% market share for _____ in these _____ specific markets in

In addition, _____ would like to establish a VIP program for approximately 10 of your travelers that basically provides for automatic upgrades to first class on all flights.

I will be in contact with _____ to see if we can schedule a meeting at a mutually convenient time to discuss this program.

Sincerely,

FIGURE 8.5. Sample Letter.

travel manager needs to be aware of the strong correlation between having a particular computer system and selling that system's airline with a preference. On the other hand, if the corporate travel department or upper management has made a decision that one carrier is better than another, the corporate travel manager may wish to seek a travel agency vendor that works with the computer system for the airline which the corporate travel manager's business has selected as the preferred airline for that business.

Summary

There are those who consider managing for profit in a business travel department to be managers concentrating on *monitoring*. Certainly, monitoring plays a large role for corporate travel departments, but many agree that monitoring travel expenses and travel service vendor suppliers is only one part of managing for profits. Accurate projections of travel budgets can save a company money by requiring less in liquid asset availability. This comes from keeping excellent records, drawing upon the knowledge of industry experts, and working closely with the head of each department budgeting for travel. Good travel expense policy formulation and the distribution of travel policies can also assist in managing for profits. Understanding tax considerations, especially as they relate to the 1986 Tax Law, staying within the tax stipulated per diem regulations, and making certain that the expense records required under the tax law are maintained, can assist in making certain that travel expense excesses subject to tax will not occur.

However, expense monitoring remains one of the best ways to save money thus effecting the overall profits of the company. This is undertaken primarily through a series of financial reports. Although a few financial reports relate to the travel department itself, corporate travel reports and travel vendor expense reports need to be designed and reviewed so that the corporate travel department is constantly aware of any problems. Exception reports are becoming more and more common, enabling the corporate travel manager to spot either potential or real problem areas right away.

One of the best ways to manage for profits is to work closely with the vendor travel agency on financial management. Before a corporate travel manager is in a position to negotiate the most profitable arrangement possible with a travel agency, it is necessary to understand how important the corporate travel account is or would be to the travel agency vendor or potential travel agency vendor. To understand this, the corporate travel manager must understand both the extent of travel volume generated within the company and how travel agencies make money. By understanding that travel agencies work on a commission basis and earn most of their commissions through the sale of airline tickets, the corporate travel manager can determine the financial effect on a travel agency of any individual trip booking. This can be extended to all travel placed with the travel agency. While travel agencies work on a base average of ten percent commission, they are expected by corporate travel departments to provide a wide range of services. They are required to always obtain the lowest air fares possible, to confirm car rental and hotel bookings at the best possible rates, deliver tickets whenever the tickets are needed, and to provide a myriad of other services.

Travel agencies can find themselves in the position of spending more money to provide travel products and services than they earn in commissions. This is especially true when there are several changes on travel documents and the average change factor is very high.

Personnel costs constitute the major expense for the average travel agency. However, it is possible for an agency to manipulate variables in order to obtain or extend profits earned from serving commercial accounts. By assigning dedicated agents to corporate accounts based upon the salary of the agent and the return on investment from the corporate account, travel agencies can often make a profit from a specific corporate account on which the agency had previously lost money. However, when less capable personnel are assigned as dedicated agents to a corporate account, the ability to obtain best fares and to serve the account may decrease. Therefore, it is important that corporate travel managers be concerned with the qualifications of the dedicated agent or agents serving their account.

An understanding of the travel agency break-even formula (and an extension of that formula to a profit formula) can provide the corporate travel manager with a tool for beginning to understand whether or not its vendor travel agency is making a profit on its account thereby giving him/her a tool for determining the approximate extent of the profit earned. This recognition can assist a corporate travel manager in negotiating for rebates or a share of override commissions. The basic formula consists of dividing expenses by average commission to determine the amount of sales needed to break-even. If one adds both figures for profits and return on investment to the expenses in this basic formula, and then divides the figure determined by combining expenses, profit, and return on investment by average commission, the resulting figure will identify the amount of sales needed to not only break-even, but to pay investors a return on investment and to provide a profit for the travel agency.

Obviously, one of the key factors in this formula is the amount of commissions. As commission levels increase, the amount of sales needed to break-even, provide a return on investment, and to provide a profit decreases. Therefore, *override* commissions can be very important to a travel agency. Travel agencies can earn greater commissions or override commissions from vendor air carriers, hotels, car rental companies, and others by either selling more total volume of these supplier vendor services or by increasing the percentage of *market share* of bookings with these vendors as compared to other vendors. For example, an override commission might be earned by a travel agency if it is able to move twenty or thirty percent of its air bookings from all other carriers to a "favored" carrier.

Override commissions can be quite extensive. They can in some cases increase the income earned per booking by as much as fifty percent. Obviously, from the standpoint of a corporate travel manager, the ability to obtain best prices and to convert sales to favored vendors may be impossible. The corporate travel manager, therefore, must constantly make certain that selling favored vendors in order to increase commissions does not raise the price per ticket or hurt the service level provided to the corporate traveler. However, when override commissions are earned by the travel agency for business that is generated from a company's corporate travel, the corporate travel manager often expects to receive a part of the override commission in what is commonly called a *commission or revenue sharing* arrangement. This can provide a substantial amount of income coming back to the corporate travel department. This income can be even more substantial if a negotiated rebate is added to the profit sharing arrangement.

When working with travel agencies, therefore, it is important for the corporate travel manager to identify a travel agency that can not only provide excellent service, but has the volume of business to negotiate for high override commissions, as well as the ability to provide rebates. Generally speaking, the larger a travel agency is, the greater its ability to negotiate for override commissions. Therefore, it is essential for the corporate travel manager to compare the pros and cons of working with large travel agencies versus small travel agencies. Even when a contractual agreement is developed with a travel agency to provide best fares, rebates, and profit sharing while still offering a high standard of service, the corporate travel manager must always be atuned to the possibility of agency bias. This is especially true as it relates to bias in booking air travel. If the base price of a ticket is considerably greater than might otherwise be possible, rebates and override "commissions or revenue sharing" commission payments to the corporate travel department will probably not be enough to make up for the difference in the base price of the tickets. Spot checks and outside audits can provide a way for the corporate travel manager to make sure that costly biases do not enter the travel agency service arrangements.

While the factors brought out in this chapter are essential for the corporate travel manager to manage for profits, there are many factors discussed in the other financial management chapters which can add to the corporate travel manager's ability to manage for profits as well. Therefore, the corporate travel manager should not look at the factors discussed in this chapter as being exclusive in terms of managing for profits, but should recognize that these factors, when combined with those brought out in the other chapters on financial management can provide the corporate travel manager with an opportunity to maximize profits.

Discussion Questions

1. In addition to cutting costs, profits can be realized by the corporate travel department by bringing money back to the company in what form?

2. Most corporate travel departments find the largest amount of vendor financial management opportunity comes in dealing with what category of vendors?

3. This chapter discussed three tools that some travel agencies utilize in obtaining profits in working with corporate travel accounts. What are these three tools?

4. Why might travel agency size be one of the major factors considered by corporate travel managers in selecting travel agency vendors?

5. Why might preferred vendor arrangements negotiated by travel agencies in working with air carriers, hotels, car rental firms, and other suppliers control a most important financial relationship between corporate travel departments and travel agencies?

6. What kind of records should a corporate travel manager maintain and where might a corporate travel manager turn for assistance in projecting travel budgets for individual departments in the business?

7. What might a corporate travel manager do to determine a very close approximation of next year's air fare costs for any single trip as well as for multiple trips?

8. Why might accurate budget projections for travel costs, in themselves, provide a substantial savings for a business?

9. What mechanics or processes might a business go through to provide its corporate travel manager with a budget that can not only give each person who will be preparing departmental budgets a good projection of travel costs, but will give the corporate travel manager a good indication of projected total corporate travel costs?

10. What costs might be reduced or eliminated by distributing travel expense policies widely within a business?

11. In what way did the 1986 Tax Reform Act affect business travelers and what can corporate travel managers do to save money and stay within the regulations of the 1986 Tax Reform Act?

12. What is meant by the statement, "Normally, monitoring is undertaken on an exception reporting basis?"

13. What are the three types of basic financial reports developed and worked with by most corporate travel departments?

14. What are three of the departmental reports prepared by many corporate travel departments?

15. What are three types of corporate travel reports? Explain the purpose of each.

16. Why is it important to understand how important one's account is to the vendor travel agency?

17. How can a corporate travel manager calculate the approximate average amount earned by the vendor travel agency for arranging a trip for a specific business traveler?

18. What are the major services provided by travel agencies in return for the commissions earned?

19. Travel agency personnel costs constitute approximately what percentage of total travel agency costs?

20. What are the two ways a travel agency has of altering the financial arrangements with a commercial account in order to create or to increase profitability?

21. How does the Commercial Account Commissions Report work and why is it important that corporate travel managers understand how it works?

22. What factors within the control of the corporate travel manager or the corporate travel manager's business affect the profitability of a dedicated agent for that agent's travel agency?

23. How might the employee cost per hour factor affect service for a corporate travel account?

24. Why might a travel agency with few corporate accounts be able to serve a business client less well than might a travel agency with a large number of corporate accounts?

25. What is the travel agency break-even formula?

26. What is the difference between *earnings* and *sales?*

27. What is an *override commission?*

28. Why does the definition of travel agency *profit* often hinge on the definition of *break-even?*

29. What is done to change the break-even formula to a profit formula?

30. Why might a corporate travel manager need to first determine whether or not the figures quoted by a travel agency are figures designed to reach true break-even point or figures designed to reach a break-even point based on having a profit, as well as breaking even in a case where an agency professes that it has difficulties in terms of meeting the financial agreements it has agreed to with a corporate travel account?

31. Why might business travel departments which participate in profit sharing arrangements be concerned with override commission levels? Explain what kind of dollars might be involved in profit sharing override commission arrangements.

32. What are the advantages and the disadvantages of working with large travel agencies?

33. What are the advantages and the disadvantages of working with small travel agencies?

34. Why can large travel agencies employ people and buy systems that will provide for true "best fare" continuous searching?

35. How has the "preferred vendor" emphasis changed and how does this affect the ability of a corporate traveler to obtain the best possible travel arrangements?

36. How might the variation of revenue sharing whereby a corporate travel manager approaches air carriers directly rather than going through a travel agency result in the receipt of greater income for the corporate travel department?

37. In what way might a saving report be biased?

38. How might agency bias be affected as it relates to selecting one air carrier as compared to another air carrier by the computer reservation system utilized by that agency?

Role Play Exercise

Two students may participate in this role play either out of class, as a fun way to review the chapter, or as an in-class exercise. One plays the role of the Travel Agency Sales Executive and the other plays the role of the Corporate Travel

Manager. Please read the script and then pick up the conversation in your own words.

Travel Agency Sales Executive: Thank you for meeting with me. We are anxious to obtain your account and I would like to spend just a few minutes familiarizing you with the services we offer.

Corporate Travel Manager: I am always interested in learning about what travel agencies have to offer. It is a very competitive industry and there are new developments all the time. Frankly, however, our major concern is financial management. What can you do for us to save money and to return some money back to the company?

Travel Agency Sales Executive: As a start, we guarantee to give you the very lowest priced air fares. In addition, our arrangements with air carriers give us higher commissions than many other travel agencies obtain and we pass on some of these extra or override commissions to our corporate accounts.

Corporate Travel Manager: We get rebates, shared, commissions, and a best fare guarantee from the travel agency we are using now. Please be specific. What do you have to offer in terms of financial benefits that we don't get now?

Travel Agency Sales Executive: It sounds like you have a good package of benefits, but we can do better. To start off with . . .

CONTINUE ON YOUR OWN

Group Discussion Situation:
The New President's Travel Agency

Two days ago Greg Grouch, the President of Hotr Humidifiers, called Ms. Primn Proper, the corporate travel manager for Hotr Humidifiers, into his office. He confidentially advised Ms. Proper that he had sold his stock and taken a position with another firm. The Board of Directors of Hotr Humidifiers had been trying very hard to get the industry's financial wizard, Slick Cosnostra, to take the position, but they could not come to terms on remuneration. Finally, last week Slick reached an agreement with the Board that he would take the position at the salary offered if the Board would agree to use Slick's travel agency (he owns 100 percent of the stock), Al Cheepo Travel, as Hotr Humidifiers' exclusive travel agency. The Board agreed. Greg advised Ms. Proper that a meeting had been set up for tomorrow. She will meet with the Chairman of the Board to discuss ways to integrate the $4.5 million travel operation at Hotr Humidifiers with Al Cheepo Travel right away so that when Slick comes on board as the new President, all travel will have been routed through Al Cheepo Travel.

You are meeting today to finalize a written set of recommendations for Ms. Proper. You are expected to reach agreement and to write a two-page summary set of recommendations designed to guide Ms. Proper in preparing for the meeting and in planning what she should say or suggest to the Chairman of the Board.

In your group session, select one person to chair the group. All will have an equal vote on decisions. In the group session you are expected to reach agree-

COMMERCIAL ACCOUNT COMMISSIONS REPORT

Period Ended_____

ACCOUNT NAME	AIR BOOKINGS	AIR COMM.	OTHER BOOKINGS	OTHER COMM.	TOTAL COMM.	# SALES HOURS	AVG. COMM. PER SLS. HR
							+
TOTAL							

FIGURE 8.6. A Blank Commercial Account Commissions Report (to be completed in the Analytical Travel Commercial Account Analysis exercise).

ment on the structure and basic content of the summary set of recommendations and to prepare the two-page paper to be presented to the entire class by the chair of your committee.

Analytical Travel Commercial Account Analysis

To practice identifying the value of the individual corporate travel accounts to travel agencies, study the four accounts that XYZ Travel is analyzing. These are:

1. New Knus, Inc.;
2. Daughters of Geriatric Undertakers;
3. The National Association of Happy Hoopers; and
4. Karl Marx Financial Management.

You may wish to use the blank *Commercial Account Commissions Report* form provided in Figure 8.6 on which to jot down data and to start an analysis of the four
accounts. After reviewing and analyzing the four accounts, answer the three
questions below the data for each of the four accounts.

ANALYTICAL TRAVEL COMMERCIAL ACCOUNT ANALYSIS

Account: New Knus, Inc.		Account: National Association of Happy Hoopers	
Air Bookings Last Quarter	$1,721	Air Bookings Last Quarter	$13,769
Average Air Commissions Last Quarter	10.2%	Average Air Commissions Last Quarter	9.7%
Other Bookings Last Quarter	$579	Other Bookings Last Quarter	$9,727
Average Other Booking Commissions	9.8%	Average Other Booking Commissions	13.6%
Sales Hours	12.40	Sales Hours	31.50
Employee Cost Per Hour	$6.73	Employee Cost Per Hour	$18.68

Account: Daughters of Geriatric Undertakers		Account: Karl Marx Financial Management	
Air Bookings Last Quarter	$7,202	Air Bookings Last Quarter	$32,200
Average Air Commissions Last Quarter	10.05%	Average Air Commissions Last Quarter	8.4%
Other Bookings Last Quarter	$2,007	Other Bookings Last Quarter	$7,201
Average Other Booking Commissions	11%	Average Other Booking Commissions	10.01%
Sales Hours	35.40	Sales Hours	91.60
Employee Cost Per Hour	$14.81	Employee Cost Per Hour	$16.42

1. Which of these accounts is of greatest value to the travel agency?

2. By changing employees (dedicated agents) who handle accounts, perhaps by
   firing some agent(s) and hiring one or more less expensive agent(s), can the
   agency turn one or more of the marginal accounts above into profitable
   accounts?

3. The corporate travel manager of which of the above accounts would have the
   best negotiating position? What might be negotiated?

CHAPTER 9

Saving Money

Introduction

In spite of the fact that travel costs are constantly increasing, corporate travel managers must still justify their positions through the ability to save money on corporate travel for their companies. Savings opportunities can be reviewed by analyzing potential savings in each component area of business travel. Because it is the largest travel expense for most companies, air travel offers the largest area for potential savings.

Best-fare guarantees are becoming one of the favorite ways of saving money on air travel. However, there are at least four types of best-fare guarantees provided by vendors in the market today. These will be discussed in detail in this chapter with the pros and cons of each presented so that the corporate travel manager can select the type of best-fare guarantee most desired.

Providing *conversion ability* is relatively new to the travel industry, but it can save companies as much as twenty percent of ticket costs.

Alternative routings present still another opportunity for air travel cost savings. These are used less often in the industry than most corporate travel managers would like.

Negotiations present an excellent chance for corporate travel managers to save money on air travel. An increasing number of corporate travel managers are taking advantage of this opportunity for saving.

Hotel savings can also be substantial. Business travelers utilize published hotel commercial rates on a regular basis. Travel-agency negotiated commercial rates, multi-corporate department consortium-negotiated commercial rates, and especially corporate travel manager-negotiated commercial rates can lower the price per room night to a level that is twenty to thirty percent less than published commerical rates in some cases.

Car rental savings offer still another opportunity to save money on corporate travel. All major national and international car rental franchisors publish corporate rates. However, travel-agency negotiated special rates and especially corporate travel manager-negotiated rates with individual franchisees can result in substantially lower costs for corporate travelers who rent cars.

Parking is a cost that is sometimes overlooked. Yet, parking charges can mount up. Negotiating reduced cost parking arrangements provides still another opportunity to save money on corporate travel. Other cost saving approaches discussed in this chapter include the management of frequent flier programs, ghost cards, and both internal computer hardware and software cost savings.

Documenting savings can be as important to corporate travel managers as creating the savings. It is often essential that documentation and reports be both precise and clear. This chapter discussed traditional savings reports and their applicability, but it also reviews annual and year-to-date reports as well as internal departmental reports.

The last part of this chapter discusses rebates. Getting cash back from suppliers provides an opportunity to not only save money, but in some cases to make money for the corporate travel department. Rebates also offer potential pitfalls which can provide hidden costs. In addition, rebates can come in both hard and soft forms. Therefore, corporate travel managers must analyze rebate opportunities carefully to determine which will present the best overall package of benefits for the company. The chapter ends with a discussion of rebates since this provides a beginning opportunity for looking at agency affiliation arrangements that hold out the possibility of the corporate travel department actually making money for the company and moving from a cost center to a profit center. These agency affiliation arrangements are discussed in the next chapter while the potential of moving from the status of a cost center to a profit center is discussed in the following chapter.

Travel Savings

One of the tasks corporate travel managers undertake is a charge to save money for the firms for which they work. When the costs of travel components go up, financial executives often look at the total annual expenditures rather than the total amount of savings. This becomes an increasing challenge for corporate travel managers who have obtained substantial savings in the past. They must continue to work with each component of the travel product to get better and better prices if, in fact, the corporate travel manager is able to show an annual budgetary saving each year in total travel costs.

The reality of economics is against the corporate travel manager in these efforts. The cost of living is constantly increasing and average travel component prices are also going up sometimes at a more rapid rate than the cost of living. Therefore, in their reports to management many corporate travel managers are quoting not only total travel costs as compared with what they were last year, but they are building in and showing a factor relating to cost-of-living increase and to average travel component increase (such as average ticket price increases in the U.S. as compared to the average ticket price increases for the tickets provided for their company). It is in ways such as this that corporate travel managers are able to identify their ability to save money for their companies.

However, saving money comes down to analyzing each component of the travel product and devising strategies for savings in each of these areas. In addition, it is possible to save money through managing frequent flier programs. And finally, corporate travel managers can save money on their own internal expenses when it comes to computer hardware and software.

Air Travel Savings

The largest area for potential savings, however, comes with air travel. There are six major management tools which the corporate travel manager may utilize in working with airline and travel agency vendors to provide air travel savings. These are:

1. best-fare guarantees;
2. discount guarantees;
3. low-fare checks;
4. the conversion ability;
5. negotiations; and
6. alternative routings.

BEST-FARE GUARANTEES

The most popular of these savings areas is the best-fare guarantee. Almost all commercial business-oriented travel agencies are offering a best-fare guarantee. This comes in several forms. The most traditional is for a travel agency in its proposals to simply say that it guarantees to provide the very lowest fare possible at the time that a reservation is made. Although this may initially sound positive, all that it is saying is that the travel agency will check and obtain a good fare if it is available when the agency is making a reservation. Every commercial account which expresses concern about costs expects its agency to obtain the best possible fare (contingent upon the limitations relating to the trip, of course). Therefore, this type of best-fare guarantee is the least beneficial of all best-fare guarantees and it is the type that saves the least amount of money.

Reimbursement Best-fare Guarantee. A slightly better best-fare guarantee is one that is backed up with a statement from the travel agency that if the agency does not obtain the very lowest fare available at the time the reservation is made consistent with the requirements for the trip, the agency will pay the difference between the best fare and the fare that it obtained. Again, this may appear on the surface to be a very positive and a very beneficial guarantee. However, seldom does an agency pay the corporate account because it is so expensive for a corporate account to go back and prove to an agency that there was a lower fare available at the time the reservation was made which the agency did not pick up. Traditionally, when a client calls an airline directly and finds a less expensive fare, the agency response is that that fare became available after the reservation was made as a result of another person cancelling. The cancelled, discounted seat becoming available again in the airline inventory created the lower fare.

Quality Control Best-fare Process. A third type of best-fare guarantee recognizes that there can be cancellations of reservations for people who have discounted fares, that airlines may lower prices on selected flights from time to time, or that for some other reason a less expensive fare might become available after the reservation is initially made. One approach toward obtaining better fares which may become available after the initial reservation is made, is a *quality control* *process.* This quality control process can be a simple one, such as having another agent recheck the initial reservation to see if something less expensive is available, or it can become sophisticated by having as many as five or ten additional checks. In reviewing proposals, it would appear that the most popular of these quality control processes is one whereby a final check to determine if there is a better fare available is made on each reservation immediately before ticketing that reservation. In other words, the agent makes an effort to obtain the best fare possible at the time the reservation is requested and the person issuing the ticket for the travel agency makes a second (or at least, a final) effort to determine whether or not a better fare has become available immediately before issuing the ticket.

Guaranteed Discount Best-fare. Still another approach toward getting best fares is the travel agency *guaranteed discount.* With a travel agency discount guarantee program, the agency guarantees to a corporate travel account in its proposals to the account that it will provide a percentage discount off of regular economy fare for all tickets provided to that business. The amount of the percentage discount is often negotiable. Obviously, if the discount is a relatively small one, the agency will have no difficulty in reaching that average discount on readily available discounted tickets provided to the corporate account most of the time. This remains true unless that corporate account makes all or almost all of its reservations at the last minute. On the other hand, if the guaranteed discount amount is substantial, the travel agency may find that it is unable to provide a sufficient number of discounted reservations to make it economically profitable for the agency to handle the account. However, from the viewpoint of the corporate travel manager, a travel agency guaranteed discount off of regular economy fares can be attractive. Quoting a Runzheimer study, *The Travel Agent* magazine (May 25, 1987, page 1 BTR) indicates that, "client satisfaction appears high," with discount guarantee programs.

Continuous Low-fare Check. In terms of economic benefit to the business, probably the optimum best-fare guarantee is that which is offered through *continuous low-fare checks.* With this system, the travel agency contracts with a reservations monitoring vendor to obtain continuous checking of availability of lower fare reservations for all current reservations for the corporate account. These checks are undertaken by a computer which can check as many as 180 records per hour. It constantly checks those records it is programmed to check. According to Carl Schwab and Richard Law of Price Waterhouse, "it may be possible to save upwards of twenty-five percent, without any loss in service or performance" using their Air Auditor system. ("Air Travel Costs: Flying Out of Control," Price Waterhouse, 1987, Number 3, p. 17). Jay Rea quotes a savings of $3,440 in one month for one corporation for which his company, CompuCheck, analyzed 338 records.

There is something of a game being played in the industry between those who provide low-fare checks and air carrier yield management departments. While the yield management departments constantly manipulate fares to obtain the highest possible income from each flight, low-fare check companies are constantly striving to identify the particular fares which yield management departments reduce in order to pick up these fares for their corporate clients before some other low-fare check company, travel agency, or traveler picks up the lowered fare seats. In a speech at the Association of Corporate Travel Executives' 1989 conference, Barbara Amster, Vice President of Pricing and Yield Management for American Airlines, pointed out that the conversion of higher priced reservations to lower priced seats made available by her yield management efforts has become one of the problems that has made her job especially hard. Although individual carriers will probably find ways of blocking corporate travel higher ticket reservation cancellations on their own carriers and rebooking yield management lowered price seat tickets through such vehicles as reservation cancellation penalties, name check blocks, and other techniques, it can be expected that both manual and computerized low fare checks will continue to be a major vehicle for taking advantage of yield management lowered fares when switching from one carrier to another carrier.

Discount Guarantees. The best-fare guarantee, that some consider to offer the best of all possible alternatives, is the *guaranteed discount fare*. Under this arrangement, travel agencies guarantee to their corporate accounts that the corporate account will receive billings for the air tickets issued for a specific percentage off of published economy fares. The travel agency risks getting fares that are at or below the guaranteed discount price, but the agency bills clients based upon a price determined by taking an agreed-upon percentage of the normal full-economy fare and subtracting the dollar amount of that discount from the full-economy fare.

There is an opportunity with this type of best-fare guarantee for mutual benefits. The travel agency has an opportunity to make more money than it might otherwise make by consistently getting tickets for its clients at prices below the guaranteed discount level. On the other hand, the corporate travel manager can guarantee to top management that a specific discount can be obtained across the board. In addition, although fares change on a regular basis, cost projections for air travel can improve when the corporate travel manager understands that those projections are based on a percentage of full-economy fares. The full-economy fares change less frequently than the discounted fares and often can be tracked historically more easily. In its "Business Travel Report" of May 25, 1987, *The Travel Agent* magazine advises that, "A recent survey of 128 corporate travel managers by Runzheimer showed twenty-one percent already involved in (obtaining agent discount guarantees)." The Runzheimer report indicated that guaranteed average discounts, ". . . go as high as thirty percent." A 1985 Air Transport Association of America study quoted in the report indicated that ". . . eighty-five percent of all revenue passenger miles were at discounted fares, with an average discount of fifty-six percent." A 1986 Topaz Enterprises audit quoted in the article indicated that, ". . . the average percentage off full-coach for tickets offered to corporate clients (was) 33.6 percent."

Although the travel agency offering guaranteed discounts may expect to track the history of the corporation before offering such guarantees, and certainly a business that orders tickets at the last minute with a substantial percentage of day-before-travel ticket changes, may provide the travel agency with a lack of opportunity to obtain a high percentage of discounted fares. Obviously, the average statistics quoted above provide the travel agency with an opportunity to earn a better than ten percent commission while providing corporate travel managers with a satisfactory guaranteed savings. *The Travel Agent* report noted that, ". . . client satisfaction appears high."

Conversion Ability

In the mid-1980s large corporate-oriented travel agencies and airlines negotiated agreements whereby the travel agency would be able to provide its corporate accounts with discounted fares at all times. This *conversion ability* offered the travel agency the ability to convert a regular economy fare to a discounted fare whenever the discounted fares were sold out and the request was within the appropriate time frame. Initially, agencies called a specially designated phone number in the reservations offices of the airline involved and a designated reservations agent would convert full-economy fares to a discounted fare. Although the most deeply discounted fares were never included in the conversion ability, utilization of this ability has been able to provide corporate travel managers with an opportunity to save in excess of $100 per ticket in some cases. Corporate travel managers report that savings are seldom less than $30 to $40 per ticket.

In exchange for this ability, the airlines expect travel agents to sell their carrier with a preference and, normally, even the largest travel agencies are provided with the conversion ability only by the air carrier with which they have contracted for computer reservations equipment. Recent trends, however, indicate that some large commercial-oriented travel agencies have obtained conversion ability from more than one carrier and in some cases from carriers that do not have or offer travel agency computerization.

Although the conversion ability virtually guarantees corporate travelers of having some type of discount on every ticket, the actual utilization of conversion ability varies from market to market, depending upon the competitiveness of that market and the degree of discounted fares available at any particular point in time in the fare inventories available. During non-peak travel times in many markets, the lack of discounted fares is seldom found. In other markets, however, and during peak travel periods (such as Christmas and New Years), discounted fares can sell out quite rapidly and the conversion ability can mean a substantial savings for corporate travel managers.

Alternative Routings

Typically, when a travel agency receives a call from a corporate account for a trip request, the travel agency pulls up availability for that trip to determine the best fare possible and the most convenient flights. However, travel agency computers are programmed to search for the most direct routings possible. In most cases, direct routings and non-stop flights are the only type that are acceptable to corporate travelers. They wish to arrive at their destinations in the most expeditious manner possible. However, on some domestic itineraries and on many international itineraries, there are no direct flights available and it is necessary for the traveler to change planes, at least once. Many travel agencies will select the easiest and most apparent route rather than search for the least expensive routing.

Although the least expensive routing may very well involve one or more hours of additional travel time, savings can be substantial. By negotiating with travel agency vendors and insisting upon having cost versus convenience alternatives provided when plane changes are involved, corporate travel managers have the opportunity of saving hundreds of dollars. Some corporate travel managers routinely work with two or more travel agencies whenever there is a complicated domestic or international flight, advising the agencies that they will be competing with one another to obtain the business for these flights. Although some agencies will refuse to enter into flight-by-flight competitive fare searches, other agencies are happy to search out alternative routings that will provide the best possible fares.

NEGOTIATIONS

With the range of opportunities available for air travel savings, corporate travel managers will find that travel agencies will select options and often will provide two or in some cases three options in their proposals. After determining which of the options or combinations of options will best fit their companies, corporate travel managers can still negotiate within the options presented. An increasing number of corporate travel managers are reviewing proposal air travel saving options, selecting the two or three potentially best vendors, and going back to those vendors with requests for additional savings. By negotiating additional travel savings programs or systems, corporate travel managers are often saving even more than the, "best deal" initially presented.

Hotel Savings

Although the bulk of travel savings often is realized through air travel savings programs, hotel prices in major cities have risen to such proportions that corporate travelers, with multi-day stays in expensive U.S. and international cities, are increasingly spending more money on hotel costs than on air travel.

COMMERCIAL RATES

Almost all hotels that cater to business clients have established commercial rates. Travel agencies normally attempt to obtain these commercial rates when booking hotels for their clients, but many corporate travel managers monitor rates to make certain that commercial rates are obtained on every booking. When a rate that is more than the published commercial rate is obtained, the corporate travel manager attempts to determine this in advance and he/she goes back requesting commercial rates.

Travel Agency-negotiated Hotel Commercial Rates. Several of the very large commercial-oriented travel agencies have joined agency consortiums which negotiate commercial rates for large numbers of corporate accounts. Because of their volume, they can often obtain commercial rates that are significantly less than published commercial rates. In some cases, these are ten percent to fifteen percent less than the published commercial rates.

Multi-corporate Department Consortium-negotiated Commercial Rates. There is a trend toward corporate travel departments working together in consortiums or in loose arrangements whereby one or more corporate travel managers negotiate on behalf of several companies to obtain corporate rates. Because the corporate travel manager has more direct control over the travelers and where they stay, hotels are sometimes more willing to provide lower commercial rates for corporate travel consortiums than for agency consortiums.

Corporate Travel Manager-negotiated Corporate Rates. Many corporate travel managers track the history of their travel and identify the number of nights travelers spend in major destination cities. By taking this data to the hotels and offering purchase guarantees based upon a percentage of history of nights of occupancy, corporate travel managers are often able to obtain substantially reduced hotel costs. The ideal arrangement for hoteliers is to have a contract guarantee. In order to obtain a guarantee, hoteliers will often reduce their commercial rates by as much as twenty to thirty percent. However, corporate travel managers need to be careful when negotiating for reduced commercial rates in order to insure that the quality of rooms provided will be as good as those offered at regular commercial rates or to the general public. Although this is usually not a problem, some corporate travel managers have found that the rooms that their travelers occupy are definitely inferior because of the very inexpensive price charged.

Car Rental Savings

As with hotels, corporate travel managers can save money on car rentals in many of the same ways. All major car rental companies have established commercial rates and it is customary for agents to book these rates. However, in many cases special rates are provided to companies simply by their asking the car rental representatives for rates for their companies. These special rates may be based on a presumption that the car rental company will be utilized wherever possible and that the car rental company will obtain a higher volume of rental throughout the U.S. and other countries than they might otherwise obtain due to their having provided this special rate for the corporate travel manager's company.

As in the case of hotels, travel agency consortiums also negotiate special rates for their clients and these special rates with many of the major car rental companies are, in some cases, less than the rates that are extended to individual companies by the same car rental firms. Larger companies have sometimes been able to negotiate with more senior executives in car rental organizations and obtain better rates than are extended by the sales representatives of the same firms. As in the case with hotels, a few groups of corporate travel managers have negotiated even better rates by having one member represent all corporations in the consortium. Again, the larger volume provides an incentive for car rental companies to negotiate a better rate.

In many cases, however, the most successful formula for getting excellent rates is to work with the individual franchisee rather than the national office of the car rental company. By identifying high-usage car rental cities (where the travelers of the corporate travel manager's firm rent cars frequently throughout the year) and the specific number of cars rented in a year (in each of these high usage cities), the corporate travel manager may approach car rental franchise owners in each of the high usage cities and negotiate directly with them for rates that tend to be considerably better than any of the nationally quoted rates. The reason for this is that those rates which are provided on a national basis must be high enough to be acceptable to the franchisee owners in each location. However, because each franchisee is not certain of the total volume that will be obtained based on these rates (even for a company that uses a very large number of cars all over the U.S.), the franchisee could be hesitant to provide the lowest possible rates. These, lowest possible rates, are offered to those who will provide a written guarantee. As in the case of hotels and hotel rooms, when the corporate travel manager will provide a written guarantee to the franchisee to purchase a specific minimum number of car rental days on a one-year or longer contract, the franchisee knows that those cars are sold at the guaranteed rate thus allowing him/her the maximum possible motivation for extending the lowest possible rates.

In obtaining the lowest possible rates under such a contract with an individual city location franchisee, the corporate travel manager should bring documentation proving past usage of car rentals in that city and should know the exact type of car preferred for corporate rental use. Contracts of this type normally specify that all renters will utilize a specific type of car or, at most, two types of cars. If possible, rental pick-up from one location (usually the airport) and return to the same location will assist in getting a better rate than rental at the airport and turn in downtown, or vice versa.

Finally, negotiating with the insurance company handling insurance for the corporate travel manager's company to cover collision damage (thus avoiding the collision damage waiver fee charged by car rental companies) will allow the corporate travel manager's company to save a substantial amount of money on car rentals. This can sometimes be as much as one fourth of the total normal daily car rental rate with collision damage waiver. Over a period of a year, with a substantial number of car rentals, the total amount of collision damage waiver fees paid by the corporation may well be several times the insurance premium charged by an insurance company on a blanket coverage for all drivers who rent cars while traveling on business trips for the company.

In addition to rates, other factors should be considered in car rental vendor negotiations. The history of maintenance is perhaps of greatest importance. A car rental company may offer excellent rates, but if travelers miss important meetings because of car break down, the savings become meaningless. Add-ons can sometimes be important too. Having a car phone can result in saving both time and money for many traveling business executives. These factors, therefore, should also be considered in negotiating for car rentals.

Parking

Parking at first may seem to be a small incidental cost as it relates to corporate travel, but adding up the parking charges incurred by business travelers, who drive their cars to the airport and leave them there until they return from their trips, can be a substantial expense for a company with a large number of business trips each year. As a result, obtaining parking cost reductions has

FIGURE 9.1. Car phones are sometimes provided for corporate travelers adding to their ability to complete their work while away from home. Photo courtesy of Hertz.

become one of the two major service "extras" requested by corporate travel managers according to a *Corporate Travel Special Report.* "In major cities, getting there—and parking—can be the toughest part of the trip," according to Harold Stevens of Stevens Travel Management in New York City.

A wide range of parking benefits are now being offered by travel agencies around the country. Some of the options offered are:

1. free parking at outlying locations with transfers on a regular basis to and from the airport, normally by shuttle bus or car;

2. reduced-rate parking at close-in airport locations (often the corporate traveler is provided with a percentage or a daily flat amount parking reimbursement after sending or presenting his parking receipt to the travel agency upon returning from a trip);

3. the agency purchase of a parking facility that may be an outlying lot, an airport hotel parking facility, or a multi-story parking garage and providing either free or discounted parking to clients; and

4. free or reduced-rate pick-up shuttles from the offices or homes of corporate travelers along with free or reduced-rate shuttle service back to their home or office when travelers return from their business trips (eliminating the need for airport parking).

In reviewing parking options, they are usually considered as extras rather than as the major reasons for selecting a travel agency vendor. Both cost reduction possibilities and service benefits or drawbacks for the traveler are important considerations in selecting parking programs. However, in addition, some agencies have installed agency branches or ticket pick-up offices in their airport parking facilities and the convenience of being able to pick up a ticket when one arrives at the point where the car is parked at the airport can provide an additional incentive for utilizing one agency as compared to another.

Frequent Flier Programs and Ghost Cards

In the early stages of deregulation air carriers recognized that they could attract more corporate travel by appealing directly to the business traveler. Frequent flier programs were introduced, providing free flights and air travel benefits to the frequent flier based on the number of air miles flown on the carrier over a period of time. The programs included such benefits as upgrades in service, reduced-rate tickets or free tickets, reduced or free airline lounge memberships, and a wide range of other benefits. To be able to obtain these benefits, the frequent flier would have to sign up for the program, thereby giving the air carrier direct contact information for those individuals who fly most often. The frequent business traveler provides his home address and airlines send frequent flier benefit information, coupons, upgrades, and free tickets directly to his home address. This effectively bypasses the corporate travel department and gives frequent fliers a wide range of air travel benefits paid for by the company through its purchase of business air travel tickets.

Many businesses have become concerned for a number of reasons. Comptrollers and other finance managers have frequently ruled that because the frequent flier program benefits and free tickets are earned as a result of tickets paid for by the company, then the free tickets, upgrades, and so forth should be the property of the company and not of the individual traveler. Others argue that the benefits provide an undue financial supplement for some company employees whereas others in the company do not receive them. Corporate travel managers and financial executives recognize that business travelers sometimes make reservations on carriers or for flights that cost the company more money than other available options in order to increase the traveler's frequent flier benefits, thereby costing the company more money in airline ticket costs.

On the other hand, there are those in business who believe that because the business traveler must fly on his own time, in many cases, and because he must put up with the hardships of travel, frequent flier benefits are a small way to compensate for this additonal effort for the company. In addition, they argue that bringing the frequent flier benefits into the company can be time consuming and will really make very little difference financially. In addition, administering a program whereby the company receives frequent flier benefits can be very difficult.

A few companies, however, have successfully taken advantage of frequent flier programs to reduce their total air travel costs. Because frequent flier programs are keyed to credit card systems, a *ghost card* is obtained in coordination with the company's travel agency and the home address for frequent fliers is shown as a post office box number or a company address. All benefit coupon vouchers or mailings are sent to the same address and are utilized by the corporate travel manager to obtain additional, but free, tickets and upgrades for those in the company who are traveling for company business. Although there has been some reluctance on the part of frequent flier corporate travelers to give up this benefit, when the frequent flier program is brought "in house" as soon as a corporate travel department is set up or in the early stages of travel by new companies, it has worked well since frequent travelers have not had the opportunity to obtain the benefits themselves since the beginning of the corporate travel program.

Saving Money on Internal Airline Computer Hardware

An increasing number of corporate travel departments are considering or have already installed reservation computers in their offices. The hardware includes CRTs (Cathode ray tube units), ticket printers, boarding pass printers, itinerary printers, and other printers for hard copy reports.

When such equipment is installed in a corporate travel department, there are costs involved as this equipment can be expensive. Traditional costs quoted by airline suppliers are in the range of $350 to $500 for each CRT, and $100 to $300 for each printer. In some cases, corporate travel managers have negotiated with their travel agency vendor to pick up the costs or some of the costs of this equipment. In other cases, the equipment is paid for by the corporate travel department. However, there have been a few cases where corporate travel departments have negotiated directly with air carriers and received airline computer reservation hardware at heavily reduced costs or in a few cases on a gratis basis.

Before negotiating with air carriers for computer reservations hardware, it is important to understand the benefits to an air carrier in having their equipment installed in a corporate travel department. There are two sources of income for an airline as it relates to having its equipment in either a travel agency or in a corporate travel department.

One source is income derived for ticket validation for other carrier ticket segments. Whenever more than one carrier is utilized on an itinerary, one of the airlines participating in the trip is considered the *sponsoring* or *validating carrier*. This means that the computer equipment validates the ticket normally on the carrier used for the first flight (on domestic trips) or for the first flight outside the U.S. (on international trips). However, since the agent can select the carrier on which the ticket is validated, frequently the airline whose hardware is being utilized is selected as the validating carrier. All monies generated from the sale of the ticket are sent to the validating carrier and it is the responsibility of the validating carrier to send payment to other participating carriers on the ticket in accordance with the cost of the air travel segments on those carriers. However, the validating carrier receives an income for the processing and accounting and this income, which is approximately $2.50 per flight segment, is considerably more than that needed to pay for actual processing and accounting. As a result, validating carriers can accrue a substantial profit for settling with the other carriers on flight segments. All of this, of course, depends upon validating on the carrier which provides the airline computer reservation hardware. However, a number of studies have identified a very strong correlation between validation preference and the carrier whose hardware is being utilized.

Airline Income for Computer Listing Other Carriers

A second, and much more important, source of income for airlines whose computers are installed in corporate travel departments comes from the sponsoring airline charging other carriers for each listing booked from listings in their reservation system. This charge accrues each time a booking is made on a carrier listed in the computer system. For example, if a corporate travel department is utilizing the United Airlines Apollo system and a booking is made for a flight segment on Delta Airlines, United Airlines charges Delta a listing fee for providing the booking through United's computer system. This charge is approximately $1.85 for each segment booking.

Calculating Your Value to an Air Carrier for Using Its Reservation System

When considering the installation of airline computer reservations hardware, the corporate travel manager may calculate the value to an air carrier for having that air carrier's computer reservations equipment installed in the corporate travel office. By looking at a sample month series of reservations and counting the number of flight segments on all segments other than the host carrier (the carrier providing the reservations system equipment), and then by multiplying this figure times $1.85, one can rapidly determine the approximate value to a host airline of having its computer reservations system installed in a corporate travel department. However, by instructing the travel agency to validate tickets with a preference to the host carrier and calculating a $2.50 charge for each ticket validation, the corporate travel manager may see a substantial increase in the total income being generated for a host carrier.

To illustrate the importance of this income for airlines, Tom Sternberg, President of Agency Management Services in Atlanta, was quoted in *Tour and Travel News* (Issue #087, July 4, 1988, p. 20) as saying, "The biggest advantage an agent (travel agency) has, if they are angry at an airline, the agent can stop paying the CRS bill and the airline won't do anything—they are happy to get the segment charge of $1.85 from a co-host." *Tour and Travel News* goes on to note that, "According to a source, the CRS vendors earn $12,000 extra per terminal during the term of the contract in segment fees from co-host airlines." *Business Travel News* (June 20, 1988, p. 1) reported that, "The airline companies that own the three largest computerized reservation systems charge other carriers booking fees that are nearly twice the cost of providing the service according to the Department of Transportation's recently released CRS industry report." Although Delta Air Lines does not charge other carriers for flights reserved through its DATAS II system, the DOT study indicates that United's "Covia Partnership (Apollo), American Airlines (Sabre) and (Eastern/Continental's) System One Corp. charge twice their costs. In fact, from the data available, System One charges booking fees equal to 276 percent of its average cost . . . ," (*Business Travel News* reporting of the DOT study).

Non-airline booking fees are even higher, according to the DOT study. They are, ". . . typically $2 to $3 per booking," *Business Travel News* reports that, ". . . the average annual revenue received by each vendor . . . ranged from $8,000 to $12,000 during 1986 . . . ." In addition, the DOT study reports that the *halo effect,* a term used to account for, ". . . the larger number of bookings received by airlines from agencies that use their systems, contributes heavily to the vendors' airline revenues . . . ," according to the study, and, in fact, the study points out that, "Indeed, our results indicate that the halo effect is larger than some vendors have estimated it to be."

Negotiating for Computer Hardware

After calculating the value to an air carrier for using its reservations system, the corporate travel manager may wish to contact competing airline representatives and negotiate directly with them for the installation of computer equipment. It should be noted, however, that negotiations need to be undertaken with an airline executive who is totally familiar with the financial benefits that can accrue to the airline by having a corporate travel department utilize its equipment. This means reaching a higher level of executive than one might customarily deal with in many cases. It is also stressed that the more accurate the data brought to the negotiation conversations, the greater the probability of obtaining reduced cost or free computer equipment. Although the initial data developed may be on any sample month, a complete study of last year bookings and a projection of future year bookings broken down by segment and by carrier will be most beneficial. It should be kept in mind that the real preference of the carrier is to have as many tickets issued on the host carrier as possible. This too, can become a bargaining point in the discussions since a complete analysis of past year ticketing and future year expected activity should identify those segments which have been booked or which otherwise would be booked on a competing carrier and which can be booked on the host carrier. In 1989 Sheryl Hansen with Hewlett-Packard utilized this type of research and the data resulting from her research to obtain full computerization of her corporate travel department on a totally gratis basis.

One approach that has been effectively used is to meet with carrier representatives from airlines that would be second or third choice host carriers for computer equipment prior to meeting with the carrier of first preference. If an offer can be obtained from the second choice carrier and/or the third choice carrier, the corporate travel manager will be in a better position to elicit an offer from the host carrier of first choice and/or to evaluate any proposal received from the host carrier of first choice as soon as the proposal is received. This should provide the corporate travel manager with a better bargaining position.

Savings Documentation and Reports

Documenting savings and preparing reports reflecting the savings is, perhaps, one of the most important tasks undertaken by corporate travel managers since saving money is, for most corporate travel departments, the reason they exist. Documenting savings usually starts with a report which is frequently called the *Corporate Air Travel Savings Report.* This traditional report has grown into reflecting more than air fare savings, however, since it now covers hotel, car rental, and other savings as well. Several types of traditional savings reports are utilized in the industry.

In addition to traditional savings reports, however, most corporate travel managers also prepare annual and year-to-year comparison reports on savings. One of the major reasons for this is to overcome any skew in a report which may occur due to a sharp increase or a sharp decrease in air fares from one year to another. Finally, several internal reports are prepared reflecting savings. These include an internal cash flow savings report and an internal float savings report.

Traditional Savings Reports

Traditional savings reports are monthly documents which show the tickets obtained for the corporate account by its travel agency throughout the preceeding month. The reports typically show the amount of the full-economy fare in the left column, the fare obtained by the travel agency for the traveler in the middle column, and the savings resulting from subtracting the fare obtained from the full-economy fare in the right hand column. While this report can be of some value to agencies in terms of documenting the fact that the company is paying less than the standard full-economy fare, many corporate travel departments have determined that they would prefer to have a report which shows another type of fare instead of the full economy fare in the left hand column. The type preferred by most is to list the least expensive fare available consistent with the constraints of the traveler. By listing this fare and comparing it with the fare obtained, a smaller savings will be realized as would be shown on the traditional savings report which listed the full economy fare and subtracted the fare obtained. In fact, by substituting the least expensive available fare consistent with the constraints of the traveler in the left-hand column, the savings report often does not show any savings, but instead shows a cost that is greater than the least expensive fare consistent with the constraints of the traveler available at the time booking occurred. The reason for this is that there are sometimes some justifiable reasons for not taking the best possible fare.

All standard traditional savings reports show exception categories so that when a fare is obtained which is more than the least expensive fare available at the time the reservation was requested consistent with the constraints of the traveler, a justification code can be entered. This justification code provides the reason why a higher fare than the best fare was selected. Some of the standard exception codes are for such considerations as:

1. a more expensive class of service was booked in order to travel with a client;

2. full economy fare was booked in order to upgrade to first class;

3. declined lowest fare, no justification provided;

4. declined because a better arrival or departure time was desired, and so forth.

When the savings report is obtained by the corporate travel manager, a rapid check of those tickets which were issued at a price higher than the best available fare can be rapidly made and a determination can be made by the corporate travel manager regarding the appropriate action to be taken consistent with the policies of the company.

Another aspect of the savings report is a report listing fare conversions and other fares obtained that were better than the fares which were originally obtained. This report lists fares obtained by the travel agency which were not in the computer at the time of original booking. Some travel agencies have an agreement with air carriers whereby an agency may switch a full economy fare to a discounted fare price when the discounted seats are sold out. This is known as having a *conversion ability*. Another aspect of this report reflects tickets that were obtained after an originally booked flight, but because of continuous fare monitoring, a less-expensive fare became available and was automatically booked. In this case, the original fare obtained will be shown and the lower-priced rebooked fare will also be shown in order to reflect the savings obtained.

Annual and Year-to-year Reports

Annual reports and year-to-year comparison reports provide top management with an understanding of comparisons regarding the progress made in travel savings. Annual financial reports will normally highlight the volume of travel (including the total number of trips taken, the total dollars paid for travel, the total number of hotel room nights of occupancy utilized, the total number of car rental days utilized, and so on. Specific savings in each category will normally be documented in paragraph form showing the specific activities that were undertaken throughout the year to reduce costs in each of the categories. Many corporate travel managers also prepare year-to-year progress reports. These reports chart progress with pie charts and/or with bar charts in each of the major cost areas.

Internal Reports

Internal reports are also prepared on a regular basis (monthly, quarterly, and annually) reflecting the savings to the business from cash flow management, as well as the savings resulting from internal float.

Making Money and Profit Centers

Historically, one of the major reasons the National Business Travel Association pushed for airline deregulation was a desire to obtain appointments as well as transferring the commissions on corporate travel from travel agencies to corporate travel departments. In this way, corporate travel departments could move from being cost centers to being profit centers. Although much was accomplished in the deregulation act, setting the stage for this type of movement, few corporate travel departments have, in fact, obtained appointments and the commisssions that come with them. However, there is a trend toward moving corporate travel departments from the status of spending money (cost centers) to the status of either making money or becoming profit centers for their businesses.

Some of the techniques utilized in doing this are related to taking advantage of travel agency rebating, establishing fee-based agency affiliations, including profit center concepts in *Requests for Proposals* and evaluating proposal options for their financial impact, establishing corporate travel department buying consortiums, buying travel agencies outright, and a group of corporate travel managers purchasing a travel agency.

Travel-agency Rebating

The practice of *rebating* by travel agencies is considered an established practice in the travel industry today. It has moved through a history beginning prior to deregulation, where it was considered bordering on illegal and violating Air Traffic Conference regulations, to a period just after deregulation when it was considered unethical by many in the industry, to a period a few years after deregulation where it was considered unprofitable, until finally, rebating has established a position of almost respectability for itself in the relationship between travel agencies and corporate travel departments. It is now an expected and accepted way of doing business. As acceptable as rebating has become, however, as it relates to international travel it continues to be illegal in the U.S. To make a cash payment back to a purchaser of an international ticket by the travel agency selling that ticket is a direct violation of U.S. federal law.

Rebating is offered in many ways in the industry. Obviously, the most direct and straightforward form of rebating is to provide a cash payment back to a company in exchange for the business that company provides to the travel agency. Perhaps at the other end of the spectrum is the relationship whereby a travel agency provides a considerable number of services on a gratis basis or at a less-than-cost basis in exchange for the business given by a corporate travel department, but no cash changes hands. There are many variations in between these two extremes.

However, it is important that the corporate travel manager understand the relationship between average ticket prices, rebates, and service. The average travel agency receives a commission of approximately ten percent for selling travel products. This includes air tickets and hotel reservations. They are also paid commissions on such other variables as car rental reservations, travel insurance, tours, cruises, and so on. Obviously, if the travel agency is to provide a high standard of service and a wide range of service options for a corporate travel department, that agency must have some money to pay for the services. If the agency gives away a substantial part of its ten percent commission, it seldom has a large amount of money with which to provide rebates.

Therefore, there is a very strong relationship between the level of cash rebates that a travel agency can make and the level of service that it can provide. If rebates are offered in the form of specific cash amounts, rather than a percentage of the ticket price, the travel agency will be taking a chance on its ability to sell a sufficient number of tickets to offset the total rebate amount promised in its proposal. However, if the travel agency hopes to keep a corporate account, it must provide a minimum amount of service. At some point, one stretches the cash available to a point whereby neither high percentage rebates nor a high level of service is possible. Many say the best possible answer is to take a small level of rebates on a percentage basis and to set up specific standards that must be met by the travel agency in terms of service.

High Rebates and High-fared Tickets

One approach to rebating, which a very few travel agencies have adopted (but an approach the corporate travel manager should be careful to look out for) is that of providing a very high cash rebate in order to obtain the business and then to increase the average ticket price over a period of time by selling full-economy fare tickets. Generally, it is the smaller or medium-sized travel agency that takes this approach. They need the business in order to stay in business or they want to obtain a contract for handling the corporate account in order to inflate the amount of business produced so that a potential sale of the travel agency will produce a higher priced sale. In many of these cases, the agency provides the high rebate and issues tickets at or close to the best fare possible in the early stages of the working relationship.

Increasingly, however, more and more full-economy fared tickets are issued in an effort to obtain a larger average ticket price so that the agency will have a sufficiently high dollar commission to earn enough money to pay the high rebate percentage and still at least break even financially after paying the costs of providing their services.

In other cases, the high, unprofitable rebate is paid simply to increase the dollar volume of business on the travel agency's books. Since travel agencies normally sell for a percentage of their gross volume, the increase of ticket volume that can come about from having another commercial account which has one-half million dollars or more in total business volume can increase the value of the travel agency in a sale by as much as $30,000 to $50,000 for each $500,000 dollars of corporate account business. Therefore, a travel agency owner can afford to pay back an unprofitably high rebate for a short period of time if the owner can show the level of business increasing sufficiently in order to command a substantially higher price for the travel agency when it sells.

Under this type of arrangement, the corporate travel manager should be wary of clauses in the contract which indicate that although a high percentage of rebate dollars will be paid to the corporate travel department, the right to sell the travel agency during the period of the contract remains with the agency. Such a clause in a contract should be treated as a red flag indicating that that is the major reason for soliciting the account in the first place. Although the corporate travel manager may not run into any difficulty with the agency until it is sold, there is a strong probability that a new owner will rapidly discover that the large rebate amount cannot be paid profitably and the new owner will either drop the account arbitrarily or come back to renegotiate for a smaller rebate.

In either case, this can be detrimental to the corporate travel department and upsetting in terms of both the quality of the service received and the nuisance of having to either settle for an arrangement that is less favorable than the originally contracted arrangement or to have to renegotiate the travel agency vendor contract. Any commission rebate of five percent or more of the gross sales should be considered in view of the possibility that few travel agencies can afford to stay in business over a long period of time and pay out such a high rebate. Of course, if the agency is a very large agency and a substantial amount of override income is being earned on a regular basis, it is feasible that the large agency can make a five percent rebate and still accrue a small profit. However, for a travel agency with a gross volume of under five million dollars, it is probable that this would be an impossible accomplishment.

Hard vs. Soft Rebates

In an age when trade-offs and bartering have regained popularity in the business community, travel agencies are now able to negotiate receiving override commissions at least partially in the form of free air tickets for utilization on the carrier issuing those tickets. These are sometimes provided to travel agencies in substantial numbers as a compensation for selling a larger percentage of air travel on the carrier involved over a period of time or for switching to and/or adopting the utilization of that carrier's computer system in the travel agency. For whatever reason they have received the free tickets, many travel agencies have more tickets than they would ordinarily use for agency staff consumption, and some agencies have in turn offered these free tickets to their corporate accounts as a form of rebating.

When a corporate account is willing to accept free tickets instead of cash, typically the value of the free tickets will be as much as two or three times as much as the value of cash. The reason for this is that cash can be utilized for any purpose whereas tickets are limited in their ability to be used (they can only be used for transportation purposes), the free tickets are always valid only on the carrier issuing the ticket, and, in some cases, the free tickets carry some restrictions with them. The corporate travel manager, therefore, has a choice of either receiving cash or receiving a substantially greater amount in terms of dollar value in airline tickets.

On the one hand, the airline ticket offer provides a much larger dollar value rebate, but on the other hand the ticket offer provides much greater restrictions in terms of how the rebate can be utilized. One corporate travel department that has made good use of this offer is a national sports team which travels substantially throughout its season playing out of town games. The team is responsible for providing not only its own air transportation to and from the out-of-town game cities, but it is also responsible for providing transportation to and from the games for a number of referees. The free tickets that are provided by the team's travel agency are utilized for referee travel since the team's contract only calls for providing transportation for the referees and does not specify that the referees be given cash with which to pay for their tickets. Although some referees are not happy with this arrangement, since their flexibility of carrier to be utilized and sometimes flights that can be taken is limited to the carrier issuing the free ticket and the flights which are not blocked against free ticket usage, nevertheless, the team has had no difficulty in getting referees to and from the out of town game cities without difficulty.

In other cases, however, businesses have had some difficulty in distributing among their employees and getting their employees to accept utilizing the free tickets received in the form of rebates. Is is suggested that corporate travel managers study the restrictions and the potentials for usage before accepting soft rebates. For some companies the arrangements will work well, but for other companies, the tickets may be so restrictive that they become unusable.

Summary

Corporate travel managers are asked to do what some believe appears to be impossible. This is to save money on corporate travel while travel expenses are increasing. By analyzing each of the travel products, it is possible for a travel manager to increasingly show excellent value for each corporate travel dollar spent.

Air travel savings is the focus spotlighted by many who analyze corporate travel expenses because it accounts for such a considerable part of total business travel costs. Air travel can be managed by requiring best-fare guarantees (and understanding each of the four types of best-fare guarantees), obtaining conversion ability (the ability to convert regular air fares to discounted seat prices), utilizing alternative routings where costs may be less expensive, and negotiating for better air travel costs.

Other areas also offer opportunities for savings. Primary among these are hotel and car rental savings. Both present opportunites for negotiation. Hotel and car rental costs tend to be the lowest possible when negotiated by corporate travel managers themselves. However, in some cases, these rates are negotiated by travel agency staff and agency or corporate travel consortiams.

Other areas that lend themselves to cost reduction management include parking fees and frequent flier management programs.

Savings reports are also possible ways of managing savings. These review actual and potential expenses and report the savings realized through cost reduction efforts.

Perhaps the most popular savings approach is to obtain rebates or other incentives. Although rebates provide the possibility of obtaining a substantial amount of money back from vendors, they also provide potential pitfalls. However, rebates open the door for potential agency affiliations that can sometimes result in changing the corporate travel department from a cost center to a profit center and actually making money for the company. These affiliation options and the profit center possibilities will be discussed in detail in the next two chapters.

Discussion Questions

1. Why is saving money on travel considered an increasing challenge for corporate travel managers?

2. What factors are built into the reports filed by corporate travel managers in order to help overcome this challenge?

3. What are the five major tools with which corporate travel managers may work to provide air travel savings?

4. Explain the differences between the several types of best-fare guarantees.

5. What are discount guarantees and how does the guarantee work?

6. How does conversion ability work and how can it save money for corporate travel managers who take advantage of it?

7. What trade-offs are sometimes involved in taking alternative routings?

8. Why might corporate travel managers negotiate better hotel and car rental rates than travel agencies are able to negotiate for them?

9. What are some of the cost saving parking options available to companies?

10. In what ways might frequent flier programs be managed in order to save money for a company?

11. What are the traditional costs quoted by airline suppliers for CRTs and printers?

12. What are the two sources of income for an airline as it relates to having its computer equipment in either a travel agency or in a corporate travel department?

13. What is meant by the term "validating carrier?"

14. What is the per flight segment dollar income paid to a validating carrier by other carriers participating on an airline ticket?

15. What is the per segment listing fee charged by a carrier's reservation system for reservations made on other carriers through that system?

16. How can a corporate travel manager calculate the value of the corporation's business to an air carrier for using its reservation system?

17. Why does the president of Agency Management Services in Atlanta maintain that the airline will not take any action if the travel agency stops paying its computer reservations bill?

18. Approximately how many dollars extra per terminal does a *computer reservation service* (CRS) vendor earn per terminal in segment fees from co-host airlines during the term of the contract?

19. According to the Department of Transportation (DOT), what are the per booking fees charged by CRS vendors for non-airline bookings (hotels, car rentals, and so on)?

20. Why might a corporate travel manager wish to meet with carrier representatives from airlines that would be second or third choice host carriers for computer equipment prior to meeting with the carrier of first preference for computer hardware equipment?

21. What is meant by the term, "exception categories" on traditional savings reports?

22. What are some of the techniques utilized in moving a corporate travel department from the status of a cost center to that of a profit center?

23. Is rebating legal in the U.S.? Explain.

24. Why is it important for corporate travel managers to understand the relationship between average ticket prices, rebates, and service?

25. Why might travel agencies providing high rebates be tempted to issue higher fared tickets than they might otherwise be able to issue?

26. What is the financial relationship between rebating and the value of a travel agency when preparing a travel agency for a potential sale?

27. What is the difference between a "hard" rebate and a "soft" rebate? Give examples of each.

Role Play Exercise

Two students may participate in this role play either out-of-class, as a fun way to review the chapter, or as an in-class exercise. One plays the role of the First Corporate Travel Manager and the other plays the role of the Second Corporate Travel Manager. Please read the script and then pick up the conversation in your own words.

First Corporate Travel Manager: Your CRTs and ticket printers are impressive. You have the latest in both types of equipment. I wish we could afford to get even just a CRT to check fares, but I can't get our comptroller to agree to the cost.

Second Corporate Travel Manager: Then negotiate with your travel agency and the airlines to provide it for you free. We aren't paying anything for our hardware, but it did take some extensive negotiation.

First Corporate Travel Manager: Are you having to cut your rebates and override profit sharing checks?

Second Corporate Travel Manager: No, let me tell you how we approached the negotiation. I calculated our total air travel volume and approached some other air carriers to get proposals. When I met with my airline of choice, our travel agency sales executive was in the meeting with us. We approached the carrier representative by saying . . .

CONTINUE ON YOUR OWN

Group Discussion Situation:
Caught Between the CFO and the CEO at Petty Parts

Pat Paulson is the part-time corporate travel manager for Patty Parts, a small partnership parts distributor. The CFO of Petty Parts doesn't like Pat and is always getting on him about reducing travel costs. Recently the new travel agency Pat has been using has provided a rebate of three percent and provided Pat with documents showing the very lowest fares have been received. Pat was very happy about all the savings he received until this morning when he got a call from the President of Petty Parts. The President advised Pat that if he (the President) ever again went out to the airport to take a flight on a plane that doesn't exist, Pat

147

Group
Discussion
Situation:
Caught
Between the
CFO and the
CEO at Petty
Parts

would be fired. In checking things out, it seems the air carrier on which the President was booked had discontinued the flight the day before the President was scheduled to fly out. The gate agent for the carrier told the President of Petty Parts that the travel agent should have known about the flight being discontinued and should have protected the President by rebooking him on another flight. Pat is sure this agency will save Petty Parts money. That will make the CFO happy. However, Pat wants to keep his job with the company and he believes the President means it when he says Pat will be fired if there is another mistake like the one yesterday.

Pat has asked several key individuals in the company to advise him as to how to proceed. You are meeting today to develop a set of recommendations for Pat. You are expected to reach agreement and to write a two-page set of recommendations. In your group session, select one person to chair the group. All will have an equal vote on decisions. In the group session you are expected to reach agreement on recommendations and to prepare the paper to be presented to the entire class by the chair of your committee.

Group Discussion Situation:
Very Bery's Hard or Soft Rebates

Nancy Nankins of Very Bery Orchards just finished chairing the committee that heard the oral proposals from the three travel agencies selected to make oral presents for the Very Bery travel business based on their written proposals. One company, Travel Services, has definitely been eliminated based on their inability to provide the services needed. However, the committee is in agreement that the other two companies are excellent. Both proposals meet and exceed Very Bery's requirements. The main difference is in the area of rebates. Traveler's Travel is offering a 1.75 percent cash rebate while Travel Destinations has offered three percent in soft dollars. Travel Destinations noted in the oral presentation that their superior service capability requires them to pay top dollar to their agents and other staff members and they will not dilute their ability to provide the best possible service by rebating hard dollars. However, as with many agencies these days, Travel Destinations pointed out, air carriers that are sold with a preference provide many free tickets to the agency. These are provided on a volume basis. By giving these tickets to Very Bery Orchards, the net effect for Very Bery will be the same as it would if Very Bery were given cash rebates and had to turn around and pay cash for their tickets. In fact, pointed out the Travel Destinations Marketing Director, the effect will be even better since the hard dollar cash rebate offered by Traveler's Travel couldn't possibly be as much as the soft dollar percentage offered by Travel Destinations.

The committee was not sure of the pros and cons between the hard dollar cash rebate offer and the soft dollar ticket provision offer. They have asked Nancy to study the two alternatives and their effect(s) on the company and especially on the company bottom line. They want Nancy to give them a specific recommendation and to back it up.

Nancy has turned to your department, the corporate travel department, and instructed you to provide her with a full briefing and a recommendation together with arguments that the committee will understand. The corporate travel manager reports to Nancy. You are meeting today to develop a concise position paper with appropriate back-up arguments for Nancy to bring back to the committee. You are expected to reach agreement and to write a position paper that will be at least two pages in length. In your group session, select one person to chair the group. All will have an equal vote on decisions. In the group session you are expected to reach agreement on the position and appropriate back-up arguments for Nancy to bring back to her committee. Be prepared to have your paper and the arguments presented orally to the entire class by the chair of your committee.

CHAPTER 10

Money-making Affiliations

Introduction

As suggested in previous chapters on financial management, the type of affiliation or contractual arrangement between a corporate travel department and its company, on the one hand, and the travel agency vendor, on the other, can make a difference as it relates to the corporate travel department being either a cost center or a profit center. Rebates were discussed in the last chapter and override commission sharing has been discussed in several previous chapters. Obviously, if the amount of rebates and override commission sharing is substantial, the combination of the two alone can exceed the costs of the corporate travel department. The result would be a profit for the corporate travel department. In other words, when the total money received by the corporate travel department for rebates and override commission sharing exceeds the total spent on administrative and other (non-travel) costs, profit is the net result.

Before identifying the financial structure that might provide the best cost or profit arrangement for a company, it is important to recognize the constraints on company travel finances and evaluate vendor agency proposals for their financial impacts. This combination of efforts can set the stage for an intelligent evaluation of potentially profitable travel agency affiliations. These profit-oriented affiliations will be discussed in this chapter.

These money-making approaches are derived from an affiliation based upon:

1. the agency billing fees for its services and all commissions being sent to the corporate travel department;
2. the business buying and operating its own travel agency; and
3. the potential for corporate travel departments to form *buying consortiums*. (This approach moves from what is considered to be the simplest profit-oriented structure to one of the most complicated structures undertaken in the corporate travel industry today.)

Government Contracted Per Diem Requirements

Federal government per diem requirements have become much more restrictive and are very specific. The result is that, in many cases, it is a challenge for the corporate travel manager and for the corporate traveler to meet per diem limitations in many locations around the country. This is especially true in some of the major locations where corporate travelers travel in order to conduct business with federal government entities. Washington, D.C. is, perhaps, a worse case situation since federal government buyers are usually headquartered in the Washington, D.C. area and, therefore, corporate travelers dealing with government businesses often make a substantial number of trips to Washington, D.C. The per diem requirements allow specific dollar reinbursement maximums for corporate travel costs when those costs are incurred while working on government-funded projects. The per diem is intended to cover hotel costs, meals, and local transportation.

Corporate travel managers are approaching government per diem limitations by managing these travel expenses in a variety of ways. One alternative is to identify hotel or motel locations in outlying areas and ask corporate travelers to drive rental cars to and from their in-town meetings. Another alternative is to negotiate with specific hotel properties for volume discounts. Many corporate travel managers make a trip to Washington D.C., and/or other locations where government per diem limitations create problems in balancing a travel budget. The corporate travel manager enters into negotiations with hoteliers, car rental franchisees, and, in some cases, with restauranteurs to negotiate volume discounts. They accomplish this armed with the statistics of the number of travelers from the company who annually travel to the destination for business. The need to stay within government per diem limitations has also spurred the interest of corporate travel department consortium negotiations and has, in some cases, resulted in price levels that still allow the corporate traveler to conduct business effectively while staying within the limitations of the government per diems.

Evaluating Proposal Options for Their Financial Impact

One of the most difficult tasks that corporate travel managers encounter is that of evaluating proposal options for their financial impact. In many cases, not only must a corporate travel manager make this type of evaluation, but in addition, he/she is often asked to factor in trade-offs between services to be received and financial advantages. This becomes a considerable challenge if it is to be calculated on a statistical basis. Most businesses, however, ask the corporate travel manager to first identify financial benefit comparisons and then to identify the service benefit comparisons.

If rankings are provided on both financial benefits and on service benefits, and if specific travel agency bidders rank very high on both scales, it is then usually possible to identify two or three potentially outstanding proposals. The customary practice is to invite those two or three agencies whose proposals do stand out to make oral presentations before a committee. Based upon the oral presentations and the written proposals, a final decision can be made.

The first step, therefore, is to determine financial comparisons. In most cases, difficulty is encountered when the agencies making proposals can provide several types of financial options. As noted earlier, these tend to be rebates (either hard or soft) or fee-based proposals. For the corporate travel manager to make comparisons, it is essential to go back to the historical data and next year's budget to determine what the specific costs as well as receivable dollars from the travel agency would be under each proposal scenerio.

This process of evaluating fee-based agency benefits is essentially the process undertaken to identify all financial benefits for fee-based proposals. However, when considering the financial benefits to be obtained through rebating, a slightly different approach is undertaken. Again, it is essential to calculate the number of transactions which took place in the previous year and to identify the number of tickets to be issued in the coming year based upon company budgets.

However, when considering rebating, it is essential to identify a history of the percentage of city pairs flown, as well as city pairs budgeted to be flown, along with projected costs for each city pair. By looking at these factors and identifying national average ticketing percentages of economy fare costs (or by identifying what travel agencies have in the past been able to obtain for your company on an average percentage of economy fare cost basis), the corporate travel manager will then be able to determine a projected total air fare cost for the coming year. This projected total air fare cost for the coming year can be multiplied by the percentage rebate offered by the travel agency. (They may be offering a *hard-dollar percentage rebate* in order to calculate the financial benefits the company would receive.) However, if the company is to receive *soft rebates* in the form of tickets, it is essential to take the formula one step further by multiplying the dollar rebate calculation figure times the ticket valuation figure to determine the total value of tickets to be received.

Obviously, in most cases, the tickets to be received will hold a greater dollar value figure than the hard-cash dollar figure. Nevertheless, in making a presentation comparing these financial advantages, the corporate travel manager normally will not only show both figures along with the appropriate figures from rebate proposals, but will also identify those proposals which offer cash and those which offer tickets as rebates. Those who decide comparative advantages will be able to see the dollar-based figures side by side. The above process can take a considerable amount of time, but the documentation will provide decision makers with a clarity of comparison which will be a mark of the professional approach utilized by the corporate travel manager.

Fee-based Agency Affiliations

One of the newer types of agency affiliation contractual arrangements is the *fee-based contract*. Under this arrangement, the travel agency agrees to provide its standard services, but will give the corporate travel client a 100 percent rebate of all commissions earned on business conducted for that client. In return, the travel agency will charge a *flat dollar annual fee*, a *flat dollar per transaction fee*, or a *percentage cost per transaction fee* which is billed directly to the corporate client as a fee for services provided. These are both advantages and disadvantages to the fee-based agency contract.

To determine the amount of potential benefit, it is necessary for the corporate travel manager to go back and measure the history of transactions occuring in the previous year. Although the corporate travel manager may not have specific data regarding the number of times any specific ticket was reissued (an increasing number of corporate travel managers are retaining this historical data for a number of years), it is possible for most corporate travel managers to identify the specific number of tickets issued for travelers over the previous twelve-month period. If they are unable to do so, the travel agency with which they have worked should be able to provide this data, since the Airline Reporting Corporation requires travel agencies to keep the agency copy of each ticket issued for a minimum of at least two years.

After calculating the total number of airline tickets purchased in the previous year (or the previous several years to get a better annual average and/or percentage of travel increase/decrease), the corporate travel manager should estimate the number of tickets to be issued during the next twelve months based on both history and on departmental budgets.

If the travel agency is offering to charge a *per transaction fee,* it should be determined whether or not this per transaction fee will be based on each ticket issued and utilized, if it includes each change of tickets (those issued and used as well as those cancelled and/or changed), or each change of data prior to the issuance of and including the issuance of tickets. If the per transaction charge is based upon only those tickets that are issued and used, the historical data and the budgeting data will provide a solid base for determining projected costs. If however, the per transaction fee is based upon tickets issued whether they were utilized, cancelled, or changed (or if the per transaction fee is based upon each record change in the computer) the corporate travel manager needs to determine an average change statistic for his/her company. This data may be hard to determine, but sampling studies can be undertaken to provide fairly accurate projections.

In what ever way the per transaction fee is determined, it is important that the corporate travel manager make a concerted effort to identify, as closely as possible, specific total transactions that will occur during the coming year based upon the interpretation of "transaction" utilized by the agency presenting the fee based option. Once this calculation has been determined, it will be possible for the corporate travel manager to compare the costs to be incurred during the coming year with the commission to be returned to the company by the travel agency as well as to calculate the dollar advantages to the company. Obviously, if there is a high amount of change and if the per transaction fee is high, it may be possible that there will be no benefit to the company by opting for a fee-based contractual arrangement. However, in most cases, the business is able to show a substantial positive difference between the amount of money received in commissions from the travel agency and the amount of money paid to the travel agency.

Some fee-based arrangements allow the company to pay either a fee or a per transaction charge, whichever is less. This type of arrangement is especially beneficial for a company since, if a company does not meet the minimum number of tickets required to offset flat fee charges, the per transaction option will normally allow the company to still show a positive return in its arrangement with the travel agency.

One of the greatest advantages to fee-based agency affiliations is the ability to move the corporate travel department from being a cost center to a profit center since the difference in the amount of money received in commissions from the travel agency as compared to the flat annual fee or per transaction fee paid to the travel agency can often be more than enough to cover all the operating costs of the corporate travel department and still return money back to the company. The major disadvantage of fee-based agency affiliations is the potential risk involved. However, if the company has a history of substantial air travel and if the travel agency has provided an option of either paying a flat dollar annual fee or a per transaction fee, whichever is less, then the risk factor is minimal. A final advantage is that fee-based agency affiliations are often easy to sell to top management since it is quite possible to prove that the company will benefit financially from such an arrangement (based upon history and budgeting projections) and that the corporate travel department will be able to show a profit after paying for all operating expenses.

In-house and In-plant Agencies

Sometimes travel agencies set up offices on the premises of a corporate account and serve both corporate and leisure travel needs. These are often referred to as *in-house agencies*. Often a split commission arrangement is worked out since the agency has a contract to handle both the corporate business and leisure travel business by company employees. Employee leisure travel is much easier to obtain when the agency is located on the company premises. This arrangement, however, is usually not a possibility unless the company is one that serves the general public and the agency is open to the general public as well as the company employees. Otherwise Airline Reporting Corporation appointment rules may be violated.

In-plant agencies are another option. This is a special form of travel agency appointment. Essentially, the travel agency is set up to operate like a branch of the travel agency. The agency is operated at the site of the business, and typically, all employees are compensated by the travel agency. However, a lower commission is paid to the travel agency by the air carriers. Sometimes this results in more compensation being obtained by the company than shared commission or other alternative income-generating alternatives, but most of the time, their *in-plants* are set up to provide better service rather than to increase the financial compensation.

Buying a Travel Agency

Historically, corporate travel managers and other corporate executives have recognized the potential benefits (to businesses with substantial air travel volume) of having full airline appointments in order to obtain full commissions on the travel purchased. The reasoning involved is that travel agencies make a commission and often receive override bonuses on top of the commission from the travel purchased by corporate travel departments. If the middle man (travel agencies) can be cut out, and if the commission and overrides can flow directly to the corporate travel department, then the corporate travel department should be able to show a definite profit. If a company's travel volume, for example, is $2 million, then, at an average ten percent commission rate, the corporate travel department would have $200,000 plus the income from overrides and other bonuses to work with in order to cover its costs. Most corporate travel managers reason that this would be more than enough to pay excellent salaries, fund all computer equipment, and other corporate travel department expenses, and still provide a substantial amount of money to put back into the company as a corporate travel department profit.

The concept of direct corporate travel department appointments by airlines as commission-earning travel sales outlets was one of the major reasons why the *National Business Travel Association* (NBTA) fought for deregulation of the airline industry. Prior to deregulation, the anti-trust waiver, under which airlines operated, allowed air carriers to avoid the issue of direct appointment of corporate travel departments. They could act in unison to avoid direct corporate travel department appointments because of the anti-trust waiver. Several options are open to air carriers under the deregulation environment.

The Airline Reporting Corporation, which appoints travel agencies on behalf of member air carriers (most airlines in the United States) has established what is generally known as the *twenty percent rule*. Under this regulation, a travel agency would not be appointed and authorized to sell airline tickets if it conducts more than twenty percent of its business with itself. This effectively eliminates corporate travel departments from receiving appointment as travel agencies.

However, there have been some moves to indirectly get around the twenty percent rule. Under deregulation a separate category of appointment was established whereby individual air carriers could appoint a category of travel sales vendors which were called *other sales vendors*. These appointments do not require meeting a twenty percent rule. Under these regulations each air carrier can appoint any business entity they wish to sell tickets on behalf of the air carrier and such *other* entities can be paid a direct commission. In the initial stages of deregulation, it was hoped by many corporate travel managers that corporate travel departments would receive appointments by individual air carriers under the *other* category. This has not been the case. Few air carriers admit to it, but the general impression is that air carriers harbor concerns in appointing corporate travel departments (paying them commissions) because if they were to do so, and knowledge of their actions was learned by a large number of travel agencies, there is a fear that the travel agencies would boycott their sales and their airline revenues would plummet. Justification for this case came about when, in the earlier stages of deregulation, one air carrier announced that it was going to reduce the commission paid to travel agencies. Within a matter of days, the carrier reconsidered its position because travel agencies stopped selling it. The potential of a travel agency boycott is a real fear for air carriers which may wish to provide direct appointments to corporate travel departments. As long as that fear exists, direct appointment under the *other* category will probably not take place.

Some efforts, however, have taken place on a *joint purchase arrangement*. In the early stages of deregulation, the NBTA sponsored the purchase of a travel agency by a large number of corporate travel departments. The agency was purchased and retained its appointments, in spite of the fact that there was general knowledge in the travel community that sole ownership of the travel agency was held by corporate travel departments.

A few other group purchases of travel agencies have been undertaken with the idea in mind that if enough corporate travel departments jointly own a travel agency, no single owner (business) would provide twenty percent or more of the total travel sold and, therefore, the twenty percent rule would not be a problem.

In May, 1988, Association World Travel received its appointments and within a year was already selling over $2 million of travel. This agency is housed in the headquarters offices of the National Cattlemen's Association in a suburb of Denver. A business plan drawn up by former agency manager and co-owner, Daniel W. Bicker, was submitted to the Airline Reporting Corporation during the appointment request phase of establishing the agency. This plan clearly identified how considerably less than twenty percent of the travel to be generated by Association Travel would come from any one of several association clients. By utilizing the assistance of Donna Conklin, a consultant in Washington D.C. who works with many applicants for airline appointments, Association World Travel was able to receive its appointment and to operate as a travel agency. Profits from the agency go directly back to the owners. The National Cattleman's Association corporate travel manager, Donna Peterson, offices out of the travel agency which is located no more than a few feet from her previous corporate travel management office. Bicker, meanwhile, has formed Classic World Travel (303-220-5444), an agency whose goal is to assist corporate travel departments in setting up their own travel agencies and getting appointed. Around the country, other joint efforts on the part of corporate travel managers are being undertaken and it can be expected that an increasing number of companies will start obtaining a major share of airline commissions as a result of joint ownership of travel agencies.

Another technique utilized to obtain the financial benefits of commissions and overrides is the purchase of a travel agency. Some of the largest travel agencies and travel agency chains in the United States, as well as in other parts of the world, are owned by other businesses which frequently mandate that all of their subsidiaries purchase travel through the travel agency owned by the parent company. Obviously, if a travel agency owned by a parent company makes money, then the benefits of owning a travel agency and putting all corporate business through that agency has paid off even though the profits may not flow back directly to the parent company (they may be retained within the agency or flow to any one of a number of subsidiary companies).

Individual companies have also purchased travel agencies in order to reap the same benefits. In some cases, these companies already had a corporate travel department and the structure becomes one whereby travel agency management reports to or through the corporate travel manager. In other cases, the company did not have a central travel management function in place prior to buying the travel agency and the company-owned travel agency is structured to perform both the roles of an external agency and a corporate travel management role.

In 1989, McDonnell Douglas Travel Company (a travel agency owned by the McDonnell Douglas Company) paid Spectrum Group Inc., what *Business*

Travel News referred to as ". . . an up-front rebate . . . ," of what, ". . . observers said . . . would be reasonable to conclude (were) between $250,000 and $300,000 in rebates under a two-year agreement." This was to handle ". . . between $5 million and $6 million of Spectrum's potential $8 million in air ticket volume . . ." (*Business Travel News,* July 10, 1989, p. 47). Some suggested that meeting the twenty percent rule was the justification for the McDonnell Douglas Travel's action. *Business Travel News* went on to say that, "since the aerospace company launched its travel agency subsidiary in 1986, industry watchers have questioned whether McDonnell Douglas attracts enough outside business to remain in compliance with airline stipulations that agencies sell at least eighty percent of their ticket volume to outside buyers." BTN went on to state, "its bid for Spectrum intensified that speculation, but brought no new facts to light." (*Business Travel News,* July 10, 1989, p. 47).

Increasingly, however, corporate travel managers are recommending the purchase of a travel agency as a vehicle for earning commissions. Some problems relate to agency purchases. In a number of cases, companies which did not have corporate travel departments prior to the purchase of a travel agency, have placed executives from the parent company in charge of the travel agency. In a number of instances, these executives did not have a sufficient background in travel management to understand the specific needs required to continue with pre-existing profits or to increase the profits. Therefore, when travel agencies are purchased, hiring a profit-proven experienced agency executive, placing a currently-employed corporate travel manager in charge of the agency or employing a profit-oriented, knowledgeable consultant will normally provide better profits for the company than will the alternative of assigning a senior executive, with little or no travel experience, to head up the travel agency.

Many are concerned with getting approval to retain the appointments of a travel agency when purchased. This is of special concern when the travel from the company which is purchasing the agency will constitute more than twenty percent of the total once that travel is integrated into the agency volume. This can be a justifiable concern. Most companies that purchase travel agencies find that the agency appointment can be maintained because, at the time of appointment request, the parent company's travel volume has not yet been integrated into the travel agency's total sales. Therefore, the documentation sent to the Airline Reporting Corporation shows a less than twenty percent total of current sales to the parent company. There have been delays in receiving appointments and there are rumors that in a few cases, some appointments have not been provided because of ARC belief that the travel agency would be doing more than twenty percent of its business with the parent company. However, "any company can become its own Airlines Reporting Company-approved travel agency, according to Donna Conklin . . . ," reports *Travel Weekly* (July 17, 1989, p. 41). Conklin stated that, ". . . in her 17 years of experience in the industry (much of it working for ARC and ATC), she had never seen an agency application which stated that more than twenty percent of the applicant's business was going to be done with itself." (*Travel Weekly,* July 17, 1989, p. 44) Conklin noted that, ". . . while ARC requires agents to indicate which tickets are written as self-sales, few agents are even aware of the self-sales requirement."

When a purchase is undertaken, therefore, it is essential that the agency be

157

Corporate
Travel
Department
Buying
Consortiums

structured in such a way that, if at all possible, the total volume of the parent company is less than twenty percent of the agency's total volume. Although it is generally recognized that the Airline Reporting Corporation seldom comes back to investigate once initial approval has been provided, a company which purposely provides a small volume of parent company travel to a travel agency that it purchases in order to receive appointment (with the idea that that small volume would be increased to include all of the company's travel once appointments have been received), is taking a chance that the Airline Reporting Corporation will not come back to investigate at a later time. While it appears that many companies have taken this risk and not suffered from it, the risk, nevertheless, continues to exist.

Corporate Travel Department Buying Consortiums

Throughout the U.S., corporate travel department buying consortiums are being formed and utilized in order to take advantage of the volume travel buying power of more than one business. These consortiums tend to range from loose buying agreements to tightly tied-together corporate buying entities. Although there are not many of them in existence throughout the country, they are growing in popularity because the financial advantages can be considerable.

Typically, buying consortiums of corporate travel departments will address the major travel products and services first. Frequently, they will concentrate on hotel and car rental purchases before addressing air negotiations. The most frequent approach is to identify the city pairs of all flyers in all member companies of the consortium. By identifying the city pairs and the overnights that are involved, (city pairs of all travelers from all businesses of the consortium members), it is possible to project the total number of hotel nights to be utilized in each major city.

If the corporate travel departments identify the destination locations of the travelers in each of the destination cities (hotels, convention centers, and so on), it will be possible to identify the geographical areas in each city where hotels need to be found. Typically, the next step is to meet with hoteliers and offer guarantees of specific numbers of room nights in exchange for specific prices and quality of services and hotel accommodations. After negotiating for the best potential arrangement, each company agrees to utilize the specified hotels. It is possible to develop specific hotel night guarantees based upon total projected usage by all involved companies. Frequently, consortiums will try to find no more than two hotels in any specific area of a city and often no more than two hotels in a specific city destination. This then provides the hotel with a guarantee of number of nights of occupancy throughout the year while providing the consortium company members with a per night/per hotel rate that is usually better than can be obtained in any other way.

The approach utilized for car rental arrangements is similar to that utilized in negotiating for hotel rates except that car rental contracts and guarantees are normally developed and worked out with the franchisee in destination cities, rather than the home office or sales representatives.

Air travel arrangements are perhaps the most difficult to develop. In some cases, consortiums have had considerable success in negotiating directly with air carriers for guaranteed utilization and obtaining considerably better than published rates specifically for their consortiums. In other cases, consortiums have not been successful in obtaining substantially reduced air rates. The key lies in reaching the appropriate level in the marketing division of an airline. However, even if one is able to negotiate with a sufficiently high level of airline executive, it is necessary to work within a situation that carries with it the potential of meeting airline marketing needs. For those routes where an air carrier is not competing with other carriers, or where an air carrier has clear superiority as compared to other much smaller carriers in the market, or for flights at times when all carriers in the market are fully booked, there is no incentive for an air carrier to provide any cost saving benefits when negotiating with corporate travel executives.

On the other hand, if there is strong competition on specific routes among three or more major carriers and flights will occur during traditionally low periods of time, air carriers will have a much greater incentive to negotiatiate for price reductions. Frank Lorenzo has stated that Continental Airlines is the only thing stopping a $1,000 air fare between New York and Los Angeles. He is basing his arguements on the concept that without the competition from Continental Air Lines, those air carriers left in the market would have no incentive to reduce costs and, therefore, would charge a considerably higher fare.

For corporate travel management consortiums, the key is to identify city pairs that most meet the needs of airline marketing executives. One way to do this is to ask air carrier representatives what their smallest load factor city pairs are and the times of year (along with the times of day) when the city pair load factors are lowest. This data is readily available to air carriers and, if they understand that there is a substantial possibility that load factors can be increased through a concerted effort on the part of corporate travel management consortiums, some air carrier executives will share the data. Once this data is obtained, corporate travel management executives need to identify the volume of travel that they have provided in the past for each city pair and to determine whether or not they can guarantee substantial increases for the particular carrier with which they are negotiating and whether or not they can move travelers to flights that have especially low load factors (usually off-peak flights) with those carriers which have serious problems in the market. If this can be done without harming company business concerns (for example, if it can be done without having the traveler arrive late for meetings or have to leave meetings too early in the day) and if the consortium can guarantee with either up front money or contractual obligations for the purchase of air travel, then the possibility exists for substantial negotiated air savings.

Unless all of the above conditions can be met, however, the opportunity to negotiate substantial savings in air fares is unlikely. Since this combination of factors is so difficult to put together, most corporate travel consortiums concentrate their efforts on the non-air negotiations, especially car rental and hotels costs.

Summary

This chapter has focused on money-making affiliations. Prior to structuring a corporate travel department as a profit-oriented department, it is important to understand the major constraints. One of these is government contract per diem requirements. With such requirements being as strict as they are, and with them increasing in limitations, it is important that corporate travel departments identify potential ways of structuring the travel department so that travelers may complete their trips as efficiently as possible. One of the more popular corporate travel structure options is to work through travel agencies. To determine the travel agencies that will provide the most lucrative financial impact for the business, as a whole, and for the corporate travel department, in specific, an evaluation of the financial impacts of proposals needs to be undertaken. Frequently this means comparing

- fee-based;
- rebate/shared override;
- travel agency ownership; and
- buying consortium membership structural options.

In order to forecast the financial impact of each option, statistical data needs to be gathered and a scenerio for each option needs to be developed as clearly as possible.

An understanding of each of the major options has been presented in this chapter. This started with an explanation of fee-based travel agency affiliation arrangements and then moved to an analysis of the impact on a business when buying a travel agency to handle the travel of the business as well as, in some cases, other businesses. An extension of this approach is that of joining corporate travel department buying consortiums. Consortiums provide an opportunity to not only share in air travel financial (and other) benefits, but to extend volume buying benefits to hotel and car rental travel purchases as well.

In the next chapter a more complete discussion of the movement from cost center structure to profit center structure will be reviewed.

Discussion Questions

1. What are some of the ways corporate travel managers are managing travel expenses in order to keep within government per diem limitations?

2. How does the approach taken in evaluating the financial benefits a company might receive under a travel agency negotiated fee-based proposal arrangement compare with the approach taken to evaluate the financial benefits the company might receive in working with a travel agency under a rebating and/or override commission sharing proposal arrangement?

3. Compare the advantages and the disadvantages of fee-based contractual arrangements based upon:

   a) a flat dollar annual fee;

   b) a flat dollar per transaction fee; and

   c) a percentage cost per transaction fee.

4. Under what circumstances might an arrangement based upon allowing the

company to pay either a fee or a per transaction charge, whichever is less, be more advantagous for a company than an annual fee charge?

5. What financial reasons might a company with an annual travel volume of $2 million have in purchasing and owning their own travel agency?

6. How do the air carrier recognized *other sales vendors* compared with travel agency vendors?

7. How might the reaction of travel agencies when a lowering of commissions was announced right after deregulation by a major carrier have affected the potential of air carriers appointing corporate travel managers, authorizing corporate travel departments to sell air tickets, and paying corporate travel departments a commission on the airline tickets issued by those departments?

8. What did Association Travel do to be able to get direct airline appointment and commissions for its association owners?

9. Why might a business which owns several other businesses also consider it a potentially good investment to purchase a travel agency as well?

10. When a company purchases a travel agency, what type of senior executive should they look for in order to manage the agency?

11. Why is it considered essential that when the company purchases a travel agency, the agency is structured in such a way that the total volume of the parent company is less than twenty percent of the agency's total volume?

12. Do corporate travel buying consortiums normally start by negotiating for large volume purchases of air travel or do they start with hotel or car rental volume purchases first? Why?

13. Which of the following volume travel purchases are the most difficult to negotiate: air, hotel, or car rental?

Role Play Exercise

Two students may participate in this role play either out-of-class, as a fun way to review the chapters or as an in-class exercise. One plays the role of the first corporate travel manager and the other plays the role of the second corporate travel manager. Please read the script and then pick up the conversation in your own words.

First Corporate Travel Manager: We have been considering opting for a fee-based travel arrangement rather than the traditional arrangement on which we have been working with our travel agency for years. I understand you made that kind of change in your company a couple of years ago. Have you found it to be beneficial.

Second Corporate Travel Manager: Definitely! Each year we pay all corporate travel department expenses including salaries, equipment costs, . . . in fact, every possible expense, and we still put back $10,000 to $20,000 a year into the coffers of the business. We are able to pay top salaries, attend educational seminars and professional meetings, and our executives are delighted with the results. We don't have the headaches normally associated with running a travel agency ourselves, but we have all the benefits. In addition, I never realized how beneficial it is to be associated with a

161

Group
Discussion
Situation: A
"Steal" for
Butcher Block
Blankets

profit center rather than a cost center. Our status in the company is considerably higher.

First Corporate Travel Manager: You really sound sold on the concept. What other alternatives might be considered at the same time we are proposing a move from our current structure and what are the pros and cons of each as you see them?

Second Corporate Travel Manager: The financial executives of your company will certainly want to see what the benefits are currently. So you will need to document what you are getting from your travel agency now. However, let's look at the other alternatives and the pros and cons of both a fee-based arrangement and the other potential arrangements that are out there. Starting with fee-based agreements, the advantages that I can see for your company are . . .

CONTINUE ON YOUR OWN

Group Discussion Situation: A "Steal" for Butcher Block Blankets

Butcher Block Blankets' corporate travel manager, Sandy Bordd, received a phone call the other day from a business broker who said, "Have I got a travel agency for you! It's a steal. If you and your fellow corporate travel managers would like to buy it, you could pay for it out of petty cash—and you will get a full ten percent commission instead of just some small rebate." He went on to explain that the owner would sell for $10 down and $40,000 over ten years. He pointed out that Butcher Block Blankets had a travel budget exceeding a million dollars a year and that other corporate travel managers Sandy knows control over twelve million dollars in travel annually. If everyone got together, the broker suggested, they could make the payments from the commissions earned on their own business, not be in violation of ARC rules, and get more savings for their companies than they ever could any other way. And, he pointed out, they would own the travel agency outright in just a few years. It sounded great to Sandy, but she started wondering what kinds of financial problems there might be.

Sandy does not want to pass up a good financial deal for herself or for her company. However, she wonders if it really is a good financial deal. She asks several corporate travel manager associates in other firms to help her to evaluate the proposal.

You are meeting today to develop a proposal evaluation for Sandy. You are expected to reach agreement and to write a two-page proposal evaluation. In your group session, select one person to chair the group. All will have an equal vote on decisions. In the group session you are expected to reach agreement on the evaluation and to prepare the evaluation paper to be presented to the entire class by the chair of your committee.

The Corporate Travel Profit Center Business Plan

Introduction

Several of the preceding chapters of the financial management section have referred to a corporate travel department as either a *cost center* or as a *profit center*. Almost all corporate travel departments are structured initially as cost centers. Before considering the change from a cost center status to a profit center status, a determination should be made as to whether or not such a change is desirable. Although one might consider that this might be taken for granted, considering the fact that most companies are in business to make a profit, there are a number of companies which have made the decision that they do not want to be in the travel business in any way. Although some of these companies have realized that they could earn a profit by starting or buying a full-service travel agency (thus creating a profit center for the company, as well as another source of diversified income for the business), the overriding decision of the executives of the company has been that the company is expert at what it does and not at travel. Therefore, having a profit center and/or owning a travel agency is not desirable.

It should be recognized, however, that profit center status does not require the purchase of or the owning of a travel agency. Profit center status can come from other business structures. In the previous chapter, it was shown that one such structure which can sometimes result in the development of a corporate travel profit center is that of working out fee-based travel arrangements with a vendor travel agency rather than traditional arrangements. There are, of course, other structures that can result in the corporate travel department being a profit center rather than a cost center as well.

A second consideration relates to whether or not the political environment in the company is appropriate for considering a move from cost center to profit center status. Companies develop through a maturity cycle. There are constant political pressures within a company. Sometimes the environment is right for a corporate travel department move from cost center to profit center, but often the environment is not appropriate. Therefore, the corporate travel manger needs to evaluate the environment before considering a proposal. It should be kept in mind that the option to consider a change in status may be available as long as that change is not suggested. However, a status change, once suggested and turned down, may not be a politically viable suggestion again in the future. In other words, in many companies, a corporate travel manager may have only one chance to obtain a structural move such as this and, therefore, the corporate travel manger should pay carefull attention to the political environment prior to making the decision to move forward.

This chapter analyses one approach toward developing a corporate travel department profit center business plan to be considered by the appropriate executives of a company. This is only one approach. Many business plan approaches are available and the corporate travel manager may wish to undertake additional research in order to develop alternative corporate travel profit center business plan structures prior to adopting a specific approach or structure. However, the business plan development process identified here is one that can be modified to fit many companies which may wish to develop a corporate travel profit center business plan.

This chapter will start with an analysis of what a corporate travel business plan is and what the ingredients are (i.e., what goes into the making of a corporate travel business plan). The management team and the financial plan needed to get a corporate travel business plan approved and to make it work are discussed in this chapter.

Financial management includes the development of profit and loss statements and three- to five-year plans. These are reviewed in this chapter, as well. Finally, policies and procedures are reviewed and the development of an implementation schedule is presented in an overview setting. Most executives who review them expect to see a considerable number of attachments to a corporate travel profit center business plan. The last part of this chapter gives some suggestions as to what items should be or could be considered for inclusion as attachments in the corporate travel profit center business plan appendix.

Profit Center Business Plan

When moving a corporate travel department from the status of a cost center to that of a profit center, it is essential to obtain the approval of top management. This is normally accomplished by developing a *profit center business plan* and presenting it through the chain of command with the expectation that a series of reviews and oral presentations will probably be expected to accompany the plan. Organizations work in various ways and the approach that works for one company is not necessarily successful for another. Therefore, the development of a profit center business plan and the approach taken to get the plan accepted will vary from one business to another. However, there are guidelines that can assist a corporate travel manager in developing a profit center business plan.

The first key to plan development is the gathering of data. It is essential that sufficient travel be handled by the company to present a potential for profit. At the very minimum, this is usually $1 million of gross travel for the business. The $1 million minimum includes air, hotel, and car rental costs. It does not include other costs, since other costs are normally non-commissionable and a percentage of the commission or the total commission is needed to obtain profitability. Companies having less than one million dollars in travel purchasing value still

164

Chapter 11:
The Corporate
Travel Profit
Center
Business Plan

have a potential for profits if an effort can be developed whereby several companies can get together and jointly develop a business plan that would provide some degree of profit for each entity. However, even under such circumstances, unless a company is doing at least $500,000 of travel or more, the probability is that a profit center cannot be developed unless several other larger travel volume entities are added to the company's volume of travel. The best that one might hope for would be the ability to offset business travel department costs to a substantial degree. Even though a profit center might not be possible, the ability to offset business travel department costs combined with the ability to lower average per trip travel costs will often be more than sufficient to justify the existence of a travel department.

The development of a profit center business plan, therefore, will presume that the business is generating at least $1 million in travel purchasing annually. Once the volume is identified, it is necessary to develop data to substantiate the travel volume and to be able to break down that volume into the commissionable categories of:

1. air travel;

2. hotel room costs; and

3. car rental charges.

Having broken down travel expenses into these three broad categories, it may be helpful to identify the total volume of air travel on a city-pair basis and on a per-carrier basis. Breakdowns of hotel expenditures should be by destination city and by hotel chain or independent property. Car rental cost breakdowns should be by rental city, rental franchise organization, and individual franchisees.

Once data has been obtained relating to annual commission paid expenses, it will be necessary to determine corporate travel department expenditures. These will include salaries, benefits, taxes, current computer expenses (lease or rent payments, if any), space rental costs, expendible supplies, printing, furnishings, and so forth. The corporate travel manager needs to recognize that the maximum amount of income that could be obtained by a corporate travel department without charging service fees would be the same as a travel agency would obtain (i.e., approximately ten percent of the gross commissionable travel expenditures). In other words, if the commissionable travel expenditures for a year (airline tickets, hotel room charges, and car rental base fees) is equal to $1 million, then by multiplying the average commission of approximately ten percent, it is possible to determine that the maximum income potential for such a business travel department would be one hundred thousand dollars. Obviously, if corporate travel department costs exceed $100,000 under such a circumstance, then the ability to create a profit center will not exist.

While this is the maximum formula, most business travel departments which are structured as profit centers do not obtain full commissions. They work on various rebate, partial commission, or fee with full commission rebated types of arrangements. This is not to suggest that an increasing number of corporate travel departments are not applying for appointments and receiving them, but currently, most corporate travel department profit centers are not structured as appointed travel agencies. Therefore, in developing a profit center business plan, most corporate travel department mangers prefer to present top management with a number of potential options.

Although one option might be to purchase a travel agency or to apply for appointment as a travel agency, other optional structures might very well be to:

1. obtain more than sufficient rebates from a full service travel agency in order to offset all corporate travel department costs and provide an additional return of *profit* to the business;

2. to operate as an *in-plant* and receive an up-front three percent commission on all air travel plus a negotiated commission on hotel and car rental expenditures; and

3. to opt for a fee-based structure under which more than sufficient income to pay corporate travel department expenses and to give the company a profit after paying the required and agreed upon contracted annual fees.

The corporate travel manager has trade-offs that provide both advantages and disadvantages. One trade-off is to present top management with a single profit center business plan, not providing options other than the one that the corporate travel manager feels will work best for the business and for the corporate travel department.

A number of corporate travel department managers present single plans rather than plans with multiple options. The advantage of such an approach is that the debate and questions can concentrate on the pros and cons of a single profit center plan, thus concentrating the effort and frequently shortening the time needed to get the necessary decisions. The disadvantage to this approach is that if top management does not like the single plan presented, it may be several years before a plan based upon another option will be considered by top management if, in fact, it will be possible to get a profit plan considered again in the future.

The advantages and disadvantages of presenting a multi-option profit center business plan are just the reverse. Executives are presented with a variety of options, each of which will provide a profit to the business. If there is some aspect of one plan which is not liked, another plan can be considered. The possibility of finding one plan among the several options which all key executives agree to is greater than the possibility of obtaining the approval of all key executives for only a single profit center proposal having no options. The danger of the multi-option plan is that executives can be split, with several executives favoring several plans. This can result in compromises or postponement of the move to the establishment of the profit center altogether. It also takes substantially longer to obtain approval than does a single option plan.

Finally, there is a danger that senior business executives will approve of a plan option which is not the one that the corporate travel manager prefers to work with and which will not be the option that would be most beneficial for the business. Top management may well be only looking at just some of the data and may not take the time to digest all data before making a decision. The corporate travel manager should analyze the political environment of the company and determine whether or not the single option plan or a multi-option plan will have a greater chance of success. The business's political environment frequently dictates

166

Chapter 11:
The Corporate
Travel Profit
Center
Business Plan

whether or not a corporate travel manager will present a single option plan or a multi-option plan.

In developing a written profit center business plan, corporate travel managers often ask how long the plan should be. There is no magic number of pages that works for all companies. However, it is generally agreed that a plan needs to be complete, but not so lengthy that it will not be read. Generally-speaking, most plans run between five and twenty pages in length. Most profit center business plans start with a summary of the proposal. It is important that the summary be convincing, direct, to the point, and concise. Often the summary is the only part of the plan that is read by senior executives, especially when they are busy.

The Ingredients of a Profit Center Business Plan

Courtney Price, Richard Buskirk, and R. Mack Davis view the development of profit entities in a company as *corporate venturing*. The organizational structure they see as ideal is one whereby the chief executive officer and top management provide approval. There is an executive and an advisory board for the profit center entity. Management team rewards are built into the establishment of the system as are incentive award programs and training programs for all involved. They stress that, ". . . the strength of corporate venturing projects relies on total commitment from the chief executive officer (CEO) and top management. A new set of entreprenurial management skills is necessary to have new ventures flourish in the corporate environment. These skills are different from the typical bureaucratic skills required in most corporate environments. Therefore, top management must be able to adjust the corporate culture to accommodate these new skills, to give their complete support for undertaking these ventures, and to nurture the corporate venturing process."

It is suggested that the corporate travel business plan incorporate at least the following sections:

1. concept;
2. corporate fit;
3. the internal market and, if there is to be one, the external market;
4. the structure;
5. price/cost analyses and profit potential;
6. plan for further action; and
7. a summary.

Throughout, one should avoid using general statements and words that are not precise. Be somewhat detail-oriented and precisely accurate in projecting concepts. Do not leave out any key aspect. Before submitting the plan to management, have someone outside the corporate travel department (better yet, someone outside the organization with no travel background) read it to see if they understand clearly and exactly what you wish to convey. Ask them to explain the plan to you. If a neophyte understands, then you are going in the right direction.

Price, Buskirk, and Davis suggest including the following points as they relate to the concept.

1. Define the important and distinct functions of the travel program(s) and travel service(s).

2. What are the unique or proprietary aspects of the travel program(s) and/or service(s)?

3. Describe any innovative technology involved with the program/services.

4. Describe the position the concept plays in the industry.

5. Who is the intended customer?

6. What benefits will be delivered to the customer?

7. How will the program(s) and services be provided to the travelers, the user departments, and other clients?

8. Who will produce/provide the travel program(s) and service(s)?

In determining how the business travel department will ". . . comply with the corporate culture or the strategic plan of the (business)," it is necessary to measure the degree of *corporate fit*. To assist in doing this, make certain that the profit plan answers the following questions.

1. What are the corporate goals for the next five years as corporate travel management may relate to those goals? Specifically, how does corporate travel management and the possibility of having a corporate travel profit center fit into the business's goals?

2. What is the present travel base for the business?

3. What is the future customer base for the corporate travel profit center and/or the business and how might this be tapped by the current business travel base and the identified future customer base?

4. How would a corporate travel profit center appeal to the present and future customer base?

5. How would this move to a profit center utilize any current assets of the business that may not be totally utilized currently?

6. Will the current corporate travel department personnel be utilized or will a move to a profit center status involve hiring additional staff or possibly utilize other personnel currently employed in the business?

7. How will the restructuring to become a profit center affect current vendor status and will this in any way alienate current business clients or others in the community served by the company and if so to what extent and how will negative aspects be handled?

Marketing questions generally will be a concern of executives considering the profit plan. Therefore, make certain that the following questions relating to the market are answered. To deal with marketing concerns, the following questions need to be considered.

1. What is the current travel base (i.e., how many annual travelers does the business travel department serve)? How many tickets are issued? How many room nights are utilized annually? How many car rental days are purchased annually, and so forth?

168

Chapter 11:
The Corporate
Travel Profit
Center
Business Plan

2. Under the profit center plan, will the market remain the same or will additional markets be developed and if additional markets are to be developed and served, what are they?

3. Will the profit center provide leisure travel benefits and services for current employees and/or others and if so, to what extent will this affect the total market and business travel services?

4. What other businesses in the community have moved to a corporate travel profit center concept providing additional services and travel benefits and can any of these be utilized as marketing models?

5. What are the demographics relating to current travelers and those who may become target market travelers if the current travel base is to become expanded?

6. Presuming that business travelers currently utilize the business travel department because it is mandated that they do so, if a broader client base is envisioned utilizing the profit center plan, why would the potential customers for the broader base prefer to work with the profit center rather than to purchase airline tickets and other travel services through current and/or more traditional routes?

7. To what extent would competitors exist as it relates to the broader market if a broader market is sought or to the current market if more freedom of choice becomes available as a result of the move toward profit center status and if there are not current competitors, to what extent might there be emerging competitors?

8. How will the services to the business travelers who are currently being provided service be changed and how will travel services and programs be sold to potential new clients if, in fact, this is envisioned?

9. What percentage of the "additional" market can the profit center capture (for example, if leisure travel is to be marketed to current employees, to what extent can it be expected that current employees will purchase leisure travel)?

Since the profit center plan, in many cases, will be the essential financial restructuring plan, identifying the financial impact is key to getting the profit plan accepted and it is essential that financial concerns be addressed thoroughly. Some of the questions that need to be addressed are as follows:

1. What costs are involved in the current mode of operation (both costs born by the business and those born by travel vendors which might be absorbed under a profit plan. These costs should include labor, computers, supplies, space costs, and so on)?

2. Who are the travel suppliers currently being utilized and what suppliers will be utilized after the move to becoming a profit center? To what extent will services and/or travel products be affected by any potential change of suppliers?

3. What equipment and materials will need to be purchased in addition to any which may currently be owned by the business?

4. What back-up supplies and equipment will be needed in order to provide at least the same level of service currently being provided and what will be the cost of this equipment and these supplies (including the storage costs, if any)?

5. Often there is a concern relating to the possible imposition of service charges when a move to profit center status is undertaken. If there is to be any increase in the price of travel products or services under the profit center status, this needs to be addressed and the reasons for it need to be addressed. Perhaps even more important, if there is to be no additional costs to user departments or to the business, which is most often the case, this needs to be clearly noted, if not highlighted.

6. The total travel commissionable sales (including airline tickets, hotel rooms, and car rentals, at least) should be estimated for the first twelve months with extensions to the first sixty months.

7. It will be essential to identify what the costs will be for providing services and these costs should include all expendible costs, labor, and capital. Normally operating costs are not included in the section relating to the costs for provided products and services, but are discussed in a separate section. Usually the cost for providing the travel services or programs are broken down by type of service provided, in other words, the cost of providing airline tickets should be identified, the cost for providing hotel bookings should be provided, and so on. Although the average travel agency commission is approximately ten percent, it is essential to discuss the expected commission and/or profit to be obtained on each type of service provided. In other words, what would be the gross profit on the provision of airline tickets? What will it be for hotel bookings? What will it be on car rentals and other services?

Operating expenses need to be detailed. These should include rent, office supplies, salaries, benefits, some allocation for corporate overhead, and marketing costs (newsletters, flyers, and so on).

Clearly identifying the potential profit is essential. Traditionally, this is identified through the following formula: *sales* minus *cost of goods* equals *gross margins* minus *operating expenses* equals *profit*, or as follows:

$$
\begin{aligned}
& \text{Sales} \\
- \ & \underline{\text{Cost of Goods}} \\
= \ & \text{Gross Margin} \\
- \ & \underline{\text{Operating Expenses}} \\
= \ & \text{Profit}
\end{aligned}
$$

Projections are an important part of profit center business plans. In a section of the plan relating to future projections, estimate total sales of all travel services and programs which should be projected on a yearly basis for the next five years. In addition, break this down to projections for each program or service provided. Identify capital expenditures which will be needed in order to reach

170

Chapter 11:
The Corporate
Travel Profit
Center
Business Plan

sales goals and break these expenditures down into the type of equipment needed and the amount of each capital expenditure. Identify personnel cost expectations listing all personnel who will be needed in the profit center by both title and job description (normally the names of individuals are not included in this section). Show personnel projections for each year up to the end of the fifth year. Identify any innovative additional services or programs that would be implemented and identify the costs for these on an annual basis up to the end of the fifth year. Indicate clearly what the benefits and costs of these innovative programs and services will be and if the innovative programs and/or services would produce an additional profit, clearly identify this as well. In addition, show how and the extent to which such innovative programs and services will have a corporate *fit*.

In the profit plan, show what role the corporate travel manager will play in the newly structured profit center if such a role can be expected to differ in any significant way from the role currently being played. Since this is a move that is sometimes made by corporate travel managers who wish to move from handling corporate travel on a part-time basis along with other duties in the organization to becoming full-time corporate travel managers, this expectation needs to be clearly identified and justified in the profit center plan.

In organizing a profit plan the following will provide a starting point for putting the pieces together. The flow is as follows:

1. summary and executive overview;
2. concept;
3. management and organization;
4. product/service;
5. production plan;
6. competition;
7. pricing;
8. the marketing plan;
9. the financial plan;
10. operating and control system;
11. schedule;
12. growth plan;
13. contingency plan;
14. the deal; and
15. appendix.

This data flow is only an initial suggestion. It should be reviewed several times and restructured to fit what the corporate travel manager believes will be most effective in the business for which it is designed and this could change drastically from one business to another. However, it is essential that a summary, frequently called the *executive overview* be included. This summary normally comes first rather than last in the profit plan and it will contain highlights relating to the following:

1. the profit center management team;

2. the current and expected market for travel programs and services;

3. marketing plans;

4. travel programs and/or service(s) processing and distribution systems;

5. relevant financial information; and

6. capital requirements.

Although the summary should be brief, remember that it is often the only part of the profit plan that is read. Therefore, it must contain enough detail to adequately describe the profit center venture.

The executive overview will state the purpose of a move to the profit center structure. Describe the current stage of development of the corporate travel department (i.e., is the current business travel department in a start-up stage, is it in the initial operations stage, is it in a stage of expansion, of rapid growth, or is the current corporate travel department operating on a stable basis). Develop a brief mission statement about the profit center. This should consist of the type of programs and services that will be provided and an overview of the pertinent aspects of the travel industry, such as the twenty percent rule and other aspects that will affect a profit center status. Identify and highlight key management personnel and their skills that will add to the potential for the success of the profit center. Briefly describe marketing aspects of the industry in a future expansion of the profit center's target market and the market penetration plan. And finally, describe the major travel programs and services and how these will fill user department and/or traveler needs better than they are currently being fulfilled.

Additional points that need to be considered in the development of the profit plan include the following:

1. Develop a personnel plan which identifies how the corporate travel manager will attract and retain competent personnel both in the short term and the long term.

2. List key internal and external advisors such as consultants, accountants, lawyers, and others who will assist in making the profit center successful. Include organization charts, both a current one and projected organization charts for a three-year and five-year future.

3. Show how the travel programs and services will better fulfill traveler and user department needs.

4. Address any future research and development efforts.

5. Indicate any government approvals (local, state, and federal) and association or semi-governmental approvals that are necessary (e.g., ARC and IATAN).

6. Identify any legal liabilities and/or insurance needs.

7. Identify the extent to which travel programs and services will be provided internally and how much of this may be provided by travel vendors and/or other subcontractors.

8. Identify significant travel purchasing contracts, especially those that commit

172

Chapter 11:
The Corporate
Travel Profit
Center
Business Plan

the business and pertain to carrying some degree of risk (for example, hotel vendor contracts guaranteeing the payment for a number of night stays annually).

9. Identify how storage and security requirements would be met.

10. Identify control systems (quality control, inventory control, and so on).

11. Describe maintenance and/or service agreements that expect to be entered.

12. Identify a break-even point (i.e., the amount of travel sales that will be needed on an annual basis to be able to cover all costs. It may be beneficial to also break out this annual break-even point into monthly sales required for break-even, a weekly break-even point, and a daily sales break-even point.

The Management Team

Anthony Coleman, Senior Consultant with Better Business Planning, Inc. stresses that the major factor considered by executives, especially chief financial executives, in considering new ventures that involve a degree of risk for companies and which appear, on the surface, to present viable profit potentials is the strength of the management team. "The management team can make or break a venture," notes Coleman. In many cases, when his company reviews a potential venture and prepares a plan to be submitted for funding, Coleman and his associates place their concentration on making certain that the management team has the background, experience, and proven ability to bring about the profits that are projected in the profit plan. It is suggested, therefore, that corporate travel managers review their own knowledge, expertise, and proven ability to produce cost savings and/or other benefits for the business and document these in the profit center business plan.

The same type of review should be undertaken for any others who may be working in the corporate travel department and who would be expected to continue to work in the restructured corporate travel department that will provide travel services after the move to profit center status is completed. This is especially true if additional employees will be hired.

For those who are considering either purchasing a travel agency, becoming a travel agency, or jointly owning a travel agency, the management team's concern may be even greater. Obviously, if the corporate travel manager has done a good job in the past, data relating to the corporate travel manager's background is available to key executives who may not know the corporate travel manager personally and certainly some, if not all, chief executives will know the corporate travel manager personally. However, if a travel agency is to be created, purchased, or jointly owned, the management team of the travel agency is totally unknown to corporate executives.

Perhaps the most unfortunate aspect relating to management teams is that, frequently, top executives are not comfortable with the management team and they will simply disapprove of a venture opportunity rather than communicate that disapproval. They may reason that the current arrangement is beneficial to the company and the management team is not strong enough to carry out a profit center venture successfully and, therefore, the best alternative is to continue with that which has been proven successful thus far (i.e., the status quo).

To offset this potential, the corporate travel manager needs to clearly identify personal and departmental strengths and weaknesses. If at all possible, an outside entity needs to be called upon to evaluate the plan as a whole, if not the strength of the management team alone. If it is determined that the management team is not as strong as the corporate travel manager believes that it should be to successfully obtain approval for the movement to a profit plan or to successfully implement a profit plan, specific weaknesses need to be identified and either internal or external resources need to be included in the overall plan to provide the strength needed.

Internal resources can come from any department within the organization. Many organizations are very comfortable with cross-utilizing experts between departments in sections of the business so that the expertise can be maximized for the benefit of the organization as a whole. Other businesses do not operate in this manner and cross-utilization is a rarity. Unless it is specifically prohibited or the corporate culture discourages such a utilization, internal consulting should be considered and included in the profit center business plan.

External consultants can be considered as well. External consultants can work on either a one-time arrangement or on a continuing basis. The most important factor here is to maximize return on investment. In order to do this, it is important to identify external consultant expertise. Once the weaknesses have been identified and external consultant expertise has been hired, a matching should be undertaken to determine exactly what an external consultant can do for the business. Although there are open-ended consulting arrangements whereby a consultant is paid a fee on a monthly, quarterly, or annual basis to provide ongoing assistance, this type of arrangement is generally less cost effective, but more rapidly responsive when specific needs arrive.

Sometimes the inclusion of consulting services in a profit center business plan can add too much to the costs and can result in a negative reaction from top management. In other cases, top management which might be concerned about the strength of the management team will consider that cost-effective consulting, which is built into the profit center business plan, will supply the additional strength needed and still allow the corporate travel department to be a profit center, thereby offering a greater chance of receiving executive approval. The corporate travel manager, therefore, will need to weigh the benefits and the drawbacks of including internal and external consultants in the management team for the corporate travel department profit center.

Financial aspects of the profit plan include *pricing*. If the corporate travel department will be purchasing tickets from a travel agency vendor, describe the pricing strategy of the vendor by each travel program or service provided. This should include unit price (per room, per car, and so on) quantity discounts, and vendor billing policies. If the corporate travel department is establishing an internal-appointed travel agency structure, describe the pricing strategy to be utilized in providing travel programs and services to each business department, leisure client, and so on. Again, include unit prices, if appropriate, quantity discounts, and billing policies. Next, compare this pricing strategy to any competition which may exist. Although the probability is that there will be no compe-

174

Chapter 11:
The Corporate
Travel Profit
Center
Business Plan

tition within the business for business travel, if leisure travel arrangements are to be provided to the employees of the business, then travel agencies in the community would probably provide competition and the extent to which this competition exists should be identified.

Describe any current or future discount policies in detail. If the corporate travel department will be purchasing travel from a travel agency and that agency is providing discount policies, these need to be identified in detail. If the corporate travel department will be acting as an appointed travel agency, then any discount policies that would apply to those either in the company or especially those who are purchasing leisure travel for their own personal use will need to be identified. Since pricing relates strongly to payment, identify what the standard payment terms will be.

The Financial Plan

There are advantages to having a distinct separate part of the profit center business plan identified as the financial plan. By clearly identifying this section of the profit plan, one is able to give executive reviewers an opportunity to skim through that which may be of less interest to them and concentrate on a section that most executives will expect to be the key section of the profit center business plan. Normally this appears as the last section of the profit center business plan. It presents the *bottom line*. The financial plan may include a number of factors, but should have at least a budget, a projected profit and loss forecast, and a three-year or a five-year financial plan projection.

Normally the budget is the first part of the financial plan. The budget is not just one budget, but it is broken down into what can be referred to as mini-budgets. There needs to be a *personnel budget*, an *expense budget*, and a *capital equipment budget*. Some organizations break out the expense budget into two seperate budgets. One of these is called a *production budget* which identifies the cost of producing travel services and programs and a second is an *expense budget*, which identifies all expenses not covered in any other category. For the purposes of this publication, a single expense budget will be utilized rather than breaking out the costs of producing travel services and programs. If the corporate travel profit center business plan is to really reflect a profit center, then the income derived by the corporate travel department will need to be more than all expenses identified in the budget (a compilation of all mini-budgets). Income projections should be modest and conservative rather than what one might like to think will happen. This helps to cushion the effect should financial results be less than anticipated. Although one should never leave out expected costs to force a paper budget profit (because this can easily backfire and create major problems), the budgets will reflect whether or not the entire business plan is indeed a profit center business plan or a business plan for a corporate travel department that remains a cost center. It is important to be accurate in reporting budget figures and projections. The probability is that the budget will be reviewed in detail and the probability is strong that corporate financial experts will be undertaking budget reviews. Therefore, it is essential to obtain exact costs as often as possible.

However, if there are costs that are not exact, good estimates should be made and a part of the financial plan should identify those parts of the budget which were based upon estimates rather than known costs. These should clearly identify how the estimates were obtained, in order to justify to the financial expert reviewers that the estimates were the best possible estimates that could be obtained with the data available. The budget development section, therefore, should not be rushed, but should be carefully researched. Normally, this is the last part of the profit center business plan to be developed because of the fact that a complete, accurate budget for all costs cannot be put together until all costs are identified.

Profit and Loss Statement

Profit and loss statements are made up of two sections. One relates to income and the other relates to expenditures. Neither can be put together in haste. Both need to be clearly identified. The income part of the profit and loss statement relates to the money which the corporate travel department expects to receive. If the corporate travel department is working with an agency vendor, the money to be received will probably come in the form of rebates. There is also the possibility that it will come in the form of commissions on travel which are paid to the travel agency for the travel services provided to the business travelers in your company. This would be the case if the arrangement with the travel agency is one whereby they would be billing for their services and providing all commissions to your business. The third option in terms of income would be for the corporate travel department that expects to be operating as an appointed travel agency. In this case, the income would come from commissions received from air carriers, hotels, and car rental firms.

In all of these cases, income projections need to be based on hard-data figures. As noted in earlier sections, this data needs to come from past history and user department travel budget projections for the next fiscal year. An exact projection on an annual basis, a monthly basis, and a weekly basis should be undertaken based on the historical data and user department travel budget projections. After the travel volume is identified, the percentage of rebate or percentage of commission needs to be applied to that total travel volume in order to identify the expected corporate travel department annual income.

The second part of the profit and loss statement relates to costs. This section should be fairly easy to complete once budgets have been completed because the cost part of the profit and loss statement will project costs in each category (i.e., personnel, capital equipment, and other expenses). After identifying all costs, a total annual cost should be calculated. The total annual cost is subtracted from the projected annual income to show projected corporate travel department profits.

Three-year or Five-year Plan

After completing the first year's plan, it will be necessary to project a three-year or a five-year plan. This should also be projected on the basis of historical data. If the travel for the business has been increasing on a regular basis, identify the total

176

Chapter 11:
The Corporate
Travel Profit
Center
Business Plan

travel volume that has been realized over the last several years and calculate an average annual travel volume increase in expenditures. This should be broken down into average annual travel volume increase in airline costs, hotel costs, and car rental costs. This figure will be the major figure to be utilized in projecting a three-year or a five-year plan, since this figure will be the foundation against which the department should plan.

Obviously, there is no guarantee that the business will continue to show the exact same percentage of business travel cost increase realized over the last three to five years, but for most businesses this is the best place to start since it shows a trend. However, it is important to modify this with expected activity within the business as a whole. For example, if the corporate travel manager knows that a new plant will be opened in the next six months or the next year which will require a substantial amount of travel from the home office to that plant, then this additional travel needs to be factored into the three-year to five-year projections. On the other hand, if the business is in a decline and the corporate travel manager knows that some of the sales offices, factories, or other sites to which the business's travelers travel frequently will be closed or phased out, then this reduction in travel needs to be factored into the projections as well.

Some of the points that need to be considered in the development of the financial plan are as follows:

1. prepare specific plans for first-year budgets for personnel, operating expenses, and capital expenditures;

2. prepare a monthly first-year profit and loss statement;

3. prepare a personnel cost projection by showing the title of each person who will be working in the corporate travel department, the salaries to be paid, and the cost of benefits to be provided;

4. prepare the three-year or the five-year plan (first year by quarters, remaining years annually), including a profit and loss statement for each of the first three or five years;

5. explain the assumptions for the projections in the profit and loss statements;

6. explain the assumptions for the projections for the three or five-year plan;

7. list the methods of purchasing capital expenditures (lease, rent, buy and so on);

8. compare fixed costs with those that vary with travel volume levels;

9. compare a break-even analysis based on the profit and loss statement.

Policy and Procedures

Some executives expect to receive at least an overview of the major policies and procedures that will be undertaken, especially if these policies and procedures will mean a radical change in the way in which the corporate travel department has been operating in the past. Other executives will not be concerned with this aspect of the operation at all, in that their total concern will be related to the potential profits that can be realized. Each corporate travel manager will need to identify the political structure in the business and determine whether or not those members of the management team who will be reviewing the profit center business plan would expect to have information relating to major policies and procedures. For those where there is a concern, this section will identify some of the most important aspects as they relate to operating the corporate travel department as a profit center and controlling corporate travel.

The first section should be a brief explanation of the procedures and any appropriate policies that will be used in receiving requests for travel services from business travelers or travel user departments. Controls relating to this procedure can be identified and policies resulting from those controls should also be identified.

The next section relates to administrative policies, procedures, and controls for:

1. receiving money in the corporate travel department for paying vendors and debiting user department travel budgets;
2. for paying travel suppliers;
3. for collecting from any individual travelers who may be traveling on leisure (non-business travel) travel trips;
4. on management reports;
5. provisions for employee training, incentives, and any special benefits that would not accrue to other employees in the company (such as familiarization trips);
6. on security of ticket stock, airline validation plates, and so on;
7. inventory control (of equipment, tickets, airline validation plates, itineraries, and so on);
8. on handling refunds and cancellations; and
9. on budget control.

Implementation Schedule

Most profit center business plans include an *implementation schedule*. Although this may be of little importance to many of the executives who will be reviewing the profit center business plan, there are executives who can be expected to review the business plan who will consider the impact on their particular department or on the business as a whole. This could be especially true as it relates to capital expenditures, the expenses for which may be expected to occur at a time when the comptroller is concerned about specific cash flow problems in the cash flow cycle of the business. Obviously, this is an event that the comptroller will want to control, if at all possible, in order to make expenditures at a time that is best for the business rather than at the very worse times. For those profit centers that are based upon receiving income from rebates, the implementation schedule may be a very simple one without involving a great many changes from the current mode of operation.

On the other hand, if the corporate travel department is joining with other

178

Chapter 11:
The Corporate
Travel Profit
Center
Business Plan

corporate travel departments to establish a jointly owned travel agency through which all travel is purchased, the implementation schedule will become a much greater factor because it will need to be coordinated with other businesses that may be members of the consortium jointly owning the travel agency. Most corporate travel departments which are moving from a cost center status to a profit center status will find themselves somewhere in between these two extremes.

Crucial to an implementation schedule is a major business travel scheduling pattern. Most companies experience a substantial drop in business travel between the second week of December and the second week of January. This means that income derived from the commissions earned on tickets or from rebates from tickets issued will fall off substantially during this period. If the corporate travel department is planning a move to profit center status whereby all costs of the corporate travel department are to be covered by commissions or rebates and the establishment of the profit center starts in early December, the corporate travel manager may suddenly find that there is no money to pay current costs because there are no business travelers taking trips. It is imperative, therefore that the date for a switchover from cost center status to profit center status be several months away from the low travel income period of late December and early January. The implementation schedule needs to be planned accordingly. Of course, for some companies there are other periods of traditionally little or no travel. If so, these "valleys" also need to be avoided in terms of the initiation date of the profit center move.

It is suggested that two different approaches be considered in developing an implementation schedule. One is a *simple planning schedule* and the other is a *critical path management plan.* The simple planning schedule will be a very simplified approach toward developing key dates. The critical path management approach is considerably more involved. It is designed to keep projects moving in the most expeditious manner possible. Since the critical path method is well documented in a number of management publications, the approach will not be described in detail here. However, it is recommended that those who are considering the establishment of a travel agency wholly owned by the business and managed by the corporate travel department, those considering the purchase of a currently-existing travel agency, again to be managed by the corporate travel department, or those considering a joint-ownership arrangement with other corporate travel departments and their businesses of a travel agency may want to study the critical path method and build the implementation schedule in accordance with the critical path method.

For developing a simple time schedule, the steps outlined below should be taken:

1. List the timing of events by month in each area. A twelve-month projection is usually more than enough. In listing the timing of events, indicate who will be responsible (by title) for seeing that the steps are accomplished. If a profit center is to be created based on agency commission or override rebates or based on working with a full rebate/fee basis travel agency, start with the request for proposal identifying when it will be developed, when it will be sent out, and what the deadline for response will be.

2. Identify deadlines for the selection of a vendor and any of the deadlines that

need to built into that selection process (such as the selection of the top three potential vendors and oral presentation schedules, if that is to be included).

3. Set down a date by which a location will be selected for the corporate travel department if the corporate travel department will need to be moved from the location where it currently exists. This may very well be the case if an expanded corporate travel department is envisioned which would serve leisure travel needs, as well as business travel needs, or if the corporate travel department will become or will own all or part of a travel agency (ARC regulations require a location that is accessible to the general public).

4. A rapid (usually one month or less) phase-out period between the current vendor and the new vendor or vendors should be built into the schedule.

5. A contract development schedule will need to be included with a projected contract starting date. The reporting relationship may or may not remain the same when a move is made from cost center status to profit center status.

6. If the internal reporting relationship is to be changed, a schedule for the orderly processing of reporting relationship changes should be included in the profit center business plan. It may very well be that management and infrastructure flow charts will be developed and included in the implementation schedule.

7. The implementation schedule should also have a section devoted to financial requirements. This will identify when monies will be needed for capital expenditures and other expenditures so that these monies will be available at the time needed. This is especially important if a travel agency is to be purchased or if the business will be part of a group travel agency purchase arrangement.

8. A personnel schedule will also be needed if the expansion of the corporate travel department is a part of the profit center business plan. This will need to identify when new personnel will need to be hired and a schedule involved in terms of interviews and the selection process.

9. Personnel incentives and personnel training schedules for implementation should be a part of the personnel implementation plan.

Appendix

The appendix to the profit center business plan can include a number of documents, but should include at a minimum the following:

1. resumes of the management team or key personnel who will be involved in the corporate travel department;

2. a copy of the organization chart if it is not already included in the body of the plan;

3. a copy of the ARC application (if a travel agency is to be purchased, partially purchased, or opened);

4. copies of the travel policy and/or the travel policy and procedures manual;

5. copies of pertinent correspondence;

180

Chapter 11:
The Corporate
Travel Profit
Center
Business Plan

6. schedules, models from other corporate travel departments that have been developed in written format, articles from trade journals, or other appropriate research data;

7. any detailed outlines of the operating and/or control systems; and

8. a time-line chart depicting significant deadlines and completion priorities.

Summary

The purpose of a corporate travel department profit center business plan can be considered to be two fold. First, obtaining the approval of top management normally requires the development of a complete plan which answers the major, if not all, questions of top management. The second purpose is to provide a framework or a guideline for developing a corporate travel profit center. This can be thought of as a map that takes the corporate travel department from cost center to profit center.

The first step is to gather data. If the data on volume indicates that the business is doing less than $1 million of travel purchasing annually, the move to a profit center will probably not be possible. However, if the volume is at least $1 million, then additional volume data will need to be determined. This includes specific information on total amounts of commissionable air travel, hotel costs, and car rental charges. Once all travel costs are identified, the corporate travel department expenditures need to be identified in detail as well. These include employee costs, computer expenses, and so on. By multiplying the total travel purchases by ten percent and comparing the resulting figure with the total corporate travel department non-travel costs, a rough determination as to whether or not a profit center is possible can be made. If the ten percent commission figure is substantially higher than the departmental costs, one can consider that profit center status might be attainable. If the figures are close or if the expenditures are greater than the commissionable income would be, then the attainment of profit center status is unlikely.

If the commission figure is several times higher than the cost of administering the corporate travel department, the corporate travel manager may have the flexibility of developing a profit center through a number of structures other than the establishment of an in-house travel agency. In other words, profit center status might be attained simply through rebates and/or override commission sharing or through fee-based travel agency contractual arrangements. Under such circumstances, some will present top executives with several alternative scenerios for the establishment of a profit center, while others will present only one plan, but point out in that plan that other scenerios are possible. The internal political factors need to be taken into consideration when making this decision.

In developing the corporate travel department profit center business plan, it should be kept in mind that most such plans start with a summary and often busy top executives read only the summary. Therefore, as the plan is developed, the summary, what it says, and how it is structured, needs to be constantly kept in mind.

Perhaps one of the most important ingredients of a successful corporate travel department profit center is the full support of chief executive officers in looking at the profit center as an important profit entity in the company with an attitude from top management that *corporate venturing*, in order to provide a maximum number of profit resources within the company, plays a vital role in maximizing potential company profits. The attitudes and approaches of all within the company will follow. Sometimes this is an attitude or approach over which the corporate travel manager has little or no control. However, if the work environment includes this type of approach, the acceptance of a corporate travel profit center business plan and the embracing of the corporate travel department as a profit center can be expected to be much more complete.

Structurally, the corporate travel profit center should have direct lines of communication to the chief executive officer and the chief financial officer or a separate executive board can be established for the corporate travel profit center. In the travel industry, one frequently encounters this type of structure in looking at travel agencies that have been purchased by business conglomerates to handle the travel of all businesses held in the conglomerate as well as to handle outside travel. The corporate travel department profit center can have a similar structure.

In addition, ideally, the corporate travel profit center business plan will identify corporate travel department executive incentives, training, and professional development activities. These entrepreneural management approaches can be beneficial in planning to maximize profits.

The corporate travel profit center business plan should include at least the following sections:

1. concept;
2. corporate fit;
3. the internal market;
4. the external market (if there is to be one);
5. the structure;
6. price/cost analyses and profit potential;
7. an action plan; and
8. a summary.

This chapter has presented eight points to consider in determining the concept. These are broad points, but each needs to be addressed.

A similar approach is taken when considering *corporate fit*. Seven points have been presented in this chapter which need to be kept in mind when considering corporate fit.

The concept of "market" is one that some tend to overlook in that there is a potential for the attitude that all corporate travelers must go through the corporate travel department and therefore there is no marketing role. Although there may very well be a "locked-in" market of travelers who must use the corporate travel department, if the department is a profit center, it needs to consider both the positive aspects related to having "satisfied clients" (company

182

Chapter 11:
The Corporate
Travel Profit
Center
Business Plan

business travelers) and the negative repercusions that might occur if the company's travelers are grossly dissatisfied or unhappy with the services of the corporate travel department. In addition, there is a potential external market if the corporate travel department as a profit center also functions as a travel agency and is able to sell leisure travel products and services to company employees and/or others outside the company. Nine points of consideration have been presented in this chapter for consideration in developing the marketing section of the corporate travel profit center business plan.

As noted earlier, several structures of the corporate travel profit center are possible and the corporate travel manager has the alternative of either presenting only one structure, noting that other alternatives are available, or presenting several potential structures.

Perhaps the most import section of the corporate travel profit center business plan is that part which addresses the finances. This is the justification for the establishment of a profit center. Therefore, clearly identifying financial ramifications is important. Six points that deal directly with the financial impact of a corporate travel profit center are presented in this chapter. In addition, a formula for clearly identifying the potential profit is presented. This, however, provides only the framework. In developing this section of the corporate travel profit center business plan it is important to be as precise, specific, and yet concise as possible including all pertinent financial ramifications.

Other points that the corporate travel manager may want to address in the corporate travel profit center business plan prior to writing the section relating to the plan for further action include an analysis of all travel products that will be provided and services that will be offered. A production plan (the process of obtaining information on travel that is needed and producing the reservations, tickets, vouchers, and other travel products needed by the traveler along with the delivery of these products and services), competition (if external marketing or the marketing of leisure travel to corporate employees is to be a part of the corporate travel profit center business plan), an operating and control system, and a contingency plan might also be included.

The plan for further action should include an overview of how the pieces discussed thus far are envisioned to come together. A schedule and a growth plan are usually a part of the plan for further action. This plan also includes a section relating to the contractual relations with suppliers.

The last major section to be written and usually considered to be the most important section from a political standpoint is the summary. Since this is often the only part of the plan that is read, it must be written in such a manner that the major questions of executives reviewing the plan will be answered in the summary and the major concerns of those executives will be addressed. It is, in essence, the selling piece of the corporate travel profit center business plan. This summary is often called the *executive overview*. Six relevant points have been identified for the summary.

The appendix to the corporate travel profit center business plan provides back-up data for those wishing to have additional information. The appendix can include such data as details regarding the statistical information on which the plan is based, a personnel plan, short-term and long-term development plans, a list of key internal and external advisors, organization charts, and other hard data.

A number of additional points can be included in the corporate travel profit center business plan. This chapter presents twelve additional points that might be considered.

Seven areas of the corporate travel profit center business plan are considered especially important. This chapter provides specific sections of recommendations in each of these seven areas. The areas include the following:

1. the management team;
2. the financial plan;
3. the profit and loss statement;
4. the three- or five-year plan;
5. policies and procedures;
6. the implementation schedule; and
7. the corporate travel profit center business plan appendix.

The financial management section of this book has moved from basic considerations through saving money to making money and establishing a profit center. There are, however, several specialized financial applications in corporate travel management. Primary among these are those applications relating to international travel financial management. The next chapter deals with this aspect of corporate travel management in detail.

Discussion Questions

1. Does having a corporate travel department structured as a profit center require the purchase of or the owning of a travel agency?
2. Why might the political environment in a company be an important factor in considering a move from cost center to profit center status?
3. Is the approval of top management important in moving the corporate travel department from its status as a cost center to that of a profit center? Explain.
4. What is the first key to profit center business plan development?
5. Why is $1 million of gross travel business an important figure in considering the possibility of establishing a corporate travel profit center?
6. What are the pros and cons of presenting single option corporate travel profit center business plans to top management for consideration versus presenting multiple-option corporate travel profit center business plans to them for consideration?
7. Generally speaking, how many pages in length do most corporate travel profit center business plans run?
8. With what section of the proposal do most corporate travel profit center business plans start?

184

Chapter 11:
The Corporate
Travel Profit
Center
Business Plan

9. What is meant by the term *corporate venturing*?

10. What are six sections often found in corporate travel profit center business plans?

11. What questions do Price, Buskirk, and Davis suggest be addressed as they relate to the corporate travel profit center business plan concept?

12. What seven points can be considered in determining the degree of *corporate fit*?

13. What nine questions should be considered in dealing with marketing concerns relating to the corporate travel profit center business plan?

14. Since it is essential that financial concerns be addressed completely, what is considered a financial key to getting the corporate travel profit plan accepted?

15. What are seven financial questions that need to be addressed in the corporate travel profit center business plan?

16. What is the traditional potential profit formula and how does this relate to the development of a corporate travel profit center business plan?

17. What are the projections that one might include in a corporate travel profit center business plan?

18. What is the order of the fifteen pieces identified as sections in a corporate travel profit center business plan? Identify the section and the order in which it is placed in the business plan?

19. Why is the corporate travel profit center business plan summary frequently called the *executive overview*?

20. What are six highlights of the corporate travel profit center business plan summary?

21. Twelve additional points that need to be considered in the development of a corporate travel profit center business plan are identified in this chapter. What are they?

22. Anthony Coleman considers the strength of what to be the major factor considered by executives when they review new ventures that involve a degree of risk for companies and which appear on the surface to present viable profit potentials?

23. Why might the management team be a greater concern for those who are considering either purchasing a travel agency, becoming a travel agency, or jointly owning a travel agency as apposed to structuring the corporate travel profit center in some other manner?

24. Why might external consultants be considered important in obtaining top management approval of a corporate travel profit center business plan?

25. What pricing considerations might be considered in corporate travel profit center business plans?

26. What is one advantage of having a distinct seperate part of the corporate travel profit center business plan identified as the financial plan?

27. What are three sections that are considered necessary in the financial plan section of a corporate travel profit center business plan?

185
Group
Discussion
Situation:
eta Prophet's
Profit Center

28. Profit and loss statements are made up of two sections. What are these two sections?

29. Three-year and/or five-year plans should be projected on the basis of what type of data?

30. What nine points need to be considered in the development of the financial plan sections of corporate travel profit center business plans?

31. Why might some executives expect to receive an overview of the major policies and procedures relating to a corporate travel profit center business plan when these policies and procedures mean a radical change from the way in which the corporate travel department has operated in the past?

32. What is an *implementation schedule*?

33. What two approaches might be considered in developing an implementation schedule?

34. What are some of the documents that might be included in a corporate travel profit center business plan appendix?

Role Play Exercise

Two students may participate in this role play either out-of-class, as a fun way to review the chapter, or as an in-class exercise. One plays the role of the company's corporate travel manager and the other plays the role of the chief financial officer of the company. Please read the script and then pick up the conversation in your own words.

Corporate Travel Manager: I appreciate your offering to help in developing a corporate travel profit center business plan proposal. I am not sure where to start. What do you suggest?

Chief Financial Officer: The first question is whether or not having a corporate travel profit center is viable. What are your departmental costs and what kind of income can you expect from commissions, overrides, override sharing, and other potential revenues? What kind of structure do you plan? What have you thought about putting into the corporate travel profit center business plan?

Corporate Travel Manager: I'll try to answer all those questions. I have given a lot of thought to each one. first, . . .

CONTINUE ON YOUR OWN

Group Discussion Situation: Neeta Prophet's Profit Center

Two years ago, Grandular Gurgles went through a cost reduction program under which a number of departments in the corporation were either eliminated or merged in order to reduce administrative costs. The initial cost reduction report on which the department elimination/merger process was based suggested the

186

Chapter 11:
The Corporate
Travel Profit
Center
Business Plan

total elimination of the corporate travel department. Neeta Prophet, the corporate travel manager, would have been without a job. Fortunately, the chair of the cost reduction committee, was a friend of Neeta and he advised her that the committee had made a recommendation to eliminate the corporate travel department. This advise came approximately five weeks before the report was released.

Neeta used the advance notice she had to work to save the department. She approached both the chief financial officer and the chief executive officer showing them details of how the corporate travel department had not only reduced costs from what they would have been had the corporate travel department not been in existence. She also showed them how rebates and override commission sharing checks provided additional income to the company. "Income . . . ," stressed Neeta, ". . . which makes a vital differences in the overall financial balances of the company when corporate losses on food products (the major source of income for Grandular Gurgles) are making the company's bottom line sway between black and red cannot be ignored." The chief executive officer stressed to Neeta that while this information was of value, the financial records showed only the expenses of the corporate travel department and did not reflect the income since income received by the corporate travel department went into general funds. Based on Neeta's arguments with both the chief executive officer and the chief financial officer, her department squeeked by and was retained, but two part-time assistants were eliminated in the department, leaving Neeta as the only employee in corporate travel.

Now that two years have gone by and the company is making reasonable profits again, Neeta wants to change the structure of the corporate travel department to make it a profit center. Last month she finished documenting an employee justification report identifying the need for at least one part-time employee to work with her in the corporate travel department. Although the justification was substantial, she was told by a friend working in salary administration that the reason the request was turned down was that the administrative costs (her salary and the overhead of the corporate travel department) are higher than several managers in the finance and personnel departments feel they should be.

Neeta has been advised that the new comptroller for the company, who came to the company just three months ago from a firm that had a corporate travel profit center, would be happy to review a corporate travel profit center proposal. However, she was warned, if the proposal is not accepted, it may be years before another proposal of this type will be considered.

For several days Neeta has been working on an outline of the executive overview (the summary) of the corporate travel profit center business plan she is preparing. Neeta has asked several executives in the company to work with her in the development of this outline in order to make sure that the proposal is both complete and precise.

You are meeting today to develop a draft outline for Neeta Prophet's consideration. You are expected to reach agreement and to write a no more than three-page sentence outline for the executive overview (summary) of the corporate travel profit center business plan proposal. In your group session, select one person to chair the group. All will have an equal vote on decisions. In the group session, you are expected to reach agreement on the outline and to prepare the outline to be presented to the entire class by the chair of your committee.

CHAPTER 12

International Travel Financial Management

Introduction

International travel financial management offers the corporate travel manager several ways to save money. These include:

1. taking advantage of exchange rate fluctuations;
2. reducing annual exchange charges; and
3. using blocked funds.

Because of the constant changes in currency exchange rates and the lag time in adjusting ticket prices to reflect these currency changes, the opportunity exists for the issuing of tickets in various currencies. In addition, variations in exchange rates between some major countries reflect patterns that tend to repeat themselves on an annual basis. By recognizing these patterns, it is sometimes possible to establish bank accounts in other countries at favorable exchange rates which can be utilized for paying hotel, car rental, and other travel bills. In addition, exchange charges can be substantial and the savings that a corporate travel department can realize has the potential of being considerable when payment is made from local bank accounts in other countries and a transfer of funds is made only once or twice a year. By recognizing and taking advantage of exchange rate patterns, it is sometimes possible to establish bank accounts in other countries at favorably exchange rates which can be utilized during less favorable exchange rate periods of the year to pay hotel, car rental, and other local travel bills from the local bank account funds held in other countries.

Blocked funds present still another opportunity to manage corporate travel finances. If a business has a substantial amount of travel internationally, the opportunity to save money through the maximum utilization of the above approaches can provide the company with substantial savings.

Pattern Identification

As with many other financial management activities, the first step is to identify patterns and to research appropriate statistics. It is important to know the volume of travel on an annual basis to each destination country. Obviously, if there is only one trip a year to a country, working with the establishment of blocked funds or going to the trouble of setting up special bank accounts in other countries can be too time consuming and too expensive to be profitable. However, on the other hand, if there is a substantial amount of travel to a destination country, the opportunity exists for savings through these and other techniques. In developing the data, it is important to identify not only the number of trips to a destination area, but also the cost of hotels, car rentals, and other expenses that are incurred in conjunction with the trips.

Ticketing Currency Decisions

Perhaps the simplist financial management approach relates to the utilization of tickets issued in currencies other than the U.S. dollar. A large number of corporate travel managers routinely identify the cost in dollars for tickets issued in a variety of currencies before making the decisions to have an international ticket issued and paid for in U.S. dollars. Usually the choice winds up being either the currency of the destination country or the U.S. dollar. However, if the trip involves stops or business in several countries for which different currencies are utilized, many corporate travel managers will evaluate the costs for the air ticket in currencies of each of the itinerary countries and select the currency that provides the best price for the ticket. Travel agencies can issue the tickets either in the U.S. using the currency involved (and this is usually the case unless exportation of the currency is illegal) or the ticket can be issued in the destination country (in the currency selected). This is sometimes the choice selected if the traveler is originating in the destination country.

Local Account Payments

Just as corporate travel managers often negotiate for special hotel rates for destination hotels in the U. S., the same approach can be undertaken for hotels in other countries. However, in some cases, the destination hotel in other countries may be hotels that may house a large number of company employees throughout the year or at specific times during the year. When this is the case, instead of having payment made by the individual traveler who normally will exchange U.S. dollars at a local bank or, in some cases, at the hotel in order to pay for the hotel room (and charge the company the exchange transaction fee), a billing arrangement can be established with the hotel whereby negotiated hotel costs are paid (this is usually the per night room cost, but sometimes includes a meal allowance in hotel restaurants) and payment can be made from funds held in local banks in local currency. This takes advantage of transfers to the account made during times of better exchange rates, allows for a reduction in the number of exchange rate transactions and the exchange rate per transaction fees that are levied in most cases, and allows for utilization of soft currencies which may be earned by the business in the destination country rather than the utilization of hard dollars when local currencies are soft currencies or the exportation of the company's profits is limited or prohibited. Of course, car rental arrangements of the same type can be negotiated in destination countries as well, resulting in similar savings.

Blocked Funds

Blocked funds present still another opportunity for financial management. In a large number of countries throughout the world there are government prohibitions or limitations on the exportation of local currencies and/or regulations prohibiting the exportation of profits by foreign (U.S.) companies. When this is the case, some companies allow the accumulation of local currency funds in local banks. These funds may be utilized by the company for expenditures within the country, but may not be exported. Corporate travel managers who have travelers traveling to these destination countries can benefit the financial management of the company as a whole by drawing on blocked funds to as great an extent as possible.

Obviously, as many of the local travel costs as possible for company employees should be paid for out of blocked funds. In addition, corporate travel managers are sometimes able to purchase tickets for travel to and from other countries by utilizing blocked funds in a country where funds are otherwise blocked, but are not restricted by the local government for the local purchase of international airline tickets. In a very few cases, this utilization of blocked funds has allowed a corporate travel manager to help the company spend a substantial percentage of blocked funds by having many airline tickets issued from the blocked fund accounts even when the tickets are to and from points not in the country where blocked funds are being utilized to purchase the tickets. In other words, the purchase of airline tickets is used as a way of exporting blocked funds. Most countries have recognized this way of using up blocked funds and have regulations limiting the issuance of air tickets with payment from blocked funds, but there are some blocked fund accounts where it is still possible to take advantage of this purchasing method.

Country restrictions on blocked fund usage vary to a considerable extent from country to country. In some countries, it is possible to utilize blocked funds for the expenditures of companies other than the company which earned the blocked funds. There are arrangements that have been undertaken within industries (for example, the film industry does this) whereby one company will utilize the blocked funds of another company when they have travel or other projects within a blocked fund destination country. Where a country limits the utilization to expenditures for the company which earned the blocked funds, there have been some cases in which employees have been temporarily assigned to the blocked-fund-earning company in order to take advantage of and to use blocked funds. Obviously, unless a substantial amount of travel is involved for a specific employee into and/or out of a country where such blocked funds are being maintained, this approach is more trouble than it is worth. However, the film industry has utilized this technique when having performers or others in the industry who have a substantial amount of business in a country where a fellow business has substantial blocked funds in order to take full advantage of the utilization of those blocked funds.

One benefit that can be provided for the company by the corporate travel manager is a search for companies that have blocked funds in destination countries and the establishment of agreements whereby fund transfers will occur in order to utilize the funds to pay for hotels, car rentals, and other local expenditures. Typically, a percentage of value of the blocked fund is determined, the using company's local bills are paid by the company which earned the blocked funds, and a percentage of fund utilization value is transferred in U.S. dollars to the U.S. bank account of the blocked fund earning company by the blocked fund user company. Although there is no master list circulated among corporate travel managers identifying all companies with blocked funds, a number of businesses that have substantial amounts of business in other countries have established informal arrangements between one another in order to utilize one another's blocked funds. Frequently, the cost of blocked fund utilization can be as little as fifty percent of the local currency value since the blocked fund earning company might easily lose any value of the blocked funds if they are not utilized.

Black Market Air Tickets

A number of corporate travel managers are, from time to time, tempted to purchase air tickets on the black market. The going rate can be substantially cheaper than the purchase of air tickets directly from air carriers or from travel agencies. However, there is substantial danger in purchasing black market air tickets. In many countries, the purchase of and/or the utilization of black market air tickets is illegal and can result in the traveler and/or other executives of the company being put in jail. Corporate travel managers are advised to avoid the temptation to purchase and/or utilize black market air tickets.

Summary

The corporate travel manager has several approaches available which can be utilized in managing the financial aspects of international travel. Perhaps the most frequently used of these is the identification of the currency which will provide the best value and having airline tickets issued in that currency rather than in U.S. dollars. For those managing travel of considerable amounts to the same destinations, the establishment of local bank accounts and the transfer of U.S. dollars into those accounts during periods of time when the exchange rate is most favorable, will provide the corporate travel manager with an opportunity to pay for travel costs at a better than exchange rate basis for many months of the year. The utilization of local bank accounts also gives the corporate travel manager an opportunity to reduce the number of exchange transactions and thereby reduce the total annual payment for currency exchanges.

One of the techniques utilized which provides a potential for considerable savings is the use of blocked funds. By having all travel expenses in the country where funds are blocked paid for with blocked funds, the corporate travel manager provides an opportunity for the company to use up some of the funds that might otherwise not be utilized at all. Sometimes blocked funds can be used for the issuance of tickets even when the tickets are to and from destinations other than the country in which the funds are blocked and in which the international airline tickets are issued and paid for. This provides still another opportunity to use up blocked funds that might not otherwise be used by the company.

Still another use of blocked funds is to take advantage of those funds accumulated by other companies which they have been unable to fully utilize. By transferring employees to the payroll of the blocked fund earning companies or by transferring blocked funds to the account of the using company and paying only a percentage of the value of the blocked funds to the blocked fund earning company, the corporate travel manager can purchase travel products and services at a fraction of the dollar value that they would otherwise cost.

One temptation facing corporate travel managers and international travelers is the opportunity to buy travel products and services on the black market of the destination countries. Black market currency exchanges and airline tickets frequently offer the buyer substantial savings. However, black market purchases are usually illegal and therefore can be very dangerous. Corporate travel managers and corporate travelers are advised not to purchase any travel services on the black market.

The last several chapters have discussed corporate travel financial management. The next chapter on automation assists the corporate travel manager in managing corporate travel finances. However, automation is of considerable value in saving time, getting the best possible fares, and recording the data needed for corporate travelers and the corporate travel department.

Discussion Questions

1. Why can corporate travel managers save money by having airline tickets issued in a currency other that U.S. dollars?

2. How can the establishment of bank accounts in other countries save money?

3. Why is it important to know the volume of travel on an annual basis to each destination country?

4. What is perhaps the most simple international financial management approach as it relates to corporate travel?

5. Why might airline tickets issued in the destination country using the currency of the destination country be more advantageous in some cases than having those tickets issued in the U.S. in U.S. dollars?

6. Why might it be financially better for a corporate travel manager to make payments to hotels in destination countries based on a billing from the hotel and utilizing money held in local banks in local currencies rather than having each company traveler pay hotel bills in local currency and show the costs on the traveler's expense report?

7. How does the use of blocked funds to pay for travel products and services benefit a company?

8. Is it ever possible for a corporate travel manager to have airline tickets issued in a country where funds are blocked for transportation starting and ending in other countries? Explain your answer and, if it is possible, explain why a corporate travel manager might want to try to utilize this approach.

9. Why might an employee be temporarily assigned to a blocked fund earning company?

10. What are some of the mechanisms used whereby blocked fund using companies can take advantage of and use the funds earned by blocked fund earning companies?

11. Why might it be better for corporate travel managers and corporate travelers to pass up the good opportunities presented by black marketeers in purchasing corporate travel products and services?

Role Play Exercise

Two students may participate in this role play either out-of-class, as a fun way to review the chapter, or as an in-class exercise. One plays the role of the first corporate travel manager and the other plays the role of the second corporate travel manager. Please read the script and then pick up the conversation in your own words.

First Corporate Travel Manager: We have just decided to establish a sales and distribution office in Cairo for our Middle East clients. Although we will be using the facilities of our franchisee, we already know that a large number of our corporate employees will be traveling to and through Cairo as a result. One of the things that has concerned our financial officers in the negotiations to undertake this arrangement has been the cost of travel. Although we have few blocked funds in Egypt, we have been able to use these for virtually all local travel expenses in Egypt. However, we can already see that there won't be enough blocked funds to pay for all our expenses in the future. You have managed international corporate travel for your company for a long time. How do you overcome the high cost of international corporate travel?

Second Corporate Travel Manager: There a number of techniques that we use consistently, but before I get into explaining these in detail, your need for Egyptian blocked funds interests me. Our company has a manufacturing base in Cairo and we are always looking for ways to use our blocked funds. Let me explain how you can manage to reduce your international corporate travel costs and at the same time help us with our problem in Egyptian blocked fund usage. Let's start by . . .

CONTINUE ON YOUR OWN

Group Discussion Situation:
International Glues' International
Travel Financial Management

International Glues has its headquarters at its largest factory in Lance Port, Wyoming. Branch offices and factories are located in Karlstadt, Germany; Cairo,

193

Group
Discussion
Situation:
International
Glues'
International
Travel Financial
Management

Egypt; and Buenos Aires, Argentina. All travel is controlled by the corporate travel manager, Greg Goings, in Lance Port. Much of the corporate travel is undertaken by technical specialists and administrators who travel between factories and small distribution offices (in ten countries throughout the world). Sales and marketing personnel also travel to cities throughout the world. The majority of sales and marketing staff are based in the factory locations in Wyoming, Germany, Egypt, and Argentina. The training department conducts training seminars throughout the year in locations all over the world. They move from one city to the next all year, but come back to Lance Port for a few days with their families about once a month.

Greg is new to his job at International Glues. He started last week. Greg was the corporate travel manager for another large company for five years, but that company had no international travel. Greg's considerable corporate travel experience is with domestic travel only. Based on the international travel of International Glues' travelers, Greg wants to identify the financial management concerns he should consider in managing International Glues' international travel. He has asked those in the company who are most involved in international travel to meet with him and help him to develop a position paper on the financial management of International Glues' international travel.

You are meeting today to draft the position paper. You are expected to reach agreement and to write a two-page position paper on the financial management of International Glues' international travel. In your group session, select one person to chair the group. All will have an equal vote on decisions. In the group session, you are expected to reach agreement on the major positions taken in the paper and to prepare the position paper to be presented to the entire class by the chair of your committee.

CHAPTER 13

Automation

Introduction

Automation has become one of the most controversial areas of corporate travel management. Prior to deregulation of the travel industry, few travel agencies in the U.S. were automated and even a number of the major airlines in the world had very little or no automation of their reservation systems. Today, however, the advancement in technology in automation, both as it relates to hardware and software, is progressing so rapidly that corporate travel managers are challenged to stay on top of the developments in automation in order to obtain the automation that is most beneficial for the business travel department and its company as it relates to corporate travel.

Reservation System Automation Limitations

Automation centers around reservation systems and it is for that reason that this chapter will concentrate on the applicability of automation in meeting the needs of corporate travelers and corporate travel departments in making reservations and generating travel documents (tickets, itineraries, boarding passes, and so on). However, the chapter will also review what is normally thought of as back office systems, the reports generated by these systems, and the tracking ability provided by back office systems for corporate travel departments.

Often corporate travel managers ask why they should be concerned with reservation systems, back office hardware, and the software that is utilized by travel agencies since the major concern of corporate travel managers is not what pieces of equipment and types of systems a travel agency uses, but the results that come from the equipment and the systems. However, while the corporate travel manager may be primarily concerned with the tickets, reports, and other end-product documents, it is essential that the corporate travel manager be aware of the fact that travel agencies are limited in what they can provide to business travel clients by the restrictions and limitations inherent in each of the major reservation systems, each unit of computer hardware, and each program that the agency may utilize.

195

Standard
Hardware Base
and Standard
or Tailored
Add-ons

Although, theoretically, an agency could buy all or most of the systems, hardware, and software on the market designed for corporate travel, the reality is that few (or no) travel agencies have all of it and even those that have a large variety of systems, hardware, and software programs, do not maintain the ability to switch from one to another with great speed and total ease. Therefore, although the corporate travel manager might prefer not to be limited in terms of the delivery of automation end products, in reality business travel clients of travel agencies are limited in that which they can obtain from a travel agency with the limitations being those tied to the equipment, systems, and software being utilized for business travel accounts by that agency. Often large corporate travel departments do not sense that they are being limited in terms of what is possible for them at any particular point in time since all automated reservation systems and back office hardware and software for travel agencies consistently strive to increase the variety and the amount of programs and reports offered to business travel managers. However, each of the five computer reservation systems has a different cost and each has specific, but somewhat different, limitations.

Standard Hardware Base and Standard or Tailored Add-ons

Travel agencies in the U.S. usually start their automation process by installing and utilizing one of five major automated reservation systems. They then tie on to these reservation systems additional hardware and software programs to provide accounting reports, business travel reports, vendor utilization reports, and so on. While small and medium-sized travel agencies will buy pre-packaged hardware and software programs to provide all of these add-on reports and benefits, the larger volume travel agencies (usually those with an annual sales level of $20 million or more) tend to purchase large pieces of computer equipment (hardware), to employ their own programmers, and to design programs tailored to the needs of specific business accounts in order to provide back office financial records and other travel-related corporate reports.

The five major automated reservation systems utilized by travel agencies in the U.S. are in alphabetical order: APOLLO, DATAS II, PARS, SABRE, and SYSTEM ONE. These systems are associated with air carriers.

The hardware to access the data and the internal software on which to run reservation programs are either leased or sold by the air carrier companies to travel agencies. The air carriers associated with the systems are as follows:

- United Air Lines—APOLLO;
- Delta AirLines—DATAS II;
- Trans World Airlines/Northwest Orient Airlines—PARS;
- American Airlines—SABRE; and
- Continental Airlines and Eastern Airlines—SYSTEM ONE.

Travel agencies that lease or purchase automated reservation systems tend to have a natural tie as well as a strong economic tie to the air carrier vendor which provides it with automation equipment and software. Therefore there is a concern in the industry relating to agency sales bias. This potential for bias is not limited to just the reservation system vendor air carrier. International alliances and networks between carriers serving destinations all over the world have resulted in almost all major international carriers tieing in with direct access to one of the five U.S. reservation systems. Booking bias, therefore, extends to reservations made to destinations far beyond the shores of America. A strong relationship between the concern for bias and a potential for bias is the fact that until recently many of the airline-associated automated reservation systems provided data on their flights in preferential order as compared with other flights. Up-to-date data, for example, last seat availablility, on other carriers in the system often was not available resulting in an agent in one travel agency sometimes believing that a flight was full when an agent in a competing travel agency working with the automation system "host" airline would find a seat available on that carrier's reservation system and would be able to book it. Worse yet, the agency's client could call the airline and find the seat available. Although recent developments in reservation direct access interfacing have resulted in a reduction in the frequency with which this happens, it nevertheless does continue to some degree.

Overrides and Hidden Bias

In addition, airline automation vendors will frequently provide financial and non-financial incentives to a travel agency to encourage the agency to sell tickets on their carrier. As pointed out in the chapter on financial management, override commissions paid to travel agencies for booking either a larger dollar volume or a larger percentage of air travel on specified carriers can provide both the travel agency and the corporate travel department (operating under the concept of revenue sharing) considerable additional income. When this occurs, a purposeful booking bias is the reason. Usually the travel agency states that it books the preferred carrier only when all other factors are equal. In other words, if the computer indicates that the flights of two or more major carriers are departing at approximately the same time, arriving at the destination at approximately the same time, and cost the same price, then the preferred carrier is booked in order to earn an override commission.

A percentage of the override commission can be shared with the corporate travel department under a revenue-sharing agreement. Theoretically, it is a way to provide additional income to both the corporate travel department and the travel agency without affecting the convenience of the traveler or the ticket cost born by the company. However, a few travel agencies, especially those which have bonus systems for agents who book *favored carriers* will sell the favored carrier even when there is a price difference or a flight departure/arrival time difference resulting in less convenience for the traveler.

Frequent less-easily-seen factors relating to reservation system booking bias have to do with reservation system differences. For example, almost all reservation systems provide considerably greater ancillery information relating to the *host carrier* (the airline which owns the reservation system being used by the travel agency to book the reservation) as compared to other carriers. Although the reservation data may be identical, information such as gate configurations at destination airports, airline refund processes and policies, and sometimes even

197

Standard
Hardware Base
and Standard
or Tailored
Add-ons

up-to-date equipment configurations may be missing for competing carriers, but available for the host carrier. This means that if, in the booking process, a client requests information on such things as type of meal, how many seats there are in a row (2, 3, 5, and so on), where the seats are that have additional leg room, how far the arrival gates of the carrier are from the main terminal building, and other similar questions, the agent will be able to answer the questions far more easily when the questions relate to the host carrier, which has probably programmed all this data (and much more) into its reservation system.

For a carrier that has simply requested that reservations be placed in the computer system, little, if any, of the ancillary information will appear in the system. Even when the data is in the host carrier's system, the agent will typcially find that several more entries will be required to access the information than to access the same information for the host carrier. This does not mean that such questions cannot be answered by the travel agency reservationist. However, the reservationist will usually have to spend additional time and take several additional steps to obtain the information. Since corporate travel reservationists are frequently paid on the volume of travel booked, they often have a preference for selecting the carrier where they have the information at hand in case a client requests additional information since they could lose an entire booking in the time it may take to research the information on a non-host carrier.

The degree of bias that exists often is a function of the knowledge, capability, and interest of the individual agent making a reservation. In a typical client booking transaction, either the traveler, the traveler's secretary, or someone from the corporate travel department will telephone the travel agency and request a reservation. Since, under this scenerio, the travel agent has access to the computer and the person calling in the reservation request does not see the computer, the three factors of agent experience, training, and interest are critical to getting both the best possible price and the most convenient, most comfortable flight arrangements. Therefore, it behooves the corporate travel manager to ensure that only the most capable travel agents handle her reservation requests.

The promotional and marketing literature that travel agencies frequently produce will often tout the number of years of experience and training that each agent has received. The reality is that in all travel agencies some agents have more experience than others and some are paid better for that experience than others. Obviously, the travel agency that has the "best" agents will pay a premium for those agents, but even if the corporate department decides to work only with agencies that pay the highest possible salaries to their agents, there will be a difference in every agency as it relates to the ability of agents to consistently provide superior service. Although an increasing number of corporate travel oriented travel agencies discourage it, the concept of having a dedicated agent or two dedicated agents is one which an increasing number of corporate travel managers are requiring in their requests for proposal.

A *dedicated agent* is an agent who works solely on one business travel account. Obviously, if the volume of business from a single account is insufficient to keep an agent busy, then a dedicated agent will be assigned to two or more accounts, but will work only on those accounts and not on any others. Also, where a single account may have too much travel for an individual agent to handle, more than one dedicated agent can be assigned by a travel agency to a business client company. Since agents do get sick on occassion, take lunch breaks, and go on vacation, a back-up agent to the dedicated agent(s) is often identified.

From the point of view of the corporate travel manager, having dedicated agents means that the preferences of travelers become known in a very short period of time since the same person is always making the travel arrangements and that person can remember the preferences rather than having to depend upon accessing computer data, which may be incomplete, relating to the preferences of a specific traveler. In addition, if the corporate travel manager shares in the selection process by which a dedicated agent is identified and specified in the contract, the corporate travel manager can take steps to make certain that the dedicated agent(s) is one of those who is highest paid, most experienced, and so on.

Finally, for a dedicated agent to handle an account solely, weaknesses can be rapidly identified and either additional training to overcome these weaknesses can be negotiated and scheduled or a change in dedicated agents can be made in order to find one or more individuals in the agency who will consistently handle the reservations for the corporate travel manager's account in a superior manner.

When selecting a dedicated agent, it is suggested that business travel managers keep in mind the frequent practice in travel agencies, often encouraged and, in some cases, even insisted upon by computer system airline suppliers, of having one agent in each agency designated as the computer system expert. Airline computer reservation system vendors strongly encourage this process so that they reduce the number of agents who attend specialized computer training programs. By identifying one agent in each travel agency to become an expert on the reservation system, the air carriers are able to make certain that at least one person is kept up to date on all new developments and can do so at a minimal amount of training cost.

Ideally, this person goes back and conducts regular training for all other agents in the agency. Obviously, if the designated computer expert in an agency is also the dedicated agent for a corporate travel manager's account, then the corporate travel manager is able to benefit from the additional, up-to-date training that the agent reservationist handling her business has received and can do so at no additional cost. Unfortunately, far too few corporate travel managers are aware of the system of designating a specific computer expert among reservationists and therefore do not require that their account be handled by such individuals.

Just having the computer expert handle the account, however, does not ensure a continuously superior reservation service. Obviously, the computer training expert in one agency who is paid one-third less than the computer training expert in another travel agency will probably have fewer years of total experience and quite possibly will have less dedication to serving an account. Therefore, having an understanding of the average salary levels as well as the top salaries of business travel reservationists (in the city in which the corporate travel manager's business is located) will assist the travel manager in identifying whether or not the person assigned as the dedicated agent is indeed one who is one of the superior travel agency reservationists in the community.

A final factor relating to the quality of a dedicated agent relates to how pressured the agent is. Agency reservationists are usually given quotas in terms of the amount of travel that they must book. It is not at all unusual for an agent to have a $1 million booking quota. Some agents can book an annual $1 million worth of travel business and still provide superior service. On the other hand, other agents may have the same quota and provide inferior service. The difference may lie in factors other than just experience and training, however. One of the reasons for the difference may be the add-on responsibilities of the agent. If the agent with a quota of $1 million dollars in sales is also the training expert and must take time out each month to attend training sessions as well as to train other agents in the agency, that agent may very well be so pushed to meet her quota of $1 million in sales during the time she is working as a reservationist that she does not have time to provide the degree of service necessary. Likewise, an agent with a $1 million sales quota who also must process tickets and accounting reports, will have less time available to provide superior service than the agent who has a $1 million sales quota, but who has no additional responsibilities. Therefore, when identifying a dedicated agent, it is important to not just know that that agent is a training specialist and a person with the highest possible salary, a person with considerable experience, but also that that individual has a reasonable quota and few ancillary responsibilities.

Automated Reservation Features

For the corporate travel manager to understand how a dedicated agent can provide superior service, it is beneficial to understand some of the special features with which travel agency reservationists are able to increase their work. While some of these features are not new, all of the automated reservation systems are consistently improving old features, making them more rapid and more user-friendly, while, at the same time, introducing new facets or totally new features. They do this partly to make the agencies utilizing their systems more marketable; in other words, to provide new or better sales points that can be emphasized when trying to win over new corporate accounts. They also do this to make certain that those travel agencies currently utilizing their system will continue to use it and so that they can win a larger share of the total number of travel agencies subscribing to their service.

Although travel agencies typically sign a five-year contract for a computer reservation system, there are many financial and non-financial incentives provided by carrier vendors to encourage agencies to change systems and an increasing number of agencies are changing systems even before the five-year contract period is up. Therefore, the race to provide additional automated reservation system features is a very real race and vendors know that if they do not provide what travel agencies and, by extension, what corporate travel managers want in new or improved features, they will fall behind and perhaps not have enough subscribers to make a profit from providing automated reservation programs. The following are some of the features that are of special interest to corporate travel managers:

1. best-fare systems;
2. multiple screens;

3. queues;

4. profiles; and

5. fact files.

Best-fare Systems

When automated reservation systems were first introduced for travel agencies, faring was not a strong consideration. This was prior to deregulation when the air travel industry was still regulated by the CAB. The Civil Aeronautics Board had to approve fare changes which resulted in a long, tedious process. Fares tended to be few in number and to stay the same for long periods of time.

Today, however, in a deregulated environment, fares change rapidly. There are literally thousands of fare changes every day. An agent wishing to find the lowest fare could spend many hours searching through the various fares available if it were not for some type of fare finding assistance built into the computer. This is especially true when searching for fares between popular city pairs. Increasingly, the reservation system vendors are providing a more and more sophisticated version of a best-fare shortcut entry. What this usually means though, is that when a travel agent requests the best fares available between two cities, the computer will provide those that are the lowest fares on a direct basis (i.e., without connections, and sometimes without stops).

There are three problems with these best fares. One is that the fares of carriers which have not been entered into the system will not be reflected. A second problem is that fares for flights requiring changes or going somewhat out of the way in terms of routings will often not be reflected. And a third problem is that the least expensive fares usually require non-refundable payment a long time in advance (sometimes as much as two or three weeks prior to the flight).

Practically speaking, few companies find that their business travelers can make reservations this far in advance. When such reservations can be made, companies often find that cancellations or changes render these non-refundable fares of no value to them. Therefore, the best fare which is provided by a reservation system may or may not be the true best fare and often will not be a fare that is a usable best fare.

A few of the systems are beginning to integrate corporate travel faring policies with a best-fare search in order to eliminate the third problem (i.e., the problem of a best fare appearing on the computer screen which is not usable by a company). In other words, if a company states that it will not consider using a fare where there is a non-refundable condition, no non-refundable fares are considered by the computer in searching for a best fare to present to the reservationist requesting best fares. This eliminates the problem of travel agents having to weed through a number of vary low fares which are unusable because of their conditions that a traveler must meet in order to use them.

In many cases, businesses will not expect their travelers to take flights where they must make a number of stops or where they must change planes several times in order to save money on the fares. Therefore, the fact that the best fare which appears on a travel agent reservationist's CRT screen when asked for best fares may not be the true best fare is not an important consideration for corporate travel managers since any lower fare's routing would require travelers to change planes (sometimes several times) or to take flights that have a large number of stops.

However, corporate travel managers should be concerned with how rapidly a computer can provide a best fare consistent with the policies of the company and how accurate the computer reservation system is in providing those best fares. The time factor is important because the reservationist ties up the time of a secretary, the traveler, or a person working in the corporate travel department during the time that a flight is being requested. The cost factor, of course, is important because savings is the justification for the existence of many corporate travel departments. It is possible to measure both time and fare.

Periodic time checks can be taken by those who call in reservation requests and compared with sample calls to other travel agencies. Independent consultants can provide periodic best-fare checks to determine whether or not the company is consistently getting the best possible fares. Both are suggested measures to undertake from time to time in order to check that the travel agency vendor is providing the service desired.

Multiple Screens

Having a multiple of screens is also a benefit to both travel agency reservationists and corporate travel managers. When automated reservations equipment was first made available to travel agencies, an agent would have to take a considerable amount of time to access flight availability data and, after leaving this data, would have to access price data. This required either writing down key information from one data base to compare (when looking at another data base) or trying to remember a considerable amount of information when moving from one data base to another. Automated reservation equipment now allows a reservationist to retain information from one data base (for example flight availability) on a portion of the CRT screen while at the same time accessing another data base (for example fare information) so that a comparison between data bases (flight availability and fares, for example) can be made rapidly without having to either remember a substantial amount of information or having to write down that information.

Some CRTs can be split into as many as six screens of information at the same time, providing the travel agent with the ability to access information and make reservations on various portions of the CRT at the same time. This has the multiple benefits of:

1. speeding up the reservation process;
2. insuring greater accuracy; and
3. providing information from which the corporate caller may request information often on an immediate basis.

Queues

A third feature of interest to corporate travel managers is *reservation queues*. Reservation queues act like tickler files for travel agency reservationists. When a reservation is made, a ticketing date is determined and after the reservation is completed, a passenger name record data from the reservation is *queued* or *referred* to the selected ticketing queue date. Each morning when a reservationist enters the agency (or in those agencies where ticketing is done by a night staff), the ticketing queue is accessed and all reservations that have been referred for ticketing on that date are then accessed on a one-by-one basis and ticketed. Although the ticketing queue is probably the most frequently used queue in most travel agencies, the queue (tickler file) system is beneficial for any number of applications within an agency.

Some of the more commonly found queues are the following:

1. *boarding pass queues;*
2. *travel document queues;*
3. *hotel and car rental queues;*
4. *wait-list clearance queues;* and
5. *pending-booking queues.*

There are also auto-drop queues, date-range queues, and queues established to monitor fares. These last three types of queues tend to be special in that they have particular working arrangements which are somewhat different than standard queues. They will be discussed after reviewing the more commonly used standard queues. Although many travel agencies have reservation systems which issue boarding passes at the same time that tickets are issued, restrictions by individual carriers on the issuance of boarding passes vary from one reservation system to another and policies vary from one airline to another. Most business travelers prefer to have a boarding pass for all flight segments of their trip prior to leaving on their trip.

Although, in some cases, airlines do not permit the issuance of advance boarding passes, this is rare to find in the U.S. other than those for which the fares are deeply discounted. Outside of the U.S. it is far more common to not have boarding passes issued in advance, but by going to the additional trouble of requesting boarding passes from air carriers (when the international airline will not allow the travel agency to issue the boarding pass), travel agencies are able to provide business travelers with boarding passes for an increasingly larger number of international flights. To do so, however, means contacting the air carrier after the reservation is confirmed. Therefore, many of the larger travel agencies utilize a queue system whereby a boarding pass request message is generated at the time an international (or other) flight is requested when the boarding pass printer(s) in the travel agency are unable to issue the required boarding pass. This series of messages is then accessed by a specialist in the travel agency who, normally in evening or off-peak hours generates computer or other messages to the carriers involved requesting the boarding passes.

A parallel boarding pass queue is often set up in the agency as a tickler file to be accessed by the boarding pass specialist to determine whether or not the boarding passes which have been requested for future flights have come in. If a boarding pass has not come in within a reasonable period of time (often ten business days), it will be identified on this additional parallel queue file so that a second written request or a telephone request can be made. By continually setting up *check dates* on the parallel boarding pass queue file, the boarding pass specialist can make certain that if a boarding pass can be obtained in advance, given enough advance time, the boarding pass will be obtained and made available to the traveler.

A similar arrangement is often worked out in large corporate travel-oriented travel agencies for hotel reservations and for car rental reservations. The reservationist taking the reservation request will frequently not handle any aspect of the reservation except the air travel request and will place hotel and car rental requests on appropriate queues. These queues are worked by hotel and/or car rental specialists in the travel agency. They normally access and work the queues on the basis of the amount of time prior to departure. In other words, if a message is received requesting a hotel for a business traveler who will need it two days later, this hotel request will be worked prior to one where a traveler is starting his trip two months later.

The queue system allows the specialist in the agency to skip the hotel or car rental requests which are for long-time future dates, to work close-in date requests first, and to then reaccess reservation request dates that are some time in the future. Some of the systems automatically place hotel or car rental requests in a date sequencing based upon *usage date*. The travel agency often finds that by using specialists to handle requests for hotels and car rentals, these requests are handled in an efficient manner and in a cost-effective manner resulting in benefits for both the corporate travel manager and for the travel agency.

If the corporate travel manager understands the queue process and recognizes that specialists within the travel agency will be handling the reservations for hotels and car rentals, the corporate travel manager will then understand that the air travel reservationists may well not know all aspects relating to reservation data for other aspects of the trip. Even though the entire reservation will be accessed and an advisory notice placed in the reservation that a hotel was obtained, requested (and on hold for confirmation) or that some other status on the hotel reservation request as, appropriate, can be read. The corporate travel manager should also understand that a phone call to the hotel or car rental specialist rather than to the air travel reservationist at the travel agency may well result in obtaining more educated information.

A fourth queue frequently found to be utilized for corporate travelers is a wait-list clearance queue. When a traveler prefers a specific flight, but that flight is fully booked, a wait-list request may be made by the travel agent. This wait-list request usually is referred to a wait-list queue which is accessed every day. If the wait-list clears, then tickets and boarding passes can be issued for the client. Normally, if the wait-list comes too close to the date of travel to jeopardize the ability of the traveler to obtain an alternative flight, the reservationist calls the traveler to obtain permission to ticket on a flight that may be the traveler's second choice.

A less-frequently utilized queue is one used for pending bookings. Some businesses obtain data from all travelers regarding the trips that they will undertake during the next fiscal year and request this data to be submitted in written form at the beginning of the fiscal year. Trip requests are then entered into the travel agency's computer for two considerations. One is to identify ticketing dates at as early a date as possible so that the least expensive fare can be obtained. In addition, when tickets are issued for flights that are a long time in advance, a continuous monitoring *best-fare search* can frequently result in lower fares being obtained. Recent studies indicate that as many as one-half of all business trips are for meetings and conventions. If these dates are known in advance and reservations made at the least expensive fare possible at the time that the reservation is originally requested, a best-fare search process that searches over a period of several months for a lower fare, will often result in cutting the fare by twenty-five percent or sometimes as much as fifty percent from the least expensive fare originally booked. This process is undertaken by interfacing reservations that have been made with a *best-fare check queue.*

The best-fare check queues automatically continuously check current reservations against fare changes on every city pair and for every reservation identified. Although there can be a considerable cost involved to provide this service automatically, the resulting savings can be as high as twenty to thirty percent.

When one considers pending bookings, the major use of this queue is to remind the corporate travel manager that a department head has budgeted for a ticket for a traveler to go to a specific meeting, but approval for the ticket has not yet been received. There could be any number of reasons for the approval to not be received by either the corporate travel department or the travel agency, but by having a cross-check, the possibility of someone simply forgetting to request the ticket is dealt with.

Fare monitoring, auto-drop, and date range queues are special types of queues that work somewhat differently than standard queues. Fare monitoring queues are different because they interface with a monitoring system which automatically searches computer data bases to find the same or similar flights at a lower price. This requires not just placing the queues in a system, but interfacing with the computers owned by an organization that provides fare monitoring services. In many instances, this involves transferring all reservations to an out-of-house contractor which provides the monitoring service. As tickets are issued and taken away from a fare monitoring queue, messages frequently need to be manually generated to show a reduction of those reservations that have been ticketed.

Auto-drop queues are frequently controlled by the air carrier rather than the travel agency. Items placed in these queues often depend on air carriers for action. An example is schedule changes. When schedules change, air carriers frequently will send a message to a schedule change queue which is accessed by travel agents each morning in order to identify all reservations that are affected by schedule changes. If the schedule change is minor (there is a flight delay of one or two minutes or perhaps the flight will leave one or two minutes earlier, the traveler is seldom advised, but the new times are noted on the traveler's itinerary. However, when the change is substantial or if a flight has been cancelled altogether, the travel agency will advise the traveler and/or the corporate travel manager in order to obtain new booking instructions, if that is what is needed. Obviously, documentation will need to be changed as well if tickets have already been issued. Other changes which are frequently advised through auto-drop queues are equipment changes, flight number changes, and wait-list confirmations.

Date range queues are different in that the items in a date range queue will appear on each date within the date range selection. Items in normal queues will appear once and will stay in the queue until they are either automatically or manually deleted. Automatic deletion can occur by an item in the queue meeting a set of circumstances whereby it will be automatically eliminated. For example, when a ticket is generated, the appearance of the item(s) dealing with that ticket in a large number of queues is automatically eliminated. Also, after the date on which a flight is to take off, many queue items for a reservation pertaining to that flight will automatically disappear (e.g., a wait-list for that flight will no longer be needed or appropriate).

Date range queues allow data to be displayed on the queue for a specific amount of time no matter what the circumstances. The items will appear from a beginning date to an ending date and will be automatically terminated from the queue at the ending date. Items that are often placed on date range queues include special meal requests that have not been confirmed, handicapped assistance requests that have not been confirmed, pending hotel or car rental confirmations, and other areas of information that will be effected up to a time near the date of departure on the trip, but will not be pertinent after the selected date.

Date range queues can be used as reminders for the corporate travel manager for contacting travelers going to meetings or for other purposes. For example, if a passport and visa will be needed for all company employees who will be attending a meeting in Japan, a date range queue can bring up the names of all who have not yet received a passport and/or a visa up to the date of the deadline for receiving both documents prior to departure. In this way, the travel agency can notify the corporate travel manager on perhaps a weekly or even a daily basis identifying those who have not yet received passports and visas. The corporate travel manager can then use personal judgement as to when to contact travelers if deadlines are getting close. The utitilization of date range queues for this type of document check can help to insure that problems of lack of notification or lack of action on the part of a key individual does not result in applying for documents so late that it is not possible to obtain them prior to scheduled departure.

The Profile System

Corporate travel managers find three major uses of the *profile system* automated reservation feature. These are:

1. client profiles;
2. corporate travel policy profiles; and
3. supplier price profiles.

The profile system is similar to a file system in that sheets or "screens" of data can be stored and brought up on the computer when needed. They were originally designed to provide individual preference information for frequent fliers. Originally limited in capacity, travel agencies assigned data information blocks to those clients who traveled most frequently. Information would be obtained and stored regarding the traveler's preferences in seating (aisle or window seat and/or smoking or non-smoking section), special meal requirements, carrier preferences (when these were appropriate), credit card numbers (or other form of payment), frequent flier program(s) in which the traveler is enrolled, contact information (such as company name, company address, company phone, home address, and home phone), billing reference information (department, cost or profit center, budget number, and so on), and other information or preferences.

In a multiscreen system, the agent reservationist can pull up *client profiles* on one screen of the CRT while reviewing flight availability and fares on other screens. When making a reservation, the data from the client profile can be automatically transferred to the reservation so that while making the original reservation preference data can guide agent choices and when reviewing the reservation at a later time client contact data, billing information, and preferences can be accessed at the same time that reservation data is accessed, simply by scrolling down the reservation data on the CRT screen.

The client profile concept was extended a few years ago to include *corporate travel policy profiles*. The simplest of these is a listing of the major company travel policies which, like the client profile, can be placed on one of the multiple screens of the CRT at the time that the reservationist is making the reservation. Like the client profile, the corporate travel policy profile can guide the agent reservationist in selecting fares, carriers, flights, and class of service in accordance with the corporate travel policy. Again like the client profiles, corporate travel policy profiles can automatically be transferred into the reservation so that future references to the reservation will also allow the agent to scroll down on the reservation to identify any appropriate travel policy data.

Additional sophistications of the corporate travel policy profiles allow the corporation to establish policies for different "classes" or "categories" of company travelers so that the policy appropriate for each individual traveler can be readily identified. This allows the company to establish several categories of travel policies depending upon the position or type of work that a traveler will be undertaking and to make sure that those policies are maintained within the guidelines of the policies determined for each particular traveler. Some travelers may fall into one category of travel policy guidelines for one type of trip (depending upon the purpose of the trip) and another travel policy for other types of trips. When this occurs, a notation to this effect can be made in the client's traveler's client profile so that the agency reservationist can be guided depending upon the nature of the trip.

In some cases, while the traveler or the traveler's secretary is on the phone making the original reservation, if the agent reservationist has pulled up the corporate travel policy profile screen and the client profile screen, a question can be asked regarding the nature of the trip to guide the agent reservationist in making a determination as to whether one travel policy or the other travel policy applies for the particular trip being booked.

The third profile of interest to an increasingly large number of corporate travel managers is a *supplier price profile*. Although most corporate travel-oriented travel agencies belong to purchasing consortiums which negotiate special hotel and car rental rates for their commercial client travelers, an increasing number of corporate travel managers are negotiating hotel and car rental price agreements themselves. In many cases, especially with hotels and car rentals in smaller cities, the corporate travel manager-negotiated prices are considerably less than the prices available through any consortium, travel agency, or nationally published corporate rate.

Where these supplier price agreements have been reached, a hotel price profile and a car rental price profile can be entered into the computer system and accessed at the same time that the traveler or the traveler's secretary is calling in a reservation. By accessing this data on one of the screens of the CRT, the travel agent can confirm with the traveler or the traveler's secretary that the hotel identified by the company as the (or one of the) hotels with which a negotiated price agreement has been reached is the hotel to be booked. If so, a notation can be made on the client reservation entry in the computer so that the booking can be made and confirmed after the traveler or the traveler's secretary has completed the reservation phone request. If another hotel is to be booked, the agent can make a note of the hotel requested and, if the travel policy requires clearing that hotel reservation request with the corporate travel department, this follow-up can be scheduled to be completed after the reservation request phone call is over. The same approach applies for car rentals and the car rental price profile. This system allows the company to take advantage of supplier price agreements to a maximum degree. It allows for hotels or car rentals other than those where negotiation agreements exist to be booked in exceptional cases. And, it allows for a smooth enforcement of corporate travel policies prior to the start of a trip (as compared with identifying variences from corporate travel policy after a trip is over).

Travel agencies also use profiles to identify promotional air fares and to flag override suppliers. Although these profile uses are of interest to corporate travel managers, they are usually less frequently involved in the development of promotional air fare and override profile data.

Fact Files

Fact files constitute still another area of interest for corporate travel managers. These are references that can be accessed easily and rapidly to provide the travel agent with the answers to questions travelers frequently ask or information they need in making travel plans. Some of the fact files that are more commonly found are files on new fare information (normally entered by airlines every two or three days), daily airline briefings, daily weather information, currently-running plays and other performances in Las Vegas, New York City, and London, airport maps, and guides for over forty countries (in most, but not all reservation systems).

The new fare information and daily airline briefings may provide travel agency reservationists with data that they will in turn want to pass on to corporate travel managers when this information relates to pending fare changes, strikes, and other pertinent data.

The weather data may be of importance to those planning a trip later in the day or wanting to know about possible weather-related delays. Travelers need only call the travel agency to have the agency reservationist access the weather information in any particular destination location and frequently this will also advise of any current flight delays or expected flight delays.

The play/performance information may be of interest to travelers who wish to attend during their leisure time. Of special interest may be the airport maps. Some travel agencies produce airport maps by printing them on hard-copy stock. They identify the gate area of the airline with which the traveler will be flying into the airport. This is of value to travelers flying to airports with which they are unfamiliar. They can transit the airport far more rapidly.

The guides are of particular importance for travelers planning trips to other countries. It is expected that the guides will be in all major airline reservation systems shortly and that they will cover as many as sixty to eighty of the more popular country destinations. Guides include data relating to departure taxies, airline service to and from major cities, transportation to and from major airports, major hotel information, car rental information, climate (average temperature each month of the year for all major cities), geography information, shopping information, tipping recommendations, and tour attractions. As with airport maps, parts or all of the guide data can be reproduced on hard copy and provided to travelers going to the destination countries.

Reports

Corporate travel departments expect to receive a variety of reports from their travel agency supplier. By far the most frequently expected report is a *cost savings report*. However, additional reports (or sometimes a part of the cost savings report) identify hotel bookings, car rental bookings, departmental bookings (by cost center, profit center, work unit, or budget number), the amount of individual traveler trips, overrides (and override profit sharing amounts from each supplier), city pairs flown, number of flights flown on each air carrier used, and the percentage of flights on each air carrier.

Since one of the primary reasons for a corporate travel department to exist within a company is to save money on corporate travel, the cost savings report is considered by many to be the single most important report generated for the corporate travel department by the vendor travel agency. Typically, this report starts by identifying air travel savings and then moves into hotel, car rental, and other savings. Variations of the report which are becoming increasingly popular are, in fact, separate reports for each of the major types of service; for example, an air travel savings report, a hotel savings report, a car rental savings report, and so on.

The *air travel savings report* is normally a monthly report which breaks down the air tickets issued by date of issuance or by date of travel (usually date of issuance). Under the date of issuance tickets are issued either numerically by ticket number (note that there will be sizeable gaps since tickets come off of computer printers in the order of issuance, but the printer will be issuing tickets for all agency clients, not just for the client whose report is being prepared. However, they will be in a numerical order. An alternative listing is alphabetical by passenger name. Still a third alternative is by budget number, cost center, or profit center number. Breakdowns by each of these categories are possible with most systems.

The air travel savings report identifies the savings provided on each air ticket issued. The customery approach is to list the normal full-economy fare for a direct flight between the city pair ticketed. Subtracted from that full-economy fare is the fare that was obtained by the travel agency. The difference between the full-economy fare and the fare obtained is shown in a column marked savings. Increasingly, this traditional type of savings report is being criticized as one that does not reflect true savings.

Gaining popularity is a savings report that, instead of identifying the full-economy fare between city pairs, identifies the least expensive fare available in keeping with the constraints of corporate travel policy. In other words, if the policy does not accept utilizing deeply discounted fares on which refund penalties are applied, then these fares are eliminated from consideration in identifying the least expensive fare available. The report goes on to identify the dollars spent over the least expensive fare possible within the constraints of the corporate travel policy. Instead of being a true savings report, therefore, it becomes an exception report.

With either type of report (savings or exception) a column is available to identify those trips where the least expensive fare (within the constraints of the corporate travel policy) was not utilized. Either a code system is used to identify the reason for the utilization of a more expensive fare or a "free-flow" description of the reason why the more expensive fare was utilized is entered.

Hotel savings reports can be prepared in much the same way as the air travel savings report. However, most hotel reports are simply tracking reports for an existing hotel program. In other words, the travel agency consortium may provide special hotel rates and the report will show the utilization of each hotel in that system and the rate provided. On the other hand, an increasing number of corporate travel departments are negotiating rates for themselves and include these as the basis on which hotel tracking is utilized.

However, a more beneficial (and less frequently utilized) hotel savings report identifies the hotel's corporate rate, the rate extended, and the savings on each hotel utilized. Whichever type of hotel report is generated, it is important to have a report that summarizes the number of nights in each hotel used as well as each hotel chain utilized. It is also beneficial to summarize cost figures. These summaries will allow the corporate travel manager to negotiate for potentially better rates based upon the volume of hotel room usage. Without this data it would be difficult for the corporate travel manager to obtain rate concessions.

Car rental savings reports are similar to hotel savings reports. Travel agency consortiums often negotiate special rates with car rental companies. Savings, usage, and tracking reports identify the volume of usage at each airport pick up location. As with hotel reports, a far less often utilized type of savings report compares the car rental company's corporate rate in each location where a car is rented by a company traveler with the discounted rate extended to the user company by the car rental franchisor. As with hotels, it is essential to provide tracking data for each rental location and each car company. The corporate travel manager can then use this data to approach individual car rental franchisees in specific high-usage locations to negotiate potentially better rates.

Far less often utilized, but of considerable potential value to corporate travel managers is a report of bookings by month, by quarter, and by year (year-to-date) for each department or unit within the user company and to compare this total with the department's annual budget. This can be done by cost center, profit center, work unit, or budget number. This allows either approximate or exact identification of the amount of travel expenses authorized versus the amount used and by subtracting provides the supervisor of the department an opportunity to identify potential cost over spendings in travel on a monthly basis. A similar report on the number of trips taken and the amount spent on travel by each individual traveler can provide supervisors with an ability to measure what has been spent versus what was budgeted and determine whether or not any overspending has occured or possibly will occur if trends continue.

The air fare savings report can provide several additional "subreports" which can be of benefit to the corporate travel manager and the travel agency in negotiating for better fares when and if direct negotiations with carriers are undertaken. One of these is a *city-pairs report*. It provides a listing of all flights between city pairs identifying the total number each month, each quarter, and annually as well as identifing the air carrier used. With this data, negotiations can be undertaken with carriers flying those particular city pairs. It is fairly easy with this data to pull out all city pairs flown which match the cities to which individual carriers fly so that during negotiations total potential volume can be discussed. A similar report identifying the number of flights flown on each air carrier used on a current month, quarterly, and on a year-to-date basis can also be beneficial in negotiating with air carriers. Of perhaps special interest in air carrier negotiation is the percentage of flights flown on each air carrier. If this comparison is identified by city pair, it is possible to show air carriers during negotiations what the possibility will be of moving travelers to a preferred air carrier and booking them on a preferred carrier basis. This holds out the potential of providing a considerable amount of additional travel for individual air carriers in some cases and thereby presents an opportunity to negotiate fares that can be particularly advantageous to the user company.

Interfacing

The above reports are provided from raw data that is obtained at the time reservations are made for travelers. This data is stored in the computer and transferred to accounting or "report" queues to either an interface system or by manually reentering the data into other agency computers. The processes, advantages, and disadvantages of interfacing affect not just reports, but also travel agency accounting, which in turn affects overrides, preferred carrier revenue sharing, and corporate travel financial management.

Before reviewing the advantages and disadvantages of interfacing, it is important to understand what interfacing is and how it works. *Interfacing* between computers is like talking between people. Basically data is transmitted from one computer to another. However, the transmission often includes a selective screening of the data so that data can be not only sorted, but identified or categorized in such a way that it provides additional bases of data or categories of data which in turn makes data analyses easier and provides more bases for analysis.

The earliest form of interfacing devised for travel agency computer reservation systems was developed in order to provide agencies with the ability to develop accounting records in general and to complete the weekly airline ticket sales report. This remains the major usage of interfacing and it is becomming an increasingly sophisticated interface. Of special value to corporate travel departments of this interfacing is the ability to draw from the accounting data information that can be pertinent to travel management.

The reports discussed above are generated primarily from the accounting data transferred through an interface system. Other reports that can be generated from and sometimes are an integral part of the accounting system include travel agency override reports. When a travel agency reaches an agreement with a preferred supplier, the agency tracks the total sales of that supplier and advises the supplier on a periodic basis regarding the override commissions due to the agency. When corporate travel departments have entered into a preferred vendor revenue sharing arrangement, the override reports determine the amount of "additional" revenue due to the travel agency. Typically, the corporate travel department agreement with the travel agency vendor is that the corporate travel department will obtain a percentage of the override commission paid to the travel agency for tickets issued for company travelers. This override commission report, therefore, provides the base against which a percentage is multiplied to determine the monies due back to the corporate travel department.

The travel agency interfaced accounting report also determines the total sales made for the business and payments received from the user business. If an agreement on delayed payment, float, or other financial management negotiated arrangement has been entered into, the interfaced accounting report often provides the foundation on which the financial management arrangements are based.

Another interfacing that can be provided is a *fare check system.* By interfacing all corporate reservations with the computer of a firm that specializes in computer fare checks, the travel agency is able to provide corporate travelers in their company with the very least expensive fares possible even under the systems used by air carriers to mazimixe revenues. All major air carriers have developed *yield management* systems to minimize the inventories of airplane seats that never get sold. These inventories are studied every evening and the inventories are manipulated by changing seat prices based on matching a history of empty seat volume to bookings and prices.

For example, if a flight is thirty percent less filled on a given day than that flight traditionally must be in order for the air carrier to make a profit on it, more seats can be given discount prices. On the other hand, if it has thirty percent more seats sold than the flight traditionally must be in order for the carrier to make a profit on it, unsold seats can be taken away from the discounted price inventory.

There are literally thousands of price changes made every day since most carriers check the status of every future flight daily and adjust their discounted inventories every day. Most of these fare changes are made early in the morning (typically between 1:00 A.M. and 4:00 A.M.) at a time when most travel agencies are closed, business travelers are not calling to make reservations, and corporate travel departments are closed. Informed leisure travelers, however, often pick up these price-change reservation opportunities by calling very early in the morning.

When a travel agency interfaces with a computerized fare check vendor, the agency sends the reservations of corporate travelers for all participating companies to the fare check company by interfacing with the fare check company's reservation computers. The individual traveler reservations are placed into an inventory of reservations that are automatically checked on an ongoing basis (usually at least once every two or three hours). These checks identify available seats on the same or similar flights that have opened up at a less expensive cost. As soon as such a seat is identified, the computer automatically rebooks the corporate traveler into the less expensive seat. The fare check vendor feeds in booking parameters to make sure that travelers are not booked on seats that are unacceptable to the business traveler or to the business traveler's company. In many cases, therefore, the rebooking is on the same flight as the traveler was originally booked, but when a change of planes or carriers is necessitated in order to get the better fare, fare check computers review the company's policy first. Again, this review is often done through an interface with the travel agency's computers. Some companies have saved as much as six percent of their initial fare costs through the utilization of fare check interface systems.

Expense account reconciliation is also a possibility through computer interfacing. Both Citicorp Diners Club and American Express are working on increasingly sophisticated systems to allow business travelers to match trip expense allocations with actual expenses on personal or home office computer screens. The expenses that are incurred through the vendor travel agency are transmitted through an interfacing to the business traveler's computer so that at least this part of the expense report is automatically reconciled.

An experimental program being conducted by Citicorp Diners Club and the Englewood, Colorado office of Rosenbluth Travel is designed to develop a potentially one-hundred percent expense account reconciliation program whereby travel advances, credit card payments, and all trip expenses are identified and reconciled on the business traveler's personal computer. By interfacing with a corporate travel manager's computer and a computer located in the company's accounting offices, it may be possible to eliminate expense account paperwork other than running a hard copy of the reconciled expense report for future reference purposes. The interfacing of computers, therefore, holds considerable promise in not only reducing paperwork, but making the task of expense account reconciliation far easier than it has been in the past.

Interfacing has also allowed for major developments in making reservations through personal computers which are interfaced with travel agency computers. By using personal computers, dialing onto a software program, and selecting travel preferences, business travelers can make airline, hotel, and car rental reservation selections and transmit their preferences to the company's travel agency through a wide variety of interfacing linkups. These include using a dedicated line to the travel agency or a dial-up/dial-back telephone interface. Not only is the wait for a reservationist at the other end of the phone line eliminated, but corporate travelers can know that the systems have the ability to automatically screen out any potential arrangements that will not be in line with the company's corporate travel policy. For example, if the company will not allow more than two executives to fly on the same plane, the interface systems know that when both places on the flight for a traveler's company have been spoken for and the system will automatically advise other travelers from the company that another flight should be selected since it would be a violation of the company's travel policy to place a third traveler on the flight.

AOS Hotel and Airport Phone Charge Automation

Just as automation has aided corporate travel management, it has also created problems in business travel management when it comes to increasing the cost of long-distance calls made from an increasing number of hotels and airports. *Alternative operator services* (AOS) companies have been linked to all hotel rooms and all airport public phones (of contracting properties) by specialized equipment that allows hotels and airports to collect either a flat fee per call or, in many cases, a percentage of telephone charges generated from their properties. Although not generally utilized by corporate travel managers in their negotiations with hoteliers, COMDIAL, the manufacturer of the telephone linking equipment, provides hotels and airports with mechanisms whereby the additional charge programming can be altered by the individual hotel property or airport administration. The hotel or airport, although, cannot currently set different add-ons for different rooms or airport phones, but can and does develop a table of phone usage rebate schedules which are negotiable. The next generation of COMDIAL equipment is expected to allow for rebating based on assigned corporate travel negotiating codes. To get more information on this and current COMDIAL equipment utilization/modification possibilities, contact Michael Murphy at COMDIAL, 1634 Northeast Seventh Court, Fort Lauderdale, Florida 33304 (305) 532-3125.

Business Travel Department Automation

Business travel departments are increasingly utilizing automation interfacing. This automation tends to be far more sophisticated than the desk-top computers used by individual business travelers to make a reservation. In many cases, direct link CRTs allow those working in the corporate travel department to make reservations and automatically transfer the reservations to the storage inventory of the travel agency. The systems are so sophisticated that it is almost as if the CRTs are located in the same office as the travel agency, since there is immediate transfer of information back and forth between the agency and the business travel department. By also having ticketing equipment located in the business travel department, it is possible for the business travel department staff person to make a reservation, transfer it to the travel agency, and transfer a request for ticketing back to the ticketing equipment in the business travel department. This results in both the reservation and the ticket appearing at the business travel department. New ticket stock is available which allows the printing of all flight coupons and the passenger receipt on the ticketing equipment located in the business travel department while at the same time printing the auditor and agency ticket coupons at the travel agency. This allows for immediate access to tickets at the business travel department, but the accounting for those tickets is undertaken at the travel agency.

FIGURE 13.1. COMDIAL's AOS telephone linkage equipment used in hotels and airports. The operator console and the room status CRT are shown. All room calls are cost evaluated and stored for retrival through a printer that correlates and details each call for a designated room/phone. The calls are totalled and can be adjusted according to the corporate traveler's company discount. With permission from COMDIAL.

Summary

Automation is allowing for an increasingly sophisticated relationship to exist between travel agencies and business travel departments facilitating both greater ease and greater economy in completing travel arrangements. Both hardware and software technological advances in automation are progressing so rapidly that corporate travel managers need to constantly investigate new advancements in order to stay abreast of all automation opportunities.

To understand automation opportunities, it is also necessary to understand automation limitations. Five major airline-affiliated reservation systems are available to travel agencies and agencies normally select only one of these systems with which to work. A very few agencies will have additional back-up units of other systems, but almost all travel agencies in the U.S. work with a single reservation system as their major system. This selection of a single system limits what a travel agency, and by extension, what the corporate travel department, is able to provide in terms of automated services and programs. Although there is considerable competition between each of the five systems, and that competition results in all five being close to equal in what they offer, each system tends to have its special benefits and drawbacks. It therefore behoves a corporate travel manager to understand the basics of each of the five major systems.

In addition to the five airline-sponsored reservation systems, a few of the very large corporate travel-oriented travel agencies have invested in purchasing their own computers and hiring their own staff to design tailored software programs for their corporate accounts. Typically, these programs provide tailored reports, but offer little in terms of other services. The limitations inherent in each of the five major systems, therefore, still carry over to those travel agencies which have their own hardware and software designed client reports.

Perhaps the strongest limitation of airline-designed and founded systems is a bias toward the sponsoring air carrier. Both economic and governmental pressures have limited the bias in recent years, but a hidden bias continues to exist in many of the systems. This hidden bias is emphasized through an override system that provides the using travel agency with financial incentives for selling the sponsoring carrier(s) with a preference. Although the overrides are sometimes shared by corporate travel departments through agreements known as *revenue sharing agreements*, the possibility of travelers flying on a *favored carrier* at a greater expense than might be possible with another carrier, or flying at a time that is less convenient or beneficial to the company than the flight times offered by another, equal-priced carrier are very real and need to be guarded aganist. A more subtle bias comes from the reservationist having a greater knowledge of the host carrier and the host carrier's reservation data being more complete than the data contained in the reservation information for other carriers. Although this may be a more subtle difference, it often results in an agent looking first to the host carrier in making a reservation and only after reviewing host carrier flight opportunities, moving to a consideration of other carriers.

Obtaining rapid reservation service often means that the corporate travel department will request a *dedicated agent*. This is an agent who handles only the single corporate account or a very few corporate accounts. Typically, this agent gets to know the preferences of the more frequent business travelers in the company and they get to know the small nuances relating to preferences without having to access the preference data screens in their computer. This makes the reservation process more rapid and more personalized. However, continuously superior reservation service is not guaranteed by just having a dedicated agent. Not all dedicated agents are equal in their knowledge and abilities. To make certain that the dedicated agent is a superior agent, the corporate travel department should investigate the background of the dedicated agent, make certain that the agent is among the most experienced agents at the travel agency, strive to be assigned the agent who has been selected to be the reservation computer training expert, and make certain that the dedicated agent has few, if any, additional or add-on responsibilities (other than reservation computer training specialist).

Automation reservation systems offer five features that are of special interest to corporate travel managers. These are *best-fare systems, multiple-screens, queues, profiles,* and *fact files.* The best-fare systems are fare request entires designed to rapidly identify the best possible air fares that fit with the best routing, as well as the policy constraints of the company. By taking periodic time checks and by utilizing outside consulting companies to determine whether or not the best possible fares were obtained, a company can determine their agency's ability to provide the best possible best-fare service.

Most reservation systems now offer CRTs with more than one screen. This allows the reservationist to bring up data from several data bases at the same time. The ideal is to have as many as six screens on which a reservationist can display data such as flight availability, client preference data, fares, and individual reservation booking data all at the same time.

The reservation queue system works like a series of tickler files allowing a travel agency to access specific file bases at any particular point in time. Date sensitive data automatically is transferred to a computer file on the date when it is needed. By accessing these queues every day, travel agencies can act on date sensitive matters without missing deadlines. Some of the more frequently utilized queues include the ticketing queue (a tickler system advising the agent when each future reservation needs to be ticketed), boarding pass queues, travel document queues, hotel and car rental queues, wait-list clearance queues, and pending booking queues. In addition, fare-check queues (monitored to determine whether or not a better fare becomes available), auto-drop queues (usually controlled by the air carrier) which provide data such as flight changes automatically from the airline or other suppliers), and date range queues (data is entered automatically on a predetermined date and keep the data on the queue as a reminder every day until a predetermined final date) are available for information such as a wait-list. Date range queues can be used to remind the agency reservationist or the corporate travel manager of tasks that need to be completed or data that needs to be compiled (for example, those people traveling in a group who have not yet received their visas).

Somewhat like the queue system, the profile system also provides file type data for the reservationist. However, this tends to be more static data. Typical profiles include client profiles (information on preferences that a frequent traveler may have), corporate travel policy profiles (data relating to the company's policy which will be important as it relates to reservations made for company employees), and supplier price profiles. The reservationist can access any profile data file on one screen while preparing a reservation and in this way can make certain that the reservation is made consistent with traveler preferences, supplier price breaks, and company policies.

Fact files are data files that are quite similar to profiles except for the fact that fact file data is usually accessed less often, normally has less of a direct bearing on an individual reservation, and is much more static data. Fact files relate to facutal data that may or may not be of benefit to a reservationist in answering the questions of a traveler or in providing greater convenience for a traveler. Fact file data can include such things as airline briefings, current and historical weather and temperature information, airport maps, plays (or other performances) in major cities, visa and immunization requirement data, guidebook information for other countries, and so on.

Reports constitute one of the major computer reservation services provided by travel agencies to corporate travel departments. The savings report is considered by most to be the most important report provided. Traditional savings reports identify air travel savings by showing the regular economy fare compared to the fare actually obtained and a savings that resulted from getting the less expensive fare. Sophistications to this traditional savings report identify the least expensive fare consistent with travel policies compared to the actual fare booked and this becomes more of an exception report than a savings report. In addition, report data relating to hotel savings and car rental savings usually is included on agency saving reports today.

All of this data is gleaned from the original reservation and ticketing information captured at the time that the travel agency makes a reservation or issues a ticket for corporate travelers. The newer reports provide increasingly sophisticated data which can include departmental travel budget summaries and identify year-to-date underspending or overspending for each department in the company. Other report data can be of benefit to the corporate travel manager in negotiating with vendors. This data can provide the travel manager with information relating to the volume of air travel on each carrier, the number of trips between each city pair, the number of room nights in each hotel chain or in each individual hotel property, the number of car rentals from each car rental franchisor or any individual car rental franchisee, and other potentially beneficial data for vendor negotiation.

Computer interfacing constitutes still another opportunity for business travel departments in interrelating with their vendor travel agencies. Interfacing is a method of transferring data from one computer to another or, as some people put it, computers talking with other computers. Accounting interfaces are utilized by more travel agencies than any other area of interfacing. This is a system whereby financial data captured during the reservation and ticketing processes is transferred to a computer loaded with software designed to provide accounting reports. These reports include the weekly ARC (Airline Reporting Corporation) ticket sales report and many of the *savings reports* provided for corporate travel departments. However, the financial information which is captured through the accounting interface can provide a wide range of additional reports of value to not only the travel agency's management, but also to corporate travel managers. Some of these include override commission reports and vendor usage reports. A *fare check interface* provides the opportunity for an outside company specializing in reservation data monitoring to search for and pick up new, less expensive reservations as they become available as the airlines reduce fares in their *yield management* efforts to obtain the best possible yield from each flight. *Expense account reconciliation* is still another opportunity to take advantage of interfacing. Individual travelers can access expense account data on their personal computers and take advantage of automatic transfers of information through interfacing between the travel agency reservation computers and their personal computers and between the credit card company computers and their personal computers. This can save considerable time in preparing expense reports.

Interfacing also provides an opportunity to automate the business travel department to a considerable extent. Direct links between the CRTs in the corporate travel department and those at the travel agency and between the printers (ticket, itinerary, and boarding pass printers) in the corporate travel department and those at the travel agency allow for a back and forth interrelationship that can provide reservation data originating with the business travel department, going to the agency for processing and verification and tickets issued with all flight coupons, passenger receipt, boarding pass, and itinerary generated

from the computers housed in the corporate travel department and all accounting documents (agent coupons and ARC auditor coupons of the tickets,
itinerary copy, and invoice data) generated on the printers housed at the travel
agency. This allows for a maximum degree of efficiency in terms of processing
documentation. Newer equipment interfacing allows individual travelers to select
flights on their personal or office computers and to transmit the data automatically to the computers housed at the travel agency.

In addition, similar interfacing is designed to speed up and more accurately
develop individual traveler expense reports that can flow from the individual
traveler's personal or desk top computer to and from the travel agency as well as
to and from the credit card company so that lengthy reviews of monthly credit
card documentation are eliminated and each expense item charged against the
credit card or the expense for documents issued by the travel agency can be
applied on a trip by trip basis directly to the data bases held in the traveler's
computer.

Automation opportunities continue to be developed at a rapid rate and
although the efficiency of the corporate travel department has increased considerably due to automation, the strides being undertaken in automating business
travel departments and interfacing between all segments in the corporate travel
arena are increasing so rapidly, it can be expected that automation will be one of
the most important developments in corporate travel management in the years to
come.

Discussion Questions

1. What aspects of travel agency automation limitations should corporate travel
   managers be aware of?

2. At what sales volume level do travel agencies usually move into purchasing
   their own pieces of computer hardware and hiring their own programmers
   in order to design corporate reports?

3. What are the names of the five major automated reservation systems utilized
   by travel agencies in the U.S. and which airlines are affiliated with each of
   these systems?

4. In what ways might a travel agency reservationist be biased toward the air
   carrier which provides automation equipment for the travel agency for which
   the agent works?

5. What is a *dedicated agent* and what criteria should corporate travel managers
   look for in the dedicated agent(s) who handle their account?

6. What are five automated reservation features that are of special interest to
   corporate travel managers?

7. What are three problems relating to obtaining the very lowest *best fares* for
   corporate travelers?

8. What types of data can be displayed simultaneously when making a reservation using a CRT having multiple screens?

9. What types of items can be placed on queues and in what ways can the queue system be of benefit to corporate travel managers?

10. How do *auto-drop* and *date range* queues work and in what way can they be of benefit to corporate travelers and the corporate travel department?

11. Corporate travel managers find three major uses of the profile system automated reservation feature. What are these three major uses of the profile system?

12. What are some of the *fact files* that can be of benefit to corporate travelers?

13. What is the most frequently expected report provided by travel agencies to corporate travel departments and what are the variations of the report which are becoming increasingly popular?

14. Why is it said that some savings reports are really exception reports?

15. What types of reports can be provided by the travel agency for the corporate travel manager which will help the corporate travel manager in negotiating with vendors?

16. What is interfacing and how does it work?

17. How is the earliest form of interfacing used by travel agencies?

18. Why might a corporate travel manager find it of interest to understand the specifics of how override commission agreements are tracked?

19. What is a *fare check interface system* and why might it be of importance to a corporate travel manager?

20. What is meant by air carrier *yield management* and what is one way that air carriers manage yield?

21. How might expense account reconciliation be benefited through the concept of computer interfacing?

22. In what ways can interfacing between the corporate travel department and a travel agency relate to and be of benefit in the total automation of business travel departments?

23. What predictions can be made regarding the future of automation and corporate travel management?

Role Play Exercise

Two students may participate in this role play either out-of-class, as a fun way to review automation, or as an in-class exercise. One student plays the role of an experienced corporate travel manager. The other student plays the role of a newer, less experienced corporate travel manager. Please read the script and then pick up the conversation in your own words.

Newer Corporate Travel Manager: We have only had our corporate travel department up and running for about two years now, but we have been thinking about moving to some type of automation. You are totally automated in your operation aren't you?

Experienced Corporate Travel Manager: We have considerable automation and we interface directly with out vendor travel agency. Automation has saved us both time and money.

Newer Corporate Travel Manager: What are the advantages of automation and what can we expect from our agency?

Experienced Corporate Travel Manager: There are a number of advantages. Perhaps the most important one is . . .

CONTINUE ON YOUR OWN

Group Discussion Situation:
Mighty Midget Widgets Meets Grieving Widows

Mighty Midget Widgets is considered to be one of the most successful Widget companies in the country. Because of its success, it has recently been purchased by Why Not Industries. Why Not has decided to merge another company, Grieving Widows, with Mighty Midget Widgets and the corporate travel department of Mighty Midget Widgets will be expected to start handling corporate travel for Grieving Widows also. In this merger and reorganization it has been decided that the corporate travel department should automate. The manager of the corporate travel department called together all employees of the department last week in order to discuss automation. A committee was formed with the task of meeting, investigating automation, and developing a two-page recommendation for automation. The recommendation is to take into consideration the following facts.

Mighty Midget Widgets has a good working relationship with its travel agency, Little Lil's Lovable Travel. Lil has visited with every corporate traveler personally and she has made a special effort to find out the special needs of each and every traveler. She makes certain that these needs are recorded and acted upon in preparing each and every trip arrangement. There have been virtually no complaints from travelers regarding the services of Little Lil's Lovable Travel.

Adding the travel of Grieving Widows will bring the total travel volume handled by the corporate travel department to approximately $9 million annually and already Mighty Midget Widgets is the largest account of Little Lil's Lovable Travel. There is already a concern that the agency will not be able to automate the corporate travel department to the extent that top management might expect.

Currently a two percent rebate is being received. One of the top executives of Mighty Midget Widgets commented recently that Lovable Little Lil confided to him that she is receiving an override commission from Cantankerous Airways in the amount of 4.5 percent commission. In the last discussion among members of the corporate travel department it was suddenly realized that an especially large number of tickets have been issued recently on Cantankerous Airways and there is some discussion about the possibility of sharing override commissions. There is also a concern about whether or not some of the tickets on Cantankerous Airways are really the least expensive fares.

Everybody in the company likes lovable little Lil and her staff. But there has been a suggestion made that Big Biggie Travel might provide more in terms of

221

Group
Discussion
Situation:
Mighty Midget
Widgets Meet
Grieving
Widows

automation and services. Big Biggie is the largest travel agency in town. In fact, at industry meetings, B. B. Biggie, the owner and manager of Big Biggie Travel, has made it very clear that lovable little Lil and her travel agency have nowhere near the automation capability that his travel agency has.

The president of Grieving Widows recently met with a sales executive from a major credit card company, which is the same credit card company used by the corporate travel department at Mighty Midget Widgets. The sales representative pointed out that many companies now are using automation interfaces to automatically reconcile expense reports. The Grieving Widows president suggested that this convenience be added to the services provided by the corporate travel department.

Since establishing a working relationship with Little Lil's Lovable Travel agency no reports have been provided to the corporate travel department. However, lovable little Lil makes a visit to the corporate travel department at least once a week and verbally discusses the status of travel. She always brings in homemade brownies when she comes in and no one has any objection to her visits or questions the data she provides.

During one of her weekly visits, lovable little Lil was asked whether she or her agents were biased toward Cantankerous Airways, the host carrier for the computerized reservation system used by lovable little Lil. She assured all involved that not only were all agents unbiased, but the system has no bias in it whatsoever. She stressed that when receiving a call from any of the company's travelers, each agent was totally knowledgeable of traveler preferences since she holds weekly meetings with agents and informs them of the results of her discussions with each traveler when she visits with the travelers each week. Therefore, whenever a call comes in, each agent is able to provide top quality service, since Lil has assured the corporate travel department that each agent remembers all details of preferences. She has even tested the agents on their ability to remember preferences. Lil has pointed out that while Cantankerous Airways has not been able to come up with more than one screen in its computer system, agent superior memories eliminate the need for having more than one screen. Although the system has queues, profiles, and fact files available to agents, Lil prefers to depend upon her agents and their excellent memories rather than to utilize these newfangled aspects of the computer system. She points out that her reservationists are far more reliable than the queues, profiles, and fact files found in the computer.

You are meeting today to finalize the report on automation recommendations. You are expected to reach agreement and to write a two page recommendations report. In your group session select a spokesperson. All will have an equal vote on decisions. In your group session you are expected to reach agreements and to prepare the two-page paper to be presented to the entire class by the spokesperson of your committee.

CHAPTER 14

The Company Travel Study

The Multi-process Major Vendor Selection/Retention Process

The major vendor for corporate travel departments is a travel agency. Although contracts may be written with air carriers (for contract fares), hotels, and car rental companies, the most important contract will be the one written with a travel agency. There is no question that the travel agency is the single most important vendor to any corporate travel department. It is also the one on which the corporate travel department and the corporate travel manager depend to the largest degree. If the agency makes a mistake and the executive has a bad trip, missed connections, or any of thousands of other potential problems, it is the corporate travel department, in general, and the corporate travel manager, in specific, that receives the blame. It is critical, therefore, that a travel agency be found that provides a high-quality service at the lowest possible cost.

The process of finding, contracting with, and retaining a travel agency starts with the company's travel study. This study is usually commissioned when one or more executives have decided that company travel should be managed. Typically, a committee is established to study the company's travel and to make recommendations as to how it might be managed better than it is currently. The company travel study looks at all aspects of the company's travel. The report developed as a result of the study discusses the current state of the company's travel and suggests "better" ways of managing the travel. Among other things, the report usually makes suggestions on the criteria to be used in selecting a company travel agency and the process to be used in selecting and retaining a travel agency.

After the travel study report has been completed and studied, the next step is to prepare and distribute a *Request for Proposal* (RFP). Although the work in developing the RFP and distributing it is often done by a staff person (often the person who has been named to the position or who will become the corporate travel manager), a company committee is usually charged with this responsibility. The committee, working with guidelines and/or directives from company executives together with the company travel study report, will prepare a Request for Proposal, set guidelines for the distribution of the RFP, conduct an initial selection process based on eliminating those proposals that are prepared incorrectly or are incomplete, set up a process for reviewing proposals, determine which travel agencies will be invited to interview for the contract, conduct oral presentations and interviews with the top several (normally about three) travel agencies, sometimes conduct a second round of interviews when the potential agency vendors are very closely ranked after the first interview, select a travel agency for the company, and notify all agencies that submitted a proposal of their selection status.

Sometimes as a part of the RFP, but usually after the selection process has been completed, a transition agreement is reached with the agency that has been selected to handle the company's account. The transition contract spells out the timing, steps, and processes to be undertaken in moving from the way in which travel for the company has been handled to working with the new travel agency vendor on an exclusive basis.

Company Travel Study

The process starts with the *company travel study*. Most of these studies are in-depth analyses of all aspects of the company's travel. The typical study starts with an executive summary giving the highlights of the study. Usually this includes a justification for the study, the major recommendations of the study, savings and other benefits that can accrue to the company if the recommendations are adopted, an overview analysis of how these savings and other benefits will be achieved if the recommendations are followed, a history of how travel has been handled (or not handled) within the company, the specifications given to the committee or person who undertook the study, the scope of the study, the methodologies used in conducting the study, statistical analysis procedures used, the findings of the study (broken down by type of vendor or service) and concluding remarks.

Specific sections of the study may include volume-buying benefits from each type of vendor, a description of how other companies in the same field or of the same travel volume size are handling their travel (and the pros and cons of their systems), policy options (including the pros and cons of each), procedures options (including the pros and cons of each), patterns that seem to appear in the handling of travel by other companies, travel (air ticket, hotel, car rental, and so on), payment options, and management reports that might be solicited. A section needs to be devoted to the expected or potential benefits to the company that could be expected with centralized travel management. This can be broken down into the financial and the non-financial benefits. Within this, a description of the benefit and service options available from travel agencies in the community can be provided.

A description of how travel is currently being handled needs to be provided. In many cases, this will mean going to each person who makes travel arrangements in each division of the company. The "current status" section could describe both the pros and the cons of how travel is currently being handled. A conclusions section needs to detail both conclusions and recommendations. In most studies, the major conclusion is that the "buying power" of the company needs to be consolidated in order to obtain maximum benefits. Justification for this, if it is the major conclusion, should be clear and concise. Recommendations need to show options. Recommendations should be both global and complete. However, the minute details of how operations should be run are seldom appropriate or appreciated. In many studies, the appendix that follows the study is longer than the study itself. The appendix may start with a table of contents followed by each appropriate attachment. If attachments are identified by tabs, they can be located much more rapidly.

The Executive Summary

The first part of the study is the *executive summary*. Because it is a summary, it should be the last section to be written. Considerable care should be spent in the writing of the executive summary since many executives can be expected to read only this section of the study. It should be outlined before writing (seldom is the outline included in the printed executive summary) and it should be concise covering only the most important aspects of the study, but covering them in a logical manner with a smooth flow from one aspect to the next. Generally, the executive summary is preceded by a cover letter and a table of contents. However, some company travel studies start out with the executive summary. There are even some that use the executive summary as the cover letter, making the summary concise enough and styled appropriately for the cover letter.

The first paragraph of the executive summary is a very brief explanation of what the study is about, who commissioned the study, why the study was initiated, and what the time parameters are relating to the study (if time constraints are an important factor). The next paragraph should briefly discuss the principal finding(s) of the study. Usually this will state that the buying power of the company has not been consolidated, resulting in a loss of benefits that might otherwise accrue to the company. Sometimes the lack of service or some services being extended to the company is also an important finding discussed in this paragraph. The next paragraph concentrates on the primary recommendation of the study and perhaps two or three (at most) strongly supporting recommendations. This primary recommendation is usually that the company's travel buying power be consolidated in a corporate travel department. Supporting recommendations are often that the full cost-saving buying power benefits should be sought by consolidating travel through a single travel agency, that a full range of free or inexpensive financial and non-financial benefits should be sought for the company and its travelers, and that a request for proposal be developed.

The fourth paragraph describes in concise detail the major cost-savings that the company can expect to receive by implementing the recommendations described in the previous paragraph. Often this is accompanied by a chart showing how these financial benefits add up to a specific dollar total in savings to the company (or in some cases in earnings for the company). The executive summary is often concluded with a large dollar figure, that figure being the cost savings to the company that can be expected if the recommendations are implemented. Prior to this large dollar savings figure should be the breakdown showing savings in each of the following categories:

- air fares;
- hotel and car rentals;

- rebates;
- float; and
- other.

These subtotals are added up to give the overall savings figure.

The Introduction of the Study

The introduction section of the study starts with history. Usually a single brief paragraph outlines the history of concern within the company regarding travel, travel benefits, and how travel has not been organized centrally within the company. If there have been moves to organize travel, these are discussed. If a specific section or division has successfully organized the travel management function in its section/division, this is discussed. Next is a sentence or two about how the study came about being commissioned, who commissioned it, and why. This paragraph also addresses what person or department has been charged with undertaking the study, the time frames given for completion of the study, and a global view of what is expected from the study.

The second paragraph discusses who will undertake, chair the committee responsible for the study, and/or write the study. If a committee has been assigned to conduct the study and write up the results, each person on the committee will be identified, reasons (if known) for their appointment to the committee will be provided, their qualifications for serving on the committee will be documented, and the chair of the committee will be identified. If one person (either in-house or out-of-house) has been selected to undertake the study and author the report, this person is identified and the individual's background and qualifications for the job are discussed.

The next section of the study usually breaks down the company into operating sections or divisions and discusses the ones whose travel has been studied in conjunction with the study (normally those having the largest amount of travel). Other companies are recognized here when they have provided copies of their travel studies, travel policies, travel procedures, and so on. Their contributions to the current study are identified and appreciation is expressed.

Overall Parameters of the Study

The overall parameters of the study are addressed next. This is composed of at least four sections that are usually very brief, but that set out the specifics of the guidelines within which the study has been undertaken. The four sections are:

1. intent of the study;
2. purpose of the study;
3. scope of the study; and
4. the methodology(ies) used in conducting the study.

The intent of the study is usually to obtain greater financial and non-financial benefits for the company. It is important to point out that the intent of the study is not to cut the travel budget, unless that is an intent outlined by the company (it usually is not).

The purpose of the study is usually to find ways of obtaining greater financial and non-financial benefits for the company as it relates to managing company travel. Greater productivity of personnel and overcoming the problems or mistakes that have occurred as a result of travel mishaps may be other purposes. The motivation for one study was to overcome the travel problems that cost the company money. The study was commissioned by the CEO after he missed a flight and by missing the flight, missed an important meeting. The airline had discontinued the flight and the president of the company had not been rebooked on another fight. The purpose of travel studies, therefore, are not always to obtain increased financial benefits alone.

The scope of the study identifies the limitations placed on the study. Most travel studies do not question why a person took a trip, for example. Instead, they are concerned with whether or not that trip was made with the maximum amount of benefits provided for the lowest beneficial price possible. Limitations often address in what parts of the company travel has been studied and/or authorized for study. If use of the company jets, for example, is not a concern, this part of the company travel should not be addressed by the study and perhaps the study will be limited to travel on commercial carriers only. Ideally, the scope of the study section identified all areas of travel that a reader might think would be a part of the study and specifically states that it either is a part of the study or is not a part of the study and why.

The methodology section of the study briefly discusses each method that was used in developing the study. Usually these methods include the following:

1. Interviews with those currently making travel arrangements.
2. Surveys of other companies regarding their travel procedures, systems, and policies.
3. Soliciting other travel studies and summarizing the pros and cons of resulting systems.
4. Collecting all company written travel systems, procedures, and policies currently being used (as well as some historical data along these lines, if such historical data is still pertinent or of potential value).
5. In-depth interviews with the CEO, CFO, and others who can be expected to have specific requirements for the travel management program.
6. A review of the published literature in corporate travel management.
7. Tracking sample travel transactions from the time the need for travel arises until all accountable documents are filed.
8. Conduct a best-fare audit on a sampling of tickets.
9. Conduct a sampling of travel payment float.
10. Interview vendors, carriers, industry consultants, corporate travel managers, and other appropriate parties,

Findings

Usually the longest section of the study and the section that requires the greatest amount of research is the section commonly referred to as *findings*. The word "findings" is an appropriate word to describe this section since the section literally is the results or the things that were "found out" as a result of the research that was conducted. After applying the methodologies described above and gathering both facts and data through the methodologies applications, the facts and data are massaged, statistical formulas are applied, and the results are reported as "findings." It is important not to confuse this section of the study report with conclusions. They are not the same. However, many treat them as the same when the written report of the results of the study is prepared. The findings are simply a straight forward report of the data and the facts that were found. It is normally summarized, though some reports include data reported exactly and completely as it is found. The results section draws conclusions from the data and facts presented in the findings and, in this regard, can be considered to be conclusions drawn from the data and facts—not the data and the facts themselves.

Annual Cost of Travel Finding

One of the first findings normally reported in the results of the travel study relates to the annual cost of travel. Three components make up this finding. These are:

1. the cost of travel calculated on an annual or "last-year" basis;
2. the components that went in to the calculation of the total cost of travel normally reported on both a percentage of total and on a gross dollar expenditures basis; and
3. a discussion of how these figures were derived (normally broken down by major type of travel cost). This section usually starts with a report on the total travel costs, proceeds to a discussion of how this figure was derived, and moves to a conclusion showing the components, percentage of total cost, and the dollar cost for each component. Frequently, a graph or chart depicting this analysis is included in this section of the study report.

Travel Authorization Study

For many companies the first step in preparing for a trip is to obtain an approved (signed) travel authorization. Normally this is initiated by the traveler and approved by the executive to whom the traveler reports. With many companies travel authorizations are not approved unless they have been budgeted in advance and there was a financial approval for the expenditure at the time the department's budget for the year was approved. In such circumstances, the executive signing the travel authorization is responsible for having checked the departmental budget to ascertain that the financial budget for the trip has been authorized and that the expected costs do not exceed the authorized costs (in the budget). This is normally done before signing the travel authorization. In other companies the travel authorization is sent to the department's or the division's financial officer prior to the "boss" signing the authorization. There it is checked against the budget and either signed by the financial officer or initialed by him.

Since obtaining approvals for the travel authorization is a first-step before travel starts for travelers in many companies, it is understandable that a study of a sampling of travel authorizations would be undertaken by the person(s) undertaking the travel study. The report on travel authorizations should include data about the study including:

1. how many authorizations were reviewed;
2. when they were reviewed (the time period over which authorizations were authorized that were reviewed);
3. departments whose travel authorizations were reviewed (and approximately how many or what percentage came from each department);
4. what the study indicates; and
5. what the study does not reveal.

Possible outcomes of the study could be:

1. what percentage of authorizations resulted in trips that were taken;
2. what percentage of authorizations resulted in trips taken at the budgeted cost and what percentage resulted in over-budget and/or under-budget trips;
3. what percentage of trips are taken by each department or division of the company;
4. how many and what percentage of trips were taken when there was no advance budget approval for the trip.

With some companies, travel authorizations must include all data regarding the trip prior to approval. This includes reservation details, all expected costs, vendor(s) to be utilized, dates of travel, frequent flier numbers (if appropriate), itineraries, hotel and car rental information, and so on. When this type of data is attached to the travel authorization, considerably greater travel study information can be obtained from a study of travel authorizations. Expected outcomes can now include:

1. the percentage of reservations made directly with air carriers and the percentage made with travel agencies;
2. the travel agencies used by the company's travelers and if there is any pattern (i.e., does one department or division use one agency only, do travelers decide for themselves which travel agency they will use, or do each of the secretaries who make reservations select a travel agency);
3. the frequency of frequent flier usage in conjunction with carriers flown (this may help to determine whether or not carriers are being selected because of their frequent flier programs rather than because of cost of ticket).

By following up on the travel authorizations and calling those who called in reservations from within the company as well as conducting an audit of the tickets written, the following data might be obtained:

1. distribution costs (what the company paid in prepaid ticket (PTA) charges, express mail charges, delivery costs, and so on);
2. how far in advance reservations were made (when two-week advanced purchase or other discounted tickets have been purchased);
3. how many changes were made to reservations and how close to flight time did these changes occur (would the company have lost money by buying advanced-purchase, no refund, and/or heavy cancellation fee tickets); and
4. if other, less expensive fares on the carrier selected or on another carrier were available when the reservation was made.

There are certain areas of information that will not be shown in a study of travel authorizations even when that study is accompanied by a phone call follow-up to the person(s) who called in reservation requests. Information not shown in such a study includes:

1. whether the person making the reservation at the airline or travel agency advised the person in the company who called in the reservation regarding less expensive fares, classes of service, or flights that might have been available at the time the reservation was made;
2. what the actual costs of the trip were and what the breakdown was between costs of air travel, hotel, car rental, meals, and so on; and
3. whether or not the fares or class of service options changed after the reservation was made resulting in what might have been a less expensive cost to the company.

This information is important and should be obtained through other studies so that it is included in the total company travel study.

Destination Analysis

A destination analysis is designed to discover identifiable travel patterns. However, it also identifies other information of value in studying the company's travel. For example, car rental usage by destination and date and hotel booking patterns can usually be reviewed at the same time and as a part of the destination analysis. Not only does the destination analysis provide data on the cities to which company travelers flew, but it provides percentages of travel to those destinations. Usually the overall destination analysis will show the percentage and raw number amounts of travel in-state versus out-of-state and out-of-country trips. In addition, it will identify key cities of travel in-state, key cities and states for out-of-state trips, and key cities and countries for out-of-country trips. Again, the data for each destination will show the number of trips and the percentage of trips to that destination.

For each destination city, an analysis of the car rental usage is conducted. The analysis identifies the number of car rental companies used, the number and type of vehicles rented, additional mileage charges, insurance charges, the number of cars rented per day/per rental company by type of car, late charges, gas refill charges, and any other charges levied by the car rental company(ies).

For each destination city, an analysis of the hotel(s) used is conducted. The analysis identifies how close the hotel was to the place where the traveler conducted business, the cost of the hotel, telephone usage charges, whether or not complimentary airport transportation was available between the hotel and the airport, room types rented, room nights rented, gratis or reduced cost items such as complimentary continental breakfast, newspaper under the door, and so on.

The air travel section of the destination analysis identifies what carriers were flown, departure and arrival times, ticket costs, ground transportation costs to and from the airport (including airport parking, if this is a reimbursable cost).

Data for the destination analysis comes from the travelers, the travelers' secretaries, airline tickets issued, expense reports, travel authorizations, the travel agency(ies) serving the company, the airlines, car rental companies, and the hotels that were utilized.

A number of potential savings can come from the information gained in conducting a destination analysis. Savings might result from:

1. car rental rate negotiations based on documented volume usage;
2. policies limiting the type of car rental that is allowed;
3. negotiating for additional free mileage;
4. negotiating a waiver in late charges to a specified (later than twenty-four hours) three or four hours after the normal twenty-four hour rental,
5. adopting a policy of limiting the type of car that can be rented based upon the traveler's company status and the purpose for which the car will be used;
6. negotiating a waiver of additional mileage costs when the need for additional mileage is known in advance;
7. negotiating an extension of the rental car turn-in time;
8. a policy requirement that rental cars are to be refilled prior to turning them in;
9. a review of other charges and the development of policies and procedures designed to mitigate or eliminate these charges as well; and
10. waiver(s) on specific city surcharges.

Hotel savings might result from:

1. negotiated rates from individual properties at frequently traveled destinations;
2. taxi and/or car rental savings by using properties that have free airport pickup and delivery and which are located within walking distance of the destination business address where the traveler will be working;
3. negotiated free airport pick up and return and/or free transfers to/from downtown;

4. free upgraded rooms;

5. rates that include breakfast; and

6. free rooms for every negotiated number of reservations.

Probably the largest amount of potential savings can come from air travel expenses. Conducting a fare comparison between the fares used and the lowest fare available will reflect the fare savings potential. If the percentage saving on the sampling study is applied to the total annual air costs of the company, this saving alone can often justify the establishment (and cost) of starting a corporate travel department. Because the potential dollar volume of savings in this area is so substantial for many companies, air fare comparisons can sometimes be the subject of lengthy debate when executives analyze the travel study report. Therefore, it will be beneficial to indicate exactly how savings potentials were determined. There are several approaches that are used. They are sometimes used within the same study. All approaches compare the actual fares paid for the tickets selected for audit comparison. These actual fares are compared to:

1. other existing lower fares on direct service flights;

2. other existing lower fares on any other routing;

3. fares paid by other company travelers flying on the same dates and to the same destinations;

4. fares paid by other travelers (not necessarily working for the company) flying on the same dates and to the same destinations, other company or government contract rates in effect between the city pairs traveled; and

5. commuter ticket or coupon book rates in effect between the two cities traveled.

In discussing fare comparisons in the travel study report, it is important to identify a range distance within which most flights take place. This could be *in-state* or it might be *in-region*. If it is in-region, identify what states or cities are encompassed within the region. The destination analysis should identify each city within the state or region to which there were multiple flights studied in the destination analysis study and should discuss:

1. how many trips to the city were reviewed in the sampling study;

2. how many were round trips and how many were one ways;

3. the number of prepaid tickets issued and what the reasons were for having prepays (contact the department authorizing the prepaid ticket) and whether or not any savings might have been possible if the ticket had been mailed or handled in some other way and if another way of handling was possible under the circumstances;

4. the number of commuter tickets issued and how the price of these commuter tickets compared with contract prices or lowest available published fares and if savings would have been better if the contract fare or lowest available published fare had been used instead;

5. the number of lowest available published fare tickets issued and if savings could have been realized if commuter tickets or the contract fare were used instead;

6. the number of contract fare tickets issued and if savings could have been realized if commuter tickets or the lowest published fare had been used instead; and

7. the number of tickets issued at any other fare, and the savings that could have been realized by issuing the ticket(s) at the lowest available published fare, the contract fare, or using a commuter ticket.

If travel agencies issued commuter tickets when another option was less expensive, call the agency to ask why and report the reasons. If they issued tickets at the contract rate and another option was less expensive, ask why and report the reason. And if they used any published fare when another option was less expensive, ask why and report the reason.

When comparing fares for destinations that are out-of-state or out-of-region a similar analysis should be undertaken for those cities to which a large percentage of company business is undertaken (for example, an overseas factory or a regional sales office). However, for most trips to destinations outside of the state or region, a comparison of the fares paid with lower existing fares is all that is appropriate in the air portion of the destination analysis.

Major Travel Expense Comparison Study

An analysis should be undertaken to compare major travel expenses incurred by the company's travelers with those reported nationally. One of the best ways to do this is to determine ratios. Compare the percentage of the total spent by the company for airfare, hotel, food, car rentals, and miscellaneous. The 1985 Diners' Club breakdown as compared with the sample company could be shown as follows:

	Diners' Club	*XYZ Company*
Air fare	40%	___%
Food/Lodging	35%	___%
Car Rental	10%	___%
Miscellaneous	15%	___%
Total	100%	100%

If there is a large discrepancy between the national percentage breakdown and the company breakdown, this should be identified, analyzed, and discussed. It may show an area in which to look for potential savings.

Air Fare Discussion

For the reader of the company travel study report to gain a knowledgeable perspective, it would be beneficial if a section of the travel study report include an overview of the air fare situation since deregulation. With as many as three hundred air fare changes a day, promotional fares being offered to the public before airline staff and travel agents know about them, and serious restrictions on discounted seat availability combined with substantial penalties for discounted fare changes or cancellations, it is difficult for the traveler, the agent, and the airline reservationist to understand and to deal with air fares, not to mention the executive who is primarily concerned with his unique areas of expertise. Therefore, briefly explaining the changes relating to air fares that results from deregulation and the relation that this has to corporate travel, potential corporate travel savings, and the need for a corporate travel department can be beneficial.

It is suggested that the air fare discussion in the company travel study report start with a one- or two-page documentation of deregulation air fare changes. This could be followed with a copy of a single-day fare sheet showing the range of fares between the company's home office and the city to which there is the greatest amount of air travel. A discussion of the lowest fares on the fare sheet should be provided, showing clearly why the company cannot use one hundred percent cancellation fee or heavy penalty fee fares, fares that require a Saturday or Sunday overnight, and other inexpensive fares designed primarily for the leisure market. How a judgment decision must often be made relating to what the least expensive fare for the company to use can usually be done by explaining the pros and cons of each of these lowest fare sheet fares.

Routings and the importance of routings needs to be clarified. One of the best approaches is to take a city pair flown frequently by the company's travelers but a city pair that has no direct flights. Next show a comparison of fares based on different routings. Identify the savings that can accrue by having a knowledgeable agent take the time to find the least expensive and convenient routing possible. At least two, and perhaps three, of these examples should be shown in order to put across the point that utilization of a dedicated, knowledgeable agent is essential if the company is to save money.

Frequent Flier Programs

Every major air carrier and many international carriers now offer frequent flier programs as incentives to get travelers to fly with them. Aimed at the business traveler, the programs have been kept and expanded because they have been effective in luring travelers onto the carriers and away from competitors who sometimes are both more convenient and who sometimes charge lower fares. The concern of many companies is that a traveler working toward a free vacation trip to an exotic destination may insist on traveling with a specific carrier in order to earn additional travel incentive points even when the trip will cost the company substantially more. This fear has proven to have a mixed degree of validity. There have been business travelers who have taken advantage of frequent flier programs at the expense of their companies and there are many more business travelers who put the company first and will fly on a preferred carrier (one offering the desired frequent flier points for the exotic trip) only if the cost to the company is the same or less.

Because of the corporate concern regarding frequent flier programs and their very real ability to increase costs to the company, the travel study report should address frequent flier programs. It is suggested that this part of the report start with an explanation of what frequent flier programs are and how they work. Next should come a discussion of each of the domestic frequent flier programs that might apply to the company's travelers (if it is one offered by a commuter airline flying between destinations in a part of the country where the company has no travel, there is no reason to include it). Finally, provide an overview of the appropriate international air carriers offering frequent flier programs. Because many of the frequent flier programs now have tie-ins with hotels and car rental companies, these tie-ins should be discussed.

After discussing the various programs, address coupon brokering and the latest position of the Internal Revenue Service regarding the taxation of the value of frequent flier incentive awards and how these two factors might affect the company.

Several positions are taken regarding frequent flier coupons. While there is uniform agreement that travelers should not select flights solely on the basis of earning frequent flier bonus points, especially when this would cost the company more money, there is disagreement as to whom the frequent flier coupons belong and how to manage frequent flier coupon programs. One position is that benefits that are paid for with company funds belong to the company. Those companies that adhere to this position will often set up post office box addresses to which all bonus point coupons on all carriers are sent and the corporate travel manager either works in the free flights for company travelers traveling on company trips or sells the coupons to coupon brokers, returning the earnings back to the company.

Another line of thinking is that managing frequent flier coupon programs is too difficult and too time consuming to be cost effective. Therefore, travelers are allowed to keep the coupons themselves and to retain the coupon program benefits for themselves. An extension of this thinking is that company travelers spend many nights away from home and family and the coupon program benefits help to compensate the traveler and his family for this additional dedication to company goals.

Whatever approach is adopted, it is beneficial when a recommended course of action is included in the company travel study report. The use of frequent flier coupons can be an emotional and a sensitive issue. To have the committee make a recommendation and to have top management make a decision regarding how frequent flier coupons will be managed takes considerable political pressure away from the corporate travel manager.

Company Travel Policies and Procedures

In most companies there has been considerable company travel extending over a period of several years prior to the undertaking of the company travel study. Since in most companies employees do not simply decide to take a trip, make travel arrangements, and leave, a history of policies and procedures for handling travel in the company exists. It is important to document this travel policy and procedures history either since the company began or at least for the last five to ten years. This historical section of the company travel study report puts change recommendations into perspective.

Sometimes the history is not very clear. There are companies that have different policies and procedures depending upon the department or the division in which the traveler works. Travel is arranged differently in one section as compared to another. Under such circumstances, the study report should point out where the differences are in terms of policies and procedures and the study should discuss the pros and cons of each system or approach toward handling travel. Finally, if one of the current sets of policies and procedures is suggested by the committee undertaking the travel study, this needs to be clearly stated and the reasons for the recommendation should be discussed. In many cases, however, the company travel study committee will suggest a set of travel policies and procedures that do not parallel any policy and procedures system currently in effect in the company. In such an event, the reasons for recommending the policy and procedures system recommended should be pointed out. In addition, the reasons for not recommending any of the policies and procedures currently in use should be pointed out in detail.

The financial flow is the foundation on which most company travel policies and procedures are based. In many cases, this financial flow is both internal and external to the company. Often the starting point is the budgeting process. In many divisions, most company travel can be projected and budgeted just as other costs can be projected and budgeted. In other divisions, there is less ability to project exact travel needs and the travel budget will be based on history and projections regarding what the company is expected to do. The company travel study report recommendations usually do not suggest major changes in the budgeting process. Normally, the only consideration here is to obtain trip cost projections from the travel agency serving the company and/or from the corporate travel manager in the hope that projections will be more accurate. This, of course, also helps the corporate travel manager to negotiate hotel and car rental contracts since the corporate travel department can start building a file of total corporate trip projections by city pairs.

Once the budgeting process has been completed, travel policies and procedures can vary considerably. It is important for the travel study report to identify how specific trips are approved, who makes the travel arrangements, who decides what travel agency or airline to phone for reservations, what the constraints are, if any, in making reservations, what reporting before and after the trip is undertaken are required, if any, and what policies guide the reservations and ticketing process. Detailing the past history with one or more travel agencies that may have served the company is important. If there has been a change in travel agencies, the reasons for making the changes are important to identify. Documenting payment procedures and refund procedures is also important. Float is important to the company, but it is also a potential trade-off for additional rebates and other immediate cash or service benefits.

Usually this part of the travel study report is detailed and lengthy as it often needs to be. Almost all recommendations of the travel study committee are presented in terms of comparisons of what is suggested as contrasted to what is currently in place or what was in place at one time with both the benefits and the detriments of the proposed approaches contrasted to those of the past or present.

Prior to the company travel study, most companies will not have had a detailed travel financial management tracking system in place. Since savings on travel is the major justification for the existence of most corporate travel departments, tracking travel expenses and documenting savings is usually a high priority with most company travel study committees. Several alternative systems need to be studied, but most companies ultimately adopt a credit card system. Major credit card systems offer the advantages of monthly detailed travel expense reporting at no cost to the company combined with excellent cash flow.

American Express, Diners' Club, enRoute, and Visa all offer corporate contract programs related specifically to a company's travel expenses and the management of those expenses. Cards can be issued to either the company or to individual travelers. If the travel volume is substantial (usually over one million dollars), there is no membership, processing, or management fee levied. No interest is charged for at least thirty days and interest and late payment charges are negotiable beyond thirty days. Lost or stolen cards, if reported right away, normally carry either limited liability or no liability. Billing is flexible. Either the company can be billed directly or a system that is popular with many company financial managers can be adopted. This system is billing the traveler directly with the traveler personally responsible for trip expenses. The traveler then submits an expense report to the company requesting trip reimbursement.

Another available benefit is free accident insurance, but before advertising this to the travelers or executives it is important to know that several of the free accident insurance programs limit payments to a maximum limit per accident, no matter how many company travelers may be traveling on the same plane. Twenty-four hour card replacement and customer assistance phone lines (usually toll-free) are normally available at no cost. Emergency overseas travel cash advances and emergency check-cashing privileges are normally extended on a no-fee basis. Foreign currency conversion at no fee and no fee travelers checks are sometimes included.

The use of the credit card system means that the company pays nothing for the trip for at least thirty days after the airline tickets are issued (giving the company good float time), only valid travel expenses are paid (reimbursing individual travelers based on their expense reports), and there is a check and balance system, thereby easing the travel accounting workload. If the traveler files expense reports immediately after returning from the trip and these are processed promptly, immediate reimbursement of individual company traveler expense payments can be accomplished after almost every trip. This means that the individual traveler does not need to carry the travel expenses and will not carry them if the processing is done in a timely manner.

The paperwork flow and the expenses of the paperwork can be reduced or eliminated with a credit card system. There is no need to obtain a formal travel expense authorization if the trip has been budgeted, the trip is not expected to exceed the budgeted amount, and all trip costs are charged to the traveler's personal credit card account. Since the travel agency can maintain a copy of signed credit cards and can report purchases as being for travelers whose signatures are "on file", the traveler only needs to phone the travel agency and make booking arrangements. The agency can process all air travel charges against the individual traveler's credit card, issue the ticket and deliver the ticket without the traveler having to sign anything after the initial credit card on file has been signed and retained by the travel agency.

One of the frequent suggestions of travel study reports regarding credit card payment systems is to adopt a credit card payment system for one department or division as a pilot study, study the results, and report back to the committee with a full list of advantages and detriments relating to the implementation of a credit card travel payment program.

Travel Agency Working Relationship History

As noted in an earlier chapter, since deregulation of the air travel industry, almost all travel arrangements made in the U.S. for corporate travel have been made through retail travel agencies. Most companies have a history of working with one or more travel agencies, but it is not unusual for companies to change agencies frequently or for a company without a corporate travel department to use several travel agencies at the same time. Individual departments and divisions may select one or two agencies for their department or division while other departments or divisions select totally different agencies. When a company has a history of changing agencies, documenting the reasons for the changes that have taken place may be beneficial in the search for an agency to handle all of the company's travel. It also may reveal major concerns that exist in specific departments of the company—concerns that the company as a whole may not share, but concerns that probably should be considered when trying to find a company-wide agency.

At the same time, when different departments or divisions have selected different agencies the reasons for the selections need to be studied. Again, it could be that the travel needs of one part of the company are different than the travel needs of other parts of the company. All travel needs should be considered, prioritized, and given appropriate weight when selecting an agency to handle all corporate business.

This study of past history and current usage of travel agencies may also indicate that having a single company-wide travel agency vendor will not be the most beneficial approach for the company. Agencies that specialize may well fit the needs of some company departments/divisions/travelers better than the agency that seems to be best for everyone else. It may very well be found that the benefits of having two or more travel agencies will far outweigh the benefits of having only one company-wide agency.

Therefore, instead of automatically assuming that having a single agency vendor will be best, a comprehensive study of department/travel agency working history should be undertaken and a portion of the study should include the pros and cons of each agency utilized or currently utilized as these pros and cons fit the travel needs of the departments, the divisions, and the travelers.

Contract Fares

A growing number of private companies and government entities have had some success with contract fares. If the travel volume of the company is substantial and/or if the travel between specific city pairs is substantial, contract fares is a partial travel management approach that the travel study and the travel study committee may want to address.

The purpose of contract fares is to get the lowest possible fare from an air carrier in exchange for dedicated usage of that carrier for all company air travel between the cities for which the fare has been contracted. The process starts by identifying the volume of air travel between all major city pairs flown by company personnel. Usually the high-volume city pairs include the company headquarters city and a company factory, plant, regional office, subsidiary, or other major entity unique to the company. Once large volume city pairs have been identified, average year usage (the number of company flights between these two cities for the last four or five years divided by the number of years) and projected next year city pair flights are calculated. If the volume is substantial (try testing volume importance by calling a few airline sales offices and asking the District Sales Manager if this volume is enough to justify consideration of developing a con-tracted fare for the company), send out invitations to bid to all air carriers serving the high-volume city pairs.

In the invitation to bid, include a statement as to whether or not commis-sionable or non-commissionable contract fares are being sought. If it is commis-sionable, you are advising the air carrier that you will be working through a travel agency and the agency commission (normally ten percent of the net, after-tax fare is included in the commissionable contract fare quoted by the air carrier. If it is non-commissionable, you are advising the air carrier that all reservations will be made with the carrier directly and the tickets will be issued by the air carrier.

In other words, you will not be working through a travel agency. Some companies have contract fares on only a few routes (their volumes not being sufficient to warrant carrier bidding on many routes) write into their requests for proposal (sent to travel agencies bidding out the handling of the company's travel) a requirement that contract fare booking and ticketing will be handled by the travel agency on a gratis basis as part of what the agency is expected to do to earn the company's commissionable ticket business. While some travel agencies may agree to do this, others will not. Much depends on the volume of both the commissionable and the non-commissionable business.

Other Company Travel Studies

In order to provide comparisons and alternatives, the approaches used by other companies in handling their travel can be included in the company's travel study. It is suggested that between five and ten other companies be included in this section of the travel study report. The selection of companies having a similar travel volume is usually considered to be the most practical approach. The president of the local chapter of the *National Business Travel Association* (NBTA) may provide a list of between ten and twenty possible companies in the same geographical area each having a similar travel volume if the chapter policies permit. The list will include the name, phone number, and address of appro-priate contact people in each company (usually the corporate travel manager). This service is usually provided on a gratis basis and normally takes a week or less to obtain.

Once the list of companies has been received, it is suggested that a phone call be made to each company on the list. Discuss the desire to obtain travel management information for your company's travel study and set up an appointment to meet the person(s) responsible for travel.

To give the readers of the company travel study an opportunity to compare options, provide about two paragraphs (approximately half a page) of information on each company in the study report. Each company's travel management review should indicate how travel is currently being handled, how it became managed and handled since formal travel management was started, concerns and problems that the company has or has had regarding travel management (and how these concerns or problems were resolved if they have been resolved), who is responsible for travel management at the company that is being studied, and any suggestions that the company being studied has for your company as you approach travel management. Most of the companies studied will be working with one or more travel agencies in some manner. Include a sentence or two, therefore, about the agency/company relationship and any history of that relationship that may be beneficial to the readers of the travel study report. Discuss the dollar travel volume of each company studied and if the studied companies have such records, include information on the amount of savings the companies have realized. If there appear to be patterns in terms of travel management and/or travel agency usage, identify the patterns and discuss what these patterns' impact on the company's travel can be expected to be (if it is felt that the pattern will affect your company as well).

Travel Agency Services

Although travel agency services have been discussed earlier, the detail and the range of these services which should be brought out in the company travel study report requires a more complete treatment. The major advantages of centralizing the management of corporate travel are to obtain cost savings, a wide range of services (either free or at low cost), and a better quality travel experience for the company's travelers. Having a full range of services, therefore, constitutes one third of the justifications or advantages of travel management. In addition, however, it can add substantially to company travel savings and to having a quality travel experience.

Computerized Traveler Profile

Sometimes the computerized traveler profile is also called the *traveler preference profile*. It is a computer-stored data sheet about key company information and travel preferences and one is kept on every frequent (as well as many infrequent) company travelers. A questionnaire, often tailor-developed by each travel agency or by the corporate travel manager (standard airline-generated questionnaires do exist), is provided to each corporate traveler when the travel account is obtained by a travel agency. This questionnaire asks a multitude of questions about the traveler and the traveler's role with his company. It also asks about his preferences regarding air travel factors (and sometimes ground arrangements as well). Whenever a reservation is requested for the traveler after the questionnaire data has been entered into the computer once, the company travel information and preferences are automatically transferred to the particular air travel reservation request. By having this information immediately at hand while working on the reservation, the travel agency reservationist will be able to request all appropriate preferences without having to have the traveler present or having to call the traveler to ask about preferences. Some of the more common information in traveler profiles include:

1. airline preference (if the traveler prefers to fly on one carrier as compared to another carrier);
2. aircraft preferences (some corporate travelers will not fly in aircraft carrying five to twenty passengers or the traveler will prefer to avoid such aircraft if at all possible);
3. airline seating preference (smoking or non-smoking section, aisle or window seat);
4. special meals (no ham, vegetarian, diet, diabetic, and so on); and
5. special medical information (information regarding the more common medical concerns, like diabetic, strongly allergic to pets, and so on).

Other information in traveler profiles has to do with ground arrangements. Examples include:

1. Prefers a four-door, not a two-door car;
2. Hertz Number One Club member (and include the membership number);
3. Provide local map with car/key pick-up;
4. No hotel room above the eighth floor (fire truck ladders only reach the lower floors of a high-rise hotel).

Many corporate travel managers adopt numerical sequences for traveler profiles. These identify profit and cost center and often identify the branch office, area, or region where the traveler is based. These code numbers make travel management report information breakouts much easier.

Automation Systems

Today corporate travel-oriented travel agencies are automated with both *front office* and *back office computer systems*. The front office systems are provided by airline vendors (except for MARS PLUS, which is independent of airline ownership, but which is found in only a very small percentage of corporate travel-oriented travel agencies). The major systems and their sponsoring air carriers, listed alphabetically, are:

• Apollo—United Airlines
• Datas II—Delta Airlines;
• PARS—Trans World Airlines/Northwest Orient Airlines;
• Sabre—American Airlines;
• System One—Eastern Airlines and Continental Airlines.

Each of these systems is designed to allow the travel agency to access a data base of reservation information and request airline, car rental, hotel, and other reservations based upon client preferences. The systems are also designed to issue airline tickets, flight boarding passes, itineraries, and ticket jackets. They record, store, and note on itineraries such essential information as car rental confirmation numbers and hotel confirmation numbers.

The front office automation systems are becoming more and more less biased toward the airlines which sponsor the systems. However, it is natural for a travel agent to prefer a sponsoring carrier for the system being used. Because of the potential for bias and preference, some travel agencies have more than one system. An additional reason for having two or more systems is the accessibility of last seat availability and up-to-date fares. Although the vendors of all systems indicate that through interfacing last seat availability is obtained, in reality this is not always the case.

Other factors also come into consideration in reviewing the front office reservation systems. One of these is the speed with which data is transmitted across or input into a reservation system. An example of the type of problem that can occur recently was reported by a travel agent who was using one of the most expensive and most sophisticated of airline-sponsored front office computer systems. She noted that she had booked a reservation for a commercial traveler and within ten minutes of completing the reservation his secretary called back. The secretary asked that a frequent flier upgrade be applied in order to change the ticket to first class since the traveler would be flying with a business associate who was also flying first class. The travel agent made the change and noted the change in the history of the transaction. When the traveler arrived at the airport, he was told that the reservation was still in the economy section of the plane, that there were no first-class seats available, and that he could not upgrade to first class. After some arguing and waiting for seat availability, the traveler was able to pay an additional fee on the spot to upgrade him to a first-class seat for which there was a no show. Needless to say, the traveler was inconvenienced and embarrassed. When the agent investigated, she found out that the airline had not transmitted the change to the carrier involved even though she had made the reservation upgrade only ten minutes after the original reservation had been made. Although all computerized reservation systems normally provide rapid interfacing with all other systems, once in a while delayed transmittals can occur. Therefore, agencies with multiple systems can provide an advantage for the corporate client and for the corporate traveler.

Front office computer systems also offer three other advantages:

1. the ability to determine the lowest air fare;
2. personalized services; and
3. computer-issued tickets, itineraries, and boarding passes.

The *fare-search* feature of all automated reservations and ticketing systems provides ability to interface the corporate policy requirements and low fare inventories in such a way that the lowest possible fare available at the time of booking can be determined consistent with corporate travel policies. Even when different sets of policies apply to different categories of travelers, the match can determine the best possible fare within any set of corporate travel restrictions, guidelines, or policies.

Personalized services for each traveler can be provided by storing the traveler's profile in a reservations computer. When the travel agent wishes to access the profile, it can be brought up on one part (screen) of the CRT while the reservation can be displayed on another screen simultaneously. Some aspects of the profile can automatically be transferred over to the reservation while the travel agent will be required to manually input other aspects of the profile. An example of the type of preference that must be manually transferred is seat selection. Seat preference has to be compared with seat availability. The availability of all unassigned seats on the flight can be displayed on yet a third screen. A choice is made based upon the preferences shown in the traveler's profile. This seat is booked and transferred from availability to the traveler's itinerary and computer booking.

Tailored itineraries can be printed with multiple copies provided for the secretary and/or spouse. Itineraries can show not only the flight information, but also car rental and hotel confirmation numbers, directions to the car rental counter, hotel addresses, and appropriate contact phone numbers. Itineraries and tickets are normally issued simultaneously either on the same or on two printers. Those tickets which are charged to a credit card can automatically include the credit card form when printed so that data on the charge form and data on the tickets are identical.

Boarding passes are issued separately on a boarding pass printer and increasingly, boarding passes can be pre-issued for all segments of an itinerary, thus saving the traveler substantial time in terms of not having to wait in airport lines.

A few travel agencies also offer back office automation systems. These may range from a low of two or three percent of the agencies in a major city to a high of twenty to twenty-five percent. The back office automation systems consist of automated accounting interface systems. Through a connecting link with the reservations/ticketing computers, accounting data is transmitted automatically to the back office computers every time a ticket is printed. Accounting data is stored and a number of reports can be generated from the stored data. The major report provided to corporate travel managers is commonly referred to as a *savings report*. Depending upon the sophistication of the back office system and the needs of the client corporations, the savings report can be tailored to meet the needs of the corporate client and other reports can be generated as well.

There are three levels of sophistication in back office computer systems. The simplest of these is a computerized system that is not linked to the reservations/ticketing computers, but because the software is designed to provide accounting reports, they are referred to as accounting interface systems. They are not interfaced automatically. The systems require that all data be hand entered. They are very time consuming compared to automated accounting interface systems and they tend to be the least sophisticated of all travel agency back office computer systems. Increasingly these are found in fewer and fewer business-travel oriented travel agencies.

The second level of back office computer systems and the one that is found most frequently in business-travel oriented agencies is the airline-sponsored automated accounting interface system. The major suppliers of reservations systems for travel agencies also have sponsored automated accounting interface systems for agencies. Again, these are the major air carriers. The simplest of the automated accounting interface systems is a system provided by Delta Airlines through its Datas II Reservations and Ticketing computer. This system is built into the Datas II and generates only the weekly Airline Reporting Corporation report. The more sophisticated automated accounting interface systems (Delta offers three levels of systems and several other airlines offer at least two levels) can provide as many as thirty to fifty different types of automated reports.

The third, and most sophisticated level, of back office systems is the system that is tailored to the travel agency. These tend to be wide in variety and to use many different software programs and integrated units of hardware. For many of these systems travel agencies employ one or more full-time staff members to write programs tailored exactly to the specifications of the agency's larger clients. Although few of these independent systems have been developed by travel agencies around the country, those which have them can offer virtually any type of report desired by client companies and they can tailor any type of existing report to the needs of their clients. This tends to be expensive and travel agencies will not normally provide this type of tailored service for any but their largest clients.

The major report around which back office systems are based is the savings report. All major systems provide this foundation report. However, computerized billing features are also popular and utilized by a large number of travel agency corporate accounts. The advantage of such billing is that bills can be interfaced with credit card statements so that automated justification can be provided. A third utilization frequently requested is a report that automatically stores all corporate travel budgets, deducts airline and/or other travel expenses from the budgets, and provides the company, department, and/or traveler with specific data related to the amount of travel expenses incurred to date versus budgeted and the balance remaining in each budget account.

Delivery Services

Travel agencies specializing in corporate travel normally offer ticket delivery service. This is usually provided on a once per day arrangement, but those corporations requesting delivery two or more times per day can often have this service provided at no cost if their volume of tickets warrants such frequent delivery. Some agencies employ part-time delivery personnel, often working only four hours per day. Others employ a full-time delivery person and still others have their own fleet of delivery vehicles. If required, most corporate travel-oriented travel agencies can deliver tickets within one hour and an increasing number provide airport pick-up service. This service varies from an arrangement with an airline insurance company, or other airport-based company to use their ticket counter for ticket pick-up service to having their own in-terminal full-service branch agency. Some of those travel agencies which provide airport parking have full-service branch agencies in the airport parking facility.

For passengers starting their trips in cities other than the headquarters city, tickets can be provided through airline pick-up services or by express mail. The express mail option is through the U.S. (or some other) postal system which guarantees delivery within twenty-four hours to most major locations throughout the U.S. The airline/airport options include utilizing the *prepaid ticket advice*

(PTA) or the airport *will-call service*. The PTA option is particularly convenient for those wishing rapid service. Under this arrangement the travel agent requests tickets from the airline and these are transmitted electronically to the airport ticket counter in the city from which the traveler will be starting his trip. When the traveler arrives at the ticket counter, he goes to the will-call desk and requests his prepaid tickets. Although sometimes (especially in emergency situations) this can be accomplished while the traveler is at the check-in counter (the whole transaction can take less than half an hour), airlines often require a twenty-four hour notice to issue prepaid tickets and levy a PTA service charge ranging from a low of fifteen dollars to a high of twenty-five dollars per ticket.

The airport will-call option provides the opportunity for a travel agency to deliver tickets to the airport for travelers to pick up. Usually there is no additional charge for this service, but the ability to provide the service in distant cities is normally limited to those travel agencies that are members of national chain operations. In such cases, they work with an associated or *other chain agency* in the city of origin. That agency issues the ticket and delivers it to the airport. The traveler picks it up at the airport will-call counter.

Emergency Assistance Options

The larger corporate travel-oriented travel agencies provide twenty-four hour emergency assistance for corporate travelers while they are away on trips. This assistance is of two types. The first, and most commonly found, is assistance in making ongoing travel arrangements or in making further travel arrangements. This is normally accomplished by calling a twenty-four hour operated national service on a toll-free 800 phone number. The travel agency subscribes to this service and therefore, since many agencies subscribe, the traveler must advise the service of the agency with which the corporation is working. The emergency assistance service will arrange to have additional tickets issued or the changes made in the itinerary for the corporate client and will transmit these to the client for pick up at the will call desk at the airport. There is no cost to the corporate traveler, but some services are designed so that tickets are transmitted in the form of one or more prepaid ticket advice(s). When this is the case, a PTA service charge is levied by the air carriers and normally is transferred by the travel agency to the corporation.

The second emergency assistance service, which is less often used, provides emergency assistance for messages back to family and/or the corporation. Those few travel agencies that provide this service normally do so in the form of an 800 number that comes back to their office and a recording machine that picks up the message. Normally, at the beginning of the next business day, all such messages are typed out and are phoned in to the corporation and/or family. A copy of the typed message is then mailed to the corporation/family if so requested. Although this emergency message service is seldom used, it is sometimes of benefit to travelers.

Meeting Planning Assistance

An increasing number of large travel agencies are employing full-time meeting planners who work with corporations and associations to assist in the planning of meetings, to advise on meeting planning options, and especially to coordinate both air and ground travel arrangements. The services of the meeting planner are normally free, but when there is considerable work relating to areas of the meeting(s) that are non-commissionable to the travel agency, the costs of the meeting planner are often negotiated. By working with a travel agency's meeting planner, coordinated travel arrangements can usually be effected and for large groups such services as VIP rooms at the arrival airport, arrival airport convention desks, group arrival and departure scheduling, negotiated hotel convention/meeting rates, negotiated meeting room rates, and negotiated car rental rates can often be realized without the need for the company or association to employ a full-time or a part-time meeting planner itself.

Even smaller meetings can be planned with the assistance of the travel agency's meeting planner, frequently resulting in having a better quality meeting from a logistics standpoint and a meeting that will cost less than it might otherwise cost.

Travel Insurance

Travel agencies offer three types of insurance to corporate travelers. These include death, accident, and baggage insurance. A fourth type, trip cancellation insurance, is also offered by most travel agencies. However, because of the need for business travelers to fly using rates other than discounted rates with time and date restrictions, the trip cancellation insurance is seldom cost effective for corporate travelers and, except for some international travel, this type of insurance is seldom used by business travelers.

Many travel agencies offer automatic insurance covering death in the case of an airplane catastrophe. In reviewing these insurance policies, it is important to recognize that this coverage may already be automatically extended to the company if payment is made for air travel on national credit cards. It is also important to recognize that some of these automatic insurance policies carry with them only limited maximums which may not cover more than one employee of the company on a single plane on which there is a catastrophe.

Most baggage insurance is provided by travel agencies at an additional cost, but this may be a negotiated factor and a savings may sometimes be realized when buying such insurance in large amounts.

Corporate Hotel and Car Rental Rate Programs

One of the major benefits that can accrue to corporations and which should be considered in the company travel study is the potential savings which might be realized by utilizing a travel agency or an in-house negotiated corporate rate program for hotels and car rental companies. Corporate travel departments often work with both in-house programs and travel agency programs. Although details of the development of these programs are discussed in a later chapter, it is important to recognize and to address in the company travel study the current amount of hotel expenditures, to compare these expenditures with the cost of hotel stays when operating under the travel agency corporate hotel rate program, and the additional savings that might be incurred if an in-house corporate travel manager negotiates corporate rates for hotels and car rentals.

Travel agencies offering corporate rate hotel programs subscribe to national services which negotiate with individual hotel properties (usually two such properties in a major city) for lower than published property corporate rates based upon a guarantee of providing a specific number of nights of occupancy in the hotel. The national services work on a basis of historical average number of nights occupied by subscribing travel agency corporate travelers and they can often obtain reductions in the published hotel corporate rate by ten to fifteen percent. In some cases, negotiated corporate rates will not be the lowest possible discounted rates, but they may be rates that offer to provide the best room at a specific, fixed cost.

By utilizing a travel agency's corporate rate hotel programs, the individual business is able to take advantage of the buying power generated by all corporations using all travel agencies that subscribe to the hotel corporate rate service. Since companies negotiating on their own must normally guarantee a high number of room nights to be occupied, the travel agency service can sometimes provide a rate that companies could never obtain on their own. On the other hand, the services that provide negotiated hotel rates on a national basis normally offer negotiated rates for a limited number of hotels in very large cities only. A corporation which has substantial travel to small towns can quite often negotiate better rates for hotels in those small towns on their own.

Ideally, corporate rate programs offer advantages beyond just cost savings. In many cases, the quality of the room is specified in the rate negotiation and the traveler is guaranteed by the hotel to receive a medium or better class room. In some cases, preferred hotel cards are issued to travelers and the traveler is given additional amenities that might not be extended to other travelers. Some of these amenities may include executive floor service, rapid registration and check out, newspaper and/or continental breakfast, and turn-down service.

Corporate rates are normally negotiated for a calendar year, but they may be extended for a longer period in some cases. This means that budgets may be prepared with a better understanding of hotel costs when hotel programs of this type are utilized since the contract with the hotel specifies that rates cannot be increased during the contract period.

The benefits noted above relating to a corporate rate hotel program are similar as they relate to a corporate rate car rental program. With car rentals, however, it must be recognized that large car rental companies work with individual franchisees at airports all over the country and these franchisees will normally not extend nationally negotiated corporate rates below a minimum that will insure a good profit for the franchisee. Although the nationally negotiated rates can often be better than published corporate rates, the quality of service, guarantees of having a car available, and convenience of rental locations are all factors that must be considered in negotiating a car rental rate on a national basis. As with the hotel negotiated rates, larger travel agencies subscribe to national services that undertake national rate negotiations. It is sometimes found that these rates offer very little cost savings as compared to the national corporate rates that would otherwise be offered to the corporation by car rental companies and some of the service programs are with car rental companies that do not provide the quality of service and convenience required by many corporations for their travelers.

On the other hand, corporate travel managers can often identify cities in which a large number of cars are rented because of frequent travel to those cities and can often negotiate much better rates with those franchisees serving those cities by providing a guaranteed number of car rental days for the length of the annual contract.

In either case, it behooves the company to identify the amount of money spent corporate wide on car rentals, the locations in which cars have been rented, and the savings that might accrue if car rental rates are negotiated either on a city-by-city basis or by utilizing a national service through a travel agency.

Training

An increasing number of travel agencies are offering training to corporations as a part of their total services. This training is normally of two types. The broadest training is provided for those in the corporation who book travel. Normally, a half-day or a full-day seminar is offered by the travel agency to explain to secretaries and others who make travel arrangements how they can obtain a reservation as rapidly as possible and what the factors are relating to getting the flights desired. They identify programmed computer information flows so that the booking secretary can have information available in the order in which it is required by reservation computers and they point out the relationship relating to the time of booking and the availability of good fares. Often they will introduce secretaries to the specific reservationist(s) who will be working in the agency and taking their reservations so that a face can be connected with a name and, in many cases, they will provide a tour of the travel agency and the reservations bay for corporate secretaries.

Special services are pointed out in the training so that the person who calls in reservation requests will understand that there is a person handling international tickets and perhaps another person handling prepaid tickets, and so on. Often quality control processes are described so that those making reservations can understand how the quality control system works and how they can interface with the quality control system to make it work even better and more efficiently. In some companies this same type of training is offered to individual travelers and when corporate travelers take advantage of the training it can often assist them in saving money and time for the corporation.

A second type of training is provided for corporate travel managers and/or those responsible for the corporate travel. Some of the larger travel agencies belong to national programs that provide such services as corporate rates for hotels and car rentals as well as emergency assistance programs. These national services sometimes hold annual or semi-annual training programs for corporate travel managers which are designed to bring the corporate travel manager up-to-date with new advances in the industry and additional services provided by the national service for member travel agencies and those corporations under contract with member travel agencies. These seminars are normally reasonable in cost and some travel agencies provide free or reduced rate air tickets and/or they pay the seminar tuition costs for corporate travel managers working with the companies they serve.

A few travel agencies extend the training service to corporate travel managers by offering to pay for membership in NBTA, ACTE, and/or the local association of corporate travel managers. This training offer is being reflected in more and more travel agency proposals and it is expected that travel agency sponsorship and payment for management education for corporate travel managers is a trend that will continue.

International Travel Services

Travel agencies provide a number of services for the business person traveling outside the U.S. The services include international fare, itinerary and ticketing specialization, documentation assistance, passport photo service, overseas emergency medical insurance, and close work with visa and passport services. Because travel to other countries can require so much close attention and specialized knowledge, some companies, especially those with significant amounts of international travel, make this area of travel a separate segment of the company travel study. As travel agencies begin to specialize, some agencies are offering special packages of international travel services to corporate clients and other agencies are specializing in handling only international business travel. As this trend continues, it can be expected that corporations will increasingly divide their contracts for handling travel by dividing their business into domestic and international and contracting with agencies that specialize in handling international business travel or that provide exclusively international business travel services, in much the same way those agencies specializing in incentive travel are awarded contracts to handle only the incentive travel of corporations. This alternative in handling international travel is often considered in the development of the company travel study and it is suggested that the pros and cons of breaking out international travel in such a manner be considered for inclusion in the company travel study.

A large number of business travel-oriented travel agencies have added *international desks* in their efforts to provide a full-range of services for their corporate clients. Often these international desks are manned by one or two agents who, depending upon the volume of international travel handled by the agency, specialize in and/or handle international travel arrangements exclusively. These agents become experts in international fares, the development of international itineraries, and the issuing of international tickets. Each of these areas (international fares, itineraries, and tickets) requires specialized knowledge, specific procedures, and differences in preparation as compared to working with domestic fares, itineraries, and tickets.

A second area of specialization is documentation assistance. A number of additional documents are required for those business people who travel in countries outside the U.S. and a travel agency needs to understand and prepare each of these documents. The documents range from international health certificates (the agency will not provide immunizations, but should be able to access immunization requirements for entering each country in which a person will be traveling), entry cards, the exit documentation requirements of countries, currency control documents, and so on.

Many travel agencies provide a passport photo service for international business travelers. Typically, this is a package program through which the U.S. Passport Service passport photo requirements are met. Two identical passport photos are taken at the same time at the travel agency in order to meet the government specifications for photos for new or renewed passports. Additional photos may be taken for visa purposes. A supply of original and renewal passport application forms is kept on hand by the agency and provided to business clients and business travelers are advised how to process passport applications through the U.S. post office or through authorized visa services. Normally, the passport and visa photos are provided at no cost when the traveler purchases international air tickets through the travel agency.

Many agencies offer overseas medical insurance policies for all international travelers and some provide several emergency medical insurance policies from which the business traveler may select.

Most travel agencies that have a significant amount of international business travel work closely with a visa and passport service to make certain that international travelers receive their passports on time and to coordinate visa processing with travel itineraries so that the international business traveler will not find himself with expired visas prior to completing his work overseas.

Incentive Travel

As is the case with international travel, incentive travel is a specialized area and a large number of companies award incentive travel contracts on a different bid or through a different *Request for Proposal* (RFP) than the bid or RFP for other travel services. Although all travel agencies may be able to provide incentive travel planning, this has developed into a distinct specialization and there are travel agencies in many cities which handle only incentive travel. As is the case with international travel, it is suggested that the company travel study address the option of awarding incentive travel contracts as separate and distinct contracts from the awards for handling other travel. In reviewing incentive travel, it is important to interface with the sales and marketing departments of the corporation to determine what has been done in the past relating to incentive programs.

Travel agencies offering incentive travel frequently have prepackaged programs with specific destinations which can be purchased by the company in a package arrangement. Most travel agencies offering incentive programs will also tailor an incentive package for business clients.

The incentive travel business is a specialized area of the travel industry and, typically, proposals are made by travel agencies to marketing and sales executives of client companies. The packages normally include a number of incentive promotions and events offered by and often undertaken by the travel agency holding the incentive travel contract.

A wide range of additional travel agency services are offered by agencies and may need to be explored in the company travel study as they relate to answering the needs of handling the company's travel. These services include coordination of new-hire travel and household goods movements, personalized baggage tags, budgeting assistance (including projections of ticket costs), travel trends, and government travel advisories (warnings put out by the U.S. State Department advising of areas of the world in which U.S. citizens who are traveling should be cautious or should avoid altogether). Other services include offering vacation packages and other vacation travel for employees, assistance in the development of a newsletter (normally prepared by the corporate travel manager and sent to all who either book travel in the company or take trips). Still additional services include the management of corporate aircraft and the scheduling of company cars.

Travel agencies will often be open to reviewing all the travel needs of the corporation and working with the business travel department as closely as the company wishes for them to do so. Many agencies will tailor prepackaged programs and services for corporations and will develop additional services to meet the specific needs of companies. This wide range of services is often considered in meeting the needs of the company when addressing those needs in the company travel study.

Rebates Versus Service

Since deregulation, the practice of rebating has been so extensive in the travel industry that today a company travel study which does not address rebating and the potential advantages to a company of receiving financial rebates is considered an incomplete study. Therefore, it is recommended that the study include a survey of the status of rebating by agencies located in the company's headquarters city and perhaps extending the rebating status study to agencies located in cities in which branch offices are located. Although some companies are selecting travel agencies strictly on the basis of amount of rebates, many companies have been disappointed by the service that has been received. Therefore, a part of the study of rebating should include a history of companies that have requested (or accepted) rebates and have returned to agencies offering services without rebates as well as companies that have been happy with agencies that offered rebates. While this may require considerable investigation and discussion with other corporate travel managers and the financial executives of these other companies, it is considered the best way to prepare for the questions relating to rebates that will arise when corporate executives review the company travel study.

Since travel agencies receive an average commission of ten percent for the domestic tickets that are issued by the agency, there is a trade-off between the amount of service that a travel agency can offer and the amount of rebates that can be provided. Although some travel agencies are naive enough to believe that they can offer both considerable service and substantial rebates, many companies have found that proposals from travel agencies offering this combination are often unrealistic and the expected results in many cases do not materialize. Therefore, the company travel study frequently prioritizes the needs of the company as determined by chief executive officers, ranking rebates and services in the priority determined by these executives. This hierarchical ranking that includes both services and rebates makes the development of a response to the request for proposal much easier.

Air Carrier Services

Deregulation has changed the role of the air carriers as they relate to corporate travel. Prior to deregulation air carriers stressed that commercial travel was theirs to handle and travel agents should limit themselves to working with leisure travel accounts. Since deregulation, a number of options have become available to travel agencies to compete for commercial business and both because of the convenience of dealing with travel agencies and the cost savings that can be realized from dealing with travel agencies, most corporate travel is now handled through travel agencies. This does not mean, however, that the attitudes and preferences of air carrier executives have changed. Many who work with airlines still believe that commercial business should be handled directly by the carriers and not through travel agencies.

Although the close relationships that have developed between travel agencies and corporations has limited the direct role played by air carriers, there still are some direct relationships that exist. When a company spends $500,000 or more on travel, air carriers take notice and wish to obtain as much of the business as possible. They work with travel agencies to obtain as large a portion (at least their *fair market share*) as possible from agencies and they call on appropriate executives in business with the intention of obtaining as much loyalty to their airline as possible. When a corporate travel department exists in a corporation, it becomes a target for certain airline marketing executives and airline sales representatives may call on corporate travel managers more frequently.

The result of the industry visibility of corporate travel managers is that often when a special need arises or when a problem occurs relating to air transportation, the corporate travel manager can contact the airline sales manager directly and resolve the problem or satisfy the need through direct negotiations. When a company's air travel business is decentralized, no such person exists and the interrelationship with air carriers can be much less powerful. The company travel study addresses this situation. The net result is that a decentralized travel configuration results in no single person in the company having enough clout with carriers to make a difference in resolving problems or in direct negotiations. On the other hand, when there is a corporate travel manager, if the travel volume is sufficient, the clout does exist and direct negotiations can bring the company more benefits.

Normally, air carrier representatives call on corporate travel managers once a month or more often, bringing a corporate travel manager up to date on the status of the airline. Information relating to new fares, routes, schedule changes, and so forth are brought to the attention of the corporate travel manager. However, when there have been problems encountered by travelers in the corporation in relationship to the airline, these can be discussed with resolutions often reached in these monthly meetings between air carrier representatives and corporate travel managers. Since many air carrier representatives call on corporate travel managers more often than they call on most travel agencies, the ability to resolve problems in these meetings is often greater than the ability of the travel agency to resolve the problems.

Perhaps of even greater importance is the ability to negotiate directly with air carriers. When the president of the company or the chairman of the board or some other executive of the company requests and needs special assistance, this can often be obtained by direct negotiation with the air carrier representative. For example, if a meeting is being held at an airport in a distant city, airlines will often provide airport meeting rooms at no cost.

Another area of direct negotiation with air carriers relates to fares. Although not all carriers offer direct negotiation opportunities relating to fares, the deregulation act opened up the opportunity for airlines to pay commissions directly to corporations. Because airlines are fearful that travel agencies will not sell their carrier if they pay commissions directly to corporations and because airlines would prefer to avoid paying any more commissions than necessary to obtain business, few direct payments by carriers to companies for their business have been made. However, barter arrangements have occurred in industry whereby airlines have traded airline tickets for company products and/or services, group travel "deals" have been struck by companies and associations with airlines to obtain preferential treatment and better fares for one-time group movements, and fare coupon packages (for example, a book of ten air tickets to single destinations for the price of nine) have been requested by companies and offered by airlines. Special meeting and/or training fares have also been negotiated with air carriers.

Although these direct negotiations have not resulted in substantial savings or benefits for most companies, the opportunity to obtain savings and benefits does exist and some companies' negotiations have resulted in their obtaining a better savings than they have been able to negotiate through travel agencies.

The company travel study identifies the negotiation power benefits that can and do accrue by working directly through air carriers when air travel is consolidated in a travel department as compared to when it is decentralized.

The Role of the Hotel Representative

As in the case of air carriers, hotels and especially hotel chains, are vitally interested in obtaining as much business as possible from companies. Although almost all hotel bookings for business travelers are made through travel agencies, when a company's travel business is centralized, the corporate travel manager becomes the focus for hotel marketing. Hotel sales representatives frequently call on corporate travel managers and provide information to them relating to rates, amenities, and benefits of potential value to the company. This normally does not occur when travel is decentralized unless there is a specific department in the company that has substantial travel and a single person in that department is responsible for the travel. Unlike airlines, however, hotel marketing executives can make direct negotiated agreements with companies for their business. This can and does result in substantial savings for many companies. When corporate travel managers identify the cities to which there are substantial trips, the ability to negotiate directly with a hotel becomes greater.

If a corporate travel manager can guarantee a large number of room nights of occupancy, hotel rebate reductions can be contracted for, resulting in better quality hotel rooms at lower rates. The company travel study identifies the relationship between a centralized corporate travel department and the ability to obtain good hotel rates and resulting hotel savings. The company travel study may also identify what takes place in relationship to booking hotels prior to centralization of the company's travel business. For those secretaries who frequently book hotels for company visitors coming to the home office or the branch office for which they work, hotels often have clubs or benefit programs to entice secretaries to call them with inbound travel bookings. This can result in higher prices and less convenient property stays when one hotel offers a series of benefits to secretaries who book with them and their benefits package is better than a competing hotel which would be more convenient and/or less expensive. The potential for upgrading quality and reducing costs by centralizing hotel bookings can be substantial for many companies.

The Role of the Car Rental Representative

As in the case of the air carrier representative and the hotel representative, car rental representatives also call on corporate travel managers directly whereas they seldom make calls on companies where travel is decentralized. Substantial savings potential exists for companies when they identify cities where a number of cars are rented throughout the year and negotiate directly for cost savings and/or improved benefits and the type of car provided. In addition, car rental representatives bring information to corporate travel managers of updated service, additional cities served, and changes in the industry that can frequently benefit the company's travelers.

Negotiation Role

The company travel study addresses the negotiation role of the corporate travel manager and the importance of that role as it relates to obtaining benefits, services, and savings for the company. Meetings with vendors (travel agencies, air carrier representatives, hotel marketing executives, and car rental vendors) represent a large amount of the work undertaken by corporate travel managers on a day-by-day basis. Although the majority of these meetings are not direct negotiation meetings, the relationships that can be established can benefit the company in many ways that are seldom seen in advance of the establishment of the corporate travel department. The primary benefits that can come from these meetings relate to the abilities to solve problems and obtain special handling when such is needed or desired. This is often difficult to portray in a corporate travel study since most studies are written in a direct, factual, statistical manner. Nevertheless, the resulting benefits are important and an editorial section of the study can convey the potential for these benefits.

Conclusions and Recommendations

The last part of the company travel study is a section that draws conclusions and makes recommendations based upon the research undertaken. Two approaches are taken in this section of company travel studies. One approach is to prioritize the importance of conclusions and recommendations, identifying each major conclusion and the recommendations drawn from it. In this approach, each major conclusion is listed in its order of priority and the recommendations from that specific conclusion are identified.

The second approach is similar to the first one in that priorities of importance are established. However, in this approach there is a section of the study that relates to conclusions alone. After all conclusions are listed and discussed, a separate part of the study relates to recommendations and recommendations are made based upon the preceding conclusions section of the study.

Both approaches have their benefits and drawbacks. The approach of listing conclusions and the recommendations drawn directly from those conclusions allows the reader to easily identify the relationship between the recommendation and the conclusions, thereby justifying the recommendations to as strong a degree as possible. On the other hand, this approach mingles conclusions and recommendations and for the reader of the study who only wants to consider the recommendations, the mingling and the additional information may become confusing and bothersome. They prefer to be selective in their reading. On the other hand, the approach of having one section which identifies the conclusions of the study and a following section that addresses study recommendations carries with it opposite benefits and drawbacks. The major drawback of this approach, of course, is the inability to rapidly relate conclusions and recommendations, but the benefit is the ability to have recommendations clearly stand out on their own.

Both approaches have merit. Whichever is used, it is important that the recommendations be based on solid conclusions from the study. It is also important that recommendations be prioritized in order of importance. In writing this section, it should be remembered that some of the company travel study readers may want to spend only a short time with the study. These readers may wish to study the recommendations rapidly and may not refer to any other part of the study unless there is a concern about a specific recommendation and the reasons for it.

The major recommendation of most company travel studies is that travel be centralized in a single department. If alternatives in terms of how this department would be structured and/or organized are presented in the recommendations section, the alternatives can often result in more rapid action than if the result is simply a brief statement that travel should be centralized in order to take advantage of volume buying benefits. The study should not present too many alternatives, but rather a reasonable set of alternatives should be made available. Basically, the options for centralizing travel buying may be to:

1. develop a request for proposal for a travel agency to handle all travel services;

2. to develop requests for proposal for travel agencies to handle portions of the

company's travel (for example, one RFP for international travel, one for incentive travel and one for all other travel);

3. develop a contract to establish an in-plant travel agency in the company; and

4. to purchase a travel agency.

After the alternatives are determined and presented, further recommendations relating to each of the alternatives can be made. Some company travel studies identify the reasons for these recommendations, tying them back to the conclusions. An alternative is to include an addendum to the study which provides the justification for each of the recommendations relating to the alternatives. The detailed recommendations relating to the alternatives need to be as detailed as possible and need to follow the process of presenting a *business plan* for the implementation of the alternatives. Although the executive or committee receiving the company travel study and making decisions based upon the study has the alternative of changing any and all details, by presenting a full set of details in the form of a business plan for implementation for each alternative, the executive or committee reviewing the company travel study can adopt a single alternative and its accompanying recommendations in total in order to rapidly implement the establishment of a corporate travel department and the benefits of centralized travel purchasing. Or, it may adopt pieces of alternative plans for implementation if it so wishes. Those who have written the company travel study have given those who will review and act upon the study the options they need.

Appendix

The appendix is the last part of the company travel study. Appendices can be lengthy. It is not at all unusual for the appendix to exceed the number of pages in the study itself. In organizing the appendix, there are several approaches that can be used. Either appendices can be added at the back of the study in the order in which reference was made to each appendix in the study itself or the appendices can be placed in alphabetical order by title of each appendix. Some travel studies have no specific order to the appendices. It is suggested that the order follow the order of reference in the travel study, however, as this approach facilitates referencing from the study to the appendix. It is also suggested that a table of contents be included for the entire appendix listing each of the appendices in the order in which they appear throughout the appendix. Another aid to rapid referencing is to have each of the appendices set off by a tab showing the starting point of the material in that appendix section.

The table of contents normally follows the appendix title page as the first item in the appendix. Unlike most tables of contents, however, this one is set out in numerical order rather than listing page numbers. Because each appendix may vary from one to several pages and because the appendices are documents that often are numbered in their original state, no new numbers are applied to the appendices. Therefore, by using a numerical listing of each appendix using either roman numerals or latin numbers and tabs identifying the starting point of each appendix, the reader is able to find the appropriate appendix documents rapidly. It is much easier to work with when the table of contents is detailed sufficiently well to fully explain what the document is that is included in the appendix. If a document is lengthy, a breakdown of important segments can be provided in the table of contents by breaking out these segments in outline form.

The appendices in every company travel study will be different, but some documents are customary and found in almost all studies. One of the earliest sections and often the first section of the documents is the glossary of terms. Although some studies do not include a glossary, defining the acronyms and the industry terms can be beneficial for readers who do not have detailed knowledge of the travel industry. As with most glossaries of terms, simply listing the term alphabetically together with its definition (and sometimes an explanation of details as this term relates to the study itself) is the customary approach.

Although all appropriate documents will be included in the company travel study, the following documents should also be included:

1. the sample ticket cost analysis study;

2. the expense report study;

3. the travel pattern analysis study (both for in the U.S. and out of the country);

4. an analysis of travel agencies (those which have been and/or are currently being used by the company and others which the company would consider using) together with descriptions of current and potential services;

5. a savings report (this is sometimes included with the cost analysis report and identifies the fares paid compared to the lowest possible fare and any savings that might have been accrued by the company);

6. an "other" expenses study which concentrates on hotel and car rental costs and any potential savings in these areas;

7. copies of any current travel policies together with policy change recommendations and an explanation of the reasons for the recommendations; and

8. copies of documents from other companies (including copies of their travel policies and procedures, their requests for proposals, and other appropriate documents).

Although it must be remembered that the appendix will not be read by most recipients of the company travel study, it can be a valuable reference and a central point from which to document positions taken in the travel study. Therefore, it is important that the appendix include all appropriate documents and studies.

Summary

Managing a company's travel usually starts with undertaking a company travel study. This study evaluates the status of travel and the way in which it is handled in the company at the time the study is undertaken. Normally, the travel study will be initiated in a company that is moving from a decentralized travel system or for a company that has no current system for or policies relating to travel management. The company travel study is normally undertaken by an appointed committee responsible for analyzing the current status of company travel and making recommendations relating to the management of the company's travel. However, often a single individual is designated as responsible for the overall conduct of the study and is expected to coordinate the development of the data, the mechanics of setting up and running committee meetings, and so forth. This is sometimes the person who will ultimately be appointed to be the corporate travel manager, but it may be an appropriate executive as well. Sometimes a chief executive officer appoints someone on his immediate staff (for example, his secretary) to handle chairing and coordinating the company travel study committee effort.

Often two major outcomes result from the company travel study. One is the development of a request for proposal to be utilized in the selection of a travel agency to handle the travel arrangements for the company. The second frequent result is the establishment of the position of corporate travel manager and/or a corporate travel department within the company.

Although it is usually the last section of the study to be written, most company travel studies start with an executive summary, giving the highlights of the study. Often the executive summary will emphasize the justifications for the study and the major recommendations resulting from the study. The executive summary also reviews the processes undertaken in developing the study, the mechanics involved and it discusses company travel policies as well as comparisons of how the company's travel is currently being handled, how other companies handle their travel, and recommended changes in the handling of the company's travel.

The introduction to the study is normally the next section to be written. This usually starts with a history of the handling of travel within the company and it is followed by a discussion of the mechanics of the workings of the committee undertaking the study. The next section often identifies how travel has been handled in specific divisions or departments of the company and often will compare this handling with similar divisions or departments in other companies and the way in which their travel is handled. The guidelines for the development of the study are presented next. This indicates the overall parameters of the study and it identifies what has been requested of the committee relating to the study as well as what has not been requested and/or is not being covered by the study (in other words, the exact scope of the study).

The study methodology section identifies the specific methods utilized in gathering, analyzing, and evaluating data and information collected for the study. It also presents how that data is processed and how recommendations are determined as a result of the conclusions drawn from the data and information.

One of the most important parts of the study is the findings. This is usually the longest section of the study and it is often broken down into several types of findings or results. One of the findings will be the annual cost of travel and will relate to how the annual cost of travel has been determined. A second finding normally relates to the travel authorization study. It analyzes how travel is authorized and the processes involved in obtaining authorizations. A third finding discusses destinations. This section is a complete destination analysis. It identifies specific travel patterns. Often this is broken down into air travel destinations, car rentals at destinations, and locations within cities where business is conducted (relating this to hotels utilized by corporate travelers). Another part of the findings is the result of a comparison study relating to major travel expenses. Most studies review air fares and the potential for savings relating to air fares. Frequent flier programs are usually reviewed as they relate to air fares and savings or potential air fare savings.

The company travel policy and procedures study findings are usually reviewed in this section of the travel study report. Credit card financial management normally constitutes a study in and of itself with the concentration being on ways to utilize credit card programs for overall travel savings. If the company has been on one or more credit card system, a comparison of the effectiveness of these systems is normally included.

Since the utilization of travel agencies is one of the most important aspects of travel management and one of the most important areas of potential travel savings, the results of or the findings resulting from a study of current travel agency utilization and potential travel agency working relationship opportunities normally constitutes a large part of the findings section of the company travel study. This travel agency section of the study reviews at least the following areas:

1. the utilization of contract fares;

2. the interrelationship between travel agencies and other companies in the handling of their travel;

3. travel agency services (including computerized travel profits, front office and back office automation systems, delivery services, emergency assistance options, meeting planning assistance, specific international travel services, and other travel services;

4. travel insurance;

5. training provided by travel agencies; and

6. incentive travel.

Rebates and the trade-offs between rebates and service is usually addressed in this section as well.

The services provided by air carrier representatives, hotel representatives, and car rental representatives are discussed and the entire negotiation role played by a corporate travel manager is reviewed together with the benefits and drawbacks that can come from negotiation with vendors.

The final section of the study relates to the conclusions and recommendations. Conclusions are drawn first with specific major recommendations discussed at length. The final part of the conclusions and recommendations section is usually a discussion of the additional recommendations (normally those of secondary importance).

Following the travel study is an appendix to the study. The appendices are frequently lengthy and often the appendix section is longer than the study itself. The appendix section needs to be organized in such a manner that references made in the study to an appendix can be easily found. This is normally accomplished by providing a table of contents and by utilizing tabs to identify each of the appendices. All appropriate complete documents as well as individual studies that have been undertaken as a part of the company travel study should be included in their entirety in the appendix section.

Overall, the company travel study provides a working document from which to justify the development of a request for proposal for undertaking a formal relationship with a travel agency vendor and it provides a justification for the establishment of a business travel department within the company.

Discussion

1. What is the major vendor for corporate travel departments?

2. How does the process of finding, contracting with, and retaining a travel agency start?

3. What does the acronym RFP stand for?

4. When does the *transition agreement* take effect?

5. What part of the company travel study is the last to be written, the first to appear, and the first to be read in the company travel study?

6. How does the *appendix* of the company travel study compare in length with the company travel study itself?

7. What is often the principle finding of a company travel study?

8. With what does the *introduction* section of the company travel study usually start?

9. What are the four sections that are usually included in the parameters discussion in the company travel study?

10. What are some of the *methodologies* used in undertaking a company travel study?

11. What is the longest section of the company travel study and why is it frequently the longest section?

12. What is studied in a *travel authorization study* and how is such a study undertaken?

13. What is studied in a *destination analysis study* and what kinds of statistical data can be developed from such a study?

14. What is meant by the terms *in-region* and *out-of-region*?

15. What is reviewed in the *major travel expense comparison study* and why is this important?

16. With what is it suggested that the *air fare discussion* in the company travel study start?

17. What is the best approach to take in showing the importance of *routings* in the company travel study?

18. What is covered and in what order is it covered in the *frequent flier program study*?

19. What is the foundation on which most company travel policies and procedures are based?

20. What are the benefits and drawbacks in utilizing credit card financial management systems in travel management?

21. Under what circumstances might *contract fares* be found to be beneficial for a company?

22. It has been suggested that other companies be contacted and a review be undertaken of how they mange their travel. How many other companies should be contacted for a review of their travel management to be undertaken in order to provide a good comparison in the company travel study?

23. What is some of the more common information included in *computerized traveler profiles*?

24. What are the five major airline automation systems and who are their airline sponsors?

25. Explain the differences between *front office computer systems* and *back office computer systems* in travel agencies.

26. What are the two ways travel agencies can arrange to have tickets issued and available to corporate travelers in cities throughout the U.S. and what are the potential cost(s) to the company(ies) for this service?

27. What are the two emergency assistance options offered by some travel agencies?

28. How can a travel agency's meeting planner save money for a company?

29. What are the three types of insurance travel agencies offer to corporate travelers?

30. Why can travel agencies offer better corporate hotel and car rental rates than companies can offer and how can companies sometimes beat the travel agency corporate rates?

31. What are the two company training audiences offered training by travel agencies for their corporate clients?

32. What are the special services, programs, and benefits that travel agencies can offer to business travelers traveling outside the U.S.?

33. Why do many companies award incentive travel contracts as separate and distinct contracts from the awards for handling their other travel?

34. What are some of the other travel services provided by travel agencies for their corporate clients?

35. What type of information is included in a rebating status study conducted by a company as part of its company travel study?

36. Why might direct negotiations with air carrier representatives be more successful in resolving air travel problems than negotiating through travel agencies?

37. Is it legal for airlines to pay commissions directly to companies for their air travel business or must commissions be paid only to travel agencies?

38. What must corporate travel managers guarantee to hotel marketing executives in order to receive contracted hotel rate reductions?

39. What must they guarantee to car rental marketing executives in order to obtain car rental rate reductions?

40. What benefit derived from corporate travel manager/vendor interrelationships is difficult to portray in a corporate travel study, but usually is beneficial to the company?

261

Group
Discussion
Situation:
Metropolitan
Industrial
Jewels

41. What are the two approaches used in developing the conclusions and recommendations section of the company travel study?
42. What is the major recommendation of most company travel studies?
43. What are the four basic options for centralizing travel buying?
44. Why is the appendix to the company travel study often longer than the study itself?

Role Play Exercise

Two students may participate in this role play either out-of-class, as a fun way to review the chapter, or as an in-class exercise. One plays the role of the chief executive officer and the other plays the role of the chair of the company travel study committee. Please read the script and then pick up the conversation in your own words.

Chief Executive Officer: I know your committee has completed a thorough study of the company's travel and that you will be making a presentation to the executive committee next week presenting the results of the study and your recommendations. We have spoken briefly about the study, but it has been several weeks. Tell me, what will your major recommendation be and what findings will you use to back it up?

Chairperson, Company Travel Study Committee: As you point out, it is an exhaustive study. We have looked at all aspects of the company's travel and I am putting the final touches on the conclusions and recommendations section of the study now. The major recommendation is the same one that I think both of us contemplated when starting the study. This is that we centralize the purchasing of travel to take advantage of volume buying benefits and that we do this through the creation of a corporate travel department. The study results back up this recommendation basically as follows:

CONTINUE ON YOUR OWN

Group Discussion Situation: Metropolitan Industrial Jewels

Metropolitan Industrial Jewels (MIJ) is one of Pullman, Washington's largest manufacturers. It manufactures jewel-tipped tools for many precision instruments and jewel-parts designed for several industries. MIJ has patents on a number of these tools and parts, making MIJ one of the largest and most unique companies of its kind in the world.

The chief financial officer at MIJ asked the purchasing director to undertake a study of the company's travel several months ago and a committee made up of representatives from each section of the company from which substantial travel has occurred has met over the last several months to develop a comprehensive study of the company's travel. Members of the committee include the staff assistant to the vice president of marketing, the purchasing director (who is directing the study), the field training director, the customer training director, the associate vice president of fine jewel purchasing, and the company president's executive secretary. Other members of the committee represent their particular departments or divisions.

From time to time, as the committee has worked on the company travel study, representatives from all company divisions have been invited to work with the committee or to make presentations to the committee especially when the committee worked on areas of the study that involved the type of travel undertaken by travelers in their division or section. Travel has been totally decentralized and each division has handled travel in any way that division executives are comfortable with. In most cases, the traveler has made all purchasing decisions himself, selecting the flight and either buying tickets at the airport or through his favorite travel agency. Some divisions have made an effort to select a travel agency for their division, but even in those cases where some work has been undertaken to centralize travel buying within a division, those travelers who preferred to not deal with the travel agency selected for the division were given the option of requesting and obtaining tickets wherever they wished.

The committee has agreed that the creation of a corporate travel department will be beneficial and should be a major recommendation of the study. However, there is strong disagreement as to who will head up the corporate travel department and where the department will be housed. Some members of the committee want the corporate travel department to be in the finance division and to report to the chief financial officer. The president's executive secretary and some other members of the committee believe that the corporate travel department should be a department housed in the presidential office suite and reporting directly to the president of the company. Still others on the committee believe that the corporate travel department should logically be housed under and report to the vice president of administration.

You are meeting today to finalize the chapter on conclusions and recommendations and you are expected to reach agreement on and write a two-page summary of conclusions and recommendations.

In your group session, select one person to play the role of each committee member. Any additional people in your group should be assigned positions as additional members of the committee representing those divisions having permanent representation on the committee. All will have an equal vote on decisions. In your group session you are expected to reach agreements and to prepare the two-page paper to be presented to the entire class by the chair of your committee.

The Proposal and Contracting Process

Introduction

One of the early tasks undertaken by most corporate travel departments is the development of a *Request for Proposal* (RFP). Generally, this comes after conducting a study of the company's travel. The study shows a need for a comprehensive travel program and describes the parameters of the program (i.e., the areas of travel needs and the areas of travel that might lend themselves to greater control and/or management). The request for proposal details the travel needs of the company as well as the expectations of the company for potential travel agency vendors. When the RFP responses come in, a committee made up of appropriate company officials (and sometimes travel experts or consultants from outside the company) reviews the proposals and selects a travel agency vendor. Next a contract, a transition plan, and a working plan are drawn up between the company and the travel agency in order to implement the interrelationship between the travel agency vendor and the company's corporate travel department.

Length and Specificity of RFP

Bid requests can be from very short to very long. Some corporate travel bid requests are so short that they are basically single-page letters. Obviously, they are very much open-ended. Other bid requests are so detailed that they are published in volumes.

There are varying philosophies among businesses relating to how specific a bid request should be. At one extreme, the business wishes to obtain as many new ideas and innovative approaches as possible. It, therefore, states only a few minimum requirements and leaves it up to the travel agency which makes a proposal to ask questions and develop a proposal that will best meet the needs of the company. The advantage of having a short, broad-based request for proposal is that if a number of travel agencies are asked to and do respond, a wide variety of proposals will be received. These may include one or two particularly appealing proposals with approaches that might not have previously been considered. On the other hand, there are advantages and disadvantages to lengthy, very

264

Chapter 15:
The Proposal
and
Contracting
Process

detailed requests for proposals. These provide the travel agency bidder with a specific understanding of the needs and desires of the business and frequently they allow those who evaluate proposals to rank them on specific numerical or other based criteria, making the final selection on a statistical calculation basis (such as a point system) which can be justified to all who might question the decision. The tendency in the industry is to develop lengthy, detail-oriented requests for proposal and these tend to be the type that are favored by most travel agencies as well.

A Hierarchy of Needs

A major complaint voiced by travel agency executives about most of the proposal requests they receive is an inability to guess the priorities assigned by those who will be evaluating the proposals. Therefore, the inclusion of a priority hierarchy ranking applied to all major aspects or sections of the request for proposal may well result in the company receiving proposals that are even more directly related to their needs and preferences.

Money and Service Considerations

In addition to the length of proposals tending to range from one extreme to another, proposals also tend to emphasize either money or service. Since the commission and override incomes received by travel agencies for the travel products they sell is based upon a very narrow percentage range, there is a trade-off between the amount of service that can be provided and the amount of money for rebates that can be offered to the agency's client. If the corporation is primarily concerned with obtaining a large rebate, this should be specified with the understanding that the larger the rebate received, the smaller the amount of money that the agency can allocate to provide services. Of course, the reverse is also true. If there is a small rebate or no rebate, a much greater amount of money is available to provide services. Therefore, the request for proposal needs to be very specific as it relates to the priorities of the company when it comes to rebates and service. If service is paramount, but the company believes that a rebate can also be provided while offering a maximum amount of service, one approach, and an approach that is frequently used, is to ask for a letter specifying the amount of rebate to be enclosed with the proposal in a sealed envelope. After proposals are evaluated on the basis of services and the top three proposals have been identified, the final choice can be made on the basis of the amount of rebates specified in the sealed envelopes. An alternative, which sometimes results in even greater amounts of service, is to make the final decision of the travel agency vendor based on services and only after that final decision is made will the envelope be opened which holds the letter specifying the amount of rebates. This type of approach encourages the travel agency to provide a maximum amount of services, but to also retain some monies for rebates.

A reverse approach is also possible. If money is the most important factor, travel agencies can be advised that an initial proposal based upon a letter indicating the amount of rebate will narrow down the selection to three companies and once this narrowing has been determined, the three companies which offer to provide the highest amount of rebates will be provided with a full request for proposal to which they may respond and on which the final selection will be made. The extreme of this position is to advise that the selection will be made strictly on the basis of the amount of rebate.

Although these opposite approaches may seem extreme, each of the scenarios described above are approaches that are actually used in the selection of travel agencies by corporations every day. Nevertheless, the average business is looking for both a financial return and services. Therefore, the average request for proposal includes a number of service factors and financial criteria. It is on this "average" that the request for proposal discussions are based in this chapter.

Cover Letter

The cover letter accompanying the proposal can either be a form with the appropriate blanks filled in or a traditional letter. In either case, it should clearly specify that the vendor to which it is sent is being invited to submit a proposal. The cover letter should be dated and a bid number or a request for proposal number should be identified if the request for proposal is only one among a number of proposal requests being processed by the purchasing department of the company. A contact name, phone number, and address should all be identified in case the bidder needs to ask for additional information. The deadline data and time for submitting a proposal should be clearly pointed out. The exact location (including room number and name of the person to receive the proposal) for the delivery of bids should be indicated. This delivery point should be both a mailing address and a hand-delivery point since proposals will be submitted in both ways.

If a pre-bid conference is scheduled (and it is recommended), the date, time, and exact location of the conference should be indicated. Some organizations hold more than one pre-bid conference to provide an opportunity for people who might otherwise be out of town or have conflicts. If attending the pre-bid conference(s) is mandatory, this should be clearly stated. A specific person within the firm should be identified to respond to inquiries. This person's name, business phone number, and exact business address should be clearly stated. In some cases, no inquiries will be accepted other than those made during the pre-bid conference. If this is the case, it should be clearly stated.

If a rebate (shared commission) or override sharing agreement is sought in a separate sealed envelope, this should be clearly stated in the cover letter. If the proposal must be signed by an authorized representative or an officer of the travel agency, this should be specified in the cover letter.

It is suggested that a specific date and time (the closing date and time for receipt of the bids) be announced as a public date and time for the recording of the proposals received and this should be done in the presence of any and all vendors who wish to attend this recording. This guarantees to the bidders that no late proposals will be considered.

Finally, all attachments to the cover letter should be identified by title and

266

Chapter 15:
The Proposal
and
Contracting
Process

listed in the order in which they are packaged for mailing. These will normally include the request for proposal itself and any appendices that are appropriate.

Terms and Conditions

Most requests for proposal will start with a section relating to terms and conditions. These are normally standard terms and conditions applicable to all who submit proposals to the company. They frequently are prepared by the purchasing department of the business and they usually apply to all bidders wishing to sell their products or services to the company. These normally state that the company abides by both state and federal legal requirements relating to the consideration of proposals. They then go on to state general requirements to be met by bidders.

Background

Often a background section of the request for proposal is the first or one of the first parts of the RFP. This section discusses the major highlights that resulted from the corporate travel study. It relates these highlights to the most important criteria contained in the request for proposal. This section is normally short and lists no more than five to ten relevant outcomes from the corporate travel study.

Request for Proposal Sections

Many of the more lengthy requests for proposal will be broken down into a number of sections, sometimes with several subsections. There are numerous ways of dividing a request for proposal into logical sections. One approach is to divide parts of the proposal into that which is for information only and that which requires a response. These can be either two major sections of the request for proposal with subsections under them or alternatively each of the main sections of the request for proposal can show a section title followed by an advisory that the section is for information only or that it requires a response. Both alternatives are followed.

Requests for proposal often start with an administrative section, usually for information only. This section provides specific contact information (address and phone number), details relating to the purpose of the request for proposal, and an overview of the scope of the proposal (i.e., pointing out that there are mandatory requirements and preferences which are not mandatory).

It is helpful to potential vendors if a schedule is included in the administrative section. This schedule should show all specific activities from the time that the request for proposal is mailed to prospective vendors. It also shows the deadlines. The schedule should include a deadline by which notice of award is sent out and a date for notifying those who were not selected. It is helpful if the schedule also includes a date by which the contract should be finished, a contract date, and a date on which operations under the contract are expected to commence.

The administrative section often includes a formal invitation to bid and inquiry contact phone numbers and addresses. It discusses how addendums or supplements to the proposal will be handled. It presents proposal submission deadlines, itemizes the specific items that are required when the proposal is submitted, and it includes a notification that late proposals will not be accepted. The manner in which proposals will be rejected is discussed. Waivers for owning RFP material submitted, considering RFP submitted material as proprietary information, and not being liable for costs incurred in the cost of proposal development and submission are all important points to include.

The administrative section often includes a subsection relating to the acceptance of a proposal. This subsection should state clearly that once the bidder is selected, its proposal statements become contractual obligations and if it fails to meet these obligations, the company has a right to cancel the award and select another bidder at any time. This section of the proposal also normally states an acceptance time. This is usually a specific number of days during which the company will make a decision on which travel agency to award the contract. Another part of this subsection relates to how the bid will be awarded. In some cases, joint proposals may be acceptable. These are proposals that are submitted by two or more travel agencies working together. If this is acceptable, it should be noted. And if joint proposals are not acceptable, this should be clearly pointed out.

Perhaps the most important part of the administrative section relates to evaluation procedures and criteria. This normally is an overview of the evaluation procedures and criteria. It can be broken down into subsections relating to the general procedures and the general criteria. Four or five sentence summaries of these procedures and criteria are normally all that is necessary in the administrative section. In other words, they should just outline the evaluation procedures and criteria.

Many companies develop contracts for a wide range of vendors and they have standard clauses that are in contracts. If this is the case, it should be pointed out. Usually when this is the case additional standard contract provisions or paragraphs will be developed from time to time. If these potential future-developed contract additions will be considered by the business to be mandatory additions without discussion or arbitration, it should be clearly pointed out that company wide contract additions will be applied without negotiation. Bidders should be made aware of this up front.

The administrative section should also point out that proposals will not be returned, unless it is the plan to return them. And, it should specify that implementation of work with the new vendor will be on a specific phase-in schedule, if this is the plan. Ideally, the phase-in schedule will be reproduced in the administrative section.

Background Section

Like the administrative section, the background section is normally for information only and this should be indicated. This section normally starts with an overview of the scope of the contract. In most cases, one aspect of the scope

268

Chapter 15:
The Proposal
and
Contracting
Process

relates to geographical coverage. If the company has offices all over the U.S. or perhaps throughout the world, some offices may be included in the contract while others may not. On the other hand, in many cases, all offices are included in the same contract. Details regarding the geographical scope of coverage are important.

In the scope of the contract part of the background section, if the utilization of only one corporate credit card will be accepted, this needs to be indicated and the name of the card system to be utilized needs to be identified. This part of the background section also usually addresses the role of the corporate travel manager and the corporate travel department as it relates to and interrelates with the successful bidder. Since this will be the department and the corporate travel manager will be the executive who can be expected to interface to the greatest degree with the successful bidder, the scope of this interface needs to be reviewed.

Another part of the background section relates to a statement of the work to be done. Again this is an overview. It relates to the major aspects of what is expected from the vendor. It should be clearly pointed out that this is only an overview and the next section of the request for proposal, normally entitled, *Scope of Work* discusses each of these areas in detail.

The most lengthy part of the background section relates to bidder requirements. Normally the bidder requirements presentation starts with an overview statement indicating that the successful bidder must meet and document all of the criteria noted in the paragraphs that follow. These paragraphs are normally broken down into specific sections relating to:

1. computer reservation system hardware;
2. personnel;
3. all other office equipment;
4. subscription services;
5. hours of operation;
6. emergency contact arrangements;
7. subcontractors and responsibility for them;
8. industry appointments and approvals;
9. financial, bank, and credit references; and
10. the ability and willingness to extend services to non-corporate travel functions such as incentive travel, leisure travel, and so on.

Each of these bidder requirement expectations need to be explained in some detail.

Scope of Work

A third major section of the request for proposal relates to the scope of work and it is normally an information only section. Although an overview of the scope of work is briefly presented in section two, it is normally detailed in section three

(Scope of Work). There are many approaches utilized in addressing the scope of work, but most companies find that they prefer to start with detailing the services expected from travel contractors. These services often start with a section on policies. The travel policies of the company are detailed as they relate to the services that need to be provided. For example, if travel on the lowest possible fare is required, this is normally stated as a specific policy. However, this can be clarified by explaining the limitations involved. For example, if the lowest possible fare between two points is available only between 2:00 A.M. and 4:00 A.M., it is probable that the company will not consider the utilization of this fare even though it is the lowest possible fare simply because it disrupts the traveler's ability to conduct business. Therefore, "lowest possible fare" can be defined by stipulating routings, delays en route, departure dates and times, arrival dates and times, any appropriate tax exemptions, and normally it will stipulate that travel scheduled to take advantage of frequent flier coupons or other awards will not be allowed if it is either more expensive or disruptive to the work schedule.

The Transportation Subsection

Policy restrictions can be qualified in even greater detail in the next subsection relating to transportation. Under this subsection it is normally pointed out that the contractor is expected to make reservations for all commercial modes of transportation, that ARC and IATAN ticket stock are the only ticket stock accepted for air transportation, that first-class travel is limited and the degree of limitation (i.e., who is allowed to fly first-class), and that full coach fares can only be used if reduced rate fares are unavailable. Travel agencies can negotiate for contract fares and these are usually the lowest possible fares. However, it is in the transportation subsection where the vendor is normally advised to use off-peak, excursion, promotional, and other discounted fares if they are lower than contract or negotiated fares. One way of insuring this is to require the travel agency contract to refund to the company any difference in cost if it fails to book the lowest available fare (within the constraints outlined in the company's travel policy).

Although many companies do not specifically state that a lowest *fare audit computer continuous check system* is required, an increasing number of companies are making this a requirement and some companies utilize such systems to check their travel agency vendors to make certain that the very lowest fare is obtained. It is usual to require the travel agency vendor to document that lowest fares were obtained (normally through a savings report) and to document the reasons for non-use of available discount fares or any other fares which might be lower than the fare actually booked and utilized.

The transportation subsection normally includes language requiring the travel agency vendor to adjust for changes in flights, train, or other transportation schedules and to alter or to reissue any tickets or billings when changes are needed. It normally points out that the agency will be required to notify travelers in the case of cancelled or delayed flights, trains, or other modes of transportation and when airports are closed. It is often stated in this subsection that a twenty-four hour toll-free number is expected to be made available to company travelers for emergency itinerary changes and any other emergency business which needs

270

Chapter 15:
The Proposal
and
Contracting
Process

to be conducted during hours when the travel agency is closed. Since the normal practice of most agencies is to subcontract this type of service, a reminder that the travel agency is responsible for the actions and the lack of actions of the subcontractor is appropriate here. Some travel agencies provide this type of service by offering to accept collect calls at home telephone numbers. If this type of arrangement is acceptable, such an alternative should be stated. In most cases, however, this option is not acceptable and that too should be stated.

An increasing number of travel agencies are allowed to make seat assignment reservations and to issue boarding passes. However, this privilege is frequently limited to specific carriers. Often this is based upon the computer reservation system(s) used by the travel agency, the type of fare booked, and the type of flight. For example, a flight that originated in a city some distance away, which may have made one or two stops prior to arriving at the city of origin, may be restricted in terms of advance seat assignment since the airline may wish to allow only open seating from the city where the corporate traveler boards. This is especially true with international flights in cities in Africa and Latin America. Also, some heavily discounted seats (especially stand-by fare tickets) are restricted from advance seat assignments.

Although most business travelers do not book these flights, the combination of reasons make it impractical for the corporation to require a travel agency to always provide advance seat assignments and advance boarding passes. The customary way of handling this in the request for proposal is to state simply that the travel agency will provide advanced seat assignments and boarding passes on all flights for which the agency is able to offer advance seat assignment and boarding passes and to require the agency to advise how and the extent to which the agency expects to provide advanced seat assignments and boarding passes.

Fare Considerations

Pre-departure fare rate verification is becoming increasingly popular with corporate travel managers. By having fare information prior to the trip and combining this data with hotel and car rental pre-departure price verification, it is possible for corporate travel managers to compare trip budgets with expected costs and to determine potential variances prior to departure. However, advance fare rate verification will not always be totally accurate if the business requires the travel agency to provide a computerized air fare audit check. Airline yield management practices today often result in near-departure fare reductions made in order to fill seats on flights that are expected to depart within twenty-four hours, forty-eight hours, or seventy-two hours with less-than-desired capacity. With the computerized fare audit check system, a certain percentage of flights (in some cases, in excess of ten percent) are rebooked within seventy-two hours of departure at lower (yield-management instituted) fares. Therefore, fare rate verification requirements in requests for proposal are increasingly being written in a manner that requires the travel agency to provide fare rates well in advance of departure, but also requires agencies to delay the issuing of tickets until the day before departure and/or to reissue tickets in the event that lower fares become available.

A third part of the services subsection of the Scope of Work section relates to international travel. This normally starts with a simple statement that the travel agency vendor will provide international travel services. These include reservations, tickets, and ticket delivery for all forms of transportation, and reservations for hotel accommodations and for car rental services. The statement also requires the travel agency vendor to provide advice and information on health requirements (including inoculations and vaccinations), required or suggested for destination areas, international destination conditions (climate, clothing required or appropriate, political concerns, if any, national holidays, religious holidays, and U.S. embassy and consulate locations). The international travel section also normally contains requirements that the agency provide technical advice on foreign currency exchange rates, insurance (car rental, additional air life insurance, excess baggage insurance, and so on), airport departure fees, other fees, visas, and passports. Frequently, the provision of a visa service and details relating to the interaction between the agency and its visa service are requested. Companies with considerable international travel sometimes require bidders to document how they will utilize blocked funds to pay for travel expenses.

Lodging

A fourth part of the services subsection of the Scope of Work section relates to lodging. Lodging requirements usually start by noting that the travel agency vendor will be expected to provide lodging reservations. This includes making recommendations based upon what would best fit the policies and price limitations of the company and the convenience of the traveler. It usually states that the travel agency will initiate the reservation, confirm reservations and the lodging rate, and provide confirmation numbers and detailed reservation data.

In many cases, businesses expect the travel agency to either subscribe to a travel agency discount rate national program or to negotiate special discount rates with hotels where company travelers and other agency clients purchase a substantial number of room nights on an annual basis. In other cases, the corporate travel manager will negotiate special rates with hotels and will expect the travel agency to book travelers with these hotels at the negotiated rates. In almost all cases, the request for proposal will stipulate that at least commercial rates be obtained by the agency. Therefore the wording will normally require the agency to book:

1. at company negotiated rates;
2. at agency negotiated rates;
3. at agency national program negotiated rates; and/or
4. at standard property commercial rates.

In most cases, a stipulation will be made that the least expensive of all these rates is the one at which travelers should be booked.

272

Chapter 15:
The Proposal
and
Contracting
Process

Rental Vehicles

Another subsection of the services part of the Scope of Work section deals with car rentals and/or the rental of other vehicles. This section normally starts by requiring the agency vendor to reserve commercial rental vehicles at the lowest possible rate. As with hotels, national chains publish commercial rates and often negotiate even lower rates. In addition, some travel agency consortiums are able to obtain better than published rates. In a few cases, large travel agencies negotiate with car rental franchisees at airport locations or at off-airport locations where a number of their clients rent cars. Their goal is to obtain even better rates through negotiation. Finally, an increasing number of corporate travel managers identify high car rental usage cities and negotiate directly with car rental companies in those cities for special *guaranteed rates*. By requiring the contractor to reserve rental vehicles at the lowest rate possible, the company expects that whichever of the above rates is the lowest, that rate will be used.

In addition to making the reservation, the RFP often requires that a confirmation be provided to the traveler and shown on the traveler's itinerary and it frequently requires that the rate be shown as well. Some requests for proposal will stipulate the type of car allowed while others will simply indicate that the vehicle size must be consistent with the minimum size of vehicle needed to achieve the traveler's mission and consistent with the company's travel policies. If a mileage cost is levied—and it usually is—there is often a stipulation that this must also be consistent with the company's travel policies. In some cases, rebate of agency commission on car rentals is also required.

Other Bookings

Although travel agencies normally are expected to provide air, hotel, and car rental bookings on a regular basis, there are occasions when companies will expect their travel agency vendors to provide other bookings as well. In many cases these have to do with seminars and meetings. In some cases, businesses will stipulate that the agency vendor must provide the services of a professional meeting planner and/or have a full-time meeting planner on their staff. Some businesses will offer to compensate the travel agency for meeting planning services. In most cases, however, it will be expected that meeting planning will be provided at no additional charge. Where these services are expected, the RFP will normally require that the vendor make all arrangements necessary for the holding of seminars and meetings for the company and for the company's personnel. It will normally point out that these arrangements should include at least the reservation of meeting or classroom space, transportation from the airport to the hotel or seminar/meeting site, transportation from the hotel to the seminar/meeting site (if it is not held at the hotel), arrangements for the lodging and meals of meeting/seminar attendees, clerical support, audio-visual support, and any related functions. Standards developed by the company will be expected to be met and it is usually expected that the lowest cost bidder will be awarded the meeting/seminar business. Normally some type of reporting, usually on a monthly basis, will also be required.

Non-service Scope of Work Areas

As noted above, in the Scope of Work section of the request for proposal, the service areas are normally detailed first. After completing these, other areas are discussed. These include both non-service items and indirect service items. They usually include, but may not be limited to, the following:

1. penalties;
2. itineraries for travelers;
3. ticket delivery;
4. management reports;
5. billing and payment requirements and data;
6. informational items;
7. internal computer hardware and software requirements;
8. unauthorized travel; and
9. bankruptcy or default protection.

Two of these sections tend to be much longer than others and tend to have several subsections. One of these relates to billing and payment and the other relates to management reports. Each area will be discussed in detail.

Penalties

Because a number of travel agency proposals indicate that the agency will provide the *best fare* or the *lowest available rate,* many requests for proposal will include a statement indicating that the vendor will be held liable for providing the best available fare and the lowest available rate. Normally a penalty will be levied against a vendor if the best fare or the lowest available rate is not obtained. The minimum penalty is normally the difference between the fare or rate that was obtained and the best fare or the lowest rate that was available. However, in some requests for proposal the penalties are greater than the difference, thus providing additional incentive for the vendor to provide the best fares and the lowest available rates.

Itineraries

Detailed itineraries in multiple copies are normally required from travel agency vendors. At a minimum, a copy is required for the traveler and the traveler's work unit (department). In addition, however, companies may, and sometimes do, require that additional itineraries be provided for the traveler's family and destination offices (or individuals who will be meeting the traveler at the trip destination). Sometimes copies are required for the corporate travel department and/or the billing and payment processing department. Whatever the number of itineraries that are required, these should be clearly specified in the request for proposal. If one or more copies of the itinerary must be delivered

274

Chapter 15:
The Proposal
and
Contracting
Process

to a point other than the traveler or to standard ticket delivery points, this should also be specified.

Data normally required on itineraries includes the following:

1. air carrier(s);
2. flight, train, bus, or other voyage number(s);
3. departure and arrival times, normally in local time, and prepared in A.M./P.M. rather than twenty-four hour clock times;
4. meals or other amenities for each flight segment;
5. ground transportation arrangements at destinations (for example, car rental, shuttle bus, or taxi);
6. contact and/or location data for meet and assist representatives who may be meeting the traveler;
7. name, phone number, and location of lodging facilities booked at each destination;
8. room rates at which each lodging facility is booked;
9. transportation to lodging facilities (if provided by the lodging vendor or other pre-arrangements for getting from the airport to the lodging facility if a car rental reservation is not made); and
10. name, local phone number, and location of rental cars and rates booked by the vendor at each destination (if appropriate).

Itineraries will usually be numbered and will show the airline ticket number so that cross reference can be made to tickets that are issued for the itinerary. However, if number cross-referencing is a need, and it usually is, a requirement stipulating this should be specified.

Ticket Delivery

The number of required ticket deliveries per day or per week should be specified. If ticket deliveries should be made before a specific time of day, this should also be specified. The items to be delivered should also be detailed. These will normally include tickets, itineraries, boarding passes (if they can be issued in advance), and any other appropriate documents. Ticket delivery requirements usually specify a minimum time by which tickets should be delivered prior to flight departure. In many cases, this will be the day before, but some corporate travel departments prefer to receive tickets two days prior to the scheduled travel date. The request for proposal should also specify to what person(s) or office(s) documents should be delivered. In large companies, delivery is often to as many as eight to ten locations whereas in smaller firms often only one person is authorized to receive ticket deliveries and they are normally delivered to that person's place of work (for example, the corporate travel department).

Many companies prefer to set up a ticket delivery system whereby the vendor is required to keep a log of all documents delivered and the log is signed and dated by the person receiving each document. This can be beneficial in tracing tickets that may not be readily located. Under such circumstances, agencies are usually required to maintain ticket delivery logs for a minimum of thirty days. If delivery logs are required, details relating to them should be specified in the request for proposal.

Emergency ticket delivery requirements are normally specified in the request for proposal as well. These normally specify that the vendor will provide emergency ticket delivery within a specific time period after receiving a call for an emergency ticket. This time varies from company to company, but one or two hours of advance notice is customary. Sometimes prepaid tickets, which can be picked up at an airline airport counter constitute an acceptable way of handling emergency ticket needs. If this is the case, it needs to be pointed out in the request for proposal that either the agency vendor will absorb prepaid ticket charges or the company will pay such charges.

For some companies, the delivery of tickets and other documents to locations some distance from the main headquarters office will be a consideration. In some cases, the company will require the travel agency vendor to maintain an office within a close enough distance that tickets can be generated and delivered on an emergency basis within an hour. In other cases, the company may allow the travel agency vendor to provide the delivery of tickets and documents by mail or by issuing prepaid tickets for travelers originating from field offices or locations other than the main office. Express services are another option sometimes allowed. As a form of pre-departure audit check many corporate travel managers require vendor travel agencies to deliver all new and changed itineraries to them every day. This is normally expected early each business day (copies of all reservations from the previous day), often by 10 A.M. In each case where a delivery cost may be involved, the request for proposal needs to identify whether the company or the travel agency vendor will be expected to absorb the delivery cost(s).

Management Reports

Almost all companies now require travel agency vendors to provide management reports on a regular basis. The frequency of the report depends upon the type of report. However, most reports are customarily requested on a monthly basis.

The most popular report is the *airline savings report.* This is sometimes referred to simply as a *savings* report. The traditional savings report compares the fare obtained with the full-economy fare and shows the savings by subtracting the difference between the full-economy fare and the fare obtained. This is done on a ticket-by-ticket basis and usually is reported either on:

1. a ticket sequencing basis;
2. an alphabetical basis by last name of the traveler; or
3. a time sequence basis, normally reporting each ticket issued each day of the time period covered.

Unfortunately, the traditional savings report does not provide management with the data it needs. A newer type of savings report requires travel agency vendors to provide a ticket by ticket analysis showing the price paid for each ticket compared with the lowest price consistent with the requirements of the company.

276

Chapter 15:
The Proposal
and
Contracting
Process

In other words, if the company refuses to utilize non-refundable tickets (and many companies do refuse to work with such tickets), then the lowest-priced possible ticket on an itinerary may well be considerably greater (sometimes as much as seventy-five percent more) than the lowest possible fare for a ticket. In addition to providing the cost of the lowest possible fare within the constraints of the company's travel policy, a column on the savings report indicates the reason why the lowest possible fare (consistent with the company's travel policy) was not obtained and the reasons why in those cases where it was not obtained. Reasons are normally reported in a code manner (usually in alpha code) which refers to a series of identifiable possible reasons why the least expensive fare available consistent with the company's travel policies was not obtained.

The savings report which provides data on air travel costs, while it is the most frequently requested savings report, is not the only type of savings report required by many companies. Similar savings reports providing similar data for car rental usage, hotel usage, and other vendor types that are used with some degree of frequency are often required on a monthly basis as well. Another frequently required report is often known as an *exception report*. This is a report that lists exceptions to rates, preferred carriers, policies, and so on which occur because of a traveler refusing to accept such rates, carriers, policies, and so on. These exception reports are usually requested on a weekly basis, but some businesses require them on a daily basis and in advance of departures (whenever possible), so that those travelers who might be planning to undertake a trip using carriers or flights that are not within the restrictions identified by policy, can be contacted prior to starting the trip. The determination can then be made as to whether or not the exception is one that management will accept. If it is not, management may receive the information early enough to opt to make a change in the reservation based upon their decision that such a change is appropriate.

To overcome possible misuse of the system by those travelers who wish to collect frequent flier awards, some companies require a report (normally monthly frequency is sufficient) advising of all travel incentives awarded by carriers or other vendors and an accumulated monthly and year-to-date total.

Global reports may include the following:

1. a report identifying total transportation charges for each department or cost/ profit center (this is normally a monthly report);
2. a report listing all tickets issued by ticket number, travel date, and/or account budget (fund) and;
3. an itemized weekly passenger listing report for each department or cost/profit center.

This department or cost/profit center report identifies the department or cost/ profit center by name, number, and/or some other accounting designation. The report lists:

1. the travel request and/or authorization number for each employee's trip;
2. the name of each traveler;
3. the name of the carrier;

4. the fare basis;

5. the origin and destination points;

6. the ticket number, the account fund, the travel dates; and often

7. any travel incentives awarded by the carrier or other vendor.

A budget summary is often required. This is a summary of sales activity data which reflects all official sales activity for each department or cost/profit center. It usually compares appropriations with actual expenditures by cost or profit center number. Usually a copy of this report will go to each individual department or cost/profit center head and another copy will go to the corporate travel department.

An increasing number of companies are asking for a concise narrative report (usually no more than two pages) which is provided on either a monthly or a quarterly basis. This report identifies problems and suggests solutions. It is an assessment of the overall operation of the contract and details relating to the specifics of the operation. Many companies ask for these reports to include suggestions to increase or enhance services by the vendor for the travelers.

Billing and Payment

Another major part of the Scope of Work section relates to billing and payment. Billing and payment considerations can be broken down into two parts; a section on compensation and a section on refunds.

The compensation requirements need to point out what is reimbursable and what is not, what cost exemptions are expected, compensation in the form of supplier commissions (if appropriate), the treatment of required advanced deposits or fees, billing and payment procedures, and the method of handling discrepancies in billings between the contractor vendor and company departments and/or cost or profit centers.

A statement is normally made that reimbursement by the company to the travel agency contractor vendor for transportation services under the contract will be limited to actual carrier rates and the fares which may be effective for the transportation vendor tickets which are issued to company travelers for official travel. The travel agency vendor is usually required to comply with the company's travel authorization requirements and procedures in order to obtain compensation.

In some cases, exemptions from standard charges or potential charges are required. The most common practice along these lines is the exemption from paying prepaid ticket charges and the exemption by tax exempt organizations from paying taxes. Most businesses accept prepaid ticket charges that are levied by the air carriers since most carriers will not waive such charges. However, the portion of prepaid ticket charges which is paid to travel agencies (often even when the prepaid ticket is cancelled) is sometimes exempt from compensation by the company.

It is the practice in the industry to provide hotel and car rental reservations, vouchers, and/or confirmations at no cost to the client. The reason these services are provided on a gratis basis is that many lodging and car rental vendors pay

278

Chapter 15:
The Proposal
and
Contracting
Process

commissions to a travel agency for selling their rooms and cars. Some requests for proposal include statements indicating that compensation for such services may be in the form of commissions received by the travel agency vendor from carriers, suppliers of rental vehicles, lodging companies, and/or other related travel providers, but that the business will not pay a service fee for lodging and car rental reservations. This is usually accompanied with a statement that the company will not accept any responsibility or a liability for collecting commissions or for the payment of commissions. An increasing number of businesses are requiring their travel agencies to rebate back to them a portion of or, in a few cases, all commissions earned in booking hotels and car rentals for their travelers.

In some cases, lodging vendors, meeting vendors, conference centers, and other suppliers require deposits or fees to be paid in advance. Frequently, requests for proposal will stipulate that such fees or advance deposits should be made by the travel agency vendor and billed to the company. Because many companies require all bills to be charged to the company's travel credit card(s), and because advance deposits and/or fees frequently must be paid by check (this is often a requirement of the facility provider), an exemption from the credit card payment requirement is usually made together with a statement indicating that the travel agency vendor contractor must submit supporting documentation together with its bill for any advanced deposits or fees which are paid and that this must be submitted on a periodic (usually monthly) basis.

Billing discrepancies can sometimes occur. This is usually noted in the request for proposal and a settlement arrangement for billing discrepancies is identified. Sometimes this settlement arrangement will be based on an arbitrary decision made by the corporate travel manager. In other cases, it will go to an identified third-party arbitrator. Whatever the arrangement, it is usually wise to identify how discrepancies will be settled and to have the travel agency vendor agree to this settlement process.

The second part of the billing and payment part of the Scope of Work section relates to the handling of refunds. Businesses usually require travel agency contractors to accept complete and unused tickets for refunds and to accept unused portions of tickets for refund. Those tickets which are clearly identified as non-refundable are customarily exempted from this requirement. Most businesses expect travel agency contractors to identify refunded tickets or portions of tickets by purchasing department, invoice, or purchase order number and/or ticket number. This assists the business in financial record-keeping and accounting. Most purchases will have been made by credit card and, therefore, credit card refunds will be the form of refund processed for most business transactions. Under such circumstances, copies of the credit card refund form, which are sent to air carriers by travel agencies when they process refunds, are normally also requested for the corporate travel department. This allows the corporate travel department to establish a tickler file and to identify when credit card refund credits have not been received by due dates so that a follow-up can be initiated.

Many businesses require refunds for exchanged tickets, cancelled tickets, and/or downgraded (and less expensive) tickets to be processed within a maximum of five business days, and when a time constraint (such as five business days) is determined, it should be identified in the request for proposal.

When credit card refunds are requested, it is normally expected that the credit will be applied to the business's credit card account. Seldom will a cash refund be offered for a credit card purchase, but to eliminate bookkeeping errors, many requests for proposal require that only credit card credits be provided for credit card charges and that no cash refunds be made.

In some cases, the travel agency contractor will be required to remit cash or check refunds (for tickets or services that were paid for in cash or by check) to the business travel department within a short period of time (seven days, ten days, or fourteen days) after receiving the refund request from the business travel department, the traveler, or the department for which the traveler works. It is recognized that the travel agency contractor may not, and probably will not, receive a refund from the airline, car rental company, or other parent vendor until many days later. However, this stipulation guarantees the client business and the corporate travel department an opportunity to clear its accounts rapidly and to utilize the refunded cash funds for float purposes.

It is usually in this section of the request for proposal where it is stipulated that the travel agency contractor will not be reimbursed if a refund is made directly to the traveler in cash, check, or in any other manner.

Expectations

Another major part of the Scope of Work section of the request for proposal relates to information. This section normally covers some of the major expectations of the business. It is expected that these expectations will be considered and addressed in the proposals received from bidders. Although a wide range of expectations can be, and often are, included in this section, a few of the standard expectations relate to information, negotiation rights, computer auditing, equipment and/or processing, payment expectations, bankruptcy and default protection, and the screening of travel requests so that the business will pay for only authorized travel.

Keeping travelers and travel managers fully informed regarding the travel management program is often considered a vendor requirement with all costs for printing and other communication expenses born by the vendor.

In this section, the business often communicates its right to negotiate contracts with others who provide travel-related services. These may include air or other services, hotels, and car rental companies. If other vendor contracts result in a need for coordination with the travel agency vendor, it is customary to state that the travel agency will be expected to administer the contracts. For example, if negotiated rates with hotels result in contracts with specific properties, travel agencies are usually expected to book only those properties in the cities where negotiated-rate-hotels are located. In fact, this section of the RFP often goes further by stating that the travel agency must utilize business-negotiated hotel, car rental, and air carrier vendors in preference to any other alternative. Another option, sometimes stated, is a requirement that negotiated hotel, car rental, and carrier vendors must be used in all cases except when a less-expensive alternative is available.

It is often noted that computerized auditing equipment, facilities, and supplies will be required. Some businesses offer to pay for the equipment, supplies,

280

Chapter 15:
The Proposal
and
Contracting
Process

and maintenance while others expect these to be provided on a gratis basis. Whether the business is willing to pay for the computerized auditing facility or it expects to receive the auditing facility at no cost, needs to be communicated clearly. In either case, it is customary for the business to require agency bidders to address all aspects of computerized auditing in their proposals. These would include equipment, operating costs, training, delivery time, and so on.

Some payments for services will relate to services which may not be charged against a business's travel credit card and, therefore, a policy relating to payments needs to be stated. Usually this includes a statement indicating the number of invoices needed and the number of days within which payment can be expected and/or the number of days before which payment must be made. The company's payment policies can be reproduced in this section so that travel agency bidders will be able to state that they will comply with the established payment policies.

The business needs to clearly state that it will only pay for authorized travel. The establishment of a procedure for identifying that which is authorized and that which is not may be either offered by the travel agency bidder in its proposal or that process may be established by the business. If a procedure is established by the business, it should be documented in this section. In either case, it is necessary to go beyond a statement that unauthorized travel will not be paid. It is essential for company executives to agree upon how authorized travel will be determined and to have an operating definition and/or process with which to work.

The same approach can be adopted as it relates to bankruptcy and default protection. Either the business may state its policies in regards to protection requirements or it may simply indicate that the bidder will be expected to address how as the vendor it would plan to protect the business in case of a bankruptcy or a default.

Overview of Bidder Required Information and Evaluation Procedures Section

Usually the final section of the request for proposal details information required from bidders and the proposal evaluation procedures. This is usually considered a required response section of the request for proposal. Some businesses take the policy that if a bidder fails to respond to one or more portions of this section, the bidder will be eliminated from consideration. It is helpful if the bidder is required to respond to items in this section in the same sequential order as the items are presented in the RFP. This will make comparisons easier for readers and will rapidly allow the reader to identify whether or not some requirement is not addressed in the proposal. Some RFPs require that the proposals be numbered and titled exactly the same as the requirements listed in this section.

Preliminary Pages

The first three items relate to preliminary pages. Normally, the first required page in the bid will be a title page. This should clearly state the name, address, telephone number, and name of contact person, (i.e., the name of the person

281

Overview of
Bidder
Required
Information
and Evaluation
Procedures
Section

responsible for the proposal). If the mailing address is different than the street address (i.e., if a post office box is utilized) this needs to be identified also.

The second page is normally a statement from the bidder accepting the invitation to bid. This is a formal indication that the responding travel agency wishes to bid and it is signed by a person from the agency who has the authority to commit the company to that which the proposal says it will undertake. This page can be either a form that is prepared by the company and included in the request for proposal or it can be drafted by the bidder in accordance with guidelines specified in the request for proposal.

The third preliminary page is a table of contents. It is suggested that a requirement of the table of contents be that all items are shown in the same numerical listing as in the RFP and with the same titles as in the RFP.

RFP Evaluation Criteria

At some point it is beneficial to clearly identify the specific evaluation criteria on which bids from travel agency vendor bidders will be evaluated. Several benefits accrue by clearly stipulating how bids will be evaluated. Perhaps the most advantageous benefit is having an agreed-upon set of criteria within the company. It is not unusual for a corporate travel manager to have one set of criteria, the CEO to have another set of criteria, and the CFO to have still another set of criteria. This can be confusing internally and disturbing externally. By establishing a published set of evaluation criteria and by getting this criteria agreed upon prior to sending out the request for proposal, the selection process will be much easier and smoother since arguments over major criteria will be reduced or, ideally, eliminated.

Some of the points which can be considered in establishing evaluation criteria include:

1. having a management plan for the project;
2. equipment and equipment capability;
3. personnel and personnel qualifications;
4. the qualifications of the travel agency bidder to manage travel;
5. financial qualifications;
6. appointments and/or accreditations;
7. shared commissions and/or override sharing;
8. a required inspection of the travel agency bidder's facilities and operations;
9. independent auditor verification;
10. having a traveler, travel coordinators, and corporate travel manager training plan;
11. enhancements;
12. financial services;
13. transportation requirements;

282

Chapter 15:
The Proposal
and
Contracting
Process

14. charge or fee exemptions;

15. information updates;

16. plans for integrating directly negotiated contracts;

17. computer terminals;

18. bankruptcy/default protection;

19. capability requirements; and

20. miscellaneous comments.

Obviously, there can be more points on which to evaluate bids (proposals) and bidders and there can be fewer points, depending upon the preferences and needs of the individual company. Each of the above twenty points deserve to be discussed in detail.

Project Management Ability Evaluation

In order to evaluate a travel agency's project management ability, the bidder should be required to submit a plan for managing the travel services it plans to deliver. This overall management plan should include a quality control plan, to plan to make sure that responses are timely, a staffing plan, and proof of ability to negotiate for air fares, lodging rates, and car rental rates. The plan should also include information relating to such areas as managing group travel, special and/or temporary tariffs, the ability to meet special travel needs, international travel resources, accounting and reporting capabilities and plans, and any other management plans the travel agency bidder wishes to include.

Evaluating Equipment Capability

The equipment capability can be addressed in several ways. Asking potential vendors to provide proof of their demonstrated ability to provide the required data processing in automated reservation and ticketing services is important. Often there is an overview section followed either immediately, or at a later point, with very specific required equipment details. The overview should discuss not only the ability to provide data processing and automated reservations and ticketing, but to provide automated and interfaced management information reports and billing reports. At the very least, specifying the systems that will be used is important. However, increasingly, it is important to require vendors to provide proof of flexibility. Since automation equipment changes rapidly in terms of its capabilities, the ability to provide up-to-date computerization and to keep it up-to-date is essential for many businesses with large travel volumes.

Evaluating Personnel Qualifications

Personnel qualifications may be difficult to measure. Evaluations of personnel, however, are critical since personnel can make the services work or they can reduce the effectiveness of even the most sophisticated equipment. Most RFPs require, at the very least, that a description of the personnel and personnel qualifications for those who will be providing services and/or assigned to the

283

Overview of
Bidder
Required
Information
and Evaluation
Procedures
Section

account must be provided. With this listing of personnel, brief biographies indicating the number of years of experience, the specific type of experience, and the kinds of accounts that the travel counselors have worked with in the past is often beneficial to require. In addition to asking for this data for travel counselors who would be assigned to one's account, this data also should be requested for those who would provide clerical, report gathering and production, ticket delivery, and other services. Specialized personnel to be used in serving the account need to be identified and descriptive background information provided as well. These include such people as incentive travel specialists, international travel specialists, on-staff meeting planners, and group travel specialists.

Business Management and Financial Qualification Evaluation

The sections on business management qualifications and financial qualifications are often closely interrelated. However, evaluation criteria relating to business management qualifications call for vendors to provide information on their past history relating to delivering volume corporate travel services, whereas financial capability documentation stresses the proven history of being able to handle financial fluctuations. Many require bidders to list either current or past travel contracts that they have obtained relating to travel, lodging, and car rentals and to show an experience-based ability in negotiating contracts for air travel, lodging, and car rentals in all destinations to which the businesses travelers travel. This is especially important if the company has a substantial amount of travel to destinations in other countries.

Financial capability can be documented by requiring financial statements, financial references, a financial plan, the documented history of payments to the Airline Reporting Corporation (ARC), a documented ability to carry the account for a period of at least thirty days (some will require up to ninety days) without interrupting services, proven ability to purchase and/or lease all needed equipment, and other financial statements which the CFO and/or others in the business may deem appropriate. In communicating these requirements it should be specified that the financial statements are deemed proprietary in nature and a statement to the effect that such documents will not be shown to or shared with others outside the organizational executives and/or consultants who will be making a decision on the selection of a travel agency vendor should be clearly made. Some businesses will require that the travel agency be bonded solely in the business's behalf (all appointed travel agencies are bonded or have an irrevocable letter of credit from a bank, but these bonds or letters of credit are on behalf of the airlines, in general, and the Airline Reporting Corporation, in specific. They do not protect the clients of travel agencies). Therefore, some businesses will make bonding on behalf of the business a requirement while others will consider it an enhancement, but not make it a requirement.

Accreditation and Appointment Criteria

Accreditation and appointment requirements should also be made a part of the evaluation process. Proof of Airline Reporting Corporation (ARC) appointments is usually mandatory. In addition, if there is considerable international

284

Chapter 15:
The Proposal
and
Contracting
Process

travel International Airlines Travel Agent Network (IATAN) appointment should also be required. Although it varies from month to month, as many as twenty percent of travel agencies in the U.S. do not maintain IATAN appointments.

AMTRAK tickets may now be sold in airline computer systems, negating major justification for direct AMTRAK appointment. Obviously, if the business has a substantial amount of domestic rail travel, it may consider requiring AMTRAK appointments. Obtaining appointments from the Cruise Lines International Association (CLIA) is of benefit only if the travel agency is selling cruises to one's business. If a substantial amount of leisure travel is handled through the corporate travel department for employees of the business, and the business expects the agency to handle a substantial number of cruise bookings for employees and their families who wish to take this type of vacation, CLIA appointments might be required. However, the requirement for appointments from AMTRAK and CLIA is rarely asked for.

Evaluating Financial Returns to the Company

Shared commissions and override revenue sharing can be treated in several ways. Prior to making decisions regarding the treatment of shared commissions and/or override revenue sharing, it is important to clarify whether financial concerns are more important than service concerns, equally important, or less important. Once this decision is made, a determination on how commissions and overrides are to be treated in the request for proposal can be made. In any case, it is wise to include a statement relating to how the business wants to deal with commission sharing and override revenue sharing. If service is of paramount importance, but having some revenue returned to the business is also important, the concept of requiring a sealed envelope with the bid is an effective way of making certain that the priorities are retained. If, however, returned revenue is more important than service, it is suggested that the business require an up-front section of the proposal documenting the amount of commissions the travel agency has historically received from all sources, the percentage of sales that these commissions represent, proof of having provided commissions and/or override revenue sharing to past or current clients, and a listing of past or current clients who may be contacted to verify this data.

In addition, the business may wish to require that the bidder allow inspections of the bidder's financial books before, during the term of, and for a specified period (approximately two years is suggested) after the term of the contract. It is suggested that shared commissions be expressed as a percentage of the airline ticket cost (less taxes), lodging cost, and/or rental vehicle cost. Tiered shared-commission proposals and tiered override revenue sharing proposals often are addressed. Some businesses, since they cannot count on tiered commission/override income, treat tiered income proposals as a zero percentage rebate. Others do not.

Site Inspections

Whether or not one plans to actually visit a travel agency under consideration, having a section in the request for proposal whereby the bidder agrees to a

285

Overview of
Bidder
Required
Information
and Evaluation
Procedures
Section

site inspection is important. It is recommended that site inspections be undertaken. Some RFPs require the bidder to work with major current clients in arranging possible site inspections at the corporate travel facilities of these clients. This is especially true if a large amount of equipment and facilities are to be maintained by the winning bidder travel agency on site or if the bidding agency has an in-plant or a staff in place in a current client's business location and a similar type of on-site equipment/staffing arrangement is contemplated in the RFP.

Independent Verification

Independent verification is a way corporate travel managers can guarantee proposal quality/quantity statements without the cost of personal investigation. The awarding of a contract to handle a company's travel comes only after a lengthy, time-consuming, and expensive process. This process may tie up hours of key executive time in reviewing written proposals, listening to oral presentations, and discussing the pros and cons of each bidder. Many of the executives who review travel agency proposals are men and women who have little or no technical expertise in the area of travel management. Although they may wish to evaluate proposals fairly and equally, they sometimes simply take the bidder's word for it when the bidder says its equipment can perform a function, its employees have a specified level of expertise, and/or that it has negotiated especially favorable rates with airlines, hotels, and car rental companies. Only after awarding the contract does the corporate travel manager, the vice president of finance, or some other executive find out that what the travel agency said it had or could do, was not totally accurate.

After experiencing the inability of its vendor to deliver, corporate travel managers and their companies have three alternatives. One is to live with the new travel vendor anyway. A second alternative is to give the contract to the travel agency that seemed to be second best. Finally, the company might send out a new request for proposal and start over. Often none of the alternatives are satisfactory. All can cost the company money. And what is worse, as proposals become increasingly longer and more complicated, the non-performance or inability to perform becomes more common and grows in proportion.

Up-front verification paid for by the bidder presents an alternative designed to give the company the best assurance possible that bidders have the ability to perform to the standards promised in their proposals. Up-front verification reports should be received by the corporate travel manager at the same time the proposal is received—not after the contract is signed.

To effect this, the RFP should state that no vendor proposal will be considered unless it is accompanied by an independent verification audit prepared and signed by an independent party selected by the company and named in the RFP. Bidders wanting to obtain the business will negotiate with the named independent party to perform a verification audit and will attach the completed audit to their proposals at the time proposals are submitted. Payment for the verification audit is rendered by the bidder directly to the independent verification specialist.

In addition to the obvious major attraction of this system (i.e., being able to know in advance that the bidder has the ability to perform to the degree and in

286

Chapter 15:
The Proposal
and
Contracting
Process

the way the proposal states), there are some nice side benefits as well. One important side benefit is the reduction of the number of proposals received being diminished to a reasonable number. Although the RFP can be mailed to all potential bidders, only the most serious and the most capable potential vendors can be expected to accept paying the cost of up-front verification. In addition, if the bidder is unable to provide the equipment, programs, and/or services called for in the RFP, it is probable that the travel agency will neither contract for independent verification nor submit a proposal. This reduces the number of proposals to be considered and it reduces both monetary and manpower costs in proposal review and vendor selection processes.

Because of the expense involved, however, some companies do not require independent verification for the consideration of written bids, but stipulate that the three bidders selected for final consideration must submit an independent verification report prior to making their in-person presentations before the selection committee. This often results in reducing the number of proposals to only those agencies which are serious, but it also results in only three bidders having to undertake the additional expense of independent verification.

Still another side benefit is that verification often results in measurable standard setting. While the verification may simply state that a vendor conforms to the RFP standard, many verification statements can be expected to go on to identify the degree to which the standard can be exceeded. Wherever the verification process provides measurable standards, the proposal evaluation process can become easier and faster.

Some companies do not require independent verification because they are unaware of individuals qualified to perform verification reviews. The major corporate travel associations can help by providing a list of those seeking consulting work who may reside in the area. *The Society of Travel and Tourism Educators* publishes a membership roster that includes travel experts in every state in the country. While many are closely associated with retail travel agencies and might be biased and/or have little expertise in corporate travel, a large number of the members have no agency affiliation and also have attained a strong degree of expertise in corporate travel.

There are several options when considering independent verification requirement wording in a RFP. It is suggested that the wording be simple and concise. A variation of or the following statement can be included:

> Verification that all of the above bidder requirements have been, will be, or can be met will be provided by the successful bidder (by those selected to make invited presentations) (by all bidders) in the form of a comprehensive evaluation of the bidder's current capability to meet these requirements. This report will be undertaken, authored, and signed by:
>
> Mr./Mrs. _____
> Address: _____
> Phone: _____

Payment for the verification report will be the responsibility of the bidder. Our firm, (name of the organization preparing the RFP) is not liable for any

287

Overview of
Bidder
Required
Information
and Evaluation
Procedures
Section

cost incurred by bidders relating to the verification report or to the preparation of the verification report.

Evaluating Training Plans

Increasingly, training plans are considered important parts of proposals and are given serious consideration in the evaluation process. Not only are the computer options and operations becoming more numerous and more complicated almost daily, but the management of travel is becoming more sophisticated all the time. Most companies expect to receive free or very low cost training for three company audiences. These include the traveler, the person making travel bookings, and the corporate travel manager. Many companies expect their travel agency to design and conduct training seminars directed to all three company audiences and to provide training on a gratis basis.

Some travel agencies are able to negotiate for free airline tickets and businesses are often including an RFP requirement that a number of free tickets be allocated to the corporate travel manager and/or other company employees to use when attending regional or national conferences or seminars relating to travel management. For several years large travel agency consortiums have held national conferences for their large corporate accounts and invite them to attend with the agency paying the conference fees. Some businesses now require agencies to provide the air transportation, to pay seminar or conference fees, and to reimburse hotel room fees for corporate travel managers attending travel management-oriented regional, national, and international functions. This is normally stipulated in the RFP as a dollar value reimbursement cost (for ground arrangements and tuition or conference fees) and a number of free tickets (for the air transportation).

Proposal Enhancements

Vendor proposal enhancements can make or break a proposal. Almost all travel agencies which respond to bid proposal requests wish to go further and add additional selling points beyond those factors specifically requested. If there is not a specific section in the request for proposal for enhancement, these enhancements will still be placed in the proposal and they may appear at various places throughout the proposal. Some agencies will make an effort to identify all enhancements and incorporate them into the most logical locations in the proposal. Others will group all enhancements together. Still others will simply place them into the proposal whenever they think about doing so or will take them from a proposal written for another potential client and will incorporate them in the same manner as in that proposal. In reading proposals, it is far easier for a corporate travel manager and a selection committee to find enhancements all listed in one specific area of the proposal.

Enhancements can be of two types. One is the type of enhancement suggested by the request for proposal and the other is the enhancement that is not considered or discussed anywhere in the RFP. The enhancement suggested in a request for proposal usually relates to a service or an equipment consideration that the company would like to have, but does not consider to be critical in terms

288

Chapter 15:
The Proposal
and
Contracting
Process

of what they must have to consider a bid. Points of this type often include such things as parking benefits and automatic insurance coverage. Unlisted enhancements may be literally anything that the travel agency bidder construes may be of benefit to the company issuing the RFP.

Financial Services

Financial services usually extend beyond a simple statement that the travel agency will work with an acceptable travel-oriented credit card. The RFP can be as broad as simply stating that any financial services or considerations which will be provided by the travel agency bidder should be documented to a detailed listing of expectations in terms of financial services. For example, clients with considerable international travel often specifically request assistance in utilizing blocked funds for travel payments.

Evaluating Transportation Services

Perhaps the most lengthy section relating to proposal evaluation deals with transportation services. It is suggested that this section be headed with a simple statement or paragraph indicating that travel agency bidders must meet minimum standard requirements in each of the domestic and international travel areas, but that they may also offer enhancements beyond the minimum requirements. Then a listing of the minimum transportation requirements can be broken down.

One of the transportation minimum requirements usually relates to fares. A statement to the effect that full-coach fares may be used only if reduced fares are not available normally appears in this section. This can be followed by a requirement that the vendor must furnish documentation to identify that the lowest possible fare within the constraints of the requirements of the company has been booked.

In some cases, conversion ability is required. This is the ability of the travel agency to convert a full-economy seat reservation to a discounted fare when all discounted seat fares are sold out. Air carriers normally extend this privilege to their largest volume travel agencies and in some cases, it is limited only to those agencies tied into the carrier's reservation system. This section also normally addresses negotiated fares, requiring the vendor to utilize these if they have been negotiated by the corporate travel manager (or someone else in the company) or to extend negotiation services in an effort on the part of the agency to negotiate lower fares. Often this section includes a statement to the effect that the vendor will refund to the company any difference between the lowest available fare (within the constraints of the company policies) and a higher fare which may have been booked if and when the agency fails to obtain the lowest available fare within the constraints of the company's policy.

The transportation section usually indicates that other evaluation criteria will be utilized. Schedule change adjustments, time alteration notifications (notifying travelers of cancelled or delayed flights), emergency ticket and reservation services (twenty-four hour toll-free reservations facilities), last seat availability booking, and the availability of boarding passes issued and delivered to the

289

Overview of
Bidder
Required
Information
and Evaluation
Procedures
Section

traveler with the ticket are all requirements that should be documented and evaluated.

Charge or Fee Exemptions

Prepaid ticket charge fee waivers are in this section. Companies may ask for either a reduction in prepaid ticket fee charges or a total elimination of prepaid ticket fee charges. Although travel agencies may have little discretion when it comes to charging air carrier-required prepaid ticket fees, all can and some do reimburse clients for their own prepaid ticket charge fees which are added to prepaid ticket costs by air carrier regulation whenever a prepaid ticket is issued.

It is in this section that many require the travel agency bidder to document how it plans to administer company-negotiated contracts. Many consider it important to stress that this will be an evaluation criteria area because the smooth coordination between vendors is often critical.

Evaluating On-site Computer Equipment and Personnel

Increasingly, on-site computer equipment and personnel are required by companies issuing requests for proposal. Most expect the bidder to document exactly what computer equipment will be maintained in the company's corporate travel department and/or at other sites belonging to the company. One way in which this is done is to require a listing of each piece of equipment by showing the following data on each piece of equipment:

1. manufacturer and model of equipment;
2. number of units;
3. location of unit of equipment;
4. hours of operation of unit of equipment; and
5. days of the week unit of equipment is operated.

If agency personnel are to operate on a full-time or a part-time basis in the corporate travel department or in some other location of the company, normally the minimal requirements for experience, education, and abilities of these individuals is requested. For example, specific experience requirements can be documented, number of years of experience can be documented, and educational attainment can be documented.

Other Evaluation Considerations

The hours of operation of required services are normally required as well as the ability to provide twenty-four hour emergency service. Many agencies will use subcontractors to provide twenty-four hour emergency service and other services. Many feel that it is important to require that subcontractors meet and comply with all conditions and standards which must be met by the vendor travel agency and that the ability of the subcontractor to meet these standards and conditions must be documented and evaluated.

290

Chapter 15:
The Proposal
and
Contracting
Process

Another evaluation area relates to professional memberships. Proof of memberships is normally required and is considered an evaluation area.

Credit and bank references constitute another evaluation area. Some will require a specific number of letters of reference. Others will require cash in bank minimum amounts. Still others make this an open requirement simply indicating that the travel agency bidder must provide bank and credit references.

Still another area considered for evaluation relates to the travel agency bidder's ability and willingness to extend the benefits and services in their proposal to others. Usually the "others" are employees and the benefits and services are for their personal leisure travel. However, some businesses require that the extension be provided to clients of the business and some go so far as requiring blanket extensions to many others in their field. For example, Eileen Wingate, the corporate travel manager at Harvard University, required and received an extension of negotiated car rental rates for all universities throughout the U.S. when she negotiated for car rental rates. Although this is unusual, there is a wide range in terms of the extension of benefits and services which can be asked for by companies. The requested extensions will often be granted. Frequently, all that is needed is to make a request.

Documenting the Evaluation Process

Normally, the final section in a request for proposal is a section relating to how the evaluation of proposals will take place and what will occur in and immediately after the selection process. This is a documentation of the procedures that will be followed. Sometimes it is accompanied by a date and even a time schedule. More often, the date and time schedule are not specifically stated, but are either left out altogether or a range of dates is provided. Although it may be impossible to eliminate all potential criticism of an especially high-volume travel bid and selection process, the documentation of evaluation and procedures helps considerably in lessening the potential for criticism and/or legal action on the part of those who may not have received the award of the travel business.

The first step for many in the evaluation process is to identify a date by which time proposals must be submitted even though this will be a repeat of the information from the preliminary pages identified earlier.

Normally, the second step is to screen proposals to identify those that are potentially acceptable and those that are not. This is often done by either a subcommittee or a staff person, but any proposal which is deemed unacceptable should have a brief statement attached to it indicating why it has been found unacceptable. This will benefit in providing a defense against those internal persons who may pressure for the acceptance of a bidder proposal for political reasons. It can provide a reason to give to the bidder if it is determined that a reason should be given. Most will not provide reasons for not accepting proposals, but in a very few cases where there are strong political or legal potential repercussions, reasons have been given.

It should be clearly stated in the evaluation procedures that after each round of reviews, those proposals which have been deemed unacceptable will not be considered further. Frequently, staff members or subcommittees continue to work through proposals to eliminate those based upon increasing criteria selectivity until no more than three or four proposals remain for consideration. Often the full committee will review proposals after they have been reduced to three or four and usually an invitation to make an oral presentation to the full committee is extended to the owners or managers of the three or four agencies under final consideration. Prior to holding oral presentations all committee members are given an opportunity to study the three to four top proposals along with the independent verification reports (if these have been required). Some selection committee chairs ask committee members to prepare written questions to be asked of bidder finalists prior to the oral presentations.

Some companies will limit the number of representatives from the bidding travel agency who may appear at the time of the oral presentation and they may also limit the amount of time provided for the presentation. It is usually better to extend the invitation to make a presentation by letter, documenting the constraints under which the bidding travel agency will be working during the oral presentation. The oral presentation normally starts with an introduction to the full committee of the travel agency bidder and then the senior executive is provided a time period during which the executive is given the ability to sell his proposal. Most will allow the senior executive to turn this over to a marketing executive, a consultant, or to some other person who may be accompanying the senior executive. The final part of the oral presentation is usually a question and answer session with questions asked by and/or all of the selection committee members or with a set of typed questions given to the travel agency spokesperson (all committee members will have copies of the typed questions).

Normally, after oral presentations have been made, a final decision is determined by the company's selection committee. The award notification is usually made by letter, but in many cases, the corporate travel manager or another senior executive may call the travel agency which is awarded the travel business to advise them that they may pick up the letter rather than wait for it in the mail if they so desire. It is considered polite and appropriate to write to all who submitted proposals advising them that their proposal was not selected. Be most careful to avoid indicating a reason for non-acceptance of a proposal in these letters.

In discussing the award procedures, it is important to identify the specific contract period for which the award extends and any renewal terms which may apply. It is also important to recognize that rumor may well occur in advance of the award and that conversations with individuals within the company during the selection process may well lead a bidder to believe that the award of business will be given to that bidder. Therefore, a disclaimer is recommended to indicate that no communication or interpretation of communication should be construed as an award or a promise of an award. The disclaimer should clearly point out that only an official letter of award signed by the contracting officer of the company (and name the officer, if possible) will be the only binding agreement to award the travel business.

Summary

The development of a request for proposal is often undertaken after the completion of a study of the company's travel. It specifies the travel needs of the

292

Chapter 15:
The Proposal
and
Contracting
Process

company and identifies how it expects those needs to be met by a particular travel agency vendor. Normally, a committee will review the proposals, select an agency bidder, prepare a contract, a transition plan, and a working plan and initiate the initial stages of implementing the interrelationship between the travel agency and the company. Bid requests, themselves, vary in length and specificity from those that are very broad (simply indicating the parameters sought by the company) to proposals that run well over one hundred pages and specify every detail of what is expected. There are advantages and disadvantages to both types. The broad-based RFP can result in receiving innovative proposals suggesting ways of handling travel which may not have been considered by the committee. On the other hand, detailed RFPs can result in receiving proposals that match the exact needs of the company and frequently these can be compared much more easily.

One of the major complaints of travel agencies receiving requests for proposal is the frequency with which RFPs do not prioritize needs. It is beneficial, therefore, if a hierarchy or a ranking of needs is included rather than just a listing of needs.

A travel agency works with a small commission compared to most retail businesses. Therefore, there is a strict limit on what an agency can afford to provide for its clients. There is often a trade-off between rebates (money given back to the company for travel handled) and services. If the company expects a high level of rebates, it will probably receive a lower level of service. On the other hand, if few dollars are rebated back to the company, a larger amount of service can be expected. It therefore behooves the company to identify where its priorities are in relation to rebates and service and to communicate these in the RFP.

Requests for proposal normally start with a cover letter formally inviting the potential bidder to submit a proposal. The cover letter normally includes a bid number and/or title, contact information (where the bidder can receive clarification of information), deadline information for submitting proposals, proposal delivery point data, prebid conference information (if a prebid conference is to be held), inquiry restriction parameters, data regarding the public recording of proposals received, and a listing of the enclosures and attachments which may be included with the RFP. Some cover letters also remind potential bidders that the proposal must be signed by an officer of the travel agency when a proposal is submitted. The cover letter should be brief and to the point. Frequently, it is one page or less in length.

Requests for proposal normally include a listing of terms and conditions. Often these are standard terms and conditions required by the purchasing department of the business of all who submit proposals to the company. However, they usually include terms and conditions relating specifically to the travel RFP as well.

Some RFPs include a background section. This provides the highlights of the results of the corporate travel study. The background assists bidders to understand how the priorities were determined and to relate priorities to one another.

Most lengthy requests for proposal are broken down into sections. This helps the writer to deal with each of the concerns and it also assists the bidder to understand needs couched different ways and from different approaches. The result may very well be a somewhat repetitive document indicating the same need or requirement sometimes two or three times. However, because the need may well be documented slightly differently each time, ideally the bidder will understand the need from the various end-user viewpoints. There is no question but that many proposal requests which are broken down into sections can result in some confusion and/or some degree of contradiction, but by holding a prebid conference these areas of potential misunderstanding can be clarified. Most travel agency marketing executives agree that requests for proposal could be more concise and more precise in clarifying the exact needs of the company. Some effort along these lines should be made in order to eliminate potential major areas of confusion.

Although there are many ways of breaking out requests for proposal into various sections, the discussion of requests for proposal in this chapter starts with an administrative section (for information only) followed by a background section (again, an information only section). Next is a Scope of Work section. This is predominantly for information only, but it may include some points for which a direct response is required. The Scope of Work section is normally the most lengthy section. It goes into great detail regarding the specifics of what is needed. The last major section is required information and evaluation procedures. This section details requirements and frequently specifies that bidders must respond in their proposals to each point in the same numerical order as the point is brought out in this part of the request for proposal.

The last major part of an RFP is an overview of the evaluation process. Following the four major sections of the request for proposal are addendums and attachments. These may range widely, but they often include copies of specific policies. Some will include standard bid policies from the purchasing department and some will include a complete listing of all corporate travel policies. A general guideline is to include those materials which would be of benefit to the bidder in understanding the needs, but to screen and not include those materials which are considered confidential within the company.

A well-written and a well-thought out request for proposal can assist the company in obtaining quality travel services. Considerable attention to the preparation of the RFP needs to be provided. Many companies will employ consultants to review their request for proposal prior to sending it to potential bidders since most companies do not have a large number of RFPs to compare with the document that they prepare. A well-written request for proposal sets the stage for a selection process that ideally will result in developing a relationship with a travel agency that will provide the company with the quality of service, timliness of service, and financial returns that will best meet the combination of company travel needs.

Discussion Questions

1. How do the study of the company's travel and the request for proposal interrelate?

2. What is the selection process that occurs after proposals are received by a company which has requested proposals?

294

Chapter 15:
The Proposal
and
Contracting
Process

3. What are the advantages and disadvantages of a short, general request for proposal and what are the advantages and disadvantages of a lengthy, specific request for proposal?

4. Why is there sometimes a trade-off between rebates and service and what are the options for a company in developing a RFP as it relates to getting the rebates and/or services that the company wants in proposals from potential vendors?

5. What points should be brought out in the RFP cover letter?

6. What are some of the major RFP section titles?

7. What points does the administrative section of the RFP address?

8. What points are made in the background section of the RFP?

9. What are the specific bidder requirements that are usually addressed in the Scope of Work part of the background section of the RFP?

10. How does the Scope of Work part of the background section of the RFP compare with the third major section of the RFP which is titled "Scope of Work?"

11. What points are raised in the transportation subsection of the Scope of Work section of the RFP?

12. International travel is frequently considered in the services subsection of the Scope of Work section of the RFP. What aspects of international travel might be considered in this subsection?

13. Lodging, rental vehicles, and other bookings are all parts of the services subsection of the Scope of Work section of the RFP. What points are discussed relating to lodging, rental vehicles, and other bookings?

14. What are the non-service Scope of Work points brought out in this section of the RFP?

15. What are some examples of penalties which might appear in the RFP?

16. What itinerary points might an RFP consider?

17. Considering that ticket delivery is one of the major complaints of both business travelers and corporate travel managers, how might ticket delivery be addressed in an RFP?

18. What management reports might a company require and what parameters relating to management reports might be discussed in the RFP?

19. How might the billing and payment part of the Scope of Work section of the RFP be broken down for consideration in the RFP?

20. What are four or five of the expectations which might be addressed in the expectations part of the Scope of Work section of the RFP?

21. Why is it considered beneficial by some companies to require bidders to respond to all portions of Section IV, Information Required from Bidders and Evaluation Procedures?

22. Why is it considered beneficial to the evaluators to require bidders to respond to items in Section IV in the same sequential order and with the same numbering order as they are presented in the RFP?

23. What preliminary pages are normally required in a bid?

24. Twenty RFP evaluation criteria were listed in this chapter. What are five of these evaluation criteria?

25. How might a bidder's equipment capability be evaluated?

26. On what bases might a bidder's personnel qualifications be evaluated?

27. How might a bidder's business management and financial qualifications be evaluated?

28. What accreditation and appointment criteria might be considered in evaluating a bidder?

29. How might shared commissions and override revenue sharing be treated in the evaluation process?

30. What might the RFP require in terms of site inspections?

31. In what ways might independent verification be beneficial to a company in its overall bidder evaluation process?

32. What training might be considered in the evaluation process and why is training important?

33. What are some examples of proposal enhancements which a bidder might provide in its proposal?

34. What are the two types of bidder enhancements?

35. What RFP options are available relating to documenting required financial services?

36. How might transportation services be treated in the evaluation section of the RFP?

37. What are some of the ways in which on site computer equipment and personnel can be evaluated?

38. What are some of the other points to be considered in evaluations?

39. What points should be brought out in the section of the RFP in which the evaluation process is documented?

Role Play Exercise

Two students may participate in this role play either out-of-class, as a fun way to review the chapter, or as an in-class exercise. One plays the role of the purchasing director and the other plays the role of the corporate travel manager. Please read the script and then pick up the conversation in your own words.

Purchasing Director: I have just come from meetings with both the CEO and the CFO. They both have concerns about the travel RFP we are developing. I know the committee is developing it, but since you are coordinating the project, I think you should know that both the CEO and the CFO expect their input and priorities to appear in the final document. And, I'm afraid their input and priorities conflict with one another.

296

Chapter 15:
The Proposal
and
Contracting
Process

Corporate Travel Manager: I'll bet the CEO is asking for a lot of service and the CFO wants rebates, cheapest prices, and a share of the overrides. Right?

Purchasing Director: You are exactly right. Now tell me, what is the committee asking for in services and exactly what are we requiring in financial benefits? How do you plan to make both the CEO and the CFO happy?

Corporate Travel Manager: From their initial input we have had a pretty good feel for where both the CEO and the CFO are coming from. We have tried to strike a balance between both services and financial returns. Let me run down what we are going to be requiring in each area. Starting with services, we . . .

CONTINUE ON YOUR OWN

Group Discussion: Multiple Mufflers and the RFP Rift

Multiple Mufflers has designed an innovative four-muffler system that exceeds the noise pollution levels of the least stringent U.S. city by at least five times. Young "dynamic" car drivers have purchased these systems as rapidly as they can be manufactured and they are growing in popularity in Europe and Japan as well. Because of the rapid expansion of Multiple Mufflers there has been an equally rapid growth in corporate travel, especially for those in the research and design, marketing, and training divisions.

Early in the fiscal year, a committee headed by the Director of Purchasing, undertook a study of the company's travel. The recommendations resulting from that study included ones to prepare a request for proposal, establish a corporate travel department, and to manage corporate travel better. The committee was asked to develop a request for proposal and the President of Multiple Mufflers has told the committee to complete the RFP within two weeks. He wants daily status reports and he has assigned deadlines for each stage in the development of the RFP. The first deadline is the day after tomorrow. He expects in this report to be advised of the overall parameters of the RFP that will be developed.

However, a serious rift in the committee has occurred. The Research and Development representatives to the committee wish to have a one-page RFP which will provide potential bidders with an opportunity to be innovative in their responses. The finance and the marketing representatives, however, wish to develop a very detailed RFP. As the chair of the committee, you are expected to develop and bring back to the committee a synopsis of the pros and cons of each type of RFP. The full committee expects this at its meeting tomorrow.

You are meeting today to finalize the synopsis. You are expected to reach agreement with the members of your sub-committee, who are assisting you in the development and writing of a two-page synopsis. In your group session, select a spokesperson. All will have an equal vote on decisions. In your group session you are expected to reach agreement and to prepare the two-page synopsis to be presented to the entire class by the spokesperson of your committee.

CHAPTER 16

Internal Considerations

Introduction

The corporate travel manager needs to consider several internal factors. These factors can be divided between those that are predominantly, if not totally, internal and those which are often predominantly internal, but also have a large component of external as well. In the first category of those that are totally independent, this chapter will consider the subjects of filing, legal matters, insurance, accounting and other record keeping. In the second category, those considerations that are both internal and external, this chapter will consider internal public relations and promotion, internal politics, and training.

Filing

Many corporate travel departments are small. They have a limited staff with which to work in setting up a filing system and in keeping files. In many cases, the person who keeps the files is also the person who uses the files. This is the corporate travel manager. Many corporate travel managers will break their file system into three basic categories. These categories are *administrative, financial,* and *vendor-related.*

The administrative files frequently are kept in alphabetical order and are prepared on an "as needed" basis. These are files related to policies and procedures, letters from superiors and those in the company who are prime travelers (or their superiors), industry update files, and so forth.

The financial files will often constitute the bulk of files kept. These are often grounded by a budget and related files kept in the ongoing development process of budgeting. Correspondence with various executives relating to financial matters are often kept here as well. Most of the financial files, however, are related to the travel budgets of each department and, in some cases, of each traveler within each department. If the corporate travel manager is responsible for reviewing expense reports, as is the case in many organizations, frequently filed expense reports will be maintained by department and by traveler over a several year period. Another section of the financial files frequently relates to ratio development and statistical data. This is utilized in the development of negotiations with vendors.

Vendor files constitute still another portion of the filing system. Vendor files are frequently broken down by type of service. In other words, there will be files for travel agency vendor(s), air carrier vendors, hotel vendors, car rental vendors, and a host of other categories of vendors. Vendor contracts may be either a part of the individual vendor file or may be separate files within the "vendor" heading or section of the file system. Of course, many corporate travel managers will maintain additional files based upon the specific needs of their companies and the specific ways in which their corporate travel department operates.

Legal

Legal matters are seldom a concern of corporate travel managers. Most companies large enough to have a corporate travel department frequently have a legal staff and almost always have legal counsel. Because of the "middle man" role played by corporate travel managers, there is often a view that there are few or no legal matters with which to be concerned. However, corporate travel managers have legal exposure. Perhaps the greatest degree of exposure is a potential of holding themselves out as being experts in the travel field, counseling a traveler on the stated basis of this expertise, and finding that the in-house client traveler, following the corporate travel manager's advise, encounters major personal harm. The exposure for a potential personal law suit may become considerable. The best way to avoid this potential, of course, is to be very careful in wording recommendations to travelers when such recommendations could have personal repercussions.

A second potential area relates closely to ethics and potential suits. Frequently this can be not directed primarily at the corporate travel manager, but indirectly by bringing in the corporate travel manager as it relates to a potential of collusion and unfair competition. This deals with the matter of handling the confidentiality of bid proposals from vendors. When a corporate travel manager is approached by a favorite vendor, a travel agency, for example, and asked to assist in developing information on competitors by sharing proposals received from other travel agencies with the favored agency so that the favored agency will have an opportunity to understand what the competitor has proposed, there is a very real potential for legal repercussions if the corporate travel manager allows an executive or appointee of the favored travel agency to sit in on or be a part of the oral presentations made during the bid process by one or more other travel agencies.

Although the majority of corporate travel managers would not entertain such a request, a minority of company travel managers have done so. By doing so they have brought upon themselves a potential legal exposure. Certainly, in every business dealing, there is some slight potential for legal exposure. If the corporate travel manager will pay careful attention to the potential and then couch that which is said and done carefully, there is a strong possibility that no legal actions will ever be brought against the corporate travel department, the parent firm, or the corporate travel manager, personally. It is beneficial, however, that corporate travel managers explore with the company's legal staff whenever the manager feels that there is or that there might be a strong potential for legal concern.

Insurance

Risk management is a concern in many companies. Insurance is the way in which risk is often transferred in business. In corporate travel, the standard business insurance, such as fire, property, business interruption, and other insurance is usually already handled by other executives of the company. In fact, in many large companies there is a separate department for handling risk management. Although travel insurance for the individual traveler may be a concern, this is frequently provided by vendors leaving little or no felt need for additional insurance concerns by the corporate travel manager. Of course, it behooves the corporate travel manager to review vendor-included insurance to make sure that it really does provide the protection that the corporate traveler and the corporate travel manager think that it provides. Frequently, this means reading through the documentation relating to automatic insurance provided by vendors. If this is forwarded to the risk management department of the company, interpretations of the sections which may be unclear may be requested.

One insurance area that an increasing number of corporate travel managers are reviewing is the *errors and omissions insurance* carried by many travel agencies. Because of the increasing frequency of suits, often considered by many in the industry to be frivolous, a large percentage of travel agencies consider this to be the most important insurance coverage they could have. What corporate travel managers frequently do not fully appreciate is that as they, individually, and as their staff take on the roles of travel counseling, they also take on the legal exposure covered by errors and omissions insurance to some degree. Therefore, it behooves corporate travel managers to review errors and omissions policies and to determine whether or not this insurance will be of potential benefit.

Accounting and Record Keeping

Some corporate travel departments maintain substantial accounting and record keeping roles while others do not. The difference often comes as a result of assigned responsibilities. If the corporate travel department is responsible for reviewing and auditing expense reports and keeping exact records of individual department, cost center/profit center, and/or project travel budgets, then a substantial accounting and record keeping role may be required. When this is the case, corporate travel departments will often keep a file on the travel budget of each work unit or project. Sometimes they will break down these budgets into subbudgets for each traveler within each work unit or project. The corporate travel manager receives a copy of the trip expense approval and will often be expected to balance this against the expense report filed after the trip is over. Frequently, it will be the responsibility of the corporate travel department to identify policy exceptions that may have occurred and to flag expenses that are greater than authorized, sometimes even taking on the responsibility of making certain that unauthorized expenses are recaptured for the company. Even when accounting and record keeping roles do not involve the corporate travel department in monitoring expense reports, the department usually has the responsibility to monitor the work of vendors and to review required vendor reports.

Savings reports are frequently required and it is usually the responsibility of the corporate travel department to make certain savings reports really do reflect savings. Periodic spot checking of itineraries reviewed before ticketing can sometimes result in a move toward reviewing all itineraries before ticketing to make certain that the best fares are being obtained. The record keeping usually goes beyond savings reports, however, and includes reviews of vendors other than airlines and travel agencies. For example, records are frequently maintained relating to the number of hotel nights utilized in each city and each hotel and the number of car rentals in each city and from each car rental vendor utilized. These records provide the corporate travel department with the tools needed to negotiate for better rates or fares. Most use manual systems to develop the accounting and record keeping, but increasingly automated systems are becoming available. It behooves corporate travel managers to periodically review what is on the market both in terms of manual and computerized systems to assist them in the accounting and record-keeping functions.

Public Relations and Promotion

While many corporate travel managers see no public relations and promotion role for their corporate travel department, others maintain a substantial and an ongoing public relations and promotion program. Within a business, a corporate travel department can be viewed in a number of ways. In many cases the view is a negative one. Business travelers often look at the corporate travel department as performing no function or role other than a policing function and role. After all, the justification for many corporate travel departments to be in existence at all, is to reduce the costs. This cost reduction, in the view of some business travelers, comes at the expense of comforts and benefits of the traveler. To help maintain policy enforcement through education is frequently felt to be a more subtle and a more effective way of obtaining policy compliance than some of the alternative approaches which might be taken. Many corporate travel managers produce a newsletter which features articles on how individual travelers have saved money for the company. However, when a corporate travel manager can provide articles in the newsletter relating to the benefits for the individual traveler or the employee that have been negotiated for with vendors and can get that message across to travelers and employees, the negative image which might have initially been in place might start changing to a more positive image.

An increasing number of corporate travel managers wish to develop a more positive image and use internal public relations and promotions in order to do so. For example, they may require hotel or car rental vendors to extend the same favored rates to company employees who are traveling for leisure purposes rather than for business purposes. By promoting and publicizing these benefits internally, the role and image of the corporate travel department starts becoming a far more positive one. A few corporate travel managers have developed annual public relations and promotion schedules and programs in order to make certain that the positive aspects of the department are well known throughout the company on an ongoing basis.

Politics

Corporate travel departments and corporate travel managers are frequently subjected to considerable internal political pressure. Not only is their prime role frequently construed to be an unpopular one (i.e., helping to develop and maintain travel policies) but often company executives bring to bear conflicting requirements on a corporate travel department. Chief financial officers and others in financial roles (comptrollers, purchasing managers, and so on) frequently expect the corporate travel department to maintain strict buying practices so that a maximum of savings will result. Sales and marketing executives expect the corporate travel department to insist on service. They want their travelers to arrive relaxed and in comfort, ready to sell. Corporate training executives, like sales and marketing executives, are concerned with getting to the destination on time, relaxed enough to either set-up for training programs, normally to start early the next day, or to conduct training right away. They want direct flights and they want to make certain that their training materials arrive with them whenever possible. While top marketing and training executives have a concern about keeping within budget, their primary concerns are with getting the job done at the destination.

Chief executive officers, meanwhile, tend to look at travel from both a cost and a service viewpoint. Since travel is such a major expense, saving money on travel is very important. However, because travel is considered to be a vehicle or a means to an end, getting the job done is also extremely important. Therefore, chief executive officers, perhaps more than any others in the company, ask for, and often demand, a combination of both top service and very low prices.

Meeting the needs of all can be difficult. If the corporate travel manager concentrates on savings and sacrifices service to some extent in order to obtain better service, then the corporate travel manager is risking the anger of those executives who need to have excellent service. On the other hand, if there is a concentration on service and costs get higher than financial executives will tolerate, the corporate travel manager runs the risk of having problems with financial executives. Since corporate travel managers often report to one of these executives, (CFO, CEO, or marketing manager), there is a strong possibility that the corporate travel manager will find a need to concentrate attention in the area of importance to the immediate supervisor. In other words, if the immediate supervisor is a financial executive, then savings tends to be of paramount importance.

If, however, the immediate supervisor is the marketing executive or another high travel use manager, concentration will often be on obtaining the best services. When this is the case, and when an immediate supervisor insists on having either strong concentration on savings or services, the corporate travel manager risks the anger of top executives, usually at the same or a higher level as the immediate supervisor, often without the ability to interact directly with those executives in order to resolve the problem. This can then become a very difficult political situation for the corporate travel manager. More than one corporate travel manager has been fired because of following the instructions of the immediate supervisor when those above and lateral to the immediate supervisor wish to have travel emphasis directed in another area of concentration.

However, the political problems can be even more severe. If the corporate travel manager performs a policing role and is required by the dictates of the job to advise travelers that they cannot take flights which are in violation of corporate policy rules, that they cannot drive rental cars that are more luxurious than corporate policy allows, or that they cannot stay in hotels that are more expensive than the travel policy allows, the traveler frequently gets upset with the corporate travel manager, sometimes either attempting to bypass the corporate travel manager or to get rid of the corporate travel manager. When several travelers in the company make the decision that the corporate travel manager is not serving their best interests and needs to be removed, the termination of employment sometimes results. Some companies go through several corporate travel managers a year, not because the corporate travel manager is not doing the job well, but because the structure is one that sets up the corporate travel manager in an intolerable political position. It, therefore, behooves the corporate travel manager who is new or the person who is considering a position of corporate travel manager to review the political environment prior to taking the job or to make certain that there are ways to offset the above potential political problems.

One of the techniques to offset such political repercussions has been discussed earlier in this chapter. This is the internal public relations and publicity role which emphasizes the benefits brought to travelers, especially for their leisure travel, by the corporate travel department and the corporate travel manager. Another approach is to discuss the potential problems openly and directly with the immediate supervisor prior to taking the position and to have a clear understanding that the immediate supervisor or the traveler's supervisor will take on the responsibility of advising travelers that they are in violation of policy. Many corporate travel managers do not view this as their responsibility and try very hard to make certain that the policing function is one in which the traveler's supervisor plays the key role of getting the traveler to comply with policy rather than the corporate travel manager having to perform that function. Of course, having a strong immediate supervisor who will take on the responsibility of handling political problems is one of the best vehicles for dealing with this potentially politically volatile situation.

Training

As pointed out earlier, there are three target audiences for training. These are the *traveler*, the *person making actual bookings*, and the *corporate travel department staff*. In all three cases, companies have come to expect vendors to provide much of the training on either a gratis basis or at a very low cost.

The training of travelers is designed primarily to assist the traveler in understanding travel documentation, reservations, and ease of transit. Often half day or one day seminars are held by vendors for travelers. These seminars may range in nature from a topic such as, "What to do if a terrorist takes over an airplane," to "How to get checked in at and through international airports in a record amount of time." These seminars are often sponsored by air carriers, travel agencies, car rental vendors, and others who have a vested interest in making the traveler happy and the trip a successful one. Sometimes corporate travel managers put together their own training for travelers and conduct this training through in-house training vehicles.

Training for those who make reservations usually is directed towards the secretaries or others who work in a clerical position in the departments where there are either many people who travel or sometimes where there are just a few travelers, but they are heavy travelers. As with the seminars which are oriented toward the traveler, the training programs for those who book travel are also frequently offered by vendors. Again, travel agency contractors will often hold short sessions to introduce those individuals at the agency who are working directly in the reservations capacity, to identify computer information flows so that those calling in a reservation request will be able to provide information in the same manner in which computers require the data, or perhaps they will provide information on how to get special meals, frequent flier program management, or how to arrange shipment of bulky, valuable, or dangerous baggage on international flights.

Perhaps the training area of prime consideration to the corporate travel manager is the training that is provided for corporate travel department staff, including the manager. Frequently, companies provide little or no budget for ongoing education and training for corporate travel managers and their staff, but not infrequently companies are more than willing to accept free or very-low-cost-training from suppliers. However, one of the problems is the ethics of asking suppliers to provide training, which is not required or agreed to in contractual arrangements outlined through an RFP, and a proposal which has been accepted. Therefore, corporate travel department staff training, even more than the training of travelers and those who make travel arrangements, needs to be spelled out in some detail in the request for proposal.

A second factor that sometimes works against obtaining top-quality training and education for corporate travel staff is the potential jealousy of others in the business when the corporate travel department flies to what is often considered an exotic location for training. Some in the business may interpret this as a violation of the corporate rules against accepting gifts. They may suggest that a training program held in Hawaii is just a bribe to get the corporate travel manager to want to continue working with the particular vendor offering the training. Those corporate travel management staff members who take familiarization trips will sometimes be accused of taking trips just to have an additional personal vacation.

The key to all training, but especially that of corporate travel staff members and the corporate travel manager is to spell out as clearly as possible that which is expected in the request for proposal. Once this has been spelled out and agreed to by the RFP development committee, training becomes one additional ingredient, and perhaps a very important ingredient, in the process of selecting a vendor which will provide the range of services and benefits expected by the company.

Corporate travel managers are urged to include in the request for proposal agreements to fund enrollment or participation of the corporate travel manager in local, regional, national, and international corporate travel training events such as conventions, specialized training programs, Association of Corporate Travel Executives (ACTE) conventions and seminars, the National Business Travel Association's CCTE (Certified Corporate Travel Executive) certification program, and special programs which may not yet have been announced. In each case, full funding by the vendor is recommended. This includes transportation costs, transfers, accommodations, meals, enrollment and training fees, and expense allowances. In addition to specifying that vendors pay for all the costs of several known annual, semiannual, or biannual meetings and conventions, an allocation, written into the request for proposal for attending training that is not known at the time of the preparation of the request for proposal is suggested. This can be handled by identifying a function cost level which will be paid for by the vendor but selected by the corporate travel manager. In this way, a total education and training program can be developed for corporate travel managers and their staff, the company can obtain increasingly knowledgeable corporate travel services, and the cost of the training and education will be born totally by vendors.

Summary

The internal factors of filing, legal matters, insurance, accounting and record keeping, public relations and promotion, politics, and training are considered in this chapter. Filing systems are kept simple. They normally fall into three categories:

1. administrative;
2. financial; and
3. vendor-related.

Administrative files include policies and procedures, letters, industry updates, and so on. Financial files can be extensive. They usually include data relating to travel budgets for all work units of the company. Financial correspondence and financial reports are often included in the financial files, as well. Vendor files are kept by vendor type and then by vendor. They include file sections for air carriers, travel agencies, hotels, and car rental vendors. In addition, other vendor files are frequently maintained. These files include data relating to volume of vendor usage, letters, and negotiated contracts.

Legal matters are usually handled by corporate legal staff or in-house lawyers. However, the corporate travel staff have exposure to two potential areas of legal concern. One is the potential for advising travelers who, on the basis of the advice, encounter difficulties and they file personal law suits. The second area relates to the ethics of disclosing vendor-confidential data. In both matters, the corporate travel staff are advised to be very careful regarding what is said to both travelers and vendors. Keeping vendor data totally confidential and remaining conservative in making travel recommendations usually protects corporate travel staff from potential legal problems.

Insurance in most large businesses is handled by an in-house risk management department. Corporate travel staff may wish to review with the in-house risk management executives potential need for errors and omissions insurance and may wish to review in detail vendor-included automatic insurance to determine exactly what is covered and what is not covered by such insurance.

Accounting and record keeping can constitute a major part of a corporate travel department's work or it can be only a minor task area depending upon the division of responsibilities. If the corporate travel department is responsible for reviewing trip requests, comparing them against budgets prior to the start of trips, and balancing expense reports against authorized pre-departure trip expenses and department-approved travel budgets, the accounting and record keeping can be substantial. If the corporate travel department also has the responsibility for assisting each work unit in the development of its budget and the monthly or quarterly reporting of budget status to each corporate work unit, the accounting and record keeping responsibilities can be even greater. Still further accounting and record keeping responsibilities can come when the corporate travel department maintains ongoing records of travel vendor usage. For example, many corporate travel departments maintain data relating to city-pair usage, hotel room/night usage, car rental franchisee vendor usage, and so forth. Although much of this data can be obtained from vendors and retained in automated computer retained records, the accumulation of the specifics needed to negotiate can sometimes be time consuming.

An increasing number of corporate travel departments are undertaking public relations and promotion activities in an effort to obtain greater compliance with travel policies through educating travelers and those who call in flight, hotel, and car rental requests. Part of the reason for public relations and promotion activities involves a desire on the part of many corporate travel managers to create a more balanced image of the corporate travel department and work toward a very positive view of the corporate travel department by all in the company. In many cases, this means bringing negotiated travel values, which can be used for employee leisure travel, to the attention of all employees.

Company politics can be a concern in many organizations. Corporate travel departments are often caught in the middle between those in the company who wish to save money on travel and those who are more concerned with maximizing travel services. Whether the corporate travel manager emphasizes savings, strikes a balance between savings and service, or emphasizes services, there is a strong likelihood that someone important in the company will not be happy. Problems can arise for the corporate travel manager when a powerful executive becomes angry with the corporate travel staff or the corporate travel manager because of policy restraints. Therefore, corporate travel managers attempt to have policy enforcement handled by immediate supervisors rather than undertaking this role themselves and they attempt to mitigate the negative image associated with travel policy maintenance by providing leisure travel benefits which may be strong enough to offset traveler concerns related to business travel limitations.

Training addresses three audiences:

1. the traveler;
2. the person making actual bookings; and
3. the corporate travel staff.

Most training is provided by vendors on a gratis or a very low-cost basis and it is required from vendors in the training section of the request for proposal. Training for travelers tends to be short, intensive seminars on very specific subjects, normally of considerable interest to the traveler. Training for those who make bookings often relates to easing the communication between the person calling in the booking and a reservationist, computer-required data information flows, and special services provided by vendors which may be available at little or no cost when requested by those calling in bookings.

Corporate travel staff training is important to consider if the department is to be maintained in a professional manner. Seldom do businesses allocate sufficient funds for corporate travel managers and their staff to obtain the ongoing, top-quality training needed to stay on top of rapidly changing developments in the field of corporate travel. Therefore, an increasing number of corporate travel managers are including corporate travel staff training expenses in requests for proposal requirements with all or most of the costs underwritten by travel agency, airline, and other vendors. Spelling out in detail in the request for proposal all required training frequently results in obtaining training that otherwise would not be available, overcoming vendor reluctance to pay for training and heading off attention to other corporate employee complaints resulting from possible jealousies. In the long run, vendor funding of local, regional, national, and international corporate travel training events and conventions can be mutually beneficial.

Discussion Questions

1. What are the three basic categories into which many corporate travel managers break their filing systems?

2. Which category of files often constitutes the bulk of the files kept?

3. What type of files are often utilized in the development of negotiations with vendors?

4. How are vendor files frequently broken down?

5. What constitutes the greatest degree of legal exposure for corporate travel managers?

6. What might a corporate travel manager do to create a potential ethical and/or legal problem as relating to the confidentiality of bid proposals from vendors?

7. Why is errors and omissions insurance carried by many travel agencies considered an insurance area that an increasing number of corporate travel managers are reviewing?

8. What internal and external accounting, record keeping, and monitoring roles might the corporate travel department perform?

9. Why might corporate travel managers produce a newsletter?

10. What are some of the political considerations with which a corporate travel manager might be concerned?

11. What are the three target audiences for training?

307

Group
Discussion
Situation:
Voodoo Dolls'
Corporate
Travel Ethics

12. What is the training area of prime consideration for the corporate travel manager?

13. What is the key to all training, especially that of corporate travel staff members and the corporate travel manager?

14. What is meant by the term *full vendor funding*?

15. What type of training for the corporate travel manager should be included as required in RFPs?

Role Play Exercise

Two students may participate in this role play either out-of-class, as a fun way to review the chapter, or as an in-class exercise. One plays the role of the corporate travel manager and the other plays the role of an experienced travel agency executive. Please read the script and then pick up the conversation in your own words.

Corporate Travel Manager: Having worked in the field of corporate travel management now for several years, I feel I understand the important day-by-day aspects of corporate travel management. However, increasingly we are getting involved in international travel. Our next RFP will require the funding of annual attendance at the ACTE international conference. What other training relating to both international and domestic needs of a specialized nature would you suggest that we include requiring in our next RFP?

Experienced Travel Agency Executive: For international training, the ACTE International Conference is certainly the best. However, there are a number of other training programs you may want to consider. Have you thought about the . . .

CONTINUE ON YOUR OWN

Group Discussion Situation: Voodoo Dolls' Corporate Travel Ethics

Jack Ripper, senior sales executive with Midnight Airways, had a conversation last week with Blanche Spider, the owner of Voodoo Travel. Jack was attempting to get Voodoo Travel to switch to the Midnight Airways computer reservation system. He pointed out that being linked to the Midnight Airways computer reservation system would be most beneficial for Voodoo Travel. Midnight Airways would refer a number of corporate travel managers to Voodoo Travel who would immediately make Voodoo Travel their agency since Midnight Airways had reached sixty percent below-the-market negotiated fare agreements with them, but requires the companies to book only Midnight Airways and to use a Midnight Airways online computer reservation system travel agency for their bookings. He pointed out that one of Voodoo Travel's major clients, Voodoo Dolls, Inc. had just gone through a request for proposal review and Jack Ripper thought that the account would be awarded to another travel agency based on the

Midnight Airways fares recently negotiated with Voodoo Dolls, Inc. However, Jack pointed out, he would approach Aunti Ethics, the corporate travel manager with Voodoo Dolls, Inc., and strongly advise that she re-sign with Voodoo Travel if Voodoo Travel decides to switch to Midnight Airways' computer reservation system.

Blanche Spider responded that she was certain Jack was wrong because she had had her senior sales representative, Secret Snooper, sit in on the Voodoo Dolls oral presentations so that she could find out exactly what the competition was offering. After the presentations were over, Secret Snooper discussed all aspects of the presentations with both Blanche Spider and Aunti Ethics in Aunti's office at Voodoo Dolls. In fact, Aunti Ethics had given Blanche a copy of all the written presentations prior to the oral presentations so that Blanche and Secret could prepare questions on any points they were not sure of and get answers during the oral presentations. "The relationship is so good," stated Blanche, "that there is no question but that the contract to handle Voodoo Dolls' travel will once again be awarded to Voodoo Travel."

Since the conversation with Jack Ripper, Jack has provided details of the conversation to Villainous Viper, the president of Vile Travel, a top contender for the Voodoo Dolls account. Viper is now planning to sue Voodoo Dolls. Aunti Ethics has just been advised by Jack Ripper that Villainous Viper's legal advisor has arranged for a subpoena to be delivered to Aunti Ethics and the president of Voodoo Dolls, Aint Swift, tomorrow afternoon.

Aunti Ethics expects that a meeting with Voodoo Dolls' in-house lawyers will be scheduled the day after tomorrow to review the matter and take a corporate position. She has asked your group to advise her in the preparation of a position paper for the meeting with the corporate lawyers. In your group session, you are expected to reach agreements and to prepare a two-page position paper to be presented to the entire class by the chair of your committee.

CHAPTER 17

Group and Leisure Travel

Introduction

Traditionally and historically, corporate travel departments have handled little group or meeting travel and almost no incentive or leisure travel. However, over the last several years, there has been a tendency for corporate travel departments to increase the areas of their responsibility and take on sometimes a considerable amount of group, meeting, incentive, and leisure travel. This chapter explores how group and leisure travel is handled and the advantages of expanding traditional corporate travel management to the group and leisure travel areas as well.

Group and Meeting Travel

The number "ten" is used as an industry figure to differentiate between several individuals traveling together and group travel. Although it is not at all unusual for several executives to accompany one another on a business trip, when two or three executives travel together this is normally considered individual travel rather than group travel. However, when ten or more are traveling together or traveling to the same function, many consider this to be group travel. The number "ten" is also the magic number utilized by most air carriers in working with their special group desks. Again, if there are ten or more people on the same flight, then the group desk in the reservations office of an air carrier will frequently handle the arrangements. When travel agencies make reservations, their airline reservation computer systems are usually programmed to consider ten or more reservation for people traveling together to be a group and to be treated as a group. On the other hand, nine or fewer reservations for the same itinerary are treated as individual bookings. Whether the nine or fewer are for several people on the same flight or for reservations on two or more flights that are cross-referenced, unless there are ten travelers, they are treated as individuals rather than as a group.

Business groups normally travel to meetings or for the purpose of meetings. Therefore, group travel and meeting travel is, to a considerable extent, the same. Of course, there are a few instances where business groups will travel for purposes other than meeting. For example, in some cases there are sales blitz' held. A large number of sales people will travel to a central location, make many sales calls during a very short period of time, and then either move to another location for a sales blitz or go back to their home territories. Although frequently with a sales blitz there are meetings involved, the meeting(s) are secondary to the sales activities. The sales blitz is only one example of a group travel movement for a purpose other than meetings. Nevertheless, in spite of the few exceptions to the rule, almost all group travel is for the purpose of attending or holding a meeting. In fact, as pointed out in the chapter on proposal and contracting processes, about half of all business travel is to attend or participate in meetings and/or conventions.

Meetings can be called by or held for any department or division within a company. Most frequently, however, meetings are held by the training department (normally they are considered training sessions), the marketing department (a wide variety of sales and other marketing meetings are held), and the executive or administrative department (also a wide variety of types of meetings are held including board meetings, stockholder meetings, and so on). Frequently, when travel is involved for a meeting there is a need for the services of a meeting planner. Increasingly, travel agencies are providing meeting planners on their staff who offer full meeting planning services, often at no additional expense for the use of the agency's professional meeting planner. In other cases a business may have a professional meeting planner employed on staff. In still other cases, contracts will be developed with independent meeting planners to handle all of the meeting arrangements.

In each case, when a meeting planner is involved in the planning of a meeting, the corporate travel department normally coordinates closely with the meeting planner to make certain that all travel arrangements fit into the total meeting plan smoothly and to insure that all participants are scheduled to arrive and leave, ideally without interrupting the meeting or missing major parts of the meeting. Because so many meetings are being held by industry, many companies are turning to corporate travel departments asking them to handle some or all of the meeting planning functions, which have traditionally not been corporate travel department responsibilities. In fact, in some cases, meeting planners are being hired and placed in the corporate travel departments of companies for administrative purposes so that the close tie that is needed between meeting planners and corporate travel departments will be much easier to facilitate.

When corporate travel departments receive a responsibility to handle meeting planning functions, one can understand the logic in making this type of responsibility allocation. Meeting planners negotiate with hoteliers for function rooms and with hotel food and beverage managers for meal and reception functions. Although these may not be the same people in a hotel with whom they have negotiated for room nights, frequently they are the same people or they work closely with those hotel individuals with whom the corporate travel department has interfaced sometimes over a long number of years. Most corporate meetings are small meetings consisting of from ten to twenty or twenty-five individuals. These meetings can normally be easily handled by a corporate travel staff at the same time that the travel arrangements are handled. Function rooms are requested at the same time as sleeping room reservations are made. Often function rooms will be given at a low price, occassionally on a gratis basis, if the sleeping rooms are booked at the same time. If meal functions are booked in the hotel, this also provides leverage for negotiating a reduction in meeting room prices.

Although few corporate travel managers have difficulty in arranging the details of small meetings and find that such arrangements can often be completed easily on the phone, arrangements for meeting of several hundred or several thousand people can become much more difficult and it can take considerably more time. When such meetings are arranged on a regular basis, it is usually found to be better to bring in a specialized person who has some meeting planning expertise or training to work on at least a part-time basis in the corporate travel department. The logistics for such meetings can be considerable and the potential cost savings and negotiations can also be considerable.

Incentive Travel

Incentive travel is expanding rapidly. While five years ago it was rare to find a travel agency that specialized in incentive travel in major cities, today all major cities in the U.S. have at least one and, in many cities, there are a number of travel agency incentive travel specialists with which a corporate travel department may work. The way of handling incentive travel is also changing for companies. In the past, marketing managers would frequently delegate this responsibility to someone in the marketing division. That person would have the responsibility of coming up with the entire incentive campaign and all of the incentive travel arrangements connected with that campaign. Recently, because of the contacts that corporate travel managers have with travel vendors, marketing executives are taking advantage of the knowledge and benefits that can be gained by their working with corporate travel departments. They, therefore, are asking corporate travel managers to take on an increasing share of coordinating the travel details associated with incentive travel. In fact, often starting from small incentive travel campaigns and sometimes growing to large campaigns, corporate travel managers are being asked to take on all aspects of incentive travel.

Often the corporate travel department will deal directly with a travel agency that specializes in incentive travel rather than the agency that may be handling all other travel for the company. There are a number of reasons for this. Agencies specializing in incentive travel tend to have packages that can be purchased as total, complete promotional units, easing many of the logistics considerations and providing continuous, but inexpensive to the company incentive promotions. Recognizing that incentive travel programs pay off for a company only if they are successful in motivating sales (and the other employees to which they are directed to increase productivity and sales) by considerable amounts, the packaging, promotion, and motivational efforts are frequently considered more important by marketing executives than the actual incentive travel award which may be earned at the end of the incentive campaign.

Although most travel agencies are in a position to put together an incentive travel program, relatively few have wide experience in doing so and those agencies which specialize in group and incentive travel tend to have the best productivity results in terms of motivating employees to produce or to sell more. Because travel incentives have been proven to produce greater productivity and sales than other forms of incentives, many companies run several incentive travel programs a year for different employee groups and sometimes for client groups. Therefore, corporate travel managers who handle incentive travel for such companies may find incentive travel can become a major part of their responsibility.

Leisure Travel

Corporate travel departments are also beginning to handle an unprecedented amount of leisure travel. Some of the larger firms in the U.S. run Saturday or Saturday to Sunday bus tours from their company headquarters almost every weekend for employees wanting an opportunity to get away on an escorted tour. In a few cases, several buses go out each Saturday morning. Although in some cases such leisure programs are offered through the company's personnel department, more often all leisure travel opportunities are provided through the corporate travel department.

From the standpoint of the corporate travel manager there are two benefits that can result from adding leisure travel to the range of corporate travel department services. One reason is to establish the image of the corporate travel department as a company unit that provides services and benefits for all employees. This may counteract the potentially negative image as the enforcer of company travel policy regulations. Certainly, as negotiations are undertaken with vendors for good car rental rates, hotel rates, and air fare rates, many of these same savings can be passed on to company employees to take advantage of when traveling for pleasure. This can reduce the cost of an employee vacation considerably and it can provide still more company benefits offered to company employees. Finally, it provides a strong, positive view of the services of the corporate travel department.

A second benefit resulting from leisure travel offerings is the ability to increase total travel volume and give the company substantially more rebate money. When corporate travel managers negotiate with vendors to reduce the costs of hotel, car rental, and air expenses, vendors become concerned with what the total purchase volume will be. There is a strong relationship between the volume of annual room nights purchased, for example, and the price per room that a hotel is willing to charge. The same volume-to-price relationship exists with car rental rates, air fares, and other travel services purchased. By adding leisure travel volume to corporate travel volume, corporate travel managers are frequently able to increase the total negotiable unit level purchased to a point that will provide the business with a considerably better rate per unit purchased than they could possibly have obtained if they were working with corporate travel business only. In some cases, the leisure usage has doubled total usage and provided corporate travel managers with substantially more powerful statistics with which to negotiate. Obviously this provides the corporate travel manager with still another tool necessary to do the job for which the corporate travel function was designed (i.e., to reduce total business travel costs).

However, the benefits of handling leisure travel do not stop with per unit cost reduction. *Revenue sharing arrangements* with travel agencies usually offer the corporate travel department a specific dollar return for each air, lodging, or ground transportation dollar of purchase. For example, if the revenue sharing is based on two percent, then a check is written to the company by the travel agency on a monthly or a quarterly basis amounting to two dollars for each one hundred dollars of purchases. If the company purchases $1 million of corporate travel annually from the travel agency, based on the two percent formula, the agency writes a check back to its client company for $20,000. If employees in the company are urged to take advantage of leisure travel opportunities and purchase their vacation travel directly from the travel agency, then the base dollar volume for revenue sharing can be increased substantially. For example, the company that purchases $1 million of business travel may also have $1 million of leisure travel purchased by their employees. Based on the two percent formula, the business now receives a check for $40,000 from its travel agency rather than the $20,000 check received from its travel agency. And, the corporate travel department has to do nothing for this doubling of revenue sharing income other than encourage employees to take advantage of the travel price discounts already negotiated for their use when the employees travel on business.

In this type of arrangement, literally everyone wins. The company gets considerably more money back from the travel agency than it otherwise would. The corporate travel department provides cost savings for employees for their vacation and other leisure travel. The travel agency obtains far more business than it otherwise would have received from the company. And, air, lodging, and ground transportation vendors receive considerably more business than they would have received if the corporate travel department handled only corporate travel.

In handling leisure travel, it is important to minimize or eliminate any administrative work on the part of the corprate travel department in booking or otherwise making leisure travel arrangements. Ideally, all travel arrangements will be made by the employee directly with the travel agency. It is also important to negotiate revenue sharing arrangements in advance and to identify exact ways of recognizing that the bookings came to the travel agency from employees of the company. Finally, it is essential to establish arrangements for getting the word out to employees on special travel opportunities and negotiated discounts so that employees will have an incentive to work with the company's travel agency rather than an alternative travel vendor. All of these details can and should be spelled out in the request for proposal and the contracts that follow. However, with very little additional work and frequently with no additional staff, adding leisure travel services can provide a substantial benefit to the corporate travel department, the company, and the company's employees.

Summary

Only recently have some corporate travel departments expanded their scope of travel management to include group and leisure travel. For ten or more travelers, airlines will offer group travel rates and arrangements. Most groups of business travelers travel for meeting purposes. Although the majority of those traveling for meetings work in the sales and marketing division, other heavy users of travel for meeting purposes are those working in the training division or department and in administration. Because meetings are becoming an important part of business life, many companies are hiring or using the services of professional meeting planners. In many cases, meeting planners work in the corporate travel department and, in a few cases, meeting planning is considered to be an equal and joint function of the corporate travel department.

Incentive travel has also expanded rapidly. Traditionally handled by the marketing department, the ability of corporate travel executives to make incentive travel arrangements and to negotiate for incentive travel prizes has resulted in a move towards corporate travel departments working closely with marketing divisions in handling all of the travel aspects of incentive travel programs.

Leisure travel is also becoming a growing part of corporate travel departmental responsibility. There are two advantages to offering leisure travel to corporate employees. The larger volume usage of air, lodging, and ground transportation vendors results in an ability to negotiate for lower per unit use prices. In addition, a more positive image of the corporate travel department often results when employees find that by using negotiated lower rates they can save substantially on their leisure and vacation travel. Additionally, those corporate travel departments which have negotiated revenue sharing arrangements find that the revenue sharing income is based on all travel purchased, including leisure travel. This often results in a sizeable increase in the total dollars received back from revenue-sharing vendors.

Because of the considerable benefits that can accrue to a company by having corporate travel departments handle group and leisure travel, it can be expected that this segment of the corporate travel area of responsibility will increase in importance during the next few years.

Discussion Questions

1. What is the minimum number of travelers who must be traveling together to be considered a *group* according to most air carriers?

2. What are some instances where a business group might travel together for purposes other than attending or holding a meeting?

3. What departments or divisions within a company most often hold meetings?

4. Why might meeting planners and corporate travel executives work closely together (sometimes in the same department)?

5. Why might a company work with a different travel agency in arranging incentive travel rather than an agency which may handle all other travel for the company?

6. Why has there been a shift in business from the marketing division or department handling all aspects of an incentive travel program to corporate travel departments handling some, if not all, travel aspects of incentive travel programs?

7. Why might companies run several incentive travel programs a year for different employee groups and sometimes for client groups?

8. What are two major benefits that can result from corporate travel departments offering leisure travel services to the employees of their businesses?

9. How might revenue sharing arrangements applied to leisure travel result in greater cash receipts for a company from its travel agency vendor on an annual basis?

10. When a company offers leisure travel to its employees, everyone wins. Explain in what way each of the following wins:

    a) The travel agency vendor.

    b) The traveler.

    c) Air carrier vendors.

    d) The corporate travel department.

    e) Lodging vendors.

    f) The company as a whole.

    g) Ground transportation vendors.

Role Play Exercise

Two students may participate in this role play either out-of-class, as a fun way to review the chapter, or as an in-class exercise. One plays the role of the chief executive officer (CEO) and the other plays the role of the corporate travel manager. Please read the script and then pick up the conversation in your own words.

Chief Executive Officer: I have reviewed your proposal for adding leisure travel offerings to our services for employees and I have mixed feelings about it. I can appreciate that our employees would be able to take advantage of some of the discounts you have negotiated with airlines, hotels, and car rental vendors, but you indicate that we will not have to add staff and that we will still come out actually making money on this kind of arrangement. It all sounds positive, but there has to be a catch somewhere. Explain to me how it works and why you think we don't have to add any additional people in your department to be able to handle it.

Corporate Travel Manager: It really is a case where everybody wins. Let me explain why we can handle it without adding any additional staff and tell you exactly how we can get a lot of money back for the company, even what should be termed a "profit." Let's look first at . . .

CONTINUE ON YOUR OWN

Group Discussion Situation:
Renewing a Ruptured Relationship

Longneker Krane, the corporate travel manager for World Wide Wonders, has felt he had an excellent working relationship with his travel agency, Truly Tops Travel, and its manager, Truly Tipsy. Two years ago, when the RFP was developed and the agency was selected to handle all travel for World Wide Wonders, Truly Tipsy took Longneker Krane out for a very expensive dinner in order to celebrate. At least once a quarter, they have had fine dinners at some of the top restaurants in town, renewing the celebration and discussing their working relationship. There has been absolutely no problem that has arisen which has not been resolved to the satisfaction of both parties practically overnight.

Although the contract signed by both parties two years ago indicated that all travel would be routed through Truly Tops Travel, Longneker advised Truly that a few very specialized trips might be handled through another agency, but that this would primarily be a transition activity until Truly Tops Travel was able to integrate their services and handle all travel. This integration was completed within the first quarter after signing the contract and since that time virtually all of World Wide Wonders' travel has been handled by Truly Tops Travel.

However, a new development occurred about a month ago. The vice president of marketing for World Wide Wonders was approached by the president of a small specialized agency, Incentive Travel Single Specialty, Inc. with an idea for an incentive travel program which the marketing vice president immediately embraced. Compared to the additional revenues which the program could be expected to generate, the cost of the incentive travel program would be minimal. He immediately brought Longneker Krane into a meeting with the president of Incentive Travel Single Specialty, Inc. and a total campaign was designed. Last week, a contract for placing the incentive travel program with Incentive Travel Single Specialty, Inc. was signed.

Yesterday Longneker Krane got a call from Truly Tipsy during which Truly expressed her anger. She said she had just learned of the incentive travel contract and considered it a violation of her contract with World Wide Wonders. She asked for an explanation. A meeting in Longneker Krane's office is scheduled for a week from Friday.

Longneker has approached several associates at World Wide Wonders and asked for your advice and assistance in drawing up a written explanation. His desire is to prepare something that will not only stand up in court in case World Wide Wonders is sued by Truly Tops Travel, but he is anxious to prepare an explanation that will make Truly Tipsy happy and reassurred about the working relationship.

You are meeting today to finalize the explanation and you are expected to reach agreement on and to write a no-longer-than two page explanation. In your group session, select one person to present your written explanation. All will have

317

Group
Discussion
Situation:
Renewing a
Ruptured
Relationship

an equal vote on decisions as to what should be included in the paper. In your group session, you are expected to reach agreement and to prepare a two-page paper to be presented to the entire class by the spokesperson selected by your group.

CHAPTER 18

Corporate Travel Policies

Introduction

Setting and maintaining policies is key to corporate travel management. Without having policies, it is doubtful that corporate travel can be managed. Travel policies are designed to save money for the company and that is their major purpose. However, they also serve a secondary purpose of allowing travelers to understand exactly what the limitations are in terms of choices and alternatives. Although many do not think about it, having policies gives the traveler the financial security of knowing what will be reimbursed and what is allowed in terms of expenditures and what is not. Policies need to be known if they are to be effective. Seldom does it work to simply put them into a manual and expect all employees to read the manual, understand all aspects of it, and remember it while they are out of town. Having a policy guide which the traveler can take on the trip can be most beneficial.

Equally important to having policies is enforcing them. Without enforcement, travelers tend to ignore policies and travel management becomes impossible. Selectively enforcing policies can also be detrimental to a company and it creates an attitude on the part of employees whereby they attempt to find ways to get around the policies if they know that others have been successful in doing so. Therefore, a policing role is needed.

But, as noted in earlier chapters, if the corporate travel department and the manager is viewed predominantly as a policing department/manager, there is frequently a desire to get rid of the corporate travel department and/or manager. Politically, the department and the manager are seldom in a position to handle the political repercussions that come with policing travel adherence. Therefore, many companies mandate that policies be policed by the immediate supervisors of travelers. While the corporate travel manager may perform the role of determining when policies are not followed, most companies feel that the corporate travel manager or preferably a higher level executive should bring this to the attention of the immediate supervisor of the employee who failed to follow the policy and the immediate supervisor should take whatever action is necessary.

The Status of Corporate Travel Policies

The *Fourth Biennial Edition of the American Express Survey of Business Travel Management,* published in late 1988, indicates that, "Forty-two percent of private companies still do not have formal, written policies, only about one-third review their policies at least annually, and nearly one-third are unsure of the degree of employee compliance with policy." The American Express Survey is based on the responses of 1,600 organizations with at least one-hundred employees and it is considered to be the most comprehensive survey ever undertaken relating to business travel in the U.S. In positive terms, the statistics mean that fifty-three percent of the survey respondents indicate that they do have a written policy manual.

Travel policy statistics have also been studied by Runzheimer International and highlights of their "1988-1989 Survey and Analysis of Business Travel Policies and Costs" was featured in the October 31, 1988 edition of *Business Travel News.* Both the American Express Survey and the Runzheimer Survey point out statistics relating to what businesses appear to consider the most important policies to affect travel cost management.

Lowest Air Fare Policy

Perhaps the policy of greatest importance is the requirement that travelers take the lowest "logical," "convenient," or "reasonable" air fare. The American Express survey uses the term *lowest logical air fare* while the Runzheimer Survey uses the term, *lowest convenient air fare.* According to the American Express Survey, eighty-six percent of the companies responding make this requirement. According to the Runzheimer Survey as reported in *Business Travel News,* seventy-one percent make this requirement.

Other Cost-limiting Travel Policy Requirements

Other requirements relating to cost management include:

1. tightening receipt requirements (seventy-four percent indicate that they have according to the American Express Survey);
2. strictly enforcing existing travel and entertainment policies (seventy-five percent indicate that they have done so according to the American Express Survey);
3. not permitting frequent flier programs to dictate travel arrangements and requiring travelers to accept the lowest convenient fares regardless of carrier preference (thirty-three percent of the Runzheimer Report respondents indicate that this is policy);
4. using stricter criteria for authorization to take international trips (seventy-three percent of the American Express respondents indicated that this is the case);

5. establishing policies on car rentals, hotel accommodations and air travel components (ninety-eight percent car rental, ninety-four percent hotel accommodations, and eighty-one percent air travel of the American Express respondents have done so); and

6. establishing per diem/spending guidelines (sixty-one percent of the American Express respondents indicated that they have done so);

Air Travel Policies

Air travel tends to be the area of greatest concern and is possibly the area with the potential of the greatest savings. The Runzheimer Report indicates that while fewer companies are requiring frequent flier bonuses to be turned over to the company and to become company property, thirty-eight percent of those responding to the 1984 survey indicated that this was a policy requirement, while only nineteen percent of the 1988 respondents indicated that it is a requirement.

The vast majority require, or strongly encourage, several controlling mechanisms as they relate to making reservations and using perhaps less convenient, but more economical flights. Policies requiring advance reservations head the list. Seventy-three percent of the Runzheimer International Survey respondents encourage and twenty percent require the making of advanced reservations. The use of non-refundable air fares, if they are cost effective, is encouraged by sixty-one percent of those responding to the Runzheimer International Survey, but the use of these fares is required by only ten percent. The use of penalty air fares, if they are cost effective, was encouraged by the policies of fifty-nine percent and required by ten percent. The use of alternative airports when flying from them would be less expensive was encouraged by the policies of forty-nine percent of the companies responding to the Runzheimer International Survey and required by five percent of the companies. Travel within specified windows of time was required in the policies of fourteen percent of the companies and encouraged by forty-eight percent. Accepting stopovers was encouraged by forty-four percent of the company policies and required by nine percent of them.

Two of the more controversial policies had fewer than fifty percent of the respondents either encouraging or requiring adherence to the policy. These policies were:

1. requiring travel during off-peak hours (forty-two percent of the companies surveyed encourage it and three percent require it); and

2. accepting one or two connections in order to obtain lower air fares (thirty-nine percent encourage accepting connections to get lower fares and eight percent require accepting connections to get lower fares).

Both of these policies, some argue, can be detrimental to the employee's ability to perform acceptably when arriving at the destination because the policies can result in trips that are both uncomfortable and lengthy.

Hotel Policies

According to the American Express survey, hotel policies that are considered include the following:

1. employees must stay in hotels with which the company or the travel agency has negotiated rates;
2. travelers must place hotel reservations through the designated travel agency;
3. the type of accommodation allowed depends on the employee's position in the firm; and
4. employees must stay at moderately priced hotels.

Of these four policies, the very high-volume travel companies (those with travel and entertainment budgets of $5 million or more) make all hotel policy requirements except the requirement of staying at moderately priced hotels to a greater degree (often to a considerably greater degree) than do those companies with lower travel and entertainment budgets. The policies required by most of the companies are to stay at hotels where the company or the agency has negotiated special rates and to stay at moderately priced hotels. Only an average of twenty-one percent of the respondents indicate that the position of the employee makes a difference in terms of the type of accommodations allowed.

Car Rental Policies

The most frequently reported car rental policies according to the American Express survey, for those employees traveling alone, are:

1. employees must use firms with which the company or its travel agency have special rates;
2. there is an imposition of a limit on the size of car the employee can rent;
3. employees are expected to refuse collision damage waiver insurance;
4. employees are expected to refuel cars before returning them; and
5. car rentals are discouraged altogther.

The high-volume travel and entertainment respondents to the survey (those with travel and expense budgets of $5 million and more) indicated that over fifty percent have policies mandating all of these requirements except the discouragement of car rentals (only six percent discourage car rentals). Interestingly, however, most of the high-volume travel and entertainment respondents indicate that the policy on the largest car size allowed is a mid-size or an intermediate, and not a compact or a sub-compact. In fact, the allowance of a mid-size or an intermediate car rather than requiring the employee to drive a smaller car is a policy maintained by all categories of respondents from the very lowest travel and

FIGURE 18.1. There is a wide choice of cars available to traveling businessmen from every vendor (in this case Hertz). The travel policies of most high-volume travel and entertainment businesses dictate that a mid-size or an intermediate-size car be the largest that is rented. (Photo courtesy of Hertz.)

entertainment volume respondents to the very highest volume travel and entertainment respondents. And, there is a substantial difference between the very low percentage of respondents requiring a compact or a sub-compact and the very high percentage that allow mid-size or intermediate-size cars as the largest car size allowed.

Other Policies

While the majority of travel policies reported in the trade press and in the surveys relate to policies concerning air travel, lodging and car rentals, many companies also have policies dealing with meal expense compensation, entertainment, and expense reporting. Frequently, companies have per diem requirements that often follow government allowed per diems. While some companies have travel policies that are quite extensive, covering almost every conceivable type of expense, the majority of companies seem to have travel policies that are limited to only the air, hotel, car rental, and, in some cases, per diem, entertainment, and reporting requirements.

The American Express survey is comprehensive in reporting the various options available to businesses. It includes an extensive travel policy model which can assist companies in devloping a complete travel and entertainment series of policies if they do not already have them.

Policy Brochure Distribution

As noted earlier, policies need to be reduced to a point where they can be easily read by, understood by, and made available to travelers. One approach that is sometimes used and is strongly recommended is to develop the policy in a booklet or a manual format narrow and thin enough to slip into the ticket jacket of travelers so that they will have a copy whenever they travel. Carol Duerr, *Business Travel News'* Corporate Travel Manager of the Year, produced a policy and procedures booklet for her travelers which is basically a legal size sheet of paper folded four times and printed on front and back. This is an inexpensive way of letting travelers know what is required of them and what is not. Some companies have very extensive travel policies which are kept in a bound volume and made available to all department heads. The highlights of these policies have been reproduced in a format similar to the one Ms. Duerr uses and enclosed with ticket jackets. Whichever approach is used, it is important to keep in mind that travelers need to have something that they can refer to while on the road if they are to be expected to comply with travel policies.

Summary

This chapter has been an overview of the policies maintained by corporate travel departments. It is designed to present the highlights of travel policies, the reasons for the development of policies, and the packaging of policies so that they will be read, understood, and followed. The importance of enforcing policies is stressed, but equally stressed is the importance of the political ramifications to corporate travel departments and corporate travel managers who try to enforce policies without the support of top management. A strong recommendation is made to have enforcement of policies undertaken by immediate supervisors. A review of the status of corporate travel policies as presented in the *American Express Survey of Business Travel Management* and the *Business Travel News* excerpts from the Runzheimer International *Survey and Analysis of Business Travel Policies and Costs* is provided.

Major policies have been discussed. These include policies dealing with air transportation, lodging, and car rentals. To a lesser extent, they include other policies as well. Air transportation policies include those requiring acceptance of the lowest "logical," "convenient," or "reasonable" air fare; not permitting frequent flier programs to dictate which carrier to use; setting standards for the approval of international airline trips; making advanced reservations; using non-refundable fares; using penalty air fares; using alternate airports to reduce air travel costs; travel at off-peak times to reduce costs; and accepting stopovers when this will lower the expense of a ticket. Most companies, it was noted, temper air cost reduction policies when cost reduction mechanisms might substantially reduce the traveler's effectiveness for which the trip is undertaken.

Hotel policies usually require the employees to stay in hotels where special rates have been negotiated, to make reservations through designated travel agencies, to use moderately priced hotels, and to select a type of accommodation in keeping with the employee's status in the organization and/or the work that is to be undertaken. Car rental policies make similar booking requirements, insisting that those franchisees be used who have extended negotiated rates and that all bookings be made through the designated travel agency. In addition, policies address the largest size of car that can be rented, the expectation that collision damage waiver insurance not be taken, and the requirement that cars be refueled before being returned. A few companies require travelers to avoid using rental cars altogether. Interestingly, medium-sized cars (sometimes called mid-size or intermediates) are usually the smallest cars allowed, not the compacts or subcompacts some expect to be the smallest cars allowed. Other policies tend to deal with factors such as meal expense compensation, entertainment expenses, expense reporting, and per diem limitations.

In conclusion, policy writers are urged to make policies comprehensive, yet concise. Publishing the policies in a booklet or brochure format that can be carried with the traveler is strongly recommended as this gives the traveler the knowledge of the policies when it is needed (i.e., while on the trip and while incurring the costs).

Discussion Questions

1. Why is setting and maintaining policies considered a key to corporate travel management?

2. In what way do policies give travelers financial security?

3. Why is enforcing policies considered to be equally important to having policies?

4. Why is selectively enforcing policies considered to be detrimental to a company?

5. Why do many companies mandate that policies be policed by the immediate supervisor of travelers?

6. Do the majority of the companies surveyed by American Express in its *1988 Survey of Business Travel Management* have formal, written policies?

7. What is considered to be perhaps the policy of greatest importance and why is it considered important?

8. What are some of the cost-limiting travel policy requirements?

9. Are more companies or fewer companies requiring frequent flier bonuses to be turned over to the company and to become company property and why might this be the case?

10. What type of air travel policies might result in less traveler convenience but greater travel savings?

325
Group
Discussion
Situation:
The Prissy
Problem

11. What are two controversial air travel policies?

12. What hotel policies are frequently adopted by companies?

13. What car rental policies are frequently adopted by companies?

14. Is the smallest car allowed usually a sub-compact, a compact, or a mid-sized car? Why might this be the case?

15. What other travel policies might one frequently encounter?

16. Why might having a policy printed and distributed in brochure or flyer format be beneficial for a company?

Role Play Exercise

Two students may participate in this role play either out-of-class, as a fun way to review the chapter, or as an in-class exercise. One plays the role of the chief financial officer (CFO) and the other plays the role of the corporate travel manager. Please read the script and then pick up the conversation in your own words.

Chief Financial Officer: I have discussed our new corporate travel department with the president of the company and we are agreed that a procedure whereby you send a note to each person who violates travel policies telling them that they will be fired if they violate the policy a second time will be the best approach to make sure policies are followed. You have the ability to monitor better than anybody else in the company. This procedure will cut through any red tape in sending memos back and forth and it will make sure that violators are put on notice right away.

Corporate Travel Manager: Will this work effectively since many of the travelers are in a higher status position than I? Might it not be better if I create a letter for your or the president's signature? Another option that might even work better would be to send a letter to the traveler's immediate boss over the signature of the president or over your signature.

Chief Financial Officer: We don't want to dilly dally on this. If you think your approach will work better, tell me why.

Corporate Travel Manager: Okay. Lets start by recognizing that . . .

CONTINUE ON YOUR OWN

Group Discussion Situation: The Prissy Problem

Prissy Prentice is a frequent traveler. She likes to leave around eight in the morning, fly to the destination, get her work done, and return on a flight around five or six in the evening so that she can get back home ". . . at a reasonable hour." However, three weeks ago Fly-By-Night Airways decided to add to its profitability by introducing special night fares. Fly-By-Night Air had traditionally operated charters during the day and shut down its equipment in the evenings. They came to a realization that using the equipment at night could add an extra measure of profitability. Therefore, they introduced new night fares that are only ten percent of the standard economy fare.

The company started requiring all travelers, including Prissy, to fly out at night (the flights usually start around eleven in the evening), get a hotel room and some sleep, conduct business during the day, have a leisurely trip back to the airport, and take an after-eleven in the evening flight back home. Even adding hotel costs, if a cheap room is rented, there will be a considerable savings for the company. And, the traveler is given a special benefit. Not only is their dinner paid for by the company in the destination city, but the chief financial officer has authorized that travelers, to compensate for their late arrival back in town, may report to work at 10:00 A.M. the morning after they arrive back rather than the 9:00 A.M. normal reporting time.

In spite of the late-reporting-back benefit, Prissy has not been happy with the arrangement since it was introduced. At 2:00 A.M. this morning Prissy returned from a business trip and, while walking from the airport terminal to her parked car, she was mugged. She is now in the hospital and threatening to sue the company because of its requirement that she must travel at night. Although the chief financial officer embraced this new Fly-By-Night concept when the corporate travel manager brought it to his attention, he told the president this morning that Prissy's mugging was totally the responsibility of the corporate travel manager, who should have considered this factor when suggesting that a policy be adopted requiring travelers to fly at night in order to save money. The president of the company has set a meeting in his office at 2:00 P.M. this afternoon. The meeting will be attended by the chief financial officer and the corporate travel manager. It is to discuss the Prissy situation and there is already a rumor among the employees in the company that the corporate travel manager will be fired.

Several friends of the corporate travel manager have gotten together to discuss this matter. Review the situation and draw up a written recommendation for the corporate travel manager. Your written recommendation will be presented to the entire class by the spokesperson selected by your group.

CHAPTER 19

Professionalism

Introduction

The concept of professionalism can be approached from many directions. It will be approached in this chapter from the direction of employment. There is a correlation between maintaining professionalism and professional standards, on the one hand, and increasing salaries and status both within a company and within an industry, on the other hand. Not only is the professional travel manager aware of salary trends and his or her position within those trends, both within the company and within the industry, but the professional corporate travel manager has found ways of gaining internal and external recognition through an increasing series of professional activities both within the organization and outside the organization for which he or she works. Many start with industry associations and other industry organizations. It is difficult to find models to follow in the corporate travel industry, but models in terms of both systems and individuals can be found through industry associations and other organizations, the trade press, and at industry gatherings (meetings and educational programs/events).

Having and building an external foundation, the professional corporate travel manager also turns inward and constantly works on building professionalism within the organization as it relates to the handling of corporate travel and within the corporate travel department as the department works with the organization as a whole and with those outside the company. This professionalism is based on:

- maintaining up-to-date approaches;
- setting, maintaining, and striving for increasingly higher ethical standards; and
- establishing and maintaining increasingly strict quality control.

Each of these areas of professionalism will be analyzed in greater detail.

Salaries and Professionalism

Corporate travel managers are among the best paid and the worst paid professionals. Although this statement may sound contradictory, clarification will explain. For the number of years that the average corporate travel manager has worked in the travel industry, the remuneration is, on average, considerably higher than most others in the industry with the same number of years of travel experience. On the other hand, compared to other corporate buyers who manage extremely large amounts of financial purchases, corporate travel managers are paid less than their counterparts.

Corporate travel managers frequently are either promoted to the position from within the business, having worked in a wide range of other jobs prior to undertaking the responsibility for corporate travel, or they came to the position from previous employment as travel agents, normally working for a corporate travel-oriented travel agency. In both cases, when they enter the ranks of corporate travel management and proceed through initial hire to several increased levels of compensation, their average salary tends to be considerably higher than that of other travel executives with the same number of years of experience in the travel field. Of course, a part of this reason, is that for many, the years of experience is in other fields and certainly, in many cases, that experience can be relevant to the corporate travel tasks being undertaken.

One of the concerns that many in the corporate travel industry have is the comparatively lower salary paid, on average, to corporate travel managers as compared to other corporate buyers whose purchasing authority and responsibility is of a similar level. Certainly many buyers must have considerable technical expertise. However, average buyer salaries can be as much as twice average corporate travel manager salaries at the same buying level in some businesses.

This contradiction in income results in several unique factors affecting the industry. The position of corporate travel manager is one that is sought after both internally and externally because often it is one of the few executive positions that is open to a person with limited formal education and to a person who has either very narrow or no experience in the travel industry. On the other hand, once a company employee performs in the role of corporate travel manager for a period of several years, that executive tends to have a different point of view and expects to have compensation more in line with that paid to others doing similar jobs or holding similar levels of responsibility in the business.

As in other areas of travel, corporate travel management is changing. There are indications that a growing number of companies expect their corporate travel managers to become more and more sophisticated in undertaking their roles—especially if there is a substantial amount of international travel involved. As an increasing number of educational institutions prepare and offer college courses and college programs oriented toward corporate travel management, and as the professional associations increase the recognition within the industry of the importance of the role of corporate travel management, it can be expected that travel buyers (i.e., business travel managers) will be hired at higher salary levels and will be given increased status and prestige within their companies. These tend to be the prerequisites for across-the-board higher salary levels. All this will take time.

For those who are currently corporate travel managers, however, and for those who are entering the field of corporate travel management, a desire for increased status and income will not wait. In order to increase salary and benefits, therefore, those currently having strong desires along these lines often set very high levels of professionalism and look for or establish models for professionalism and career development.

There are only two ways to obtain greater compensation and status in the field of corporate travel management for those who are currently working in the field. One of these ways is to increase the personal and/or departmental status within one's own company. By obtaining a recognition of what can or is being done in the area of corporate travel management, some corporate travel managers have been able to work with corporate salary administrators to upgrade the classifications of their positions so that, in some cases, considerable increases in income are realized. In other cases, the effort has been to increase a corporate travel manager's personal recognition as a professional and to thereby negotiate for increased compensation. Although in most instances there are no promises, the performance of an exceptional job, once corporate travel savings are recognized and the benefits of professional corporate travel management are understood by top management, appropriate compensation realignments can result.

A second approach to obtaining increased compensation is to move to other businesses, making a lateral move, often with the same title, but at a higher compensation level. This approach has not been undertaken as often in the corporate travel area as it has in many other areas of travel management. For example, many who work with travel agencies and obtain their two years of experience required to meet airline qualifier requirements for travel agencies will, immediately after the two year experience criterion has been met, start sending out resumes and working toward getting an offer to be a qualifier at often significantly higher levels of compensation. Part of the reason for the difference, of course, is the number of jobs involved. There are many more travel agencies than there are corporate travel departments. There is also an identifiable position within an identifiable career ladder in the retail travel industry. In corporate travel, however, the openings for corporate travel manager are not widely advertised and the decision makers who select a person to fulfill the role of corporate travel manager frequently have different titles. In addition, there usually is no internal career ladder promising future higher level, better paid jobs for corporate travel managers.

While this means that it may be more difficult for a corporate travel manager to move up or to move laterally (from one business to another), it does not mean that it is impossible. And, in fact, there are an increasing number of corporate travel managers who do move up and who do move from one business to another. But to attain any movement, corporate travel managers may feel that models for professionalism are needed. There are certainly models that exist to assist them in their efforts to set high standards of professionalism and career development.

External Professional Development and Models

In every industry there are people who are models to follow. It behooves the new corporate travel manager to look for models, those whose work in corporate travel management set professional standards that can be emulated. This is especially true in a field as new as corporate travel management. In this field, where little has been documented, finding others who have accomplished corporate travel management feats in their business, feats which serve as patterns or models for reaching the same goals in other companies, is one of the few techniques a new corporate travel manager must achieve. He has to find management strategies that will work and to set professionalism goals that are attainable. In searching out models, one looks for people and systems that are exceptional. It is also necessary to search for models that provide a high standard of professionalism, clear cut ethics, and quality services and products.

The Associations

One of the best ways to find models is to attend functions with other corporate travel managers and to become involved in corporate travel-oriented associations. There are associations for corporate travel managers that provide high standards of professionalism and quality as well as educational benefits on a local, regional, national, and even on an international level. Some of these associations are devoted solely to corporate travel and corporate travel management while others address a broader spectrum of concerns, but include corporate travel and corporate travel management.

Those national associations dedicated primarily to corporate travel managers are the Association of Corporate Travel Executives (ACTE) and the National Business Travel Association (NBTA). Both strive for professionalism and many corporate travel managers belong to both associations. Upon request and the completion of an appropriate application form, ACTE provides free membership for students currently enrolled in a travel-oriented program or business students who plan to enter the field of corporate travel management upon graduation. NBTA provides a listing of local organizations serving corporate travel managers. Local membership will vary widely in terms of its national association affiliation. Local association corporate travel managers may also be members of ACTE, NBTA, both national associations, or neither of the national associations. However, many of the most professional corporate travel members believe that at least one national association membership is important.

The Institute of Certified Travel Agents and the American Society of Travel Agents predominantly serve a travel agency clientele, but both associations provide some educational programs of benefit to corporate travel managers as well. For example, many corporate travel managers have completed the ICTA certification program and are Certified Travel Counselors (CTC). The American Society of Travel Agents (ASTA) holds a number of seminars oriented toward marketing to corporate travel managers.

The Association of Corporate Travel Executives' meetings are primarily on a national and an international level, but they have made a concerted effort to hold educational and other meetings in major cities throughout the U.S. so that corporate travel managers with limited budgets can attend. In addition, they are in the process of putting together a series of videotape training programs which corporate travel managers can review in the privacy of their homes or offices. The ACTE also works closely with a large number of universities, colleges, and other institutions of higher learning to provide educational programming on local, regional, national, and international levels.

Like the ACTE, the National Business Travel Association offers educational presentations during their annual national convention. They also have a certification program (the Certified Corporate Travel Executive) which, while it has certified few corporate travel managers, some in the industry feel provides a different perspective.

The associations also offer educational materials in print. Two books have been authored by industry experts associated closely with ACTE. The Association of Corporate Travel Executives also publishes a quarterly journal, edited under the leadership of corporate travel expert, Robert Vaiden, with Ciba-Geigy Pharmaceuticals. The *Wall Street Journal* reproduced one issue of the *ACTE Journal* in its entirety as a supplement to the *Wall Street Journal*. The NBTA has a monthly news magazine which sometimes offers educational features. Another ACTE publication of interest to those seeking professionalism in corporate travel management is the *ACTE Journal*. The Association of Corporate Travel Executives also honors publishers with annual awards in corporate travel journalism and corporate travel publishing.

The NBTA holds an annual convention and educational presentations are included on the convention schedule each year. The Association of Corporate Travel Executives' Annual Convention and Trade Show, held in February each year, combines a strong educational format with an opportunity to exchange ideas and ask questions from industry experts. A trade show is held in conjunction with the convention, providing corporate travel managers with an opportunity to interface with suppliers and others in the field and thereby providing still another format for increasing one's education in corporate travel management.

The Association of Corporate Travel Executives is also closely associated with academia. It provides research topics for university and college-based corporate travel research studies, thereby building a research base in corporate travel management. Several of these studies can be accessed through university and college computer-aided literature reviews. The ACTE Foundation Inc. plans to maintain a corporate travel resource center and a corporate travel library at the New School for Social Research headed up under the direction of Cord Hansen-Sturm, director of the New School's Tourism, Travel and Transportation Management program. The Foundation works with educational consultants from institutions of higher education throughout the U.S. While its senior consultant is affiliated with Harvard University, its corporate travel resource center and corporate travel library are on the campus of the New School for Social Research in New York City.

The Association of Corporate Travel Executives Foundation encourages scholarship, conducts and encourages research, and provides the foundation with the educational resources for ACTE's educational conferences and video home study programming. In addition, it is in the process of starting a college and university accreditation program.

The educational and other association opportunities for increasing one's knowledge and professionalism have grown substantially in the last several years. Plans indicate that these opportunities will grow even greater in the near future. As more and more corporate travel managers take advantage of these opportunities and as the associations continue to develop raw research and interface with strength with chief executive officers and chief financial officers, it can be expected that the professional status of corporate travel management will grow proportionally. However, with the growth of the professional status of corporate travel management will come a need for a growth in individual professionalism among the practitioners of corporate travel management.

The Trade Press and Suppliers

The trade press and suppliers also offer opportunities to grow professionally and to keep up-to-date with industry developments. Both *Business Travel News* (a CMP Publication) and *Corporate Travel Management* offer regular opportunities to find out what is happening in the industry. Subscriptions are provided on a gratis basis for corporate travel managers. Both publications not only provide news information, but they also provide detailed analyses of new trends and developments in the industry. They run their own seminars for corporate travel managers and they publish the results of not only their own surveys of corporate travel managers, but the surveys conducted by other organizations as well. Many feel that there is no better way to keep up-to-date with what is happening in the industry than to read the trade publications.

Some go even further and read the publications oriented toward travel agencies and airlines. Chief among these is *Travel Weekly,* a publication oriented primarily for travel agents. *Travel Weekly* comes out twice a week and often includes either features or supplements relating to corporate travel and corporate travel management. *Travel Agent,* another twice-a-week publication, has been featuring corporate travel information, too.

Suppliers also help corporate travel managers to stay educated and to become increasingly professional. Supplier-offered seminars are available throughout the year and those that are dedicated toward new technologies and new technological developments can be especially beneficial for corporate travel managers. Many corporate travel executives feel that meeting with industry sales executives, attending industry functions, and participating in industry-sponsored educational events keeps them more up-to-date than any alternative process and assists them in developing a standard of professionalism that would not be possible without substantial industry input.

Internal and External Ethics

Ethics relates directly to professionalism. There is a wide range of corporate travel ethical concerns. The vast majority of ethical concerns, however, can be placed into one of two broad categories. One of these is the confidentiality of supplier data, information, and material. The other is the acceptance of any supplier-provided benefit that can be construed to be of a personal nature or that might be of benefit to the corporate travel manager (or other corporate travel staff person(s)) personally.

Corporate travel managers receive a large volume of information and material from suppliers. This is especially true when they are evaluating proposals in

SECOND CLASS MAIL

POSTMASTER NEWSPAPER HANDLING

Business Travel NEWS

A CMP PUBLICATION

Issue 131   *The Newspaper Of The Business Travel Industry*   CWE   January 16, 1989

What Industry Leaders Are Saying About '89

"**D**ue to the new laws, car rental companies will absorb the cost of protection that they did not previously provide, and it is expected that there will be a corresponding rate increase."
—Avis' Joe Vittoria

"**T**he globalization of the economy and the forthcoming deregulation of the European airline industry will spur the demand for worldwide travel management expertise."
—Carlson's Curt Carlson

"**T**he realization will come to many corporations that a 1, 2, or 3 percent rebate is not as meaningful as care and responsiveness on the part of a travel counselor."
—USTS' Peter Sontag

"**A**s commercial air traffic continues to increase, a growing portion of DOT resources surely will be aimed at maintaining and continuing to improve the safety standards."
—DOT's James Burnley

For more on what to expect in the year ahead, see Outlook '89 on page 15.

System One Shakes Up Sales Effort, Cuts 250

BY MARY BRISSON

HOUSTON — System One Corp. last week said it will give up primary sales responsibility for its computerized reservation system and cut its work force as the company shifts its focus from expanding market share to maintaining its subscriber base.

Field sales responsibility for the CRS will shift from the Texas Air Corp. automation subsidiary to the sales forces of its affiliated carriers:

Continued on Page 42

American Renews Deal With PacBell

Discounts Apply 'For 2 Or 2,000,' Says Res Agent

BY JEANETTE BORZO

SAN RAMON, CALIF. — American Airlines has renewed through July 5 a controversial deal that gives Pacific Bell travelers up to 50 percent discounts off full-coach fares.

When details of the original agreement surfaced (*BTN*, Sept. 12), American contended that the discounts were available for meetings only. However, industry observers suggested the deal—and others like it—are merely masks for direct corporate discounts usable on virtually all business trips.

American's commercial sales director, Jim Marsicano, last week said the lower fares still apply only when at least 10 employees fly to the same city. But a call placed to American's 800-number meetings services desk suggested otherwise.

Asked about the PacBell fare for a trip from San Jose to Los Angeles, for just one employee to meet with another, an American reservationist said, "It can be two, it can be 2,000. You're still entitled to the discount."

Asked specifically about the minimum attendee requirement, the reservationist said, "One person could show or a million. There are no specific requirements."

Marsicano said meeting fares are not regulated by the reservation desk, but by local American sales

Continued on Page 42

Travel Manager To Exit Tandem

BY MARY BRISSON

CUPERTINO, CALIF. — Ruthanne Mulvihill, the travel manager whose public stand against a Continental Airlines promotion last fall led the carrier to foreswear similar future programs, has resigned her position at Tandem Computers Inc. to become a consultant.

She said her decision, effective Jan. 31, had nothing to do with the flap over the Continental Cash Back program. Tandem's upper manage-

Continued on Page 42

USTS Moves Threaten Consortia

Puts Offer On Table To Buy Out ATN; Faces Competing Bid From Wagon-lits

BY DON MUNRO

CHICAGO — The "For Sale" sign affixed to Associated Travel Network Inc. marks a major step in the decline of travel agency consortia in North America, according to ATN executives and members.

ATN board members last month voted 7-4 to recommend that stockholders accept a buyout plan—worth about $1 million—from USTravel Systems Inc., Rockville, Md., which owns some of ATN's key members.

The board also voted to present to stockholders a proposal by Belgium-based mega-agency Wagon-lits to buy ATN and restructure it into a franchise organization.

"Although I don't agree, there appears to be a perception

Continued on Page 43

Seals Deal To Acquire $70 Million Member Of Hickory Travel Systems

ROCKVILLE, MD. — Fresh from a proposal to buy one major national travel agency consortium, USTravel Systems Inc. last week purchased a key member of another.

The newest USTS-owned agency is Hickory Travel Systems Houston, which had 1988 air sales of $70 million. It had been part of Hickory Travel Systems Inc., the Saddle Brook, N.J., consortium.

The acquisition closely follows a USTS bid to purchase the Chicago-based Associated Travel Network consortium.

USTS also recently completed the purchase of Hartford, Conn.-based Travelrama, an agency that does $50 million in annual air sales. Over the past year, USTS has roamed the United States acquiring regional agencies, and now has 18 units representing about $760 million in air sales.

Continued on Page 43

FIGURE 19.1. A basic part of professionalism is keeping up to date with industry trends and events. A wide range of publications are available to the professional corporate travel manager. These include *Business Travel News,* a publication devoted to news about corporate travel and corporate travel management. (Reprinted with permission from *Business Travel News.*)

the process of selecting a travel agency vendor. Vendors expect their material to be treated as confidential and it is considered unethical to share trade secrets, rebate figures, and other data that is provided in confidence. Although most corporate travel managers are very careful about not revealing any detail of supplier-provided confidential data and material, there are a very few who violate these ethical standards. It is considered unethical to send travel agents copies of other agency's proposals, to allow representatives from one agency to sit in on oral presentations made by representatives from another travel agency, or to tell a preferred vendor that it will be able to obtain one's business if they can beat the proposal received from another supplier, providing the details that must be exceeded. All corporate travel managers wish to obtain the best "deal" for their companies. However, it is not considered ethical to have several rounds of bids with all participants being advised of the top bidding arrangements unless the request for proposal specifically states that this is the way in which a decision will be made.

The second area of ethical concern is not as clear cut as the first one. This relates to internally determined ethical standards. It is generally recognized that corporate travel managers wield considerable power in selecting and working with travel industry vendors. Travel agencies, airlines, car rental companies, and hotel firms stand to gain or lose a considerable amount of business based on the decisions and actions of corporate travel managers. Therefore, it is not unusual for a vendor to provide a benefit for the client company which may be construed to be more beneficial to the corporate travel manager personally or to one of the corporate travel staff persons.

Many companies have policies against receiving gifts from vendors. However, even when such policies exist, interpreting what is a gift and what is not can sometimes be difficult. Most companies accept the vendor paying for a lunch or a dinner when a meeting is set up over lunch or dinner. Most companies also accept vendors buying drinks for corporate travel managers at industry functions. However, when it comes to accepting holiday gifts (even very small ones), free or reduced air tickets from air carriers or travel agencies, better-than-paid-for rooms or free accommodations from hoteliers, bigger-than-paid-for cars or free cars from car rental firms, and so forth many companies are adamant in their expectation that corporate travel managers should turn down such offers. More than many others in the travel industry, corporate travel managers and their staff must be very careful when it comes to accepting anything that has a monetary value.

It is strongly recommended that the corporate travel manager evaluate and project the areas of potential need in working with travel vendors and include even the smallest item in the request for proposal. For example, many companies have no objection to vendors paying for all costs in attending educational and professional development programs when this is stipulated as a condition for contract in the request for proposal, a proposal is tendered offering to provide these services, and the entire proposal, including the benefits section, is accepted by the company. On the other hand, if these same educational benefits are offered outside of the request for proposal/proposal acceptance process, many companies consider the benefits to be bribes or personal compensation for corporate travel managers and consider the acceptance by the corporate travel manager to be unethical. It is always wise for the corporate travel manager to review with upper management the exact parameters of the gifts policies and to know exactly what is accepted by the company and what is not. Once the parameters are determined, corporate travel managers should strive to stay within them.

Quality Control

With the emphasis in the industry on saving money, corporate travel managers sometimes lose sight of quality control. However, consistently maintaining high quality in the services and products over which one has control is a hallmark of professionalism. To obtain top quality, continuous monitoring and feedback is necessary. The larger, professional, travel agencies employ quality control specialists who review documents prior to their distribution to clients and reservations prior to the issuing of tickets. Corporate travel managers can learn from quality control specialists in travel agencies. By following similar procedures, the corporate travel manager can make certain that reservations are not only the least expensive, but the most convenient possible within the constraints of cost limitations and that all ground arrangements are documented and processed with a high degree of quality.

In order to make certain that quality services are being provided, some corporate travel managers include questionaire forms with each ticket with a request that when the trip expense report is filed, the questionnaire be completed and returned as well. By reviewing these on a weekly basis, corporate travel managers are rapidly able to determine whether or not there is a pattern of problems. Other corporate travel managers prepare periodic surveys asking travelers to describe their concerns and problems when traveling, but also asking what the most important services are as well. They seek out suggestions on improving quality. A continuous effort to upgrade the quality of products and services is one of the best assurances a corporate travel manager has that the company's travelers will recognize the corporate travel manager as a professional.

Summary

Striving for professionalism means constantly increasing one's knowledge and professional expertise. It means engaging in professional activities both internally (within the company) and externally (outside the company). It means keeping up to date with new developments in the industry, setting strict ethical guidelines and staying within those guidelines, and it means establishing quality controls and maintaining those controls.

Some in the industry equate salaries to professionalism and certainly salaries are an indication of how the corporate travel function and role are perceived by decision makers within the company. The salaries of corporate travel managers tend to be good compared to the salaries of others with similar amounts of experience in the travel industry. However, compared with others with similar buying responsibility in business, the salaries tend to be low. This discourages some corporate travel managers, but others treat it as a challenge. Because of the work of the corporate travel associations and others in the industry with both academia and corporate officers in America, there is a strong probability that considerably higher salary levels will be paid to corporate travel managers in future years. However, for those corporate travel managers who are currently working in the industry only two approaches are possible. One is to upgrade salary and compensation in the company with which they are currently working and the other is to move to another firm. Setting and maintaining high professional standards is one of the few ways corporate travel managers have of obtaining the recognition needed to encourage greater compensation to be provided in their own companies. It is also an excellent way of making a move to other companies and increasing their income by changing firms.

For the new corporate travel manager one of the approaches often taken is to look for models in the form of individuals who have demonstrated expertise in the field and models in the form of systems that provide outcomes of excellence. One of the best ways of finding these models is through the professional associations. Although several associations provide services and assistance to corporate travel managers, the two major ones are the Association of Corporate Travel Executives and the National Business Travel Association. Both provide educational opportunities in both print and seminar format and both provide opportunities to find models in the form of both individual experts and expert systems. The trade press and suppliers also offer opportunities to learn and to keep up-to-date on the industry. Attending supplier seminars and discussing problems with supplier experts provides the corporate travel manager with still another opportunity to gain and/or to increase professionalism.

Ethics relate directly to professionalism. There are two major areas of ethical concerns in the industry. One is the concern over the confidentiality of supplier data, information, and material. The other is the acceptance of anything that can be construed to be of a personal nature which is offered by vendors or suppliers. By setting very specific standards of not revealing any supplier confidential information or data and not accepting any supplier or vendor gift in any format, the corporate travel manager can avoid many of the potential ethical problems. However, the professionalism of maintaining high ethical standards is the responsibility of the corporate travel manager and the manager should not expect vendors, suppliers, or internal company associates to establish or maintain the ethical standards for the corporate travel department.

Maintaining a high level of quality control is still another hallmark of professionalism. Corporate travel managers can learn from travel agency and other supplier experts in quality control, but many also survey their travelers on a regular basis to determine what aspects can be improved and what additional services the traveler would like to have provided.

The combination of striving for excellence in all of these areas is a mark of professionalism. The ability to become professional and to maintain a high standard of professionalism requires an effort that is a continuing, and in many ways, a very difficult one.

Discussion Questions

1. Why is it accurate to say that corporate travel managers are among the best paid and the worst paid?

2. What factors are occuring that indicate a probability of future better salaries for corporate travel managers?

3. What are two ways to obtain greater compensation and status in the field of corporate travel management for those who are currently working in the field.

4. What two kinds of models are often sought by those entering the field of corporate travel management?

5. What are the two major associations serving corporate travel managers?

6. How do the services and programs of each of these associations compare with one another?

7. What are two major trade publications oriented primarily to the field of corporate travel management and what services are provided by these publications other than the reporting of news?

8. In what ways do suppliers help corporate travel managers to stay educated and to become increasingly professional?

9. What are the two major ethical concerns in the field of corporate travel management?

10. What steps might a corporate travel manager take to institute a high degree of quality control in corporate travel management?

Role Play Exercise

Two students may participate in this role play either out-of-class, as a fun way to review the chapter, or as an in-class exercise. One plays the role of the director of administrative services and the other plays the role of the corporate travel manager. Please read the script and then pick up the conversation in your own words.

Director of Administrative Services: I realize that you are new to corporate travel management and it is going to be necessary to do a lot of training and education in the field. However, I am in a bind. I have to keep training allocations in the budgets for executives at your rank pretty much equal or the total cost figures can get out of hand fast. I just can't let a cost allocation go through for the kind of money that I know we have to spend to get you the training you need. Do you have any suggestions?

Corporate Travel Manager: You are on the committee developing the request for proposal. Much of the kind of training we are talking about is often provided by or paid for by vendors. It is in their interest that they work with knowledgeable, well-educated corporate travel managers.

Director of Administrative Services: But isn't it unethical to take checks from them paying for seminar tuitions and that kind of thing? And what about hotel costs, meals, transportation, . . . all the other costs that are involved?

Corporate Travel Manager: If we spell out what's needed in the RFP and the agency agrees to fund it, we won't be violating any industry ethics. Let me explain how we can word the RFP. First, . . .

CONTINUE ON YOUR OWN

Group Discussion Situation:
Konservatif vs. Greedy

Busy Bee Beehives is the world's largest Queen Bee supplier for the raw honey industry. Travel needs are unique in that Queen Bees are shipped all over the world. Because of the fragile nature of Queen Bees, they often are carried in the airplane cabin in specially prepared containers.

Brood Greedy is the Director of Internal Affairs for Busy Bee Beehives and Karl Konservatif is the corporate travel manager for the company. Brood prides himself on uncovering violators of the company's ethics policies and getting them fired. He has stated at conventions of the National Internal Security Directors' Association that there are virtually no ethics violators at Busy Bee. His security mechanisms have been perfected to such a degree that he discovers violations almost before they happen and he gets rid of the perpetrator right away.

Brood Greedy has gone right to the president with his latest finding. He has discovered that Karl Konservatif, who is a member of the Board of Directors of the National Association of Corporate Travel Managers, accepted a free ticket from Totally Free Travel, the travel agency having the contract to handle all Busy Bee Beehives' travel, in order to attend a Board of Directors' meeting of the National Association of Corporate Travel Managers last year. He has also discovered that Karl Konservatif got the travel agency to pay for his transfer costs from the airport to the downtown hotel meeting site, two meals during the time he was away for the meeting, and the hotel room expenses. Greedy gave the president documentation taken directly from Totally Free Travel. Although he did not explain how this documentation was obtained, the documentation clearly shows that all these expenses were paid for by Totally Free Travel. Brood Greedy told the president, "This is a clear violation of our gifts policy. Karl Konservatif should be fired immediately."

Karl has been dating the president's secretary, Saalees Sympathetic. Karl received a call from Brood Greedy at ten o'clock this morning telling him to be at a meeting in the president's office at two o'clock tomorrow afternoon. Greedy gave no explanation of the reason. A few minutes later, however, Karl got a call from Ms. Sympathetic advising him that she had overheard the conversation between Brood Greedy and the president. She filled Karl in on the exact details.

Karl has decided to bring in copies of the request for proposal developed by the company eighteen months ago when the travel contract came up for bid and a copy of the Totally Free Travel bid proposal which was ultimately accepted by Busy Bee Beehives. He believes that the specific RFP requirements and the accepted bid proposal will protect him in this situation, but he has approached several friends in the company and asked for advice on how to present his defence.

Your group is meeting today to prepare a recommendation for Karl Konservatif. You are expected to reach agreement and to write a two-page defence based on the attached RFP and proposal excerpts. In your group session, select one person to chair the group. All will have an equal vote on decisions. In your group session you are expected to reach agreement on the structure and to prepare the two-page paper to be presented to the entire class by the chair of your committee.

Excerpt from Busy Bee Beehives' Request for Proposal

IV.3.a. Recognizing that travel agencies negotiate with air carriers for free tickets and often receive vouchers for free or reduced-cost hotel rooms in major chain hotels, and vouchers for free or reduced-cost car rentals with major car rental franchisees and recognizing that the professional development and the professional expertise of corporate travel managers and corporate travel staff is mutually beneficial providing benefit for the travel agency as well as the corporation, the following requirements are expected from the travel agency that will be selected to handle this account:

1. Ten trips per year will be totally funded by the travel agency for the corporate travel manager and/or the corporate travel staff. These trips will be for the purpose of familiarization, attending travel industry functions, educational seminars, or other activities that will increase the professionalism or be of educational benefit for the corporate travel manager and/or the corporate travel staff.
2. The compensation funded by the travel agency in item IV.3.a.1 will cover the traveler's airline tickets, ground transfers or car rental, accommodation costs, meals and incidentals, and airport parking charges. If tuition or other fees are charged, the travel agency will pay for these as well.

Excerpt from Totally Free Travel's Bid Proposal

Totally Free Travel will fund a minimum of twelve trips per year for the corporate travel manager and/or the corporate travel staff of Busy Bee Beehives. These trips may be for the purpose of one or more of the following:

1. familiarization;
2. attending travel industry functions;
3. attending educational seminars; or
4. participating in other activities that will or may increase the professionalism or be of educational benefit for the corporate travel manager and/or the corporate travel staff.

The compensation reimbursement funded by Totally Free Travel for these trips will cover at least the following, but will not necessarily be limited to the following:

1. the traveler's airline tickets;
2. ground transfers and/or a car rental;
3. all accommodation costs (including three phone calls home);
4. meals and incidentals;
5. airport parking charges;
6. mileage costs for driving to and from the airport of departure; and
7. any tuition or other fees charged for attending the event.

Index